Spring Dynamic Modules in Action

Spring Dynamic Modules in Action

ARNAUD COGOLUÈGNES
THIERRY TEMPLIER
ANDY PIPER

MANNING

Greenwich
(74° w. long.)

For online information and ordering of this and other Manning books, please visit
www.manning.com. The publisher offers discounts on this book when ordered in quantity.
For more information, please contact

> Special Sales Department
> Manning Publications Co.
> 180 Broad Street
> Suite 1323
> Stamford, CT 06901
> Email: orders@manning.com

♾ Recognizing the importance of preserving what has been written, it is Manning's policy to have
the books we publish printed on acid-free paper, and we exert our best efforts to that end.
Recognizing also our responsibility to conserve the resources of our planet, Manning books are
printed on paper that is at least 15 percent recycled and processed without the use of elemental
chlorine.

Manning Publications Co.
180 Broad Street, Suite 1323
Stamford, CT 06901

Development editor: Cynthia Kane
Copyeditor: Andy Carroll
Cover designer: Marija Tudor
Typesetter: Gordan Salinovic

ISBN 9781935182306
Printed in the United States of America
1 2 3 4 5 6 7 8 9 10 – MAL – 15 14 13 12 11 10

brief contents

contents

12 The Blueprint specification 374

foreword

It must have been in 2006 that I got a call as OSGi's Technical Director from Adrian Colyer, CTO of Interface21, the company that was the source of the Spring Framework. Yes, I'd heard of the Spring Framework, and I understood that it was a great improvement over existing techniques for writing software for the enterprise. As a developer who had gained most of his experience in developing embedded and middleware applications, I found all that XML rather foreign. However, I'd noticed the enterprise world's interest in OSGi, so I too was interested.

It turned out that Interface 21, BEA, and Oracle were considering creating support for OSGi in the Spring Framework. Spring is very good at configuring an application built out of simple objects that use, among other things, the simplified Spring interfaces to communicate with the world. However, Spring did not provide any support for modularity. In contrast, OSGi provides strong modularity support but it's not strong in configuration and it had no services in the enterprise space. This was a match made in heaven!

To discuss supporting OSGi in Spring, Adrian proposed a conference call with Hal Hildebrand (Oracle), John Wells (BEA), and one of the authors of this book: Andy Piper (BEA). B.J. Hargrave (IBM) also attended as OSGi's CTO. The initial conference call was followed by a meeting in London at the offices of BEA. It was a meeting I'll always remember, it was the start of what became Spring DM. At first, I felt that the group saw OSGi as something that needed to be supported by Spring; that is, as one of many things to be supported. As the meeting progressed, it became clear how nice the combination of Spring and OSGi could be; there was a lot of synergy and surprisingly little overlap. At the end of the meeting, we were thrilled with this project's potential.

The Spring DM project became crucial for the adoption of OSGi in the enterprise space. At that time, OSGi had been adopted by Eclipse, which made it acceptable for general programming. However, the enterprise space is conservative and was hesitant about adopting OSGi. The fact that Interface21 people started to sell OSGi at the many conferences they visited helped to give OSGi a place in the enterprise world. That said, it was a surprise for me when Interface21 changed their name to SpringSource and put a lot of emphasis on the OSGi connection. They quickly became a member of the OSGi Alliance and started RFC 124, as an endeavor to put Spring DM under the OSGi flag. This RFC later turned into the Blueprint specification. SpringSource also introduced the dm Server (now project Gemini in Eclipse) and more importantly, they launched the OSGi Bundle Repository, filling a crucial gap for the acceptance of OSGi in the enterprise. This repository contained bundles based on open source projects. Before this repository, developers were forced to create their own bundles from open source projects, and this was not always painless.

Alas, it still is not always painless. The core principle of OSGi is modularity, creating inside and outside spaces with well-defined ports. The advantages of modularity are numerous and well proven. However, OSGi enforces those rules strictly on all levels. Unfortunately, it turns out that many open source libraries do not live well inside modules—thay need global visibility of all classes. Over the past decade, mainstream Java has given rise to a number of patterns that appear to be modular but are not so in reality.

That's why this book about Spring DM and Blueprint is so crucial. First, it provides an excellent introduction to OSGi and what the guiding principles are. As one of the participants of the OSGi specification, I do not think I could have improved on this description. The book then explains how you should structure your projects with Spring DM, but it doesn't stop there. It doesn't hide the complexities of today's reality, which is that you have to use existing (open source) libraries. It provides an extensive description of what you should do when you need to use libraries that do not play well in a modular world.

If you're already building applications using Spring, then read this book and take the leap into the OSGi world. Although you might run into some hurdles, this book will help you solve them, and the rewards are well worth it.

PETER KRIENS
OSGi TECHNICAL DIRECTOR

preface

We all dream of the perfect software program.

You know the one—it's composed of multiple modules, each in charge of a specific, tightly defined set of tasks, each uniquely simple and elegant, interacting harmoniously to achieve the complex ends required by the user. We are taught in school how to build these perfect programs using techniques such as object-oriented programming and aspect-oriented programming. These techniques work well, but the end goal is always to make the system more reliable, more testable, more complete, and more flexible by making it more modular so that the whole is greater than the sum of the parts.

Of course, most of the software programs we work with are not perfect—have you encountered any of these issues?

- *The big, bad application problem* Your application is 600 MB in size and it takes 10 minutes to repackage one Java class and 20 minutes to deploy to your favorite application server. When you do finally get it to deploy, you find you've made a mistake and now you have to undeploy, fix, and redeploy—all outside of office hours—missing the soccer and poker night with your mates.

- *The brittle-change problem* A high-profile customer reports a problem, so you quickly fix the code and try to rebuild the application, only to find that the application won't build because another component is using the internal function you just changed. When you finally get the application built and deployed, you start getting reports of other parts of the application that are malfunctioning. Working into the night—again missing the soccer game—you discover that the change you made had unforeseen consequences that could only be discovered by running the full QA suite—a process that takes 48 hours.

- *The build-the-world problem* Your development team is in Beijing, Mumbai, and San Ramon, and each subteam works on different parts of the application in different time zones and on different development schedules. As the team and application grow, you find that it becomes increasingly hard to keep the different parts of the product separate—any time you make a change, you find it impossible to tell which teams will be affected by your changes. The only solution is to keep all the teams on exactly the same version of the application, and to rebuild and retest the entire product every time any change is made. You eventually spend all of your time building and testing the product and none actually developing it. The company goes bankrupt, you lose your job, and now you have plenty of time to watch soccer—if only your widescreen TV hadn't been repossessed.

These problems are all symptoms of unmodular applications.

As authors, we come from different but related, backgrounds. Arnaud and Thierry come from the enterprise application development sphere, and Andy comes from a middleware product development background, thanks to his jobs at BEA and then Oracle. But we all share the same enthusiasm and passion for Spring technologies and for anything that can help us build better software. Arnaud remembers his first contact with Spring Dynamic Modules—he attended Costin Leau's (Spring Dynamic Modules' project lead) talk at SpringOne Europe in 2008. What could be more exciting for a Spring enthusiast than to be able to use Spring on the OSGi platform? At last, real, run-time modularity meets Spring! Unfortunately, there was not, at the time, much in the way of resources around Spring Dynamic Modules. That was when he met Thierry and they both went on to write a French book on Spring. In contrast, Andy in 2008 had already been working with Spring Dynamic Modules for a couple of years, having been involved with its original development and having used it extensively on several BEA products. It was later in 2009 that Manning Publications contacted Arnaud and Thierry to suggest writing a proposal for a Spring Dynamic Modules in Action book.

Working with Manning can be difficult: they have high standards for their books, and we had no idea how high the mountain would turn out to be when we wrote that proposal, which then passed a succession of reviews. Some reviewers were happy with it, but others were tough, like that Oracle guy, Andy Piper. But his remarks were constructive, and based on his feedback Manning suggested that he be involved in the writing process. After all, if you want something done right, you do it yourself! Having a native English speaker on the writing team also proved useful, as some say that the French accent comes across even in written text.

We have done our best to make this book as comprehensive and accessible as possible. We hope you'll benefit from our experience with the Spring Framework, OSGi, and in making both worlds cohabit as harmoniously as possible using Spring DM. We believe that these technologies are an important piece of the puzzle in bringing your applications closer to the mythical "perfect" program.

acknowledgments

We thank the team at Manning for their hard work through the process of writing the book. Michael Stephens first contacted us and helped us create the book proposal. Marjan Bace gave us the opportunity to write the book and provided us with valuable advice about its structure. Karen Tegtmeyer organized the reviews, which resulted in further improvements. Last, but not least, thanks to our development editor, Cynthia Kane, who helped us improve the book's writing and structure.

Thanks to all the reviewers who took the time to read the book and make constructive remarks about its content. Their feedback was essential in keeping us on the right track: David Dossot, Gildas Cuisinier, Jawher Moussa, John Guthrie, Peter Pavlovich, Jos Dirksen, Denys Kurylenko, Dmitry Sklyut, Edmon Begoli, Marco Ughetti, Deepak Vohra, Rob Harrop, and Jeroen Benckhuijsen.

This book is about an open source project, so it would not exist were it not for the efforts of the people who spent their time creating and making Spring Dynamic Modules live. Thanks to all the Spring DM team: Adrian Colyer, Hal Hildebrand, and, of course, Costin Leau, the project's lead. An open source project is also a community project, so thanks to everyone who contributed to the project by answering questions on the forum or by participating in the bug-tracking process. This also helped us to learn more about how people use Spring DM.

A very special thanks to Peter Kriens, the director of technology at the OSGi Alliance, who carefully reviewed the book and wrote the foreword.

Our technical proofreader, Loïc Simon, helped us produce a more accurate and polished book. Thank you for your contribution Loïc!

ARNAUD COGOLUÈGNES

Many thanks to all the people around me for their patience and understanding once I got absorbed in this project. Thanks to my manager at Zenika, Carl Azoury, who provided me with some time during my day-to-day job to work on the book. And thanks to Claire, who had the patience to put up with my writing two books in a row.

THIERRY TEMPLIER

I am grateful to my beloved wife Séverine for her confidence and her support and for being by my side in life.

ANDY PIPER

Being involved in Spring DM from the start has been a wild ride, and I thank (again) the gang at SpringSource for their help and patience with my sometimes strange requirements, in particular Rod Johnson and Adrian Colyer, who have always been professional, courteous, and friendly in our interactions. My fellow authors, Arnaud and Thierry—who did the bulk of the writing—were invaluable with their contributions and intelligent insight; I could not have done it without them. Thanks also to Oracle for giving me sufficient time for the project. Finally, my gratitude extends to my long-suffering family for putting up with my many projects, although I can't promise this will be my last book!

about this book

Spring Dynamic Modules is a technology that bridges the gap between the Spring Framework and OSGi, combining the simplicity and power of Spring with the modularity, flexibility, and dynamism of OSGi. Spring hardly needs any introduction, being the framework of choice for a significant segment of the Enterprise Java development market. OSGi, in contrast, although not a new technology is one that is just becoming mainstream, helped in no small part by Spring DM.

Spring Dynamic Modules in Action is a cookbook for using Spring DM, but it also serves as a primer for both of the technologies that Spring DM combines. Deciding what we thought you should know, what we thought you might not know but which was essential to further understanding, and what you didn't know (you are reading this book, after all!) proved quite tricky. In the end, we decided to cover the basics of Spring, because some readers will be OSGi users wanting to understand Spring DM, and we decided to provide a little more detail on OSGi, because many more readers will be Spring users wanting to understand Spring DM. If you are comfortable with either or both of these technologies, you can safely skip over the first couple of chapters.

Another problem for us was the breadth of technologies covered by Spring that could be supported in an OSGi environment. There are already numerous books covering Spring in general, and also particular elements of the "Spring portfolio." As a result, in chapters dealing with these technologies we've focused on *how to make them work* using Spring DM, rather than offering a more general discussion of the features offered by the technologies. Likewise, some of the features of Spring DM support OSGi features (such as compendium services), the scope of which is too broad to be covered in this book. So again we have limited ourselves to describing the feature briefly and then focusing on its use in Spring DM. If you read these sections and find you want to know more, rest assured that further information is freely available in the various Spring reference manuals (www.springframework.org) and the OSGi set of specifications (www.osgi.org).

The main exception to this general approach is the discussion of web applications. Spring DM 1.2 includes extensive support for web applications, and we felt that the topic deserved a greater depth of coverage. But as with all new technologies, the state of the art can move very quickly, and when we were halfway through writing this book, the web support was deprecated for Spring DM 2.0 in favor of RFC 66 as implemented by Spring dm Server. Then, toward the end of the writing process, the Eclipse Gemini project was started, with Spring DM moving to this project; right at the end, dm Server itself was transitioned to Gemini as the Eclipse Virgo project. This technological shape-shifting would have been impossible to track accurately in the book, so we finally decided to stay with our discussion of Spring DM 1.2.

Because this is an "in Action" book, we have striven to provide code and configuration examples throughout, both to illustrate the concepts and to provide a template for successful operation.

Who should read this book

Our primary target audience for this book is Spring developers and architects who want to discover what OSGi can do. Spring Dynamic Modules is about using Spring in an OSGi runtime environment, so if you want to write Spring-based applications on the OSGi platform, this is the book for you.

But we aren't so naive as to assume that everyone is working on enterprise applications using Spring; some people have been using OSGi for years, creating all kinds of applications, and they may have barely heard about the Spring Framework—the popular dependency-injection framework that has helped developers build so many applications. So the reverse is also true: if you want to build OSGi applications using the Spring Framework, this book is also for you!

Roadmap

The book is divided into three parts. The first covers the basics of Spring DM, Spring, and OSGi. The second part forms the core of the discussion of Spring DM's features. The final part covers more advanced topics, including advanced configuration, testing, and the Blueprint specification. We also included several appendixes covering tooling support for Spring DM development.

Chapter 1 discusses Java modularity in general—after all, OSGi and Spring DM are primarily technologies that enable modularity—and also Spring, OSGI, and Spring DM. The concepts covered are reinforced in later chapters, so if you want to get the flavor of the whole book, chapter 1 is a good place to start.

Chapter 2 is an OSGi primer, and it introduces the main building blocks of OSGi: bundles, wiring, and services. It also covers topics such as native code and error handling.

Chapter 3 then relates OSGi concepts to an overview of Spring DM features, covering the main facets such as the application context, dependencies, Spring extender, osgi namespace, container provisioning, fragment configuration, and application development using Maven.

Chapter 4 covers the operation of the two extenders that Spring DM provides: the standard extender and the web extender.

Chapter 5 covers the use of OSGi services with Spring DM. Because service support is integral to the feature set provided by Spring DM, this chapter is one of the pivotal chapters of the book.

Chapter 6 covers the development of enterprise applications using Spring DM and, in particular, how to design and structure applications of this type to take advantage of all the power that Spring DM and OSGi provide. The chapter also covers the integration of third-party enterprise libraries into an OSGi environment.

Chapter 7 covers the use of JDBC and JPA in Spring DM-enabled applications.

Chapter 8 covers the use of common web frameworks in Spring DM-enabled applications.

Chapter 9 covers some advanced topics, including configuration of the Spring DM container and some Spring DM patterns that have proved useful in real products that use Spring DM.

Chapter 10 covers the testing of OSGi applications that use Spring DM.

Chapter 11 discusses Spring DM's support for OSGi compendium services, in particular configuration admin and eventing.

Chapter 12 covers the OSGi Blueprint specification and its relationship to Spring DM.

Code

The source code for the example applications in this book has been donated to the Apache Software Foundation. This source code is available at http://code.google.com/p/springdm-in-action/ and is also freely available from Manning's website, www.manning.com/SpringDynamicModulesinAction.

Much of the source code shown in the book consists of fragments designed to illustrate the text. When a complete segment of code is given, it is shown as a numbered listing; code annotations accompany some listings. When we present source code, we sometimes use a bold font to draw attention to specific elements.

In the text, Courier typeface is used to denote code (Java and XML) as well as Java methods, XML element names, and other source code identifiers:

- A reference to a method in the text will generally not include the signature, because there may be more than one form of the method call.
- A reference to an XML element in the text will include the braces but not the properties or closing tag (for example, <action>).

Author online

Purchase of *Spring Dynamic Modules in Action* includes free access to a private web forum run by Manning Publications where you can make comments about the book, ask technical questions, and receive help from the lead author and from other users. To access the forum and subscribe to it, point your web browser to www.manning.com/SpringDynamicModulesinAction. This page provides information on how to get on the forum once you are registered, what kind of help is available, and the rules of conduct on the forum.

Manning's commitment to our readers is to provide a venue where a meaningful dialogue between individual readers and between readers and the author can take place. It is not a commitment to any specific amount of participation on the part of the author, whose contribution to the AO remains voluntary (and unpaid). We suggest you try asking the author some challenging questions lest his interest stray! The Author Online forum and the archives of previous discussions will be accessible from the publisher's website as long as the book is in print.

about the authors

ARNAUD COGOLUÈGNES is a software developer, Java EE architect, and author with deep expertise in middleware, software engineering, and Spring technologies. Arnaud spent a number of years developing complex business applications, integrating Java-based products, and dispensing training on the Java platform.

THIERRY TEMPLIER is coauthor of two French books on Spring and JavaScript and contributed to the Spring Framework through its support for JCA and Lucene. He is a Java EE and Web2 architect and MDE expert with 10 years of experience. He develops rich internet applications combining Spring, OSGi, JPA, and GWT based on Spring DM.

ANDY PIPER is a software architect with Oracle Corporation working on Oracle's event-driven suite of products, a Java software stack based on OSGi, Spring, and Spring DM technologies. Prior to working for Oracle, Andy was open source architect at BEA systems looking at open source technologies such as Spring and core architect for WebLogic Server. Andy was responsible for many of WebLogic's enterprise-class features, such as clustering, RMI, IIOP, and HA technologies. Andy is a committer on the Spring DM project and holds a PhD in distributed computing from Cambridge University, England.

about the title

By combining introductions, overviews, and how-to examples, the *In Action* books are designed to help learning and remembering. According to research in cognitive science, the things people remember best are the things they discover during self-motivated exploration.

Although no one at Manning is a cognitive scientist, we are convinced that for learning to become permanent, it must pass through stages of exploration, play, and, interestingly, retelling of what is being learned. People understand and remember new things, which is to say they master them, only after actively exploring them. Humans learn in action. An essential part of an *In Action* book is that it is example-driven. It encourages the reader to try things out, play with new code, and explore new ideas.

There is another, more mundane, reason for the title of this book: our readers are busy. They use books to do a job or solve a problem. They need books that allow them to jump in and jump out easily and learn just what they want just when they want it. They need books that aid them in action. The books in this series are designed for such readers.

about the cover illustration

The figure on the cover of *Spring Dynamic Modules in Action* is an "Alkar" from the small town of Sinj in Croatia. The Alka is an equestrian tournament held in Sinj every first Sunday in August since 1715, commemorating the definitive victory of the region over the invasions of the Ottoman Empire. Alka is also the name of the object used in the tournament, which is made of concentric iron rings connected with three bars, and hung on a rope above the race track. Over a course of three rounds, the ceremonially dressed contestants, called alkars, ride their horses down the track at full gallop and attempt to thread the central ring of the alka with their spears. Points are scored depending on precision and which part of the alka the contestant pins. The victor is celebrated as a bold hero and knight.

The illustration is from a recent reproduction of a book of Croatian dress customs, *Characterization and Description of Southwestern Wende, Illyrians and Slavs*, by Balthasar Hacquet, originally published around 1800. The illustrations were obtained from a helpful librarian at the Ethnographic Museum in Split, Croatia, located in the Roman core of the medieval center of the town, amid the ruins of Emperor Diocletian's retirement palace built circa AD 304.

Dress codes and lifestyles have changed over the last 200 years, and the diversity by region, so rich at the time, has faded. It is now hard to distinguish the inhabitants of different continents, let alone of hamlets or towns separated by a few miles. Perhaps we have traded cultural diversity for a more varied personal life—certainly for a more varied and fast-paced technological life.

Manning celebrates the inventiveness and initiative of the computer business with book covers based on the rich diversity of regional life of two centuries ago, brought alive by illustrations from old books like this one.

Part 1

Spring DM basics

Welcome to *Spring Dynamic Modules in Action*. Spring Dynamic Modules—a synthesis of Spring and OSGi-is the technology that can help you write better, more beautiful, programs. In these first three chapters, we are going to discuss the basics of all three technologies—Spring, OSGi, and Spring DM—and by the end you should have a good idea of why these technologies can help address the thorny problems associated with unmodular applications.

In chapter 1, we cover the concepts of Java modularity in general—since Spring DM and OSGi are primarily technologies that enabled modularity—the specifics of the Spring Framework, and the features of OSGi. We then move on to show you where Spring DM fits in, and how its approach and its features simplify the development of standard Java applications in an OSGi environment. The concepts covered are reinforced in later chapters, so if you want to get the flavor of the whole book, chapter 1 is a good place to start.

Chapter 2 is an OSGi primer, focusing on how you can take advantage of OSGi technology within your Java applications. It introduces the main building blocks of OSGi: bundles, wiring, and services.

At last, in chapter 3, we are ready to get down to the main business of Spring DM. There is a lot to learn and we introduce all of the main features and concepts here—dependency injection, extenders, writing bundles container provisioning, fragment configuration, and application development using Maven.

In part 2 we delve deeper into the main features of core Spring DM, covering each in a good amount of detail.

In part 3 we look at some more advanced topics surrounding the use of Spring DM.

Modular development with Spring and OSGi

This chapter covers

- Java's limitations regarding modularity
- How OSGi builds on Java for better modularity
- How OSGi and Spring are complementary solutions

Spring DM—or Spring Dynamic Modules for OSGi Service Platforms, as it's more formally called—is about using the Spring programming model in OSGi applications. If you're a Java programmer, you have probably heard of, or used, Spring—the dependency injection framework for Java. But what about OSGi? This dynamic module system for Java may be less familiar; but no matter, Spring DM is about OSGi for the masses, providing OSGi's modularity features in a neat Spring-shaped package. You don't need to get too involved in the nitty-gritty of OSGi to benefit from its features.

In this book, we'll describe what Spring DM is, how to use it, and more importantly how to *benefit* from it. Because Spring DM is not only about using modular Java systems to get things to work—it's about getting them to work well. We'll also look at some of the implementation challenges involved in using Spring DM, challenges that boil down to OSGi's strict classloading model. For instance, using object/relational mapping (ORM) tools or creating web applications can seem daunting in an OSGi environment, but never fear—we're here to help!

In this chapter, after having covered the concepts of modularity, the specifics of the Spring Framework, and the features of OSGi, we'll show you where Spring DM fits in, and how its approach and its features simplify the development of standard Java applications in an OSGi environment. If you're already familiar with OSGi and Spring, you can skip the next few sections and go to section 1.4, which introduces Spring DM.

1.1 Java modularity

We all fall in love with abstraction sooner or later. Abstract data types, polymorphism, and encapsulation—these are all ideas that appeal to the engineers in us and mesh neatly with the old adage of keeping it simple, stupid. No man is an island, however, and code is no different. No matter how beautiful your code—and let's face it, we all like to think we write beautiful code—it eventually has to interact with other code.

In this book, you'll learn how Spring DM and its OSGi substrate can be used to address the problems caused by unmanageable spaghetti code. But before we get to the cool technology, it's worth reviewing what we mean by modularity and the kind of problems modular software is designed to solve.

1.1.1 What is modularity and what is it good for?

A modular application is, in essence, one that's divided into several pieces with the connections between the pieces being controlled and well defined. It's this limit on connections that reduces the impact of change and markedly improves things like testability.

But what is a *connection*? What creates connections, and how do you reduce them? The answers are clearly contingent upon technology, which in our case is Java.

1.1.2 Java—the end and the beginning

Java is great. We would argue it's the best general-purpose programming language ever developed, for it addresses many of the deficiencies of languages that went before it. The first step toward modularity lies in the object-oriented features that the Java language offers: splitting applications into classes and enforcing encapsulation with interfaces and visibility modifiers (`private`, `protected`, and so on). That's a good step, but it isn't enough.

Java EE also acknowledged the need for composite applications by introducing several kinds of deployment units: the Java Archive (JAR), which is the most common, but also the Web Archive (WAR) and the Enterprise Archive (EAR). But these archives, particularly the web and the enterprise ones, only allow you to split your application into coarse-grained components; they do nothing to enforce the program architecture that you know is required. This is a good step, but, again, it isn't enough, especially for large, complex systems and systems that need to be extensible or that want to promote reusability.

Are we facing a hopeless situation? We've been using Java for years, telling ourselves we're developing well-designed applications. Was that a lie, or were we just daydreaming?

1.1.3   Are your applications really modular?

Why should we care about *real* modularity? Isn't there enough modularity in plain Java? And what would be the value proposition of modularity in any shape or form?

At stake is building robust, maintainable systems. Anyone can write and maintain Hello World, but no system is as simple as Hello World, and many are at the opposite extreme in terms of complexity. The drive toward ever more complex systems is inevitable in the digitally connected world that we now live in, but that complexity is now not something any individual can handle. Just as there are really no "renaissance men" today—the world of science is simply too broad and deep—complete understanding of today's systems is beyond even the most talented.

So for the question, "Are your applications really modular?" you should already know the answer—it will be defined by the degree of pain you feel when trying to make changes, or the degree of slippage you experience when trying to develop new functionality. If you don't know, the answer is almost certainly "no." That may not matter if you're a lone developer or part of a small team, but beware—small programs have a funny way of getting bigger quickly, and it's much easier to keep things in order than it is to untangle them after the fact.

By now you should understand what we mean by modularity and appreciate the need for modularity in Java systems. But, practically speaking, how do we make Java systems more modular? Part of the answer is in their design: finding the correct granularity, creating the components, and making them work together in a loosely coupled way. This is what the Spring Framework is all about: decoupling and assembling components.

1.2   The Spring Framework

Spring is a layered application framework and lightweight container, the foundations of which are described in *Expert One-on-One J2EE Design and Development* by Rod Johnson (Wrox, 2002). The Spring project itself started in 2003.

The lightweight container and the *aspect-oriented programming* (AOP) system are the main building blocks of Spring. Besides these, Spring provides a common abstraction layer for transaction management, integration with various persistence solutions (plain JDBC, Hibernate, JPA) as well as with Java enterprise technologies (JMS and JMX). The Spring Framework isn't an all-or-nothing solution; you can choose the modules according to your needs, the lightweight container being the glue for the application and the Spring classes.

The Spring Framework is now widely used in Java enterprise applications and well documented in books like Manning's *Spring in Action* by Craig Walls, a third edition of which will be published in fall 2010. We'll see in this section the building blocks of the Spring Framework: its lightweight container, which makes dependency injection a breeze, and its support for AOP and for the development of enterprise applications.

We'll start immediately by looking at the loosely coupled component model the Spring Framework promotes.

1.2.1   *Loose coupling of classes*

Loose coupling is the first step on the road that leads to true modular programming. Any object-oriented system is made up of components interacting with each other. They must be as independent as possible, or one change in the system can trigger cascading changes.

Imagine one of your business services needs to notify other components that a new user has been created. The following snippet illustrates a tightly coupled solution (you should not do this!):

```
public class BusinessServiceImpl implements BusinessService {
  private JmsNotifier jmsNotifier;

  public void createUser(User user) {
    ...
    jmsNotifier.notify("User created");
  }

}
```

Why can the previous snippet be considered tightly coupled? The reason is that the notification technology is concretely defined using the JmsNotifier property. This tells us that the BusinessServiceImpl class can't be used or even tested without a Java Message Service (JMS) container. Reuse of the BusinessService with another type of notification technology or even without notification at all wouldn't be an easy task.

The BusinessServiceImpl class can easily be decoupled from the notification by introducing a Notifier interface instead of using an implementation. The following snippet shows this solution:

```
public class BusinessServiceImpl implements BusinessService {
  private Notifier notifier;

  public void createUser(User user) {
    ...
    notifier.notify("User created");
  }

}
```

In this snippet, the notification concept is embodied by the Notifier interface, without any reference to the underlying technology. Thanks to this abstraction, the BusinessServiceImpl can now easily be reused with any kind of notification (email, JMS, and so on), the only requirement being to implement the Notifier interface. Figure 1.1 shows how we moved from a tightly coupled solution to a loosely coupled one.

Now in BusinessServiceImpl, the notification concept is a simple dependency. The next problem is to assign the right Notifier implementation. This is where dependency injection comes in and we let an external system assemble all the application components.

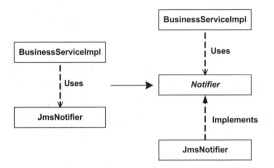

Figure 1.1 Introducing an interface helps in moving from a tightly to a loosely coupled solution. The question now is how can we get the right implementation and stay loosely coupled?

1.2.2 *Dependency injection*

Dependency injection is all about creating, configuring, and wiring components. The system in charge of doing this assembling is called a lightweight container. With a container managing their dependencies for them, components don't need to concern themselves with lookups. Rod Johnson calls it the *Hollywood Principle*—"don't call us, we'll call you."

Figure 1.2 illustrates how this container can manage and wire together our components. Notice that the container API doesn't leak to our application classes.

Typically, there are a number of ways to configure the component wiring, ranging from XML files to Java annotations to plain text. The Spring lightweight container offers a rich set of features to do the wiring; the following snippet illustrates the XML-based configuration for our business service and its `Notifier` dependency.

```
<beans (...)>
  <bean id="notifier"
        class="foo.bar.notify.JmsNotifier" />

  <bean id="businessService"
    class="for.bar.service.impl.BusinessServiceImpl">
    <property name="notifier" ref="notifier" />
  </bean>
</beans>
```

Injects notifier into business service

The container takes care of each step of a component's creation (instantiation and wiring), leaving it with no dependencies on any callable class or interface such as a

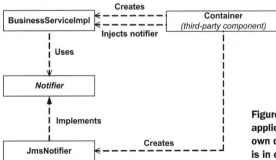

Figure 1.2 When using dependency injection, application classes don't need to look up their own dependencies—the lightweight container is in charge of assembling the components.

factory. In Spring terminology, the container is referred to as the *application context* or simply the *context*.

Dependency injection is a simple yet rather powerful pattern. Combined with interface-based programming, it allows you to write more testable and less tightly coupled code. Component management (creation and wiring) can then be delegated to lightweight containers, such as Spring. The Spring Framework can be a great help in your OSGi development: the lightweight container assembles the inner elements of your modules, and Spring DM will take over to make them interact easily with the OSGi platform.

The POJO programming model set me free!

The acronym POJO stands for *Plain Old Java Object*. A POJO is a regular Java object without any dependencies on framework interfaces or classes. Frameworks like Spring and Hibernate promoted the POJO programming model when standards like EJB 2.x were heavily relying on technical APIs. The main benefits of using POJO are simplicity and testability. In a way, POJO set us free from intrusive technical frameworks.

With full control over the component lifecycle, lightweight containers can do much more than wire components together. We'll see this in a second with AOP.

1.2.3   *Aspect-oriented programming (AOP)*

In traditional object-oriented programming (OOP), components are loosely coupled and each has its own responsibilities. Nevertheless, components often require additional features beyond the basic ones they're meant to provide. These features are usually related to system services, such as security, logging, or resource management and are called *cross-cutting concerns* because they tend to cut across components or application layers. You can deal modularly with these cross-cutting concerns by using aspect-oriented programming and transparently relieving your OOP components from dealing with them directly.

In AOP, the unit of modularity is called an *aspect* and deals with one cross-cutting concern (the unit of modularity in OOP is the class). Figure 1.3 illustrates the transition from a pure object-oriented solution to a solution using both object- and aspect-oriented programming. Notice how the business code is tangled up with cross-cutting concerns such as logging and security in the completely object-oriented solution. By using AOP, cross-cutting concerns are deported to dedicated aspects, and application code doesn't have to deal with them anymore.

With AOP components, the developer can focus on their core tasks, then the aspects can be easily reused in any situation. In this way, AOP isn't meant to replace OOP but rather complements it.

By managing components, Spring is able to apply aspects to them. The action of applying aspects is called *weaving*. Different ways of weaving exist, the simplest being using a proxy in place of the target component. Proxy weaving can be achieved with

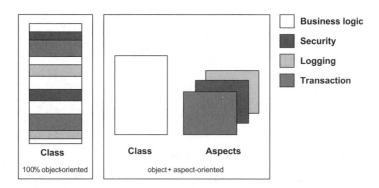

Figure 1.3 With a completely object-oriented solution, business code becomes tangled and cross-cutting concerns are scattered all through the application. AOP helps modularize cross-cutting concerns in their own programming units, allowing for cleaner business code.

standard Java features, as long as you stick to interface programming. Each call to the target is intercepted by the proxy, and any aspect can be called before or after the call is delegated to the target.

AOP pushes modularization a step further, but in a different way than traditional OOP does. AOP appears tricky at first glance, but, in a Spring-managed environment, it's just a matter of XML (or annotation) configuration. The Spring Framework provides AOP features out of the box: the lightweight container has full control over the components, so it can weave them with aspects after their initialization. Because Spring DM builds a bridge between the Spring Framework and OSGi, you'll get AOP automatically in your OSGi developments.

Now that you've seen the main benefits of the Spring lightweight container, we'll study what the framework can bring to enterprise developments.

1.2.4 Enterprise support

Besides its lightweight container and AOP features, the Spring Framework provides support for a number of Java and Java EE standards and frameworks. Although these libraries are self-sufficient, configuring and combining them in an application can turn out to be tricky, largely due to their configuration subtleties; Spring is able to handle configuration for the most common cases, leaving you with very simple configuration steps to perform. If you're more comfortable with the target framework or use less conventional features, all the regular configuration settings are still available through Spring configuration.

Spring support is particularly useful in the data access area, with its common abstraction layer for transactions and its template-based approach to persistence. Spring deals with common resource management "plumbing" code and allows for declarative transaction management in various situations ranging from managed environments with JTA (Java Transaction API, the transaction standard in Java) to native database transaction with plain JDBC. Declarative transaction management is made possible through Spring AOP support and can be applied to any kind of component.

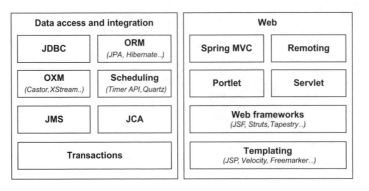

Figure 1.4   In addition to supplying the lightweight container, Spring provides support for classic enterprise application scenarios and supports many Java frameworks in a consistent way.

It has no impact on application code, and switching from one environment to another is a matter of configuration. Application components can focus on their primary task and don't even know they're fully transactional.

Transaction management and data access are only a few of the common use cases that the Spring Framework provides support for. Figure 1.4 shows that Spring support extends to a number of other technologies.

Spring and its philosophy should no longer be a stranger to you, and it should be clear that Spring is the first step toward modularity. We'll see in the next section how the OSGi technology pushes the Java platform to its limits to offer *true* modularity.

1.3   *A new approach to modular development with OSGi*

As we asserted at the beginning of the chapter, modularity and reusability are key issues in the development of any reasonably sized application, but the Java platform doesn't provide complete support at this level. OSGi is a technology that makes it possible to tackle these problems head-on in Java applications. OSGi relies heavily on Java's different features and operating mechanisms, and in particular the classloader feature.

This section provides an overview of OSGi, and chapter 2 gives a more comprehensive introduction. But if you want in-depth coverage of OSGi, you should read Manning's *OSGi in Action*, by Richard S. Hall, Karl Pauls, Stuart McCulloch, and David Savage, to be published in fall 2010.

We understand that you're stamping with impatience to learn about Spring DM, but if you're totally new to OSGi, you'll first need to understand the benefit of the bridge that Spring DM provides.

1.3.1   *Aims of OSGi*

OSGi addresses Java's limitations regarding modularity in four ways:

- It defines exactly what a module is (Java defines only deployment units, like JAR or WAR).
- It provides ways to finely set visibility rules between modules.
- It defines the lifecycle of a module (a module can be installed, started, stopped, and so on).
- It lets modules interact with each other via services.

OSGi is divided into a set of layers, each of which provides a brick in the modularity wall. The next section gives an overview of this layered architecture.

1.3.2 *OSGi layers*

OSGi provides a standardized environment that is divided into different layers, as shown in figure 1.5. Each layer has a role in making the OSGi platform modular: enforcing visibility rules between modules, making modules evolve through a set of states, and providing a broker for modules to communicate with each other. Every OSGi container is based on the Java virtual machine (JVM) and specifically implements three layers that enable support for dynamic modularity.

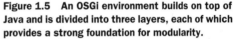

Figure 1.5   An OSGi environment builds on top of Java and is divided into three layers, each of which provides a strong foundation for modularity.

MODULE LAYER

The first container layer, the modules layer, is responsible for handling components. Its main goal is to provide modularity based on the Java platform. The key building block for this layer is the module or component, which in OSGi is called a *bundle*.

The module layer enforces visibility rules between modules, and it achieves this thanks to strict classloader isolation. By default, a component is really a black box in OSGi. If you want to make things visible, you need to specify them explicitly; conversely, when using classes, the required packages must be specified as being visible before you can reference them from other bundles.

OSGi bundles are standard JAR files, with additional metadata in their manifest file that aims at (among other things) identifying them and configuring the visibility rules. The following snippet shows an excerpt of the manifest file of an OSGi bundle, with OSGi headers that identify the module (`Bundle-Name`, `Bundle-Version`, and `Bundle-SymbolicName`) and set visibility rules between the current module and the other modules (`Export-Package` and `Import-Package`):

```
Bundle-Name: Spring OSGi Bundle
Bundle-Version: 1.0
Bundle-SymbolicName: com.manning.spring.osgi.simple
Export-Package: com.manning.spring.osgi.simple.service
Import-Package: com.manning.spring.osgi.utils
```

So the module layer enforces modularity; now let's see how the lifecycle layer defines a set of states the modules can evolve through.

LIFECYCLE LAYER

A developer can install a bundle in an OSGi container; this is the first state a bundle can take: "installed". Then, based on the container's default settings, commands issued through an administration console, or even programmatic calls, the newly installed bundle can transition through different states. It can, for example, be resolved, meaning that all its dependencies are met and that it can now make some its own Java packages visible to other modules. There are several states available in OSGi, and section 2.1.4 of chapter 2 describes them all.

The lifecycle layer relies on the module layer for classloading and provides a dynamic approach to bundle management, making it possible to update parts of an application without stopping it. When a bundle gets to the active state, it's then able to interact with the service registry, powered by the top layer of OSGi.

SERVICE REGISTRY LAYER

The service registry is an important part of OSGi because it allows bundles to be used and to interact in a way that takes the dynamic nature of the system into account. Through the service registry, OSGi offers the ability to register one or several access points to components through services. Figure 1.6 shows how modules can communicate by registering and consuming services.

The service layer programming model is POJO- and interface-driven: modules only expose what they need to expose in terms of services, making them more loosely coupled.

1.3.3   *What OSGi offers*

To summarize, OSGi provides a foundation for developing component- and service-based solutions. It implements components through a strict classloader and dependency versioning scheme. It also provides a platform that follows all the principles of service-oriented architectures in a particularly lightweight way and directly within a JVM.

The strength of this solution is that OSGi enables the implementation of all these mechanisms in a dynamic way. Indeed, the platform provides the mechanisms necessary to manage components at runtime and to dynamically interact with the service registry to both publish and consume services without stopping and restarting the

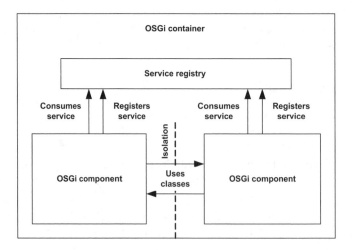

Figure 1.6   Thanks to the service registry, modules can publish and consume services. They can then communicate in a loosely coupled manner, which enforces modularity.

whole container. By using OSGi, monolithic Java EE applications can be split into modules and can leverage the dynamic updates of some of their inner parts. These dynamic aspects also create new issues, because application features must now take into account the varying presence of entities or services.

The OSGi technology fills the lack of modularity in Java applications by providing a complete and lightweight platform for implementing component-based and service-oriented applications within a JVM. Let's see now how Spring DM fits into that.

1.4 *Using Spring in an OSGi environment with Spring DM*

We described in the previous section the characteristics of Spring and OSGi and saw that they address a complementary set of features. That background is important for understanding where Spring DM fits into the mix. Now we're ready to see how it's possible to use Spring technologies in an OSGi environment.

1.4.1 *What is Spring DM?*

Spring DM provides a powerful modular solution for developing Spring-based applications that can be deployed in an OSGi execution environment. The aim of the technology is both to make Spring and OSGi work together in a simple way as well as addressing the limitations of the two technologies.

Figure 1.7 shows where Spring DM fits in and how it's the bridge between components, the service registry, and embedded web containers. This figure gives a high-level picture of how Spring DM both allows the embedding of the Spring container within OSGi components and the use of web technology inside an OSGi container.

Why would we want to use Spring DM? Namely to make two different but complementary technologies work together. Let's discuss the limitations of both to justify their complementarity.

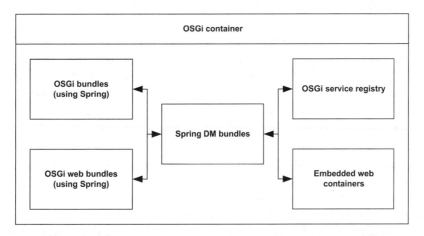

Figure 1.7   Spring DM is composed of a set of OSGi bundles that become part of the infrastructure when installed in an OSGi container. They can then manage a Spring application context for bundles or even start a web container inside the OSGi container.

Despite the benefits of the Spring Framework described in section 1.2, it suffers from several drawbacks in particular use cases. The first one occurs when trying to scale up to large and complex applications. In this case, a lot of beans need to be configured within the Spring container, making its configuration more difficult to maintain. In addition, Spring suffers from a lack of modularity and provides no real support to improve this. For example, there's no way to limit the visibility of a bean in Spring; any other bean can use it, and it can be looked up from the application context even if it should not be used directly. Although you can divide your configuration into several XML files, they all serve to configure a single application context, and the alternative—integrating several Spring containers—can be difficult to achieve. (Using more than one application context could allow you to split an application into modules more easily, creating clearer boundaries between these modules.)

Another limitation of Spring is the static nature of its dependency graph configured using dependency injection. As soon as bean A is injected into bean B, bean B depends on A. An application may have hundreds of beans, and these dependencies between beans form a dependency graph. The limitation arises because the links between beans are created once, mainly at the startup of the container, and there is no built-in support to update them at runtime. To reload the dependency graph and take any updates into account, the whole application needs to be restarted.

This problem of static coupling is made worse by issues with the instantiation order of beans. Spring computes a complex dependency graph to determine the order in which beans will be instantiated and injected. This computation is internal to Spring, and application developers can't get their hands on it. If something goes wrong, debugging can be particularly complex, especially when you have a lot of dependencies. Furthermore, there is very limited support for circular dependencies, putting an even heavier burden on developers to configure their beans correctly.

On the other side of the table, the OSGi core specification doesn't provide any support for patterns or tools in the design and implementation of bundles. This is by design, leaving the developer free to choose a suitable architecture and the framework. Using a framework like Spring can really enhance the power of the platform because it enables the use of dependency injection, AOP, and other modern paradigms. But "here be dragons" because there are obvious challenges in managing the disparate lifecycles of both Spring and OSGi bundles.

Another challenge in using OSGi relates to the explicit configuration and dynamic behavior of services. Services are essential in creating any OSGi application because they're the only safe way to access functionality across bundle boundaries. But using the service management API is tedious, and managing the dynamic nature of services in user code is extremely error prone.

We can see that the two technologies appear to be mutually complementary, with the whole being potentially greater than the sum of the parts. This is where Spring DM fits in.

Spring DM and SpringSource dm Server

We should mention in passing that Spring DM is *not* SpringSource dm Server, although the names sound similar. dm Server is a full-stack application server that leverages Spring DM and OSGi as its modular kernel, but provides many more features on top of these, including tooling, deployment, and management. Spring DM is a *framework*, not a runtime environment.

1.4.2 Embedding Spring within an OSGi container

Spring DM is a framework, made of a set of OSGi bundles that can be deployed in any OSGi container. These bundles don't bring any business features to an OSGi application; instead, they aim at watching other bundles and creating Spring application contexts for them. This is why Spring DM is sometimes called a bridge between Spring applications and OSGi. Let's see more about how Spring DM achieves that.

SPRING MANAGEMENT WITH SPRING DM

Let's now focus on how Spring DM makes it easy to work with Spring within OSGi. In a classical Spring application, a dedicated Spring container is used, and the framework is configured from its enclosing contexts (from the classpath or web environment). The framework also provides a hierarchical relationship between application contexts while tying them together. With Spring DM, things work slightly differently. A dedicated Spring container is associated with each Spring DM–powered bundle. Each container is unconnected with the rest and is internal to its enclosing bundle. Logically speaking, having separate containers is mandatory because each bundle has its own lifecycle and can appear or disappear at any time.

Spring DM manages all of these containers in a convenient and nonintrusive way. No code or configuration is required inside a bundle to configure, start, or destroy a Spring container. All that's required is that Spring DM's bundles are installed in the OSGi container, and that the bundle includes a Spring application context configuration file. The Spring DM bundle in charge of managing Spring-powered bundles is called the Spring DM *extender.* Figure 1.8 illustrates these mechanisms.

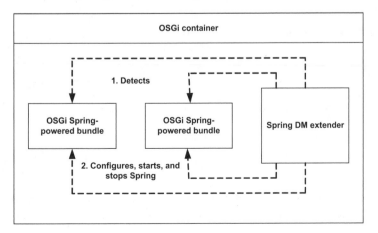

Figure 1.8 The Spring DM extender is an OSGi bundle that scans bundles for Spring configuration files and manages (creates, destroys, and updates) a Spring application context on their behalf.

Spring DM monitors the bundle lifecycle in order to determine when to trigger the appropriate actions. Once Spring DM is deployed inside an OSGi container, it can automatically detect Spring-powered components based on the presence of the Spring application context configuration file as well as through certain dedicated headers in the manifest file of the bundle. When a bundle with the appropriate configuration is started, a Spring container is also configured and embedded inside the component. By doing this, Spring DM implements the Extender pattern.

OSGI SERVICE SUPPORT WITHIN SPRING DM

As well as managing the creation of Spring containers, Spring DM also provides a convenient way to link bundles using the OSGi service registry. In any OSGi application, simply using package imports and exports isn't sufficient because these only specify the behavior of class *linkages* within the application; they do nothing to manage the lifecycle of object *instances* created from these classes. This is what makes the OSGi service registry so essential—it provides a well-defined boundary through which object instances can be accessed while still maintaining appropriate class and lifecycle boundaries.

Think of it as being a bit like the old English class system: servants were never allowed to speak directly with the master of the house; instead they had to interact through the butler or another go-between. It did not matter what the servants looked like, or even whether they were the same servants from one day to the next; the facilities provided to the master of the house were always the same, and hidden behind the austere demeanor of Jeeves or his counterpart. Where Spring DM improves upon the services of the butler—or the service registry, in our case—is that it provides a very easy and declarative way to configure and reference services from within the Spring configuration itself, even allowing dependency injection of artifacts from the service registry.

The heart of this configuration is a dedicated Spring XML namespace. Thanks to this mechanism, simple POJOs can be exposed as OSGi services, and OSGi services can be injected into regular Spring beans by using the appropriate elements. The following code snippet shows how to expose a bean named `myService` as an OSGi service using the `<osgi:service>` element. At the startup of the corresponding Spring container, the service is automatically registered, and it's unregistered when it's destroyed.

```
<?xml version="1.0" encoding="UTF-8"?>
<beans xmlns="http://www.springframework.org/schema/beans"           Exposes
    xmlns:osgi="http://www.springframework.org/schema/osgi"          myService
    (...)>                                                           bean as
                                                                    OSGi service
  <osgi:service ref="myService"
        interface="com.manning.spring.osgi.simple.MyService"/>       <┘
  <bean id="myService"
        class="com.manning.spring.osgi.simple.impl.MyServiceImpl"/>  <┐
</beans>
                                                          Defines POJO in Spring
                                                             XML configuration
```

The following snippet shows the other side of the service coin—referencing and using an OSGi service in a classic Spring bean through the use of the `<osgi:reference>`

element. This example shows a service named com.manning.spring.osgi.simple.
MyService being made available as a bean called myService and then being injected
into myBean.

```xml
<?xml version="1.0" encoding="UTF-8"?>
<beans xmlns="http://www.springframework.org/schema/beans"
       xmlns:osgi="http://www.springframework.org/schema/osgi"
       (...)>

  <osgi:reference id="myOSGIService"
        interface="com.manning.spring.osgi.simple.MyService"/>
  <bean id="myBean" class="com.manning.spring.osgi.simple.MyBean">
      <property name="service" ref="myOSGIService"/>
  </bean>
</beans>
```

> **Configures reference to OSGi service**

> **Injects OSGi service reference into service property**

Now you have a better idea of what Spring DM is. Let's see the benefits of using it
when writing OSGi applications.

1.4.3 Benefits of Spring DM for real-life OSGi applications

Spring DM allows Spring-based applications to be deployed as OSGi bundles. This
allows for true application modularity while still harnessing the power of the Spring
Framework. Spring DM also provides a semantically rich and user-friendly way of linking components by declaratively providing and consuming OSGi services. All these
aspects allow applications to take advantage of the dynamic nature of OSGi.

Spring DM addresses several issues in order to make it easier to use Spring within
an OSGi container:

- Enforces module boundaries and adds dynamics at runtime
- Detects and manages Spring-powered and web-powered bundles
- Enables transparent configuration, starting and stopping Spring containers
  inside Spring-powered bundles
- Provides facilities related to service management and use
- Transparently handles the dynamic aspects of OSGi

Another important thing to understand is that you aren't tied to a specific tool when
developing your OSGi components, not even Spring DM! You can interact with existing bundles using a variety of different technologies. Because links between bundles
are based on the OSGi-standard service registry, the service consumer doesn't know—
and doesn't care—what technology was used in the creation of the service.

In the same spirit as the design of the Spring Framework, Spring DM provides a
programming model based on best practices and patterns that enable you to use the
OSGi technology in an optimal and efficient way. This is especially true if you have an
enterprise application background: you'll be able to use your favorite libraries and
frameworks and the corresponding Spring support in your OSGi bundles.

Now that we've introduced all the background of Spring DM and the technologies
it leverages, it's time to see how to implement your first application.

1.5   *Spring DM Hello World*

Let's stick to old programming traditions by providing a Hello World example using Spring DM! Like any other Hello World application, the example will be simplistic but it'll show you enough of Spring DM to get the concepts.

The example consists of declaring a simple Java bean in a Spring application context and letting Spring DM handle the context creation when the bundle is deployed. The bean will emit the "Hello World" message at its creation. You'll see that Spring DM handles most of the dirty work—application context discovery and bean creation—and that you'll only have to write the bean class and create XML configuration files.

Before starting the example, take a look at table 1.1, which gives an overview of the various versions of Spring DM and their corresponding requirements and main features.

Table 1.1   Overview of Spring DM versions

Version	Requirements	Supported OSGi platforms	Description
2.0	Java 1.5+ Spring 3.0	OSGi R4 versions 4.0, 4.1, 4.2 Equinox 3.5.x Felix 2.x Knopflerfish 3.x	Blueprint (RFC 121) reference implementation
1.2	Java 1.4+ Spring 2.5.6	OSGi R4 versions 4.0, 4.1 Equinox 3.3.x Felix 1.4.x Knopflerfish 2.2.x	Support for compendium services
1.1	Java 1.4+ Spring 2.5.5	OSGi R4 versions 4.0, 4.1 Equinox 3.2.x Felix 1.0.x Knopflerfish 2.1.x	Web support
1.0	Java 1.4+ Spring 2.5.1	OSGi R4 versions 4.0, 4.1 Equinox 3.2.x Felix 1.0.x Knopflerfish 2.0.x	Standard extender for embedding a Spring application container in an OSGi bundle

You can choose the version that best suits your target environment (version of Java or Spring or supported OSGi platform). If you don't have any constraints, you should choose Spring DM 2.0 (the latest version at the time of this writing) because it provides the most features and benefits from the latest bug fixes. This is the version we'll be using throughout this book. Nevertheless, the Hello World example should work with any version.

1.5.1   *Provisioning the OSGi container*

The Hello World example will run in an OSGi container, and as you want to use Spring DM, you need to provision the container with Spring DM's bundles before creating your Spring-powered bundle. Most of the necessary bundles are in the Spring DM distribution, which you can download from http://www.springsource.org/osgi (be careful to download the "with-dependencies" version of the distribution). Once the download is complete, create a `hello-world-springdm` directory and copy org.eclipse.osgi-3.5.1.R35x_v20090827.jar from the lib directory of Spring DM distribution.

What does Eclipse, the famous Java IDE, have to do with an OSGi Hello World example? A lot, actually. Eclipse is *based* on OSGi and is built upon Equinox, the Eclipse Foundation OSGi container. The org.eclipse.osgi-3.5.1.R35x_v20090827.jar file contains Equinox and not the whole Eclipse IDE.

To launch Equinox, open a command line, go to the hello-world-springdm directory, and type the following command:

```
java -jar org.eclipse.osgi-3.5.1.R35x_v20090827.jar -console
```

An `osgi` command prompt appears. You can type the `ss` command (for *short status*) to learn about the container state and the installed bundles:

```
osgi> ss

Framework is launched.

id      State       Bundle
0       ACTIVE      org.eclipse.osgi_3.5.1.R35x_v20090827

osgi>
```

The only bundle is the container itself; it's now time to provision it with the Spring DM bundles. Type `exit` to stop Equinox.

Create a `bundles` directory at the root of your project, and copy all the necessary bundles listed in table 1.2.

Table 1.2 OSGi bundles for the Hello World project

JAR file	Origin
org.springframework.aop-3.0.0.RC1.jar	Spring DM distribution lib directory
org.springframework.asm-3.0.0.RC1.jar	Spring DM distribution lib directory
org.springframework.beans-3.0.0.RC1.jar	Spring DM distribution lib directory
org.springframework.context-3.0.0.RC1.jar	Spring DM distribution lib directory
org.springframework.context.support-3.0.0.RC1.jar	Spring DM distribution lib directory
org.springframework.core-3.0.0.RC1.jar	Spring DM distribution lib directory
org.springframework.expression-3.0.0.RC1.jar	Spring DM distribution lib directory
com.springsource.slf4j.api-1.5.6.jar	Spring DM distribution lib directory
com.springsource.slf4j.org.apache.commons.logging-1.5.6.jar	Spring DM distribution lib directory

Table 1.2   OSGi bundles for the Hello World project *(continued)*

JAR file	Origin
com.springsource.slf4j.nop-1.5.6.jar	SpringSource Enterprise Bundle Repository
com.springsource.org.aopalliance-1.0.0.jar	Spring DM distribution lib directory
spring-osgi-core-2.0.0.M1.jar	Spring DM distribution dist directory
spring-osgi-extender-2.0.0.M1.jar	Spring DM distribution dist directory
spring-osgi-io-2.0.0.M1.jar	Spring DM distribution dist directory

All bundles can be found in the Spring DM distribution except for one, the NOP SLF4J implementation. You can download it from the SpringSource Enterprise Bundle Repository (EBR) by following these steps:

1   Go to http://www.springsource.com/repository/app/.
2   Choose Advanced Search in the menu on the left.
3   Enter `slf4j.nop` in the Search field and `1.5.6` in the Version Range field.
4   Click on the Search button to launch the search.
5   Choose the "com.springsource.slf4j.nop 1.5.6" library in the search results.
6   In the Details page, click on the Binary Jar link to download the JAR file of the library.

When you first launched Equinox, it created a `configuration` directory, where it keeps runtime information between executions. It's now time to tell Equinox which bundles it has to install each time it starts. In the configuration directory, create a config.ini file with the following content:

```
osgi.bundles=bundles/org.springframework.aop-3.0.0.RC1.jar@start, \
bundles/org.springframework.asm-3.0.0.RC1.jar@start, \
bundles/org.springframework.beans-3.0.0.RC1.jar@start, \
bundles/org.springframework.context-3.0.0.RC1.jar@start, \
bundles/org.springframework.core-3.0.0.RC1.jar@start, \
bundles/org.springframework.expression-3.0.0.RC1.jar@start, \
bundles/spring-osgi-core-2.0.0.M1.jar@start, \
bundles/spring-osgi-extender-2.0.0.M1.jar@start, \
bundles/spring-osgi-io-2.0.0.M1.jar@start, \
bundles/com.springsource.org.aopalliance-1.0.0.jar@start, \
bundles/com.springsource.slf4j.api-1.5.6.jar@start, \
bundles/com.springsource.slf4j.nop-1.5.6.jar, \
bundles/com.springsource.slf4j.org.apache.commons.logging-1.5.6.jar@start
```

Be careful to enter the trailing backslash (\) at the end of each line and add `@start` at the end of each filename. Careful readers perhaps noticed that the NOP SLF4J bundle doesn't use `@start`; it's because it's a *fragment* (more on this in chapter 3).

Equinox is now properly provisioned. You can start it and check that all the bundles have been resolved and some of them started:

```
osgi> ss

Framework is launched.

id        State        Bundle
0         ACTIVE       org.eclipse.osgi_3.5.1.R35x_v20090827
1         ACTIVE       org.springframework.aop_3.0.0.RC1
2         ACTIVE       org.springframework.asm_3.0.0.RC1
3         ACTIVE       org.springframework.beans_3.0.0.RC1
4         ACTIVE       org.springframework.context_3.0.0.RC1
5         ACTIVE       org.springframework.core_3.0.0.RC1
6         ACTIVE       org.springframework.expression_3.0.0.RC1
7         ACTIVE       org.springframework.osgi.core_2.0.0.M1
8         ACTIVE       org.springframework.osgi.extender_2.0.0.M1
9         ACTIVE       org.springframework.osgi.io_2.0.0.M1
10        ACTIVE       com.springsource.org.aopalliance_1.0.0
11        ACTIVE       com.springsource.slf4j.api_1.5.6
                       Fragments=12
12        RESOLVED     com.springsource.slf4j.nop_1.5.6
                       Master=11
13        ACTIVE       com.springsource.slf4j.org.apache.commons.logging_1.5.6
```

Don't worry if the NOP SLF4J is RESOLVED and not ACTIVE. Again, it's a fragment and fragments cannot be started. The point is that now the Spring DM extender (bundle 8) keeps an eye on each bundle installation to create Spring application contexts for those powered by Spring DM. Exit from Equinox and get ready to write your first Spring DM OSGi bundle.

1.5.2 *Writing the Spring DM–powered bundle*

Our first bundle will be minimal, because it will contain only one Java class and the necessary configuration files (JAR manifest and Spring DM XML configuration).

Create an src directory at the root of the project and create the following Java class (be careful to create it in the corresponding directory, following Java package conventions):

```java
package com.manning.sdmia;

public class HelloWorld {

  public HelloWorld() {
    System.out.println("Hello world, I'm being created!");
  }

}
```

This class is obviously not useful, but it will emit our Hello World message in the console when Spring DM instantiates it, which is the point of this exercise.

Create a bin directory and compile the class:

```
javac -d bin src/com/manning/sdmia/HelloWorld.java
```

OSGi bundles are standard JAR files with additional headers in the manifest. The OSGi container uses these headers to identify the bundle: identity, description, version, and so on.

In the src directory, create a META-INF directory with a MANIFEST.MF file in it. The manifest should have the following content:

```
Manifest-Version: 1.0
Bundle-ManifestVersion: 2
Bundle-Name: Spring DM Hello World
Bundle-SymbolicName: com.manning.sdmia.helloworld
Bundle-Version: 1.0.0
Export-Package: com.manning.sdmia
```

Note that the manifest *must* contain an empty line at the end (which is hard to illustrate in a book). On top of the description headers (`Bundle-Name`, `Bundle-SymbolicName`, and `Bundle-Version`), the manifest contains an `Export-Package` header, which tells the OSGi container to make the corresponding package available to other bundles. By this means, bundles will be able to import classes from our bundle package.

So far, so modular. The bundle is a usual OSGi bundle and you'll never see the Hello World message if you deploy it as is in Equinox. You want Spring DM to create an instance of the `HelloWorld` class, and this implies creating a configuration file in the location expected by the Spring DM extender. Create a spring directory in META-INF and create a hello-world-context.xml file in it. The following snippet shows the content you need to add to the file.

```xml
<?xml version="1.0" encoding="UTF-8"?>
<beans xmlns="http://www.springframework.org/schema/beans"
  xmlns:xsi="http://www.w3.org/2001/XMLSchema-instance"      Declares
  xsi:schemaLocation="http://www.springframework.org/        Spring beans
     schema/beans                                             namespace
    http://www.springframework.org/schema/beans/
     spring-beans.xsd">

  <bean id="helloWorld"                                       Declares Hello
      class="com.manning.sdmia.HelloWorld" />                 World bean

</beans>
```

Those familiar with Spring will see no difference between declaring the `helloWorld` bean in an OSGi environment and declaring it in a Spring-based application, mainly because there is no difference at all. Every feature of the Spring Framework—dependency injection, AOP, utilities classes—are available and can be leveraged to properly initialize our bundle.

You now have all the pieces of your bundle; you only need to package it before installing it in Equinox. Copy the whole META-INF directory to the bin directory, and use the jar program to create the archive:

```
jar cvfm helloworld.jar src/META-INF/MANIFEST.MF -C bin .
```

This creates a helloworld.jar file, ready to be deployed in Equinox.

1.5.3 *Deploying the bundle*

It's time to install the bundle into Equinox and see how Spring DM handles it. Launch Equinox and type `install file:helloworld.jar` to install the bundle. Equinox answers by giving the bundle ID in the runtime environment, so the console should output something like this:

```
osgi> install file:helloworld.jar
Bundle id is 14
```

The bundle ID in your environment can be different from what you see in this text. Remember this ID because it will be used in subsequent commands. Check the bundle status by launching the `ss` command; this bundle appears at the end and is in the `INSTALLED` state:

```
14      INSTALLED   com.manning.sdmia.helloworld_1.0.0
```

The bundle is installed, but there's no Hello World message on the console yet. We didn't miss anything—the bean has not been created yet. The bundle needs to be started, which will trigger the Spring DM extender and your bundle's Spring context creation. Start the bundle, and you should see the long-expected message (use the correct bundle ID after the `start` command):

```
osgi> start 14

osgi> Hello world, I'm being created!
```

Congratulations! You've just finished the Spring DM Hello World example!

This rather simplistic example shows one of the strengths of Spring DM: you're able to interact with the OSGi container without manipulating any OSGi API—everything is done declaratively. This follows the Spring philosophy: the framework handles technical concerns, letting the developer concentrate on the application code.

1.6 *Summary*

All Java applications eventually have to deal with issues of modularity, both at build time and at runtime. Making regular Java SE or Java EE applications modular, however, isn't an easy task; you really need something else to do the heavy lifting. That "something else" is OSGi. OSGi is an open and lightweight technology for implementing truly modular Java applications.

Despite the power of this technology, it remains difficult to use, thanks to both the strictness of its classloader isolation model and its lack of support for modern application frameworks such as Spring. All is not lost, however, because Spring DM is available to address these issues, making it easier to develop Java applications based on the Spring Framework, and web applications in an OSGi environment. The power of both the Spring Framework and OSGi are harnessed by Spring DM to provide a rich framework for developing component-based and service-oriented applications. Spring DM allows you to embed a Spring container inside OSGi components and manage these containers using the standard OSGi lifecycle. Each component, or bundle, can use dependency injection, aspect-oriented programming, and other enterprise support provided by the framework like in any regular Java application outside an OSGi container.

In the next chapter, we'll describe the key concepts of OSGi in a Spring DM perspective. Because the tool runs inside an OSGi container, you need to understand how this platform works and become comfortable with OSGi mechanisms. The next chapter will help you understand the features and mechanisms of Spring DM.

Understanding
OSGi technology

This chapter covers

- Describing concepts involved in OSGi
- Describing how to use the key parts of OSGi
- Providing all OSGi skills to be able use Spring DM

Perhaps you're wondering how a dedicated chapter on OSGi technology is appropriate to a Spring DM book? As we saw in chapter 1, Spring DM enables the use of the Spring Framework within an OSGi environment. Spring is really popular at the moment, and many Java developers know of its features: dependency injection, AOP, and its approach to structuring Java applications and simplifying development of enterprise Java applications. In contrast, the term "OSGi" is reasonably well known, but its features are much less so. Most developers and architects probably know that the technology addresses the modularity of applications but little else.

We're strongly convinced that some OSGi features need to be understood in detail before you can understand and fully utilize Spring DM correctly. As this book is about Spring DM, we'll focus our discussion of the OSGi technology to the context of the framework and emphasize the most important aspects to make learning it easier.

Let's now look at the OSGi technology and how you can take advantage of it within your Java applications. Because we provided a high-level description of OSGi's features in chapter 1, we won't describe those key concepts again. We'll go ahead and show, in more detail, how the technology works and how to use its features.

2.1 OSGi components

As emphasized in chapter 1, the core concept of OSGi is the *component*, called a *bundle* in this context. OSGI enables advanced management of bundles and their relationships. It leverages the existing Java packaging support and uses only elements, concepts, and mechanisms present in this Java technology.

In this section, we'll describe what an OSGi component is and how to configure it, and we'll introduce the concept of the OSGi *container*, which manages components based on a specific lifecycle.

2.1.1 Component structure

The structure of OSGi components is quite similar to that of traditional Java JAR files. This kind of component can contain the following elements:

- Java class files.
- Text files and other resources used by classic Java applications.
- A MANIFEST.MF file, as required by the JAR standard, located in the META-INF directory of the component. It enables you to configure the different properties of a component and its behavior within the OSGi container.
- Other JAR files, allowing for the inclusion of libraries and frameworks in a bundle. Unlike classic JAR files, these files can be used internally by the component by specifying them within the OSGi `Bundle-Classpath` header.
- Native libraries that are required by the component.

Figure 2.1 sums up all the possible content of an OSGi bundle. Note that embedded JARs are acknowledged as first-class participants in the makeup of the JAR.

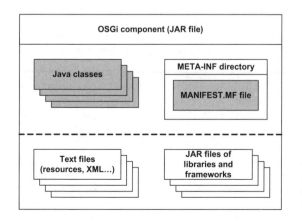

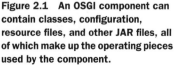

Figure 2.1 An OSGI component can contain classes, configuration, resource files, and other JAR files, all of which make up the operating pieces used by the component.

The main way in which a bundle differs from a JAR file can be found in the new headers within the manifest file used to configure the bundle. Let's look at these different headers and what they allow you to configure.

2.1.2 Component configuration

Unlike classic JAR files, each OSGi component needs to specify information that's used to identify it and describe its behavior inside the OSGi container. The entire bundle configuration must be provided in the manifest file contained in the bundle JAR file. OSGi technology defines additional manifest headers.

Table 2.1 lists the main OSGi headers usable in a bundle's manifest file. You'll notice that this list contains no headers for describing OSGi services. The core specification only allows services to be defined using the OSGi API, as described in section 2.4.

Table 2.1 The main OSGi headers used in a bundle's manifest file

Header	Description
Bundle-ManifestVersion	Corresponds to the version of the manifest file of the component. This must be 2 for OSGi R4.x-based bundles. OSGi implementations should support bundle manifests without a Bundle-ManifestVersion header and assume compatibility with OSGi R3.
Bundle-SymbolicName	Specifies the symbolic name of the component. This name must be unique for the same Bundle-Version number, and using the reverse domain name of the root package of the classes in the bundle is recommended. With the value 2 for the Bundle-ManifestVersion header, this attribute must be specified.
Bundle-Name	Specifies a human-readable name for the component.
Bundle-Version	Specifies the component version.
Bundle-DocURL	Specifies the documentation address for the component.
Bundle-Category	Specifies the component category.
Import-Package	Specifies the names and versions of class packages that the component is dependent on. The components providing packages don't need to be specified here. This header forms part of OSGi's dependency management and will be described in section 2.2.
Export-Package	Specifies the names and versions of packages contained in the component that should be made available to other components. This header also forms part of OSGi's dependency management and will be described in section 2.2.
DynamicImport-Package	Specifies the names and versions of class packages that the component is dependent on. The main difference between this and Import-Package is when the resolution of specified dependencies occurs. Dependencies aren't resolved when the OSGi container tries to change the bundle state to resolved but when a class from the package is actually used. This header also forms part of OSGi's dependency management and will be described in section 2.2.

Table 2.1 The main OSGi headers used in a bundle's manifest file *(continued)*

Header	Description
`Bundle-NativeCode`	Lists all native libraries of the component.
`Require-Bundle`	Specifies the `Bundle-SymbolicName` of components that are used by this component. In this case, all the packages provided by the specified components are automatically imported. This header also forms part of OSGi's dependency management and will be described in section 2.2.
`Bundle-Activator`	Corresponds to the class name that will be used to initialize and finalize the bundle when it's started and stopped. Note that this class must implement the `BundleActivator` interface. This feature will be described in section 2.3.
`Bundle-Classpath`	Specifies the internal classpath, based on elements present in the component JAR file. By default, when the header is omitted, the value corresponds to ".", meaning that all the classes in the bundle are taken into account. If needed, you can specify your own value. In this case, remember to add the value "." to use the classes within the bundles.

Using extra manifest headers to configure a JAR file is quite common in other Java technologies. For OSGi, you have to learn the new OSGi headers and their meanings. The name and value of a header must be separated by the a colon and a space character (:). Listing 2.1 shows a simple manifest configuration for a bundle with the symbolic name com.manning.spring.osgi.simple and named "Spring OSGi Bundle".

Listing 2.1 Simple manifest configuration for an OSGi component

```
Manifest-Version: 1.0
Bundle-Name: Spring OSGi Bundle
Bundle-Version: 1.0                                          Bundle information
Bundle-ManifestVersion: 2                                    headers
Bundle-SymbolicName: com.manning.spring.osgi.simple
Export-Package: com.manning.spring.osgi.simple.service        Dependency
Import-Package: org.osgi.framework,                           configuration headers
 com.manning.spring.osgi.utils,
 com.manning.spring.osgi.annotation;resolution:=optional,
 org.osgi.framework;version="1.3.0"                           Configuration
Bundle-Activator:                                             header of activator
     com.manning.spring.osgi.simple.SimpleActivator
```

Listing 2.1 shows that OSGi makes it possible to specify a collection of values for a header with the comma (,) separator character. Moreover, the technology allows you to apply much more complex configuration by specifying additional parameters for these values. This kind of parameter is called a *directive*, and it usually modifies the meaning of the header.

A directive consists of a key and a value separated by the colon and equal characters (:=), and you can specify several directives for the same header value by using the semicolon (;) separator character. The value of a directive can itself contain a list of values, making the whole header value quite difficult to read. When specifying a value for a directive that contains a list, you need to enclose the value between two double-quote characters (") and to separate items from each other with a comma (,).

In addition to directives, additional *attributes* can be added. An attribute also consists of a key and a value, but in this case they're separated by the equal character (=). Attributes play an important role in the matching between exported and imported package configuration.

The configuration of a header follows the syntax illustrated in the following snippet:

```
Header-Name:
 header-value1;directive1:=value1;directive2:=value2,
 header-value2;directive1:="item1, item2, item3";attribute1=value4,
 header-value3;directive1:=value1;directive3:=value3...
```

This kind of configuration using headers and their associated directives and attributes is particularly useful when configuring dependencies for versions and resolution strategies. The following snippet shows a real use case of directives and attributes in the configuration of Spring's spring-beans.jar file. Notice that this declaration uses the `resolution` directive and the `version` attribute.

```
Import-Package:
 javax.xml.parsers;resolution:=optional,net.sf.cglib.proxy;
 resolution:=optional,org.apache.commons.logging,org.springframework.beans;
 resolution:=optional;version=2.5.0,org.springframework.beans.annotation;
 resolution:=optional;version=2.5.0,...
```

Now that you know what an OSGi component is, what it can contain, and what rules must be followed to configure it, let's see what an OSGi container looks like and what mechanisms and lifecycles it provides for managing these components.

2.1.3   *OSGi containers*

The OSGi specification describes a platform for managing components and services. An implementation of the specification is generally called an OSGi container, and using OSGi usually requires using such a container.

Because the OSGi specification is freely accessible through the OSGi Alliance website (http://www.osgi.org), several open source implementations are available. Table 2.2 sums up the three main implementations of the R4 version of OSGi.

These containers provide the basic OSGi platform components as described in the OSGi Alliance specification, but most of them also provide convenient administration tools for interacting with the container. The more popular ones have console- and web-based interfaces, allowing you to see the details of all the components inside the container and allowing for convenient management and error diagnosis.

Equinox also extends the specification specifically to suit the needs of the IDE by providing *extension points*. These allow enhanced component-based features, making it possible for components to register for the services of the extended features of a component. This feature is widely used to extend the UI of the Eclipse platform.

Table 2.2 The main open source OSGi containers

OSGi container	Description
Equinox	The OSGi implementation from the Eclipse platform, which is the foundation for the plug-in model of the Eclipse IDE. This container can be used outside Eclipse and is available at http://www.eclipse.org/equinox/.
Felix	The OSGi implementation from the Apache Software Foundation and the successor to Oscar, an implementation of OSGi R3. The container can be found at http://felix. apache.org.
Knopflerfish	An OSGi implementation by the Makewave company, available at http://www. knopflerfish.org/.

We've seen in this section that an OSGi container is responsible for component management. Let's look now in more detail at the lifecycle services they provide to components.

2.1.4 OSGi component lifecycle

We looked at the component lifecycle briefly in chapter 1, and we'll expand on that now. Each OSGi container manages components, also called bundles, and their lifecycles with associated states, transitions, and events. This mechanism has some similarities to the way the Spring lightweight container uses events to initialize and finalize POJOs. With OSGi technology, the component lifecycle is more tightly linked to the availability of components within the container and the resolution of their dependencies.

Let's take a high-level look at the management of an OSGi component from cradle to grave. The OSGi component lifecycle has two main parts.

In the first part, the component is installed into the container without trying to resolve its dependencies. The resolution of dependencies takes place next, when the component tries to reach the resolved state. If errors occur during the resolution of dependencies, the component remains in the installed state. You'll notice that OSGi allows the refreshing of components, and when this happens, dependency resolution must be performed again. During these steps, other components in the container can't use the component. Figure 2.2 shows the different states, transitions, and events in the first part of the lifecycle.

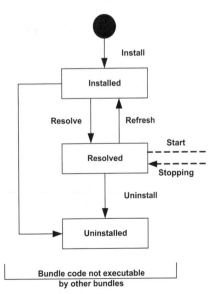

Figure 2.2 The first part of the OSGi component lifecycle: components are installed and their dependencies resolved.

The second part of the lifecycle involves making components available in the container for execution and making their code executable by other components. The main state here is the active state, which is reached thanks to a start event. The component first passes through a transitional state called starting. When returning to the resolved state, OSGi triggers a stop event on the component, which then passes through another transitional state called stopping. Figure 2.3 shows the different states of the second part of this lifecycle.

As you can see, understanding the OSGi lifecycle is important because it's tightly tied to the bundle's availability. We'll also see in section 2.2 that the resolution of dependencies is done according to this lifecycle. When trying to diagnose problems, understanding the states of components is fundamental (as described later in section 2.6).

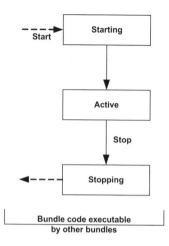

Figure 2.3   The second part of the OSGi component lifecycle corresponding to states handling component execution for other components

We've seen the core concepts relating to OSGi components, the key elements of the OSGi technology, and how they're managed by the OSGi container. Components form the core of OSGi, but because components are intended to work together and interact, OSGi provides complete support for managing component dependencies and controlling the visibility of component internals.

2.2   Component dependencies

Having structured an application based on OSGi components, the next step is to orchestrate their interactions using the mechanisms provided by OSGi to control the versioning and visibility of component internals. OSGi provides sophisticated support for dependency management at runtime through classloader management.

In the following sections, we'll focus on the features related to dependency management. We'll see how OSGi applications are different from classic Java applications, though they bear similarities to container-managed enterprise applications because of the classloader management. We'll then deal with the configuration of components and how they reference each other. Finally we'll see how OSGi handles the matching of producer to consumer components and the management of their versioning.

> **NOTE**   In section 6.3, we'll explain how to organize enterprise applications based on OSGi components using enterprise-specific OSGi techniques.

In OSGi, components are black boxes by default. Nothing is visible from outside except packages getting configured as boot delegation packages within the container, like the java package. The component can only use resources that it contains; OSGi enables private classes to be scoped to a component. Although this is useful in itself, our real interest here is in arranging these components into applications within the container. This is done with the dependency-management features of OSGi, which allow you to declaratively link components and relax the default visibility constraints.

This visibility feature is implemented and enforced using the classloader feature of Java. It's essential to have a clear understanding of how the OSGi technology handles classloading in order to understand what is going on in the OSGi container and to resolve errors when they occur.

2.2.1 Classloader isolation and chaining

Java lacks first-class support for developing truly modular applications and managing fine-grained dependencies, although work is under way to change this under the auspices of JSR 294. Imagine you want to use several Java libraries or frameworks that use different and incompatible versions of the same library. It will result in exceptions such as `ClassNotFoundException` or `NoSuchMethodException`, depending on the library version loaded by Java. This problem is commonly called "JAR hell," and there is currently no built-in solution in the Java platform to address this problem.

Classloaders are used in Java to dynamically load classes and correspond to the entities that throw `ClassNotFoundExceptions` when classes can't be found. This processing is done on demand by the JVM when a class needs to be used. The appropriate classloader searches the known location of classes, reads their contents, and loads them.

Before describing the way OSGi uses classloaders, let's recap how default classloaders work in Java. Classloader technology is based on a *hierarchical* approach to handling class resolutions, and Java integrates three types of classloaders:

- *Bootstrap classloader*—Loads classes from the core Java libraries present in the lib directory of your java home directory
- *Extension classloader*—Loads classes from the lib/ext directory of your Java platform or any directory specified in the `java.ext.dirs` system property
- *Application classloader*—Loads classes based on the elements specified in the application classpath

These three classloaders are linked in a hierarchical relationship. In order to load a class, a classloader first asks its parent if it's able to load the class. If not, it tries to load the class itself. This mechanism is used at each classloader level. Figure 2.4 shows this mechanism and the relationship between the three classloaders.

As you can see, in Java the same classloaders are used to resolve all the classes of an application, which makes it difficult to isolate the resolution of different classes.

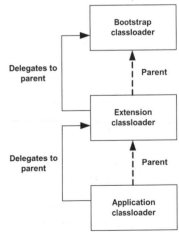

Figure 2.4 Traditional use of classloaders in Java

OSGi technology provides a different approach to using classloaders; it's not based on a hierarchical approach but on the concept of classloader *chaining*, which allows fined-grained control of the visibility of classes from each other. In this context, each component is associated with a dedicated classloader. According to the component configuration, this classloader is linked to other components' classloaders for the resolution of classes outside the current component. Having classloaders dedicated to components makes isolation between components possible, and, by default, no class can be seen outside a component. Instead, you need to explicitly import and export them by configuring the corresponding packages in the manifest files.

Figure 2.5 sums up this resolution process, called *classloader chaining*, by showing the links between component class loaders. For the sake of simplicity, we associated a class loader with each component, but the implementation can differ depending on the configuration of the OSGi container.

We stated earlier that we must specify the required packages in the manifest file. This configuration can be accomplished in two ways: declaring which packages—and hence classes—are visible and usable within the container, or declaring which OSGi components should be used. Let's focus on these two options.

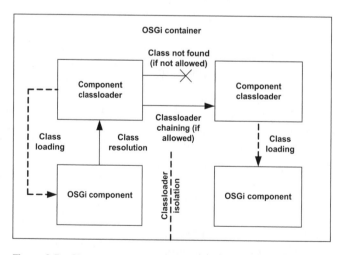

Figure 2.5   Class resolution using the classloader chaining feature, according to configurations in OSGi headers

2.2.2 *Providing dependencies*

Before you can use the classes of other components, you must first make these classes visible. OSGi doesn't allow you to specify class visibility at the class level, but instead at the level of the containing package.

When specifying a package, the subpackages aren't exported by default, which means you need to explicitly specify each one if you want to export them all. This also means that when using this mechanism, the way you organize your classes becomes very important, because truly public and internal classes must be located in separate packages. Of course, classes within private packages still have a role to play and can be used to hide classes in a package from other components.

Making the classes of a package visible from a bundle is an easy task. You simply have to add the fully qualified package name to the value of the `Export-Package` header in the bundle's manifest file, as shown in the following snippet:

```
Bundle-Name: Spring OSGi Bundle
(...)
Export-Package: com.manning.spring.osgi.simple,
 com.manning.spring.osgi.simple.service
(...)
```

If you only specify a list of packages, the default properties and behavior are used, but the header can provide finer-grained configuration thanks to dedicated directives that can be associated with each package name. Table 2.3 summarizes these directives and their purposes.

Table 2.3   Directives for the `Export-Package` header

Directive	Description
exclude	Specifies a list of packages that must be invisible to the component importing the package.
include	Specifies a list of packages that must be visible to the component importing the package.
mandatory	Specifies a list of mandatory properties that must be specified when using the exported package in other components.
uses	Specifies a list of packages that an exported package uses. This directive is used by the dependency resolver to ensure that imported package versions correspond to those specified here.

In addition to these directives, the `version` attribute can be added to specify the version of the exported package. Specific user attributes can also be used, and the OSGi framework automatically adds the `bundle-symbolic-name` attribute corresponding to the bundle identifier that exports the package, and the `bundle-version` for the version of this bundle. All these attributes can take part in the matching algorithm, which will be described in section 2.2.5.

The following snippet shows an extract of the manifest file from the spring-beans.jar file, showing its use of the `Export-Package` header together with the `uses` directive and the `version` attribute.

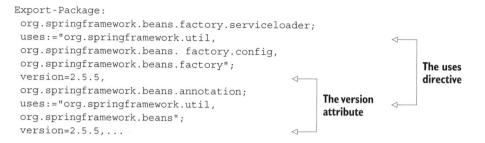

```
Export-Package:
  org.springframework.beans.factory.serviceloader;
  uses:="org.springframework.util,
  org.springframework.beans. factory.config,
  org.springframework.beans.factory";
  version=2.5.5,
  org.springframework.beans.annotation;
  uses:="org.springframework.util,
  org.springframework.beans";
  version=2.5.5,...
```

The previous snippet makes visible the packages `org.springframework.beans.`
`factory.serviceloader` and `org.springframework.beans.annotation` outside the
component.

The use of the `Export-Package` header provides other components with access to
component classes. When using those classes, the components need to explicitly specify that they want to consume them. OSGi provides several different ways to do this,
again through dedicated headers specifying packages or components. The following
sections describe these approaches and their configuration.

2.2.3 *Consuming dependencies with the Import-Package header*

OSGi provides several approaches for using previously exported packages. The most
common—and recommended—way is to specify `Import-Package` in the manifest,
which makes it possible to use classes from the specified package in a component. If this
package has been exported by another component, the package is made visible to the
consumer using the matching mechanism (which will be described in section 2.2.5). By
using this header, the package consumer doesn't need to know which bundle exported
it because the container handles the matching.

For the `Import-Package` header, the OSGi specification defines the standard attributes listed in table 2.4.

Table 2.4   Standard attributes usable with the `Import-Package` header

Attribute	Description
version	Specifies the version range for matching exported packages. If this attri-bute isn't specified, the default value is `[0.0.0, ∞)`. For more details, see section 2.2.5.
bundle-symbolic-name	Specifies the symbolic name of the component that exports the pack-ages. In the case of a fragment bundle, the name will correspond to the host bundle's symbolic name instead. A fragment is a special bundle that allows extending an existing bundle. We'll describe this feature of OSGi in section 3.3.
bundle-version	Specifies the version of the component that exports the packages. As with `version`, the default value is `[0.0.0, ∞)` and the fragment behavior is as for `bundle-symbolic-name`.

All these attributes make possible fine-grained selection of the packages. The following snippet shows how you can use the version attribute in the Import-Package header.

```
Bundle-Name: Spring OSGi Bundle
(...)
Import-Package:
 com.manning.spring.osgi.utils;version=1.0.0,
 com.manning.spring.osgi.service;version=1.0.0
```

By default, the processing of the header content corresponds to the mechanism described in section 2.1.4. As we saw, the resolution is performed immediately prior to the bundle transitioning to the resolved state. If problems occur during dependency resolution, the component remains in the installed state.

In addition to the previous attribute, the resolution directive of the Import-Package header makes it possible to change the behavior of this resolution mechanism. The first possible value of the directive is mandatory, which is also the default. When a package is marked as mandatory, it means that if the package can't be resolved, the component itself can't be resolved. The other value is optional. In this case, if the package isn't present during the resolution phase, the package isn't considered imported by the component.

To better understand the behavior of this feature, imagine you want to use the spring-beans.jar file from the Spring Framework. For your application, using a small number of the classes in the JAR file may be enough, so you only need to specify the packages of the classes you use. Additionally, you don't require features of the component that require additional dependencies. In order for your application to resolve without these dependencies being present in the container, Spring specifies them using the optional value for the resolution directive.

The following snippet shows an extract of the Import-Package header for the org.springframework.beans component corresponding to the spring-beans.jar file:

```
Import-Package: javax.el;version="[2.1.0, 3.0.0)";resolution:=optional
 net.sf.cglib.proxy;version="[2.1.3, 2.2.0)";resolution:=optional,
 org.apache.commons.logging;version="[1.0.4, 2.0.0)",
 org.springframework.core;version="[2.5.6, 2.5.6]";resolution:=optional,
 org.springframework.core.annotation;version="[2.5.6, 2.5.6]";
 resolution:=optional
```

Classes of these packages are now visible and usable within the components.

Figure 2.6 describes links between the components involved in the previous snippet. You can see that the javax.xml.parsers package is provided by the OSGi container itself.

A variant of the Import-Package header is the DynamicImport-Package header. It makes it possible to bypass the regular class-resolution mechanism we have described and instead allows classes to be loaded on demand at runtime. Dependencies specified in this way are ignored during the transition between the installed and resolved states.

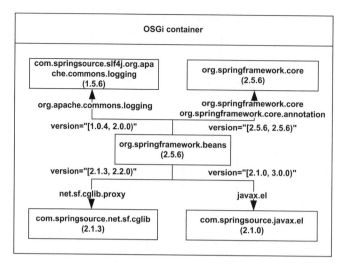

Figure 2.6   **Links between the components involved in the previous snippet**

The `DynamicImport-Package` header can contain a list of packages, but it also supports two wildcards for specifying package names. Moreover, these imports are searched for in the order in which they are specified. This ordering is important, especially when using wildcards, because it determines the order in which matching occurs. In the following snippet, packages with the value `test` for the attribute `myattribute` will be preferred over other packages.

```
DynamicImport-Package: *;myattribute=test, *
```

No directives are defined for this header, but the standard `version`, `bundle-symbolic-name`, and `bundle-version` attributes can all be used for package matching with the same semantics as `Import-Package`.

> **NOTE**   You should try to avoid using the `DynamicImport-Package` header as much as possible, because it provides less control over the classes that the importing bundle will use (these classes will be resolved at runtime, depending on what is available in the OSGi container). The `DynamicImport-Package` header was introduced to solve problems in legacy code, and real OSGi applications should not use it.

The `Import-Package` and `DynamicImport-Package` headers allow components to specify which packages they need to import for their dependencies to be satisfied. OSGi also provides another approach, based on the `Require-Bundle` header, to directly import all the exported packages of a component.

2.2.4 *Consuming dependencies with the Require-Bundle header*

The `Require-Bundle` header is provided by the OSGi specification so you can consume all exported packages from other components based on component symbolic names. In this case, you directly specify the bundle you need, and the OSGi container gives you access to all packages it exports, regardless of whether or not you need them. Whereas the configuration using this header is much less verbose, it has the disadvantage of tying the component to the specific dependency that exports the packages. Although its use is recommended for developing Eclipse plug-ins, using the Import-Package header is generally preferable because it more effectively decouples providers from consumers.

As with the previously described headers for consuming packages, the value of this header contains a list of element names, but this time they aren't package names but rather bundle symbolic names. The matching between exported and imported entities is still based on attributes, but only one standard attribute is defined by the OSGi specification: the bundle-version attribute. The bundle-version attribute uses the same semantics as the version attribute of the Import-Package header and specifies the component version of the dependency. For more details, see section 2.2.5. The following snippet shows a simple use of the Require-Bundle header.

```
Manifest-Version: 1.0
(...)
Import-Package: javax.servlet;version="2.5.0",
 javax.servlet.http;version="2.5.0",
 javax.servlet.jsp;version="2.0.0",
 (...)
Require-Bundle: com.springsource.javax.servlet.jsp.jstl;
 bundle-version=1.1.2,com.springsource.org.apache.taglibs.standard;
 bundle-version=1.1.2
```

Import-Package and Require-Bundle headers can both be specified in the manifest configuration of a bundle, but the Import-Package header takes priority over the Require-Bundle header. Moreover, packages that are implicitly exported by a Require-Bundle header and imported via an Import-Package header must not be treated as split packages.

Split packages

You saw that referencing bundles with the Require-Bundle header is equivalent to importing all of their exported packages. A problematic case occurs when two different required bundles export the same package. Such packages are named *split packages* because their content comes from several bundles.

Although OSGi allows split packages, you'll notice that they have several obvious drawbacks. When different bundles provide the same classes, unpredictable shadowing of classes can arise.

When using the Require-Bundle header, the directive mechanism can be used to adapt the handling of the header. Table 2.5 lists the directives associated with the header.

Now that we've described how to provide and consume dependencies within OSGi components using the Import-Package, DynamicImport-Package, and Require-Bundle headers, let's explore in more detail the mechanisms responsible for matching and version management.

Table 2.5   Directives usable with the `Require-Bundle` header

Attribute	Description
`visibility`	When set to `private` (the default value), the exported packages of the corresponding bundles aren't re-exported. Setting this to `reexport` will achieve the opposite.
`resolution`	Controls dependency resolution. If set to `mandatory` (the default value), the dependency must be successfully resolved for the bundle to resolve. With the `optional` value, dependencies are only resolved if they're present, and the bundle will resolve regardless.

2.2.5   *Matching and versioning*

In describing the headers for importing and exporting packages, we introduced the matching mechanism of OSGi. This mechanism is powerful and flexible because it gives very fined-grained control over the individual elements specified in `Export-Package`, `Import-Package`, and `Require-Bundle`. We'll now dive into the details of the matching and versioning mechanisms provided by OSGi and describe the matching of versions and attributes and the handling of optional dependencies.

VERSION MATCHING

The version concept is a key feature of OSGi dependency management. As a matter of fact, OSGi allows several versions of the same bundle or of the same package to coexist within a container. The version makes it possible to select which dependency to use.

Table 2.6 shows the parts that make up a version value. These parts are separated by the period (`.`) character and are listed in order of appearance in the value.

Table 2.6   The different parts of a version value

Part	Description
Major number	For major updates with no provision for compatibility with previous major versions.
Minor number	For functional updates compatible with the current major version (compatible for clients using an interface, but not for implementers).
Micro number	For bug fixes.
Qualifier	Values like "–SNAPSHOT" for the current development version can also be added at the end of the value. The version number with a qualifier is lower than the number without.

You'll notice that this format isn't specific to OSGi and is generally used by libraries and frameworks. The following values correspond to valid versions as described in the OSGi specification: `1.5.3`, `1.0.0`, and `1.0.0.SNAPSHOT`. These values can be used, for instance, in the `version` attribute, as shown in the following snippet:

```
Import-Package: javax.servlet;version="2.5.0",
 javax.servlet.http;version="2.5.0",
 javax.servlet.jsp;version="2.0.0",
 (...)
```

When matching packages, the OSGi container tries to find an exported package with a version number equal to or greater than the one specified in the importing component. Specifying nothing when exporting a package means that the default version `0.0.0` is used.

For importing packages or components, OSGi allows you to specify either specific versions or a range of versions as the value for the `version` or `bundle-version` attributes. These attributes define the compatibility range of a component when using a dependency.

The OSGi specification uses a mathematical convention for interval notation, used to define a range. The notation contains two parts separated by the comma (`,`) character: the *floor* and *ceiling* values. These values must be enclosed by the opening bracket characters "(" or "[" and the closing bracket characters ")" or "]". The parentheses, ( ), specify that the end value of the range must not be included; the opposite is true with the bracket characters, [ ]. The following values correspond to valid versions as defined by the OSGi specification: `[1.5.3, 2)` and `[2.1.0, 2.5.0]`. When using a range with the `version` or `bundle-version` attributes, it must be enclosed between two double-quote characters (`"`). You'll notice that a single version value is equivalent to the interval `[version,?)` and no version to the interval `[0.0.0,?)`.

> **NOTE** All through the book, we'll show you how to manage dependencies and versions with OSGi. This implies handling specific entries in the manifest file of your bundles, but you should be aware that you usually won't maintain the manifest file by hand. Tools (such as Eclipse PDE, Bnd, and Bundlor) can help you easily and efficiently manage the manifest file, and they can easily be integrated with building tools like Ant or Maven.

Table 2.7 shows examples of common version expressions and their matching characteristics.

Table 2.7 Common version expressions and their matching characteristics

Version expression	Matching
No version specified	Matches to versions above or equal to 0.0.0 (0.0.0 ≤ version)
1.2.3	Matches to versions above and including 1.2.3 (1.2.3 ≤ version)
[1.2.3, 4.5.6]	Matches to versions above 1.2.3 and below 4.5.6, including these two versions (1.2.3 ≤ version ≤ 4.5.6)
[1.2.3, 4.5.6)	Matches to versions above 1.2.3 and below 4.5.6; the first version is included and the last excluded (1.2.3 ≤ version < 4.5.6)
(1.2.3, 4.5.6]	Matches to versions above 1.2.3 and below 4.5.6; the first version is excluded and the last included (1.2.3 < version ≤ 4.5.6)
(1.2.3, 4.5.6)	Matches to versions above 1.2.3 and below 4.5.6, exclusive of these two versions (1.2.3 < version < 4.5.6)

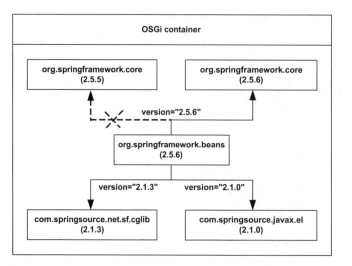

Figure 2.7 Relationships between components at the version level in the spring-beans.jar configuration

The following code snippet from the Spring Framework's spring-beans.jar file shows how to specify version ranges within the `Import-Package` header:

```
Import-Package: javax.el;version="[2.1.0, 3.0.0)";resolution:=optional
 ,net.sf.cglib.proxy;version="[2.1.3, 2.2.0)";resolution:=optional,
 org.springframework.core;version="[2.5.6, 2.5.6]";resolution:=optional,
 (...)
```

Figure 2.7 shows the relationships between components at the version levels specified in the previous snippet.

OSGi also allows you to match packages by selecting a specific provider; for instance, if several components provide the same package with the same version. This selection can be done by adding the `symbolic-name` and `bundle-version` attributes. As a matter of fact, when packages are exported, these attributes are automatically added by the container and can then be used for matching. The main drawback to using this approach is that you're tying yourself to a specific component. The following snippet shows the use of these attributes:

```
Import-Package: org.springframework.core;
 bundle-symbolic-name=org.springframework.beans;
 bundle-version="[2.5.6, 2.5.6]";resolution:=optional,
 (...)
```

OPTIONAL DEPENDENCIES

A dependency can be tagged as optional in the dependency configuration of a component with the `optional` value for the `resolution` directive. The dependency is then not considered mandatory and will be used and imported if present and not otherwise. A missing dependency won't prevent the component from resolving.

OSGi supports this mechanism on both packages and bundles with the `Import-Package` and `Require-Bundle` headers. This feature is particularly useful for frameworks and libraries that have associated tooling. When you're not using the tooling, the tool components don't need to be present in the OSGi container for the components to be used.

For example, Spring components import all packages corresponding to third-party libraries for all parts of the framework. You commonly only use a part of the framework and its related libraries, so all the imported packages are marked as optional. You only need to specify libraries as mandatory for the parts of the Spring Framework you use within the container. These components can be successfully started without the other dependencies.

ATTRIBUTE MATCHING

The last feature related to matching is support for attributes. Although the OSGi specification defines standard attributes like `version` and `bundle-version`, you're also free to specify your own. OSGi provides a generic mechanism for using all attributes when handling dependency matching. Note that you should use this feature as a last resort—the standard attributes can usually handle dependencies in OSGi applications.

As described earlier, an attribute consists of a key and a value separated by the equal character (=), and which can be applied at the end of a header value separated with the semicolon (;). Zero or more attributes can be specified in this way jointly with directives, as shown in this snippet:

```
Header-Name: header-value1;directive-name1:=directive-value1;
  attribute-name1= attribute-value1;attribute-name2=attribute-value2,
  (...)
```

When exporting packages with the `Export-Package` header, custom attributes can be added for each package. These attributes can also be used when importing packages for fine-grained matching. The use of attributes isn't mandatory except if they're specified in the value of the `mandatory` directive.

Let's take an example component that exports the `com.manning.osgi.simple` package with an attribute named `criteria`.

```
Export-Package: com.manning.osgi.simple;criteria="Manning"
```

A package import without the attribute, or with this one and the value "Manning", will resolve successfully, as shown in the following snippet:

```
Import-Package: com.manning.osgi.simple;criteria="Manning"
```

If, in the export configuration, the `mandatory` directive is added with the `criteria` value, as shown in the following snippet, the use of this attribute is then mandatory for resolution to be successful:

```
Export-Package: com.manning.osgi.simple;
  criteria="Manning";mandatory:="criteria"
```

Figure 2.8 summarizes the attribute-matching mechanism according to the presence of attributes and the `mandatory` attribute.

Now that we've described how OSGi manages dependencies of components, we'll focus on how the technology allows interaction with the corresponding container.

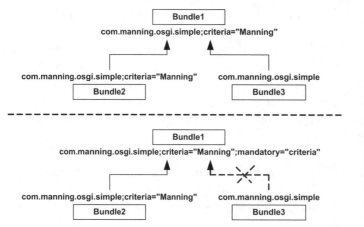

Figure 2.8   Summary of the attribute-matching mechanism. When using the mandatory attribute, the specified attribute (criteria, in this example) is required for a successful match.

2.3   *Interacting with the OSGi container*

Because OSGi is intrinsically dynamic, it offers ways to interact with containers and manage the lifecycle of components and services through the use of a dedicated API. This is very important, as it enables components to adapt their behavior based on updates to other components.

The bundle context, encapsulated in the BundleContext interface, is the central entity that makes it possible to interact with the container in different ways:

- *Managing and using bundles*—You can access every bundle in the container, regardless of status, and manipulate them using the Bundle interface. Even installing and uninstalling bundles is possible.
- *Handling bundle lifecycles*—You can get the current state of the bundle and eventually update it.
- *Accessing container and system properties*—You can get various properties.
- *Listening for events*—OSGi allows you to listen to all the events occurring in the container at different levels.
- *Interacting with persistent storage*—This is provided for the bundle by the container in order to store data.
- *Managing and using services*—The bundle context allows you to both register and unregister services and obtain instances of them. This is described in detail in section 2.4.

The following subsections will cover all the features in this list (except for services, which will be discussed in section 2.4). In the last subsection (2.3.6), we'll describe how to obtain an instance of BundleContext by using the bundle activator.

The OSGi API observes the same class visibility rules as other APIs, and you need to import the corresponding package in order to use it. This package name is org.osgi.framework and must be specified as in the following snippet:

```
Import-Package: org.osgi.framework;version="1.3.0", (...)
```

NOTE The OSGi API version depends on the OSGi implementation version provided by the OSGi container. For R4.0, R4.1, and R4.2, the API versions are 1.3, 1.4, and 1.5 respectively. Specifying version 1.3.0 makes it possible to use the OSGi API corresponding to R4.0+.

2.3.1 Bundles

You can interact with bundles at several levels both to get information about the bundles' configuration and contents and to manage them.

The first step consists of obtaining references to the bundles you want to interact with. The `BundleContext` interface provides three methods for doing this:

- The `getBundles` method returns an array containing all the bundles installed in the container.
- The `getBundle` method returns a particular instance of a bundle using its internal identifier within the container, which must be passed as a parameter. This identifier is managed by the container and is different from the bundle's symbolic name defined in the manifest file.
- The `getBundle` method without parameters returns the current bundle associated with the context, which usually turns out to be the bundle in which the method is called.

The following snippet shows how to use these methods from a `BundleContext` instance to obtain references to the bundles present in the container:

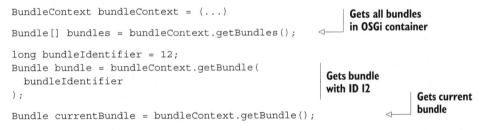

```
BundleContext bundleContext = (...)

Bundle[] bundles = bundleContext.getBundles();          Gets all bundles
                                                        in OSGi container
long bundleIdentifier = 12;
Bundle bundle = bundleContext.getBundle(
  bundleIdentifier                                      Gets bundle
);                                                      with ID 12
                                                                      Gets current
Bundle currentBundle = bundleContext.getBundle();                     bundle
```

Once you have obtained an instance of a bundle, the `Bundle` interface allows you access to the general information about the bundle and more generally to its whole configuration, which is defined in the manifest file. The identifier, the install location, and the symbolic name of a bundle can be accessed using the `getBundleId`, `getLocation`, and `getSymbolicName` methods. And the `getHeaders` method can be used to access all the headers present in the manifest file of a bundle. Listing 2.2 shows how to use these methods.

Listing 2.2 Accessing general and configuration information about a bundle

```
Bundle bundle = (...)

Long bundleId = bundle.getBundleId();
String location = bundle.getLocation();
String symbolicName = bundle.getSymbolicName();
```

```
Dictionary<String,String> headers
          = bundleContext.getBundle().getHeaders();
String bundleName = headers.get(Constants.BUNDLE_NAME);
String bundleVersion = headers.get(Constants.BUNDLE_VERSION);
```

The `Bundle` interface also allows you to access the content of a particular bundle. When accessing this content, OSGi bypasses the classloader and its visibility mechanisms. You should be aware that accessing bundle resources this way can retrieve content from both the bundle and its attached fragments.

> **NOTE** A fragment is a special kind of bundle that is incomplete and allows an existing bundle's content or configuration to be extended. We'll discuss this concept in chapter 3.

You can directly access a particular resource using the `getResource` method and providing its path. The path is always relative to the root of the bundle classpath and may begin with the slash (/) character. With this method, you must know the exact resource path in advance, but this isn't always possible for applications. This method also allows you to see resources present in imported packages.

Suppose you wanted to retrieve all the resources present under the META-INF/spring folder of a bundle—the `findEntries` method would be preferable in this case. Its first parameter is the root directory for the search, with the path following the same rules as for `getResource`. The second parameter specifies a pattern for matching resource names, and you can use the asterisk (*) wildcard character; a null value is equivalent to `"*"`. The last parameter allows you to enable recursion for the search.

The following snippet shows how to use the `getResource` and `findEntries` methods:

```
Bundle bundle = (...);

URL specificConfigurationFile = bundle.getResource(
                        "META-INF/spring/osgi-context.xml");

Enumeration configurationFiles = bundle.findEntries(
                        "META-INF/spring", "*.xml", false);
```

In this example, `getResource` gets a particular file in the bundle, and `findEntries` gets all files inside a directory in the bundle.

> **TIP** Spring DM uses these resource-accessing mechanisms to detect bundles that its extender must manage, identifying elements both in the manifest file and on the bundle content. We'll cover the Spring DM extender in chapters 3 and 4.

2.3.2 *Lifecycle management*

The `Bundle` interface includes a set of constants corresponding to all the possible states of a bundle. Those states were described in section 2.1.4, which discussed the OSGi component lifecycle, and they're listed in table 2.8.

Table 2.8   States in a bundle's lifecycle

State	Description
Installed	Bundle is installed within the OSGi container.
Uninstalled	Bundle is uninstalled from the OSGi container.
Resolved	Bundle is installed and all dependencies are resolved.
Starting	Bundle is starting, moving from the resolved to the active state.
Active	Bundle is available to do work within the OSGi container.
Stopping	Bundle is stopping, moving from the active to the resolved state.

A component can be installed in the current OSGi container using one of the installBundle methods of the BundleContext interface. After the method's execution returns, the component is present in the container in an installed state. The following snippet shows how to install a component using the OSGi API.

```
BundleContext bundleContext = (...);

String absoluteBundlePath = (...);
Bundle bundle = bundleContext.installBundle(absoluteBundlePath);

int state = bundle.getState();
```

After having set the absolute path to locate the bundle JAR file, the installBundle method can be used to install the bundle. After this task done, the state of the bundle is Bundle.INSTALLED.

The Bundle interface allows you to manage the component states programmatically, using the methods listed in table 2.9.

Table 2.9   Bundle interface methods related to component state management

Method	Description
start	Tries to start the bundle and put it in the active state.
stop	Tries to stop the bundle and return it to the resolved state.
uninstall	Tries to uninstall the bundle. After a successful execution of this method, the component can no longer be seen in the container.
update	Tries to update the bundle contents, assuming the bundle is already installed and not in an uninstalled state. If the initial state of the bundle is active, starting, or stopping, the method attempts to stop it before trying to update. After the update, the bundle state is set to installed.

Once a bundle is installed, using the start method tries to move the component into the active state via the resolved state. The bundle reaches the active state if no exception occurs during its dependency resolution and activation. The following snippet shows how to use the start method.

```
Bundle bundle = (...)

bundle.start();
int state = bundle.getState();
```

After you've started the bundle using the start method, the bundle state moves to Bundle.ACTIVE.

2.3.3   Properties

Several global properties are defined by the OSGi container, and you can access their values via the BundleContext's getProperty method. Several property keys are standardized in the OSGi specification and are present in the Constants interface—these constants can be used as parameters of the getProperty method:

- Constants.FRAMEWORK_VERSION and Constants.FRAMEWORK_VENDOR—The version and name of the OSGi container used
- Constants.FRAMEWORK_LANGUAGE—The language used by the container to implement components
- Constants.FRAMEWORK_OS_NAME and Constants.FRAMEWORK_OS_VERSION—The name and version of the operating system that's running the container
- Constants.FRAMEWORK_PROCESSOR—The name of the processor corresponding to the host computer

Listing 2.3 shows how to use the getProperty method to access to the name and version of the OSGi container.

Listing 2.3   Accessing properties using the BundleContext interface

```
String containerName
        = bundleContext.getProperty(Constants.FRAMEWORK_VENDOR);
String containerVersion
        = bundleContext.getProperty(Constants.FRAMEWORK_VERSION);

String usedLanguage
        = bundleContext.getProperty(Constants.FRAMEWORK_LANGUAGE);

String osName
        = bundleContext.getProperty(Constants.FRAMEWORK_OS_NAME);
String osVersion
        = bundleContext.getProperty(Constants.FRAMEWORK_OS_VERSION);
```

Note that if the key searched for isn't found in the OSGi container's properties, it's then searched for in the JVM's system properties.

2.3.4   Event support

OSGi provides first-class event support, which is useful for handling the dynamic aspects of the technology. Imagine that a dependency disappears from the OSGi container—all the components using it need to be notified in order to change their behavior and avoid errors. OSGi's event support allows you to achieve this regardless of whether the event occurs because of changes in the OSGi container itself, in bundles present in the container, or in changes to services. We'll focus here on support for events at the bundle level; we'll cover service support in section 2.4.

OSGi's event support at the bundle level allows code to be notified of every update to the state of a component during its lifetime. Once the event listener is notified, it can change the behavior of the system according to the new state. OSGi provides two ways to handle these events:

- An *asynchronous* method using the BundleListener interface
- A *synchronous* method using the SynchronousBundleLister interface

The BundleListener interface is shown in the following snippet:

```
public interface BundleListener {
  void bundleChanged(BundleEvent event);
}
```

The SynchronousBundleListener interface extends BundleListener without adding anything more. Only the way the container handles this interface changes.

Both interfaces contain a bundleChanged method that provides the triggering event object itself. This event object is of type BundleEvent, and it includes both the event type and the component triggering the event, as shown in the following snippet:

```
public interface BundleEvent {
  static final int INSTALLED = 0x00000001;
  static final int STARTED = 0x00000002;
  static final int STOPPED = 0x00000004;
  static final int UPDATED = 0x00000008;
  static final int UNINSTALLED = 0x00000010;
  static final int RESOLVED = 0x00000020;
  static final int UNRESOLVED = 0x00000040;
  static final int STARTING = 0x00000080;
  static final int STOPPING = 0x00000100;
  static final int LAZY_ACTIVATION = 0x00000200;

  Bundle getBundle();
  int getType();
}
```

Listing 2.4 shows a simple use of the BundleListener interface to detect asynchronously the start and the stop of components within the OSGi container. When such events occur, the listener prints the information in the standard console.

Listing 2.4 Handling a bundle event in an asynchronous listener

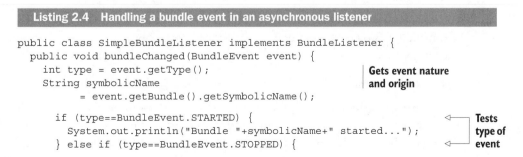

```
public class SimpleBundleListener implements BundleListener {
  public void bundleChanged(BundleEvent event) {
    int type = event.getType();                          Gets event nature
    String symbolicName                                  and origin
        = event.getBundle().getSymbolicName();

    if (type==BundleEvent.STARTED) {                           Tests
      System.out.println("Bundle "+symbolicName+" started..."); type of
    } else if (type==BundleEvent.STOPPED) {                     event
```

```
        System.out.println("Bundle "+symbolicName+" stopped...");
    }
  }
}
```

Once you have implemented one of these listeners, you need to register it with the container by using the `BundleContext` instance and its `addBundleListener` method. The `addBundleListener` method supports both asynchronous and synchronous listeners.

> **NOTE** Spring DM uses all these event mechanisms to manage instances of the Spring lightweight container. This work is handled by a special listener bundle, also called an *extender*.

2.3.5   *Persistent storage area*

Each OSGi container has a dedicated area where it stores persistent information, and this area is accessible through the `BundleContext` interface's `getDataFile` method. The parameter of the method is the relative path of the file within the area. If the file doesn't exist, it is automatically created by the OSGi container the first time information is written to it. The `getDataFile` method returns a `File` object, so the Java IO API can be used to manage persistent data as for any regular Java application.

Listing 2.5 shows how to write to a file located in the persistent storage area.

Listing 2.5   Interacting with the persistent storage area of a component

```
BundleContext bundleContext = (...)

File directory = bundleContext.getDataFile("/data");
if (!directory.exists()) {                              ⊲─┐ Creates data directory
  directory.mkdir();                                        if one doesn't exist
}

File file = bundleContext.getDataFile("/data/test.txt");  ⊲─┐ References
FileWriter writer = null;                                      test.txt file
try {
  writer = new FileWriter(file, true);
  writer.write("my content");
} catch(IOException ex) {
  (...)
} finally {
  closeWriter(writer);
}
```

The persistent storage area for a component is destroyed when the component is uninstalled, but OSGi containers preserve these areas between restarts and updates for a component.

2.3.6   *Bundle activator*

As we've seen, the entry point for using the OSGi API is the `BundleContext` interface. It gives you access to all the entities and interfaces in the container and allows you to manage the current bundle as well as others. You might now be wondering how you obtain an instance of this class. Because bundles are managed within an OSGi container, the container will provide an instance of BundleContext at a specific point in the component lifecycle, thanks to an entity called an *activator.*.

An activator is registered on a per-bundle basis and is notified when its bundle starts and stops. It's responsible for initializing and finalizing its bundle. Activators implement the BundleActivator interface, which requires two methods to be implemented, corresponding to the start and stop events, as shown in the following snippet:

```
public interface BundleActivator {
  void start(BundleContext context);
  void stop(BundleContext context);
}
```

The start method is called when the bundle is started; stop is called when the bundle is stopped.

The OSGi container ensures that the stop method will only be called if the start method successfully executes. The container also guarantees that the same instance of the activator is used in both cases, making it possible to share instance attributes between the methods. Figure 2.9 shows when the OSGi container triggers the methods of an activator in the context of the lifecycle of a bundle. As you can see, the bundle activator provides a convenient way to initialize and finalize a bundle.

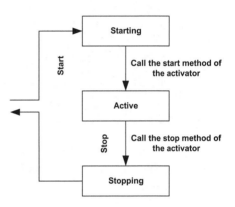

Figure 2.9 Execution of activator methods in the context of the bundle lifecycle

Listing 2.6 shows a simple implementation of the BundleActivator interface, which registers services on component startup and unregisters them at shutdown.

Listing 2.6 Registering and unregistering services with a BundleActivator

```
public class SimpleActivator implements BundleActivator {
  (...)

  public void start(BundleContext context) {
    registerServices(context);
  }

  public void stop(BundleContext context) {
    unregisterServices(context);
  }
}
```

Because the framework can't automatically detect the activator use, the activator's class for your bundle must be explicitly specified. Only one class of this kind can be used by a bundle, and this class must be contained inside the bundle.

The activator is configured in the manifest file for the bundle by using the `Bundle-Activator` header. The header's value is the fully qualified name of the activator class, as shown in the following snippet:

```
Manifest-Version: 1.0
Bundle-Version: 1.0
Bundle-Name: Simple OSGi Bundle
Bundle-ManifestVersion: 2
Bundle-SymbolicName: com.manning.osgi.simple.bundle
Bundle-Activator: com.manning.osgi.simple.SimpleActivator
```

⟵ Specifies activator for the bundle

> **Activator mechanism and Spring DM**
>
> Spring DM made the choice not to use the activator mechanism to manage Spring DM–powered components because this approach is intrusive for bundle configuration and can't be configured globally. Each bundle activator would have to have been configured explicitly in each Spring DM–powered bundle. Instead, Spring DM chose the extender pattern to manage the initialization and finalization operations; this pattern allows Spring DM–powered bundles to be handled consistently without using activators. This mechanism is described in more detail in chapter 3.

Now that we've described how to implement and use bundle activators, let's see how the service support works within OSGi and how it handles the dynamic nature of the technology.

2.4   *Service support in OSGi*

Having described the characteristics of OSGi components, how they're managed by OSGi containers, and how OSGi handles the visibility of component content and component dependencies, we'll now deal with OSGi's last main core feature, the support for services. OSGi services provide a robust way for components to interact with each other in an OSGi container, taking into account the dynamic nature of the OSGi technology (described in chapter 1).

The OSGi services feature is based on the service registry, which provides name- and property-based lookup, registration, and management of all service instances registered in the container. It also can be used to notify components when changes occur, to prevent errors from occurring. Figure 2.10 summarizes the possible interactions between the service registry and OSGi components.

OSGi services are a feature of the OSGi container, so the same rules of class visibility apply. The component providing a service must also make sure that the packages required by the service are available. This is a common requirement, as the bundle providing a service and the bundle providing the service *type* are usually different bundles (to provide better decoupling).

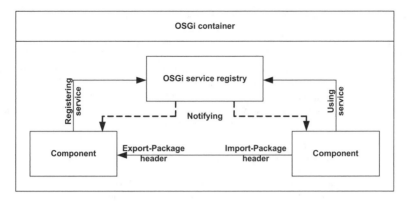

Figure 2.10 Possible interactions between OSGi components and the service registry

2.4.1 *Providing services*

OSGi services are implemented as regular POJOs—they don't need to implement the OSGi APIs. Interface-based programming is recommended when defining services, but it's not mandatory.

Once you've developed a service, the only thing you need to do to make it usable is to register it in the OSGi service registry. This is done with OSGi APIs present in the BundleContext interface.

When implementing a service using interface-based programming, it's important to put the service interface and its implementation into separate packages. Although this separation isn't required, because services reside inside the OSGi container, the package visibility features allow you to expose only the contract of the service while hiding its implementation. To achieve this, only the package containing the interface must be exported; that way nobody can see the implementation and become tightly coupled with the bundle internals by using the implementation directly.

To demonstrate this structuring, let's consider a simple Hello World service that takes a string parameter and returns it embedded in a new string. The service interface named SimpleService contains a single method named test. The following snippet shows a simple POJO implementation of this interface:

```
public class SimpleServiceImpl implements SimpleService {
  public String test(String s) {
    return "parameter: " + s;
  }
}
```

Once the service is implemented, you can register it with the OSGi service registry by using one of the two registerService methods on the BundleContext interface. These two methods take three parameters and have similar parameters, as listed in table 2.10. Only the first parameter changes, depending on the number of classes or interfaces specified. If several classes or interfaces must be specified, the type of the parameter is an array of objects instead of a single object.

Table 2.10 Parameters for the `registerService` methods

Method	Description
`clazz` or `clazzes`	One or several names used to register and identify the service. In OSGi, these names correspond to the names of the service classes or, if interface-based programming is used, the names of the implementing interfaces. Type checks are performed using these names. Several services with the same name can coexist within the OSGi service registry.
`service`	The implementation of the service itself, or an instance of the `ServiceFactory` interface.
`properties`	A set of properties to associate with the service. These properties must be of type `String`. The value can be `null` if there are no properties.

The `registerService` methods return an instance of type `ServiceRegistration`, which is dedicated to managing the registration or update of the service properties, and it must be kept for future use—typically to unregister the service.

Concerning service properties, the OSGi container automatically inserts two additional properties that are related to the service identifier (`service.id`) and the classes used for the registration (`objectClass`).

Listing 2.7 shows a typical usage of one `registerService` method to register and unregister a service within an OSGi activator.

Listing 2.7 Simple implementation of the `HelloWorldService` interface

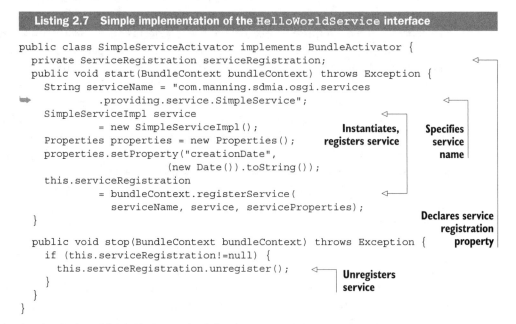

```
public class SimpleServiceActivator implements BundleActivator {
  private ServiceRegistration serviceRegistration;
  public void start(BundleContext bundleContext) throws Exception {
    String serviceName = "com.manning.sdmia.osgi.services
           .providing.service.SimpleService";
    SimpleServiceImpl service
           = new SimpleServiceImpl();
    Properties properties = new Properties();
    properties.setProperty("creationDate",
                   (new Date()).toString());
    this.serviceRegistration
           = bundleContext.registerService(
             serviceName, service, serviceProperties);
  }
  public void stop(BundleContext bundleContext) throws Exception {
    if (this.serviceRegistration!=null) {
      this.serviceRegistration.unregister();
    }
  }
}
```

Specifies service name

Instantiates, registers service

Declares service registration property

Unregisters service

As shown in table 2.10, instead of the instance of the service itself, an instance of the `ServiceFactory` interface can be registered. This allows you more flexibility in providing the service. As a matter of fact, this mechanism allows you to provide different

Service registration with Spring DM

As you can see in listing 2.7, when using only core OSGi, service registration must be done programmatically. Conversely Spring DM provides a dedicated Spring XML namespace for registering services declaratively. This feature makes it possible to expose Spring beans as OSGi services by encapsulating the use of the `registerService` method and the `ServiceRegistration` interface. During the registration, Spring DM adds additional information to the service properties. Note that other frameworks like Declarative Services or iPOJO also offer a declarative way to interact with the OSGi environment, but they're not backed up by the Spring Framework the way Spring DM is.

service instance types according to the bundle using the service or to maintain state per bundle. When a bundle tries to obtain an instance of this service, the `getService` method , which is responsible for creating the real service instance, is called. When the service instance is no longer used by the bundle, the `ungetService` method is called to clear resources stored in the service factory. The following snippet shows the content of `ServiceFactory` interface.

```
public interface ServiceFactory {
  Object getService(Bundle bundle, ServiceRegistration registration);
  void ungetService(Bundle bundle,
                ServiceRegistration registration, Object service);
```

To demonstrate the use of a service factory, imagine you want to provide particular service instances for bundles whose names begin with "com.manning". Listing 2.8 shows the implementation of such a class, called `SimpleServiceFactory`.

Listing 2.8 Simple implementation of the `ServiceFactory` interface

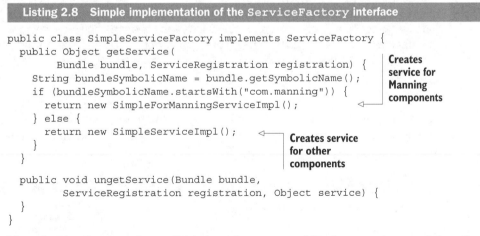

```
public class SimpleServiceFactory implements ServiceFactory {
  public Object getService(
        Bundle bundle, ServiceRegistration registration) {        Creates
    String bundleSymbolicName = bundle.getSymbolicName();         service for
    if (bundleSymbolicName.startsWith("com.manning")) {           Manning
      return new SimpleForManningServiceImpl();         ◁         components
    } else {
      return new SimpleServiceImpl();      ◁    Creates service
    }                                              for other
  }                                                components
  public void ungetService(Bundle bundle,
        ServiceRegistration registration, Object service) {
  }
}
```

Note that implementations of this interface are used by the container and therefore must be thread-safe. The instance returned by the `getService` method is cached by the framework until the bundle releases the service.

2.4.2   *Using services*

The OSGi API provides access to all services present in the OSGi service registry. As explained in chapter 1, the service registry is the feature that makes it possible for bundles to interact with each other in a way that takes the dynamic nature of the system into account. As with registering services, the OSGi API must be used to obtain, and then use, service instances. The OSGi technology offers two specific approaches for accomplishing this.

BASIC APPROACH

The first, and lowest-level, method of using services requires that you explicitly manage instances of service references yourself. OSGi provides a two-step approach to obtaining service instances:

1   Get a `ServiceReference` instance for the service, based on the service name from the `BundleContext` instance. Either the `getServiceReference` or `getService-References` method can be used. The `ServiceReference` interface makes it possible to add one level of indirection between bundles and service instances, because when you want to use the service, you must get the service instance from the corresponding `ServiceReference` instance.

2   Get the service instance itself, based on the `BundleContext` instance and the previously obtained `ServiceReference` instance.

> ### Service names
>
> When registering a service, the convention is to use the interface that the service implements as the name in the service registry. The OSGi framework requires the name to match an interface that is implemented or the name of the registered object's class or one of its superclasses. But if you register an implementation name, then look up the interface name, the lookup will fail unless you have physically registered both interface and implementation names. Fortunately, Spring DM has some schemes for making the matching of class names within a hierarchy more natural.

Listing 2.9 shows a typical approach to getting, using, and freeing a service instance. The `ungetService` method is called at the end to notify the container that we've finished using the service.

Listing 2.9   Consuming an OSGi service

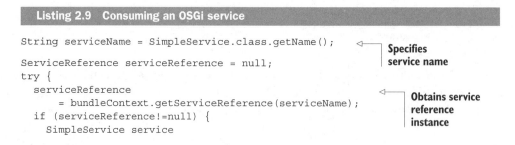

```
String serviceName = SimpleService.class.getName();          Specifies
                                                             service name
ServiceReference serviceReference = null;
try {
  serviceReference
     = bundleContext.getServiceReference(serviceName);        Obtains service
  if (serviceReference!=null) {                               reference
    SimpleService service                                     instance
```

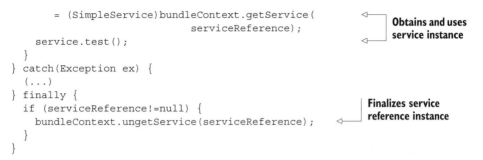

```
            = (SimpleService)bundleContext.getService(
                            serviceReference);
    service.test();
  }
} catch(Exception ex) {
  (...)
} finally {
  if (serviceReference!=null) {
    bundleContext.ungetService(serviceReference);
  }
}
```

Obtains and uses service instance

Finalizes service reference instance

`ServiceReference` instances can also be obtained by using bundle instances, which provide the following methods:

- `getRegisteredServices`—Returns the list of services registered by the bundle
- `getServicesInUse`—Returns the list of the bundle services used by other bundles

SERVICETRACKER

In addition to providing these low level APIs for accessing services, OSGi offers a utility class named `ServiceTracker`. To use it, its package, `org.osgi.util.tracker`, must be imported in the manifest file of your component. `ServiceTracker` correctly and transparently gets and ungets services based on service events, greatly simplifying the handling of service lifecycles. When using `ServiceTracker`, you no longer need to manipulate instances of `ServiceReference` type.

> ## OSGi and generics
>
> You'll notice that many of the OSGi APIs have a distinctly "old Java" feel to them, leveraging none of the ease-of-use features introduced in Java 5, such as generics and covariant return types. Service registration even takes a `Dictionary` object (a class that was made obsolete in Java SE 1.2) rather than a `Map`! This is because OSGi is designed with maximum portability in mind, being targeted at not just enterprise systems, but also embedded and Java ME-style applications, where the JVM version typically trails the state of the art significantly. Fortunately this restriction is likely to be lifted in OSGi R5.

The first step in using `ServiceTracker` is to create a `ServiceTracker` instance for a service or set of services, then call its `open` method. Then you can obtain service instances using its `getService` method. Because the class is generic, you need to cast the return instance. When you have finished using the `ServiceTracker` instance, you only have to close it.

Listing 2.10 shows the way to use this class.

Listing 2.10   Using the `ServiceTracker`

```
String serviceName = SimpleService.class.getName();

ServiceTracker serviceTracker = null;
```

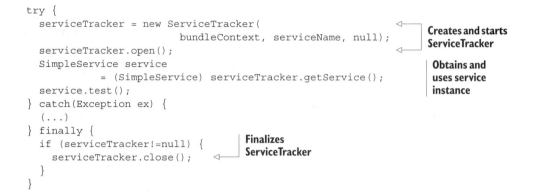

```
try {
  serviceTracker = new ServiceTracker(
                        bundleContext, serviceName, null);        Creates and starts
  serviceTracker.open();                                          ServiceTracker
  SimpleService service                                           Obtains and
          = (SimpleService) serviceTracker.getService();          uses service
  service.test();                                                 instance
} catch(Exception ex) {
  (...)
} finally {
  if (serviceTracker!=null) {        Finalizes
    serviceTracker.close();          ServiceTracker
  }
}
```

Referencing services with Spring DM

Spring DM allows you to reference an OSGi service directly by configuring dependencies, thanks to its custom namespace. The reference is then treated by Spring as a regular Java bean. The referencing mechanisms are directly integrated into the Spring DM Framework itself, and the tricky work of handling OSGi dynamics is done transparently for you (assuming that the dynamics don't involve services with state, especially state that can depend on the clients using the services).

2.4.3   Service event support

Like other OSGi features, OSGi services are dynamic. Applications using OSGi services likewise need to take account of service availability. OSGi will notify registered observers when events are triggered, providing information such as the service properties, the registering bundle, and the bundles that use the service.

The OSGi API

The core of the OSGi API consists of 27 interfaces and classes (as of OSGi 4.2, in the `org.osgi.framework` package), making it a good-sized API to learn. Throughout this book, we say that the use of this API is tedious and error-prone, but this is mainly a matter of point of view. The OSGi API is tedious and error-prone for application developers who would use it every day to build enterprise applications, but we don't blame the OSGi Alliance for the API they designed, because it's well suited for middleware development. We're sure that the teams who developed tools like Spring DM, iPOJO, and Declarative Services implementations have been happy to work with such an efficient API.

OSGi provides the `ServiceListener` interface, shown in the following snippet, to handle these events:

```
public interface ServiceListener {
  void serviceChanged(ServiceEvent event);
}
```

This interface contains a serviceChanged method, which provides the event object, of type ServiceEvent. This event object contains both the event type and the relevant ServiceReference, as shown in the following snippet:

```
public interface ServiceEvent {
  public static final int REGISTERED = 0x00000001;
  public static final int MODIFIED= 0x00000002;
  public static final int UNREGISTERING = 0x00000004;

  ServiceReference getServiceReference();
  int getType()
}
```

Listing 2.11 shows a simple example of using of this interface to print a message whenever a service is registered, unregistered, or updated.

Listing 2.11   A ServiceListener implementation handling service events

```
public class SimpleServiceListener implements ServiceListener {

  private String getServiceName(ServiceEvent event) {
    String[] objectClass = (String[])
        event.getServiceReference().getProperty("objectClass");
    return objectClass[0];
  }

  public void serviceChanged(ServiceEvent event) {
    int type = event.getType();                              Gets service name
    String serviceName = getServiceName(event);    ◁─────   from event
    String symbolicName
        = event.getServiceReference()               ◁──     Gets bundle
          .getBundle().getSymbolicName();                    symbolic name

    if (type==ServiceEvent.REGISTERED) {                              ◁─┐
      System.out.println("Service " + serviceName
          + " registred by the bundle " + symbolicName + "...");      ◁─
    } else if (type==ServiceEvent.UNREGISTERING) {            Handles service
      System.out.println("Service " + serviceName                    event
          + " being unregistered by the bundle "
          + symbolicName + "...");                                   ◁─┘
    } else if (type==ServiceEvent.MODIFIED) {
      System.out.println("Service " + serviceName
          + " modified by the bundle " + symbolicName + "...");
    }
  }
}
```

Once you've implemented a listener, it needs to be registered with the container using BundleContext.addServiceListener as shown in the following snippet:

```
BundleContext context = (...)
SimpleServiceListener listener = new SimpleServiceListener();
Context.adServiceListener(listener);
```

That's it for OSGi services. Let's now see the last big feature of the OSGi technology—how it handles native code within components.

2.5   *Handling native code*

OSGi provides support for loading native libraries from components. This support includes loading the correct library based on the OS of the target host. Each component's classloader intercepts calls to System.loadLibrary and loads libraries based on the configuration in the component's manifest file. As with any Java program, JNI must be used within the Java code wishing to call a native library.

> ### Java Native Interface (JNI)
>
> JNI is a framework in the Java platform that makes it possible for Java code running in a JVM to call, and to be called by, native libraries. This framework is particularly useful when applications can't be written entirely in Java. For such applications, JNI provides interfaces to map native code structures to Java classes. Note that a single native library can only be used by one class loader.

This configuration of native libraries is done using the Bundle-NativeCode header, which defines the location of native libraries inside components and supports the set of attributes listed in table 2.11.

Table 2.11   Attributes of the Bundle-NativeCode header

Attribute	Description
osname	The name of the target OS for the native library
osversion	The target OS version for the native library
processor	The target processor architecture for the native library
language	The ISO code for a language associated with the library
selection-filter	A selection filter that must be a valid filter expression indicating whether or not the native code should be enabled

> ### Filter expressions
>
> A filter expression is an OSGi-defined construct that provides a concise description of constraints based on attributes. Its syntax is based upon the string representation of Lightweight Directory Access Protocol (LDAP) search filters. This kind of expression must be enclosed between opening and closing parentheses, (and), and it accepts characters like the ampersand and pipe (& and |) for combining expressions, the exclamation mark (!) for negation, and the equal sign (=) for comparisons of attribute values. Filter expressions also accept wildcards. In the context of the Bundle-NativeCode header, the selection-filter attribute can have the value (com.acme.windowing=win32) in order to enable native code having the property com.acme.windowing with the value win32.

> **(continued)**
> This kind of expression can be used either in the attributes of headers like `selection-filter` for `Bundle-NativeCode` or as parameters to methods. For example, the `getServiceReferences` method takes a filter to obtain a subset of service instances.

Suppose you want to use a math library that provides a set of high-performance math functions for a component. Your OSGi container runs under the Linux OS, and its developers provide a shared library called `libmathematical.so` for this environment. You can create a `lib` directory in the structure of your component and make your configuration point to this directory, as shown in the following snippet:

```
Bundle-ManifestVersion: 2
Bundle-SymbolicName: com.manning.osgi.native.code
Bundle-NativeCode: lib/libmathematical.so
(...)
```

In this example, your component is tied to the target execution environment. OSGi also can load the right library for the environment, as shown in the following snippet, by using the `osname` and `processor` attributes:

```
Bundle-ManifestVersion: 2
Bundle-SymbolicName: com.manning.osgi.native.code
Bundle-NativeCode: lib/libmathematical.so;osname=Linux;processor=i686,
    lib/mathematical.dd;osname=Windows;processor=x86
(...)
```

Finally, it's time to look at how to diagnose errors when implementing and executing OSGi components. Developers new to OSGi can find errors difficult to understand and resolve because OSGi provides slightly different mechanisms than classic Java applications.

2.6 Diagnosing errors

OSGi works quite differently from classic Java applications, but no technology always works perfectly, so you need to know how to diagnose errors and isolate their root cause. This section describes how to diagnose and resolve basic errors, but it certainly isn't exhaustive.

As we have explained OSGi relies on Java but provides a completely new approach for implementing modular Java applications. The technology implements a strict classloader model and dependency management for components. Most of the errors you'll encounter in OSGi development come from these two features.

We'll describe how to diagnose errors using the Equinox console, which provides a set of commands to inspect entities in the container. Other containers provide similar kinds of tools, but the command names can vary.

Let's look at an example. Suppose we have a container that includes two components with the following behavior:

- `com.manning.osgi.bundle1`—Provides and registers a simple service in the OSGi service registry
- `com.manning.osgi.bundle2`—Consumes the registered service from `com.manning.osgi.bundle1`

We purposefully left some errors in the configuration and coding of these two components. Figure 2.11 shows the dependencies between the bundles and their interactions with the OSGi service registry.

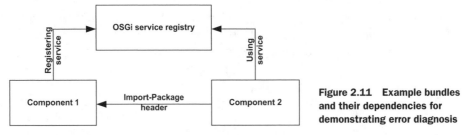

Figure 2.11 Example bundles and their dependencies for demonstrating error diagnosis

2.6.1   *Detecting components with problems*

When you notice problems in your application, the first step is to determine which components seem to have problems. Problems can obviously come from internal execution—and you'll need to debug the code if this is the case—but they can also be caused by issues preventing components becoming available in the container.

By having a look at bundle states, you can get a first hint of where the problem lies. If the autostart mode of your container is enabled, all the bundles should be in the active state except for fragment bundles in the resolved state. Fragment bundles are necessarily linked to the host bundle they extend, which makes it easy to identify them. (Fragment bundles are discussed in chapter 3.)

We can display component states within the Equinox container with the `ss` (short status) command, which gives the following output when components have started successfully:

```
osgi> ss
id  State       Bundle
0   ACTIVE      system.bundle_3.2.2.R32x_v20070118
5   ACTIVE      com.manning.osgi.bundle1_1.0.0
6   ACTIVE      com.manning.osgi.bundle2_1.0.0
```

If all your bundles are in autostart mode, and problems occur during their processing by the container, these components will remain in either the installed or resolved state. These component states offer interesting hints, enabling you to diagnose where errors may be coming from. For instance, if a problem occurs during the resolution of dependencies for bundle2, the output of the `ss` command would be as follows:

```
osgi> ss
id  State       Bundle
0   ACTIVE      system.bundle_3.2.2.R32x_v20070118       Bundle has a
5   ACTIVE      com.manning.osgi.bundle1_1.0.0           problem resolving
6   INSTALL     com.manning.osgi.bundle2_1.0.0           dependencies
```

2.6.2 Detecting different kinds of problems

After you've identified the component with problems, the important thing is to identify in which part of the component lifecycle the error occurred. We'll describe a set of basic problems here. We'll describe other problems in more depth in subsequent chapters.

MISSING IMPORT-PACKAGE

First, we'll introduce an error in the manifest of bundle2 by removing the `Import-Package` header related to the bundle1 packages. The component state is installed, and when a user tries to manually start it, a `BundleException` exception occurs, indicating that a constraint is missing, as shown in listing 2.12.

Listing 2.12   Exception related to a missing constraint exception

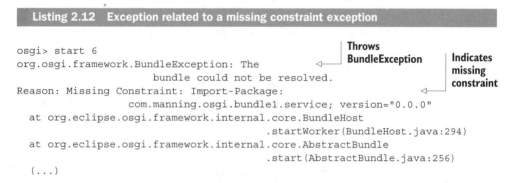

```
osgi> start 6
org.osgi.framework.BundleException: The
                    bundle could not be resolved.
Reason: Missing Constraint: Import-Package:
                com.manning.osgi.bundle1.service; version="0.0.0"
  at org.eclipse.osgi.framework.internal.core.BundleHost
                            .startWorker(BundleHost.java:294)
  at org.eclipse.osgi.framework.internal.core.AbstractBundle
                            .start(AbstractBundle.java:256)
  (...)
```

The name of the missing package is visible in the content of the exception—the package `com.manning.osgi.bundle1.service` in this example. Adding this package in the `Import-Package` header of bundle2 solves the problem.

ERROR DURING COMPONENT INITIALIZATION

Errors can also occur when the component is started by a user. To illustrate, we'll manually throw a `RuntimeException` exception in the `start` method of the component activator. The component can be resolved, but when trying to start it manually, a `BundleException` exception is still thrown. Listing 2.13 shows the throwing of such an exception.

Listing 2.13   Exception during component initialization

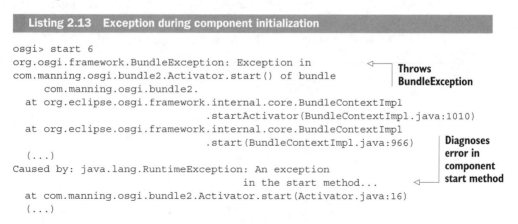

```
osgi> start 6
org.osgi.framework.BundleException: Exception in
com.manning.osgi.bundle2.Activator.start() of bundle
    com.manning.osgi.bundle2.
  at org.eclipse.osgi.framework.internal.core.BundleContextImpl
                        .startActivator(BundleContextImpl.java:1010)
  at org.eclipse.osgi.framework.internal.core.BundleContextImpl
                        .start(BundleContextImpl.java:966)
  (...)
Caused by: java.lang.RuntimeException: An exception
                        in the start method...
  at com.manning.osgi.bundle2.Activator.start(Activator.java:16)
  (...)
```

For more details on this error, you'd need to have a look in the activator to see what happened and how to solve it.

2.7 *Summary*

OSGi fills the modularity void in the Java platform by providing first-class component support and strict classloader isolation. The technology introduces a new approach to developing Java applications, requiring developers to explicitly specify which dependencies and dependency versions must be used. All these features must be configured for each component via the component's manifest file and a set of specific headers defined by OSGi. Components are black boxes by default and can completely control what parts are visible and what classes and services can be used from other components.

OSGi also provides a very lightweight in-JVM service-oriented framework. Each component in the container can both provide and consume services by interacting with the service registry. This feature allows components to interact in predictable ways while remaining dynamic. The service registry allows components to be notified when updates occur and to adapt accordingly.

Fine-grained interactions between components and the container itself are made possible thanks to the OSGi API. Implementing advanced mechanisms for managing and update components and services is possible, thanks to the ability to inspect installed components and their contents and to handle update notifications. This API makes the dynamic nature of the OSGi platform possible.

OSGi is a fairly low-level framework for implementing modular applications in Java. Indeed, application developers can find that some features, such as services, are tedious to use through the OSGi API. On the other hand, whereas OSGi provides a complete and dynamic component platform, it doesn't place constraints on the implementation of components. It's up to additional tools to provide appropriate abstractions and help developers adhere to best practices when using OSGi. Spring DM aims to address all these aspects by making OSGi development simpler, more convenient, and more efficient. In this chapter, we gave some hints about OSGi features that Spring DM supports or leverages.

If you want to go deeper into the OSGi technology, we recommend reading Manning's *OSGi in Action*, by Richard S. Hall, Karl Pauls, Stuart McCulloch, and David Savage, which is dedicated to this technology. It is to be published in fall 2010.

Getting started
with Spring DM

3

This chapter covers

- Spring DM extender basic operation
- Installing Spring DM in an OSGi container
- Creating, packaging, running, and testing
  Spring DM–powered bundles

So far you've seen little of Spring DM itself, except in chapter 1, where we built our very first Spring DM–powered bundle. Spring DM is indeed a bridge between the OSGi and Spring worlds, and that's why we provided introductions to both in chapters 1 and 2. Now you're all set to get started with Spring DM!

Spring DM offers a lot of features, such as dependency injection and its ability to handle the dynamic nature of an OSGi environment, but before we dive into all that, you need a practical understanding of Spring DM's mechanisms, especially its extender, which is at the heart of the framework. Working with OSGi isn't an easy task, and it can appear daunting when you don't know exactly how to manage your workspace. We'll do our best to navigate you through this difficult path by explaining how to install Spring DM in an OSGi container from the very beginning. You'll also learn how to write your first bundles, including a web bundle, with a little help from Maven 2 to automate packaging. Last, but not least, we'll take our first steps with the Spring DM integration test framework.

By the end of this chapter, you'll know about the basics of Spring DM, including how to install it in an OSGi container and how to set up a Spring DM project with Maven 2.

3.1   Using Spring in OSGi components

Good news: with Spring DM, you can now use the power of the Spring Framework in your OSGi development. This means that Spring DM is able to scan bundles and manage a dedicated Spring application context for them.

Perhaps you know the Spring Framework for its lightweight container, and you'll see that it will help you in assembling the inner parts of your OSGi bundles. But don't forget that Spring also comes with an AOP framework and support for a large set of enterprise frameworks, like Hibernate or JPA.

This section introduces you to the basic mechanics of Spring DM: how the framework scans OSGi bundles, how it associates a Spring application context with each of them, and how it manages this application context for the bundles, unleashing the full power of the Spring Framework into OSGi.

3.1.1   Embedding the Spring application context within components

Spring DM introduces a new kind of OSGi bundle: Spring-powered bundles. This marketing-sounding expression means that a bundle can automatically have a dedicated Spring application context managed by Spring DM, and so can benefit from all the features of the Spring lightweight container. A Spring-powered bundle is still a traditional OSGi bundle and can import or export Java packages, but it doesn't need to worry about initializing and exporting its services or looking up its dependencies, as shown in figure 3.1. For these tedious tasks that normally imply the use of the OSGi

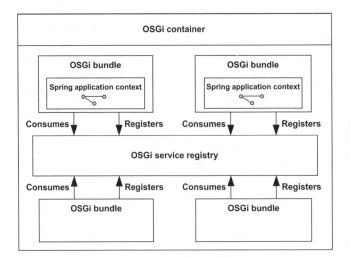

Figure 3.1   **Spring-powered bundles benefit from the Spring Framework features (dependency injection, AOP, and so on) but can also benefit from the OSGi environment like any other OSGi bundle. Spring DM helps them with tasks like interacting with the OSGi service registry.**

API, a Spring-powered bundle can rely on the Spring lightweight container and on Spring DM's capability to communicate with the OSGi platform, using an XML configuration or annotations.

You saw in the previous chapter how a bundle can do initialization through its `BundleActivator`. Usually, bundles use a `BundleActivator` to create and initialize their inner parts, and to consume and export some services. To do this, you need to know how to use the OSGi API, which seems logical when developing OSGi applications, but manipulating this API over and over, for each of your bundles, is tedious; component initialization and OSGi service handling imply complex and error-prone API-driven programming, in particular when dealing with OSGi's dynamic nature.

A Spring-powered bundle automagically has an instance of the Spring container tied to itself. The container handles declaratively all the initialization and wiring of the bundle's internal artifacts. You can leverage all the features of the Spring lightweight container—dependency injection, AOP, enterprise support, and so on—and you don't need to write a bundle activator: the Spring container instance is automatically bootstrapped by Spring DM.

When it comes to interacting with the OSGi platform, Spring DM offers configuration features to consume and export services, listen to OSGi events, and reliably handle some of the dynamic aspects of OSGi. These OSGi configuration features follow the Spring philosophy: they can be part of an XML Spring configuration file (with a dedicated OSGi namespace) or they can be annotations. Table 3.1 summarizes how plain OSGi and Spring DM compare regarding the handling of some OSGi-specific aspects.

Table 3.1 Comparing plain OSGi and Spring DM bundles

Action	Plain OSGi	Spring DM
Initialization	Manual; done within a `BundleActivator` that needs to be written and explicitly declared.	Declarative; powered by the Spring container (dependency injection, AOP). Bootstrapping is automatically handled by Spring DM.
Finalization	Manual; done within a `BundleActivator` that needs to be written and explicitly declared.	Declarative; powered by the Spring container. Destruction is automatically handled by Spring DM.
OSGi service registry interaction	Manual; done by using the `BundleContext` interface.	Declarative; uses Spring DM dedicated XML namespace or annotations.
Dynamic updates	Manual; code must handle all the dynamic updates in a safe way.	Automatic; Spring DM handles service appearance and disappearance in a reliable way.

At the heart of the Spring lightweight container is the `ApplicationContext` interface, which represents an instance of the container. There are several implementations of `ApplicationContext`, depending on the environment the Spring container is running in; OSGi is no exception, as Spring DM provides its own implementation.

3.1.2   *Spring DM's OSGi-aware application context*

Spring DM introduces its own OSGi-specific application context with the `Osgi-BundleXmlApplicationContext` class. Through a bunch of internal interfaces and abstract classes, the `OsgiBundleXmlApplicationContext` class offers the following functionality:

- Access to the owning `Bundle` and its corresponding `BundleContext`, because there is a one-to-one relation between a Spring DM application context and an OSGi bundle
- Conditional publication of the application context in the OSGi service registry
- Specific resource search strategies
- New bundle scope
- Application context lifecycle broken into steps to allow asynchronous startup, initialization, and destruction

> ### Spring bean factory and application context
>
> At the heart of the Spring lightweight container are its mechanisms to manage any kind of Java object. These mechanisms range from object instantiation and dependency injection to behavior addition through AOP and destruction (and even more!). The `BeanFactory` interface handles most of the bean lifecycle operations (creation, injection, and destruction). The `ApplicationContext` is built on the `BeanFactory` and adds other functionality, such as easier integration with Spring AOP, event propagation, and context inheritance.
>
> In short, `ApplicationContext` provides a lot of enterprise-specific features, and its use should always be preferred to `BeanFactory`. Spring containers in Spring DM are built on standard Spring `ApplicationContext` implementations.

The `OsgiBundleXmlApplicationContext` class implements all OSGi-specific behaviors required for proper Spring application context startup. Spring DM uses it for standard OSGi bundles and turns to its little sister, `OsgiBundleXmlWebApplicationContext`, for web OSGi bundles.

    The handling of the OSGi application context lifecycle isn't part of a developer's day-to-day job; everything is done transparently by the Spring DM extender bundle, which we'll describe in the next section.

> ### Bean scopes in Spring
>
> Bean configurations in Spring XML files can be thought of as recipes, and as such are often referred to as bean definitions. Based on these definitions or recipes, the Spring lightweight container creates bean instances.

(continued)

The definition controls not only the bean configuration and dependencies but also its *scope*. Each time you ask for a bean from the lightweight container, the container checks the bean scope to decide which instance of the bean to return. The simplest scope is the *singleton* scope: the bean is created once, and for each request, the lightweight container returns the same instance. Singleton beans are usually thread-safe objects, like data access objects or business services. Another commonly used scope is the *prototype*: a new bean is created each time you ask for it. Prototypes are usually not thread-safe or single-use objects.

Singleton and prototype scopes were the only two scopes allowed in Spring 1. Spring 2 introduced new web-based bean scopes. With web-based scopes, beans can be tied to the HTTP request or session and even injected into singleton or prototype beans, with the lightweight container taking care of the wiring.

The Spring 2 (and above) bean-scoping mechanism is extensible, and Spring DM takes advantage of this feature by providing the *bundle* scope. When a bundle-scoped bean is exported to the OSGi service registry, one instance of the bean will be created for each bundle importing it.

3.1.3 *Spring DM's extender mechanisms*

Spring DM provides an extender bundle, which listens for bundle installation events, detects Spring DM–powered bundles, and creates corresponding Spring application contexts. For those familiar with Spring in a web environment, the Spring DM extender is the equivalent of the `ContextLoaderListener`, which loads the root application context of a web application. Spring DM extender's in-depth mechanisms and configuration are covered in chapter 4, but you'll see the basics in this subsection. Figure 3.2 shows how the Spring DM extender fits into an OSGi container, along with Spring-powered bundles.

The extender pattern in OSGi

As Peter Kriens has stated, "the extender pattern allows other bundles to extend the functionality [of OSGi] in a specific domain".[1] In OSGi, an extender listens to bundle lifecycle events and reacts to them according to predefined conventions. Often, these conventions are identified by specific headers in the bundle manifest, like a header indicating the path to a Spring configuration file.

Let's look at an example. OSGi provides a basic HTTP service, which allows for registering servlets in a web container.

---

[1] Peter Kriens, aQute Software Consultancy, "Extender Pattern with Automatic Servlet Registration," http://www.aqute.biz/Snippets/Extender.

(continued)

Any bundle can plug a servlet into the web container, but this requires a complex programmatic registration, and this cumbersome and error-prone code snippet must be written (usually in the `BundleActivator` of the bundle) each time a servlet is registered. Wouldn't it be simpler to have a dedicated header, whose value corresponds to the servlet class. Then a dedicated bundle could track this header and, when a bundle is installed, do all the registration dirty work in a reliable way. This is possible, and this dedicated bundle would be called an extender.

In Spring DM, the extender pattern can be achieved with the `BundleListener` interface. The `BundleActivator` of the extender bundle registers a `BundleListener`, which listens to bundle events and creates or destroys Spring application contexts depending on the bundle content. Other key contributions of the extender pattern implementation are the ability to inspect bundle content and to act on behalf of the inspected bundle (such as for service publications). The extender pattern is particularly important in Spring DM because application contexts are only started when service dependencies have been satisfied. This management would be onerous in the extreme for a programmer to handle by hand.

In OSGi 4.2, the new `BundleTracker` class provides additional support for implementing the extender pattern. Also in OSGi 4.2, the extender pattern is the subject of the OSGi standardization process.

The Spring DM extender creates application contexts asynchronously, on a different thread than the one handling the bundle start event. This ensures that bundle startup is fast and doesn't block the entire OSGi container. The asynchronous creation of application contexts is also vital to the ability of the extender to handle dependent bundles, especially if there are cycles. This is the default behavior, and it can be overridden.

The Spring DM extender also takes care of application context destruction when the corresponding bundle is being shut down. In contrast to creation, destruction is done synchronously.

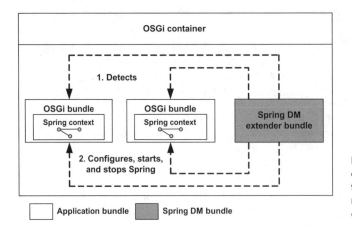

Figure 3.2 The Spring DM extender bundle scans bundles for Spring configuration files and manages a Spring application context on their behalf.

Spring application context management in OSGi environments is an example of the inversion of control (IoC) pattern: Spring DM–powered bundles wait for the extender to inspect them and create their application context; no application code is needed for this task. The Spring DM extender is familiar with the OSGi-specific application context classes presented in the previous section and uses them to properly load lightweight container instances.

How does the extender determine that a bundle is indeed Spring DM–powered? To be Spring DM–powered, a bundle must meet one these conditions:

- Contain a META-INF/spring directory with Spring XML files in it. Spring DM will scan all files with an .xml extension in lexical order and try to create a single application context from them.
- Contain a `Spring-Context` header in its META-INF/MANIFEST.MF file. The header value specifies the configuration file location and can use the Spring resource syntax.

We'll stick with the first alternative in this chapter, as this is the simplest and the most commonly used. All the details of the discovery of Spring DM–powered bundles are covered in chapter 4.

3.1.4 *Kinds of supported bundles*

Spring DM supports two different kinds of bundles: standard Spring-powered bundles and web bundles. In the previous section, we introduced the Spring DM extender, which tracks bundles with specific content or headers to start up Spring application contexts. This extender supports the first kind of bundle. Spring DM also provides a web extender, which supports deploying web applications, packaged as standard OSGi bundles, in a dedicated web container.

Figure 3.3 illustrates the two kinds of supported bundles, along with their corresponding Spring DM extenders, and a web container packaged as an OSGi bundle.

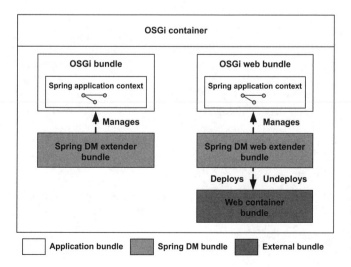

Figure 3.3 Spring DM supports standard Spring-powered bundles, but is also able to deploy web bundles, thanks to its web extender.

The two Spring DM–powered bundles are referred to as application bundles because they're created for an application, unlike other bundles (Spring DM extenders and the web container), which serve infrastructure purposes.

Thanks to its Spring application context, a Spring-powered bundle can leverage the Spring Framework for its internal wiring, but that's only half of the work. Spring DM doesn't only manage the Spring context according to the bundle lifecycle; it also helps the context interact with the OSGi environment, especially with the service registry.

3.1.5   Spring DM's osgi namespace

Spring DM provides an `osgi` namespace whose primary goal is to interact with the OSGi service registry. Before listing the namespace tags, let's look at how to declare the namespace in an XML Spring configuration file.

The `osgi` namespace can be used nested in another top-level namespace (usually the `beans` namespace), as shown in listing 3.1.

> **Listing 3.1   Spring DM `osgi` namespace declaration nested in Spring `beans` namespace**

```
<?xml version="1.0" encoding="UTF-8"?>
<beans
   xmlns="http://www.springframework.org/schema/beans"          ⟵  Uses beans
   xmlns:xsi="http://www.w3.org/2001/XMLSchema-instance"             namespace as default
   xmlns:osgi="http://www.springframework.org/schema/
       osgi"                                                     Declares Spring DM name-
   xsi:schemaLocation="http://www.springframework.org/schema/beans   space with osgi prefix
      http://www.springframework.org/schema/beans/spring-beans.xsd
      http://www.springframework.org/schema/osgi
      http://www.springframework.org/schema/osgi/spring-osgi.xsd">

   <osgi:service id="myServiceOsgi" ref="myService"             Uses Spring DM name-
          interface="com.manning.sdmia.MyService" />            space with osgi prefix

</beans>
```

Spring XML schema-based configuration

Spring has used XML schema-based configuration since its 2.0 version. XML schemas replaced a more generic DTD-driven approach, using mainly two tags: `bean` for declaring a bean and `property` to inject dependencies. (Our apologies to the Spring creators for this quick-and-dirty summary!) This approach worked perfectly well for creating beans and injecting their dependencies, but this was not sufficient from a developer point of view. The bean/property division was unable to hide complex bean creation, and this was a real shortcoming for advanced features like AOP or security (former Acegi Security users will understand!): XML configuration used to be nonintuitive and very verbose.

Spring 2.0 came with a new, extensible, schema-based XML configuration system. XML schemas describe the syntax and corresponding Java namespace handlers encapsulate the bean-creation logic.

> **(continued)**
>
> The Spring Framework provides namespaces for its modules (AOP, transaction, JMS, and so on) and other Spring-based projects can benefit from the namespace-extension mechanism to provide their own namespaces. Each Spring portfolio project comes with one or more dedicated namespaces to provide the most natural and appropriate configuration using specific tags. Spring DM is no exception, with its `osgi` and `compendium` schemas.

The Spring DM namespace can also be declared as the top-level namespace, and so can be used without any prefix, as shown in listing 3.2.

Listing 3.2 Spring DM `osgi` namespace declared as the top-level namespace

```
<?xml version="1.0" encoding="UTF-8"?>
<beans:beans
   xmlns="http://www.springframework.org/schema/osgi"          Uses osgi namespace
   xmlns:xsi="http://www.w3.org/2001/XMLSchema-instance"        as default
   xmlns:beans="http://www.springframework.org/schema/          Declares beans name-
       beans"                                                    space with beans prefix
   xsi:schemaLocation="http://www.springframework.org/schema/osgi
      http://www.springframework.org/schema/osgi/spring-osgi.xsd
      http://www.springframework.org/schema/beans
      http://www.springframework.org/schema/beans/spring-beans.xsd">

   <service id="myServiceOsgi" ref="myService"                 Uses Spring DM name-
           interface="com.manning.sdmia.MyService" />          space without prefix

</beans:beans>
```

You'll use the `osgi` namespace to publish your Spring beans in the OSGi service registry, as well as to consume other services from this same registry. Imported services can then be used as standard Spring beans and injected into your bundle beans. Table 3.2 lists the main tags available in the `osgi` namespace. Publishing and consuming services with Spring DM is covered in depth in chapter 5.

Table 3.2 The main Spring DM `osgi` namespace tags

Tag name	Description
service	Publishes a bean in the OSGi service registry
reference	Retrieves a service from the OSGi service registry
list/set	Retrieves a list or set of services published in the OSGi service registry, matching a predefined criteria
bundle	Defines a bean representing a bundle object

By tying a Spring application context to a bundle and allowing declarative interaction with the OSGi registry, Spring DM deserves its title of *bridge* between OSGi and Spring.

This is the main goal of Spring DM—applying the Spring application model to OSGi without much pain and effort—and that's what we introduced in this section. This was the theory you needed to fully understand the installation and first use of Spring DM, which we'll cover in the next section.

3.2   Installing Spring DM

In this section, we'll look at how you can prepare an OSGi environment to host your Spring DM–powered bundles. You already got a glimpse of this in chapter 1, with the Hello World bundle, but in this chapter we'll dive deeper into the details of container configuration and provisioning, and we'll also take a look at Spring DM's web support.

3.2.1   Configuring a container

You should know by now that OSGi is a specification, so several OSGi container implementations exist in this competitive market. Spring DM is tested on three of these, which appear to be the most popular because they're feature-rich, reliable, and open source: Eclipse Equinox, Apache Felix, and Knopflerfish. To keep things simple, we'll stick to Equinox—the most popular one—but the vast majority of what we'll look at is also valid on the other OSGi platforms.

For now, we'll assume we're working in a dedicated directory, where we'll build our Spring DM samples.

The Equinox binary is available in the Spring DM distribution (org.eclipse. osgi-3.5.1.R35x_v20090827.jar). Create a container directory in your working directory, and copy the Equinox binary to it. The Equinox binary contains its own classes but also the OSGi API classes, which explains its ease of installation.

You saw in chapter 1 that Equinox can be easily started using this command:

```
java -jar org.eclipse.osgi-3.5.1.R35x_v20090827.jar –console
```

We also saw that some diagnostic information is accessible using the `ss` (short status) command:

```
osgi> ss

Framework is launched.

id      State      Bundle
0       ACTIVE     org.eclipse.osgi_3.5.1.R35x_v20090827

osgi>
```

You can shut down Equinox with the `exit` command.

Equinox creates a `configuration` directory, where it keeps working files (container state, log, and so on). If you look in this directory, you'll find a log file with a scary error message saying Equinox cannot find an application service. That's because Equinox is integrated with Eclipse and, by default, it tries to start an Eclipse application. As we'll be sticking with plain vanilla OSGi, we don't need an Eclipse application, and this default behavior can be overridden using a dedicated option; to do this we need to create an Equinox configuration file, config.ini, in the configuration directory. Here is the content of an appropriate config.ini to prevent Equinox from trying to start an application:

```
eclipse.ignoreApp=true
```

With this option set, the scary error message should be gone. Your working directory should now have the following structure:

```
container/
  org.eclipse.osgi-3.5.1.R35x_v20090827.jar
  configuration/
    config.ini
    (Equinox's own files)
```

Your container is now ready to receive Spring DM bundles!

3.2.2 *Provisioning a container for simple use*

Once the OSGi container is ready, you need to copy the bundles Spring DM needs from the Spring DM distribution, and organize them in the `container` directory in a dedicated `bundles` directory.

As we saw earlier, Spring DM's central component is its extender, which detects Spring-powered bundles and bootstraps their corresponding Spring application contexts. The extender is an OSGi-compliant bundle and relies on two other Spring DM bundles. Table 3.3 lists the main Spring DM bundles.

Table 3.3   The main Spring DM bundles

Bundle	Filename	Description
Spring DM I/O support	spring-osgi-io-2.0.0.M1.jar	Provides support for resource loading in OSGi environments
Spring DM core	spring-osgi-core-2.0.0.M1.jar	Provides OSGi-based Spring application contexts and service publishing/consuming facilities
Spring DM extender	spring-osgi-extender-2.0.0.M1.jar	Detects and bootstraps Spring-powered bundles

Spring DM application contexts and AOP features are built on top of the Spring Framework and, as such, Spring DM depends on some of its modules. As of Spring 2.5, all Spring modules are packaged as OSGi bundles and can be used in an OSGi container. Table 3.4 lists the Spring modules Spring DM needs and their transitive dependencies.

Table 3.4   Spring dependencies needed by Spring DM

Bundle	Filename	Description
Spring Core	org.springframework.core-3.0.0.RC1.jar	Provides utility, I/O, and exception classes
Spring Beans	org.springframework.beans-3.0.0.RC1.jar	Provides basic lightweight container features and the bean factory

Table 3.4   Spring dependencies needed by Spring DM *(continued)*

Bundle	Filename	Description
Spring Context	org.springframework.context-3.0.0.RC1.jar	Provides more advanced light-weight container features and the application context
Spring Context Support	org.springframework.context.support-3.0.0.RC1.jar	Provides integration classes for common third-party libraries
Spring Expression Language	org.springframework.expression-3.0.0.RC1.jar	Defines Spring Expression Language parser
Spring ASM	org.springframework.asm-3.0.0.RC1.jar	Repackaged version of the ASM library
Spring AOP	org.springframework.aop-3.0.0.RC1.jar	Provides Spring AOP API and AspectJ integration
AOP Alliance	com.springsource.org.aopalliance-1.0.0.jar	Defines AOP API used in Spring AOP
CGLIB	com.springsource.net.sf.cglib-2.1.3.jar	Allows class proxying, needed by Spring AOP

Note that some library filenames in table 3.4 start with "com.springsource", but that doesn't mean they're SpringSource-specific; they're the same libraries as the originals but packaged as OSGi bundles *by* SpringSource. You could also use any other OSGi-ified version of these libraries.

The last kind of bundles we need are log libraries. The Spring Framework and Spring DM use Commons Logging as their log library, but logging must be boot-strapped from a custom log factory. The SLF4J library (Simple Logging Framework 4 Java) will act as a facade, and Log4j will do the actual logging. This complexity is necessary because of Commons Logging's bad behavior in OSGi environments.

Don't worry about these gory details, because the Spring DM distribution contains the OSGi-ified versions of all these log libraries. Table 3.5 lists the log libraries (with the com.springsource prefix removed from the SLF4J filenames for better readability).

Table 3.5   Log libraries needed by Spring DM

Bundle	Filename	Description
SLF4J API	slf4j.api-1.5.6.jar	Contains SLF4J API and internal implementation classes
SLF4J Commons Logging adapter	slf4j.org.apache.commons.logging-1.5.6.jar	Contains Commons Logging API and adapts it to SLF4J
SLF4J binding for Log4j	slf4j.log4j-1.5.6.jar	Binds the use of SLF4J to Log4j
Log4j	log4j.osgi-1.2.15.jar	Log implementation (can log to the console, files, and so on)

We're going to organize the bundles into three different categories: springdm, spring, and log. Create a corresponding directory in the bundles directory for each category, and copy each bundle from the Spring DM dist and lib directories to its appropriate directory. Your working directory should now have the following structure:

```
container/
  org.eclipse.osgi-3.5.1.R35x_v20090827.jar
  configuration/
    config.ini
    (Equinox own files)
  bundles/
    springdm/
      (Spring DM bundles)
    spring/
      (Spring Framework bundles)
    log/
      (Log bundles)
```

We could now launch Equinox and install each bundle manually, but this would be cumbersome and tedious! Instead, we'll do exactly as we did in chapter 1 and use the `osgi.bundles` option in the config.ini file to tell Equinox which bundles to install and start when the platform is launched:

```
osgi.bundles=bundles/springdm/spring-osgi-io-2.0.0.M1.jar@start, \
bundles/springdm/spring-osgi-core-2.0.0.M1.jar@start, \
bundles/springdm/spring-osgi-extender-2.0.0.M1.jar@start, \
bundles/spring/org.springframework.aop-3.0.0.RC1.jar@start, \
bundles/spring/org.springframework.asm-3.0.0.RC1.jar@start, \
bundles/spring/org.springframework.beans-3.0.0.RC1.jar@start, \
bundles/spring/org.springframework.context-3.0.0.RC1.jar@start, \
bundles/spring/org.springframework.context.support-3.0.0.RC1.jar@start, \
bundles/spring/org.springframework.core-3.0.0.RC1.jar@start, \
bundles/spring/org.springframework.expression-3.0.0.RC1.jar@start, \
bundles/spring/com.springsource.org.aopalliance-1.0.0.jar@start, \
bundles/spring/com.springsource.net.sf.cglib-2.1.3.jar@start, \
bundles/log/com.springsource.slf4j.api-1.5.6.jar@start, \
bundles/log/com.springsource.slf4j.log4j-1.5.6.jar, \
bundles/log/com.springsource.slf4j.org.apache.commons.
➥    logging-1.5.6.jar@start, \
bundles/log/com.springsource.org.apache.log4j-1.2.15.jar@start
```

You can now launch Equinox. But alas! A disagreeable warning will take the luster off your sense of triumph:

```
osgi> log4j:WARN No appenders could be found for logger
(org.springframework.osgi.extender.internal.boot.ChainActivator).
log4j:WARN Please initialize the log4j system properly.
```

This message comes from Log4j, which could not find an appropriate configuration file to configure itself. Log4j configuration will be our use case for the upcoming section about fragments, and we'll see how to fix that then. At least this message tells us that the log libraries started correctly!

We can check the container provisioning with the `ss` command:

```
ss
Framework is launched.

id       State        Bundle
0        ACTIVE       org.eclipse.osgi_3.5.1.R35x_v20090827
1        ACTIVE       org.springframework.osgi.io_2.0.0.M1
2        ACTIVE       org.springframework.osgi.core_2.0.0.M1
3        ACTIVE       org.springframework.osgi.extender_2.0.0.M1
4        ACTIVE       org.springframework.aop_3.0.0.RC1
5        ACTIVE       org.springframework.asm_3.0.0.RC1
6        ACTIVE       org.springframework.beans_3.0.0.RC1
7        ACTIVE       org.springframework.context_3.0.0.RC1
8        ACTIVE       org.springframework.context.support_3.0.0.RC1
9        ACTIVE       org.springframework.core_3.0.0.RC1
10       ACTIVE       org.springframework.expression_3.0.0.RC1
11       ACTIVE       com.springsource.org.aopalliance_1.0.0
12       ACTIVE       com.springsource.net.sf.cglib_2.1.3
13       ACTIVE       com.springsource.slf4j.api_1.5.6
                      Fragments=14
14       RESOLVED     com.springsource.slf4j.log4j_1.5.6
                      Master=13
15       ACTIVE       com.springsource.slf4j.org.apache.commons.logging_1.5.6
16       ACTIVE       com.springsource.org.apache.log4j_1.2.15
osgi>
```

Notice that all bundles are in active state except for one—the SLF4J Log4j binding. This bundle is actually not a bundle on its own, but a fragment, whose master bundle is the SLF4J API bundle. Because fragments can't be started, the SLF4J Log4j fragment will always stay in the resolved state. Shortly, we'll develop our own fragment to configure the Log4j library, which will eliminate the startup warning message as well.

For now, the container is ready to accept Spring-powered bundles; in the next section, we'll prepare a container to accept web bundles.

3.2.3   *Provisioning a container for web use*

As of version 1.1, Spring DM supports web application deployment in OSGi environments. Web applications differ from plain vanilla OSGi bundles in resource and class loading, which web containers handle in traditional deployment scenarios. Spring DM provides a bridge between the web container and the OSGi environment so that loading is no longer a concern. The web container still handles most of its usual jobs: deployment, specification support (Servlet/JSP (JavaServer Pages) request handling (I/O, thread pool), web.xml parsing, and so on. Spring DM doesn't provide a replacement web container; instead it delegates all the web application management by deploying applications to the web container and connecting its resource-loading facilities to the OSGi platform. By doing it this way, web applications don't suffer from any particular limitations, except ones introduced by the web container itself, as long as they're correctly packaged as OSGi bundles.

Spring DM web support is also based on the extender pattern, through the web extender, which detects and installs web bundles. The web extender relies on another

Spring DM bundle, which acts as the bridge between the web container and the OSGi world. Table 3.6 lists these two mandatory bundles for activating web support.

Table 3.6   Spring DM web bundles

Bundle	Filename	Description
Spring DM web	spring-osgi-web-2.0.0.M1.jar	Provides deployment support for Tomcat and Jetty web containers, and a web application context class for OSGi environments
Spring DM web extender	spring-osgi-web-extender-2.0.0.M1.jar	Detects and deploys/undeploys web bundles

The Spring DM web bundles aren't sufficient for web support because Spring DM relies on a true web container to handle web applications. Spring DM supports two web containers, Apache Tomcat and Jetty (from Mort Bay), and provides all the necessary bundles for the basic use of each in its distribution. Tomcat is the default container in Spring DM, and we'll stick to using it to keep things simple. (We'll see in chapter 9 how to configure the web extender to use Jetty.) Table 3.7 lists the bundles for the simplest web support with Spring DM.

Table 3.7   Web bundles for minimal support of Tomcat

Bundle name	Filename	Description
Servlet API	com.springsource.javax.servlet-2.4.0.jar	OSGi-ified version of the 2.4 Servlet API
Apache Tomcat	catalina.osgi-5.5.23-SNAPSHOT.jar	OSGi-ified version of Apache Tomcat
Tomcat activator	catalina.start.osgi-1.0.0.jar	OSGi activator; bootstraps Tomcat

NOTE   We use Tomcat 5.5 here because it's part of Spring DM's distribution. Chapter 9 covers how to upgrade to Tomcat 6.0 and how to use Jetty as the embedded web container.

With the bundles listed in tables 3.6 and 3.7, you'll be able to deploy simplistic web applications—ones that are servlet-based or that carry only static resources. Java web applications usually use a dedicated view technology to deliver the user interface, and JSP) is the Java EE standard for this. You can embed Java code in JSPs, but the preferred way to handle logic in views is by using *taglibs*—reusable components that encapsulate some presentation logic. We'll add JSP support to our basic container configuration by providing a JSP compiler, because JSPs are compiled to Java classes, and use the JSP Standard Tag Library (JSTL) for our tag library. Table 3.8 lists the necessary bundles.

Bundles for JSP and taglib support aren't available in Spring DM, but you can retrieve them from the Spring DM OSGi repository or from this book's source code.

Table 3.8   Bundles for JSP and taglib support

Bundle	Filename	Description
JSP API	jsp-api.osgi-2.0-SNAPSHOT.jar	JSP standard API definition
Tomcat Jasper 2	jasper.osgi-5.5.23-SNAPSHOT.jar	Tomcat JSP engine; compiles JSP
Commons EL	commons-el.osgi-1.0-SNAPSHOT.jar	JSP 2.0 Expression Language interpreter
JSTL	jstl.osgi-1.1.2-SNAPSHOT.jar	Specific OSGi bundle with JSTL API and Apache Standard implementation

Spring DM OSGi repository

Not all libraries are packaged as OSGi bundles, which makes them unusable as first-class components in an OSGi environment (although they can be packaged as part of an individual bundle's classpath). To address this problem, SpringSource has re-packaged a large number of open source libraries and made them available through its EBR (http://www.springsource.com/repository/app/). You can use this repository with Maven 2 or Ivy, or by browsing it and downloading the bundles you need.

Spring DM also has its own OSGi repository because not all dependencies can be downloaded from SpringSource's EBR. Spring DM's repository is hosted at Amazon S3, so you need an S3 client to browse it (we'll see later that you can download the JAR files with Maven 2 just like for any repository).

Most of the OSGi-ified libraries available in Spring DM's OSGi repository are marked as *SNAPSHOT* (meaning they can change at any moment) and have an .osgi suffix.

We now need to provision the container. Copy the Spring DM web bundles to the springdm directory and create a web directory for the remaining web bundles. Your working directory should now have the following structure:

```
container/
  org.eclipse.osgi-3.5.1.R35x_v20090827.jar
  configuration/
    config.ini
    (Equinox own files)
  bundles/
    springdm/
      (Spring DM bundles)
    spring/
      (Spring Framework bundles)
    log/
      (Log bundles)
    web/
      (Web bundles)
```

We also have to modify the config.ini file to include these new bundles:

```
eclipse.ignoreApp=true
osgi.bundles=bundles/springdm/spring-osgi-io-2.0.0.M1.jar@start, \
(...)
bundles/log/com.springsource.org.apache.log4j-1.2.15.jar@start, \
bundles/springdm/spring-osgi-web-2.0.0.M1.jar@start, \
bundles/springdm/spring-osgi-web-extender-2.0.0.M1.jar@start, \
bundles/web/com.springsource.javax.servlet-2.4.0.jar@start, \
bundles/web/catalina.osgi-5.5.23-SNAPSHOT.jar@start, \
bundles/web/catalina.start.osgi-1.0.0.jar@start, \
bundles/web/jsp-api.osgi-2.0-SNAPSHOT.jar@start, \
bundles/web/jasper.osgi-5.5.23-SNAPSHOT.jar@start, \
bundles/web/commons-el.osgi-1.0-SNAPSHOT.jar@start, \
bundles/web/jstl.osgi-1.1.2-SNAPSHOT.jar@start
```

Before launching Equinox, be aware that you must not have any kind of server listening on port 8080, because that's Tomcat's default port. Once Equinox has been launched, you can check your installation with the ss command:

```
osgi> ss

Framework is launched.

id      State       Bundle
0       ACTIVE      org.eclipse.osgi_3.5.1.R35x_v20090827
1       ACTIVE      org.springframework.osgi.io_2.0.0.M1
2       ACTIVE      org.springframework.osgi.core_2.0.0.M1
3       ACTIVE      org.springframework.osgi.extender_2.0.0.M1
4       ACTIVE      org.springframework.aop_3.0.0.RC1
5       ACTIVE      org.springframework.asm_3.0.0.RC1
6       ACTIVE      org.springframework.beans_3.0.0.RC1
7       ACTIVE      org.springframework.context_3.0.0.RC1
8       ACTIVE      org.springframework.context.support_3.0.0.RC1
9       ACTIVE      org.springframework.core_3.0.0.RC1
10      ACTIVE      org.springframework.expression_3.0.0.RC1
11      ACTIVE      com.springsource.org.aopalliance_1.0.0
12      ACTIVE      com.springsource.net.sf.cglib_2.1.3
13      ACTIVE      com.springsource.slf4j.api_1.5.6
                    Fragments=14
14      RESOLVED    com.springsource.slf4j.log4j_1.5.6
                    Master=13
15      ACTIVE      com.springsource.slf4j.org.apache.commons.logging_1.5.6
16      ACTIVE      com.springsource.org.apache.log4j_1.2.15
17      ACTIVE      org.springframework.osgi.web_2.0.0.M1
18      ACTIVE      org.springframework.osgi.web.extender_2.0.0.M1
19      ACTIVE      com.springsource.javax.servlet_2.4.0
20      ACTIVE      org.springframework.osgi.catalina.osgi_5.5.23.SNAPSHOT
21      ACTIVE      org.springframework.osgi.catalina.start.osgi_1.0.0
22      ACTIVE      org.springframework.osgi.jsp-api.osgi_2.0.0.SNAPSHOT
23      ACTIVE      org.springframework.osgi.jasper.osgi_5.5.23.SNAPSHOT
24      ACTIVE      org.springframework.osgi.commons-el.osgi_1.0.0.SNAPSHOT
25      ACTIVE      org.springframework.osgi.jstl.osgi_1.1.2.SNAPSHOT

osgi>
```

As everything looks fine, you should have a Tomcat server running on your computer. You can check this by launching a web browser, typing http://localhost:8080 in the address bar, and finding that you get ... a blank page! This might seem disappointing, but it means you successfully provisioned Equinox for web support, and that you'll be able to deploy the web application we'll be developing later!

That's enough provisioning for now. We'll see in the next section how to configure logs using an OSGi fragment.

3.3   *Using a fragment to configure the LOG4J bundle*

You probably remember the nasty warning message we received after the installation of the Spring DM bundles. It was coming from Log4j, complaining that it couldn't find its configuration file. This section explains how to get rid of this warning by properly configuring Log4j by using an OSGi feature: fragments.

3.3.1   *Using the fragment configuration pattern*

A fragment is an incomplete bundle; it can't exist on its own and must be attached to a *host* bundle. The host bundle can't itself be a fragment and must be a full-fledged bundle, even if it relies on its fragment to add classes or resources. A fragment can serve many purposes, such as completing its host bundle with specific classes or providing configuration through resources (property or XML files).

Imagine a component of your system is composed of portable, platform-independent code, but it also needs some platform-specific code. The portable part could be provided by a bundle, *bundle A*, and the platform-specific code could be provided in a bundle fragment for each platform. The fragment pattern is especially useful here because platform-specific fragments will generally be tied to internal features of bundle A, and they could not be deployed as regular bundles without exporting bundle A's internal features. Instead, classes and resources contained in a fragment are merged into the host bundle classpath without requiring export.

> **WARNING** Apache Felix has long been known for being the OSGi platform that doesn't support fragments. As of version 1.8.0, Apache Felix *does* support fragments.

Configuration is another application for the fragment pattern: the host bundle can use a resource provided by one of its fragments as a configuration file. You could use the host bundle without modification, then create a fragment that serves to configure the bundle. Figure 3.4 illustrates this process, with Log4j as the library being configured.

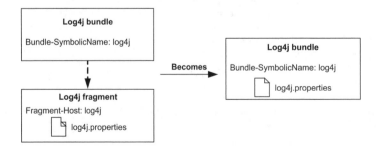

Figure 3.4   A fragment complements a host bundle, as the fragment content is available to the host bundle. The host bundle (generic) can then use the content of the fragment (specific) for retrieving configuration artifacts.

Now you're aware of the fragment feature and how it can be leveraged to configure a host bundle, so let's discuss how to create a fragment to configure Log4j.

3.3.2 Implementing a fragment

A fragment is like any other OSGi bundle: a JAR file with specific headers in its manifest. Even though a fragment is only part of a regular bundle, it must identify itself and the host bundle to which it must be attached.

The following snippet shows the manifest file for the Log4j configuration fragment:

```
Manifest-Version: 1.0
Bundle-ManifestVersion: 2
Bundle-Name: Log4J Configuration
Bundle-SymbolicName:
    org.springframework.osgi.log4j.config
Bundle-Version: 1.0.0
Fragment-Host: org.springframework.osgi.log4j.osgi
```

❶ Identifies fragment
❷ Identifies fragment's host bundle

A fragment provides its identity with the OSGi `Bundle-SymbolicName` header ❶ and references its bundle host with the `Fragment-Host` header ❷. This fragment host bundle is the Log4j bundle we installed while provisioning the OSGi container for standard use.

This fragment isn't very useful without providing a resource for configuring Log4j. We'll stick to Log4j's default configuration mechanism by providing a log4j.properties file at the root of the classpath. The following snippet shows the content of this configuration file:

```
log4j.rootLogger=INFO, FILE

log4j.appender.FILE=org.apache.log4j.FileAppender
log4j.appender.FILE.File=equinox.log
log4j.appender.FILE.layout=org.apache.log4j.PatternLayout
log4j.appender.FILE.layout.ConversionPattern=%-4r [%t] %-5p %c %x - %m%n%M
```

If you're familiar with Log4j, you'll have noticed that we configured the log output to an equinox.log file, with information like seconds from startup, thread name, log level, and log message for each log entry.

Now we have all the pieces, so let's put them together. The fragment structure should be the following:

```
log4j-config/
  src/
    log4j.properties
  MANIFEST.MF
```

To package these fragment as a JAR file, launch the following command:

```
jar cvfm log4j-config.jar MANIFEST.MF -C src .
```

This will produce a log4j-config.jar file that we'll install in Equinox next.

3.3.3   *Installing a fragment into the OSGi container*

You declare fragments in an OSGi container as you would any regular bundle, except that they can't be started. Copy the log4j-config.jar file to the bundles/log directory with the other log bundles, and modify the Equinox config.ini file to provision the container with the fragment:

```
osgi.bundles=bundles/springdm/spring-osgi-io-2.0.0.M1.jar@start, \
(...)
bundles/log/log4j-config.jar
```

After starting Equinox, you'll notice that the Log4j warning has disappeared and that an equinox.log file has been created. You'll also notice that Spring DM has emitted some log messages:

```
0    [Start Level Event Dispatcher] INFO
 org.springframework.osgi.extender.internal.boot.ChainActivator
 - Blueprint API detected; enabling Blueprint Container functionality
<init>0    [Start Level Event Dispatcher] INFO
 org.springframework.osgi.extender.internal.activator.ContextLoaderListener
 - Starting [org.springframework.osgi.extender] bundle v.[2.0.0.M1]
(...)
```

The ss command also reflects the relation between the Log4j bundle and its fragment:

```
16    ACTIVE      com.springsource.org.apache.log4j_1.2.15
                  Fragments=26
(...)
26    RESOLVED    com.springsource.org.apache.log4j.config_1.0.0
                  Master=16
```

Congrats! You've just configured logging in your OSGi container! With logs enabled, we'll be able to follow what Spring DM is doing and diagnose any problems. It's time now to create some Spring DM–powered bundles!

3.4   *Developing Spring DM bundles*

You took your first steps with Spring DM in chapter 1 by implementing a simple bundle. We made the creation of this bundle as simple as possible, using the JDK tools, but if we keep on using them we'll be hindered by their lack of productivity as we get into more advanced usage. Instead, we'll see in this section how to create, manage, and package a bundle with Maven 2. We'll keep using the old-fashioned way to test our bundle, by deploying it manually to Equinox, but we'll also see how to use the Spring DM integration test framework for testing purposes.

3.4.1   *Creating and configuring a bundle*

OSGi bundles need careful packaging because their manifest contains key information about dependencies and exported classes. Spring DM–powered bundles also contain some configuration files that we need to maintain and include in bundles, so we need to maintain a neat and precise organization of our bundle projects.

To do so, we'll use the standard Maven 2 file structure. Our bundle will consist of a single Java class and a corresponding Spring context file to create one instance of that class.

Maven 2

Maven 2 is a powerful tool that can be used to build and manage any Java-based project. Maven 2 is based on the concept of a Project Object Model (POM), and for each project managed by Maven 2, all the information is gathered in one place, the pom.xml file. Maven 2 consists of a core system, and plug-ins expand its features (nearly all Maven 2 features are provided by plug-ins). Maven 2 relies heavily on the convention over configuration pattern, so Maven 2 projects use a standardized structure. Most Java IDEs support Maven 2—the M2Eclipse plug-in for Eclipse for example.

Appendix B gives an introduction to Maven 2, from its installation to advanced features like multimodules projects. If you're new to Maven 2, don't hesitate to read this appendix, which also covers how to leverage plug-ins for OSGi development. If you prefer Ant, appendix C explains how to adapt this chapter's examples for that tool.

Why would we want to use Maven 2 for OSGi projects? Maven 2 is (among others) a build tool and, as such, it can automate most of the cumbersome and error-prone tasks (such as compiling, running tests, and packaging). This is obviously not a particularly compelling reason, because a tool like Ant can do the same (except that, if we follow Maven 2's standardized project structure, we'll have to do a little less work to accomplish tasks with Maven 2 than with Ant). However, the pom.xml file is a unique, central location for gathering information such as the project group, name, and version, which we can then use to identify the resulting OSGi bundle. Maven 2 also comes with a built-in dependency and versioning management system, which turns out to be very useful for OSGi-based development. Dependencies are declared in the POM, and Maven takes care of downloading them from public repositories and storing them in the user's local repository.

The Spring DM project build is based on Maven 2, as is its integration test framework, which uses the Maven 2 local repository to provision, on the fly, the OSGi container. These are other good reasons why using Maven 2 makes sense for the source code of a Spring DM book.

Nevertheless, using Maven 2 isn't compulsory when working with Spring DM. If you're already familiar with tools like Ant or Apache Ivy, you can use them to develop Spring DM bundles or adapt the examples from this book. Use the tools that best suit you!

The Maven 2 archetype mechanism will help us create a bundle skeleton. This will create a standard Maven 2 Java project that we'll modify slightly to shape the bundle. To create the project skeleton, type this command:

```
mvn archetype:create -DgroupId=com.manning.sdmia -DartifactId=springdm-sample
```

Our project is created in a springdm-sample directory, and the archetype command created the POM file and all its associated structure for us. From now on, our work will only consist of creating a Java class and the Spring configuration file.

NOTE If you're using Eclipse, you can type the `mvn eclipse:eclipse` command in the project directory to create Eclipse project configuration files and then import the project into your workspace. You'll also need to create a `M2_REPO` classpath variable pointing to the Maven 2 local repository (which defaults to .m2/repository in the user directory).

Here is the project structure (with our two files in bold):

```
springdm-sample
  src/
    main/
      java/
        com/manning/springdmia/
          SpringDmSample.java
      resources/
        META-INF/
          spring/
            springdm-sample.xml
    test/
    (...)
  pom.xml
```

The following snippet shows the `SpringDmSample` class, which is very simple, displaying only a message on the console when an instance is created:

```
package com.manning.sdmia;

public class SpringDmSample {

  public SpringDmSample() {
    System.out.println("Spring DM sample created");
  }

}
```

We placed the Spring configuration file in META-INF/spring, which Spring DM scans to bootstrap application contexts. The following snippet shows the content of springdm-sample.xml, which creates an instance of `SpringDmSample`.

```
<?xml version="1.0" encoding="UTF-8"?>
<beans xmlns="http://www.springframework.org/schema/beans"
  xmlns:xsi="http://www.w3.org/2001/XMLSchema-instance"
  xsi:schemaLocation="http://www.springframework.org/schema/beans
  http://www.springframework.org/schema/beans/spring-beans.xsd">

  <bean id="springDmSampleBean" class="com.manning.sdmia.SpringDmSample" />

</beans>
```

The Spring configuration is now complete; the next step is to package the bundle!

3.4.2 *Packaging a bundle*

Even if our bundle is simple, it needs proper OSGi packaging. In chapter 1, we created a manifest file ourselves, and although this solution is sufficient for a Hello World application, it becomes cumbersome and error-prone for bigger bundles. Maven 2 can package the bundle for us, and its JAR packaging mechanism supports a customization of the manifest (for OSGi-specific headers). This is a more user-friendly solution than manually editing the whole manifest, but it still isn't well-suited to complex OSGi bundles. Even though our bundle isn't that complex, we'll use a more powerful dedicated packaging mechanism, the Felix Bundle Plugin for Maven.

> **NOTE** The Felix Bundle Plugin for Maven is part of the Apache Felix project, but it generates manifests for any OSGi container. Under the covers, it uses the Bnd packaging tool (http://www.aqute.biz/Code/Bnd). We're using this plug-in only for packaging; its usage doesn't imply the use of the Apache Felix OSGi platform! You'll learn more about Bnd in chapter 6, where we cover how to package an existing library as an OSGi bundle. Appendix B also provides more in-depth coverage of the Felix Bundle Plugin.

To use the Felix Bundle Plugin, we need to modify the pom.xml file as shown in listing 3.3.

Listing 3.3 POM modification for packaging with Felix Bundle Plugin

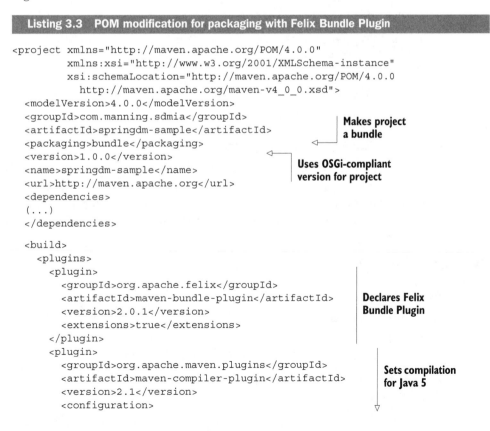

```
<project xmlns="http://maven.apache.org/POM/4.0.0"
        xmlns:xsi="http://www.w3.org/2001/XMLSchema-instance"
        xsi:schemaLocation="http://maven.apache.org/POM/4.0.0
          http://maven.apache.org/maven-v4_0_0.xsd">
  <modelVersion>4.0.0</modelVersion>
  <groupId>com.manning.sdmia</groupId>
  <artifactId>springdm-sample</artifactId>
  <packaging>bundle</packaging>                 ← Makes project a bundle
  <version>1.0.0</version>                      ← Uses OSGi-compliant version for project
  <name>springdm-sample</name>
  <url>http://maven.apache.org</url>
  <dependencies>
  (...)
  </dependencies>

  <build>
    <plugins>
      <plugin>
        <groupId>org.apache.felix</groupId>
        <artifactId>maven-bundle-plugin</artifactId>      Declares Felix
        <version>2.0.1</version>                          Bundle Plugin
        <extensions>true</extensions>
      </plugin>
      <plugin>
        <groupId>org.apache.maven.plugins</groupId>
        <artifactId>maven-compiler-plugin</artifactId>    Sets compilation
        <version>2.1</version>                            for Java 5
        <configuration>
```

```
            <source>1.5</source>
            <target>1.5</target>
        </configuration>
      </plugin>
    </plugins>
  </build>

</project>
```

> Sets compilation
> for Java 5

The Felix Bundle Plugin provides another packaging mechanism to Maven 2: the bundle. The plug-in will now take care of the packaging and generate the manifest file, with OSGi headers retrieved from the project information contained in pom.xml. Launch the packaging step with the following command:

```
mvn package
```

It produces a springdm-sample-1.0.0.jar file in the target directory. You can open the archive to read the manifest and check that the plug-in retrieved the correct information from the POM (bundle name, version, and so on):

```
Manifest-Version: 1.0
Export-Package: com.manning.sdmia
Bundle-Version: 1.0.0
Build-Jdk: 1.6.0_13
Built-By: acogoluegnes
Tool: Bnd-0.0.357
Bnd-LastModified: 1256764353375
Bundle-Name: springdm-sample
Bundle-ManifestVersion: 2
Created-By: Apache Maven Bundle Plugin
Import-Package: com.manning.sdmia
Bundle-SymbolicName: com.manning.sdmia.springdm-sample
```

The bundle is now ready to be deployed.

3.4.3   *Checking a bundle within a container*

With the Equinox container provisioned with all the required Spring DM bundles, we can safely install the bundle. The Spring DM extender scans bundles only when they reach the active state, so we need to start the bundle after its installation. We'll then see the message from the bean, and we can check the bundle status with the ss command:

```
osgi> start 27

osgi> Spring DM sample created
ss

Framework is launched.

id      State       Bundle
0       ACTIVE      org.eclipse.osgi_3.5.1.R35x_v20090827
(...)
27      ACTIVE      com.manning.sdmia.springdm-sample_1.0.0

osgi>
```

We just ran an integration test: we tested that the bundle could be properly installed and started in an OSGi container. Even if this activity can be somewhat entertaining, it involves manual steps and is limited to one type of container. In the next section, we'll start to use the Spring DM integration test framework, to automate the bundle integration test.

3.4.4 Developing an integration test

Spring DM provides an integration test framework to check if bundles can be successfully deployed on the three OSGi containers it supports. The main benefit of the testing framework for the developer is it safely tests bundles without requiring any change in testing habits: the testing framework is based on JUnit, and tests can be launched as usual using Eclipse, Maven 2, or Ant.

When launching an OSGi-based integration test, Spring DM launches an OSGi container (Equinox is the default), provisions it from the local Maven 2 repository, and runs the test methods. The test itself is deployed on the fly as a bundle. All this makes the Spring DM integration test framework a fantastic tool for testing not only Spring DM–powered bundles but any kind of OSGi bundle. In this chapter, we'll only explore the basics of this test framework; the whole of chapter 10 is dedicated to its use.

As we described earlier, Spring DM uses the local Maven 2 repository to provision the OSGi container it launches for running tests. Spring DM won't download the dependencies itself, or even ask Maven 2 to do it, so we need to reference them in our project POM and invoke a Maven 2 command to download them. Then they will be in our local repository and will be used each time we launch an integration test using the Spring DM testing framework. Listing 3.4 shows the dependencies in the POM.

> **Listing 3.4   Maven 2 dependencies for OSGi integration tests**

```
<project xmlns="http://maven.apache.org/POM/4.0.0"
        xmlns:xsi="http://www.w3.org/2001/XMLSchema-instance"
        xsi:schemaLocation="http://maven.apache.org/POM/4.0.0
          http://maven.apache.org/maven-v4_0_0.xsd">
  <modelVersion>4.0.0</modelVersion>
  <groupId>com.manning.sdmia</groupId>
  <artifactId>springdm-sample</artifactId>
  <packaging>bundle</packaging>
  <version>1.0.0</version>
  <name>springdm-sample</name>
  <url>http://maven.apache.org</url>

  <properties>
    <springdm.version>2.0.0.M1</springdm.version>
    <equinox.version>
    3.5.1.R35x_v20090827
    </equinox.version>
  </properties>

  <dependencies>
    <dependency>
      <groupId>org.springframework.osgi</groupId>
```

Uses property for artifact version

Adds Spring DM runtime bundles

```
      <artifactId>spring-osgi-core</artifactId>
      <version>${springdm.version}</version>
      <scope>test</scope>
    </dependency>
    <dependency>
      <groupId>org.springframework.osgi</groupId>
      <artifactId>spring-osgi-annotation</artifactId>      Adds Spring DM
      <version>${springdm.version}</version>                runtime bundles
      <scope>test</scope>
    </dependency>
    <dependency>
      <groupId>org.springframework.osgi</groupId>
      <artifactId>spring-osgi-extender</artifactId>
      <version>${springdm.version}</version>
      <scope>test</scope>
    </dependency>
    <dependency>
      <groupId>org.springframework.osgi</groupId>            Adds Spring DM
      <artifactId>spring-osgi-test</artifactId>             integration test
      <version>${springdm.version}</version>                bundle
      <scope>test</scope>
    </dependency>
    <dependency>
      <groupId>org.eclipse.osgi</groupId>
      <artifactId>org.eclipse.osgi</artifactId>            Adds OSGi
      <version>${equinox.version}</version>                container
      <scope>test</scope>
    </dependency>
  </dependencies>
  (...)
</project>
```

What we're doing now is the equivalent of the manual provisioning we did in section 3.2.2. Notice that we didn't reference any Spring Framework dependencies, because Spring DM's own POMs reference them and Maven will download them too as it handles *transitive dependencies*.

Unfortunately, Spring 2.0.0.M1 references a development version of the Spring Framework that is no longer available in Maven 2 repositories, so we have to explicitly add the dependencies to a stable version of Spring. Listing 3.5 shows how to do that.

Listing 3.5   Spring's dependencies

```
(...)
<properties>
  <springdm.version>2.0.0.M1</springdm.version>
  <equinox.version>3.5.1.R35x_v20090827</equinox.version>     Uses property for
  <spring.version>3.0.2.RELEASE</spring.version>              Spring version
</properties>
<dependencies>
  (...)
  <dependency>
    <groupId>org.springframework</groupId>                    Adds Spring
    <artifactId>org.springframework.core</artifactId>         bundles
```

```
        <version>${spring.version}</version>
        <scope>test</scope>
      </dependency>
      <dependency>
        <groupId>org.springframework</groupId>
        <artifactId>org.springframework.beans</artifactId>
        <version>${spring.version}</version>
        <scope>test</scope>
    </dependency>
    <dependency>
      <groupId>org.springframework</groupId>
      <artifactId>
        org.springframework.context
      </artifactId>
      <version>${spring.version}</version>
      <scope>test</scope>
    </dependency>
    <dependency>
      <groupId>org.springframework</groupId>
      <artifactId>org.springframework.aop</artifactId>
      <version>${spring.version}</version>
      <scope>test</scope>
    </dependency>
    <dependency>
      <groupId>org.springframework</groupId>
      <artifactId>org.springframework.test</artifactId>
      <version>${spring.version}</version>
      <scope>test</scope>
    </dependency>
</dependencies>
```

Adds Spring bundles

NOTE We stuck to the Spring Framework development release in the manual provisioning for simplicity's sake, because it's provided with Spring DM's distribution. Feel free to download the Spring distribution separately and use it, as long as it's a 3.0.x distribution.

We also need to add extra dependencies on AOP and log, as shown in listing 3.6.

Listing 3.6　Extra dependencies for OSGi integration test

```
<dependencies>
  (...)
  <dependency>
    <groupId>org.aopalliance</groupId>
    <artifactId>
      com.springsource.org.aopalliance
    </artifactId>
    <version>1.0.0</version>
    <scope>test</scope>
  </dependency>
  <dependency>
    <groupId>net.sourceforge.cglib</groupId>
    <artifactId>
      com.springsource.net.sf.cglib
```

Adds Spring Framework dependencies

```
      </artifactId>
      <version>2.1.3</version>
      <scope>test</scope>
   </dependency>

   <dependency>
      <groupId>org.slf4j</groupId>
      <artifactId>com.springsource.slf4j.api</artifactId>
      <version>1.5.6</version>
      <scope>test</scope>
   </dependency>
   <dependency>
      <groupId>org.slf4j</groupId>
      <artifactId>
        com.springsource.slf4j.log4j
      </artifactId>
      <version>1.5.6</version>
      <scope>test</scope>
   </dependency>
   <dependency>
      <groupId>org.slf4j</groupId>
      <artifactId>
       com.springsource.slf4j.org.apache.commons.logging
      </artifactId>
      <version>1.5.6</version>
      <scope>test</scope>
   </dependency>
   <dependency>
      <groupId>org.apache.log4j</groupId>
      <artifactId>
        com.springsource.org.apache.log4j
      </artifactId>
      <version>1.2.15</version>
      <scope>test</scope>
   </dependency>
</dependencies>
```

Adds Spring Framework dependencies

Adds log dependencies

That's a lot of dependencies! Fortunately, Maven 2 will download them all for us, but to do this, it needs a nudge in the right direction. Maven 2 downloads dependencies from public repositories, which contain most of the open source libraries, but our case is a little bit special: we need OSGi bundles and some very specific dependencies. Spring DM and the Spring Framework binaries are available from public repositories and are packaged as OSGi bundles, so they aren't a problem. But the other dependencies can only be found on specific repositories, which we must register in our POM, as shown in listing 3.7.

Listing 3.7 Maven 2 repositories for OSGi bundles

```
<project>
(...)
  <repositories>
    <repository>
      <id>com.springsource.repository.bundles.release</id>
      <name>SpringSource EBR - SpringSource Bundle Releases</name>
```

```
      <url>http://repository.springsource.com/maven/bundles/release</url>
   </repository>

   <repository>
      <id>com.springsource.repository.bundles.external</id>
      <name>SpringSource EBR - External Bundle Releases</name>
      <url>http://repository.springsource.com/maven/bundles/external</url>
   </repository>

   <repository>
      <id>spring-maven-milestone</id>
      <name>Springframework Maven Repository</name>
     <url>http://s3.amazonaws.com/maven.springframework.org/milestone</url>
   </repository>

   <repository>
      <id>spring-osgified-artifacts</id>
      <snapshots>
         <enabled>true</enabled>
      </snapshots>
      <name>Springframework Maven OSGified Artifacts Repository</name>
      <url>http://maven.springframework.org/osgi</url>
   </repository>
 </repositories>
</project>
```

Almost set! For the integration test, the bundle must also be in the local repository, so we need to install it. This also has the side effect of downloading all of its dependencies. Type the following command to compile, package, and install the bundle:

```
mvn install
```

Now that the Maven 2 local repository has all the pieces we need, we can create the integration test in the src/test/java directory following Maven 2 conventions. You can see in listing 3.8 that the integration test doesn't differ much from a standard unit test.

Listing 3.8   The bundle integration test

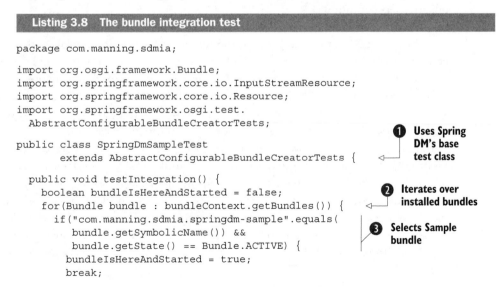

```
package com.manning.sdmia;

import org.osgi.framework.Bundle;
import org.springframework.core.io.InputStreamResource;
import org.springframework.core.io.Resource;
import org.springframework.osgi.test.
   AbstractConfigurableBundleCreatorTests;

public class SpringDmSampleTest
      extends AbstractConfigurableBundleCreatorTests {        ◁——①  Uses Spring
                                                                      DM's base
                                                                      test class
   public void testIntegration() {
      boolean bundleIsHereAndStarted = false;
      for(Bundle bundle : bundleContext.getBundles()) {       ◁——②  Iterates over
                                                                      installed bundles
         if("com.manning.sdmia.springdm-sample".equals(
            bundle.getSymbolicName()) &&                       ③  Selects Sample
            bundle.getState() == Bundle.ACTIVE) {                  bundle
         bundleIsHereAndStarted = true;
         break;
```

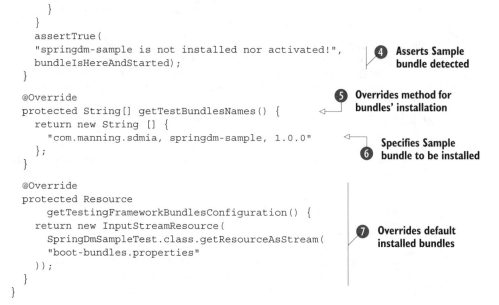

```
      }
    }
    assertTrue(
    "springdm-sample is not installed nor activated!",       ④ Asserts Sample
    bundleIsHereAndStarted);                                     bundle detected
  }

  @Override                                                   ⑤ Overrides method for
  protected String[] getTestBundlesNames() {                     bundles' installation
    return new String [] {
      "com.manning.sdmia, springdm-sample, 1.0.0"            ⑥ Specifies Sample
    };                                                          bundle to be installed
  }

  @Override
  protected Resource
      getTestingFrameworkBundlesConfiguration() {
    return new InputStreamResource(                          ⑦ Overrides default
      SpringDmSampleTest.class.getResourceAsStream(             installed bundles
      "boot-bundles.properties"
    ));
  }
}
```

This integration test is simple but functional: it checks that the Spring DM Sample bundle has been correctly started. The Spring DM integration test framework provides a handy abstract class that provides hooks for the OSGi container configuration, and this test uses it as its parent class ❶. The test framework is based on JUnit 3.8, so test methods must have the `test` prefix. Once in a test method, we're running inside an OSGi container and we can work with the bundle context, because the test *is* a bundle deployed in the container ❷. We could scan all the installed bundles and check their states, but we're particularly interested in *our* bundle, whose name is com.manning. sdmia.springdm-sample ❸. As we're also in a JUnit test, we can use `TestCase` methods to assert conditions ❹.

OK, so our test is running in an OSGi container and we can scan other bundles, but how does Spring DM provision this container? Spring DM automatically provisions the container with its own bundles and dependencies (core, extender, Spring Framework, and some log libraries) but we can add our own extra bundles with the `getTestBundlesNames` method ❺. If we want our Spring DM Sample to be installed and started, we must provide it with its Maven 2 identity (group, artifact IDs, and version) as shown at ❻, and Spring DM will retrieve it from the local repository.

Finally, we need to override the `getTestingFrameworkBundlesConfiguration` method ❼, because we want to customize the bundles that Spring DM's test framework installed by default. As we mentioned earlier in this section, Spring DM depends on a development release of the Spring Framework, so it uses it by default in its test environment. We need to specify in the overridden method the path to a properties file where we list all the bundles we want to be installed in the OSGi container during the test.

Here's an excerpt of this file (take a look at the book's source code if you want all the details):

```
ignore.spring.version=3.0.2.RELEASE
ignore.spring.osgi.version=2.0.0.M1
ignore.spring.groupId=org.springframework
ignore.spring.osgi.groupId=org.springframework.osgi
(...)
${ignore.spring.osgi.groupId},spring-osgi-io,${ignore.spring.osgi.version}=
${ignore.spring.osgi.groupId},
➥    spring-osgi-core,${ignore.spring.osgi.version}=
(...)
${ignore.spring.groupId},org.springframework.asm,${ignore.spring.version}=
${ignore.spring.groupId},org.springframework.beans,${ignore.spring.version}
```

NOTE We should have created our integration test in a dedicated project, but we've tried to keep things as simple as possible for now. We'll cover OSGi test best practices with Spring DM in chapter 10.

You can launch the test from Eclipse by right-clicking on the test file from the Package Explorer view, selecting Run As and then JUnit Test. To launch the test with Maven 2, type the following command:

```
mvn test
```

The console should output something like the following:

```
-------------------------------------------------------
 T E S T S
-------------------------------------------------------
Running com.manning.sdmia.SpringDmSampleTest
Spring DM sample created
Tests run: 1, Failures: 0, Errors: 0, Skipped: 0, Time elapsed: 1.171 sec

Results :

Tests run: 1, Failures: 0, Errors: 0, Skipped: 0

[INFO] ----------------------------------------------------------------
[INFO] BUILD SUCCESSFUL
[INFO] ----------------------------------------------------------------
[INFO] Total time: 3 seconds
[INFO] Finished at: Wed Oct 28 22:42:39 CET 2009
[INFO] Final Memory: 11M/19M
[INFO] ----------------------------------------------------------------
```

Notice the message that confirms that the bean has been created. This means the bundle has been correctly installed and started, and that the Spring DM extender properly bootstrapped the Spring application context. All this took about 3 seconds, including the OSGi container startup time!

NOTE We did not refer to any OSGi platform in our integration test. By default, Spring DM uses Equinox in its integration tests. You can check the platform used in the test with the getPlatformName method. The Spring DM test framework can launch tests on Equinox, Felix, or Knopflerfish; we'll see in chapter 10 how to switch from one platform to another.

Although it may seem somewhat involved to write this first integration test, every subsequent test should be much easier because all your OSGi integration tests can now be written as usual, from Eclipse, from the command line, or even through your continuous integration process.

That's all there is to using Spring DM for standard bundles; we'll now see what Spring DM can do for us when deploying web bundles.

3.5   Developing Spring DM web bundles

So far, Spring DM has brought a lot of benefit to our OSGi development process: we can use the Spring lightweight container to wire up all the inner parts of our bundles, and we can even write OSGi-based integration tests. We'll continue to see in this book how it can bring many more benefits. To illustrate, we'll take a first look at its web application support. We're now going to develop and deploy a web bundle with a static page and JSP, using the same tools and approach we used for our previous bundle.

3.5.1   Creating and configuring a web bundle

The web bundle will be created and packaged as a standard OSGi bundle, with OSGi entries in its manifest file. But some of its content (a web.xml file and resources like JSP files) will indicate that the bundle is a web bundle, and Spring DM will treat it accordingly, by deploying it in a web container.

We'll still use a Maven 2 archetype to create the project skeleton:

```
mvn archetype:create -DgroupId=com.manning.sdmia
       -DartifactId=springdm-web-sample
```

As before, we have only a basic Maven 2 structure and we need to create some files to complete our web bundle. The following snippet shows the project structure with our files in bold:

```
springdm-web-sample\
  src/
    main/
      java/
      webapp/
        WEB-INF/
          web.xml
        index.html
        index.jsp
    test/
  pom.xml
```

You can see from the structure that our web bundle doesn't contain a Spring context file. Web bundles are a special case; they don't usually contain any Spring-specific file that the Spring DM extender will load. Instead, the Spring application context bootstrapping is delegated to the web application, with a dedicated servlet listener.

Spring DM provides an OSGi-aware web application context, which we'll discuss in chapter 8, but we won't be using it here. Instead, we'll stick to a simple web application, with its web.xml file, a static "hello" page, and a hello JSP to check that the JSP compiler works properly. Here is the content of the web.xml file:

```
<?xml version="1.0" encoding="ISO-8859-1"?>
<web-app xmlns="http://java.sun.com/xml/ns/j2ee"
         xmlns:xsi="http://www.w3.org/2001/XMLSchema-instance"
         xsi:schemaLocation="http://java.sun.com/xml/ns/j2ee
         http://java.sun.com/xml/ns/j2ee/web-app_2_4.xsd"
         version="2.4">
  <display-name>Spring DM web sample</display-name>
  <description>Spring DM web sample</description>
  <welcome-file-list>
    <welcome-file>index.html</welcome-file>
  </welcome-file-list>
</web-app>
```

The index.html file is as simple as possible:

```
<html>
  <head><title>Spring DM web sample</title></head>
  <body>
    <h1>Hello Spring DM world! (HTML)</h1>
  </body>
</html>
```

The index.jsp page uses an expression element for the Hello World message:

```
<html>
  <head><title>Spring DM web sample</title></head>
  <body>
    <h1><%="Hello Spring DM world! (JSP)"%></h1>
  </body>
</html>
```

The writing of the web application is finished. Let's move on to the packaging.

3.5.2 Packaging a web bundle

How do we package our web bundle? Can the Felix Bundle Plugin really package this unusual kind of bundle? Well, yes it can. Our bundle will be a standard OSGi bundle, except for additional information to help Spring DM deploy it.

Our bundle will be deployed in two steps: it will be deployed as a bundle in the OSGi container, then the Spring DM web extender will react to its registration with OSGi by deploying it to the web container. To be deployed by the web extender, a bundle needs to meet one of two conditions:

- Its filename ends with .war.
- It contains a WEB-INF directory at its root.

Our bundle meets the second condition, so the Spring DM web extender will deploy it to the web container. All we have to do is properly configure the Felix Bundle Plugin to include the webapp directory in the bundle, as shown in listing 3.9.

Listing 3.9 POM modification to package the web bundle

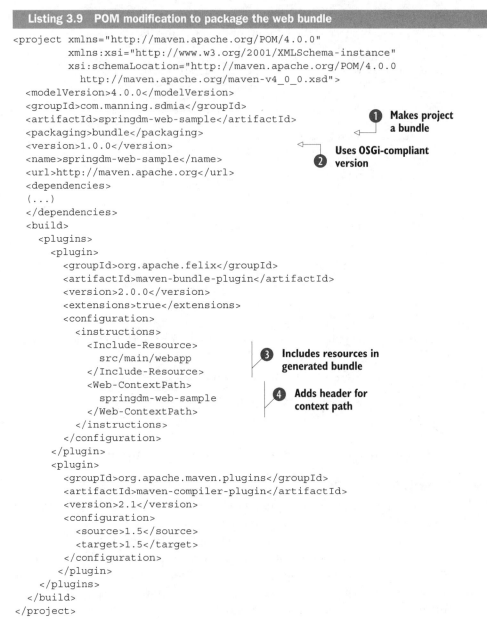

```
<project xmlns="http://maven.apache.org/POM/4.0.0"
         xmlns:xsi="http://www.w3.org/2001/XMLSchema-instance"
         xsi:schemaLocation="http://maven.apache.org/POM/4.0.0
           http://maven.apache.org/maven-v4_0_0.xsd">
  <modelVersion>4.0.0</modelVersion>
  <groupId>com.manning.sdmia</groupId>
  <artifactId>springdm-web-sample</artifactId>          ❶ Makes project
  <packaging>bundle</packaging>                             a bundle
  <version>1.0.0</version>                               ❷ Uses OSGi-compliant
  <name>springdm-web-sample</name>                          version
  <url>http://maven.apache.org</url>
  <dependencies>
  (...)
  </dependencies>
  <build>
    <plugins>
      <plugin>
        <groupId>org.apache.felix</groupId>
        <artifactId>maven-bundle-plugin</artifactId>
        <version>2.0.0</version>
        <extensions>true</extensions>
        <configuration>
          <instructions>
            <Include-Resource>
              src/main/webapp                           ❸ Includes resources in
            </Include-Resource>                             generated bundle
            <Web-ContextPath>
              springdm-web-sample                       ❹ Adds header for
            </Web-ContextPath>                              context path
          </instructions>
        </configuration>
      </plugin>
      <plugin>
        <groupId>org.apache.maven.plugins</groupId>
        <artifactId>maven-compiler-plugin</artifactId>
        <version>2.1</version>
        <configuration>
          <source>1.5</source>
          <target>1.5</target>
        </configuration>
      </plugin>
    </plugins>
  </build>
</project>
```

The Felix Bundle Plugin is activated because we switched the packaging from `jar` to
`bundle` at ❶. We use an OSGi-compliant version number for the bundle at ❷. We added
extra configuration with the `instructions` tag. First, to include the web application
files, we used the `Include-Resource` tag at ❸. Second, the Spring DM web extender can
use the `Web-ContextPath` header specified in a bundle's manifest to deploy the web
application under this context name; we added this header by using `Web-ContextPath`
tag at ❹, so the Felix Bundle Plugin will include it in the generated manifest.

The bundle is now ready to be packaged with the Maven 2 `package` target.

3.5.3   *Checking the operation of a web bundle in a container*

Because we provisioned Equinox with Spring DM web bundles and with the other necessary web bundles, our own web bundle can now easily be deployed. Once installed, we need to start it, and the now familiar `ss` command assures us that everything is fine:

```
osgi> ss

Framework is launched.

id      State       Bundle
0       ACTIVE      org.eclipse.osgi_3.5.1.R35x_v20090827
(...)
27      ACTIVE      com.manning.sdmia.springdm-web-sample_1.0.0.SNAPSHOT

osgi>
```

The short status isn't very verbose, and for once we have a graphical result. You can check the two pages with a browser:

- http://localhost:8080/springdm-web-sample/
- http://localhost:8080/springdm-web-sample/index.jsp

If you see web pages corresponding to the index.html and index.jsp pages we wrote previously, congrats! You successfully installed Spring DM web support and deployed a web application.

The next section covers how to write an integration test for our web application.

3.5.4   *Developing an integration test for a web bundle*

Developing an integration test for a web bundle is nearly the same as for a standard bundle, except that you need to add more bundles as dependencies. Listing 3.10 shows the minimal dependencies for web support that we can add to the POM.

Listing 3.10   Minimal Maven 2 dependencies for web support

```
<project>
  (...)
  <properties>
    <springdm.version>2.0.0.M1</springdm.version>
    <equinox.version>3.5.1.R35x_v20090827</equinox.version>
    <spring.version>3.0.2.RELEASE</spring.version>
  </properties>

  <dependencies>
    (...)
    <dependency>
      <groupId>org.springframework.osgi</groupId>
      <artifactId>spring-osgi-web</artifactId>
      <version>${springdm.version}</version>
      <scope>test</scope>
    </dependency>
    <dependency>
      <groupId>org.springframework.osgi</groupId>
      <artifactId>spring-osgi-web-extender</artifactId>
```

Needs standard bundle dependencies

Adds Spring DM bundles for web support

```
            <version>${springdm.version}</version>
            <scope>test</scope>
        </dependency>
        <dependency>
            <groupId>org.springframework.osgi</groupId>
            <artifactId>catalina.osgi</artifactId>
            <version>5.5.23-SNAPSHOT</version>
            <scope>test</scope>
        </dependency>
        <dependency>
            <groupId>org.springframework.osgi</groupId>
            <artifactId>catalina.start.osgi</artifactId>
            <version>1.0.0</version>
            <scope>test</scope>
        </dependency>
    </dependencies>
    (...)
</project>
```

Adds Spring DM bundles for web support

Adds Tomcat support

Listing 3.10 shows the dependencies for minimal web support, but our web bundle needs more than that because it includes a JSP. We must add a JSP compiler, as shown in listing 3.11.

Listing 3.11   Dependencies for JSP and taglib support

```
<dependency>
    <groupId>org.springframework.osgi</groupId>
    <artifactId>jsp-api.osgi</artifactId>
    <version>2.0-SNAPSHOT</version>
    <scope>test</scope>
</dependency>
<dependency>
    <groupId>org.springframework.osgi</groupId>
    <artifactId>jasper.osgi</artifactId>
    <version>5.5.23-SNAPSHOT</version>
    <scope>test</scope>
</dependency>
<dependency>
    <groupId>org.springframework.osgi</groupId>
    <artifactId>commons-el.osgi</artifactId>
    <version>1.0-SNAPSHOT</version>
    <scope>test</scope>
</dependency>
<dependency>
    <groupId>org.springframework.osgi</groupId>
    <artifactId>jstl.osgi</artifactId>
    <version>1.1.2-SNAPSHOT</version>
    <scope>test</scope>
</dependency>
```

As described previously, Spring DM will use all these dependencies to provision the container it launches from the Maven 2 local repository; so we must invoke a Maven 2 command to download them. The `mvn install` command, for example, will do this and also install our bundle in the repository.

The integration test, shown in listing 3.12, is more complex than our first one. It not only checks our bundle installation but also launches HTTP requests against the application.

Listing 3.12 Integration test for the web bundle

```
package com.manning.sdmia;

import java.net.HttpURLConnection;
import java.net.URL;
import org.osgi.framework.Bundle;
import org.springframework.core.io.InputStreamResource;
import org.springframework.core.io.Resource;
import org.springframework.osgi.test.
    AbstractConfigurableBundleCreatorTests;

public class SpringDmWebSampleTest
            extends AbstractConfigurableBundleCreatorTests {

  public void testIntegration() throws Exception {
    boolean bundleIsHereAndStarted = false;
    for(Bundle bundle : bundleContext.getBundles()) {
      if("com.manning.sdmia.springdm-web-sample".equals(
        bundle.getSymbolicName()) &&
        bundle.getState() == Bundle.ACTIVE) {
      bundleIsHereAndStarted = true;
      break;
      }
    }
    assertTrue(
"springdm-web-sample is not installed nor activated!",
bundleIsHereAndStarted);
    Thread.sleep(10 * 1000);
    testConnection(
      "http://localhost:8080/springdm-web-sample/
    index.html");
    testConnection(
      "http://localhost:8080/springdm-web-sample/
    index.jsp");
  }

  @Override
  protected String[] getTestBundlesNames() {
    return new String [] {
"org.springframework.osgi, spring-osgi-web," +
      getSpringDMVersion(),
"org.springframework.osgi, spring-osgi-web-extender," +
      getSpringDMVersion(),
"javax.servlet, com.springsource.javax.servlet, 2.4.0",
"org.springframework.osgi, catalina.osgi, 5.5.23-SNAPSHOT",
"org.springframework.osgi, catalina.start.osgi, 1.0.0",
"org.springframework.osgi, jsp-api.osgi, 2.0-SNAPSHOT",
"org.springframework.osgi, jasper.osgi, 5.5.23-SNAPSHOT",
"org.springframework.osgi, commons-el.osgi, 1.0-SNAPSHOT",
"org.springframework.osgi, jstl.osgi, 1.1.2-SNAPSHOT",
"com.manning.sdmia, springdm-web-sample, 1.0.0"
```

❶ Asserts web bundle is active

❷ Waits until everything is deployed

❸ Tests web pages

❹ Provisions test container

```
      };
    }
    (...)
}
```

This test checks that the bundle is properly started ❶ and puts the thread to sleep ❷ to allow time for the web container to deploy the web application. At ❸ we connect to the two pages of the application (the code of the testConnection method isn't shown in listing 3.12; it just ensures that the container returns a 200 status code). We still need to tell Spring DM which bundles we want it to include for our test, and we do this by overriding the getTestBundlesNames method ❹.

> **NOTE** Starting the web container on port 8080 can be problematic on a busy integration server, because this port would probably be already used. We'll see in chapter 9 how to change the default configuration of the embedded Tomcat.

By executing the test with Maven 2, you should get output something like the following:

```
-------------------------------------------------------
 T E S T S
-------------------------------------------------------
Running com.manning.sdmia.SpringDmWebSampleTest
Tests run: 1, Failures: 0, Errors: 0, Skipped: 0, Time elapsed: 12.453 sec

Results :

Tests run: 1, Failures: 0, Errors: 0, Skipped: 0

[INFO] ------------------------------------------------------------------
[INFO] BUILD SUCCESSFUL
[INFO] ------------------------------------------------------------------
[INFO] Total time: 20 seconds
[INFO] Finished at: Thu Oct 29 22:06:31 CET 2009
[INFO] Final Memory: 6M/12M
[INFO] ------------------------------------------------------ --------------
```

Great work! Deploying a web application on OSGi platforms isn't an easy task, and we achieved it in a pretty straightforward way, thanks to Spring DM.

3.6   *Summary*

This concludes our overview of Spring DM. There are many ways to start with OSGi frameworks, and we've tried to take you through the installation of all the basic Spring DM elements that you'll need when tackling OSGi development. We covered how to develop standard and web bundles using a popular build tool, Maven 2. This will undoubtedly help you to manage dependencies and package your bundles. We also saw two ways to test OSGi bundles: the manual approach, where you launch the OSGi container from the command line, and the integration testing approach, where you take advantage of Spring DM's testing support.

We're about to dive into Spring DM's features in more detail in the next chapters, and you should be ready to develop, package, and test all that you'll learn or apply it directly to your own applications.

Part 2

Core Spring DM

In part 1 we discussed the building blocks of Spring DM, and you should now have more than a superficial understanding of what each piece does and why it's important. We're now going to get into the nitty-gritty details of using Spring DM and its associated technologies in a variety of enterprise development contexts.

This part forms the meat of the book, so if you are going to read anything, read this!

In chapter 4 we look at the operation of the two extenders that Spring DM provides: the standard extender and the web extender.

Chapter 5 covers the definition and use of OSGi services with Spring DM. Service support is at the core of the feature set provided by Spring DM and thus this chapter is one of the key chapters of the book.

Chapter 6 looks at the development of enterprise applications using Spring DM and, in particular, how to design and structure applications of this type to take advantage of all the power that Spring DM and OSGi provide. The chapter also covers the integration of third-party enterprise libraries into an OSGi environment.

Chapter 7 covers the use of data access through JDBC and JPA in Spring DM-enabled applications.

Chapter 8, the last in part 2, covers the use of common web frameworks in Spring DM-enabled applications.

Using Spring
DM extenders

This chapter covers

- The standard Spring DM and web extender
  mechanisms
- The lifecycle of Spring application contexts in
  Spring-powered bundles
- How to structure and configure Spring-powered
  bundles

Spring DM brings new powers to your OSGi bundles; namely, all the power available in the Spring Framework, which means a great deal! We saw in the previous chapter how Spring DM can automatically create an application context on behalf of a bundle, assuming this bundle contains Spring configuration files in a specific location. With the availability of the Spring lightweight container, a bundle can build and wire all of its constituent components and let Spring DM interact with the OSGi platform to register Spring beans in the service registry. All this can be driven declaratively, without any of your Java code depending on the OSGi APIs.

As a result, writing Spring-powered bundles becomes very easy thanks to Spring DM. The extender hides most of the complexity of the process from us. Nevertheless, a good understanding of the inner mechanics of what is going on, and of all of the available options, is bound to come in handy. The standard Spring DM extender presents opportunities to tune the structure of Spring-powered bundles and the way that their application contexts are created. In this chapter, we'll cover these options as well as how Spring DM manages the whole lifecycle of application contexts. We'll also see that Spring DM is truly simple, as it set us free from the vagaries of the OSGi API, but that it doesn't sacrifice any features of OSGi.

Furthermore, Spring DM brings its web support to OSGi, making it possible to deploy bundles as web applications to an embedded web container. We'll see in this chapter how this web support is unique to an OSGi environment, because web bundles are treated like any other OSGi bundle and can consume services available in the OSGi service registry. At the heart of the Spring DM web support is its web extender, which contains a WAR deployer, which we'll take a look at to see how it differs from a standard web deployer.

This may sound like a lot for a single chapter, but this is because Spring DM offers a lot of options when managing Spring application contexts for OSGi bundles. Spring DM has reasonable defaults, which makes it easy to use, but sometimes defaults aren't appropriate, and that's when you'll come to this chapter.

4.1   *Unleashing Spring DM's standard extender*

As explained in previous chapters, the Spring DM standard extender is a special bundle that listens for bundle installations in the OSGi container. What is so special about it? Extender-based bundles, if you'll forgive the pun, spring into action when the kind of bundles they're interested in change state or are deployed. The Spring DM extender scans bundles looking for Spring configuration files and creates Spring application contexts on behalf of these Spring-powered bundles. As an extender, it primarily listens for bundle starting events, but it also looks for Spring-powered bundles that are already in the active state when it is itself started. This means that your Spring-powered bundles go from passive to real active OSGi components as soon as the extender discovers them, and this without any additional work from you.

In this section, we'll cover the Spring DM standard extender mechanisms for creating and destroying Spring application contexts, as well as the lifecycle hooks it provides for these contexts. We'll also see what entry points Spring DM offers for interacting directly with the enclosing OSGi environment. All this information will be valuable in understanding the way the extender works and when its default behavior won't suit your needs.

We'll start with a section that may look off-topic, but it's at the heart of Spring DM's extender: dependencies between Spring-powered bundles.

4.1.1   *A word about dependencies*

When working with Spring DM, you'll hear a lot about dependencies between Spring-powered bundles. The word "dependency" includes a lot of notions, so let's make it crystal clear at the beginning.

In the case of Spring-powered bundles, *dependencies* means that the application contexts of these bundles share some beans, thanks to the registering and consumption mechanisms of the OSGi service registry. Figure 4.1 illustrates this.

By looking at figure 4.1, you can easily see that bundle B's and bundle C's Spring application contexts *depend* on bundle A's application context, because the latter registers one of its beans on the OSGi registry. Bundle B's and bundle C's application contexts consume this OSGi service through Spring DM and it becomes one of their beans. This service can become one of the key parts of these application contexts, so much so that they can't work properly or even start without it.

You'll learn everything about Spring DM's declarative way of interacting with the OSGi service registry in chapter 5, but here is an overview. The following snippet shows how bundle A first defines a service as a standard Spring bean and registers it in the OSGi registry:

```
<bean id="myService"
      class="com.manning.sdmia.impl.MyServiceImpl"/>

<osgi:service ref="myService"
              interface="com.manning.sdmia.MyService"/>
```

To consume and use the service, bundle B or C would use the `reference` element from the `osgi` namespace and then use the OSGi service like any other Spring bean, as shown in the following snippet:

```
<osgi:reference id="myService"
                interface="com.manning.sdmia.MyService"/>

<bean id="webController"
      class="com.manning.sdmia.web.MyController">
  <property name="service" ref="myService"/>
</bean>
```

In real-world applications, dependencies between Spring-powered bundles can become complex and have deep impacts on the way Spring application contexts must be managed: their start and stop order, event propagation, and so on. Luckily, it's Spring DM's job to deal with this concern. We'll see in this chapter that most of the behavior of Spring DM's extender is driven by dependencies.

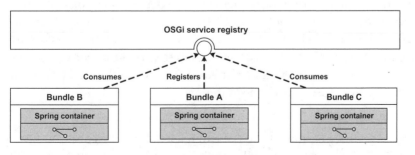

Figure 4.1   Bundles register and consume OSGi services with Spring DM. Their Spring application contexts *depend* on each other.

It's time now to dive into the real topic. We'll begin with the structure of Spring-powered bundles.

4.1.2   *Structure of standard Spring OSGi components*

From the OSGi container's perspective, Spring-powered bundles don't differ from vanilla OSGi bundles. They use the same packaging—a JAR file with a META-INF/MAN-IFEST.MF file containing OSGi-specific headers—but they also contain Spring XML configuration files that the Spring DM extender will use to bootstrap an application context. As we explained earlier, a Spring-powered bundle needs to contain either a META-INF/spring folder or a `Spring-Context` manifest header.

DEFAULT BEHAVIOR FOR LOCATING SPRING CONFIGURATION FILES

If it contains a META-INF/spring folder, a Spring-powered bundle doesn't need to contain non-OSGi manifest headers, and its packaging and manifest generation remain the same as any regular bundle (except that Spring configuration files must be included in the right place). Its structure would look like the following:

```
my-springpowered-bundle.jar
  META-INF/                            OSGi-compliant
    MANIFEST.MF          ◁──┘          manifest file
    spring/
      application-context-1.xml        Spring configuration
      application-context-2.xml        files
  com/
    manning/                           Bundle classes
      sdmia/                           and resources
        ...
```

This packaging is particularly convenient for its simplicity, and this default behavior follows the convention over configuration pattern, but there are drawbacks.

First, the Spring DM extender scans for any XML files in the META-INF/spring folder, which means any files with .xml extensions. If an XML file that has nothing to do with Spring is found in the META-INF/spring folder, the Spring DM extender will try to use it to bootstrap the application context, and this will usually result in an exception. Luckily non-Spring configuration files should not usually be found in the META-INF/spring folder, because its name makes clear its specific purpose.

Second, and more serious, is the fact that the default behavior will also create the application context with default settings. Fortunately, the default settings are suitable for most Spring-powered bundles. The alternative is to use the `Spring-Context` header.

DEFINING THE LOCATION OF SPRING CONFIGURATION FILES WITH THE SPRING-CONTEXT HEADER

The `Spring-Context` header can be used to specify the Spring configuration files' location. Its primary use is as simple as this:

```
Spring-Context: config/application-context.xml
```

In the previous snippet, the Spring DM extender will use the config/application-context.xml file to bootstrap the bundle application context. Any XML file in the META-INF/spring folder will be ignored, because the `Spring-Context` header overrides the default configuration file detection behavior. You can specify more than one file by separating their names with commas:

```
Spring-Context: config/app-context-1.xml, config/app-context-2.xml
```

When using the `Spring-Context` header, where exactly are the XML files retrieved from? The default extender behavior is to retrieve the Spring configuration files from the *bundle space*, as it's defined in the OSGi specification (section 4.4.14 for version 4.2 of the spec[1]). To quickly summarize, when using the bundle space, the extender scans the bundle JAR and all of its fragments.

With the `Spring-Context` header, locations can use wildcards to define file patterns. For example, consider the following header value:

```
Spring-Context: config/*.xml
```

With the preceding header, the Spring DM extender would use all the files ending with .xml in the config folder of the bundle space.

The Spring DM extender understands Ant-style syntax for files and directories, so it can recursively scan directories. Imagine your bundle contains a config directory with the following content:

```
config/
  dao-context.xml
  business-context.xml
  web/
    web-backoffice-context.xml
    web-frontoffice-context.xml
```

If you used the following header value, the Spring DM extender would use all the preceding files to create the bundle application context:

```
Spring-Context: config/**/*.xml
```

Considering the bundle space consists of the bundle JAR and all its fragments, a bundle can have its application context augmented by any XML file contained in a fragment, as long as the XML file matches the `Spring-Context` header value. This is a convenient way to facilitate the configuration of a Spring-powered bundle, as shown in figure 4.2. The `MyApp` bundle has its own Spring configuration files and lets some

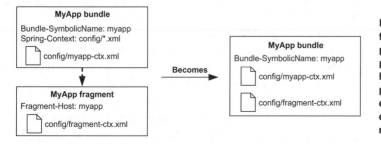

Figure 4.2 Applying the fragment configuration pattern to a Spring-powered bundle. The host bundle contains the static part of the application context and the fragment complements it with the remaining variable parts.

---

[1] Available at http://www.osgi.org/Specifications/HomePage.

options be tuned by fragments. The latter can override the default behavior by providing their own bean definitions.

Spring DM isn't only able to look in the bundle space; it has its own way to locate resources in bundles or from any other location.

SPRING DM'S RESOURCE LOCATION BEHAVIOR

In our previous examples, locations refer to resources, and, without any prefix, locations are interpreted as *relative* resource paths. This is directly related to the Spring Framework resource abstraction and the way that Spring DM extends this mechanism. Spring DM introduces a new `Resource` implementation, `OsgiBundleResource`, which encapsulates all the necessary logic for proper resource loading from a bundle in an OSGi environment.

Spring resource abstraction

The Spring Framework defines an abstraction to load resources from an application context. This abstraction is based on the `Resource` interface, which represents the access to a resource and is agnostic to the underlying resource medium (filesystem, classpath, URL, and so on). Spring defines the `ResourceLoader` interface, which is meant to be implemented by objects that can load resources (a Spring application context always implements this interface).

For a resource loader, a resource is defined by its path, which can be relative or explicit. A relative resource path doesn't contain any prefix and its loading (and origin) will depend on the resource loader's nature. Let's imagine we want to load a resource with the following path: path/to/resource.txt. A classpath-based application context will load this resource from the classpath, and a file-based application context will load it from the filesystem.

A resource path is said to be explicit when its starts with a prefix that describes the resource origin or medium. If we're sure our previous resource comes from the classpath, its path could be explicit thanks to the `classpath` prefix: `classpath:path/to/resource.txt`. Spring supports several prefixes: `classpath`, `file`, `http`.

In OSGi environments, class and resource loading are carefully controlled. Spring DM application contexts have specific behavior and extend the resource management mechanisms of regular Spring application context implementations.

Spring DM also has its own interpretation of some resource prefixes: for example, there is quite a bit of difference between `classpath` in the web environment and `classpath` in a regular OSGi environment. This can seem odd at first, but it's consistent with the Spring resource abstraction: the final behavior is defined by the underlying application context implementation. Developers used to traditional, non-OSGi, Spring applications should be aware that commonly used prefixes, such as `classpath`, don't behave the same way in an OSGi environment. Table 4.1 summarizes the Spring DM resource abstraction specifics and how it honors OSGi spaces, as defined in the 4.4.14 section of the 4.2 OSGi specification.

Table 4.1 OSGi resource search strategies with Spring DM

OSGi search strategy	Prefixes	Description
Class space	`classpath:` `classpath*:`	Search is delegated to the bundle classloader. The bundle itself, imported packages, and required bundles are then scanned using the same semantics as the `Bundle.getResource` method.
JAR file	`osgibundlejar:`	Only the bundle itself is scanned, using the same semantics as the `Bundle.getEntry` method.
Bundle space	`osgibundle:`	The bundle and its fragments (if any) are scanned. Delegates internally to the `Bundle.findEntries` method. This is Spring DM's default resource-loading strategy.

The demonstrated flexibility of resource loading has some important implications. For example, the two following lines are equivalent because resource-abstraction mechanisms also operate in the Spring configuration files:

```
Spring-Context: config/application-context.xml
Spring-Context: osgibundle:config/application-context.xml
```

If one of your beans has a `Resource` property, you can use any prefix and Spring DM will load it, applying, as appropriate, any of the specific behaviors we've just described. In the following snippet, the `resource` property is of type `Resource`:

```
<bean id="someBean" class="com.manning.sdmia.SomeBean">
  <property name="resource"
            value="classpath:help/section1.html" />
</bean>
```

Spring DM supports all conventional prefixes, such as `file:` and `http:`. These prefixes don't imply any interaction with the classpath and behave identically in an OSGi environment as in any other context. You can use them in your `Spring-Context` header if you'd like to configure your bundles from the filesystem:

```
Spring-Context: file:/etc/spring/application-context.xml
```

This feature is quite handy, as it allows you to configure a Spring DM bundle without cracking the JAR and without having to generate a fragment. This is especially valuable if you want to change configuration attributes at runtime.

ORGANIZING SPRING CONFIGURATION FILES IN A BUNDLE

A suggested practice regarding Spring configuration files in a bundle is to split the traditional Spring and OSGi configurations into two separate files. The traditional Spring configuration would contain bean declarations, wiring, and technical concerns, such as transaction and AOP (AOP) configuration entries. The OSGi configuration would mainly deal with the interaction between the bundle and the OSGi environment. Spring DM comes with a dedicated namespace for interacting with the OSGi platform, and this namespace should not be used in the files used for wiring the bundle's inner beans.

A typical Spring-powered bundle of this sort would have the following structure:

```
my-springpowered-bundle.jar
  META-INF/
    MANIFEST.MF
    spring/
      modulename-context.xml
      modulename-osgi-context.xml
  com/
    manning/
      sdmia/
        ...
```

◁ **Declares regular Spring beans**

◁ **Configures bundle interactions with OSGi platform**

You can choose not to use the default location for Spring files (and use the Spring-Context header) but you should at least respect the convention of keeping the regular bean declarations free from any OSGi-specific configuration.

> ### How should you organize your Spring configuration files?
>
> The Spring lightweight container can create an application context from multiple files, as long as these files define a consistent set of beans and their dependencies. Thus, bean B from file 2 can reference bean A, which is defined in file 1.
>
> For a typical Spring-based web application, the Spring configuration files can be split by abstraction layer (datasource-context.xml, dao-context.xml, business-context.xml, and so on). For really big applications, another level of division becomes necessary; namely, splitting on a business module basis (dao-frontoffice-context.xml, dao-back-office-context.xml). Splitting Spring files makes them easier to maintain and improves modularity by allowing only one layer of an application to be bootstrapped—to unit test it, for example.
>
> OSGi is all about modular programming so a module should not need dozens of Spring configuration files. You can split the bundle application context definition into several files, but if one of your bundles needs a large and complex Spring configuration, you should consider splitting the bundle itself into more fine-grained bundles.

The structure of Spring-powered bundles holds no secrets for you now. You know how to tell Spring DM where to find Spring configuration files, how Spring DM handles file discovery, and how to properly package and organize your bundles. In the next section, we'll see how Spring DM manages application contexts, which is important for understanding the various options the framework provides.

4.1.3   *Initializing and destroying the Spring container*

A Spring-powered bundle doesn't have to worry about its application context's creation and destruction; the Spring DM extender handles this process on behalf of the bundle. Nevertheless, it's useful to have some knowledge of the application context lifecycle because it can have implications for the OSGi platform itself. In this section, we'll describe Spring DM's default behavior for handling application contexts. We'll also describe why you might want to override the default behavior, and how.

The Spring DM extender does for bundles exactly what the `ContextLoaderListener` does for Spring-based web applications: it creates and destroys Spring application contexts. In fact, the activator of the Spring DM extender bundle is also called `ContextLoaderListener` and implements all the logic for the management of a bundle's application context.

HOW SPRING DM CREATES APPLICATION CONTEXTS

When the Spring DM extender is started, it scans the OSGi container for bundles in the active state and bootstraps the application contexts for those it identifies as Spring-powered. It doesn't often find any, because the extender is an infrastructure bundle and is usually among the first bundles to be started. Nevertheless, it's worth noting that the Spring DM extender is able to create application contexts even for bundles that were started *before* it was.

Usually, Spring-powered bundles are deployed *after* the Spring extender. The extender tries to bootstrap application contexts only from bundles that manage to reach the active state. Therefore, an application context is created *after* its owning bundle has been started (in OSGi terms, the extender initiates application context creation on the started event).

The Spring DM extender creates application contexts *asynchronously*; application contexts are started in a different thread than the one that started the bundle (usually a thread owned by the OSGi platform). Spring DM behaves in this way primarily for two reasons:

- The OSGi specification recommends that event processing complete in a short, finite time so that other event handlers are dealt with in a timely manner, and, depending on its content, creating an application context can take some time. If the creation happened in the OSGi event thread, it could prevent other platform tasks from running and slow the whole container.

- The extender bundle waits for application context service dependencies to be satisfied before starting a bundle's application context. If this task were performed synchronously, the bundle start order would have to be carefully managed to ensure that a bundle would not cause a deadlock by waiting for a service that had not yet been started (and could not be started because of the synchronous usage of the event thread). For the same reasons, synchronous creation would make it impossible to start bundles with service dependencies involving cycles.

Thanks to asynchronous application context creation, starting Spring-powered bundles has virtually no impact on the OSGi container's responsiveness, as shown in figure 4.3.

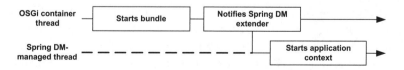

Figure 4.3 Spring DM's extender bootstraps Spring application contexts asynchronously to avoid blocking OSGi containers.

The Spring DM extender is a bundle listener!

In Spring DM 1.2, the extender is a synchronous bundle listener, registered by the activator of the Spring DM extender bundle. What exactly is a synchronous bundle listener? It's an implementation of the observer pattern, which allows code to react to bundle events, such as activation, startup, or stopping. There are two kinds of bundle listeners, synchronous and asynchronous (represented by two interfaces, `SynchronousBundleListener` and `BundleListener` respectively), and the way the OSGi platform notifies them is slightly different.

Synchronous listeners receive more events than their asynchronous brethren, as they're notified of starting and stopping events (the targeted bundle is on the way to being started or stopped, respectively). Second, they're called *during* the processing of the event. In the case of bundle startup, the caller asks the platform to start the bundle, the platform notifies the synchronous listeners, each does its work, and the bundle is started (and then the platform broadcasts a started event, but that's another story). With the synchronous method, listeners are always notified during the processing of the event.

Asynchronous bundle listener notification isn't as straightforward as the synchronous case. The OSGi platform doesn't place any constraints on the timeliness of notification and can add events to a queue and let a background thread dispatch them to the asynchronous listeners. There is no guarantee that event ordering is respected (the started event of the bundle could be delivered after the corresponding stopped event). This doesn't make asynchronous listeners useless, but the dispatch mechanism needs to be understood when writing listeners of this type!

The `BundleListener` and `SynchronousBundleListener` interfaces define the same method, the synchronous flavor being simply a marker-based extension of the asynchronous interface. Synchronous bundle listeners must be used with caution, because they can slow the whole platform if their processing takes too much time. The Spring DM extender is a synchronous bundle listener but it delegates the creation of Spring application contexts to different threads by default.

Asynchronous context creation is the default behavior, but we'll see that it can be easily overridden.

FAILURES DURING CREATION AND THE EXTENDER MODEL

What if the creation of an application context fails? Because an application context can contain a complex set of beans, it can easily fail to start. If this happens, it will definitely have consequences for the bundle's interaction with the OSGi container (for service registration, for instance) but it won't affect the bundle's state; it'll still remain in active state. Spring DM would, however, log the cause of the failure, which is another good reason to properly set up log reporting.

This illustrates another facet of the extender pattern; an extender should not modify the state of a bundle, but rather should react to bundle state changes. It's tempting to think that the extender should shut down the bundle itself in the case of failure, but this would result in an inconsistent state machine—one that other dependent OSGi framework services would find impossible to accommodate coherently.

HOW SPRING DM DESTROYS APPLICATION CONTEXTS

There is a one-to-one relationship between a Spring-powered bundle and an application context, so when a bundle is stopped, its application context is destroyed. The Spring DM extender takes care of the destruction of application contexts (on stopping bundle events) and accomplishes this crucial operation in a managed and safe way.

Why should application contexts need to be destroyed properly? In standard, non-OSGi applications, Spring application contexts have many infrastructure-related responsibilities: they can, for instance, manage connections to databases. All these kinds of resources need to be properly released. Application beans can also have specific shutdown requirements, and it's the application context's responsibility to call the appropriate methods, because it's in charge of the lifecycle of the beans. The Spring Framework offers various hooks (interfaces to implement, annotations, and declarative configurations) for beans to register initialization or destruction methods.

OSGi applications have further requirements: each bundle can interact with the service registry, and because Spring DM handles this interaction (service publication and consumption), it must handle the interaction through the full lifecycle of the bundle. So, when a bundle is stopped, all the services it exported must be unregistered and the services it imported disposed of.

To summarize, through application context destruction, Spring DM accomplishes the following things:

- Calls the shutdown method on Spring beans
- Unregisters exported services
- Informs the OSGi container that imported services are no longer used

In contrast to the asynchronous creation of an application context, the destruction is handled synchronously : the OSGi container is told to stop a Spring-powered bundle, it sends a stopping event, the Spring DM extender receives the event and stops the bundle application context (in the same thread), and then control returns to the container, which then stops the bundle. This is illustrated in figure 4.4.

The destruction is done synchronously because the application context must be destroyed *before* the bundle is stopped. Once stopped, a bundle—and in particular, its bundle context—can't be used anymore. A stopped bundle would thus prevent its application context from performing tasks such as unregistering.

The destruction of an application context isn't always an isolated event, and it can be part of the shutdown of the whole OSGi platform or the Spring DM extender itself.

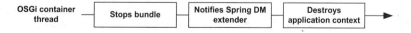

Figure 4.4   Spring DM's extender shuts down Spring application contexts synchronously because the context needs to be shut down before the bundle itself.

What's the deal with application context creation and destruction?

Creating or destroying a Spring application context can be slow, so does this mean Spring is slow?

No, the Spring lightweight container is powerful and accomplishes many things when it creates and manages Java objects, but it isn't intrinsically slow. What takes more time when starting a Spring application context is the initialization of the beans themselves, which are usually not Spring classes. Creating a database connection involves network traffic and the creation of a security context, and this can take some time; creating an ORM context involves the scanning of classes and configuration files to load metadata, and this can take some time too.

That's why loading a Spring application context can take a long time. If you try to load a Spring application context with only one simple JavaBean in it, you'll see it starts up pretty quickly.

In the next section, we'll see that this implies the destruction of all extender-started application contexts and how the extender handles this.

STOPPING THE EXTENDER

When the extender is stopped, either explicitly or due to the shutdown of the OSGi platform, it has a lot of work to accomplish before it's finished. The extender bundle must obviously deal with its own internal housekeeping, which isn't really our concern; what really matters is the way the extender destroys the application context of each Spring-powered bundle. The good news is that it handles this gracefully—we have nothing to worry about! Nevertheless, let's see exactly what the extender does for us.

The challenge mainly consists of destroying the application contexts in the right order. Why must there be a "right" order? Well, application contexts can have dependencies on each other; some can export services that others consume. The right order is therefore based on the way bundles are connected through the service registry. Spring DM must compute the dependency graph of Spring-powered bundles by analyzing their service relationships.

Let's look at the simple example of the Spring-powered bundles shown in figure 4.5.

Figure 4.5 shows bundles as they would be organized in a typical, layered enterprise application. By looking at the diagram, you could easily compute the dependency graph:

```
web -> businessservices -> dataaccess -> datasource
```

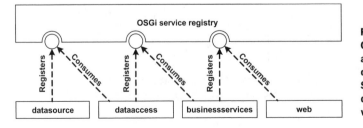

Figure 4.5 Because of OSGi service registration and consumption, bundles depend on each other, and Spring DM takes these dependencies into account when it stops its extender.

Bundles should be stopped in this order.

Let's see how Spring DM's algorithm would lead us to this dependency ordering. Spring DM would first track bundles that either don't export any services, or export services that aren't referenced (used). These bundles are destroyed immediately (although Spring DM will additionally attempt to do this in the reverse order of their creation) and whatever services they're using are released. The services these bundles were using might then no longer be referenced, and Spring DM would find their owning bundles and destroy their application contexts. This cycle continues until there are no more application contexts left to shut down.

By applying the algorithm to our sample bundles, the web bundle would come first, as it doesn't export any services. By destroying its application context, Spring DM would release the service references to businessservices, making the application context of the businessservices bundle available for destruction. The same scenario applies to the dataaccess and then the datasource bundles; all the application contexts are properly destroyed without breaking service reference integrity!

Unfortunately, things aren't always as simple as this: the algorithm will loop until there are no remaining bundles that export unreferenced services, but some application contexts may remain because of a cyclic dependency between service references. Figure 4.6 illustrates this using three bundles with a cyclic dependency (A -> B -> C -> A).

In this case, Spring DM has no choice other than to break the cycle by trying to find the most appropriate bundle to stop first. Spring DM bases its choice on an OSGi property of services: the service ranking. Services are looked up from the service registry by their interface. In the case that there are several services implementing the same interface, the one with the highest service ranking is returned by the OSGi platform. For each remaining bundle, Spring DM finds the highest service ranking number and destroys the application context whose bundle has the lowest service ranking among the set just calculated. If there is a tie in lowest ranking, Spring DM uses the bundle ID (an indicator of start order) as a tiebreaker, stopping the bundle with the highest ID (which was thus started last). This will hopefully break the cycle, and Spring DM can restart its algorithm at the beginning to find other application contexts to destroy.

Now you know all of the dirty work the Spring DM extender does for you! It handles application context creation and destruction, which ends up being much more complex (at least internally!) than it appears at first blush. We also saw in this section

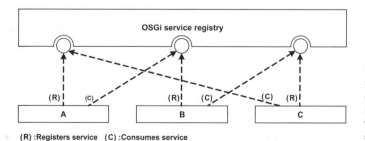

(R) :Registers service   (C) :Consumes service

Figure 4.6   At shutdown, when there are cyclic dependencies between bundles, Spring DM tries to break them by using a specific shutdown algorithm.

the default behavior of the Spring DM extender. Now it's time to take a look at the settings that Spring DM provides for customizing application context creation.

4.1.4 *Customizing application context creation*

We saw earlier that a Spring-powered bundle can use a dedicated Spring DM header in its manifest to tell it where to find its Spring configuration files. You can use this header to override the default location of these files. The `Spring-Context` header can contain more than configuration files—it accepts *directives*, using a syntax that conforms to the common header syntax, as defined in the OSGi Platform Core Specification (section 3.2.3 for version 4.2 of the spec).

With these directives, we can tell the extender precisely how to create the application context of a bundle. As they're part of the manifest of a bundle, they're interpreted by Spring DM on a per-bundle basis; they can't be used to globally modify the creation of application contexts for all the Spring-powered bundles (we'll see in chapter 9 how to configure the extender itself). Table 4.2 lists the available directives for the `Spring-Context` header and their respective default values. The following subsections discuss them each in turn.

Table 4.2   Directives for the `Spring-Context` header

Directive	Possible values	Description
`create-asynchronously`	`true, false`	Tells the extender to create the bundle application context asynchronously or synchronously. Default is `true` (asynchronously).
`wait-for-dependencies`	`true, false`	Controls whether application context creation should wait for all mandatory imported services to be available. Default is `true`.
`timeout`	`integer`	Indicates the time (in seconds) to wait for mandatory imported services to become available before failing the creation of the application context. Default is `300` seconds (5 minutes).
`publish-context`	`true, false`	Controls whether the bundle application context is published in the OSGi service registry. Default is `true`.

CREATE-ASYNCHRONOUSLY

By setting the `create-asynchronously` directive to `false`, the creation of the application context occurs in a thread managed by the OSGi platform, as shown in Figure 4.7. The following snippet shows how to set the `create-asynchronously` directive:

```
Spring-Context: config/application-context.xml;create-asynchronously:=false
```

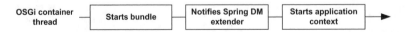

Figure 4.7   Synchronous application context creation using the `create-asynchronously` directive

WAIT-FOR-DEPENDENCIES

With the `wait-for-dependencies` directive, the creation of an application context can be delayed until all its mandatory service dependencies are available. The following snippet shows how to force the creation of the application context even if some of its dependencies aren't yet available:

```
Spring-Context: config/application-context.xml;wait-for-dependencies:=false
```

With this setting, mandatory dependencies are treated as optional, and Spring beans using them will be injected with a service proxy that isn't currently backed by an actual service retrieved from the service registry. You should stick to the default behavior (waiting for dependencies before starting the application context creation) if your bundle dependencies are truly mandatory and if it can't work properly without them.

Thanks to this mechanism, bundles can be started in any order by the OSGi platform, and Spring DM will take care of creating application contexts in the correct order.

TIMEOUT

A dependency can *really* be missing, compromising seriously the creation of an application context. To avoid having the application context creation hanging forever, Spring DM maintains a timeout, which can be set through the `timeout` directive shown in the following snippet:

```
Spring-Context: config/application-context.xml;timeout:=120
```

With this setting, an application context will wait for its mandatory dependencies for 120 seconds before the creation attempt fails. The `timeout` directive makes sense only when application contexts wait for their mandatory dependencies, so it's ignored when the `wait-for-dependencies` directive is set to `false`.

PUBLISH-CONTEXT

The last directive, `publish-context`, controls whether the application context of a Spring-powered bundle should be published in the OSGi service registry. The default is to publish the application context. If you use the `bundle <id>` command under Equinox, where `<id>` is the ID of a Spring-powered bundle, you should get something like this:

```
Registered Services
    {org.springframework.osgi.context.
  DelegatedExecutionOsgiBundleApplicationContext,
    org.springframework.osgi.context.ConfigurableOsgiBundleApplicationContex
    t, org.springframework.context.ConfigurableApplicationContext,
    org.springframework.context.ApplicationContext,
    org.springframework.context.Lifecycle,
    org.springframework.beans.factory.ListableBeanFactory,
    org.springframework.beans.factory.HierarchicalBeanFactory,
    org.springframework.context.MessageSource,
    org.springframework.context.ApplicationEventPublisher,
    org.springframework.core.io.support.ResourcePatternResolver,
    org.springframework.beans.factory.BeanFactory,
    org.springframework.core.io.ResourceLoader,
    org.springframework.beans.factory.DisposableBean}=
```

```
{org.springframework.context.service.name=com.manning.sdmia.
➡    springdm-sample,
➡    Bundle-SymbolicName=com.manning.sdmia.springdm-sample,
➡    Bundle-Version=1.0.0.SNAPSHOT, service.id=24}
```

This tells us that the bundle exported its application context to the service registry. If you don't want this to happen, you can do the following:

```
Spring-Context: config/application-context.xml;publish-context:=false
```

This concludes our exploration of the options available for tuning the creation of application contexts with Spring DM. All these options act on a per-bundle basis; we'll see in chapter 9 how to tune the extender itself, using fragments.

We're now done with context creation and destruction—the next section covers another facet of the lifecycle: how to react to events with the extender event system.

4.1.5   *Listening to extender events with the whiteboard pattern*

Spring DM has a built-in event mechanism that it uses to notify third parties of the application context lifecycle of Spring-powered bundles. We'll describe in this section how to take advantage of this event system and see that it's implemented using a common OSGi pattern: the whiteboard pattern.

THE SPRING DM EVENT MECHANISM

So far we've seen that the Spring DM extender does a lot of work in the background, taking care of the whole lifecycle of application contexts. You'll sometimes need to know about the success or failure of application context startup, for logging purposes for example, and that's why Spring DM offers an event mechanism, through which application contexts send events about their lifecycle to interested parties. The available events are Java classes in the `org.springframework.osgi.context.event` package and they're listed in table 4.3.

Table 4.3   Application context events in Spring DM

Event class	Description
OsgiBundleContextRefreshedEvent	Published when an application context is successfully started or refreshed
OsgiBundleContextFailedEvent	Published when the creation of an application context fails
OsgiBundleContextClosedEvent	Published when an application context is closed, usually when a Spring-powered bundle is stopped

People used to the Spring lightweight container know that standard, non-OSGi application contexts also have an event mechanism. Events of both systems have similar semantics; for example, Spring DM's `OsgiBundleContextRefreshedEvent` is raised when the `refresh` method of the `ConfigurableApplicationContext` interface is called, which is the same point in the lifecycle that the Spring `ContextRefreshedEvent` is raised.

Both systems also have important differences. Spring's standard event system propagates container events to interested beans in the *same* application context (figure 4.8), whereas Spring DM propagates events *outside* the containing application context (figure 4.9).

How does one register listeners for Spring DM events? Simply by declaring a bean that implements the `OsgiBundleApplicationContextListener` interface and then publishing it as an OSGi service. Spring DM will automatically detect it and add it to the list of managed listeners.

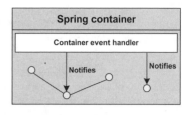

Figure 4.8   Spring's container (non-OSGi) event system: container events are propagated to beans in the *same* application context.

Spring's standard event mechanism

The Spring lightweight container comes with a built-in event mechanism that allows beans to be notified of lifecycle steps in their parent application context. Beans interested in receiving events need to implement the `ApplicationListener` interface, and the application context will register them as listeners when it creates them. They will be notified of events such as the application context starting, stopping, or closing. Spring also allows beans to raise their own events, which will be propagated the same way as built-in ones. This makes it easy to use an event-driven approach in Spring applications, which would normally be enough for simple use cases.

Even though Spring DM offers its own event mechanism, the scope is quite different from that of the standard Spring one, which is, of course, still honored by Spring DM applications.

The listener interface declares only one method, `onOsgiApplicationEvent`, with the event as the only parameter. From the event (an `OsgiBundleApplicationContext-Event`, the base class of the three events we saw previously), the source application context, its enclosing bundle, and the timestamp of the event are available. Depending on the nature of the event, more information can be available (such as the cause of the failure for an `OsgiBundleContextFailedEvent`).

Listing 4.1 shows an implementation of a listener that counts refresh and closing events.

Figure 4.9   Spring DM's event system: events are propagated *outside* the containing application context, possibly *between* bundles.

Listing 4.1   An OSGi bundle application listener

```
package com.manning.sdmia.ch04;

import org.springframework.osgi.context.event.
  OsgiBundleApplicationContextEvent;
import org.springframework.osgi.context.event.
  OsgiBundleApplicationContextListener;
import org.springframework.osgi.context.event.
  OsgiBundleContextClosedEvent;
import org.springframework.osgi.context.event.
  OsgiBundleContextRefreshedEvent;

public class ApplicationContextObserver implements
  OsgiBundleApplicationContextListener<OsgiBundleApplicationContextEvent> {

  private transient int countRefreshed = 0;          Declares event
  private transient int countClosed = 0;             counters

  public void onOsgiApplicationEvent(                 Implements interface
      OsgiBundleApplicationContextEvent evt) {        method
    if(evt instanceof
       OsgiBundleContextRefreshedEvent) {
      countRefreshed++;
    } else if(evt instanceof                          Handles event
       OsgiBundleContextClosedEvent) {
      countClosed++;
    }
  }

  public int getCountRefreshed() {
    return countRefreshed;
  }

  public int getCountClosed() {
    return countClosed;
  }
}
```

To take effect, an `OsgiBundleApplicationContextListener` must be declared in a Spring-powered bundle and exported as an OSGi service. Listing 4.2 shows how to declare a listener and export it as an OSGi service, using Spring configuration for the declaration and the Spring DM namespace for the export.

Listing 4.2   Declaring and exporting a listener

```
<?xml version="1.0" encoding="UTF-8"?>
<beans xmlns="http://www.springframework.org/schema/beans"
  xmlns:xsi="http://www.w3.org/2001/XMLSchema-instance"
  xmlns:osgi="http://www.springframework.org/schema/osgi"
  xsi:schemaLocation="http://www.springframework.org/schema/beans
    http://www.springframework.org/schema/beans/spring-beans.xsd
    http://www.springframework.org/schema/osgi
    http://www.springframework.org/schema/osgi/spring-osgi.xsd">

  <bean id="observer"                                 Declares
        class="com.manning.sdmia.ch04.               listener
            ApplicationContextObserver" />
```

```
<osgi:service ref="observer"
              interface="org.springframework.osgi.
    context.event.
    OsgiBundleApplicationContextListener"/>
```

Exports listener as OSGi service

```
</beans>
```

Thanks to this small amount of configuration, our listener bean will be notified of all relevant application context lifecycle events for all Spring-powered bundles in the container.

Figure 4.10 illustrates this mechanism: the configuration we've just seen would take place in bundle C, and the listener bean would be notified of the lifecycle events of bundle A's and bundle B's application contexts. In this scenario, the Spring DM extender acts as a kind of event broker (the Spring DM OSGi implementation of application context is actually responsible for a good part of the event system, but this metaphor is sufficient for understanding the basic principles). What is remarkable about this process is that Spring DM hides the required manipulation of the OSGi service registry, so that you, as an OSGi developer, don't have to worry about it: write your listener, declare it, and export it. You're done, without even having to reference the OSGi API!

When the listeners don't get called

If you try the preceding example to monitor a number of different Spring DM–powered bundles, you may notice that you don't see events for some of the bundles. Why is this?

Remember that Spring DM creates application contexts asynchronously in their own threads by default, so their start order can't be precisely determined. In the example in figure 4.10, Bundle C will only receive notifications if its application context is started *before* that of bundles A and B. Because bundles A and B don't have any dependencies on bundle C (remember, only dependencies impose any order on startup) there is no guarantee that this will be the case, unless you, for example, start bundle C first manually and wait some period before starting bundles A and B. A better way to ensure the behavior you desire is by introducing synthetic dependencies from bundles A and B to C. In any case, caveat emptor!

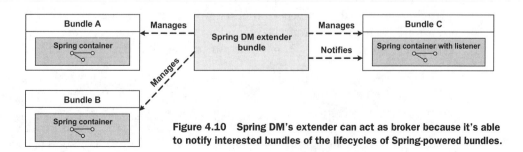

Figure 4.10 Spring DM's extender can act as broker because it's able to notify interested bundles of the lifecycles of Spring-powered bundles.

The event mechanism is a simple example of what Spring DM can do for you when you want to interact with the OSGi platform, especially with the service registry. You'll see more of this in the next chapter, but don't worry, we're going to satisfy your thirst for knowledge by first exploring the pattern behind the Spring DM event system: the whiteboard pattern.

THE WHITEBOARD PATTERN

Event-based communication is a common way to decouple components, especially when they can be split in two categories: producers and consumers. Think of the observer pattern: some components (observers) are interested in other components (observables), because the observers want to react when the observables' state changes or when the observables take some specific action. The observer components could be directly embedded in the observable components (or the latter could even implement some of the operations of observers), but that would then definitely tie them to each other and would not represent a very extensible design. To avoid that, observable components usually maintain a list of observers and notify these observers when some events occur (a state update, for example).

In an OSGi environment, event-based communication between components can be implemented by following the observer pattern, but the dynamic nature of OSGi becomes a real hindrance to its use. The difficulty mainly consists in maintaining consistent linkages between producers and consumers, because to provide modular inter-bundle connections, they should be OSGi services, and as such, they can disappear or reappear at any moment. A producer would have to maintain its own collection of listeners, usually with the use of a `ServiceTracker`. Even if this solution could work well, it would be cumbersome and error prone.

> **NOTE**   The whiteboard pattern is more about "event-based" communication, so that's why we don't use the exact same vocabulary as with the observer pattern: observables become event producers, and observers become listeners or consumers.

Another solution might consist of using some kind of middle tier to decouple producers and listeners. Listeners would register with this middle tier, and producers could retrieve listeners from it in a totally safe manner. The intricacies we described previously would now be handled by this middle tier. Luckily for us, this middleware already exists in OSGi, in the shape of the service registry!

In the whiteboard pattern, each time a producer wants to send an event to its listeners, it retrieves it from the whiteboard and proceeds with the event dispatch. The collection of listeners it receives from the registry can be seen as a snapshot of the listeners

Why "whiteboard"?

The whiteboard pattern takes its name from the analogy of subscribing to something by writing your name on a whiteboard. You don't have to find out who is in charge of subscriptions, and this person knows who is subscribed by reading the whiteboard.

that are registered at the moment the event is dispatched. The producer relies on the service registry to correctly maintain the collection of listeners. The usual way to retrieve listeners is to track them through their interface with a `ServiceTracker` and use the `getServices` method.

Figure 4.11 illustrates the whiteboard pattern, where the two bundles on the right register listeners; the producer (bundle on the left) retrieves them through the service registry and notifies each of them.

The Spring DM system for propagating application context events is an implementation of the whiteboard pattern, but Spring DM does so much for us that registering a listener ends up requiring writing a single line of XML! This is one of the major benefits of Spring DM: OSGi's dynamic nature is taken care of, and application code doesn't need to use the OSGi API at all.

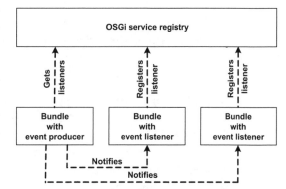

Figure 4.11 In the whiteboard pattern, the OSGi service registry acts as a middle tier to connect event listeners to event producers.

Sometimes, however, we still need a way to interact more intimately with the OSGi platform, and that's why Spring DM offers entry points to the OSGi API itself. We'll see in the next section how to access these entry points.

4.1.6   Hard dependencies on the OSGi environment

When using Spring DM, your application code should not depend on the OSGi API, because Spring DM is able to handle all the necessary interactions with the OSGi platform. Nevertheless, Spring DM lets you access some of the low-level APIs of OSGi if you really need to.

USING THE OSGI BUNDLE CONTEXT IN SPRING BEANS

Any bean in a Spring DM application context can easily get a reference to its bundle context by implementing the `BundleContextAware` interface (located in the `org.springframework.osgi.context` package). When instantiating the bean, the Spring DM application context implementation detects that it implements this special interface and automatically hands the bundle context to the bean by calling the sole method of the interface, `setBundleContext`. The bean can implement any logic it likes when it gets passed the bundle context: it can work directly with it or just keep a reference to it and interact with it later. The following snippet shows a class implementing the `BundleContextAware` interface:

```
package com.manning.sdmia.ch04;

import org.osgi.framework.BundleContext;
import org.springframework.osgi.context.BundleContextAware;
```

```
public class OsgiAddict implements BundleContextAware {
  public void setBundleContext(BundleContext bundleContext) {
    ...
  }
}
```

**Does any
operation on
bundle context**

The bean can be declared as any other bean is, without making any reference to the bundle context, because Spring DM automatically passes the bundle context:

```
<bean id="osgiAddict"
      class="com.manning.sdmia.ch04.OsgiAddict" />
```

By implementing the `BundleContextAware` interface, our OSGi-addicted bean has a direct dependency on the Spring DM API. That could be problematic, because if some OSGi-specific classes require a reference to the OSGi API, they can't support references to other frameworks. Fortunately, in each Spring DM application context, Spring DM automatically inserts the bundle context as a Spring bean with the name `bundleContext`.

The following snippet shows another kind of OSGi-specific bean, which keeps a reference to the bundle context (notice it doesn't depend on the Spring DM API in any way):

```
package com.manning.sdmia.ch04;

import org.osgi.framework.BundleContext;

public class PojoOsgiAddict {

  private BundleContext bundleContext;

  public void setBundleContext(BundleContext bundleContext) {
    this.bundleContext = bundleContext;
  }
}
```

**Doesn't implement any
Spring DM–specific interface**

This time, the bundle context must be explicitly injected by using the implicit `bundleContext` bean when we declare the `PojoOsgiAddict` bean:

```
<bean id="pojoOsgiAddict" class="com.manning.sdmia.ch04.PojoOsgiAddict">
  <property name="bundleContext"
            ref="bundleContext" />
</bean>
```

Thanks to Spring DM, you can easily enjoy the best of both Spring and OSGi worlds! Let's move on to the next section, where we'll see how to interact declaratively with bundles.

WORKING WITH BUNDLES

The Spring DM `osgi` namespace comes with a `bundle` element that makes it possible to get references to OSGi bundles and even manipulate them. By using the `bundle` element in an application context, you define an `org.osgi.framework.Bundle` bean in it. You can then use this bundle bean like any other bean.

For example, you can make a reference to any *already installed* bundle in the OSGi platform by using the `symbolic-name` attribute, just as in the following snippet, which retrieves the Spring DM extender bundle directly:

```
<osgi:bundle
  id="springDmExtenderBundle"
  symbolic-name="org.springframework.osgi.extender" />
```

The `bundle` element is not limited to only Spring DM bundles; it works for any OSGi-compliant bundle. You can also use the `bundle` element with bundles that aren't yet deployed to the OSGi platform, thanks to the `location` attribute. With this attribute, you can indicate where to find a bundle by using the Spring resource syntax. You can also choose an action to be performed when the bundle is loaded by Spring DM. The following snippet shows how to create a bundle bean from the filesystem and then start it:

```
<osgi:bundle
  id="myBundle"
  location="file:/my/bundle/repo/somebundle.jar"
  action="start" />
```

The `action` attribute supports five values that are the equivalent of the methods of the `Bundle` interface: `install`, `start`, `update`, `stop`, and `uninstall`. They have the same semantics, but Spring DM makes their use easier than in a pure OSGi environment. If you take a look at the Javadoc for these methods, you'll notice that they have strict preconditions. For example, you can't call the `start` method on a bundle that isn't in the resolved state yet. With the `action` attribute of `bundle`, Spring DM handles these kinds of implicit transitions, and no OSGi exceptions will be thrown.

Table 4.4 lists all the attributes available in the `bundle` element. Notice the `destroy-action` attribute, which can tie an action to a bundle when the application context is destroyed, providing an easy way to stop bundles in a cascade, for example.

This ends our study of the Spring DM standard extender. You have learned a lot about its mechanics and how to tune the way it handles application contexts; this

Table 4.4　Attributes of the `bundle` element

Attribute name	Values	Description
`id`	Any XML-valid ID	Unique ID of the bean in the application context.
`symbolic-name`	Any valid OSGi symbolic-name	The symbolic name of an already installed bundle.
`location`	Spring resource syntax	The location to load the bundle from, usually to interact with and call some lifecycle methods.
`start-level`	Integer	The bundle start level.
`action`	`install`, `start`, `update`, `stop`, `uninstall`	An action executed on the bundle. This uses the same semantics as the methods from the `Bundle` interface, with preconditions weakened.
`destroy-action`	`install`, `start`, `update`, `stop`, `uninstall`	An action executed on the bundle when the application context is destroyed. This uses the same semantics as the methods from the `Bundle` interface, with preconditions weakened.

should be enough for most of your needs. In chapter 9, we'll see advanced techniques to tune the extender itself, by changing its global behavior.

If you're interested in the web support that Spring DM provides, move on to the next section, as it gives information about the web extender and how web applications can fit into an OSGi environment.

4.2   *Unleashing Spring DM's web extender*

From reading the previous chapter, you'll already know that you can deploy web applications on an OSGi platform thanks to the Spring DM web extender. When using the web extender, OSGi bundles are installed on the OSGi platform the same way as usual, but they will also be deployed to the embedded web container if they're detected as being web-enabled. Spring DM defines its own structure for web OSGi bundles, but we'll see that it doesn't really differ from the structure of traditional bundles.

We'll also see in this section that Spring DM web support opens up a realm of possibilities for web applications. They will now be able to interact with the OSGi platform and will no longer have to be packaged as big, monolithic WAR files.

4.2.1   *Structure of Spring DM web OSGi components*

When started on the OSGi platform, the Spring DM web extender will try to deploy a bundle to the embedded web container if it meets one of the following conditions:

- The bundle location (filename) ends with .war
- The bundle contains a WEB-INF directory

When a bundle is detected as a web bundle, the web extender will trigger its deployment to the web container, letting the latter handle everything.

> **WARNING** Because the web container handles the application context creation, as it does for any standard Spring-based web application, most of the behavior of the Spring DM extender that we saw earlier doesn't apply to the web extender. This includes placing configuration in the META-INF/ spring/ directory, using the `Spring-Context` header, and mechanisms like asynchronous startup or waiting for dependencies to bootstrap the application context.

The structure of the simplest web bundle ever is the following:

```
my-web-bundle
  META-INF/
    MANIFEST.MF
  WEB-INF/
    web.xml
```

This bundle could be packaged as a my-web-bundle.jar file and then be installed and started on an OSGi platform. The Spring DM web extender would then deploy it to the web container (assuming the platform is correctly provisioned, as explained in chapter 3). The web bundle would be deployed under a web context named `my-web-bundle`.

How are context paths associated with bundles? The default behavior of the Spring DM web extender, with respect to the definition of context paths, is dictated by a context path strategy, the default being the `DefaultContextPathStrategy` class (in the `org.springframework.osgi.web.deployer.support` package). This default strategy bases its decision first on the presence of the `Web-ContextPath` header, and then, if the header isn't present, on the location of the bundle, by removing the trailing .war or .jar (just like in our example). After that it falls back on some of the other bundle metadata (name, symbolic name, or identity) if it can't use the bundle location. You can consult the Javadoc to see the exact algorithm.

In most cases, the truncated bundle location would make a nice context path, but if this doesn't suit you, you can override it by using the `Web-ContextPath` header in the bundle manifest:

```
Web-ContextPath: mycontext
```

This makes the deployment of web bundles easy, but you may be wondering, "Where are my WEB-INF/lib and WEB-INF/classes directories"? That's a pertinent question, related to classloading, which happens to be the topic of the next section.

4.2.2 Classloading in web bundles

A web application is usually made up of its own classes, which can use other classes (frameworks, for example). All these classes must be available on the web application's classpath, which is structured like this:

- WEB-INF/classes directory—Contains application classes (web controllers, such as servlets). They're under their `.class` file form (not packaged) and organized following the traditional tree-like structure of Java packages.
- WEB-INF/lib directory—Contains third-party libraries, packaged as JAR files.

Figure 4.12 illustrates this organization for two web applications in a web container. They both come with their application classes (in WEB-INF/classes) and their libraries (in WEB-INF/lib).

What we've just seen is the usual way to make classes available for loading in a traditional, Java EE standard web application, and it isn't valid for web applications deployed with Spring DM on an OSGi platform.

When you deploy a web application using the Spring DM web extender, OSGi-specific classloading mechanisms take precedence. Remember that before being a web application, your application was also an OSGi bundle; as such, its classpath is the OSGi classpath. It

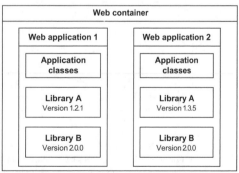

Figure 4.12 In standard Java EE deployment scenarios, web applications come with their third-party libraries embedded in their archives.

benefits from everything OSGi provides for handling classloading (class visibility, versioning, reloading, and so on).

Your web application will be able to load classes from the following locations:

- Its bundle space (classes in the JAR or WAR and classes from all the associated bundle fragments)
- Classes from the packages imported with the `Import-Package` header
- All the exported classes from bundles appearing in the `Require-Bundle` header

Figure 4.13 shows the new scenario for web applications deployed with Spring DM in an OSGi environment. Notice that web applications contain only their application classes and can rely on OSGi's mechanisms for classloading (to be able to use bundle A and bundle B classes). This scenario is possible thanks to Spring DM, because it builds a bridge between OSGi and the web container, so that web applications can use the OSGi classpath as if they were ordinary bundles.

If needed, you can still make your web bundles look like standard WARs, thanks to the `Bundle-Classpath` header, which indicates to the OSGi platform where to find classes and resources in the bundle. This header defaults to ".", meaning the root of the bundle. You can override this default value and set it to the traditional locations of classes and libraries in WARs (you should not forget to include the default location):

```
Bundle-Classpath: .,WEB-INF/classes,WEB-INF/lib/libA.jar,
➥   WEB-INF/lib/libB.jar
```

You now know the nuts and bolts of Spring DM's unique web support. It's time to see how Spring DM allows you to interact with the OSGi platform from your OSGi web applications.

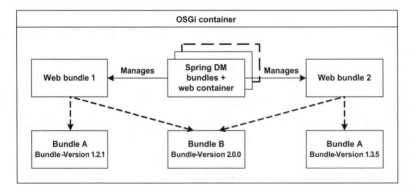

Figure 4.13   In an OSGi environment, web applications can rely on OSGi classloading mechanism for their third-party libraries. This is especially useful when different versions of the same library must cohabit.

4.2.3 OSGi-aware Spring web container

When studying Spring DM's standard extender, we spoke a lot about the application context lifecycle, but so far we've avoided this topic for web bundles. We'll see in this section how Spring DM extends the behavior of traditional Spring web applications. Let's start with a little refresher about the way this kind of application works.

Standard (web) Spring applications have only one Spring application context, which contains all the beans necessary for the application: data source, data access objects, business services, and even web controllers (if you don't want to use servlets). In a web container, web applications can't share their Spring beans (there's a way to make this possible, but it's more of a hack and is beyond the scope of this book).

Figure 4.14 shows how Spring-based web applications are usually deployed to a web container. Notice how the two applications and their respective Spring containers look isolated and can't communicate with each other to share Spring beans as services.

What do we really want in our OSGi web applications? We want them to be able to consume backend services from the OSGi registry and use them as black-box components in their web controllers. This scenario is shown in figure 4.15:

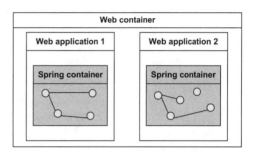

Figure 4.14 Traditional Spring web applications can't make their Spring containers communicate with each other.

three bundles together build a backend layer (at the top of the diagram; their interconnections aren't shown for clarity) and one of them exposes this layer by registering business services in the OSGi service registry. Our web bundles (at the bottom) then consume

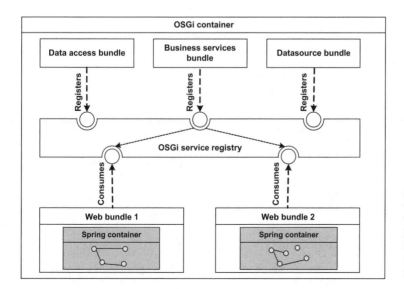

Figure 4.15 In an OSGi environment, web applications powered by Spring DM can interact with the OSGi service registry.

these business services. Note that the backend bundles can be ordinary or Spring-powered bundles, as they interact normally with the service registry; in contrast, the web bundles are backed by Spring DM. This scenario isn't science-fiction and can become a reality thanks to the OSGi-enabled web application context Spring DM provides!

The trick to making the scenario in figure 4.15 reality is to ask the web container to bootstrap an OSGi-enabled application context. In standard Spring-based web applications, the Spring container is started and stopped by the web container itself, usually through a dedicated servlet listener, the `ContextLoaderListener`. (Don't confuse this servlet listener with the Spring DM extender, which has the same class name but is an internal class and isn't meant to be used directly.)

The `ContextLoaderListener` we're interested in is part of the web module of the Spring Framework. You declare it in the web.xml file of your web application, and in it you can set the location of your Spring configuration files and, more importantly in our case, the implementation of `ApplicationContext` you want to use.

Spring DM comes with a specific application context implementation, `Osgi-BundleXmlWebApplicationContext`, which can communicate with the OSGi platform even though its instances are created by a web container. Listing 4.3 shows how to configure the context loader listener in the web.xml file of the web application to use this new class.

Listing 4.3   Configuring a web application to use the OSGi web application context

```
<web-app (...)>
  (...)
  <context-param>
    <param-name>contextClass</param-name>        ❶ Declares context
                                                     class parameter
    <param-value>
      org.springframework.osgi.web.context.support.   ❷ Sets OSGi web
          OsgiBundleXmlWebApplicationContext             application context
    </param-value>
  </context-param>

  <context-param>
    <param-name>contextConfigLocation</param-name>   ❸ Declares context
                                                        location parameter
    <param-value>
      WEB-INF/applicationContext.xml,                ❹ Sets
      WEB-INF/applicationContext-osgi.xml               configuration files
    </param-value>
  </context-param>

  <listener>
    <listener-class>
      org.springframework.web.context.             ❺ Declares context
          ContextLoaderListener                       loader listener
    </listener-class>
  </listener>
  (...)
</web-app>
```

The context loader listener uses a context parameter so that it knows which type of web application context ❶ it must use. The parameter value defaults to

XmlWebApplicationContext, so we must override it to use Spring DM's OSGi web application context implementation ❷. We also customize the location of the XML configuration files with the contextConfigLocation context parameter ❸. This is optional, and the default is to use a WEB-INF/applicationContext.xml file, but we decided to split the context definition into two files: one specific to OSGi (usually using the Spring DM osgi namespace) and another for standard, non-OSGi bean definitions ❹. We set the context loader listener at ❺. That's it, your web application is OSGi-enabled and can share OSGi services with other bundles!

> **WARNING** If you use the ContextLoaderListener and the OsgiBundleXmlWeb-ApplicationContext in your web applications, you must include their respective packages in the Import-Package header of your web bundle manifest.

You now know more about Spring DM web support in OSGi environments and should be able to see the possibilities it brings to web, as well as to OSGi, applications. You'll learn more about developing OSGi web applications in chapter 6, where you'll learn how to structure them, and in chapter 8, where we'll cover topics like Spring MVC, Ajax, and Web Services. In the next section, we'll see how Spring DM makes the scenarios we presented possible by discovering how it deploys and undeploys web applications.

4.2.4 *Spring DM web deployer*

Just like the standard extender, the Spring DM web extender is implemented as a synchronous bundle listener, which is registered by the activator of the bundle. The bundle listener doesn't itself handle the deployment of web bundles; it delegates this perilous task to a WAR deployer. Figure 4.16 illustrates the relation between the activator, the extender, and the WAR deployer (class or interface names appear in parentheses).

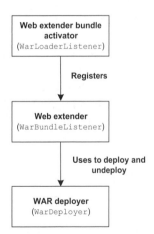

Even though the activator of the web extender bundle coordinates and performs some of the work (scanning of incoming bundles, thread management for deployment and undeployment), the WAR deployer is in charge of truly deploying (or undeploying) web applications to the embedded web container. Through the WarDeployer interface, Spring DM abstracts the action of deploying and undeploying WAR files, allowing a separation of concerns, because WarDeployer implementations just handle the deployment process for their web container, whereas the

Figure 4.16 The Spring DM web extender delegates the handling of WAR files to a WAR deployer.

web extender sticks to its primary goal: listening for bundles starting or stopping.

Spring DM provides two implementations of WarDeployer: one for Apache Tomcat (the default) and one for Jetty. We'll see in chapter 9 how to switch from one web container to another. Figure 4.17 shows the WarDeployer class hierarchy in Spring DM.

WAR deployers interact directly with the underlying web container instance when the web extender hands them a WAR bundle. They can manage their own instance of the web container, but the usual way is to look it up in the OSGi service registry. By "instance of web container," we mean an instance of the core class of the web container—`org.apache.catalina.Service` for Tomcat and `org.mortbay.jetty.Server` for Jetty. Remember that in chapter 3, when we made our first web bundle, we added a Tomcat activator bundle. Its role is to bootstrap a Tomcat `Service` instance and register it as an OSGi service. This `Service` is then con-

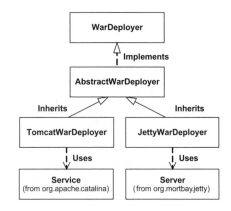

Figure 4.17 The class hierarchy of WAR deployers in Spring DM

sumed by the default `TomcatWarDeployer`. We'll also see in chapter 9 how to publish our Tomcat `Service` or Jetty `Server` instances to be used by the corresponding WAR deployer.

This ends our tour of Spring DM's web extender, which allows us to leverage the power of OSGi in web applications, mainly by making web applications rely on the OSGi classloading and letting them interact with the OSGi registry, just like any other bundle.

4.3 Summary

Spring DM extenders should no longer be a mystery to you, almost! By now you should understand that behind the term "Spring-powered bundle" lies complex mechanisms. Fortunately, Spring DM is here to handle them and fill the gap between OSGi and the programming model of Spring. Nevertheless, even though Spring DM does a lot for us in the management of Spring application contexts, we need a basic understanding of its extenders to use them appropriately; that's why we dived into their functionality in this chapter.

From this chapter, the main takeaways are that Spring DM

- is able to track the dependencies between bundles and start and destroy their respective application contexts in the right order
- allows you to set numerous options on a per-bundle basis (asynchronous or synchronous startup, application context publication, and so on)
- has unique web support that offers a whole new perspective for structuring your web applications

Now you know that your bundles are backed by the Spring container, a new OSGi world has opened up to you: you can leverage all the features of the Spring Framework in your OSGi bundles that were so empty before.

Your Spring-powered bundles can benefit from the Spring Framework for their own, inner components, but we're also interested in the help Spring DM can provide for interacting with the OSGi service registry. That's the topic of the next chapter, where you'll see how to declaratively export and import services, and let Spring DM handle the dynamic nature of OSGi for you.

Working
with OSGi services

This chapter covers

- Using dependency injection with OSGi services
- Registering and referencing services with Spring DM
- Handling service dynamics with Spring DM
- Handling service collections with Spring DM

In the previous chapter, we described how Spring DM provides support for managing Spring-powered OSGi components as well as web components. We showed that the framework doesn't actually use OSGi's activator feature but instead provides an implementation of the extender pattern to decouple components' implementation from the enabling technology and to configure bundles globally by providing a single point of management. These mechanisms allow components to use classic Spring features, such as dependency injection, AOP, and support for enterprise applications.

In this chapter, we'll focus on Spring DM's support of OSGi services. As we emphasized in chapter 1, services are a key OSGi feature because they allow you to define entry points for component interactions, and they provide a robust way to take into account the dynamic nature of OSGi.

Unfortunately, the core OSGi specification only provides low-level API-based support for implementing services. Its use may initially seem simple, but the work becomes more tedious when you want to support OSGi dynamics in a robust fashion. Moreover, you're tied to the OSGi API when registering and using services, even if these services are POJO-based. Fortunately Spring DM provides an abstraction layer that integrates service support with the dependency injection mechanisms of the Spring container.

5.1 Dependency injection and OSGi services

In this section, we'll describe all the concepts that Spring DM uses to integrate OSGi services with Spring's support for dependency injection. We'll also provide examples to illustrate these concepts. As we explained in chapter 2, OSGi doesn't provide declarative support for services and, by default, you need to access them via the OSGi API.

We'll also describe Spring DM's mechanisms for managing services and how to configure those services with XML and annotations.

5.1.1 Combining OSGi services and dependency injection

Before describing how to use Spring DM's support for OSGi services, we'll first describe the concepts underlying Spring DM's support for services, then focus on its internal operation.

GENERAL CONCEPTS

When it comes to services, Spring DM's aim is to shield users from using the OSGi service API and enable users to easily support dynamic OSGi services in a robust manner. Spring DM's support for services is completely declarative and is done using XML configuration or annotations. Spring DM also transparently supports service dynamics for you by managing a service's availability at runtime. In addition, Spring DM allows these dynamic mechanisms to be directly handled within dependency injection and decoration using AOP as if they were configured by the Spring container.

Spring DM provides the ability to define OSGi services directly in the Spring configuration. The Spring DM container is responsible for interacting with the OSGi service registry according to the stages of the Spring DM lifecycle. Beans configured as services are registered and unregistered when the Spring container starts and stops, respectively. Because Spring DM is responsible for bootstrapping the Spring container when an owning bundle starts up, and for stopping it when the bundle is stopped, configured services are also registered and unregistered at these times.

Spring DM also allows you to reference an OSGi service as if it were a regular bean. This service can then be injected into other beans configured within Spring.

Figure 5.1 describes the ways Spring DM lets you interact with the OSGi service registry. When referencing OSGi services, Spring DM offers a bridge between beans and services and allows dependency injection with services. It also provides a simple way to

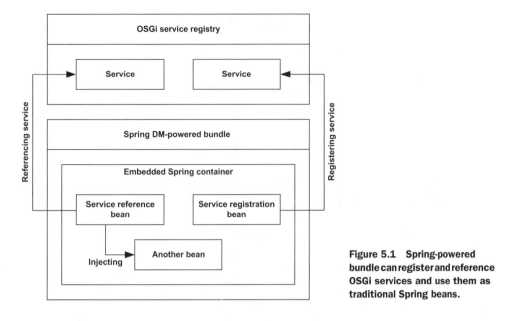

Figure 5.1 Spring-powered bundle can register and reference OSGi services and use them as traditional Spring beans.

register beans as services. In both cases, Spring DM handles all internal OSGi mechanisms and manages OSGI dynamics.

SERVICE PROXYING

Spring DM's service support is powerful and takes care of a lot of things under the hood by using a proxy mechanism between the service and the user of the service as a level of indirection for the service.

Because OSGi is dynamic and services can come and go at any time, directly injecting a service instance into another bean isn't a good idea. The instance could become stale over time if the underlying service becomes unavailable. Instead, Spring DM uses a proxy that passes itself off as the target OSGi service, so the service user isn't tied to the service. Figure 5.2 illustrates the proxy mechanism used to inject OSGi services and shows how Spring DM provides a proxy between the service and its user.

Spring DM's proxy behavior can be configured to modify the way service dynamics are handled: references can be configured as mandatory or optional. For a single instance, Spring DM will automatically look for a replacement when the current service referent disappears. For mandatory services, this lookup must always be successful, but this isn't essential for optional services. For service collections, Spring DM will automatically add and remove services when service registrations and unregistrations

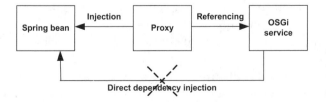

Figure 5.2 The proxy mechanism of Spring DM references services and provides a level of indirection between service instance and service user.

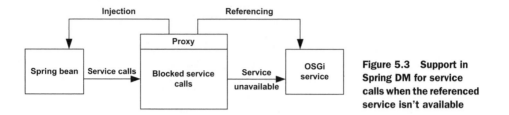

Figure 5.3 Support in Spring DM for service calls when the referenced service isn't available

occur. If the service collection is configured as mandatory, an empty collection won't be allowed.

Spring DM also provides support for when services become temporarily unavailable, such as during component updates. The framework makes it possible not to lose requests by making them block. When the service becomes available again, blocked calls will be executed on the target service. In addition, Spring DM provides a timeout-based mechanism for when services remain unavailable for an extended period. If services remain unavailable longer than the timeout, a `ServiceUnavailableException` exception is thrown. Figure 5.3 illustrates Spring DM's blocking support for service calls.

The service proxy resolves one last important issue—it provides a flexible solution for controlling the classes that are visible in the context classloader. We'll look at the context classloader in section 5.2, and see how to configure the appropriate strategy in sections 5.3.1 and 5.3.2.

That covers how Spring DM relates to OSGi services. We'll now take a first look at how Spring DM allows you to configure services through XML configuration and annotations. (We'll describe more advanced usage later in the chapter.) These features of Spring DM make it possible to leverage OSGi services together with dependency injection. They provide a convenient way to allow components to communicate while transparently handling OSGi dynamics at runtime.

5.1.2 *XML-based registration and referencing*

In this section, we'll see how to use XML to configure OSGi services with Spring DM within Spring configuration files and we'll describe the XML tags and their main attributes. Spring DM also offers the ability to specify other attributes that allow fine-grained configuration of the registration and lifecycle of OSGi services, and we'll describe that sort of advanced configuration in sections 5.3.1 and 5.3.2.

Although Spring DM offers an annotation-driven approach to service configuration (which we'll cover in section 5.1.3), the XML approach remains the main one, and it supports all of the mechanisms described in section 5.1.1. We'll use the same `osgi` XML namespace we introduced in chapter 3—the configuration of this namespace was described in section 3.1.5.

The XML-based approach supports both registering and referencing services as shown in figure 5.4.

Spring DM supports services directly from Spring's XML configuration, thanks to its dedicated `osgi` namespace. Figure 5.4 emphasizes that Spring DM allows both the

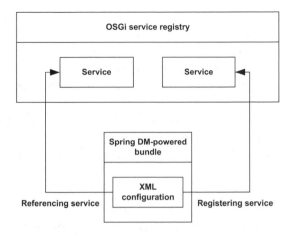

Figure 5.4 Spring DM allows you to both reference and register OSGi services from within XML-based configuration files.

registration and referencing of services directly from within a Spring XML configuration file. In following sections, we'll describe how to configure and use these registering and referencing features of Spring DM.

EXPORTING SERVICES

Spring DM permits you to define OSGi services by using the `osgi` namespace's `service` tag. This tag allows you to register a Spring bean in the OSGi service registry. When the Spring container for the bundle is started, all the services declared through the `service` tag are registered in the service registry. Similarly, when the bundle—and hence the Spring container—is stopped, the services are unregistered. The service bean that's created by this process is an instance of `ServiceRegistration`.

Listing 5.1 shows the most common way to configure an OSGi service using the `service` XML element. As with a classic bean, an `id` attribute can be specified to identify the service. The value of the `ref` attribute is the identifier of the bean to be registered, and the value of the `interface` attribute is the name of the interface to be advertised in the service registry.

Listing 5.1 Simple service configuration within Spring XML configuration

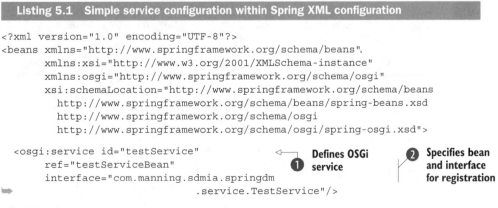

```
<?xml version="1.0" encoding="UTF-8"?>
<beans xmlns="http://www.springframework.org/schema/beans",
       xmlns:xsi="http://www.w3.org/2001/XMLSchema-instance"
       xmlns:osgi="http://www.springframework.org/schema/osgi"
       xsi:schemaLocation="http://www.springframework.org/schema/beans
         http://www.springframework.org/schema/beans/spring-beans.xsd
         http://www.springframework.org/schema/osgi
         http://www.springframework.org/schema/osgi/spring-osgi.xsd">

  <osgi:service id="testService"
       ref="testServiceBean"
       interface="com.manning.sdmia.springdm
                       .service.TestService"/>

</beans>
```

❶ Defines OSGi service

❷ Specifies bean and interface for registration

The `service` XML element allows you to set an `id` attribute ❶ to reference the bean from within the Spring configuration. You'll notice that this bean is of type `Service-Registration` and corresponds to the registration object of the service. You can then use the `ref` attribute ❷ to specify the bean that implements your OSGi service. Finally, the `interface` attribute ❷ allows you to specify the interface you need to expose for the OSGi service.

You'll notice that in listing 5.1, any bean configured within Spring can be used in the `ref` attribute because a Spring-declared OSGi service is simply a POJO. Spring DM provides additional configuration possibilities at this level, which we'll describe in section 5.3.1.

REFERENCING SERVICES

Spring DM also enables you to obtain OSGi service references. In this section, we'll describe how to use XML to configure a bean that references an OSGi service from within Spring DM.

Using OSGi services from Spring DM is very simple. Thanks to the `osgi` namespace, Spring DM provides the `reference` XML element, which transparently configures a proxy for the underlying service. The configured entity can be thought of as a service instance and used directly as a simple bean. Spring DM automagically handles all the dynamic behavior of OSGi for you.

Listing 5.2 shows a common way of referencing an OSGi service using the `reference` tag. As with a classic bean, an `id` attribute can be specified to identify the service reference. The `interface` attribute is used to specify the required service from the OSGi registry. This attribute corresponds to the identifier stored in the registry and is usually the interface name that the service exposes.

> **OSGi service identifiers and Spring DM**
>
> OSGi uses class names to locate services within the service registry. Even though the identifier is a string, the OSGi container ensures that the service object is an instance of each of the specified service interfaces or classes unless the object is an instance of `ServiceFactory`. Although we use the term "identifier" for this concept, you should remember that this identifier must represent an actual class.

Listing 5.2 Simple service referral within Spring XML configuration

```xml
<?xml version="1.0" encoding="UTF-8"?>
<beans xmlns="http://www.springframework.org/schema/beans"
    xmlns:xsi="http://www.w3.org/2001/XMLSchema-instance"
    xmlns:osgi="http://www.springframework.org/schema/osgi"
    xsi:schemaLocation="http://www.springframework.org/schema/beans
      http://www.springframework.org/schema/beans/spring-beans.xsd
      http://www.springframework.org/schema/osgi
      http://www.springframework.org/schema/osgi/spring-osgi.xsd">

  <osgi:reference id="testService"
      interface="com.manning.sdmia.springdm
```

❶ **References OSGi service and specifies interface**

➥   `.service.TestService"/>`

```
<bean id="testBean" class="com.manning.sdmia.springdm.SimpleTestBean">
  <property name="testService"
            ref="testService"/>
</bean>
```
❷ Injects service in bean

`</beans>`

The `reference` XML element allows you to configure a reference to an OSGi service. The corresponding bean is identified with the `id` attribute ❶ and can be used as a regular bean. The service is selected by specifying its exposed interface in the `interface` attribute ❶. Once the reference is correctly configured, it can be injected ❷ into any other bean using the normal dependency injection mechanisms of Spring.

The entity configured with the `reference` element can only be used as an instance of the type specified in its `interface` attribute. When configuring OSGi services with Spring DM and injecting them in beans, the beans aren't aware that they're actually using OSGi services. Spring beans see OSGi services configured with Spring DM as regular beans.

In this section, we saw how to use the OSGi service support of Spring DM using its Spring DM `osgi` XML namespace. This support allows you to both register and reference services from within a Spring XML configuration file using dependency injection. Let's now take a look at the alternative approach that Spring DM provides for referencing OSGi services—one based on Java annotations.

5.1.3 Annotation-based service referral

Spring DM also provides annotation-based support for referencing and using services, as shown in figure 5.5; service registration isn't supported by this approach. Annotation-based service lookup provides a less verbose way to configure service references because it gleans some of the required information from the class itself.

To reference a service, you need to annotate a property of your bean (by annotating its setter in the Java class) with the `ServiceReference` annotation. If the annotation-driven strategy is activated in the Spring XML configuration, services are automatically looked up and injected as proxies into the target bean. They're then usable directly

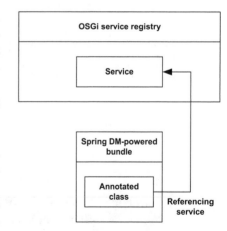

Figure 5.5 Spring DM allows OSGi services to be referenced by annotations in the Java class.

within the bean. With annotation-based referencing, Spring DM uses the same underlying mechanisms as it does for XML configuration.

The `ServiceReference` annotation must be specified on the setter corresponding to the service, as shown in the following snippet. The identifier for the service is deduced from the type of the corresponding class property—the `TestService` interface in this example.

```
public class AnnotatedTestBean {                    ❶ Property corresponding
  private TestService testService;              ⟵      to service

  (...)

  @ServiceReference                                 ❷ Annotation and setter
  public void setTestService(                          for service injection
                TestService testService) {
    this.testService = testService;
  }

}
```

With annotations, you can reference services directly from within classes configured by Spring. You generally need to have a property ❶ corresponding to the exposed interface of the OSGi service. To implement the injection, you need to set a `ServiceReference` annotation on the setter method of the property ❷. When detecting such an annotation, Spring DM will automatically inject an instance of the service.

The `ServiceReference` annotation accepts the same attributes as the `service` tag we described previously. We'll describe these attributes in section 5.3.2.

Annotation-based injection isn't enabled by default in Spring DM. To activate it, two approaches can be used. The first uses Spring DM's extender-based configuration by setting the `process.annotations` property. Such advanced configuration will be described in chapter 9.

The other solution is based on Spring's bean post-processor feature. This feature is commonly used by the Spring web MVC framework with its annotation-based programming model. The `ServiceReferenceInjectionBeanPostProcessor` class must be configured as a bean in the Spring XML configuration of the bundle, as shown in the following snippet:

```
<beans (...)>
  (...)
  <bean class="org.springframework.osgi.extensions
➥             .annotation.ServiceReferenceInjectionBeanPostProcessor"/>
</beans>
```

Dependency management with annotations

We've discussed how mandatory dependencies configured in a Spring-powered bundle's XML file cause the application context to be suspended until the dependencies are satisfied. Spring DM achieves this by preinstantiating `service` beans, then deciding whether or not they're mandatory. But instantiating mandatory service references declared through annotations gets quite tricky because the actual bean class is required, and mandatory dependencies don't cause the application context startup to be suspended. Instead, the application context is created as usual, but any subsequent calls to mandatory dependencies will block.

> **(continued)**
> Spring DM provides support for dependency management with annotations through the use of the `ServiceReferenceDependencyBeanFactoryPostProcessor` class, but this class is package-protected and can only be used through extender-based configuration. For this reason, we recommend that you use the extender-based configuration mechanism (discussed in chapter 9) if you want to use annotation-based service injection.

The most common approach to using services is to use Spring XML configuration, so we'll focus on it in the following sections of the chapter. Annotation-based support will suit people who prefer using Spring with annotations rather than with XML. You'll notice that both types of support are equal when referencing services, and the same configuration properties are available in both.

Before going further into advanced uses of Spring DM's service support, we'll focus on the context classloader and how it can be used within OSGi context. Spring DM integrates context classloader management in its service support to make class resolution easier.

5.2 The thread context classloader and its use in OSGi

As we described in chapters 1 and 2, OSGi provides strict classloader management that controls the visibility of classes in bundles. For some specific enterprise use cases, this strict behavior isn't particularly convenient (such as when dynamic classloading is involved). Luckily, Java provides a *thread context classloader* (TCCL) that allows the classloading of an implementation to delegate classloading to the caller, and vice versa, without having to specify an `Import-Package` declaration.

The next section describes what this classloader is, how to use it, and why it's particularly important in the context of OSGi. We'll need to look at Java's context classloader feature to understand how Spring DM uses this feature within an OSGi environment.

5.2.1 Using the thread context classloader

The TCCL was introduced in Java version 1.2 to allow code to associate a particular classloader with the current thread. Java frameworks regularly use it for loading classes they need, and callers of these frameworks are expected to set the TCCL appropriately. By default, this classloader is the application's classloader, but Java gives you the ability to change it according to your needs.

The classloader can be accessed through the `getContextClassLoader` method of the current thread, as shown in the following snippet:

```
ClassLoader currentTccl = Thread.currentThread().getContextClassLoader();
```

To specify a different classloader, use the `setContextClassLoader` method of the current thread, as shown in this snippet:

```
Thread.currentThread().setContextClassLoader(
            TcclActivator.class.getClassLoader());
```

5.2.2   *Using the thread context classloader with OSGi*

Using the TCCL within OSGi makes it possible to solve some problems without having to export and import packages. In particular, it helps frameworks that don't know until runtime which classes they need to use. Frameworks usually look at several class-loaders, including the context classloader, when trying to load classes dynamically.

Resolving classes using TCCL is particularly useful for frameworks implementing dependency injection, such as Spring, and ORM, such as Hibernate. With Spring, you can configure bean instances to be managed, and the framework will instantiate them according to the XML configuration. If the bundles corresponding to the framework don't declare the right imports in their manifest, `ClassNotFoundExceptions` will be thrown when the framework tries to load the bean's classes. Hibernate, in contrast, will instantiate persistent instances corresponding to mapped classes. `ClassNotFound-Exceptions` will also occur if the classes aren't visible to Hibernate bundles because Hibernate is a generic ORM framework without dependencies on user applications. By default, implementation bundles for these kinds of frameworks don't import application classes.

Figure 5.6 illustrates the problem when a Hibernate component tries to load mapped classes for an application component. Hibernate can't load the mapped classes because they're user-defined classes and aren't specified in the `Import-Package` header of the Hibernate component. The framework tries to discover the required classes through configuration.

> **NOTE** The preceding Hibernate use case is typical when using ORM tools within OSGi. The way to best address these issues is described in detail in chapter 7 in the context of JPA.

Specifying packages directly within the bundles of frameworks isn't practical because you would then need to update the manifest contents of third-party bundles. Alternatively, you could use fragments to extend these bundles, but that's also somewhat limiting because it requires you to implement a bundle and limits you to a single extension of the framework bundle.

This is where the TCCL comes into play, because most frameworks are smart enough to look for classes in several classloaders, including the TCCL. If the caller's bundle has set the context classloader with its associated classloader, the framework bundle will be capable of instantiating classes that are visible only to the caller's bundle.

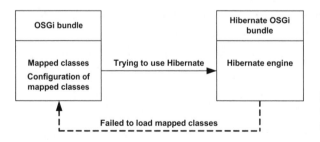

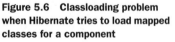

Figure 5.6   Classloading problem when Hibernate tries to load mapped classes for a component

Consider a bundle trying to instantiate a Spring context using the `FileSystemXml-Application` class, as shown in the following snippet:

```
FileSystemXmlApplicationContext context = null;     Instantiates and
try {                                               loads Spring
  context = new FileSystemXmlApplicationContext(    ◄─── container
                    "resources/bundle-context.xml");
} finally {
  if (context!=null) {
    context.close();
  }
}
```

In this example, the bundle-context.xml file is a Spring XML configuration file that contains a bean of a type visible to the current bundle. With this code, the attempt to load the Spring container throws a `ClassNotFoundException` exception because it can't find the bean's class. But if the caller sets the context classloader appropriately, Spring would be able to see the class and load it. No exception would be thrown in this case.

Listing 5.3 shows how to set the context classloader.

Listing 5.3 Using the context classloader when creating a Spring container

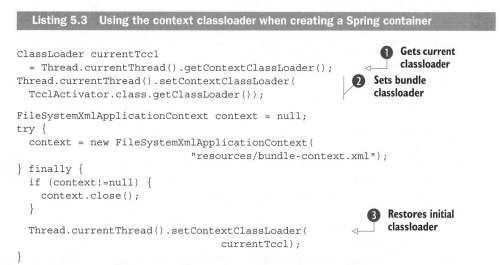

```
ClassLoader currentTccl                              ❶ Gets current
  = Thread.currentThread().getContextClassLoader();  ◄─┘   classloader
Thread.currentThread().setContextClassLoader(        ❷ Sets bundle
  TcclActivator.class.getClassLoader());                 classloader

FileSystemXmlApplicationContext context = null;
try {
  context = new FileSystemXmlApplicationContext(
                    "resources/bundle-context.xml");
} finally {
  if (context!=null) {
    context.close();
  }                                                  ❸ Restores initial
                                                        classloader
  Thread.currentThread().setContextClassLoader(      ◄─┘
                    currentTccl);
}
```

In listing 5.3, we first obtain and save the previous classloader ❶ contained in the context classloader in order to restore it later. We then set the bundle classloader as the context classloader ❷. After executing our processing, we restore the initial classloader as the context classloader ❸. By adjusting the context classloader this way, the implementation will be able to see the classes of the current bundle.

We've seen how Java's context classloader can help in an OSGi environment to solve class visibility problems without adding packages to the `Import-Package` headers of components. This mechanism can also be used to allow service implementations to see and use the classes of the caller. We'll see in section 3.2 that Spring DM makes it possible to directly configure this in the XML configuration file.

In the next section, we'll discuss advanced configuration when registering and referencing OSGi services using Spring DM.

5.3   *Advanced OSGi service configuration*

In section 5.1, we discussed Spring DM's support for services. Spring DM also provides a flexible way of registering and referencing services by declaring specific properties. In this section, we'll discuss these advanced settings in detail.

5.3.1   *Configuration for registering services*

In this section, we'll look at the advanced settings related to the `service` tag. Spring DM provides different advanced configurations when registering beans as OSGI services. It allows you to specify a variety of options:

- Referencing beans that register services
- Registering service identifiers based on service interfaces
- Specifying properties used during registration
- Managing classloaders related to services
- Ranking services
- Configuring the service factory feature with bundle scope

All these kinds of configurations are described in detail in following sections.

BEAN REFERENCE

Spring DM supports several ways to specify which bean is used for registration. We've already seen the most common one—the `ref` attribute. It allows you to reference a bean via its Spring identifier.

Spring DM also supports the use of an anonymous bean within the `service` tag, as shown in the following snippet:

Specifies inner ❶
bean for service

```
<osgi:service id="testService"
    interface="com.manning.sdmia.springdm.service.TestService">
  <bean
     class="com.manning.sdmia.springdm.service.impl.TestServiceImpl"/>      ◁──────┘
</osgi:service>
```

You can use anonymous beans when registering a service by directly specifying a `bean` tag ❶ inside the `service` tag. In this case, the bean doesn't need to have an `id` attribute and can't be used elsewhere in the Spring configuration.

SERVICE INTERFACE SUPPORT

When you use the `service` tag's `interface` attribute, Spring DM registers the service with an identifier corresponding to the value of this attribute. Because OSGi allows you to register services under several identifiers, Spring DM also provides an inner `interfaces` tag that accepts a list of values, as shown in the following snippet. Note that the `interface` attribute and the `interfaces` tag can't be used at the same time in a `service` tag.

```
<osgi:service id="testService" ref="testServiceBean">
  <osgi:interfaces>
    <value>
      com.manning.sdmia.springdm.service.TestService
    </value>
    <value>(...)</value>
  </osgi:interfaces>
</osgi:service>
```

◁─┐ **Uses multiple**
   identifiers for
◁─┘ **registration**

In addition to this explicit configuration of interfaces, Spring DM provides a mechanism to detect values used for the `interface` attribute and `interfaces` tag. This mechanism is configured through the `auto-export` attribute and provides alternative strategies to autodetect interfaces when the `interface` attribute and `interfaces` tag are not specified, as described in the table 5.1.

Table 5.1 Auto-export strategies for the `interface` attribute and `interfaces` tag

Strategy	Description
`disabled`	Default strategy where you need to explicitly specify values of the `interface` attribute and `interfaces` tag
`interfaces`	Strategy using all the interfaces implemented by the service
`class-hierarchy`	Strategy using the class and all parent classes of the service
`all-classes`	Corresponds to both the `interfaces` and `class-hierarchy` strategies

The following snippet shows how to use the `auto-export` attribute with the `interfaces` strategy. Because the class corresponding to the `testServiceBean` bean implements the `TestService` interface, its qualified name will be used as its identifier during the service registration:

```
<osgi:service id="testService" ref="testServiceBean"
              auto-export="interfaces"/>
```

When using a strategy other than `disabled`, you don't have to specify values for the `interface` attribute and `interfaces` tag. However, you can combine both explicit settings with the `interface` attribute and `interfaces` tag and autodetection to specify the identifiers to use when exporting a service. Note that only visible types of the bundle will be used in autodetection.

SERVICE PROPERTY SUPPORT

Spring DM's `service` tag allows properties to be specified when services are registered. These properties can be used in a filter expression in combination with the service identifier when looking up a service. Spring DM provides a `service-properties` tag to be used as an inner tag; it accepts a list of key/value pairs, as shown in the following snippet:

```
<osgi:service id="testService" ref="testServiceBean"
          interface="com.manning.sdmia.springdm.service.TestService">
  <osgi:service-properties>
```

```
    <entry key="creationDate" value="2009-12-12"/>
    (...)
  </osgi:service-properties>
</osgi:service>
```

The snippet first defines a block for properties using the `service-properties` XML tag and then specifies a property for the service with the key `creationDate`.

Specified properties correspond to the `properties` parameter of the `registerService` method in the `BundleContext` interface, and this `properties` map is of type `Dictionary`. The values specified in the `service` tag are automatically passed to this `registerService` method by Spring DM when registering the corresponding service.

MANAGING THE CLASSLOADING CONTEXT

Spring DM lets you manage a service's classloading context by setting a classloader as the TCCL during the call of a service method. If specified in the service registration configuration, Spring DM makes it possible during the service call to see all the classes of the bundle that registers the service, as shown in figure 5.7.

When exporting a bean as an OSGi service, Spring DM allows you to specify which classes are reachable from this service based on the TCCL managed by Spring DM. At this level, either no classes, or classes present in the bundle that registers service, will be reachable.

This behavior can be configured using the `context-class-loader` attribute of the service tag. Table 5.2 lists the strategies for this attribute.

Table 5.2   Context classloading strategies for the `context-class-loader` attribute

Strategy	Description
unmanaged	This is the default strategy, where no context classloader management is done.
service-provider	This strategy allows the service implementation, during the service call, to see all the classes of the bundle that registered the service.

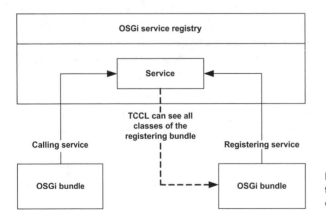

Figure 5.7   Configuring the TCCL from service registration to manage class visibility during a service call

This snippet shows how to use the `service` tag to configure the `service-provider` strategy when the service is registered:

```
<osgi:service id="testService" ref="testServiceBean"
              interface="com.manning.sdmia.springdm.service.TestService"
              context-class-loader="service-provider"/>
```

Internally, Spring DM adds a proxy in front of the target service to transparently manage the TCCL. Adding this proxy is supported for both interface-based and concrete classes, but for the latter you'll need to use CGLib.

SERVICE-RANKING SUPPORT

Spring DM allows you to specify a rank for a service through the `service` tag's `ranking` attribute. This attribute is optional and its default value is 0. The following snippet shows how to use this attribute:

```
<osgi:service id="testService" ref="testServiceBean"
              interface="com.manning.sdmia.springdm.service.TestService"
              ranking="5"/>
```

OSGi's ranking feature is used when you're trying to obtain a service reference and there's more than one service match. In this situation, the service with the highest ranking will match. The ranking of services is also used by Spring DM as a tiebreaker in its shutdown algorithm.

BUNDLE SCOPE

The Spring Framework provides the `scope` attribute of bean tags to control the instantiation of beans. Spring DM provides a dedicated `bundle` scope, which allows you to finely manage the creation of service instances by calling components.

> ### Spring's scope support
>
> The Spring Framework allows you to manage bean creation through the `bean` tag's `scope` attribute. Two native scopes, `singleton` and `prototype`, were originally supported. The default, `singleton`, guarantees that only one instance of a bean is provided; `prototype` allows you to obtain a new instance when requesting the bean from the container.
>
> With Spring 2, scope support became open—you can define your own scopes with the `Scope` interface and the `CustomScopeConfigurer` class. Basing on this new scope support, several new scopes (`request`, `session`, and `globalsession`) related to web technologies were also added.

The OSGi specification also describes the `ServiceFactory` interface, which allows you to create a unique service instance for each bundle that requests the service. Spring DM can implement this mechanism without using the related OSGi `ServiceFactory` interface, based on the `bundle` scope. For the `bundle` scope, Spring DM transparently enables service instantiation per component.

The configuration of the service factory feature using `bundle` scope must be done on the bean (in the `bean` tag) in order to export the bean as a service. It is not done on the service exporter (the `service` tag of the `osgi` namespace). The following snippet shows this:

❶ Defines OSGi service

```
<osgi:service id="testService"          ◄──┘
        ref="testServiceBean"
        interface="com.manning.sdmia.springdm.service.TestService"/>

<bean id=" testServiceBean"                          ❷ Defines bean, specifies
        scope="bundle"                                  bundle scope
        class="com.manning.sdmia.springdm.service.impl.TestServiceImpl">
    (...)
</bean>
```

The registration of an OSGi service using the `service` tag ❶ can be based on a bean definition using the `bundle` scope ❷. This configuration automatically enables the service factory feature when accessing and using the service.

5.3.2 Configuration for referencing services

We've seen how to register services with Spring DM through its `service` tag. Now we'll look at the how to reference services with Spring DM's `reference` tag.

> **NOTE** These advanced configurations are applicable only when using a single service. Section 5.5 will address the support that Spring DM provides for using a collection of services.

Spring DM allows you to specify different advanced configurations when referencing OSGI services:

- Specifying service identifiers based on service interfaces
- Managing service availability
- Managing classloaders
- Selecting services

In the following sections, we'll describe all the possible advanced configurations when referencing a service through Spring DM.

SERVICE INTERFACE SUPPORT

You can specify identifiers when referencing services in the same way as when registering services. The `interfaces` tag is available and must be used as an inner tag. It accepts a list of values, as shown in the following snippet:

```
<osgi:reference id="testService">
  <osgi:interfaces>
    <value>
      com.manning.sdmia.springdm.service.TestService    ◄──┐ Specifies
    </value>                                                  several
    <value>(...)</value>                                 ◄──┘ interfaces
  </osgi:interfaces>
</osgi:reference>
```

Like the service tag, the interface attribute and interfaces tag can't be used at the same time.

SERVICE AVAILABILITY IN REFERENCING

Spring DM includes sophisticated support for links between components made using OSGi services. It allows you to define what happens when a service isn't available or when one becomes unavailable.

The availability attribute of the reference tag allows you to configure whether or not service is optional, and it accepts the values listed in table 5.3.

Table 5.3 Values for the availability attribute

Value	Description
optional	This value specifies that the service is optional and doesn't need to be available all the time.
mandatory	This is the default value, which specifies that the service is mandatory for the component to function correctly. The service must always be present for the component's execution.

NOTE Before Spring DM version 2, the availability attribute was named cardinality. In that context, the value 0..1 was the equivalent of the optional value, and 1.. was the equivalent of mandatory.

Setting the value for the availability attribute specifies how Spring DM should behave during service matching and, more particularly, when the service can't be immediately resolved. Table 5.4 lists all the possible cases.

Table 5.4 Different behaviors of Spring DM depending on service availability

Availability	When	Description
mandatory	On Spring container startup	The container waits until the service is available before completing its startup. If the service isn't available after the specified timeout, the container throws a ServiceUnavailableException exception and the container isn't started.
optional	On Spring container startup	The container starts even if the referenced service isn't available.
mandatory	Spring container started	On a service call, if the service isn't available, the container waits until the service becomes available to execute the call. If the service isn't available after the specified timeout, the container throws a ServiceUnavailableException exception.
optional	Spring container started	It behaves in the same way as on Spring container startup.

The following snippet shows how to use the availability attribute to specify that the service is optional for the component:

```
<osgi:reference id="testService"
        interface="com.manning.sdmia.springdm.service.TestService"
        availability="optional"/>
```

The timeout attribute allows you to specify the amount of time, in milliseconds, to wait for a service to become available when an operation is invoked on it. The depends-on attribute specifies that the service reference must not be resolved until the specified bean has been initialized by the Spring container. The following snippet illustrates how to use these two attributes:

```
<osgi:reference id="testService"
        interface="com.manning.sdmia.springdm.service.TestService"
        timeout="1000" depends-on="anotherBean"/>
```

CLASSLOADER MANAGEMENT

As with service exporting, Spring DM provides support to automatically manage the TCCL when calling a referenced service. Spring DM allows a service call invocation to see all the classes of the calling bundle, or of the bundle that registered the service, through the setting of the TCCL, as shown in figure 5.8.

When referencing an OSGi service, Spring DM allows you to specify which classes are reachable from this service by setting the context classloader. At this level, either no classes, or classes present in the bundle that either registers or calls the service, will be reachable.

The class visibility can be configured using the context-class-loader attribute of the service tag. Table 5.5 lists the available strategies for this attribute.

Table 5.5 Context classloading strategies for the context-class-loader attribute

Strategy	Description
client	This default strategy allows the implementation to see all the classes of the calling component during the service call. This strategy provides a robust solution for the problems described in section 5.2.2.
service-provider	This strategy allows the service implementation to see all the classes of the bundle that registered the service during its call.
unmanaged	This strategy performs no context classloader management.

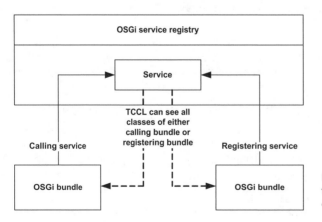

Figure 5.8 Configuring the TCCL from service referencing to manage class visibility during a service call

The following snippet shows how to configure the `service-provider` strategy during the service referral through the `reference` tag.

```
<osgi:reference id="testService"
            interface="com.manning.sdmia.springdm.service.TestService"
            context-class-loader="service-provider"/>
```

As you'll have noticed, classloader management for services can be configured both when registering and referencing services. Spring DM will always override the reference setting if the service setting is configured.

SERVICE SELECTION

Spring DM allows you to specify fine-grained selection of services at the level of the `reference` element. Two attributes are available:

- `filter` can be used as an expression to select a subset of services to be matched.
- `bean-name` allows you to select the service with the `bean-name` property set. For this to work, the service must have been registered using Spring DM or a tool that also uses the `bean-name` property.

The following snippet shows how to select the service corresponding to the `TestService` interface and having a `creationDate` attribute with the value `2009-12-12`:

```
<osgi:reference id="testService"
        interface="com.manning.sdmia.springdm.service.TestService"
        filter="(creationDate='2009-12-12')"/>
```

We've now seen how to configure OSGi service support in Spring DM. Next we'll tackle Spring DM's support for OSGi dynamics. As we'll see, Spring DM can handle all the tedious processing necessary to keep your system consistent.

5.4 *Handling OSGi service dynamics*

Because OSGi is intrinsically dynamic, Spring DM allows you to configure listeners that are notified when services are updated. Although Spring DM internally handles OSGi's dynamics for you, you'll probably need to add your own dynamic logic at times to make your system work the way you want. For instance, unregistering a service can affect components that use it, and those components need to be notified so they can adapt their processing.

Spring DM can send notifications both when a service is registered and referenced, depending on the Spring DM configuration, as shown in figure 5.9. You can even register user components as listeners for these events. Spring DM provides a bridge between events triggered by the OSGi container and these listeners configured as beans. It also provides an abstraction over the OSGi API and enables the use of POJOs as listeners.

Figure 5.9 summarizes the notifications that can be triggered by Spring DM regarding services. Notifications can be handled on the referencing bundle side and the registering bundle side. Spring DM is responsible to dispatch events to entities registered as listeners.

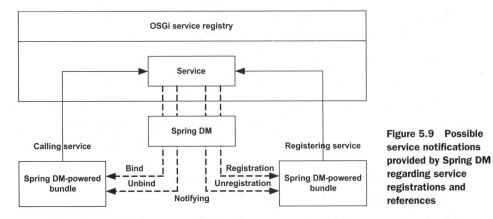

Figure 5.9   Possible service notifications provided by Spring DM regarding service registrations and references

Let's look now at how we can listen for these two kinds of events when exporting and referencing services.

5.4.1   Service registration and unregistration events

Spring DM allows you to configure listeners in the `service` tag when exporting a service. Like the Spring Framework, with its support for bean lifecycle notification, Spring DM provides two ways to implement and configure listeners:

- *Make the service implement the* `OsgiServiceRegistrationListener` *interface.* When this interface is present, Spring DM will automatically register the bean as a listener of the service's lifecycle. This is a reasonable approach, but it ties your implementation to the Spring DM API.
- *Specify a service listener configuration in the service tag.*   This approach is preferred because it allows you to use a POJO as a listener. The association between events and callback methods is specified through the service listener configuration.

We'll focus on the latter and recommended approach, using the `osgi` XML namespace to configure the service listener.

Spring DM provides a `registration-listener` element to be used as an inner tag of the `service` tag. Table 5.6 lists the available attributes for that XML element.

Table 5.6   Attributes of the `registration-listener` element

Attribute	Description
`ref`	Specifies the identifier of the bean to be used as a service listener.
`registration-method`	Specifies the method of the listener bean to be called when the service is registered. The method must have exactly two parameters: One of the type of the service and corresponds to the service that's being listened to. A second which corresponds to the service's properties and can be of type `Map` or `Dictionary`.
`unregistration-method`	Specifies the method of the listener bean to be called when the service is unregistered. The method signature follows the same rules as for `registration-method`.

Listing 5.4 shows the contents of a registration service listener that has an `onService-Registered` method to handle the service registration event and an `onServiceUnregistered` method for the service unregistration event.

Listing 5.4   Contents of a registration service listener

```
public class TestRegistrationServiceListener {
  public void onServiceRegistered(
                TestService service, Map properties) {
    (...)                                                    Method for
  }                                                   registration event

  public void onServiceUnregistered(
                TestService service, Map properties) {
    (...)                                                    Method for
  }                                                 unregistration event
}
```

Once the listener is implemented, it can be configured as a bean and referenced from the service definition using the `ref` attribute of the `registration-listener` tag. The following snippet shows how you can specify the previous bean as a service listener for the `testService` service.

```
                                                      Definition of and    ❶
                                                   reference to listener

<bean id="testListener"
        class="com.manning.sdmia.springdm
                .service.impl.TestRegistrationServiceListener"/>

<osgi:service id="testService" ref="testServiceBean"
          interface="com.manning.sdmia.springdm.service.TestService">
  <registration-listener ref="testListener"
      registration-method="onServiceRegistered"
      unregistration-method="onServiceUnregistered"/>         ❷ Methods for
</osgi:service>                                                  service registration
                                                                 and unregistration
```

The listener is defined as a simple bean ❶. It's then referenced as a listener for the service in the `ref` attribute of the `registration-listener` tag, within the `service` tag. Within the `registration-listener` tag, you can use the `registration-method` attribute to specify which methods must be used on service registration and use the `unregistration-method` attribute to specify the methods used on service unregistration ❷.

Let's now look at how to register for notifications when a service is bound to and unbound from a service reference, and how to handle these events.

5.4.2   Service bind and unbind events

Spring DM allows you to configure beans that reference services to receive notifications when the configured service is bound or unbound by Spring DM. Like its support for registration events, Spring DM provides two different methods for configuring beans:

- *Make the listener implement the* `OsgiServiceLifecyleListener` *interface.* When this interface is present, Spring DM will automatically use the interface's methods when binding and unbinding occur.
- *Specify a service reference listener configuration in the reference tag.* This approach is preferred because it allows you to use a POJO as a listener. The association between events and callback methods is specified through the service reference listener's configuration.

These two approaches are equivalent because the listener can be configured as a dedicated entity in both cases and it's separate from the service itself. Which you choose depends on your preference for implementing an interface or using a declarative approach.

The first approach requires you to implement the Spring DM `OsgiServiceLifecycleListener` interface in the listener. The following snippet shows the content of this interface:

```
public interface OsgiServiceLifecycleListener {
  void bind(Object service, Map properties);
  void unbind(Object service, Map properties);
}
```

This interface has methods corresponding to the bind and unbind events: `bind` is called on a service bind event, and `unbind` is called on an unbind event. The first parameter is the instance of the related service, and the second is the associated service properties.

The bean implementing `OsgiServiceLifecycleListener` must be configured as a simple bean, and it can be referenced within the `reference` tag with a `listener` nested element, as shown in the following snippet:

```
<bean id="testListener"                          ⟵┐ Declares
              class="com.manning.sdmia.springdm    │ listener as bean
                    .service.impl.TestServiceListener"/>

<osgi:reference id="testService"
              interface="com.manning.sdmia.springdm.service.TestService">
  <osgi:listener ref="testListener"/>            ⟵┐ References listener
</osgi:service>                                    │ when importing service
```

The second approach is declarative, so the listener class doesn't need to implement any interface. Any POJO can be used, but the methods used when events occur must follow simple rules in the declaration of their signatures. To configure the link between events and the methods to call, Spring DM provides the attributes listed in table 5.7 for the `listener` nested tag of the `service` tag.

Listing 5.5 shows the content of a service listener with an `onServiceBound` method for the service bind event and an `onServiceUnbound` method for the service unbind event. You'll notice that the method parameters are now typed.

Table 5.7 Attributes of the `listener` tag

Attribute	Description
ref	Specifies the identifier of the bean to be used as a service listener.
bind-method	Specifies the method of the listener to be called when a reference to the service is bound. The method must have two parameters: The first is of the type of the service and corresponds to the service. The second corresponds to the service properties and can be of type Map or Dictionary.
unbind-method	Specifies the method of the listener to be called when a reference to the service is unbound. The method signature follows the same rules as for the bind-method attribute.

Listing 5.5   Contents of a service listener

```
public class TestServiceListener {
  public void onServiceBound(
                TestService service, Map properties) {
    (...)                                                    Method for
  }                                                       registration event

  public void onServiceUnbound(
                TestService service, Map properties) {
    (...)                                                    Method for
  }                                                      unregistration event
}
```

Once the listener is implemented, it can be configured as a bean and referenced from the service reference definition using the `ref` attribute of the `listener` element. The following snippet shows how you can specify the `TestRegistrationServiceListener` class as a service listener for the `testService` service.

❶ Defines and references listener

```
<bean id="testListener"
            class="com.manning.sdmia.springdm
                    .service.impl.TestRegistrationServiceListener"/>

<osgi:reference id="testService"
            interface="com.manning.sdmia.springdm.service.TestService">
  <listener ref="testListener"
            bind-method="onServiceBound"
            unbind-method="onServiceUnbound"/>
</osgi:service>
```

❷ Methods for service bind and unbind

The listener is defined as a simple bean ❶, and it's then referenced as a listener of the service reference through the `ref` attribute of the `listener` element ❶ within the reference element. Within the `listener` element, you can use the `bind-method` attribute to specify which methods must be used on the service bind event and use the `unbind-method` attribute to specify the methods used on the service unbind event ❷.

Spring DM also supports the use of a nested bean for the listener instead of using the `ref` attribute of the `listener` tag to refer to another bean.

We've now covered Spring DM's core support for OSGi services. You have learned all the concepts and seen how to register and reference single services. You also know how Spring DM handles the dynamics of OSGi.

The next feature we'll look at is Spring DM's support for service collections. This powerful and useful feature allows you to handle a set of services and easily implement the OSGi whiteboard pattern.

5.5   *Handling collections of OSGi services*

OSGi allows you to register several services using the same identifier, but when you do a lookup on the OSGi service registry, you usually want to refer to a single instance of a service. The OSGi service registry finds all the services that match the requirements and choose one to be returned (as determined by an algorithm).

> **NOTE**   The OSGi specification defines the algorithm that is used to select the service that's returned.

Nevertheless, you may be interested in all the services that implement a given interface and that meet some criteria. Collections of services can be useful in parts of an application that can be *extended*, like entries in a menu, tabs in the UI that provide access to different modules of an application, and so on. Imagine removing a bundle that registers such a service in your OSGi container, and the UI is immediately updated with the new functionality. (This is exactly what we'll do in chapter 6, section 6.4.1.) Collections of services can also be used in variants of the observer pattern, like the whiteboard pattern, where the listeners are services.

You can manipulate collections of services with plain OSGi, but this can lead to complex, cumbersome, and error-prone code; Spring DM provides a flexible way to transparently handle them. Moreover, Spring DM internally deals with all the dynamic features of OSGi to provide an up-to-date collection at any given moment.

5.5.1   *Configuring collections*

Spring DM provides two tags for configuring collections of OSGi services within the Spring configuration of components: the `list` tag for lists and the `set` tag for sets. The difference between lists and sets is the uniqueness of contained elements, based on the returned value of the `equals` method of these elements. This method must be overridden in this case and its return value is determined using the attribute values of the elements. This mechanism is integrated within the Java Collections framework and isn't specific to OSGi.

These tags accept the same attributes as the `reference` tag, described previously in section 5.3.1, along with a few others. The `comparator-ref`, `greedy-proxying`, and `member-type` attributes are specific to `list` and `set` tags. These attributes are listed in table 5.8.

The use of the `comparator-ref` and `greedy-proxying` attributes is described in sections 5.5.2 and 5.5.3.

Table 5.8 Attributes of the `list` and `set` tags

Attribute	Description
`interface`	Specifies the identifier for the service and must correspond to a class or interface name. This is the same use as for the `reference` tag.
`filter`	Can be used as an expression to select a subset of services to be matched. This is the same use as for the `reference` tag.
`bean-name`	Allows you to select the service with the `bean-name` property set. This is the same use as for the `reference` tag.
`context-class-loader`	Can be used to automatically manage the TCCL when calling a referenced service. This is the same use as for the `reference` tag.
`availability`	Specifies whether the collection can be empty. A value of `optional` means that the collection can be empty and services are optional; a value of `mandatory` (which is the default) requires at least one service in the collection.
`comparator-ref`	Specifies the comparator to be used to sort collection.
`greedy-proxying`	Specifies whether service proxies within the collection can be seen only as service classes (value `false`) or as all classes exported by service (value `true`).
`member-type`	`Specifies` which type of object may be added to the collection. With a value of `service-object` (the default), Spring DM service proxies are present in the collection; with a value of `service-reference`, the collection contains `ServiceReference` objects.

The following snippet shows how to use the `list` tag to reference a service collection for a given identifier and make it available within the Spring container as a `java.util.List`.

```
<beans (...)>

  <osgi:list id="testServices"            Specifies collection of
        interface="com.manning.sdmia      services by identifier
                 .springdm.service.TestService"/>

</beans>
```

You've now seen the basic configuration of service collections. Let's look at how to configure and use advanced features, such as collection sorting, greedy proxying, and integrated support when collections are updated.

5.5.2 Sorting collections

Spring DM allows you to sort service collections within `list` and `set` tags by using the `Comparator` interface. Comparators can be configured directly within the Spring container and referenced when configuring service-based collections. These two ways to configure comparators are supported by Spring DM:

- Referencing an existing comparator bean by its identifier through the `comparator-ref` attribute
- Configuring a comparator as a nested bean through the nested `comparator` element

A comparator is a class implementing the Java `Comparator` interface and its `compare` method to compare two objects, as shown in the following snippet:

```
public class MyCustomComparator implements Comparator<TestService> {
  public int compare(TestService o1, TestService o2) {
      //Implementing the compare processing
      (...)
  }
}
```

Now that you know how to implement a comparator, we'll see how to configure them within Spring DM to sort service collections. Listing 5.6 demonstrates how to configure sorting using both the comparator reference and a nested element for comparator.

Listing 5.6   Configuring custom comparators for service collections

```
<bean id="customComparator"
    class="com.manning.sdmia.springdm.service.sorting.MyCustomComparator"/>

<osgi:set id="testServiceSet"
    interface="com.manning.sdmia.springdm.service.TestService"
    comparator-ref="customComparator"/>

<osgi:list id="testServiceList"
    interface="com.manning.sdmia.springdm.service.TestService">
  <osgi:comparator>
    <bean class="com.manning.sdmia.springdm.service
        .sorting.MyCustomComparator"/>
  </osgi:comparator>
</osgi:list>
```

Defines comparator bean ❶

Specifies comparator by reference ❷

Specifies comparator with inner bean ❸

A custom comparator needs to be defined first as a regular Spring bean ❶, and it can then be referenced within the service collection configuration by using the Spring DM `comparator-ref` attribute ❷. The comparator can be defined as a nested bean within service collection configuration by using the `comparator` tag ❸ within the `list` and `set` tags.

Instead of providing your own comparators, Spring DM allows you to use natural comparators, through the `natural` tag of the `osgi` namespace. This tag has a `basis` attribute that accepts one of two values, specifying which sorting strategy you want to use:

- `services`—The ordering is based on the service instances, which must implement the `Comparable` interface.
- `service-references`—The ordering is based on the `ServiceReferences` (which are automatically `Comparable`)

Listing 5.7 shows how to use Spring DM's natural comparators within `comparator` tags.

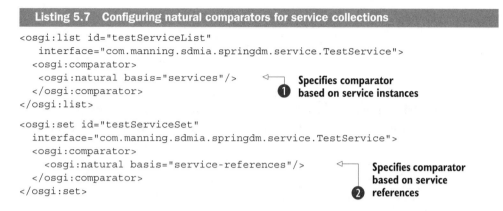

Listing 5.7   Configuring natural comparators for service collections

```
<osgi:list id="testServiceList"
   interface="com.manning.sdmia.springdm.service.TestService">
  <osgi:comparator>
   <osgi:natural basis="services"/>
  </osgi:comparator>
</osgi:list>
```
❶ Specifies comparator based on service instances

```
<osgi:set id="testServiceSet"
   interface="com.manning.sdmia.springdm.service.TestService">
   <osgi:comparator>
     <osgi:natural basis="service-references"/>
   </osgi:comparator>
</osgi:set>
```
❷ Specifies comparator based on service references

Both strategies for using a natural comparator can be specified through the `basis` attribute of the `natural` tag within the `comparator` tag. For the service-instance approach, the `services` value must be specified ❶, whereas the `service-references` value is used for the service-reference approach ❷.

Now that you know how to configure service collection references with Spring DM and how to sort them, let's look at their more advanced features.

5.5.3   Greedy proxying

When configuring service collections, Spring DM allows you to use one or several interfaces to determine the services that will be present in the collection. However, services can expose interfaces other than the specified ones, and applications sometimes need to use these additional interfaces. By default, Spring DM doesn't allow you to cast services in collections to other types than those set in the `interface` attribute or `interfaces` tag.

The greedy proxy feature of Spring DM makes it possible to cast services in collections to all of the exposed interfaces that a service supports. The only restriction is that the interfaces used must be visible to the component within OSGi.

The following snippet shows how to enable the greedy proxy feature on `list` and set tags through the `greedy-proxying` attribute.

```
<osgi:list id="testServiceList"
    interface="com.manning.sdmia.springdm.service.TestService"
    greedy-proxying="true"/>
```

Once greedy proxying is enabled, you can cast your service reference to any of the exposed interfaces and classes visible to your component. Listing 5.8 shows how to use this mechanism when iterating through the service collection configured in the previous section.

Listing 5.8   Using the greedy proxying feature in code

```
for (Iterator iterator = testServiceList.iterator(); iterator.hasNext();) {
  TestService service = (TestService) iterator.next();
  (...)
```
Gets service instance with declared type ❶

```
if (service instanceof AnotherInterface) {
  AnotherInterface anotherServiceInterface
                           = (AnotherInterface)service;
}
}
```
Gets service instance with other type ❷

As usual, the service elements can be accessed as the type specified when configuring the service collection reference ❶. When enabling the greedy proxying feature of Spring, you're able to see these elements as other types corresponding to other exposed interfaces for the service ❷.

As emphasized in chapters 1 and 2, OSGi is a dynamic technology in which services can come and go at any time. Let's now look at how Spring DM handles service collection references in this context.

5.5.4 *Integrated support when collections are updated*

Spring DM supports the dynamic update of service collections and guarantees that the collections are always up to date according to the service registry.

Service collections managed by Spring DM follow these rules:

- For mandatory service collections, an empty collection throws a Service-UnavailableException exception when trying to use an iterator.
- For optional service collections, an empty collection throws no exception and is simply empty.

When parsing collections, the Iterator interface must be used as in standard Java applications. Spring DM automatically updates iterators when services disappear, to avoid dealing with the resulting stale service references. Note that this feature has no impact on unregistered service instances that have been obtained from an iterator. Using them will result in a ServiceUnavailableException because they no longer exist in the service registry.

That's all there is to say about service collection management within Spring DM. In the last sections of this chapter, we'll describe how to programmatically use Spring DM to register and reference services. This approach can be particularly useful when developing unit tests or implementing processing not configurable by using Spring DM's XML and annotation support.

5.6 *Programmatic service support*

In some advanced scenarios, you'll need to use Spring DM's service support programmatically. This part of the support is hidden by the osgi XML namespace and unfortunately is not publicly documented. Fortunately, Spring's FactoryBean feature makes it quite easy to use. This programmatic support can be very useful when implementing test cases or building Spring configurations.

This approach is particularly suitable for bundles that can't use the osgi XML namespace and must work directly with the underlying Spring DM abstractions.

> ### Spring's FactoryBean feature
> Spring `FactoryBean`s allow you to configure beans that can't be created by simply using a `new` operator. For example, this is the case when using the factory design pattern, which hides how you instantiate classes. Once the `FactoryBean` is initialized, the target bean instance can be obtained through the `getObject` method.

5.6.1   Registering a service programmatically

The dedicated abstraction for registering OSGi services is the `OsgiServiceFactory-Bean` class located in the `org.springframework.osgi.service.exporter.support` package. As this class is directly used by the `osgi` XML namespace, you'll find it has the same configuration properties as the `service` tag.

Listing 5.9 shows how to register a service using the `OsgiServiceFactoryBean` class. This configuration is similar to that shown in listing 5.1 and described in section 5.1.2, where we used the `service` tag to register an OSGi service with Spring DM.

Listing 5.9   Programmatically service registration configuration

```
TestService testServiceBean = new TestServiceImpl();          Instantiates
(...)                                                       ❶ service bean

OsgiServiceFactoryBean factoryBean
            = new OsgiServiceFactoryBean();
factoryBean.setBundleContext(bundleContext);
factoryBean.setTarget(testServiceBean);
factoryBean.setInterfaces(
            new Class[] { TestService.class });            Instantiates     ❷
factoryBean.setContextClassLoader(                        and configures
            ExportContextClassLoader.UNMANAGED);          Spring DM's
factoryBean.afterPropertiesSet();                        service factory

ServiceRegistration registration
            = (ServiceRegistration)factory.getObject();
                                                         Gets service
(...)                          ❹ Destroys service       registration  ❸
factoryBean.destroy();            factory
```

The first step is to instantiate the bean ❶ and the dedicated Spring DM `FactoryBean` service abstraction ❷. The `FactoryBean` then needs to be configured with the same elements that are used when configuring a service reference through the Spring DM XML namespace: the exported interfaces of the service, the target bean reference for the service, and the context classloader strategy must all be set. The `afterPropertiesSet` method must then be called to check whether the `FactoryBean` is correctly configured, and the method also initializes it. If no errors occur, the service is now successfully registered. A valid `ServiceRegistration` instance can be obtained through the `getObject` method ❸. In order to finalize the `FactoryBean`, the `destroy` method must be called ❹.

You can similarly reference a service programmatically with the Spring `Factory-Bean` feature.

5.6.2   *Referencing services programmatically*

For referencing services, Spring DM provides two FactoryBean implementations: the OsgiServiceProxyFactoryBean class for referencing a single service and the OsgiServiceCollectionProxyFactoryBean class for a collection of services. Both classes are located in the org.springframework.osgi.service.importer.support package.

Listing 5.10 shows how to reference a service using the OsgiServiceFactoryBean class. This configuration is similar to that in listing 5.2 and described in section 5.1.2, where we used the reference tag to reference an OSGi service with Spring DM.

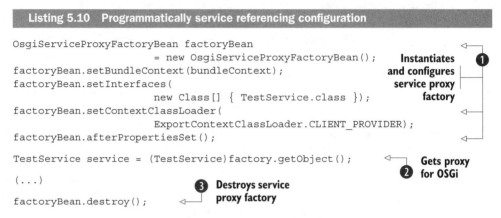

Listing 5.10   Programmatically service referencing configuration

```
OsgiServiceProxyFactoryBean factoryBean
                = new OsgiServiceProxyFactoryBean();    Instantiates ❶
factoryBean.setBundleContext(bundleContext);          and configures
factoryBean.setInterfaces(                             service proxy
                new Class[] { TestService.class });    factory
factoryBean.setContextClassLoader(
                ExportContextClassLoader.CLIENT_PROVIDER);
factoryBean.afterPropertiesSet();

TestService service = (TestService)factory.getObject();    Gets proxy
                                                      ❷   for OSGi
(...)                            ❸  Destroys service
factoryBean.destroy();              proxy factory
```

The first step is to instantiate the dedicated Spring DM FactoryBean abstraction for referencing a service ❶. The object then needs to be configured with the same elements required when configuring a service reference using the Spring DM XML namespace: the required interfaces of the service and the context classloader strategy must be set. The afterPropertiesSet method must then be called to check whether the FactoryBean is correctly configured and to initialize it. A valid service reference instance can then be obtained by using the getObject method ❷. In order to finalize the FactoryBean, the destroy method must be called ❸.

Programmatically configuring a service collection is similar, but it's done with the OsgiServiceCollectionProxyFactoryBean class. That's why we won't describe it here, but we'll show how Spring DM allows you to get native service references from service proxy management.

5.6.3   *ServiceReference support*

Spring DM supports injecting a service's ServiceReference instance into a bean instead of injecting the service instance itself. Nothing special needs to be done except for injecting the configured reference into a property of type ServiceReference. Spring DM will automatically inject the ServiceReference instance.

You'll notice that the injected instance corresponds to a proxy and not the target reference of type ServiceReference. If the underlying reference is needed, you can access it using the proxy's `getTargetServiceReference` method, as shown in the following snippet:

```
ServiceReference serviceReference = getServiceReference();
ServiceReference nativeReference =
  ((ServiceReferenceProxy)serviceReference).getTargetServiceReference();
```

Having injected the `ServiceReference` for the referenced service, the instance can be used within the application, as in the first of the preceding code lines. Spring DM allows the native reference given by the OSGi container to be accessed through the proxy via the `getTargetServiceReference` method (as in the second of the code lines).

A typical use case for this technique is when you want to get hold of a real OSGi service because an OSGi container implementation expects a native `ServiceReference` instance instead of a Spring DM proxy.

5.7   *Summary*

The core OSGi specification doesn't provide declarative support for managing and using services; it requires that you use the low-level OSGi API. To do so, you have to handle OSGi dynamics by hand, which can be tedious and error-prone.

Together with the extender mechanism, service support is the most powerful feature of Spring DM as it allows both registering and referencing services transparently without having to use the OSGI API at all. The `osgi` XML namespace, which allows you to manage and use services like regular beans in a Spring application context, is commonly used. Annotation-based support is also provided. These two approaches for to managing OSGi services provide a flexible way to register and reference services using Spring DM.

Another powerful aspect of Spring DM's service support is its management of OSGi dynamics: all the instances Spring DM manages adapt automatically to the registration and unregistration of services. Spring DM also allows you to customize what happens when services are, or become, unavailable, by specifying services as mandatory or optional.

Spring DM also provides built-in support for managing the TCCL when calling services. This allows you to solve classic problems of class visibility in a simple and straightforward way, without adding `Import-Package` entries in the manifests of framework-based components.

This chapter ends our discussion of the core features of Spring DM. We'll see in the next chapter how to apply them to develop enterprise, OSGi-based applications.

OSGi and Spring DM
for enterprise applications

This chapter covers

- Using the traditional Java EE framework in OSGi
  environments
- Creating OSGi bundles from existing Java artifacts
- Designing OSGi-based enterprise applications
- Handling OSGi's dynamic nature

You saw in the previous chapter that OSGi lets its modules communicate only by way of services. This helps decouple them and promotes a more modular programming model than in standard Java. Modularity is good for applications, but, as enterprise application developers, we've become negligent when developing enterprise applications in the last few years. These applications grew big and monolithic, did not have particularly strict dependency management, and sometimes used Java introspection or classloaders in fancy ways. Now that we have discovered OSGi and want to build our enterprise applications on top of this wonderful platform, we need to eliminate these bad habits. There is no place for approximation in OSGi.

Don't feel guilty or desperate: OSGi is a welcoming world, even for enterprise application developers. Throughout this chapter, we'll show you how to adapt your development to OSGi by choosing good frameworks and libraries that are OSGi-compliant, by getting existing Java artifacts ready for use in OSGi environments, and by designing your own applications to leverage the features of OSGi. This may look like a tortuous path, but you'll be surprised at how much OSGi has already become part of day-to-day development work. You may well discover that you've been using OSGi-compliant frameworks for months without knowing it.

In this chapter, we'll guide you along the OSGi path. We'll start by showing you that you can still use your favorite libraries and frameworks in OSGi: some of them are already OSGi bundles, and you'll learn how to make the others compatible. Because OSGi brings a new modularity paradigm to Java, we'll also show you how to leverage it and design applications with OSGi, backed up by Spring DM.

This may seem off topic in a Spring DM book, but it will show you that introducing OSGi in enterprise applications isn't difficult. Spring DM will be the bridge between your applications and the OSGi runtime; we'll discuss this in section 6.3, which provides guidelines about application design with OSGi. Spring DM can help you follow and implement these guidelines. You'll learn how Spring DM can assemble and communicate with your OSGi bundles easily, and how it can help you handle the powerful but tricky dynamic aspect of OSGi.

Let's start by looking at how traditional Java libraries and frameworks react within an OSGi environment.

6.1 Building an OSGi repository for enterprise applications

The deployment unit in OSGi is the bundle, which is a standard JAR file, enhanced with metadata that (among other things) informs the OSGi platform of the bundle's dependencies and what it can provide to other bundles in terms of Java packages. Having all of your libraries, frameworks, modules, and applications packaged as bundles is essential for successfully using OSGi.

In sections 6.1.1 and 6.1.2, we'll look at how to use these kinds of Java frameworks and libraries, and in section 6.1.3 we'll see how to get them easily from repositories dedicated to OSGi. Note that this section isn't specific to Spring DM; the information it covers is valid for any OSGi-based application.

6.1.1 Using Java and Java EE frameworks in OSGi environments

As a developer of enterprise applications, you'll know that you never start a new project from scratch. You know you can rely on your pet frameworks, which relieve some of the recurrent technical concerns. Indeed, that's what enterprise application development is all about—not reinventing the wheel, and reusing existing code as much as possible. But in developing OSGi applications, you'll soon notice that not all Java and Java EE libraries or frameworks are packaged as OSGi bundles. Even worse, some aren't OSGi-friendly in their use and execution.

Fortunately, some projects are aware of the growing popularity of OSGi in Java enterprise middleware and applications, so becoming OSGi-compliant, from their design to their packaging, became one of their priorities. Don't abandon OSGi because you're afraid you'll have to start your project from scratch. There are a lot of enterprise frameworks and libraries that work in OSGi environments. If you decide to develop OSGi applications, the biggest changes will be in the structure of your applications rather than in the frameworks you use.

If you're lucky, your favorite frameworks and libraries will work out of the box. If you aren't so lucky, you'll have to make their packaging OSGi-aware. We'll cover both cases, starting by describing what's known to work in an OSGi environment.

6.1.2   *Choosing the right frameworks for OSGi*

So you're an enterprise application veteran and you want to try out OSGi? Or you're an old hand at OSGi and are eager to exercise your skills in large-scale enterprise applications? In any case, you'll have to make both the OSGi and enterprise-application worlds work together, and you know that some Java libraries and frameworks are more suited to OSGi than others. For example, Jakarta Commons Logging (JCL)is known to be OSGi-unfriendly because of its dynamic discovery process (see the sidebar for more details). Some functions like dynamic loading of classes are sensitive within OSGi, so you should ensure that your favorite libraries and frameworks handle them in a safe and reliable way before using them in an OSGi environment.

Jakarta Commons Logging and OSGi

JCL is probably the most popular logging facade, but despite its large adoption, JCL is very OSGi-unfriendly. How can a good library become a bad egg in OSGi?

JCL is a thin wrapper around several logging implementations, Log4j being the most popular. This means you can use the JCL API in your applications and simply plug in your favorite implementation, as long as it's supported.

JCL initializes itself when the first call to the logging system is made. This initialization consists of dynamically finding which implementations are available on the classpath, choosing one, and redirecting all subsequent calls to it. In theory, this sounds simple: you drop JCL and Log4j JAR files into your applications and the latter will be used automatically in most cases. If you're unlucky, you won't get any log messages and will fight for hours trying to diagnose cryptic classloader issues.

JCL's discovery process is dynamic and relies on the use of the TCCL. Corresponding JCL implementation classes (such as `Log4jLogger`) are also loaded by the TCCL, but when it comes to instantiating one of these logging objects, JCL uses the *current* classloader, which doesn't always see the same implementation classes (because it can be different from the TCCL). This dynamic discovery process can be problematic in some servlet containers, and it makes the use of JCL in an OSGi environment very difficult, if not impossible.

(continued)

To learn more about the pitfalls of JCL's discovery process, you should read the article, "Taxonomy of class loader problems encountered when using Jakarta Commons Logging" (http://www.qos.ch/logging/classloader.jsp), by Ceki Gülcü, the founder of Log4j, SLF4J, and Logback.

You must now be wondering how Spring DM and the Spring Framework both use the Jakarta Commons Logging API. Recall that we also deploy SLF4J bundles when we use Spring DM. SLF4J is another logging facade, which strives to address JCL's pitfalls by using a static discovery process. Using SLF4J is quite similar to using JCL: you use its API, and you drop into its classpath the API's JAR, the JAR of one (and only one!) of its bindings (the bridge between SLF4J and the target logging framework), and the JAR of the logging implementations. Unlike JCL, SLF4J's discovery process is static: the SLF4J API just expects a binding class, `StaticLoggerBinder`, which is made available by the sole SLF4J binding JAR that you generally should provide on the classpath.

But still, Spring and Spring DM use Jakarta Commons Logging! Yes, they do, and that's why we also deploy a special JCL bundle, which is a library provided by SLF4J. It defines the exact same API as JCL but it's backed up by SLF4J. This library has the appearance and smell of JCL, but it's actually SLF4J. That's the trick for making Spring and OSGi happy about logging.

To help you find appropriate libraries and frameworks, table 6.1 offers a nonexhaustive list of those that are known to be OSGi-compliant.

Table 6.1   OSGi-compliant enterprise frameworks and libraries

Name	Type	Note
Spring Framework	Lightweight container and dependency-injection framework, enterprise support	The Spring Framework binaries have been packaged as OSGi bundles since version 2.5. For use in OSGi, prefer the "A" versions.
Spring Portfolio projects	Miscellaneous (security, web, batch, integration, ...)	All binaries are OSGi bundles, and most of the projects have been tested in OSGi environments.
Google Guice	Lightweight dependency-injection framework	Distributed as OSGi bundles since version 2.0.
Groovy	Java-based dynamic language	Distributed as an OSGi bundle.
Jetty	Web container	Distributed as an OSGi bundle and used as an implementation of OSGi's HTTP service.
Apache Commons	Reusable Java components	Most of the projects are OSGi-compliant thanks to the Felix Commons effort.
EclipseLink	ORM	Distributed as OSGi bundles.
OpenEJB	EJB 3.0 container	Distributed as OSGi bundles and used in several application servers.

Table 6.1   **OSGi-compliant enterprise frameworks and libraries** *(continued)*

Name	Type	Note
SLF4J	Logging facade	Distributed as OSGi bundles and tested in OSGi environments.
Logback	Logging implementation	OSGi-compliant; intended to be successor to Log4j.
Wicket	Web framework	Wicket binaries have been packaged as OSGi bundles since version 1.4.
MINA	NIO framework	MINA binaries have been packaged as OSGi bundles since version 2.0. Apache server-based projects use MINA for their NIO layer.
H2	Pure Java database engine	Distributed as an OSGi bundle.

In the next section, we'll introduce you to several repositories where you can download ready-to-use OSGi bundles.

6.1.3 Getting OSGi-ready artifacts

We saw that some projects distribute their binaries as OSGi bundles. If one of your dependencies happens to not be a part of these projects, there's still a small chance you won't end up wrapping it yourself, because there are some projects targeted at making OSGi bundles available. Here is a list of some of these OSGi repositories:

- *OSGi Bundle Repository* (http://www.osgi.org/Repository/HomePage) Maintained by the OSGi Alliance, this repository hosts more OSGi-centric bundles than OSGi-ified versions of enterprise frameworks. You can search bundles by keyword or category and get precise information from the web interface. The format of the repository follows a standard described in the "OSGi RFC 112 Bundle Repository," making the repository usable remotely by any OSGi container.
- *Apache Felix Commons* (http://felix.apache.org/site/apache-felix-commons.html) This isn't exactly a repository, but a community effort to popularize the distribution of Java projects as OSGi bundles. Some volunteers OSGi-ify standard Java artifacts and make them available, hoping original developers will then include the OSGi-ification process in the build of their frameworks and libraries. Contributions include most of the Apache Commons projects, ANTLR, and cglib.
- *Eclipse Orbit* (http://www.eclipse.org/orbit/) This repository includes bundles that have been used and approved in one or more projects from the Eclipse Foundation. These bundles can contain some Equinox-specific metadata because they're meant to be used with this particular OSGi container.
- *SpringSource Enterprise Bundle Repository* (http://www.springsource.com/repository/app/) This repository hosts hundreds of open source enterprise libraries, usually OSGi-ified by SpringSource employees. It features a search engine and precise information about bundles. Artifacts are made available for use with Maven 2 and Ivy.

You should find what you need from among these repositories. But if you don't find a library, you'll have to do the dirty work yourself, and in the next section we'll describe techniques that make this relatively painless.

6.2 OSGi-ifying libraries and frameworks

Before diving into the design of enterprise applications with OSGi and Spring DM (which we'll do in section 6.3), we need to have all our dependencies be OSGi-compliant. Developing applications for an OSGi environment should not prevent you from using your favorite Java and Java EE libraries and frameworks. More and more libraries are now OSGi-friendly, because packaging them as an OSGi bundle is part of their build; but bad things happen, and perhaps one day you'll find that your best-loved Java framework is packaged as a normal JAR and is absolutely useless in your OSGi application.

This isn't a desperate situation. You're about to learn everything you need to know about transforming a non-OSGi JAR file into a 100 percent OSGi-compliant bundle, a process that we decided to qualify with the barbarism "OSGi-ification" for brevity. We'll start with a little bit of theory, and then we'll dive into the transformation. We'll first try to do it by hand and then use tools like Bnd. We'll do our experimenting on the Apache Commons DBCP library.

6.2.1 How to create OSGi-ified versions of libraries

The main issue in the OSGi-ification of an existing library is visibility. From the library's point of view, it means being able to see external dependencies but also making its own classes visible to other bundles if necessary. You may have figured out that we'll have to juggle the `Import-Package` and `Export-Package` manifest headers.

When a library is built upon other libraries, it uses their classes and imports some of their packages into its own classes. In a standard Java environment, you can add these libraries on the classpath, and any class can import their packages and use their classes. The story is different in an OSGi environment: libraries must explicitly *export* the packages they want to share, and modules that want to use them must explicitly *import* these packages. The whole export/import process is managed by the OSGi platform with metadata contained in the bundle's manifest file.

IMPORTING PACKAGES

Let's talk first about the process of importing: a library needs to use some classes defined in another library (we'll assume the other library properly exports these classes, making them visible to other bundles). As an example, consider the ORM module in the Spring Framework: this module includes support for popular ORM tools such as Hibernate, iBATIS, and OpenJPA. If we focus on Hibernate, the `Import-Package` of the ORM module might look like the following:

```
Import-Package: org.hibernate,org.hibernate.cache,org.hibernate.cfg
(...)
```

Hibernate has a lot of packages, and Spring ORM uses most of them, so we didn't include the whole list.

The previous snippet is fine regarding what Spring ORM can see (some of Hibernate's packages) but it isn't precise enough regarding *versions*. In its 2.5.6.A version, Spring ORM's Hibernate support is only tested against Hibernate 3.2, so this should appear in the manifest. The `Import-Package` header can use the `version` attribute to specify the exact version or version range the bundle needs. This attribute defaults to the range [0.0.0, ?), and because we didn't use the `version` attribute in our first manifest declaration, the ORM module would use any available version installed in the OSGi container. This could make a 3.0 Hibernate bundle eligible for use, whereas the ORM module isn't compatible with Hibernate 3.0.

As you can see, when OSGi-ifying a library, good practice consists of indicating the version of each package in the `Import-Package` header. Spring ORM declares that it works with Hibernate from version 3.2.6.ga, inclusive, to 4.0.0, exclusive:

```
Import-Package: org.hibernate;version="[3.2.6.ga,
4.0.0)",org.hibernate.cache;version="[3.2.6.ga, 4.0.0)",
org.hibernate.cfg;version="[3.2.6.ga, 4.0.0)"
(...)
```

> **NOTE** The "ga" version qualifier stands for "General Availability" and denotes a stable, production-ready version of the software.

Spring ORM not only includes support for Hibernate, but also for iBATIS, amongst others, so the Spring ORM bundle can apply the same pattern for declaring dependencies on iBATIS:

```
Import-Package: org.hibernate;version="[3.2.6.ga,
4.0.0)",org.hibernate.cache;version="[3.2.6.ga, 4.0.0)",
org.hibernate.cfg;version="[3.2.6.ga, 4.0.0)",
(...)
com.ibatis.common.util;version="[2.3.0.677, 3.0.0)",
com.ibatis.common.xml;version="[2.3.0.677, 3.0.0)",
com.ibatis.sqlmap.client;version="[2.3.0.677, 3.0.0)"
(...)
```

Nice, but let's imagine you're working on an application that uses Hibernate and the support provided by Spring ORM. You provision your OSGi container with the corresponding bundles, but you soon notice that if you want the Spring ORM bundle to be resolved, you need all of its dependencies in your container, like iBATIS or OpenJPA, even if you only use Hibernate. That's a real pain, because you'll have to get all these dependencies as OSGi bundles and deal with their dependencies—all for nothing because you don't even use them!

Don't panic, there's a solution: these kinds of dependencies can be marked as optional in the manifest, by using the `resolution` directive. This directive defaults to `mandatory`, meaning that the bundle won't be able to resolve successfully if the imported package isn't present in the container. The `resolution` directive can also take the `optional` value, to indicate that the importing bundle can successfully resolve even if the imported package isn't present. Of course, if some code that relies on the missing import is called at runtime, it will fail.

Spring ORM declares its dependencies on ORM tools as optional, because there is little chance that all these libraries will be used at the same time in an application:

```
Import-Package: org.hibernate;version="[3.2.6.ga,
4.0.0)";resolution:=optional,
org.hibernate.cache;version="[3.2.6.ga,
4.0.0)";resolution:=optional,org.hibernate.cfg;version="[3.2.6.ga,
4.0.0)";resolution:=optional,
(...)
com.ibatis.common.util;version="[2.3.0.677, 3.0.0)";resolution:=optional,
com.ibatis.common.xml;version="[2.3.0.677, 3.0.0)";resolution:=optional,
com.ibatis.sqlmap.client;version="[2.3.0.677, 3.0.0)";resolution:=optional
(...)
```

To sum up, when OSGi-ifying libraries or frameworks, you should remember the following guidelines with respect to the `Import-Package` header:

- Import the packages that the library or framework uses, and don't import unused packages, which would tie the bundle to unnecessary dependencies.
- Specify the version of the packages, so the library or framework won't use classes that it isn't meant to use, which could lead to unexpected behavior.
- Specify the difference between mandatory and optional dependencies by using the `resolution` directive.

That's enough about importing from other bundles; let's see now how a library can make its classes visible in the OSGi platform.

EXPORTING PACKAGES

Which packages need to be exported by a library depend on its design. Some libraries clearly make the distinction between their API and their implementation classes, through some kind of special structuring of their packages. For example, interfaces (the API) may be located in one package and internal classes (implementation, utilities) in an `impl` or `internal` subpackage.

> **NOTE** Generally speaking, splitting API and implementation packages is a good design practice, not only in OSGi.

Nevertheless, the export declarations will usually end up exporting all the packages of a bundle because even if we follow the programming through interface pattern, we'll usually need an implementation that's provided by the same library as the API.

> **NOTE** We'll see more about design in section 6.3, so we'll keep things simple for now. Just remember that OSGi services are a good way to expose what other bundles need to use. This keep implementation details from leaking through the whole system.

In the `Export-Package` header, you should always specify the version of the exported package. The following snippet shows the first line of the `Export-Package` header from the Spring ORM module manifest (notice the use of the `version` attribute):

```
Export-Package: org.springframework.orm;version="2.5.6.A",
(...)
```

The `version` value can be different for each exported package, but usually all the exported packages will share the same version as the owning bundle. There are some exceptions, but this generalization covers most cases.

`Import-Package` and `Export-Package` are the most important headers to specify when OSGi-ifying libraries, but there are a few others to take note of, especially those used to identify a bundle.

GIVING AN IDENTITY TO A BUNDLE

In an OSGi environment, a library must be properly identified, because dependency resolution in OSGi builds on bundle-identity mechanisms. We've looked at many manifest headers already, especially in chapter 2, so we won't describe all of them again. We'll focus on three here.

The following snippet (part of the Spring Core 2.5.6.A bundle manifest) shows these three manifest headers:

```
Bundle-SymbolicName: org.springframework.core
Bundle-Version: 2.5.6.A
Bundle-Name: Spring Core
```

The `Bundle-SymbolicName` header specifies a unique name for a bundle, usually based on the reverse package (or domain) convention. The header value can't contain any whitespace—only alphanumeric characters, periods (`.`), underscores (`_`), and hyphens (`-`). The `Bundle-SymbolicName` header is compulsory, it doesn't take a default value, and it must be set carefully because it's the main component of your bundle identity.

The other aspect of a bundle identity is its version, set with the `Bundle-Version` header. Unlike the `Bundle-SymbolicName` header, the version header isn't compulsory and it defaults to `0.0.0`, but it should *always* be explicitly set. When setting the bundle version, you should follow the format and semantics of OSGi versioning (major, minor, and micro numbers, and qualifier), as explained in chapter 2. The symbolic name and version tuple comprises the identity of your bundle: there can't be two bundles with the same symbolic name and version number installed at the same time in an OSGi container.

`Bundle-Name` isn't meant to be used directly by the OSGi platform but rather by developers, because it defines a human-readable name for the bundle. Its value can contain spaces and doesn't have to be unique (even though it should be, to avoid confusion). It needs to be explanatory enough.

Now that you've seen the theory behind the OSGi-ification of libraries, let's discuss putting this into practice and see the different ways to convert a plain JAR file into an OSGi bundle.

6.2.2   Converting by hand

Because the deployment unit in OSGi is the JAR file along with some metadata, the conversion boils down to carefully editing the MANIFEST.MF file. We've already discussed the manifest headers, but we should not forget the specifics of the JAR packaging:[1]

---

[1] You can find more about these requirements from the JAR file specification: http://java.sun.com/j2se/1.5.0/docs/guide/jar/jar.html.

- The META-INF/MANIFEST.MF file must be the first entry in the JAR, and the `jar` command enforces this rule (so you shouldn't try to package your OSGi bundles manually).

- The manifest format has strict requirements. For instance, lines can't be longer than 72 characters and the file should end with an empty line.

Given these requirements and the sensitive needs of OSGi metadata, manually editing an OSGi manifest can end up being a nightmare. A typo or extra space can break the manifest and be difficult to track down. Take a look at the manifest of each module in the Spring Framework and imagine the daunting task of maintaining each manually. Imagine doing this for a bunch of Java EE frameworks, like Hibernate or JavaServer Faces!

Manually editing manifests, without any support from tools, isn't a realistic or desirable undertaking. In the next section, we'll discuss tools that can help you to reliably package your OSGi bundles.

6.2.3 Converting using tools

You can't deny that your life as a developer wouldn't be the same without the tools you rely on every day. You'll also probably have strong opinions on tooling: developers should not become too dependent on their tools and should know exactly what these tools do for them under the covers.

Java and Java EE have a large set of tools, both commercial and open source: IDEs (for content assistance, debugging, and so on), build tools, continuous integration servers, and many more. The good news is that OSGi tooling is getting better and better. We'll focus in this section on tools that can help you package Java libraries into OSGi-compliant JAR files. We'll adopt a progressive approach: we'll start by using a command line tool, Bnd, and we'll end up including the OSGi-ification process into a Maven 2 build. The Apache Commons DBCP, the database connection pool library, will be our candidate library.

THE BND TOOL

Bnd (http://www.aqute.biz/Code/Bnd) is a tool created by Peter Kriens to help to analyze JAR files and to diagnose and create OSGi R4 bundles. It's used internally by the OSGi Alliance to create OSGi libraries for the various OSGi reference implementations and Technology Compatibility Kits (TCKs). Bnd consists of a unique JAR file but it can be used from the command line, as an Eclipse plug-in, or from Ant (yes, a JAR can be all of this). You already know from chapter 3 that the Felix Bundle Plugin for Maven is based on Bnd.

Are there any other tools than Bnd?

Bnd is arguably the most popular tool for packaging JARs as OSGi bundles, but OSGi tooling is getting more and more widespread. The latest rival for Bnd is Bundlor (http://www.springsource.org/bundlor), a tool created by the SpringSource team to automate the creation of OSGi bundles.

(continued)

Like Bnd, Bundlor analyzes class files to detect dependencies, but it's also able to parse different kinds of files to detect *more* dependencies: Spring application context XML files, JPA's persistence.xml, Hibernate mapping files, and even property files. Bundlor follows a template-based approach, which consists of giving hints for the manifest generation in the guise of a property file (the same approach used by Bnd). At the time of this writing, Bundlor is still quite new, but it can already be used with Ant and Maven 2. The use of Bundlor with Maven 2 is covered in appendix B.

OSGi also gets into your development environment: there has always been the Plug-in Development Environment (PDE) in Eclipse (http://www.eclipse.org/pde/), which enables the development of Eclipse plug-ins and offers some nice support for OSGi (such as a dedicated editor for manifest files). More recent is the SpringSource Tool Suite (STS), http://www.springsource.com/products/sts) a dedicated Eclipse distribution targeting the development of Spring- and SpringSource dm Server–based applications. As SpringSource dm Server applications rely heavily on OSGi, STS offers some support for OSGi. STS was once a commercial product but has been free since mid-2009.

In this section, we'll use Bnd from the command line to OSGi-ify Apache Commons DBCP 1.2.2. So let's get down to business! Download Bnd from http://www.aqute.biz/Code/Bnd, DBCP 1.2.2 from http://commons.apache.org/dbcp/, and copy the two JARs into a working directory (both JAR files are also available in the code samples for this book).

Why Apache Commons DBCP?

Commons DBCP is a very popular database connection pool: Apache Tomcat uses it to provide its data sources, and a lot of applications embed a DBCP connection pool (often as a Spring bean). Unfortunately, DBCP isn't yet among the OSGi-ified libraries of the Apache Commons family. Converting Commons DBCP is a good exercise, and it will prove to be useful, because we'll use our brand new OSGi-ified version in chapter 7.

Note that you should stick to the version of DBCP (and of its dependency, Commons Pool) that we're using in this book, because it's likely they will be distributed as OSGi bundles one day!

You can't convert a plain JAR file into an OSGi-compliant bundle without knowing a little about it. That's why Bnd comes with the print command:

```
java -jar bnd-0.0.313.jar print commons-dbcp-1.2.2.jar
```

Don't be overwhelmed by the output. It's divided into sections, and we're going to analyze the most important ones.

The first section provides information taken from the manifest:

```
[MANIFEST commons-dbcp-1.2.2.jar]
Ant-Version                             Apache Ant 1.5.3
Build-Jdk                               1.4.2_10
Built-By                                psteitz
Created-By                              Apache Maven
Extension-Name                          commons-dbcp
Implementation-Title                    org.apache.commons.dbcp
Implementation-Vendor                   The Apache Software Foundation
Implementation-Vendor-Id                org.apache
Implementation-Version                  1.2.2
Manifest-Version                        1.0
Package                                 org.apache.commons.dbcp
Specification-Title                     Commons Database Connection Pooling
Specification-Vendor                    The Apache Software Foundation
X-Compile-Source-JDK                    1.3
X-Compile-Target-JDK                    1.3
```

The more interesting section is the one starting with [USES], which delivers information about the Java packages of the target JAR:

```
[USES]
org.apache.commons.dbcp                 java.sql
                                        javax.naming
                                        javax.naming.spi
                                        javax.sql
                                        org.apache.commons.jocl
                                        org.apache.commons.pool
                                        org.apache.commons.pool.impl
                                        org.xml.sax
org.apache.commons.dbcp.cpdsadapter     java.sql
                                        javax.naming
                                        javax.naming.spi
                                        javax.sql
                                        org.apache.commons.dbcp
                                        org.apache.commons.pool
                                        org.apache.commons.pool.impl
(...)
```

We now know which packages our library depends on. The output ends with an error section:

```
One error
1 : Unresolved references to [javax.naming, javax.naming.spi,
javax.sql, org.apache.commons.pool, org.apache.commons.pool.im
pl, org.xml.sax, org.xml.sax.helpers] by class(es) on the Bund
le-Classpath[Jar:commons-dbcp-1.2.2.jar]: [org/apache/commons/
dbcp/datasources/PerUserPoolDataSource.class,(...)
```

With this monolithic block of text, Bnd tells us that, with respect to the current classpath, some packages that our library needs to work are missing. We can also see that Commons DBCP depends on the org.apache.commons.pool and org.apache.commons.pool.impl packages. Indeed, Commons DBCP relies on the Commons Pool library to handle its pooling algorithm and adds a thin layer on top of it for database connections.

This dependency means that we'll need to do two things in the OSGi-ification of Commons DBCP:

- Properly import packages from Commons Pool
- Have Commons Pool packaged as an OSGi bundle

We can immediately start the OSGi-ification with Bnd's `wrap` command:

```
java -jar bnd-0.0.313.jar wrap commons-dbcp-1.2.2.jar
```

This creates a `commons-dbcp-1.2.2.bar` file in the same directory, with an OSGi-compliant manifest and all the defaults for OSGi manifest headers. Unfortunately, Bnd can't guess the proper values for some important headers, and default values aren't always appropriate. That's why Bnd uses a configuration file to supply this information: version, symbolic name, imports, and exports can be defined in a way that's similar to the manifest format but more editor-friendly and more powerful, thanks to the use of variable substitutions and pattern matching.

Where do the .class files come from?

Bnd isn't a traditional packaging tool; it doesn't need as an input a directory containing `.class` files that it will compress in a JAR file. It directly locates `.class` files in the classpath and packages them into a JAR file. You can potentially include in your OSGi bundle all the `.class` files from the classpath you specified when launching Bnd from the command line.

The following snippet shows the Bnd configuration file for converting Commons DBCP into an OSGi bundle:

```
version=1.2.2                                              ❶
Bundle-SymbolicName: org.apache.commons.dbcp                   ❷
Bundle-Version: ${version}                                 ❸
Bundle-Name: Commons DBCP
Bundle-Description: DBCP connection pool
Export-Package: org.apache.commons.dbcp.*;                        ❹
⇨      version=${version}
Import-Package:org.apache.commons.pool.*;version=1.3.0,
⇨      org.apache.commons.dbcp*;version=${version},*;             ❺
⇨      resolution:=optional
```

Bnd allows variable substitution, so we use this feature for the version ❶ because it's needed at several places in the template. We then specify the bundle's symbolic name ❷ and the version ❸, using the `version` variable, with the `${variableName}` pattern. We also specify which packages the bundle will export ❹: notice that we use a wildcard (*) to specify that we want to export the `org.apache.commons.dbcp` package and all its subpackages. We use the `version` variable again to specify the version of the exported packages. Finally, we specify that the bundle imports version 1.3.0 of all the Commons Pool packages it references ❺. Notice that we import the

Commons DBCP packages with the same version, to ensure a consistent class space. The last wildcard refers to all the remaining packages used by Commons DBCP, and we mark them as optional.

> **NOTE** With Bnd, you should always define configurations from the most specific to the most general. If an element is matched twice, the first match always takes precedence. That's why the instruction to mark the dependencies as optional in our `Import-Package` header comes last.

Let's issue the `wrap` command again, but now with the `properties` option, to specify the Bnd configuration file:

```
java -jar bnd-0.0.313.jar wrap -properties commons-dbcp-1.2.2.bnd
➥    commons-dbcp-1.2.2.jar
```

We can now look at the manifest file of the generated OSGi bundle. Here's an excerpt showing the `Export-Package` and `Import-Package` headers:

```
(...)
Export-Package: org.apache.commons.dbcp.cpdsadapter;uses:="javax.namin
 g,javax.sql,org.apache.commons.pool.impl,org.apache.commons.pool,java
 x.naming.spi,org.apache.commons.dbcp";version="1.2.2",org.apache.comm
 ons.dbcp;uses:="org.apache.commons.pool.impl,org.apache.commons.pool,
 javax.sql,javax.naming,javax.naming.spi,org.xml.sax";version="1.2.2",
 org.apache.commons.dbcp.datasources;uses:="org.apache.commons.dbcp,ja
 vax.sql,org.apache.commons.pool,javax.naming,javax.naming.spi,org.apa
 che.commons.pool.impl";version="1.2.2"
(...)
Import-Package: javax.naming;resolution:=optional,javax.naming.spi;res
 olution:=optional,javax.sql;resolution:=optional,org.apache.commons.d
 bcp;version="1.2.2",org.apache.commons.dbcp.cpdsadapter;version="1.2.
 2",org.apache.commons.dbcp.datasources;version="1.2.2",org.apache.com
 mons.pool;version="1.3.0",org.apache.commons.pool.impl;version="1.3.0
 ",org.xml.sax;resolution:=optional,org.xml.sax.helpers;resolution:=op
 tional
```

Now you can compare the end result with the instructions we specified in the Bnd configuration file. As you can see, Bnd is a very convenient tool. You now have an OSGi-compliant version of Commons DBCP.

> **TIP** Because Commons DBCP isn't distributed as an OSGi bundle, a good practice is to include "osgi" in the filename: commons-dbcp-osgi-1.2.2.jar. If your bundle turns out to be distributed and is used by third parties, you can also prefix it with your company name: com.manning.commons-dbcp-osgi-1.2.2.jar.

We mentioned that we also need an OSGi-compliant version of Commons Pool, because Commons DBCP is built on this library. Unfortunately, Commons Pool isn't distributed as an OSGi bundle either, so we have to again do the conversion ourselves. It turns out to be fairly simple, because we can follow the same process as for Commons DBCP. The following snippet shows the Bnd configuration file for Commons Pool:

```
version=1.3.0
Bundle-SymbolicName=org.apache.commons.pool
Bundle-Version: ${version}
Export-Package: org.apache.commons.pool*;version=${version}
Bundle-Name: Commons Pool
```

Congratulations, you can now create database connection pools with Commons DBCP in an OSGi environment! But perhaps you're fond of automation; we'll look now at how to make the OSGi-ification part of a Maven build.

THE FELIX BUNDLE PLUGIN FOR MAVEN 2

You met the Felix Bundle Plugin in chapter 3, where we used it to package our first Spring DM bundles. We relied on Maven 2 to provision the Spring DM OSGi test framework. You'll get to know it better in this section, because we'll repeat the OSGi-ification of Commons DBCP, but in a 100 percent Maven 2 style this time.

The Felix Bundle Plugin provides integration between Bnd and Maven 2: the plug-in uses Bnd under the covers, providing it with information from the POM file. By using this plug-in, you can take advantage of all of Maven 2's features (automation, dependency management, standard project structure, and so on) and still package your project as OSGi-compliant bundles. The plug-in has reasonable default behavior, making the configuration simple for simple needs.

For the OSGi-ification of Commons DBCP, we start by creating a simple pom.xml file:

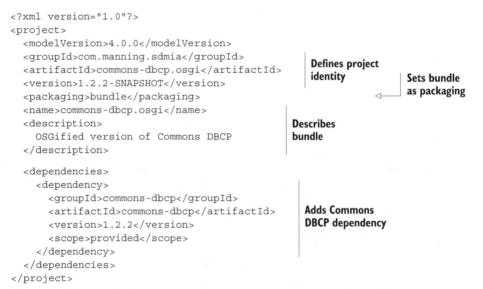

```
<?xml version="1.0"?>
<project>
  <modelVersion>4.0.0</modelVersion>
  <groupId>com.manning.sdmia</groupId>          Defines project
  <artifactId>commons-dbcp.osgi</artifactId>    identity        Sets bundle
  <version>1.2.2-SNAPSHOT</version>                              as packaging
  <packaging>bundle</packaging>
  <name>commons-dbcp.osgi</name>
  <description>                                  Describes
    OSGified version of Commons DBCP            bundle
  </description>

  <dependencies>
    <dependency>
      <groupId>commons-dbcp</groupId>
      <artifactId>commons-dbcp</artifactId>      Adds Commons
      <version>1.2.2</version>                   DBCP dependency
      <scope>provided</scope>
    </dependency>
  </dependencies>
</project>
```

Notice how we clearly state that the project is our own distribution of an OSGi bundle:

- The groupId refers to our company
- The artifactId is postfixed with osgi

Even if Bnd is wrapped in a Maven plug-in, it still bases its search for classes on the classpath, so we add Commons DBCP as a Maven dependency.

We now need to explicitly reference the Felix Bundle Plugin; otherwise the bundle packaging doesn't have any meaning for Maven 2. We do this inside the `build` tag (just before the `dependencies` tag), where we usually configure Maven 2 plug-ins. Listing 6.1 shows the configuration of the Felix Bundle Plugin for OSGi-ifying Commons DBCP.

Listing 6.1   Felix Bundle Plugin configuration for OSGi-ifying Commons DBCP

```
<build>
  <plugins>
    <plugin>
      <groupId>org.apache.felix</groupId>
      <artifactId>maven-bundle-plugin</artifactId>          ❶ Declares plug-in
      <version>2.0.1</version>
      <extensions>true</extensions>
      <configuration>
        <instructions>
          <Bundle-SymbolicName>                             ❷ Sets bundle's
            org.apache.commons.dbcp                            symbolic name
          </Bundle-SymbolicName>
          <Export-Package>
  org.apache.commons.dbcp*;version=${project.version}
          </Export-Package>
          <Import-Package>                                   ❸ Sets packages to
            org.apache.commons.pool*;version="1.3.0",          export and import
            *;resolution:=optional
          </Import-Package>
          <Embed-Dependency>                                 ❹ Instructs how to
            *;scope=provided;type=!pom;inline=true             handle dependencies
          </Embed-Dependency>
        </instructions>
      </configuration>
    </plugin>
  </plugins>
</build>
```

We start by declaring the plug-in ❶. Never omit the version of a plug-in with Maven 2 unless you want your build to break unpredictably.

The configuration starts with the `configuration` and `instructions` elements. We use the `Bundle-SymbolicName` tag to set the manifest header ❷. We then use the `Export-Package` instruction to define the Java packages the bundle will export ❸. Notice that we can use the same syntax as in Bnd files to include subpackages. This time, we didn't define a variable for the version, because we can refer to the project version directly with the `${project.version}` variable. We define imported packages the same way as in plain Bnd ❸. Finally, we use the `Embed-Dependency` tag to tell the plug-in how to handle dependencies ❹: include all dependencies with `provided` scope (but exclude dependencies of type POM) and copy them inline in the JAR.

All set! Any Maven packaging goal (`install` or `package`) will generate a 100 percent OSGi-compliant bundle.

NOTE   The Commons Pool library can also be easily OSGi-ified with the Felix Bundle Plugin.

OSGi-ifying a library and making the process part of a traditional build is fairly simple, thanks to the Felix Bundle Plugin. You just need to be careful with the generated OSGi metadata, and Bnd will handle the rest.

We've now talked a lot about converting existing libraries, but what about packaging our own modules and applications? We'll discuss this topic in the next section.

6.2.4   *Packaging your own modules as OSGi bundles*

If you understand how to OSGi-ify existing libraries, making your own Java applications and modules into OSGi bundles should not be a problem for you. You can apply all the OSGi-ification techniques we've covered so far to your own modules. You can stick to Bnd, choosing the mechanism that suits you best:

- Command line—Straight and simple, but difficult to automate
- Eclipse plug-in—Embedded in your development environment, but still difficult to automate
- Ant task—Included in your build, and perfect if Ant is your tool of choice for all your builds (this is covered in appendix C)
- Maven 2 plug-in—Included in your build, and fits perfectly with any Maven 2–based project

Packaging existing libraries or your own modules as OSGi bundles should not cause you any trouble now. Nevertheless, OSGi isn't only about packaging. It's also about *modularity*, and without good design, you'll have a hard time packaging your modules. That's why we'll discuss how to design OSGi enterprise applications and how to leverage Spring DM in the next section.

6.3   *Designing OSGi enterprise applications*

Designing OSGi enterprise applications isn't so different from developing "standard" enterprise applications: OSGi people don't pretend that the world was waiting for them in order to write modular applications. Nevertheless, anyone can learn from the strict modular approach of OSGi.

With plain Java, we can't really encapsulate our classes and interfaces; they can be used as long as they're on the classpath. The standard deployment unit in Java, the JAR file, is a convenient kind of packaging, but Java doesn't provide us with real dynamic deployment capabilities. Web (WAR) and enterprise (EAR) deployment units usually end up being monolithic, hard to split entities; they're too coarse-grained.

We, as enterprise application developers, have learned to get along with these pitfalls. But even if we managed to write well-designed, layered applications with Spring, we can still improve them and even take advantage—especially at runtime—of the way we designed them.

To see how OSGi can help to improve the design of a Java application, we'll progressively transform a standard web application packaged as a monolithic WAR file into a modular web application. Along the way, we'll also see how to introduce Spring DM into our OSGi design.

6.3.1 Organizing OSGi components

Let's start with a standard web application and reorganize it to obtain a truly modular, OSGi-compliant application.

ORGANIZING THE DEPENDENCIES

In Java, web applications are packaged as WAR files. The WAR structure is quite simple:

- It's a ZIP file
- Downloadable resources (images, JavaScript files) are located at the root of the WAR
- Application classes (servlet, web controllers) are located in WEB-INF/classes
- Libraries and frameworks (packaged as JAR files) are in WEB-INF/lib

Let's focus first on libraries and frameworks; this is the first place where OSGi can help, because the WAR packaging has some pitfalls. Web applications can embed these JAR files or let the application server provide them, as shown in figure 6.1. If the application server provides them, WAR files are smaller, and depending on the application server, the global memory footprint is also smaller.

This scenario, where the application server provides the libraries and frameworks, works well because both web applications depend on the same versions of the frameworks they use.

Figure 6.2 shows another scenario, where the production team said to the developing team: "Spring and Hibernate are provided by the application server, so don't embed them in the WAR." Unfortunately, application 2 needs different versions of Spring and Hibernate than those provided by the application server.

What would happen in figure 6.2, when the application server provides the libraries? Nobody knows. We'd have to cross our fingers and see. Application 1 has no reason not

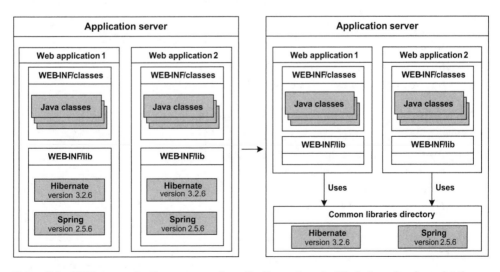

Figure 6.1 Within an application server, web applications can embed their dependencies or let the application server provide them.

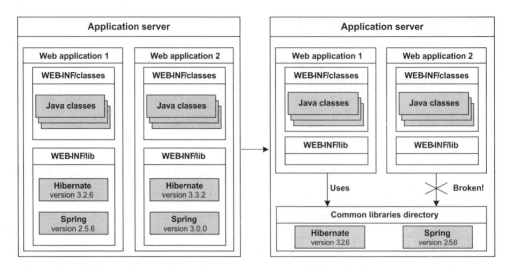

Figure 6.2   Application 2 uses different versions of Spring and Hibernate than those provided by the application server. It can't safely rely on these versions.

to work, but we can't know about application 2: perhaps it won't start, or maybe it'll fail when a user triggers an action that relies on Spring 3.0 or Hibernate 3.3.

On standard Java EE application servers, applications have no standard way to indicate that they depend on a particular version of a framework; these kinds of metadata don't exist in Java EE standards. We could try to check the version when the application starts, but this would be cumbersome, especially if we had to do the check for all of the dependencies. We could embed the libraries in the WAR (as shown in figure 6.3), but this could lead to unpredictable behavior, depending on the application server's classloading strategy and the version of the WAR-embedded and server-provided frameworks: classes could be partially loaded from different JAR files, or frameworks could try to dynamically detect some libraries (Hibernate does that with Hibernate Validator). We usually call this "JAR hell."

With OSGi, there is no room for approximation. Modules declare their dependencies, and the OSGi container is in charge of their resolution. We

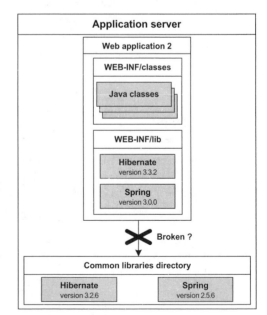

Figure 6.3   Application 2 tries to embed its dependencies. This can lead to unexpected behavior and hard-to-debug issues.

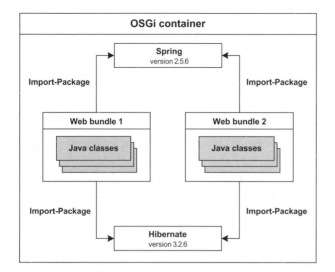

Figure 6.4 **In OSGi environments, modules explicitly declare their dependencies and don't embed them.**

don't need to write our own checks; the platform does it for us. If we fail to properly declare our module dependencies, shame on us.

The OSGi world is harsh, but in the end you'll benefit from this. Figure 6.4 shows how the two web applications can use the same libraries in an OSGi environment. Applications declare their dependencies, and the OSGi container does the classloader wiring to the respective dependency bundles.

Figure 6.4 demonstrates a simple scenario, so let's look at a more complex one, where applications don't rely on the same versions of frameworks, and we still want to share the dependencies among modules. This scenario is shown in figure 6.5.

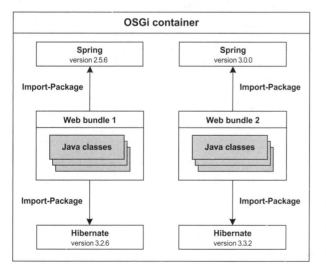

Figure 6.5 **In OSGi environments, different versions of the same modules can be deployed, and dependent modules declare which version they want to use.**

Thanks to its sophisticated classloading mechanisms, OSGi supports this scenario out of the box:
different versions of the same library can coexist in a
container.

We've looked at dependencies, so let's move on
and see how we can organize our application.

ORGANIZING THE APPLICATION

Enterprise applications are usually organized as a
stack of layers, where each layer has its own responsibilities and relies on the layer immediately below.
This layer organization encourages best programming practices, such as separation of concerns and
unit testing. The so-called domain layer is an exception: it represents business entities (customers, con-
tracts, and so on), which mainly carry data across the
layers. As such, domain entities are used in all the layers. Figure 6.6 pictures a layered application.

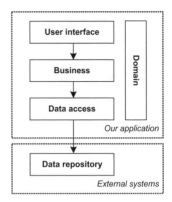

**Figure 6.6 Enterprise
applications are layered, for a
better separation of concerns.**

Domain-driven design versus the anemic domain model

Saying that domain classes carry only data is a bold statement—they can also contain behavior in the form of business-oriented methods. Layering applications is
good, but, applied in a simplistic way, it can lead to poorly designed enterprise applications, whose structure becomes closer to procedural programming than real OOP.
This is especially true for the domain classes, which are then limited to data-transfer
tasks. Such a domain layer is commonly referred to as an *anemic domain model*. Domain-driven design promotes rich domain models, where some parts of the business
logic are embedded in the domain classes.

OSGi, layered applications, and domain-driven design can cohabit, but comprehensive
coverage of these topics is far beyond the scope of this book. If you want to learn
more about the common pitfalls that too-strict layering can lead to, we recommend
Martin Fowler's article about the anemic domain model (http://www.martinfowler.
com/bliki/AnemicDomainModel.html).

How can we translate the layer concept into Java? We accomplish this by using the simplest constructs of Java—classes and interfaces—as shown in the UML diagram in figure 6.7. (This is about the design; at runtime, we'll need a little help from a
lightweight container like Spring.)

The next question is how to split our OSGi bundles, now that our design tells us
more about our dependencies? The answer is the one we usually don't like: it
depends. It depends on various factors, such as these:

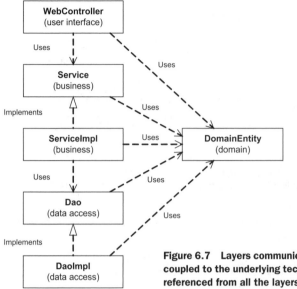

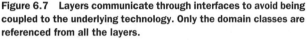

Figure 6.7   **Layers communicate through interfaces to avoid being coupled to the underlying technology. Only the domain classes are referenced from all the layers.**

- How we organize development and teams (this isn't related to OSGi)
- How modules are designed to evolve and be developed, updated, and refactored
- How modules are meant to be reused by other modules
- How we want to expose services (business services, data access objects, and so on), and how we want to encapsulate and hide inner mechanisms
- How many implementations of the same service are going to be deployed

OSGi static and dynamic features offer so much power that we have a choice of virtually unlimited combinations! Some combinations are good, but others should be avoided, so let's see some guidelines.

The first tip when developing OSGi applications is to separate the static components from the dynamic components.

- *Static components* are bundles that define APIs by exporting interface-based Java packages. These bundles don't contain a Spring application context (or a `BundleActivator`) and don't register or reference any OSGi services.
- *Dynamic components* are bundles that import Java packages from static bundles, provide implementations, and usually register OSGi services. As this is a Spring DM book, these bundles are Spring-powered.

Figure 6.8 illustrates the pattern of splitting static and dynamic components.

Generally, static components should be stable, changing infrequently, whereas dynamic components can be frequently updated and benefit from OSGi dynamic features such as on-the-fly service updating. Section 6.4, which deals with Spring DM and OSGi dynamic features, will explain just how using Spring DM is relevant to

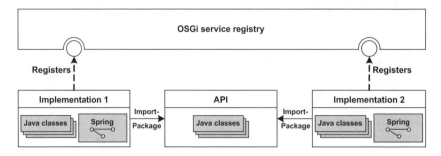

Figure 6.8   Static parts of an application (such as the API) and dynamic parts (the implementations) should always be deployed in different bundles within an OSGi environment. This helps the application to benefit from the dynamic features of OSGi.

implementing those dynamic components—the framework takes care of all the dirty work during bundle updates.

Now, let's see how we can apply this pattern to our enterprise application. The most extreme modular approach would consist in developing

- One bundle for each layer that has only classes (the domain and web layers)
- Two bundles for each layer that has interfaces and class implementations (the data access and business layers)

This approach could be labeled the "So you want modularity" approach, and it's shown in figure 6.9.

The approach shown in figure 6.9 is the most flexible: you can update any part of your application, and other modules can be built on top of any of yours by importing your packages and defining other implementations. Also note that by using Spring

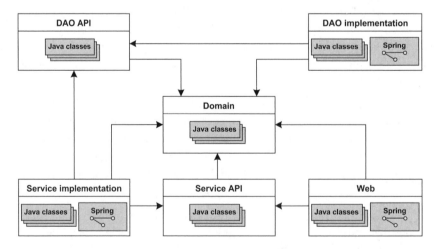

Figure 6.9   Organizing bundles in the "So you want modularity" way. There's at least one bundle for each layer, and two bundles if the layer has an API and implementation classes. (Arrows represent the `Import-Package` manifest header.)

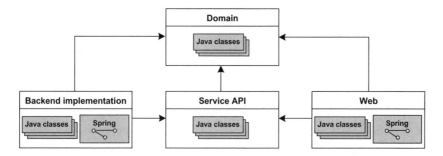

Figure 6.10 Organizing the bundles in a SOA way, the backend bundle hides its internal functioning. (Arrows represent the `Import-Package` manifest header.)

DM for implementation bundles, you benefit from dependency injection and all the enterprise support of the Spring Framework (data access, transaction management, and so on). One of the drawbacks of this approach is that you have to maintain of lot of bundles, usually as separate projects.

That approach gives us flexibility, but what if we don't want or don't need it? Perhaps exporting the packages of data access object (DAO) interfaces is useless, because what we're really interested in is the business services. Remember, OSGi is sometimes referred to as a service-oriented architecture (SOA) in a JVM. We can still define the service API, but the implementation can hide its inner workings. We can then reorganize our bundles in a simpler way and gather the service implementation and data access layer in the same bundle—the backend bundle.

Taking this approach doesn't change the logical organization of our application, as it's still a layered application; we just changed its physical organization. Figure 6.10 illustrates this new organization.

The SOA approach is no less flexible than the extremely modular approach. If DAOs and business services follow the same development and deployment cycles, there is no point in splitting them into different bundles.

We know now that the way we organize bundles is a question of balance. We've mainly discussed how bundles are *statically* linked by their dependencies, but we haven't considered how bundles communicate with each other using OSGi's service layer. That's the topic of the next section.

6.3.2 Defining interactions between application bundles

In our enterprise application, Java packages can be shared between bundles because of the `Export-Package` and `Import-Package` headers in their manifests. Nevertheless, Java packages aren't enough; an application needs real Java objects to run, and these objects must be registered as services in the OSGi registry. That's where Spring DM comes in.

Spring DM will instantiate and wire beans in our bundles and register them in the registry based on declarations in the context file. We'll end up not writing a single line

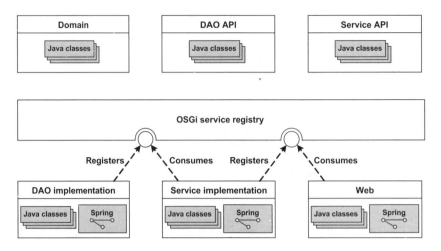

Figure 6.11   Spring DM helps implementation bundles to share OSGi services.

of code related to OSGi. (We'll see later that Spring DM will even handle OSGi's dynamic behavior for us.)

Let's again take our extreme modular approach from the previous section and focus on the service dependencies—we'll ignore dependencies related to Java packages for now. The implementation bundles are backed by Spring DM and can easily register or consume services (see figure 6.11).

In this scenario, if other bundles need to use our DAOs, they can easily consume them, regardless of whether or not they're Spring-powered bundles. Remember that our OSGi services are created by the Spring lightweight container, and as such, they can benefit from dependency injection or AOP. They can become transactional or get automatic database-connection handling with a few lines of XML or by inserting a couple of Java annotations. These are some of the benefits of using Spring DM.

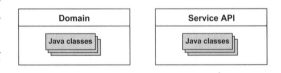

Now, let's fall back to our simpler SOA approach. It works in much the same way, but the backend bundle has a bigger Spring application context because it hosts DAOs and business services. In this scenario, DAOs can't be consumed by other bundles, because the only entry point is embodied by the business services. The SOA scenario from the OSGi service layer's point of view is shown in figure 6.12.

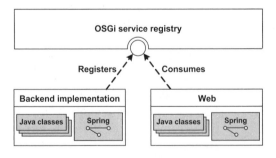

Figure 6.12   The SOA approach implies fewer registered services and offers better encapsulation.

What should we remember about the way bundles communicate? Mainly that there is still no simple answer and that we need to find a compromise between what we want to offer and what we want to hide. Generally speaking, we should only expose what is useful and is *prepared* to be used as a service: you should not let your system be compromised because a poorly written service isn't used the way it was meant to be.

In any event, Spring DM will be your friend when it comes to registering or consuming services. You'll like Spring DM even more when you see in the next section how it helps you handle dynamic behavior in OSGi.

6.4 How Spring DM handles OSGi applications' dynamic behavior

Within OSGi, services can appear and disappear at any time. This dynamic behavior is specific to OSGi; it's sophisticated and powerful but more complicated to deal with than static services.

Tracking services using plain OSGi is quite painful and error prone. The best tool OSGi offers for this task is the `ServiceTracker`, which accomplishes a lot, but we want more! When using the `ServiceTracker`, we still need to write code, and we're tied to the OSGi API. Moreover, we have to write the same kind of tracking code over and over.

That's where Spring DM comes in. You saw in the previous chapter that with Spring DM you can register and consume services declaratively. This looks static at first sight, but Spring DM handles all the dynamics for you, adopting a reasonable default behavior in most cases—default behavior that you can override.

In this section, we'll discuss typical cases related to OSGi's dynamic behavior and how Spring DM can help you deal properly and reliably with them. These cases range from the appearance and disappearance of a service or collection of services to the dynamic update of your modules.

6.4.1 Dealing with the appearance or disappearance of services

Spring DM's support for referencing services comes in two flavors: *individual,* when you need only one service matching a given description, and *collection,* when you want to have all the services that match some criteria. In enterprise applications, the individual case is the most common: a business service needs only one OSGi service implementing a given DAO interface. Spring DM is able to transparently handle service appearance and disappearance for both individual and collections of service references. We'll cover the mechanics of both flavors here.

When Spring DM's transparent management isn't enough, because you need to track services more carefully, Spring DM offers a simple POJO-oriented solution to react to the binding and unbinding of services. We'll also cover this topic, using a Swing application to illustrate it.

DEALING WITH AN INDIVIDUAL SERVICE REFERENCE

Let's go back to our enterprise application, using the extreme modular approach. Imagine it involves retrieving users from the database, so we'll have a user DAO, created and wired in a Spring-powered bundle, and registered as an OSGi service by Spring DM:

```
<bean id="contactDao"
      class="com.manning.sdmia.directory.dao.jdbc.
    ContactDaoJdbc">
  <property name="dataSource" ref="dataSource" />
</bean>
```

Creates and injects DAO

```
<osgi:service
  id="contactDaoOsgi"
  interface="com.manning.sdmia.directory.dao.
    ContactDao"
  ref="contactDao" />
```

Registers DAO as OSGi service

This contact DAO is meant to be imported and used by business services, such as the contact business service, defined in another Spring-powered bundle:

```
<osgi:reference
  id="contactDao"
  interface="com.manning.sdmia.directory.dao.
    ContactDao">
```

Imports DAO from OSGi registry

```
<bean id="contactService"
      class="com.manning.sdmia.directory.service.impl.
                ContactServiceImpl">
  <property name="contactDao" ref="contactDao" />
</bean>
```

Injects DAO into business service

In this scenario, there is only one OSGi service implementing the `ContactDao` interface, and it will be imported by the service. If there is more than one, Spring DM will pick one by following a predetermined strategy. If the choice doesn't suit the business service, that's too bad. It should have given Spring DM enough information to pick the right service.

But what happens if there's no OSGi service implementing the `ContactDao` interface? This could happen if the business service bundle is deployed in the OSGi container and the data access bundle isn't. In this scenario, Spring DM will figure out that the Spring application context of the business service bundle has a missing dependency, and it will defer the application context startup until the dependency is satisfied, which means when an OSGi service implementing the `ContactDao` interface is registered. If this condition isn't met after 5 minutes, Spring DM will throw an exception. This is the Spring DM default behavior: references are mandatory, and all mandatory references must be resolved before an application context can start. We covered how to change this default behavior in chapter 4, by using the `timeout` directive of the `Spring-Context` header.

This is reasonable default behavior, but what if the business service bundle doesn't contain only the user business service but critical business services that need to be available as soon as possible? They would be unavailable because the user business service doesn't have this unique dependency.

You can resolve this issue by making the reference to the contact DAO optional, by using the `availability` attribute of the `reference` tag:

```
<osgi:reference
  id="contactDao"
  interface="com.manning.sdmia.directory.dao.ContactDao"
  availability="optional" />
```

Now the business service application context will start up even if there is no contact DAO available in the OSGi service registry.

The user business service delegates data access operations to the `contactDao`, so what happens if the user business service handles an incoming request and calls the `contactDao`? Well, nothing. The call will block until a contact DAO service is registered. This behavior makes sense: the overall system isn't in a nominal state, and the missing dependency should not be missing for long, so we can wait until it appears.

All of this is handled by Spring DM, which injected a proxy into the user business service in place of the user DAO. This proxy blocks when someone tries to call it, but as soon as the target OSGi service (the contact DAO, in this example) appears on the service registry, the proxy delegates all the calls to it.

So far we've been talking about startup, but services can appear and disappear after the OSGi container has been started. Let's imagine the container reached its steady state a long time ago and that the DAO service then disappears. Any reference to it can be replaced on the fly if Spring DM finds a replacement for it. Finding this replacement will depend on the filter the importing bundle declared when it imported the DAO and on the availability of a matching service.

As you can see, in the case of an individual service reference, Spring DM handles most of the dynamic behavior. It does provide some opportunity for tuning, but the defaults should fit in most cases.

Let's now discuss the case of a collection of service references.

DEALING WITH A COLLECTION OF SERVICE REFERENCES

We learned in chapter 5 that with Spring DM we can declaratively reference collections of OSGi services, thanks to the `list` and `set` tags of the `osgi` namespace. Collections of services are interesting for the parts of an application that can be extended with additional services or for implementing observer-based patterns like the whiteboard pattern, where a central component (the whiteboard) periodically needs a snapshot of all the available services that meet some requirements (the listeners). What can Spring DM do about the content of these collections when services appear or disappear?

In fact, Spring DM populates the collections as needed. It adds matching services to the collection, and when one of the services referenced in the collection is unregistered from the OSGi registry, Spring DM automatically removes the reference from the collection. Note, though, that this is only valid for collections (java.util.List and java.util.Set) that are managed by Spring DM. Indeed, Spring DM can't track service appearances and disappearances and update collections that it doesn't totally control.

This is good news: we can use our collections of service references as any other collections. We usually use collections by iterating over them, using `Iterators`, but there's one important thing to know when iterating over a collection of service references managed by Spring DM: even the `Iterator` is dynamic. Imagine you start iterating over a collection of service references, and its content changes during the iteration because some services were unregistered and some matching services were registered. With Spring DM, you'll be aware of this immediately, because the `Iterator` will reflect these changes dynamically.

Thanks to Spring DM's transparent dynamic management, we're now well prepared to deal with the appearance or disappearance of services. Nevertheless, the support for the dynamic side of OSGi would be incomplete if we could not easily *track* services and react accordingly.

REACTING TO THE APPEARANCE AND DISAPPEARANCE OF SERVICES

In plain OSGi, the `ServiceTracker` is the Holy Grail for the developer who wants to track services. But despite its unquestionable usefulness, the `ServiceTracker` implies the use of the OSGi API and needs to be registered programmatically, which means writing a `BundleActivator`. This quickly becomes cumbersome, especially if we need to track services in many bundles.

We saw in chapter 5 that, when referencing a service (either with the `reference`, `list`, or `set` tags), we can attach a listener that will be warned when a matching service is registered or unregistered. This can be done with the `listener` tag of the `osgi` namespace. This is powerful, because an importing bundle can easily react to the appearance or disappearance of one or more matching services.

The next question is how do we deal with the generated events? Let's take as an example a Swing program, the Paint application.

> **NOTE**   The Paint application is the "official" Apache Felix demonstration application, used to illustrate how OSGi helps to create dynamic and extensible applications. It was written by Richard S. Hall, the founder of the Apache Felix project and co-author of *OSGi in Action.*

The Paint application is a Swing application that allows you to choose shapes from a toolbar and lay them on a painting area. The different kinds of shapes are represented by the `SimpleShape` interface, which has several implementations: `CircleShape`, `SquareShape`, `TriangleShape`, and so on. Figure 6.13 shows the UI of the Paint application.

The design of the Paint application is simple: a `DrawingFrame` handles the

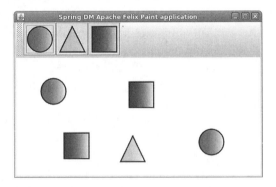

Figure 6.13   The Paint application

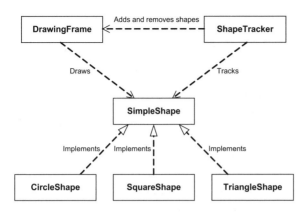

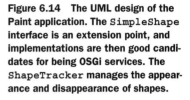

Figure 6.14 The UML design of the Paint application. The `SimpleShape` interface is an extension point, and implementations are then good candidates for being OSGi services. The `ShapeTracker` manages the appearance and disappearance of shapes.

user interaction and the drawing of the shapes, and a `ShapeTracker` tracks the different kinds of shapes available and notifies the `DrawingFrame` of their appearance or disappearance. Figure 6.14 illustrates the design of the Paint application with a UML diagram.

The dynamic part of the Paint application rests in the availability or unavailability of shapes. If a new shape implementation appears in the system, it should be automatically added to the toolbar. Conversely, if a shape disappears from the system, it should be automatically removed from the toolbar. Shapes can be seen as contributions to an extension point and are therefore good candidates for OSGi services. We can easily infer the organization of our application as OSGi bundles, as shown in figure 6.15.

If a bundle wants to contribute to the Paint application, it has to define an implementation of the `SimpleShape` interface and publish the instance in the OSGi registry. Here is the `SimpleShape` interface:

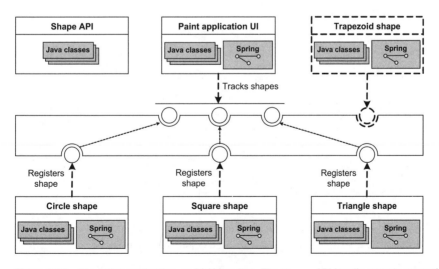

Figure 6.15 The Paint application as OSGi bundles. The `Shape` API bundle exports essential packages; the Paint application UI and `Shape` implementation bundles are Spring-powered.

```
package com.manning.sdmia.paint.shape;

import java.awt.Graphics2D;
import java.awt.Point;

public interface SimpleShape {

  public static final String NAME_PROPERTY =
      "simple.shape.name";
  public static final String ICON_PROPERTY =
      "simple.shape.icon";

  public void draw(Graphics2D g2, Point p);
}
```

Service property key for the shape name

Service property key for the shape icon

Method to implement to draw shape

The bundle of a `SimpleShape` implementation leverages the Spring lightweight container to declare the shape as a bean and Spring DM to export the bean to the service registry. Here is an excerpt from the book's code samples, which shows how to export the square shape implementation as an OSGi service:

```
<osgi:service
    ref="squareShape"
    interface="com.manning.sdmia.paint.shape.
      SimpleShape">
  <osgi:service-properties>
    <entry key-ref="nameProperty" value="square"/>
    <entry key-ref="iconProperty"
          value-ref="squareIcon"/>
  </osgi:service-properties>
</osgi:service>
```

Exports squareShape bean to OSGi service registry

Defines name and icon property

The bundle of the Paint application is interested in `SimpleShape` services and wants to know when some are registered or unregistered. It then uses the `list` tag to import `SimpleShape` services and the inner `listener` tag with the callback methods plugged into its `ShapeTracker`:

```
<osgi:list
    id="shapes"
    availability="optional"
    interface="com.manning.sdmia.paint.shape.
      SimpleShape" >
  <osgi:listener ref="shapeTracker"
              bind-method="addingShape"
              unbind-method="removedShape" />
</osgi:list>

<bean id="shapeTracker"
      class="com.manning.sdmia.paint.ShapeTracker">
  <property name="drawingFrame" ref="drawingFrame" />
</bean>
```

Imports SimpleShape services

Registers shape tracker as listener

With this configuration, Spring DM calls the `addingShape` or `removedShape` method of the `ShapeTracker` when a shape service is registered or unregistered respectively.

The `ShapeTracker` will have to do all the dirty work, but OSGi dynamics are no longer part of its concern; it can focus on the update of the UI. Here are the two callback methods, free from any reference to the OSGi API:

```
public class ShapeTracker {
  (...)
  public Object addingShape(
      SimpleShape shape, Map properties) {
    processShapeOnEventThread(ADDED, properties, shape);        Bind method
    return shape;
  }

  public void removedShape(
      SimpleShape shape, Map properties) {
    processShapeOnEventThread(REMOVED, properties,             Unbind method
      shape);
  }
  (...)
}
```

This means that the application will work properly and can be tested outside of an OSGi environment, which is very convenient. Moreover, the application class (the `ShapeTracker`) is relieved of the burden of OSGi dynamics, because Spring DM handles most of the complex plumbing. `Shape` services can appear or disappear, and the UI is updated on the fly, as shown in figure 6.16, where the square shape service has been removed from the registry.

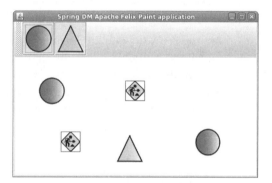

Figure 6.16   The square shape service has been unregistered. It's removed from the toolbar and drawn squares are replaced by "under construction" icons, all of this on the fly.

The Paint application is the perfect example of using OSGi services as an extension mechanism. With the dynamic features of OSGi and a little help from Spring DM, tracking services becomes easy, without any references to the OSGi API.

In the next section, we'll continue with dynamics and see how Spring DM handles the updating of bundles.

6.4.2   *Providing a new version of a component*

One of the major features of OSGi is its capacity to dynamically update components, without stopping the container. If we take our application in its extreme modular form, we can stop the DAO implementation bundle, install a new version, update the bundle, and restart it without redeploying or updating dependant bundles.

As you saw previously, if calls are made on the DAO service reference, Spring DM lets them block until it reappears, and as soon as Spring DM registers the new version

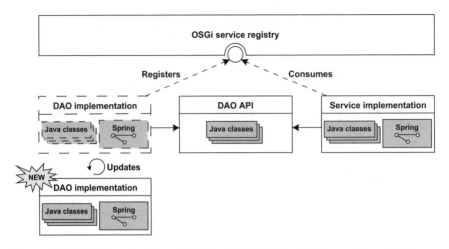

Figure 6.17   Updating an implementation bundle. With Spring DM, the service update happens transparently, and dependant bundles don't need to be restarted.

of the DAO, dependant Spring-powered bundles will import the new reference. This is a common update operation, and the dynamic, on-the-fly service replacement works out of the box with Spring DM. This is one benefit of following the pattern of splitting static and dynamic parts of an application. Figure 6.17 illustrates this kind of update.

How can you update a service like this? Let's do it with Equinox. You start by issuing the ss command to find the DAO implementation bundle:

```
osgi> ss

Framework is launched.

id  State        Bundle
0   ACTIVE       org.eclipse.osgi_3.5.0.v20090520
1   ACTIVE       com.manning.sdmia.ch06.directory-datasource_1.0.0
2   ACTIVE       com.manning.sdmia.ch06.directory-domain_1.0.0
3   ACTIVE       com.manning.sdmia.ch06.directory-modular-dao_1.0.0
4   ACTIVE       com.manning.sdmia.ch06.directory-modular-dao-jdbc_1.0.0
5   ACTIVE       com.manning.sdmia.ch06.directory-service_1.0.0
6   ACTIVE       com.manning.sdmia.ch06.directory-modular-service-impl_1.0.0
7   ACTIVE       com.manning.sdmia.ch06.directory-web_1.0.0
(...)
```

As you can see, the DAO implementation bundle is bundle number 4 (shown in bold). Let's stop it and uninstall it:

```
osgi> stop 4

osgi> uninstall 4
```

This is the point at which Spring DM blocks calls on OSGi services that were registered by the bundle and imported by Spring-powered bundles (the business service implementation bundle, for example). You can then install a new version of the DAO implementation bundle and start it:

```
osgi> install
        file:./com.manning.sdmia.ch06.directory-modular-dao-jdbc_1.0.1.jar
Bundle id is 44

osgi> start 44
```

As soon as the new version of the bundle registers a `contactDao` OSGi service, Spring DM will send it the blocked calls, so that the waiting incoming requests can be processed.

A less common but still relevant situation is what happens when the DAO disappears but can be replaced. This means that there are one or more OSGi services that can suit the importing bundles. In this case, Spring DM will automatically switch to the next best replacement, observing the filters of the dependant bundles.

This kind of update works well for black-box components, meaning components that don't export any packages and just provide services. These are what we previously called the *dynamic components* of our OSGi applications. But what about the static components of an application? In our DAO-based example, the static part is the DAO API, which the DAO implementation and service implementation bundles depend on. Usually, if we ship a new version of the DAO API bundle, it will come with a new version of the DAO implementation and the service implementation bundles, which benefit from the API updates. Simple update operations won't be enough in this case, because implementation bundles need to be wired to the new version of the API bundle classes. For this wiring to happen, you need to *refresh* the DAO API bundle, and the OSGi framework will handle the refresh of dependant bundles.

To summarize, when updating the DAO API bundle, we'll have to go through these steps:

1 Stop the DAO API, DAO implementation, and service implementation bundles.
2 Install the new versions.
3 Update the bundles.
4 Refresh the DAO API bundle (the OSGi framework will then automatically refresh all the bundles that import Java packages exported by the DAO API bundle).
5 Start the DAO API bundle.

Figure 6.18 illustrates this procedure.

When updating an API bundle, the precise procedure is the hardest part, because Spring DM handles the Spring application context startup order, service registration, and importing. If you carefully design and organize your OSGi application components, Spring DM will manage the complex technical jobs.

That's it for dealing with OSGi dynamics. You now know all the techniques and tricks to benefit from this unique OSGi feature!

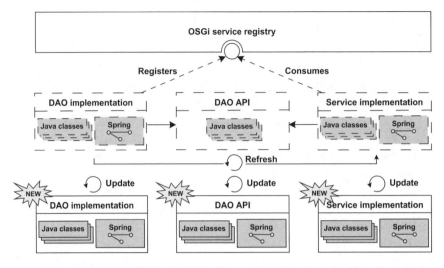

Figure 6.18   Updating an API bundle. It implies updating, but also refreshing, dependant bundles to wire them with the new classes.

6.5   *Summary*

You should now have a good understanding of the right way to write OSGi-based enterprise applications.

The first step is to have OSGi-compliant JAR files. More and more libraries and frameworks are packaged as OSGi bundles, but alternatively you can rely on OSGi repositories or handle the OSGi-ification yourself, building your own repository or even making your OSGi bundles available to the global OSGi-ification effort.

The second step is to properly design your OSGi applications and understand how to benefit from OSGi specificities. If you're on your own for the design, Spring DM is a great help for filling in the gap between OSGi and traditional application development. It's able to handle transparently most of the dynamics-related issues, and it allows you to retain a POJO-based development style.

We'll continue with enterprise application development, as the next chapter is dedicated to a topic without which enterprise applications wouldn't be the same: access to relational databases with Spring DM.

Data access
in OSGi with Spring DM

7

This chapter covers

- Accessing data from relational databases with Spring DM
- Using JDBC and JPA with Spring DM
- Avoiding specific pitfalls and resolving problems when using JPA with Spring DM
- Implementing transactions within OSGi applications with Spring DM
- Using the "open element in view" pattern, within OSGi applications with Spring DM

In the previous chapter, we showed you how to prepare third-party frameworks and libraries for use in an OSGi environment and how to organize the bundles of your enterprise applications. You also saw that developing enterprise applications with OSGi is slightly different than for classical Java applications, especially with regards to data access.

In this chapter, we'll focus on this last topic and describe how to implement data access components using standard Java technologies, such as Java Database Connectivity (JDBC) and Java Persistence API (JPA), within an OSGi environment using Spring DM. OSGi has some constraints regarding the implementation of these technologies, and we'll look at how to address them and the pitfalls to avoid.

The last subject we'll tackle in this chapter is that of transactions. We'll see how to use Spring DM and the OSGi service registry to make transactions work smoothly.

7.1 Using JDBC within OSGi with Spring DM

JDBC is the foundation for accessing relational databases from Java applications. It provides an abstraction that hides the specifics of interacting with different kinds of databases, and it allows you to specify SQL queries to get or update data. JDBC provides a robust foundation for applications to persist their data.

Using JDBC within OSGi has particular constraints, especially with respect to the JDBC driver. In this section, we'll describe how to make JDBC work in OSGi and how to organize OSGi applications that use it.

7.1.1 JDBC concepts

JDBC is a Java technology that makes it possible to interact with relational databases using the SQL language for querying and updating data. The technology was designed to keep things simple and provide an independent way of interacting with databases. It provides an abstraction over the specifics of different databases by using a driver to implement the actual communication with a specific database, as shown in figure 7.1. But JDBC doesn't provide solutions to handle the specifics of SQL—this is left up to the client application.

The public API for interacting with databases is provided directly in Java SE within the `java.sql` package. This package provides the key abstractions corresponding to connections, statements, result sets, and metadata, as listed in table 7.1.

Listing 7.1 shows an example of using JDBC to execute a SQL select request from a Java application. This listing implements best practices to correctly release resources. JDBC leaves the release of resources up to the application rather than trying to handle it transparently.

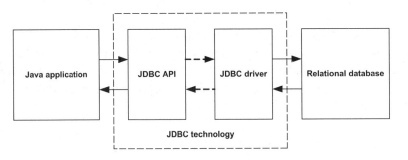

Figure 7.1 The general JDBC architecture, illustrating how the JDBC API uses a driver when accessing a relational database

Table 7.1 Common entities provided by JDBC

JDBC abstraction	Description
Connection	Corresponds to the connection to the database, allowing the execution of SQL requests and being responsible for handling local transactions
Statement	Corresponds to the core abstraction for executing all kinds of SQL requests
PreparedStatement	Corresponds to an advanced statement that supports precompiled SQL queries and parameter specification
CallableStatement	Corresponds to a kind of statement enabling you to execute stored procedures with JDBC
ResultSet	Allows for the parsing of data received on the execution of a SQL query
DatabaseMetaData	Provides access to metadata of the target database
ResultSetMetaData	Provides access to metadata about the types and properties of the columns contained in a result set

Listing 7.1 Using JDBC to execute a SQL select request

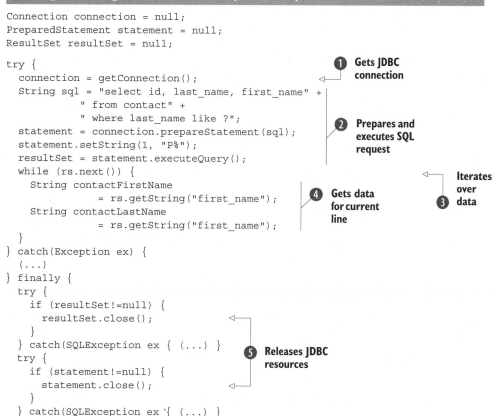

```
Connection connection = null;
PreparedStatement statement = null;
ResultSet resultSet = null;

try {
  connection = getConnection();                        ❶ Gets JDBC
  String sql = "select id, last_name, first_name" +       connection
          " from contact" +
          " where last_name like ?";
  statement = connection.prepareStatement(sql);        ❷ Prepares and
  statement.setString(1, "P%");                           executes SQL
  resultSet = statement.executeQuery();                   request
  while (rs.next()) {                                                    ❸ Iterates
    String contactFirstName                                                over
            = rs.getString("first_name");    ❹ Gets data                   data
    String contactLastName                      for current
            = rs.getString("first_name");       line
  }
} catch(Exception ex) {
  (...)
} finally {
  try {
    if (resultSet!=null) {
      resultSet.close();
    }
  } catch(SQLException ex { (...) }        ❺ Releases JDBC
  try {                                       resources
    if (statement!=null) {
      statement.close();
    }
  } catch(SQLException ex { (...) }
  try {
```

```
    if (connection!=null) {                    ⑤  Releases JDBC
      connection.close();                          resources
    }
  } catch(SQLException ex { (...) }
}
```

Listing 7.1 shows a classic way of using JDBC to execute SQL requests for both querying and updating data. We first obtain a JDBC connection ❶ enabling us to create a statement to execute SQL requests ❷. We create a JDBC prepared statement, allowing us to use a parameterized SQL request. In our example, the request gets contacts whose names begin with the letter *P.* We also set parameters on the prepared statement. We can then execute the request, get the corresponding result set, and iterate over it ❸ to get data contained in its current line ❹. Finally we need to release all the JDBC resources ❺.

An extension to JDBC is also available to provide additional support for server-side usage through the `javax.sql` package. The more well-known interface of this extension is the `DataSource` interface, which corresponds to a connection factory and is commonly used by pool implementations. The Spring Framework also provides implementations of the `DataSource` interface within its JDBC support.

We won't discuss the details of JDBC any further, because it's beyond the scope of this book, but we will concentrate on using it within an OSGi environment. We'll also look at how to use JDBC within enterprise applications when using Spring DM.

7.1.2 *JDBC issues when used within OSGi*

The underlying implementation of JDBC is the driver, which consists of the middleware between the Java application and the target database. This driver is database-specific and implements communication protocols necessary to communicate with the database server. The driver contract is specified in the JDBC specification through the `Driver` interface, as shown in the following snippet:

```
public interface Driver {                              Checks if driver can
  boolean acceptsURL(String url);                       handle JDBC URL
  Connection connect(String url, Properties info);  ◄─┐
  int getMajorVersion();                                │  Creates connection
  int getMinorVersion();                                │  with database
  DriverPropertyInfo[] getPropertyInfo(String url, Properties info);
  boolean jdbcCompliant();
}
```

But what, then, is the issue with using JDBC in OSGi and Spring DM?

The central class when using JDBC in common Java applications is the `DriverManager` class. You've probably written code similar to the following snippet many times:

```
Class.forName("org.h2.Driver");
Connection connection = DriverManager.getConnection(
                        "jdbc:h2:tcp://localhost/springdm-directory",
                        "sa", "");
```

The driver class name is loaded using the static `forName` method of the `Class` class. The driver can then be used to create a JDBC connection using the `DriverManager` class's static `getConnection` method.

How does `DriverManager` know about the specific JDBC driver code? The driver automatically registers with the `DriverManager` class using a static code block in the driver's implementation class.

The problem is that the `DriverManager` class uses classloaders in a specific way that can have strange side effects within an OSGi container. The class internally checks whether the caller class is able to instantiate the driver class, and if the caller doesn't have the required package imports in its manifest configuration, unexpected `Class-NotFoundException` exceptions can occur. To avoid this check, it's better to not use the `DriverManager` class within an OSGi container.

The alternative is to use the driver interface directly to obtain a JDBC connection, as shown in the following snippet. Note that Spring's `ClassUtils` and `BeanUtils` classes can be used to safely instantiate a JDBC driver from within an OSGi container.

```
Class driverClass = ClassUtils.resolveClassName(          ⟵┐ Loads and
            driverClassName, ClassUtils.getDefaultClassLoader());   ⟩ obtains
Driver driver = (Driver) BeanUtils.instantiateClass(      ⟵┘ driver
                               driverClass);

Properties properties = new Properties();
properties.put("user", userName);
properties.put("password", password);                     │ Sets properties and
Connection connection = driver.connect(                   │ obtains connection
                  jdbcUrl, properties);
```

Moreover, when using a pool, you should ensure that it doesn't use the `DriverMan-ager` class. The C3P0 library partially uses the `DriverManager` class to get a driver and then directly works with the returned class. In this way, C3P0 uses classloaders correctly from the perspective of an OSGi container.

In the following sections, we'll provide more details on configuring a JDBC data source from within an OSGi environment using Spring DM.

7.1.3 Configuring JDBC data sources

There are different strategies for managing JDBC connections within applications. JDBC provides an abstraction named `DataSource`, which defines a contract for providing connections. A `DataSource` supports provider implementations according to your required resource management strategy (direct use of driver, pools, and so on). Applications, however, are completely independent of the chosen strategy, which can be varied according to the target environment (test or production), as shown in figure 7.2.

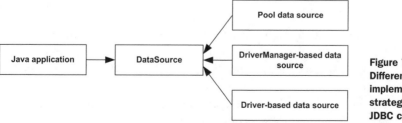

**Figure 7.2
Different data source
implementation
strategies for creating
JDBC connections**

You must choose which data source implementation you need according to your requirements. If you aren't in a multithreaded environment, implementations that manage or provide a single connection can be used. Alternatively, for performance reasons, pools should be used to manage a group of preopened connections.

In this section, we'll only describe the configuration of a pool within an OSGi environment using Spring DM. For other approaches, Spring's `SimpleDriverDataSource` class can be used instead of pool implementations.

CONFIGURING A POOL BUNDLE

Database connection pool classes need to see driver packages because the classes contained in these packages manage the connection resources. By default, the components corresponding to the pools don't have the correct OSGi package configuration in their JAR manifest entries. Several strategies exist to address this issue:

- During the packaging or OSGi-ification of the pool component, you can add optional import entries for each package for the possible drivers that you might use.
- You can implement a fragment bundle that will add the package containing the driver class that's used to the pool component's manifest configuration. This approach corresponds to the fragment configuration pattern described in section 3.3.

The OSGi-ification of existing third-party libraries with Bnd is described in section 6.2.3. As we explained, you can use a configuration file to parameterize information that will be specified in the manifest configuration of the generated OSGi component. We can add most of the JDBC driver packages as optional packages to the Bnd configuration file. That's shown in listing 7.2. Only the drivers available at runtime in the OSGi container will be resolved.

Listing 7.2   Specifying driver packages within the Bnd configuration

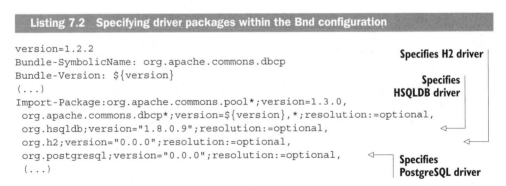

```
version=1.2.2
Bundle-SymbolicName: org.apache.commons.dbcp
Bundle-Version: ${version}
(...)
Import-Package:org.apache.commons.pool*;version=1.3.0,
  org.apache.commons.dbcp*;version=${version},*;resolution:=optional,
  org.hsqldb;version="1.8.0.9";resolution:=optional,
  org.h2;version="0.0.0";resolution:=optional,
  org.postgresql;version="0.0.0";resolution:=optional,
  (...)
```

Specifies H2 driver

Specifies HSQLDB driver

Specifies PostgreSQL driver

A less intrusive way to configure driver visibility within pool components is to use the fragment configuration pattern by creating a fragment responsible for extending the `Import-Package` specification. In the fragment, this header will only specify the package of the driver.

The following snippet shows the manifest configuration of a fragment bundle that adds the H2 package to the C3P0 component:

```
Manifest-Version: 1.0
Bundle-ManifestVersion: 2
Bundle-Name: C3P0 Configuration Fragment
Bundle-SymbolicName:
➡ com.springsource.com.mchange.v2.c3p0.config
Bundle-Version: 1.0.0
Bundle-Vendor: Manning
Fragment-Host:
➡ com.springsource.com.mchange.v2.c3p0;bundle-version="0.9.1"
Import-Package: org.h2;version="0.0.0"
```

Specifies H2 package to add

Specifies fragment and target component

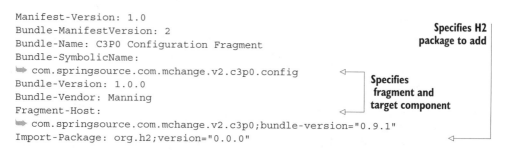

The fragment is linked to the C3P0 component through its symbolic name com.springsource.com.mchange.v2.c3p0 specified in the Fragment-Host header. The fragment doesn't have any content and only adds an Import-Package entry.

> **TIP** The SpringSource repository provides a modified version of DBCP that also looks for drivers in the context classloader. When using this version, you don't need to add such a fragment, because the driver will be present in this classloader during the pool's initialization.

CONFIGURING A DATA SOURCE WITH SPRING DM

Once the driver has been added in the pool component, we can focus on the data source configuration itself. For OSGi, best practice consists of defining a dedicated bundle to configure the data source. Within this bundle, Spring DM facilities can be used to configure a DataSource instance and register it as an OSGi service. This service can then be referenced by data access components to interact with the database.

In this section, we'll describe how to configure a C3P0 pool with the ComboPooled-DataSource class. A similar configuration can be done for DBCP using its BasicData-SourceFactory class. Figure 7.3 shows the elements involved in the configuration of a C3P0 pool.

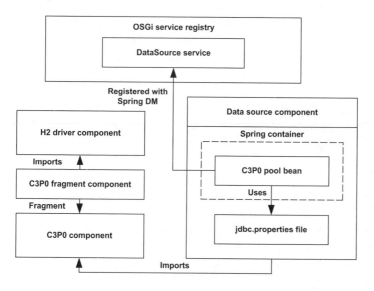

Figure 7.3 The elements involved in creating a data source and configuring OSGi within a data source component using Spring DM

The C3P0 pool is configured as a simple bean within the Spring container. Standard JDBC properties like driver class name, JDBC URL, username, and password are specified in this bean. The driver class can be used because its package has been added to the pool component by using a dedicated fragment, as described in the previous section. Best practice here also consists of using a properties file through Spring's `PropertyPlaceholderConfigurer` feature. It allows you to gather configuration parameters into a property file.

Listing 7.3 shows how to configure a C3P0 pool as a bean with Spring DM.

Listing 7.3 Configuring a C3P0 pool with Spring DM

```
                                                Specifies JDBC
                                           configuration file  ◁──┐
<bean id="propertyConfigurer"                                     │
            class="org.springframework.beans                      │
                  .factory.config.PropertyPlaceholderConfigurer">  ❶
  <property name="location"                                  ◁────┘
          value="classpath:/jdbc.properties"/>
</bean>

<bean id="dataSource"
      class="com.mchange.v2.c3p0.ComboPooledDataSource">
  <property name="driverClass"
          value="${jdbc.driverClassName}"/>
  <property name="jdbcUrl" value="${jdbc.url}"/>         Defines data  ❷
  <property name="user" value="${jdbc.username}"/>       source bean
  <property name="password"                              with properties
          value="${jdbc.password}"/>
</bean>
                                            ❸ Exports data source
<osgi:service ref="dataSource"        ◁──┘    as OSGi service
          interface="javax.sql.DataSource"/>
```

When specifying JDBC information for a data source, best practice for Spring consists of externalizing JDBC configuration properties through a properties file using the Spring `PropertyPlaceholderConfigurer` class ❶. This allows us to specify the properties file's location in the classpath. We can then configure the C3P0 pool using the JDBC properties of the configuration file ❷. Finally, the pool must be registered as a service ❸ in the OSGi service registry.

Because we're in an OSGi environment, all the required packages must be added to the manifest configuration of the bundle, as shown in the following snippet. These packages correspond to the pool itself, the JDBC driver used, and Spring itself regarding the `PropertyPlaceHolderConfigurer`, which uses the configuration properties file.

```
Import-Package: com.mchange.v2.c3p0;version="0.9.1.2",
 org.hsqldb;version="1.8.0.9",
 org.springframework.beans.factory.config;version="3.0.0.M1",
 org.springframework.context;version="3.0.0.M1"
```

We saw in previous sections how to use Spring DM to organize and configure JDBC data sources in an OSGi environment. In the next sections, we'll focus on how to provision the OSGi container to use Spring's JDBC support, then how to use it with Spring DM.

7.1.4 Provisioning the OSGi container for JDBC

At the JDBC level, nothing specific to Spring DM needs be added, other than its common components. Table 7.2 lists the Spring components you need to add to the OSGi container along with the core Spring components to use Spring's JDBC support within an OSGi environment.

> **NOTE** All the bundles we'll be discussing come from the SpringSource EBR.

Table 7.2 Common bundles for Spring JDBC support from SpringSource EBR

Group ID	Artifact ID	Version
org.springframework	org.springframework.transaction	3.0.0.RC1
org.springframework	org.springframework.jdbc	3.0.0.RC1

You're now ready to implement bundles that use the JDBC technology together with Spring and Spring DM.

7.1.5 Using JDBC within OSGi with Spring DM

In the previous sections, we described how to correctly initialize JDBC in an OSGi environment in order to follow OSGi best practice for bundle structuring and classloading. We'll now see how to build a Spring-powered bundle that relies on Spring JDBC support to access a database.

If you exclusively rely on ORM tools for you persistence layer, feel free to skip this section.

SPRING JDBC SUPPORT

JDBC isn't hard to use, but it requires a lot of repetitive and error-prone code: forget to close a connection and your application will become unstable, and diagnosing the cause can be very difficult.

Spring JDBC support addresses this limitation by providing abstractions integrating all this complicated plumbing. These classes provide a high-level abstraction over the JDBC API, which manages JDBC resources for you and allows you to concentrate on your application's logic. The support provides call-back interfaces that allow you to customize the behavior, and it also handles JDBC-specific exceptions by encapsulating them into unchecked, generic data exceptions with exception chaining.

We won't describe this support in detail because books like *Spring in Action* by Craig Walls provide complete and in-depth coverage of Spring JDBC. We will, however, show the basic use of Spring JDBC support through its `JdbcTemplate` class.

Let's see now how to configure and use JDBC with Spring DM.

REFERENCING JDBC DATA SOURCES IN SPRING DM

Referencing a data source is like referencing any other OSGi service—you use Spring DM's service support and its `reference` element. All data sources implement the `DataSource` interface and are registered under this interface, so the value `javax.sql.DataSource` must be used for the `interface` attribute, as shown in the following snippet:

```
<osgi:reference id="dataSource" interface="javax.sql.DataSource"/>
```

If several data source services are available in the OSGi service registry, you must specify an expression for the `filter` attribute of Spring DM's `reference` element to be sure you select the right one. All of these data sources must be registered as services and have properties that makes it possible to distinguish them. The `filter` attribute can be used as shown here:

```
<osgi:reference id="dataSource" interface="javax.sql.DataSource"
                filter="(source='database1')"/>
```

In the preceding snippet, the `filter` attribute specifies a custom `source` property to select the correct data source. This data source can then be injected into your data access objects, just as you would do in a classic Spring application:

```
<bean id="contactsDao"
  class="com.manning.sdmia.dataaccess.domain.dao.jdbc.ContactsDaoImpl">
  <property name="dataSource" ref="dataSource"/>
</bean>
```

We've now correctly configured our beans by using Spring DM to reference the requisite data source in the OSGi service registry and injecting the data source into our DAO beans. It's time now to implement the beans using Spring's JDBC support.

USING THE JDBCTEMPLATE CLASS

The `JdbcTemplate` class is the central class of Spring's JDBC support. This class encapsulates all the repetitive and error-prone logic of JDBC and makes it possible for you to concentrate on your own application logic.

Spring provides a convenient class for configuring this template, the `JdbcDaoSupport` class. Having specified this class as the superclass for your DAO, you can inject an instance of type `DataSource` into your DAO and access a correctly configured instance of `JdbcTemplate` through the `getJdbcTemplate` method. Listing 7.4 shows how to use this class with the `ContactsDaoImpl` class.

> **Listing 7.4   DAO structure using the Spring JDBC support**

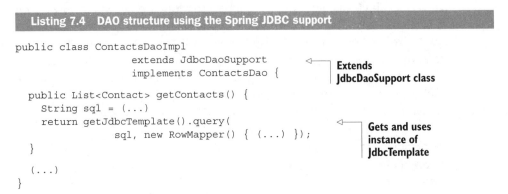

```
public class ContactsDaoImpl
                extends JdbcDaoSupport          ◁──┐ Extends
                implements ContactsDao {            │ JdbcDaoSupport class

  public List<Contact> getContacts() {
    String sql = (...)
    return getJdbcTemplate().query(               ◁──┐ Gets and uses
            sql, new RowMapper() { (...) });          │ instance of
  }                                                    │ JdbcTemplate

  (...)
}
```

When using Spring's JDBC support and the corresponding template, you need to specify all the required packages in the manifest configuration. The following snippet shows the packages you need to specify for the `Import-Package` header in the bundle's manifest file.

```
Import-Package: (...)
  org.springframework.beans.factory;version="3.0.0.M1",
  org.springframework.core;version="3.0.0.M1",
  org.springframework.dao;version="3.0.0.M1",
  org.springframework.jdbc.core;version="3.0.0.M1",
  org.springframework.jdbc.core.support;version="3.0.0.M1"
```

Imports Spring's dao package

Imports Spring's core packages

Imports Spring's JDBC support packages

> **Bootstrap packages**
>
> The `javax.sql` package is provided by the OSGi container as a bootstrap package, which means that you don't have to specify it explicitly in a bundle. You can specify which of the packages already present in Java you want by setting your OSGi container's configuration.
>
> This configuration is specific to the container. For example, the Equinox container requires the use of the `org.osgi.framework.bootdelegation` configuration property with a value such as `sun.*,com.sun.*,java.*,javax.*,org.w3c.*`.

Once the JDBC template is correctly configured, you can use its methods to develop your DAO implementations. We won't discuss this further because this isn't specific to OSGi and Spring DM.

To summarize, JDBC technology isn't difficult to use within an OSGi environment when you have Spring DM. The key enabler is the dedicated data source component, which makes the data source available as an OSGi service. Although packages related to Spring JDBC support must be added in the manifest configuration, this support can subsequently be used in the same way as any classic Spring application.

When we look at implementing JPA, you'll see that some parts of the configuration can be reused. That's because the Spring JPA support is based on a `DataSource` bean.

We'll now look at another aspect of data access, namely how to use ORM technologies with Spring DM. We'll focus first on concepts of JPA that are specified in the Java EE 5 specification.

7.2   *Using ORM within OSGi with Spring DM*

Although JDBC represents the foundations of data access using relational databases within Java applications (and OSGi applications), the technology has inherent limitations because you need to tackle different SQL dialects and convert between relational structures and object-oriented applications.

That's why most complex enterprise applications don't usually use JDBC directly but instead use transparent persistence through ORM tools. In contrast to JDBC, which isn't too hard to use with OSGi, ORM tools can be much more complex to implement.

First we'll discuss the key ORM concepts, then we'll focus on how to use Java EE's JPA within an OSGi container using Spring DM. To that end, we'll look at what load-time weaving is, how you can use it within an OSGi container, and what its relationship is with JPA.

We'll then look at the steps involved in making JPA work in an OSGi environment with Spring DM:

1 *Provision the OSGi container*   You need to provision the OSGi container with the bundles needed by your chosen JPA implementation. All of these components can be found in the SpringSource EBR. (This is discussed in section 7.2.3.)

2 *Configure JPA entities with Spring JPA support*   You must configure the chosen JPA implementation using Spring's JPA support. Here you can distinguish between configurations of the `EntityManagerFactory` entity and the JPA provider. (This is discussed in section 7.2.4.)

3 *Configure global packages in the OSGi configuration*   Having configured the JPA entities, you need to add the related packages to the OSGi configuration of the component. This configuration is common to all JPA implementations, because it corresponds to client JPA and Spring JPA support APIs. (This is discussed in section 7.2.4.)

4 *Implement DAO classes*   The next step is implementing JPA DAO classes using the configured entities and Spring's JPA support. (This is discussed in section 7.2.4.)

5 *Address issues specific to JPA implementations*   Finally, you need to configure the OSGi environment for the chosen JPA implementations, such as the underlying mechanisms required to configure packages of classes used at runtime, and also LTW. (This is discussed in section 7.2.5.)

We'll describe each of these steps in turn and concentrate on the specific issues that occur in an OSGi environment. We'll also look at what facilities are provided by Spring DM for using this technology in this context.

7.2.1   *Object/relational mapping*

In this section, we'll introduce the concepts of ORM technologies and how to use the Java EE ORM standard, the JPA. We'll give you everything you need to develop basic application logic using JPA. If you want a more in-depth discussion of JPA, we recommend *Java Persistence with Hibernate*, by Christian Bauer and Gavin King (Manning, 2006).

JPA CONCEPTS

JDBC allows you to access relational databases in a generic way using Java because it provides an abstraction layer above the vendor-specific database drivers. Although any database-based Java application must rely on JDBC, there's a structural mismatch between object-oriented applications, which are based on objects, and relational databases, which are based on rows, tables, and relations. This structural mismatch causes some issues that are difficult to resolve when directly using JDBC:

- *Handling specific SQL dialects*—Although SQL is a specification, every database engine has its own extensions. If a Java application wants to be compliant with several databases, it needs to support all of their dialects. Because ORM tools handle SQL internally, they provide the necessary SQL dialect support for the target database.
- *N+1 selects*—When applications use entity relationships, a vastly different number of SQL requests can be executed (than when they don't use entity relationships) depending on the chosen loading strategy. This can quickly have a large impact on performance.
- *Object graph handling*—JDBC doesn't provide an easy way to handle object graphs because you need to build this graph using data contained in result sets. Implementing this is generally very tedious.
- *Object mapping*—Entity mapping with table and inheritance support must be handled by the application.

ORM tools are aimed squarely at addressing these issues and sit at a higher abstraction level than raw JDBC, as shown in figure 7.4. They provide an abstraction above the SQL language so that applications can interact with relational databases using only the object-oriented paradigm.

ORM allows you to manage entities through corresponding tables in the database: that's the structural part of ORM. It also has a conversational part, in which the lifecycle of entities is introduced through several states. Transitions between these states allow the JPA engine to detect the operations that trigger the persistence context to be flushed or synchronized.

> **NOTE** The persistence context contains all the persistence instances currently manipulated by JPA. This context can be thought of as a first-level cache for the calling code. In enterprise applications, this context is commonly associated with a transaction or a web request and is flushed at the end of each.

Figure 7.5 depicts the possible transitions. Note that the transition names are those specified in the JPA specification.

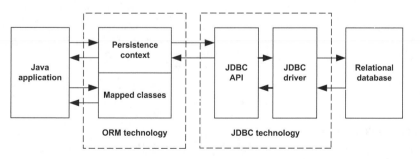

Figure 7.4   The general ORM architecture, showing that the ORM technology is based on JDBC and implements mapped classes and a persistence context for execution.

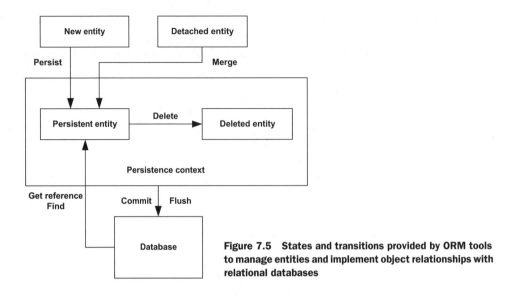

Figure 7.5   **States and transitions provided by ORM tools to manage entities and implement object relationships with relational databases**

You'll notice that entities that aren't in the persistence context have no correspondence with the database. Table 7.3 lists the JPA methods that cause the transitions shown in figure 7.5.

Table 7.3   **JPA methods controlling transitions in the mapped object lifecycle**

Method	Description
`getReference` and `find`	Allow you to get persistent entities from the database. Updates to these entities are automatically synchronized with the database on a flush operation. Related SQL requests correspond to `SELECT` requests.
`persist`	Allows you to create persistent entities in order to add them to the database. Related SQL requests correspond to `INSERT` requests.
`merge`	Allows you to attach detached entities. This operation results in persistent entities. Related SQL requests correspond to `UPDATE` requests.
`delete`	Allows you to remove persistent entities from the database. Related SQL requests correspond to `DELETE` requests.
`flush and commit`	Allow you to execute SQL requests corresponding to operations done on the persistent context. All pending transitions on managed entities, except for loading, are done at this point.

Now that we've described the concepts of JPA, let's see how to configure and use it based on its API.

JAVA PERSISTENCE API

Java EE 5's support for ORM is included in JSR 220 (EJB 3) and is named the Java Persistence API (JPA). Its aim is to provide a standardized layer so that ORM tools are merely specific implementations of this specification.

The specification describes how to map managed entities to database tables and how to use JPA to interact with the database. New features include the ability to use this technology outside of an Enterprise JavaBeans (EJB) container and to use local transactions instead of global transactions through the use of the JTA.

These are the main JPA implementations available in the open source community:

- *Hibernate JPA*—JPA implementation based on Hibernate.
- *OpenJPA*—The Apache Foundation's JPA implementation.
- *EclipseLink*—The Eclipse Foundation's JPA implementation. This implementation is based on the TopLink product, for which Oracle donated the codebase.

The recommended way to configure the mapping between objects and tables is to use annotations within managed entities. A set of annotations is provided by JPA to map classes, properties, and different kinds of relationships and inheritance. Listing 7.5 shows some examples.

Listing 7.5 Implementation of the `Contact` class using JPA annotations for mapping

```
@Entity
public class Contact {
  @Id
  @Column(name="id")
  @GeneratedValue(strategy = GenerationType.AUTO)
  private int id;

  @Column(name="last_name")
  private String lastName;

  @Column(name="first_name")
  private String firstName;

  @OneToMany(mappedBy = "contact",fetch = FetchType.EAGER,
             cascade = CascadeType.ALL)
  private List<Address> addresses;

  (...)
}
```

NOTE An XML-based approach is also available in JPA.

Once mapping is complete, you need to configure the persistence unit by creating a persistence.xml file. This file allows you to specify which classes to manage and the type of transactions the application uses, and it's commonly located under the META-INF directory. The following snippet shows a sample of a persistence.xml file:

```
<persistence xmlns="http://java.sun.com/xml/ns/persistence" version="1.0">
  <persistence-unit name="directoryUnit"           Configures persistence
              transaction-type="RESOURCE_LOCAL">   unit and transaction type
    <class>com.manning.sdmia.dataaccess
              .domain.model.Contact</class>         Specifies mapped
    <class> com.manning.sdmia.dataaccess            classes
              .domain.model.Address</class>
```

```
    (...)
  </persistence-unit>
</persistence>
```

Once this configuration is complete, you can use the JPA API to interact with the database. The main abstractions of this API are the `EntityManager` and `EntityManager-Factory` interfaces:

- The `EntityManager` is associated with a persistence context and provides a set of methods to interact with it. This interface is responsible for loading data and updating the states of managed entities.
- The `EntityManagerFactory` interface corresponds to the `EntityManager`'s factory and is in charge of loading the persistence.xml file as part of its creation.

Listing 7.6 shows how to use the `EntityManager` instance to store and access data.

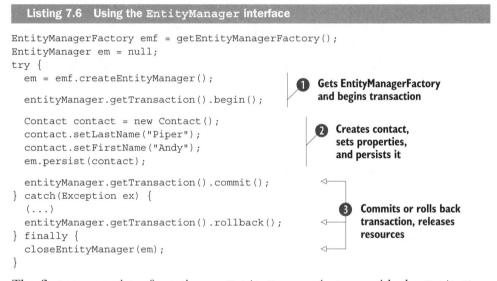

Listing 7.6   Using the `EntityManager` interface

```
EntityManagerFactory emf = getEntityManagerFactory();
EntityManager em = null;
try {
  em = emf.createEntityManager();                          ❶ Gets EntityManagerFactory
                                                              and begins transaction
  entityManager.getTransaction().begin();

  Contact contact = new Contact();                         ❷ Creates contact,
  contact.setLastName("Piper");                              sets properties,
  contact.setFirstName("Andy");                              and persists it
  em.persist(contact);

  entityManager.getTransaction().commit();
} catch(Exception ex) {
  (...)                                                    ❸ Commits or rolls back
  entityManager.getTransaction().rollback();                 transaction, releases
} finally {                                                   resources
  closeEntityManager(em);
}
```

The first step consists of creating an `EntityManager` instance with the `EntityManagerFactory` ❶. The `EntityManager` allows you to interact with the JPA persistence context. If you want to insert data contained in a `Contact` instance, you can instantiate and configure a plain `Contact` instance ❷. This can then be persisted using the `EntityManager` instance. In order to flush modifications back to the database, you need to validate the corresponding transaction ❸, which was started previously ❶. If an exception occurs, the transaction is rolled back ❸. Finally, we must close all resources we used as with JDBC. The `getEntityManagerFactory` and `closeEntityManager` methods come from a utility class implemented for this example.

JPA also provides an object-oriented language to execute queries against the database: JPQL (Java Persistence Query Language). This language allows you to query mapped objects with all their object-oriented features. The JPA implementation is responsible for converting these queries to native SQL `SELECT` statements for the target database.

Listing 7.7 shows how to execute queries using the `EntityManager` interface.

Listing 7.7 Using the `EntityManager` interface

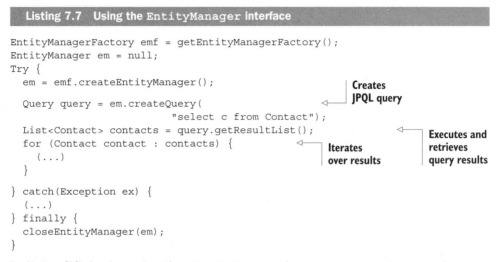

```
EntityManagerFactory emf = getEntityManagerFactory();
EntityManager em = null;
Try {
  em = emf.createEntityManager();
                                                          Creates
  Query query = em.createQuery(                           JPQL query
                     "select c from Contact");
  List<Contact> contacts = query.getResultList();         Executes and
  for (Contact contact : contacts) {        Iterates      retrieves
    (...)                                    over results  query results
  }
} catch(Exception ex) {
  (...)
} finally {
  closeEntityManager(em);
}
```

In listing 7.7, having created an `EntityManager` instance, we create a `Query` instance from an object query string. We then execute it and get the corresponding result list, which can be iterated through to access the data.

We've introduced ORM and JPA. Next, we'll describe how to use this technology in an OSGi environment with Spring DM. We'll start by explaining *load-time weaving* because JPA can use this technique to instrument managed classes.

7.2.2 Load-time weaving

Some JPA implementations have made the choice to use load-time weaving (LTW) to instrument managed entities. Because LTW is tied to classloading, using it in OSGi can be tedious and depends on support from the underlying OSGi container.

We'll start by outlining the main concepts, and then we'll focus on how to use it inside Equinox and discuss which JPA implementations need this feature.

LOAD-TIME WEAVING CONCEPTS

Load-time weaving (LTW) is related to AOP. Without going into details, the term "weaving" refers to the way aspects are applied to the application code. The weaving mechanism isn't standardized and several approaches exist:

- Compilation-time weaving—Java code is updated to add aspects before its compilation
- Binary weaving—Updates bytecode to add aspects after its compilation
- Load-time weaving—Modifies the bytecode of classes as they're loaded into a JVM

LTW updates class content as classes are loaded. Several mechanisms in Java can be used to implement it:

- *Dedicated classloader*—A dedicated classloader is used to update classes as they're loaded.
- *Java 5 agent*—Java 5 introduced the concept of a Java agent, which makes it possible to instrument classes while loading them. This mechanism is based on the `Instrumentation` and `ClassFileTransformer` interfaces. The latter specifies how to transform classes and must be registered through the `Instrumentation` interface.
- *Java 6 class redefinition*—Java 6 allows you to redefine classes to update their logic after JVM startup. In this case, the `ClassDefinition` interface can be defined and registered through the `Instrumentation` interface.
- *Class enhancer tools*—Such tools work by putting a proxy in front of instances to add logic around method execution. Usually these tools create subclasses dynamically. This approach isn't transparent to the application because it must use the tools' API to obtain updated instances.

As you can see, LTW can be implemented in different ways and is usually tied to class-loaders. That's why there are implications for its use in an OSGi container. Moreover, there is no universal solution to the class instrumentation problem at the moment in OSGi because it would require updates to the OSGi specification itself.

In the following sections, we'll describe how to use LTW with the Equinox container and Spring, and we'll describe its interaction with JPA. Be aware that LTW isn't supported by all OSGi containers.

The Equinox Aspects tool is dedicated to leveraging AOP across all present OSGi components within an Equinox instance, and it enables LTW using the container's hooks.

EQUINOX ASPECTS

A dedicated project named Equinox Aspects allows you to use LTW and AspectJ within the Equinox container. This project is available at http://www.eclipse.org/equinox/incubator/aspects/. AspectJ is a tool that implements AOP concepts for Java. It provides several ways to weave aspect in code including LTW.

Equinox Aspects takes advantage of the extensible nature of the Equinox Framework: the Equinox Framework adaptor hooks are responsible for handling internal mechanisms like classloading. This feature allows you to hook into the framework through the hookable adaptor, which allows you to add extensions to insert additional functionality into the framework itself. For example, `ClassLoadingHook` makes possible various classloader extensions, most specifically bytecode weaving.

These extensions must be defined as fragments for the system bundle org.eclipse.osgi. To enable their loading, the container must be launched using the `osgi.framework.extensions` system property. These fragments aren't considered regular bundles because they must be discovered before the platform is launched.

To use Equinox Aspects, the components listed in table 7.4 must be present within your Equinox container.

Table 7.4   Required components for using Equinox Aspects

Component	Description
org.eclipse.equinox.weaving.hook	Equinox hook implementation
org.eclipse.equinox.weaving.aspectj	Bridge between Equinox Aspects and AspectJ
org.eclipse.equinox.weaving.caching	Optional component for caching
org.eclipse.equinox.weaving.caching.j9	Optional component for caching
com.springsource.org.aspectj.runtime	AspectJ runtime component
com.springsource.org.aspectj.weaver	AspectJ weaver component

Equinox Aspects is a powerful tool that can used to weave aspects into components with AspectJ. Because the workings of Equinox Aspects are outside the scope of the book, we won't delve any deeper. Instead we'll concentrate on how it can help us in using JPA with Spring DM in an OSGi environment.

EQUINOX ASPECTS ADAPTER FOR SPRING

The Spring Framework includes LTW support based on the `LoadTimeWeaver` interface. The support follows the style of AspectJ (despite it not being tied to this framework). The main difference consists in the ability to apply LTW to only one specific class-loader instance (as opposed to applying it to every classloader in a JVM process). Because the support is open and interface-driven, Spring comes with several built-in implementations, and you can choose the best one for your needs, such as the best one for the application server you use.

As OSGi has a specific way of using classloaders, none of Spring's built-in LTW implementations are quite suitable for OSGi. We need an implementation dedicated to Equinox (based on Equinox Aspects) enabling instrumentation of classes through all components in OSGi. Martin Lippert, the most active developer of Equinox Aspects, has developed an LTW implementation for Equinox Aspects, but it's only available to be downloaded in the Spring DM forum at http://forum.springsource.org/showthread.php?t=60253&page=2.

Once the `org.eclipse.equinox.weaving.springweaver` package is imported in the manifest configuration, along with the other packages required by Equinox Aspects, the implementation can be configured in a Spring container as shown in the following snippet:

```
<bean class="org.eclipse.equinox.weaving.springweaver
                              .EquinoxAspectsLoadTimeWeaver"/>
```

You can also use the `load-time-weaver` element of Spring's `context` XML namespace to register this implementation, as shown in the following snippet. The `EquinoxAspectsLoadTimeWeaver` class will be considered the default LTW for the Spring container.

```
<context:load-time-weaver
      weaver-class="org.eclipse.equinox.weaving.springweaver
                              .EquinoxAspectsLoadTimeWeaver"/>
```

You now have LTW enabled within our Equinox container, so you're able to use JPA implementations that rely on it. Let's focus on using this support in an OSGi environment with Spring DM. First, you need to provision the container according to the JPA implementation that you use.

7.2.3 Provisioning a container for JPA implementations

Before being able to use Spring's JPA support, you need to provision the OSGi container with the necessary components. These include common components for Spring JPA support and JPA implementation components and their dependencies.

> **NOTE** The components listed in the following sections can be added to your OSGi container as described in sections 3.2.2 and 3.2.3. All bundles referred to here come from the SpringSource EBR.

COMMON SPRING JPA COMPONENTS

At this level, nothing specific to Spring DM needs to be added to the OSGi container. Table 7.5 lists the components that need to be added to the OSGi container in order to use Spring's JPA support. The core Spring components also need to be added.

Table 7.5   Common bundles for Spring JPA support from the SpringSource EBR

Group ID	Artifact ID	Version
javax.persistence	com.springsource.javax.persistence	1.0.0
org.springframework	org.springframework.transaction	3.0.0.M1
org.springframework	org.springframework.jdbc	3.0.0.M1
org.springframework	org.springframework.orm	3.0.0.M1

In addition, you need to add components related to JPA implementations and their dependencies. We'll describe the provisioning for the three main JPA implementations: Hibernate JPA, OpenJPA, and EclipseLink.

PROVISIONING FOR HIBERNATE JPA

Hibernate JPA was developed to sit above Hibernate itself. As a result, you need to provision your container with OSGi-ified versions of both the Hibernate bundles and their dependencies. You also need to add the Hibernate JPA bundles listed in table 7.6.

Table 7.6   Hibernate JPA bundles and their dependencies from the SpringSource EBR

Group ID	Artifact ID	Version
org.hibernate	com.springsource.org.hibernate.ejb	3.4.0.GA
org.hibernate	com.springsource.org.hibernate.annotations.common	3.3.0.ga
org.hibernate	com.springsource.org.hibernate.annotations	3.4.0.GA
org.hibernate	com.springsource.org.hibernate	3.3.1.GA
org.apache.commons	com.springsource.org.apache.commons.beanutils	1.7.0

Table 7.6 Hibernate JPA bundles and their dependencies from the SpringSource EBR *(continued)*

Group ID	Artifact ID	Version
org.apache.commons	com.springsource.org.apache.commons.codec	1.3.0
org.apache.commons	com.springsource.org.apache.commons.collections	3.2.0
org.apache.commons	com.springsource.org.apache.commons.digester	1.8.0
org.apache.commons	com.springsource.org.apache.commons.io	1.4.0
org.apache.commons	com.springsource.org.apache.commons.lang	2.4.0
org.apache.commons	com.springsource.org.apache.commons.pool	1.4.0
org.antlr	com.springsource.antlr	2.7.7
org.jboss.javassist	com.springsource.javassist	3.3.0.ga
javax.xml.stream	com.springsource.javax.xml.stream	1.0.1
org.dom4j	com.springsource.org.dom4j	1.6.1
org.jgroups	com.springsource.org.jgroups	2.5.1
org.objectweb.asm	com.springsource.org.objectweb.asm	1.5.3
org.objectweb.asm	com.springsource.org.objectweb.asm.attrs	1.5.3
javax.transaction	com.springsource.javax.transaction	1.1.0

Hibernate JPA consists of the `com.springsource.org.hibernate.ejb` component, which corresponds to a wrapper around the Hibernate tool, and the `com.spring-source.org.hibernate.annotations` component, which provides support for JPA compatible annotations. These components require a large set of dependencies to work; dependencies that are inherited from Hibernate itself.

PROVISIONING FOR OPENJPA

OpenJPA requires a much shorter set of bundles. All the needed components are listed in table 7.7.

Table 7.7 OpenJPA bundles and their dependencies from the SpringSource EBR

Group ID	Artifact ID	Version
org.apache.openjpa	com.springsource.org.apache.openjpa	1.1.0
org.apache.commons	com.springsource.org.apache.commons.lang	2.4.0
org.apache.commons	com.springsource.org.apache.commons.collections	3.2.1
org.apache.commons	com.springsource.org.apache.commons.pool	1.4.0
org.objectweb.asm	com.springsource.org.objectweb.asm	2.2.3
net.sourceforge.serp	com.springsource.serp	1.13.1
javax.transaction	com.springsource.javax.transaction	1.1.0

Like Hibernate JPA, OpenJPA requires a set of dependencies that must be present in the OSGi container in order to work correctly.

PROVISIONING FOR ECLIPSELINK

EclipseLink requires two bundles with two external dependency packages for its use. All the required components are listed in table 7.8.

Table 7.8   EclipseLink bundles and their dependencies from the SpringSource EBR

Group ID	Artifact ID	Version
org.eclipse.persistence	com.springsource.org.eclipse.persistence	1.0.0
org.eclipse.persistence	com.springsource.org.eclipse.persistence.jpa	1.0.0
org.eclipse.persistence	com.springsource.org.eclipse.persistence.asm	1.0.0
org.eclipse.persistence	com.springsource.org.eclipse.persistence.antlr	1.0.0

Having provisioned the container, you're now ready to implement bundles that use JPA with Spring and Spring DM. We'll first describe the generic way to configure and implement DAO components using the JPA, and then we'll look at specific OSGi configurations necessary at runtime.

7.2.4   *Using JPA in OSGi with Spring DM*

We've now covered all the issues with using JPA in an OSGi environment, and you have correctly provisioned your container according to your chosen JPA implementation. You can now implement your bundle logic using Spring JPA support.

In much the same way as Spring provides JDBC support, Spring provides support for JPA technology that simplifies the use of this technology. It provides a thin layer over the JPA API and transparently manages resources. It also allows you to configure implementations with XML.

> **NOTE**   The OSGi Enterprise Expert Group (EEG) will soon provide the OSGi JPA RFC 143, which will introduce a standard for making JPA work within an OSGi environment.

We'll first describe how to configure and use this support, and then we'll discuss the issues involved in using JPA in an OSGi environment.

CONFIGURING JPA WITH SPRING SUPPORT

Spring's JPA support provides two classes to configure JPA and its underlying implementation: `LocalEntityManagerFactoryBean` and `LocalContainerEntityManagerFactoryBean`. These classes implement Spring's `FactoryBean` interface and allow you to configure a JPA factory of type `EntityManagerFactory`.

The `LocalEntityManagerFactoryBean` class is the simplest way to configure JPA in Spring. It uses an autodetection mechanism to discover the configured JPA implementation from the persistence.xml file located in the META-INF directory in the classpath, but it provides no way to link to an existing JDBC data source configured in Spring. This makes it impossible to use this abstraction in an OSGi environment, because data sources are registered as OSGi services.

The `LocalContainerEntityManagerFactoryBean` class is more flexible and particularly suitable when using JPA with OSGi. It allows you to inject a data source and specify a chosen JPA implementation.

The `LocalContainerEntityManagerFactoryBean` class is based on implementations of the `JpaVendorAdapter` interface. Implementations of this interface can be injected in this class to select the JPA implementation to use. Built-in implementations of this interface are listed in table 7.9. All these implementations are located in the `org.springframework.orm.jpa.vendor` package.

Table 7.9   Built-in implementations of Spring's `JpaVendorAdapter` interface

Vendor	Implementation
Hibernate JPA	`org.springframework.orm.jpa.vendor.HibernateJpaVendorAdapter`
OpenJPA	`org.springframework.orm.jpa.vendor.OpenJpaVendorAdapter`
EclipseLink	`org.springframework.orm.jpa.vendor.EclipseLinkJpaVendorAdapter`

Listing 7.8 illustrates how you can configure JPA and its Hibernate implementation in Spring by using the `LocalContainerEntityManagerFactoryBean` class and a data source bean. (This bean can either be defined in the same application context or retrieved from the OSGi service registry, as we saw in section 7.1.)

Listing 7.8   Configuration of the Hibernate JPA implementation with Spring

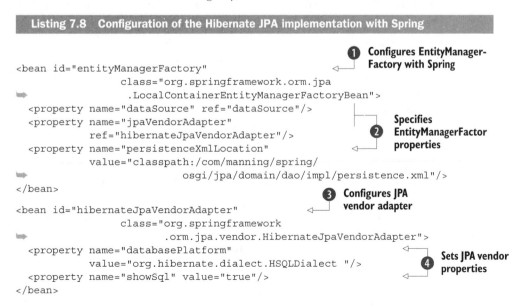

```
<bean id="entityManagerFactory"                          ① Configures EntityManager-
              class="org.springframework.orm.jpa            Factory with Spring
                 .LocalContainerEntityManagerFactoryBean">
  <property name="dataSource" ref="dataSource"/>
  <property name="jpaVendorAdapter"                       ② Specifies
           ref="hibernateJpaVendorAdapter"/>                 EntityManagerFactor
  <property name="persistenceXmlLocation"                    properties
           value="classpath:/com/manning/spring/
                        osgi/jpa/domain/dao/impl/persistence.xml"/>
</bean>
                                                         ③ Configures JPA
<bean id="hibernateJpaVendorAdapter"                        vendor adapter
              class="org.springframework
                     .orm.jpa.vendor.HibernateJpaVendorAdapter">
  <property name="databasePlatform"                       ④ Sets JPA vendor
           value="org.hibernate.dialect.HSQLDialect "/>      properties
  <property name="showSql" value="true"/>
</bean>
```

The configuration of an `EntityManagerFactory` instance is done using Spring's JPA support and its `LocalContainerEntityManagerFactoryBean` class ➊. This allows us to inject necessary beans and specify properties ➋. The first one consists in injecting the data source. The configuration of JPA continues with the specification of the JPA implementation and of the persistence.xml file to use. We then configure the Hibernate JPA implementation ➌ by specifying some properties ➍, like the target database and by activating traces for the generated SQL queries.

NOTE The `persistenceXmlLocation` property is optional. If this property isn't specified, the `LocalContainerEntityManagerFactoryBean` class uses the persistence.xml file under the META-INF directory.

You need to specify in the manifest configuration all of the packages used. Some correspond to the JPA API; others correspond to Spring's JPA support and are common whatever the implementation used. The following snippet shows the packages you need to specify in the `Import-Package` header in the component's manifest file:

```
Import-Package: (...)
 javax.persistence;version="1.0.0",
 org.springframework.beans.factory;version="3.0.0.M1",
 org.springframework.core;version="3.0.0.M1",
 org.springframework.dao.support;version="3.0.0.M1",
 org.springframework.orm.jpa;version="3.0.0.M1",
 org.springframework.orm.jpa.support;version="3.0.0.M1",
 org.springframework.orm.jpa.vendor;version="3.0.0.M1"
```

Vendor adapter configurations can also require specific classes, depending on the chosen JPA implementation. In that case, additional packages must be added to the manifest configuration. We'll describe the specifics of JPA implementations in section 7.2.5.

USING JPA WITH JPATEMPLATE AND SPRING DM

After configuring JPA in your bundle's manifest file and Spring configuration files, you can use the central class of Spring's JPA support, the `JpaTemplate` class, in your DAO implementations. This class allows you to implement all your data access logic by providing an abstraction layer over the JPA API.

Spring's JPA support provides the `JpaDaoSupport` class as a base class for all DAOs using the JPA technology. Having specified this class as a superclass for your DAO, you can inject an instance of `EntityManagerFactory` into your DAO and access a correctly configured instance of the template with the `getJpaTemplate` method.

Listing 7.9 shows how to use this abstraction with the `ContactsDaoImpl` class.

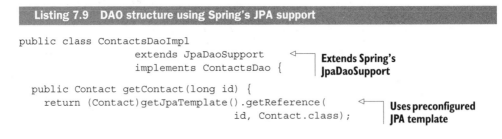

Listing 7.9   DAO structure using Spring's JPA support

```
public class ContactsDaoImpl
               extends JpaDaoSupport            ◁─┐ Extends Spring's
               implements ContactsDao {            │ JpaDaoSupport
  public Contact getContact(long id) {
    return (Contact)getJpaTemplate().getReference(     ◁─┐ Uses preconfigured
                          id, Contact.class);             │ JPA template
```

```
    }
    (...)
}
```

Once the JPA template is correctly configured, you can use its methods, which closely follow those of the `EntityManager` interface. The `EntityManagerFactory` instance previously configured only needs to be injected into JPA DAO classes using Spring's JPA support. The following snippet shows how to configure the `ContactsDaoImpl` class:

```
<bean id="entityManagerFactory" (...)>
    (...)
</bean>
                                          Configures bean
                                          instance of DAO
<bean id="contactsDao"                 ◁
    class="com.manning.sdmia.directory.dao.impl.ContactsDaoImpl">
    <property name="entityManagerFactory"    ◁
        ref="entityManagerFactory"/>          Injects entity manager
</bean>                                        factory into DAO
```

All these elements are universal to all JPA implementations. But, because each JPA implementation uses slightly different mechanisms internally, some configuration specific to the implementation must be done for bundles using them, both in the manifest configuration and Spring configuration files. We'll dig into these specifics in the next section.

7.2.5 *JPA implementation specifics when used with Spring DM*

In previous sections, we described the general concepts and configuration necessary to use JPA in an OSGi environment with Spring's JPA support. Although JPA is a specification, specific implementations can have their own requirements for configuration and use. These requirements may have more impact in an OSGi environment, depending on the way they manage classloading and proxies for managed entities.

These are the requirements when using JPA in an OSGi environment:

- *Visibility of mapped classes*—When configuring JPA implementations at runtime, the mapped classes must be visible.
- *Automatic discovery of mapped classes*—JPA implementations provide support to autodiscover mapped classes. This feature has implications when used within an OSGi environment.
- *LTW*—JPA implementations require or have the option for load-time class instrumentation. This feature has a big impact on components and the OSGi container itself, especially when using LTW.
- *Specific OSGi imports*—In addition to the common packages described in section 7.2.4, packages must be specified according to the chosen JPA implementation.

We'll discuss each of these points in this section. We'll also describe how you can make the three main JPA implementations work in an OSGi container with Spring DM and Spring's JPA support.

GENERAL ISSUES WITH OSGI

You'll probably recognize by now that the first issue when using JPA in OSGi is a class visibility one: mapped classes must be visible to the JPA implementation when creating the `EntityManagerFactory` entity. Spring DM is smart enough to make these classes visible to components of the JPA implementation. Thanks to Spring DM's TCCL support, the mapped classes only have to be visible to the component creating the `EntityManagerFactory` (that's a DAO implementation bundle in most cases).

Another class visibility issue occurs when using classes enhanced (decorated) by the JPA implementation. JPA implementations tend to transparently instrument classes, and these "unexpected" classes must also be visible to the implementation as per OSGi visibility rules. These classes will obviously depend on the chosen JPA implementation and we'll detail each in the following sections specific to each implementation.

Moreover, some JPA implementations try to autodetect classes through classpath scanning for the `Entity` annotation. In an OSGi environment, this feature can cause exceptions, as shown in the following snippet:

```
Caused by: java.io.FileNotFoundException: /home/[...] /
    com.manning.sdmia.service.jpa.openjpa/bin/ (Is a directory)
```

This happens because inspecting JAR files in OSGi doesn't work the same way it does in classic Java applications. As a matter of fact, this inspecting is based on URLs using the `bundlesource` protocol. Because this isn't handled by all JPA implementations, the JPA implementation may not be able to browse the contents of a component.

Best practice is to deactivate this feature and to explicitly define which classes must be used by the JPA implementation. This can be done in the persistence.xml file, as shown in the following snippet:

```
<persistence xmlns=http://java.sun.com/xml/ns/persistence version="1.0">
  <persistence-unit name="directoryUnit"
                transaction-type="RESOURCE_LOCAL">    Specifies using
    (...)                                             explicitly defined
    <exclude-unlisted-classes>                        mapped classes
                true</exclude-unlisted-classes>
  </persistence-unit>
</persistence>
```

Forgetting to set the `exclude-unlisted-classes` parameter to `true` can cause some JPA implementations to crash (such as OpenJPA).

As stated earlier, some JPA implementations need LTW to work properly, and this can be the biggest problem when using JPA in OSGi. We described LTW in section 7.2.2, and we'll see in the next section how to configure it with JPA.

Depending on the JPA implementation used, additional packages must be added to the manifest configuration file of the components. This configuration is described in the following sections discussing specific implementations.

Strange behavior can also sometimes occur when using JPA implementations within an OSGi environment. For instance, we encountered a JPQL problem when using Hibernate JPA. Using a request like the one shown in the following snippet raises a strange ClassCastException:

```
from com.manning.sdmia.service.jpa.model.Author a left join a.books
```

The exception it raised was this:

```
java.lang.ClassCastException: [Ljava.lang.Object; can't be cast to
    com.manning.sdmia.service.jpa.model.Author
```

Adding a select clause solves the problem, as shown in following snippet:

```
select a from com.manning.sdmia.service.jpa.model.Author a left join a.books
```

This isn't an obvious solution at first sight! This problem seems to be a bug caused by the use of Hibernate JPA in an OSGi environment.

USING SPRING LTW AND JPA

The JPA specification defines the contract for class transformation through the ClassTransformer interface. This interface must be implemented by persistence providers that want to transform entities and managed classes at class load time or at class redefinition time. This feature isn't mandatory, and implementations are free to use or ignore it.

The following JPA implementations behave differently regarding LTW:

- *Hibernate JPA*—Doesn't require LTW because the implementation provides a ClassTransformer implementation based on Javassist.
- *OpenJPA*—Leaves the choice to the application about whether or not to use LTW. OpenJPA detects whether it can register a ClassTransformer. If this registration is successful, LTW is enabled; otherwise it's not.
- *EclipseLink*—Requires LTW to enable features such as lazy loading, transparent fetch groups and optimized change tracking.

Spring enables you to integrate ClassTransformer entities into its generic LTW support when their use is required for a JPA implementation. To use this support, you need to configure the LTW implementation that you want to use. In our case, that's Equinox Aspects. This configuration can either be done globally through the load-time-weaver facility of Spring's context XML namespace or directly on the Entity-ManagerFactory, as shown in the following snippet:

```
<bean id="entityManagerFactory" class="org.springframework.orm.jpa
                   .LocalContainerEntityManagerFactoryBean">
  (...)
  <property name="loadTimeWeaver">
    <bean class="org.eclipse.equinox.weaving.springweaver
                       .EquinoxAspectsLoadTimeWeaver"/>
  </property>
</bean>
```

Remember that you must specify the osgi.framework.extensions system property with the value org.eclipse.equinox.weaving.hook to enable Equinox Aspects for

LTW. Tracing can be activated for this feature by setting the `org.aspectj.osgi.ver-bose` system property to `true`.

SPECIFIC CONFIGURATION FOR HIBERNATE JPA

As emphasized in the previous section, the Hibernate JPA implementation doesn't use LTW to instrument managed entities. Instead, the framework uses Javassist to manipulate Java bytecode on the fly.

Although these tools aren't explicitly used by the application developer, some of their packages need to be specified in the manifest configuration of the bundle that creates the `EntityManageFactory` entity. The following snippet shows the packages that need to be added:

```
Import-Package: (...)
 javassist.util.proxy;version="3.3.0.ga",
 org.hibernate.proxy;version="3.3.1.GA",
 org.hibernate.jdbc;version="3.3.1.GA",
 (...)
```

Moreover, if you want to use JPQL requests, the `org.hibernate.hql.ast` package must be present in the context classloader. This package must be added to the manifest configuration of the bundle whose classloader corresponds to the context classloader. Because OSGi doesn't explicitly set the context classloader, Spring DM's context classloader support can be used to address this issue by setting it on the service that exports the DAO entity.

SPECIFIC CONFIGURATION FOR OPENJPA

Like Hibernate, OpenJPA requires you to set additional packages in the manifest configuration.

First of all, the `org.apache.openjpa.jdbc.kernel` package must be specified in the manifest configuration of the component creating the `EntityManageFactory` entity.

Moreover, you need to add some other packages related to the instrumentation runtime of mapped classes for both proxy-based and LTW strategies, as shown in the following snippet:

```
Import-Package: (...)
 org.apache.openjpa.enhance;version="1.1.0",
 org.apache.openjpa.jdbc.kernel;version="1.1.0",
 org.apache.openjpa.util;version="1.1.0"
```

7.2.6   *A JPA summary*

This ends our tour through the intricacies of using JPA with Spring DM. Unlike the use of JDBC, using JPA in an OSGi environment can be quite tedious. The technology implements several advanced concepts to overcome the structural mismatch between object-oriented applications and relational databases, and this comes at a price when using it in OSGi. Implementing transparent persistence implies that many things have to be configured correctly for implementations to work, as summarized here:

- *Visibility of mapped classes*—Use the built-in support provided by Spring DM for making mapped classes visible when configuring JPA entities at runtime.
- *Automatic discovery of mapped classes*—Deactivate the automatic discovery of mapped classes using the `exclude-unlisted-classes` tag in the persistence.xml configuration file. This feature isn't commonly supported within an OSGi environment.
- *LTW*—Configure LTW if needed by the JPA implementation or if you want to use it and your JPA implementation allows it. In the Equinox container, LTW requires the use of Equinox Aspects and its integration with Spring's LTW support.
- *Specific OSGi imports*—Specify all the additional packages in the `Import-Package` header for the chosen JPA implementation. These packages correspond to hidden classes used at runtime by implementations.

Having described the use of several data access technologies in an OSGi environment with Spring DM, we now need to address the associated issue of using transactions. This is important, as it guarantees data consistency. By using Spring data access support, we've already included support for transactions (in the shape of the Spring Transaction module), so we only need now to configure it.

7.3 Transactions

Spring provides powerful, generic, and portable transaction support. It consists of managing transactions declaratively using AOP or annotations, and it can be used with a large set of data access technologies, including JDBC and JPA. Moreover, all the required resource management is directly integrated into the corresponding Spring templates, which makes the demarcation of transactions transparent when using Spring's data access support.

In this section, we'll describe how the transaction support works and how you can set up and configure Spring transactional support for JPA in an OSGi environment with Spring DM. We won't cover JDBC here because its configuration is relatively straightforward.

7.3.1 Spring's transactional support

Spring's transactional support consists of two main parts for managing transactions on beans that are managed by the container:

- *Transactional synchronization*—This manages resources used to handle transactions. This mechanism is directly integrated into Spring's data access support and is based on a transactional context stored in a variable of type `ThreadLocal`.
- *Transaction demarcation*—This allows you to apply transactions to application logic. Although an API is available, Spring also provides features to declaratively apply them to Spring-managed beans through AOP and annotations.

The key abstraction for this support is the `PlatformTransactionManager` interface, which provides a contract for transaction demarcation. The following snippet shows the content of this interface:

```
public interface PlatformTransactionManager {
  TransactionStatus getTransaction(TransactionDefinition definition);
  void commit(TransactionStatus status);
  void rollback(TransactionStatus status);
}
```

In the `PlatformTransactionManager` interface, the `getTransaction` method allows you to initialize and start a transaction. The `commit` method successfully finalizes a transaction; the `rollback` one cancels it.

Implementations of this interface are provided for each data access implementation in Spring. These implementations are commonly based on factories for the corresponding technology (because they must be able to access resources to manage transactions), or, in the case of JTA, on the Java transaction manager.

With respect to transaction propagation, Spring defaults to transactions being `REQUIRED` on beans, which allows application components to participate in the current transaction or to create it if it doesn't exist. In addition, Spring introduces read-only transactions, which can help improve performance in ORM tools.

We won't discuss the generic use of transactions any further here. We recommend reading *Spring in Action*, by Craig Walls, for more details. (A third edition will be published by Manning in fall 2010

You can configure transactions in Spring by following these steps:

- Create and configure all your POJOs in the Spring container. They will correspond to abstractions for data access, DAO entities, and business services.
- Configure a transaction manager bean, whose implementation depends on the underlying persistence technology.
- Apply transactional behaviors to business services using either XML or transaction annotations.

The last point can be implemented in Spring by using Spring AOP support and a dedicated transaction XML namespace, as shown in listing 7.10.

Listing 7.10   Transaction configuration using AOP and XML

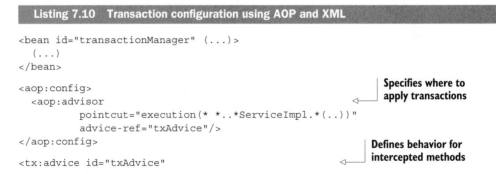

```
<bean id="transactionManager" (...)>
  (...)
</bean>

<aop:config>                                          Specifies where to
  <aop:advisor                                   ◁──  apply transactions
          pointcut="execution(* *..*ServiceImpl.*(..))"
          advice-ref="txAdvice"/>
</aop:config>                                         Defines behavior for
                                               ◁──  intercepted methods
<tx:advice id="txAdvice"
```

```
            transaction-manager="transactionManager">
    <tx:attributes>
      <tx:method name="add*"/>
      <tx:method name="update*"/>                    Specifies
      <tx:method name="delete*"/>                    behavior for
      <tx:method name="*" read-only="true"/>         methods
    </tx:attributes>
  </tx:advice>
```

Another possibility is to use the `Transactional` annotation to specify transactional behavior directly in interfaces and classes. Information specified on interfaces is automatically used in corresponding implementations and can be overridden if necessary. The annotation can be specified both at the class level or method level. At the class level, it provides global configuration for all methods, which can then be overridden if another configuration is required.

The following snippet shows how to specify transactional behavior using the `Transactional` annotation.

```
@Transactional                              Specifies transactional
public interface ContactsService {          behavior for whole interface
  @Transactional(readOnly=true)
  List<Contact> getContacts();              Overloads default
                                            behavior to be read-only
  void addContact(Contact contact);
}
```

Transactional annotation support isn't activated by default and must be enabled through the `annotation-driven` element of Spring's `tx` namespace, as shown in the following snippet:

```
<bean id="transactionManager" (...)>
  (...)                                      Enables annotation-based
</bean>                                      transaction support

<tx:annotation-driven transaction-manager="transactionManager"/>
```

We'll discuss annotation-based support in the following sections because it's easier to use.

7.3.2 *Using JPA transactions with Spring DM*

As emphasized in the previous section, the central abstraction of Spring's transactional support is the `PlatformTransactionManager`. When using local transactions, the transaction manager implementation depends on the underlying data access technology, whereas for global transactions Spring provides a specific implementation that interacts with the underlying JTA transaction manager (which is usually hosted by an application server). We'll describe here only the local transaction approach and use the annotation-driven method of configuring transactions.

We can identify two use cases for configuring transaction management, depending on the organization of bundles within an application:

- *Services and DAOs are in the same component.*   In this case, Spring's transaction support can be used as in regular Spring applications. The `EntityManagerEntity` entity, services, DAO, and Spring transaction manager are all located in the same Spring container.
- *Services and DAOs are in different components.*   In this case, services, the `EntityManagerEntity` entity, and the Spring transaction manager are located in different components. Because you need a transaction manager to apply transactions to services, this must be registered as an OSGi service. The service component is then able to reference and use it.

In the first use case, bundles are autonomous, containing both services and DAO entities, and they embed their own transaction managers. Transactions are managed within these components, and transactions are already applied to entities registered as OSGi services. Figure 7.6 illustrates bean interactions in this case.

In the use case where services and DAOs are separated, the Spring transaction manager can be provided as an OSGi service to a service component by the DAO component. In the service component, this service is used to apply transactions to services. Figure 7.7 depicts this organization and shows the interactions between these components.

As illustrated in figure 7.7, the service for the Spring transaction manager is registered under the `PlatformTransactionManager` interface, which is the root interface for all transaction managers within Spring. That makes this service independent from the underlying data access technology.

The following snippet shows how to register the transaction manager as an OSGi service from the DAO component:

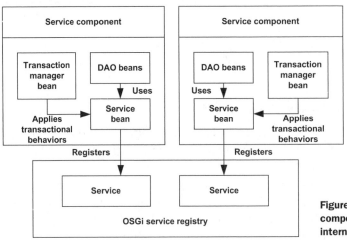

Figure 7.6   Autonomous service components manage transactions internally.

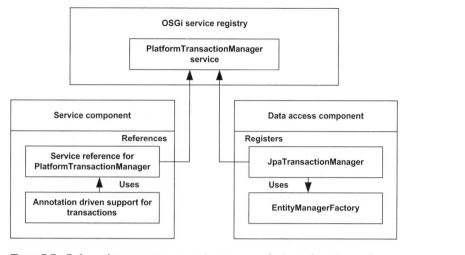

Figure 7.7 Referencing a `JpaTransactionManager` instance from the service component using the OSGi service registry

```
<bean id="entityManagerFactory" class="(...)">        Configures
  (...)                                                EntityManager-
</bean>                                                 Factory bean

<bean id="transactionManager"           Configures Spring JPA    Registers transaction
    class="org.springframework.orm.jpa.JpaTransactionManager">   manager as OSGi
  <property name="entityManagerFactory" ref="entityManagerFactory"/>    service
</bean>

<osgi:service ref="transactionManager"
  interface="org.springframework.transaction.PlatformTransactionManager"/>
```

The following snippet shows how to use the transaction manager to apply transactions to the service component:

```
<osgi:reference id="transactionManager"
    interface="org.springframework.transaction.PlatformTransactionManager"/>

<tx:annotation-driven transaction-manager="transactionManager"/>
```

Here the transaction manager is provided as an OSGi service and is then used in the configuration of Spring's annotation-based transaction support.

Because Spring transactional support requires more classes than just the transaction manager, new packages must be added in the manifest configuration for bundles that decorate their beans with transactional behavior. That's shown in the following snippet:

```
Import-Package: (...)
 javax.persistence.spi;version="1.0.0",
 org.aopalliance.aop;version="1.0",
 org.springframework.aop;version="3.0.0.M1",
 org.springframework.aop.framework;version="3.0.0.M1",
 org.springframework.transaction.annotation;version="3.0.0.M1 "
```

Once all this is configured, you can apply transactional behavior directly within classes and interfaces to specify which methods are transactional, how they behave in the presence of an existing transaction, and whether their behavior is read-only.

We saw that Spring provides the `Transactional` annotation for describing transactional behavior. A good practice consists of using this annotation on *service* interfaces. All the implementation classes will then directly benefit from the definition of transactional behavior at the interface level.

It's now time to look at a different aspect of transactions. In the next section we'll look at how to implement the "open `EntityManager` in view" pattern, which consists of extending the scope of ORM sessions to the web layer.

7.4   *Using the open EntityManager in view pattern*

Using ORM tools can induce some problems, especially when building views such as JSP pages, because some parts of managed entities can only be partially loaded. One solution used by ORM tools to improve performance is to lazily load entities, by using an on-demand approach. This optimization becomes a problem when we need to use data that hasn't been loaded, but we're out of the scope of the ORM session. In fact, by this point the session has already been closed at the level of the service.

The open element in view pattern (where the element is `EntityManager` in JPA) exists to address this problem. In this section, we'll describe the concepts behind this pattern and how to set it up and use it in an OSGi environment using Spring DM.

7.4.1   *The open EntityManager in view pattern*

The open `EntityManager` in view pattern is useful; every ORM framework makes it possible to lazily load entities during view construction.

To do so, you need to keep hold of the `EntityManager` instance that loaded the entity. If the associated `EntityManager` instance is closed when using lazy loading on an entity, you'll encounter some exceptions, as shown in the following snippet using Hibernate:

```
org.hibernate.LazyInitializationException:
   failed to lazily initialize a collection of role:
   com.manning.sdmia.dataacces.domain.model.Contact.adresses,
   no session or session was closed
```

The end of this error message specifies that the error occurred because the associated session was closed.

With Spring, the lazy loading is tied to its resource management within its data access support. According to the data access configuration, Spring is responsible for obtaining and releasing the underlying resources of the JPA implementation. This implies that the scope of the resource transparently changes. These are the impacts on resources scope in two use cases.

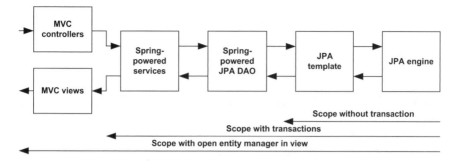

Figure 7.8 `EntityManager` **scope according to chosen strategy**

- *No transaction configured*—Spring obtains an `EntityManager` instance before the call of every `JpaTemplate` method and releases it after each call. `EntityManager` instances aren't gathered and every call uses a different `EntityManager`.
- *Transaction applied on service methods*—Spring obtains an `EntityManager` instance and uses it for all the nested calls within the service method logic. The resource is obtained before the call of every service method, stored in a variable of type `ThreadLocal`, and released when the service method exits.

As you can see, using lazy loading of entities instrumented by the ORM tool after calling transactional services isn't possible because these entities are outside the scope of transactions. As a matter of fact, the underlying resource is closed after the service method returns. This isn't particularly convenient because applications commonly use entities managed by the ORM within their UI after service calls, and they can't generally load data lazily, according to their needs, as shown in figure 7.8.

The Spring Framework provides implementations of the open element (or `EntityManager`) in view pattern for each of the supported ORM technologies.

7.4.2 Using the open EntityManager in view pattern with Spring DM

Components using the open `EntityManager` in view pattern and data access components are typically separated, because the former implement the UI of applications. Moreover, data access components must make their `EntityManagerFactory` entities accessible as OSGi services so that the user interface component can get at them, as shown in figure 7.9.

Exporting the `EntityManagerFactory` bean as an OSGi service can be done with Spring DM facilities, as shown in the following snippet:

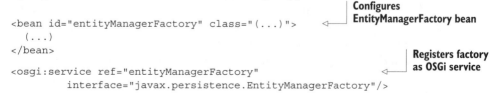

```
<bean id="entityManagerFactory" class="(...)">      ⟵   Configures
  (...)                                                   EntityManagerFactory bean
</bean>
                                                        Registers factory
<osgi:service ref="entityManagerFactory"           ⟵   as OSGi service
        interface="javax.persistence.EntityManagerFactory"/>
```

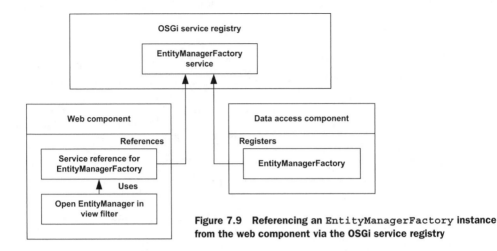

Figure 7.9 Referencing an `EntityManagerFactory` instance from the web component via the OSGi service registry

The UI component must then reference this `EntityManagerFactory` service in its Spring configuration, as demonstrated in the following snippet:

```
<osgi:reference id="entityManagerFactory"
                interface="javax.persistence.EntityManagerFactory"/>
```

In this example, the component is tied to JPA and must specify the javax.persistence package in its manifest configuration.

The web filter implementing the open `EntityManager` in view pattern can then be configured in the web.xml of the web application, as follows:

Configures filter class

```
<filter>
  <filter-name>openEntityManagerInViewFilter</filter-name>
  <filter-class>
      org.springframework.orm.jpa.support.OpenEntityManagerInViewFilter
  </filter-class>
</filter>
```

Configures filter mapping

```
<filter-mapping>
  <filter-name>openEntityManagerInViewFilter</filter-name>
  <url-pattern>/*</url-pattern>
</filter-mapping>
```

You'll notice that the filter is, by default, based on the `EntityManagerFactory` bean with the identifier `entityManagerFactory`. This configuration can be changed with the `entityManagerFactoryBeanName` filter initialization parameter. After performing this configuration, your web application can lazily load data to build its views.

To summarize, the open `EntityManager` in view pattern provides a workable solution to using lazy loading in JPA. This feature isn't difficult to implement in an OSGi environment using Spring DM, but it requires the sharing of `EntityManagerFactory`. Components using this pattern are then tied to the underlying technology both through the service type and by the packages needed in the manifest configuration.

7.5 *Summary*

Implementing data access components is complex even in regular Java applications, and it requires avoiding a lot of potential pitfalls. This is even more true in an OSGi environment. Components need to be specifically organized, and some components, like pools, need to be extended to allow them to see the JDBC drivers. The more complex the technology used, the more numerous the issues to address.

Once you've correctly configured drivers, pools, and data sources, using JDBC with Spring DM is straightforward. If you decide to use Spring's JDBC support with Spring DM, you need to provision the container with the related bundles and then import the packages corresponding to JDBC and Spring JDBC you want to use.

When developing enterprise applications, using JDBC alone isn't sufficient in most cases because of the mismatch between object-oriented applications and relational databases. Using ORM tools is a good solution to this problem, but it can be tricky to implement because the logic of such tools is much more complex. They commonly use class instrumentation to transparently manage mapped entities, but what is completely transparent to classic Java applications isn't at all transparent with OSGi. The classes used must be visible to the component, and these classes are often difficult to determine beforehand. But with a few hints, using JPA with Spring DM turns out to be much less difficult than you might have expected.

Finally, transactions aren't difficult to implement in an OSGi environment, but they can require the sharing of resources using the OSGi service registry, depending on how your bundles are organized.

In the next chapter, we'll tackle one of the main aspects of enterprise applications: implementing the web layer. We'll show you how to use servlet and JSP technologies with Spring DM, and how to use web frameworks like Spring MVC, JSF, and GWT to implement real web applications. We'll also describe how to connect these kinds of components to the data access components described in this chapter.

Developing OSGi web components with Spring DM and web frameworks

This chapter covers

- Using Spring DM in a web environment
- Integrating Spring DM with different kinds of web frameworks (action-based, component-driven, AJAX, web services)
- Taking advantage of Spring support for these frameworks to make using Spring DM simple

In the previous chapter, we described how to use data access technologies such as JDBC and JPA with Spring DM to handle data for non-OSGi applications. In this chapter, we'll focus on another aspect of enterprise applications: developing web components. Although Java EE provides servlets and JSPs (JavaServer Pages) to address these issues, using them on their own is generally considered tricky. One solution is to use a dedicated framework that leverages the Model-View-Controller

(MVC) pattern. When implementing web bundles with Spring DM, these issues—and their solutions—are largely unchanged. The key is knowing how to use web frameworks in an OSGI environment and how to integrate them with Spring DM.

In the following sections we'll describe how to integrate Spring DM with various web technologies and frameworks to create web UIs or expose web services. We'll describe each in the context of the framework family they belong to:

- Action-based web frameworks
- Component-driven frameworks
- AJAX-based frameworks
- Web services

For each, we'll explain how to optimize their integration with Spring DM. Let's get started!

8.1   Using action-based web frameworks with Spring DM

Action-based web frameworks are responsible for selecting the appropriate actions to handle requests. Actions are responsible for extracting parameters from requests, executing the requests, and building responses. Most frameworks of this kind provide integration with Spring and can also use Spring DM in an OSGi environment.

In this section, we'll look at the general concepts of how to integrate such frameworks with Spring DM and how to do this integration using Spring MVC.

8.1.1   Using Spring DM with action-based frameworks

The central entity of action-based web frameworks is the *action* entity. This kind of entity is responsible for handling requests and executing functionality based on the requests, typically by using external components. Integrating Spring DM with action-based frameworks involves using OSGi services, configured through Spring DM, in action implementations. These actions use OSGi services to execute business functionality.

When configuring Spring support for this kind of framework, there are two main steps:

1   Specify the OSGi web application context from Spring DM to use the `osgi` namespace. This allows you to define and reference OSGi services from within Spring application contexts.

2   Inject OSGi services configured through Spring DM info the actions of the application. This can be done using classic or annotation-based dependency injection.

Figure 8.1 shows the integration of action-based web frameworks with Spring DM. By using Spring DM's OSGi-aware web application contexts and its service support, we can reference business services from actions.

That's the general concept behind integrating Spring DM with action-based web frameworks. Now let's take a detailed look at how to implement this concept using Spring MVC.

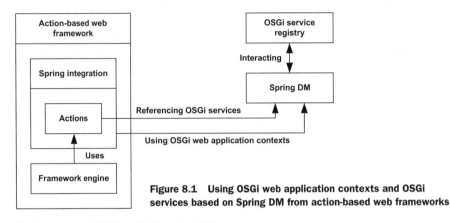

Figure 8.1   Using OSGi web application contexts and OSGi services based on Spring DM from action-based web frameworks

8.1.2   Using Spring MVC with Spring DM

Spring MVC is an action-based web framework shipped with Spring itself. It takes advantage of dependency injection and annotations to implement and configure the MVC 2 pattern. Spring DM can be used easily with Spring MVC by taking advantage of the extensibility of Spring application contexts. This feature allows you to specify OSGi-aware application contexts from Spring DM.

> **MVC 2 pattern**
>
> The MVC pattern aims to keep responsibilities separate when implementing UIs. The *model* corresponds to the data to be displayed, and the *view* to the UI. The *controller* intercepts user requests, executes business services, and then forwards the results to the view.
>
> Although this pattern is convenient, it can be cumbersome to implement. That's why a new version has been developed based on a controller called the *front controller*, which is responsible for forwarding requests to the right handling entity. The rest of the pattern remains as it was before. All current Java web frameworks base their implementations on the second version of this pattern.

In the following sections, we'll describe how to configure Spring MVC for Spring DM, how to use an OSGi service configured with Spring DM within a Spring MVC controller and how to display data returned from an OSGi service in a JSP page. We know this may sound confusing, but in the next section we hope to clear things up.

INSTALLING SPRING MVC

Spring MVC is part of Spring itself, and, like other parts of the framework, it's available as OSGi components directly in the Spring distribution. Some additional components need to be present in the OSGi container if JSP and JSTL are used.

Table 8.1 shows all the components necessary for installing Spring MVC in an OSGi container and using it with JSP and JSTL views.

NOTE   All the bundles we'll be discussing come from the SpringSource EBR.

Table 8.1 Bundles related to Spring MVC, available from the SpringSource EBR

Group ID	Artifact ID	Version
org.springframework	org.springframework.web.servlet	2.5.6
javax.servlet	com.springsource.javax.servlet	2.5.0
javax.servlet	com.springsource.javax.servlet.jsp	2.1.0
javax.servlet	com.springsource.javax.servlet.jsp.jstl	1.1.2
org.apache.taglibs	com.springsource.org.apache.taglibs.standard	1.1.2
org.springframework.osgi	spring-osgi-web	1.2.0

To install Spring MVC, all these components need to be provided to the OSGi container.

Once you have Spring MVC installed in the OSGi container, the next step is to configure the framework to use it with Spring DM.

CONFIGURING SPRING MVC FOR SPRING DM

Spring MVC uses two Spring application contexts for its configuration.

The first one corresponds to Spring MVC's association with the web application; it's used to configure entities independent of web-related concerns, such as logic or business entities. If you're using Spring DM, this context is also where you'd put OSGi service references to business services. To use Spring DM's service support, we need to specify OsgiBundleXmlWebApplicationContext, which is the OSGi-aware application context provided by Spring DM.

Listing 8.1 shows how to configure OsgiBundleXmlWebApplicationContext as Spring's web application context in the web bundle's web.xml file.

Listing 8.1 Configuring the Spring web application context

```
<web-app (...)>
  (...)
                                              Configures Spring XML  ❶
                                                 configuration file
  <context-param>                                       locations
    <param-name>contextConfigLocation</param-name>
    <param-value>/WEB-INF/osgi-context.xml</param-value>
  </context-param>

  <context-param>                          ❷ Configures OSGi-aware
    <param-name>contextClass</param-name>     web application context
    <param-value>
        org.springframework.osgi.web.context.support
         .OsgiBundleXmlWebApplicationContext
      </param-value>
  </context-param>

  <listener>                                   ❸ Configures
    <listener-class>                              web listener
        org.springframework.web.context.ContextLoaderListener
    </listener-class>
```

```
</listener>
(...)
</web-app>
```

Spring's `ContextLoaderListener` class supports the loading and managing of an application context within a web environment. This class must be set with the `listener` XML element ❸ in the web.xml file. The behavior of this listener can be configured using context parameters. The first uses the `contextConfigLocation` XML element ❶ to specify the location of the configuration file for the listener. The last, in this example, configures Spring DM—it adds an OSGi-aware behavior to the context through the `OsgiBundleXmlWebApplicationContext` class by specifying the `context-Class` XML element ❷.

The other Spring application context corresponds to the Spring frontend controller, the `DispatcherServlet`. This context is a child context of the web application context, and it has access to all artifacts configured in its parent. We can also use Spring DM at this level to reference services by specifying an OSGi-aware application context class.

Listing 8.2 shows how to configure the `DispatcherServlet` by using the `context-Class` init parameter of the `DispatcherServlet` class in the web.xml file.

> **Listing 8.2   Configuring the Spring MVC front controller**

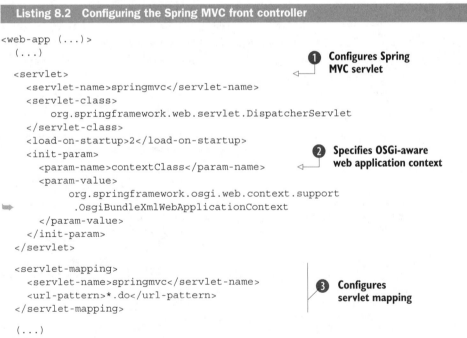

```
<web-app (...)>
  (...)

  <servlet>                                          ❶ Configures Spring
    <servlet-name>springmvc</servlet-name>              MVC servlet
    <servlet-class>
        org.springframework.web.servlet.DispatcherServlet
    </servlet-class>
    <load-on-startup>2</load-on-startup>
    <init-param>                                     ❷ Specifies OSGi-aware
      <param-name>contextClass</param-name>             web application context
      <param-value>
          org.springframework.osgi.web.context.support
          .OsgiBundleXmlWebApplicationContext
      </param-value>
    </init-param>
  </servlet>

  <servlet-mapping>
    <servlet-name>springmvc</servlet-name>           ❸ Configures
    <url-pattern>*.do</url-pattern>                      servlet mapping
  </servlet-mapping>

  (...)
</web-app>
```

The configuration of the `DispatcherServlet` servlet consists of two parts.

The first part involves the configuration of the servlet properties using the `servlet` XML element ❶. Here we can specify the servlet's name, its class name, and its init parameters. We use the `contextClass` parameter ❷ to specify OSGi-aware behavior for this context with the `OsgiBundleXmlWebApplicationContext` class.

The second part is the configuration of the servlet mapping, by using the `servlet-mapping` XML element ❸. This specifies the criteria for calling Spring MVC controllers. In our example, their URLs must end with the `.do` string.

We've finished configuring Spring MVC for use with Spring DM. This combination allows us to use OSGi services in the MVC framework. We'll now deal with implementing Spring MVC entities that use services configured with Spring DM.

USING ANNOTATION-BASED SUPPORT

The programming model for version 2.5 of the Spring Framework has changed: it's based on using annotations to define and configure MVC controllers. Because Spring DM provides annotation-based support for referencing OSGi services, this approach should be preferred (over the XML-based approach) when implementing MVC controllers. In fact, everything will be configured using annotations within controllers.

Listing 8.3 shows how to configure Spring MVC with annotations for both Spring and Spring DM and how to specify a view resolver based on JSP.

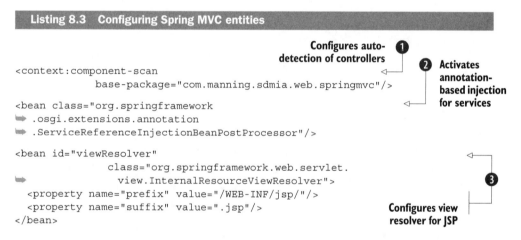

Listing 8.3   Configuring Spring MVC entities

```
                                        Configures auto-   ❶
                                  detection of controllers
<context:component-scan                              ❷  Activates
            base-package="com.manning.sdmia.web.springmvc"/>   annotation-
                                                         based injection
<bean class="org.springframework                         for services
➡ .osgi.extensions.annotation
➡ .ServiceReferenceInjectionBeanPostProcessor"/>

<bean id="viewResolver"
            class="org.springframework.web.servlet.
➡           view.InternalResourceViewResolver">    ❸
  <property name="prefix" value="/WEB-INF/jsp/"/>
  <property name="suffix" value=".jsp"/>         Configures view
</bean>                                           resolver for JSP
```

The first line of code uses Spring's `component-scan` XML element ❶ to specify in which packages Spring will find Spring MVC annotated controllers. The framework automatically detects and configures such entities.

The second XML element of the code activates Spring DM's annotation support to reference OSGi services via the `ServiceReferenceInjectionBeanPostProcessor` class ❷. Section 5.1.3 of chapter 5 details all the ways to configure the annotation-based support for services referencing in Spring DM.

The last XML element in listing 8.3 configures the Spring MVC view resolver to find the right view for a view identifier. For simplicity, we've configured a JSP view resolver ❸ in order to use JSP for our views. Spring MVC builds JSP URIs based on the view identifier and then forwards request handling to the corresponding JSP resource.

With this configuration done, we can implement our controller classes. As emphasized previously, Spring MVC uses an annotation-based programming model for parameterizing controller properties. Annotations allow you to define a class as the controller and specify rules for accessing it with HTTP. For controllers that want to use OSGi services for their processing, Spring DM's annotation support can be used to follow the same programming model.

Listing 8.4 shows how to use these different kinds of annotations within a controller implementation.

Listing 8.4   Implementing the Spring MVC controller

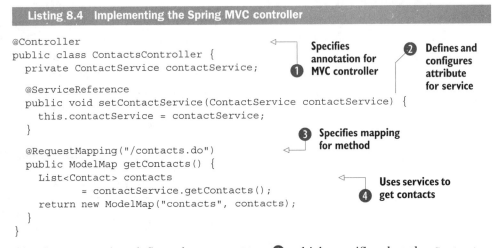

```
@Controller
public class ContactsController {
  private ContactService contactService;

  @ServiceReference
  public void setContactService(ContactService contactService) {
    this.contactService = contactService;
  }

  @RequestMapping("/contacts.do")
  public ModelMap getContacts() {
    List<Contact> contacts
        = contactService.getContacts();
    return new ModelMap("contacts", contacts);
  }
}
```

① Specifies annotation for MVC controller
② Defines and configures attribute for service
③ Specifies mapping for method
④ Uses services to get contacts

The first annotation defines the `Controller` ①, which specifies that the `Contacts-Controller` class is a Spring MVC controller. A `RequestMapping` annotation ③ is associated with each method of the class to specify that they're entry points for the controller. We also specify the URI to access these entry points. The OSGI service that's used must be defined as a property ② in the class with a corresponding setter method, and the `ServiceReference` annotation must be specified on this setter method to let Spring DM transparently inject the corresponding OSGi service instance. The instance can then be used to request processing using the service ④ and, in our example, get a list of contacts.

Only a few packages need to be added to the `Import-Package` header of the bundle's manifest file. They correspond to Spring MVC itself, Spring annotation definitions, and UI classes. The following snippet shows these additional packages:

```
Import-Package: (...)
 org.springframework.stereotype;version="2.5.6",
 org.springframework.ui;version="2.5.6",
 org.springframework.web.bind.annotation;version="2.5.6",
 org.springframework.web.servlet.view;version="2.5.6"
```

Let's now look at how to implement a Spring MVC view based on JSP and JSTL.

CONFIGURING AND USING JSTL

JSTL is a powerful extension of the JSP specification. It provides a standard tag library for common tasks in JSP pages.

When using this technology in an OSGi environment, some packages need to be added to the `Import-Package` header of the manifest file. These packages are related to servlet, JSP, and JSTL extensions and also to the specific JSTL implementation, in our case the one from Apache.

Listing 8.5 shows the specification of these packages in the web bundle's manifest file.

Listing 8.5 Packages to import for Spring MVC

```
Import-Package: (...)
  javax.servlet.http;version="2.4.0",           Packages
  javax.servlet.resources;version="2.0.0",      for servlets
  javax.servlet.jsp;version="2.0.0",
  javax.servlet.jsp.jstl.core;version="1.1.2",        Packages for
  javax.servlet.jsp.jstl.fmt;version="1.1.2",         JSP and JSTL
  javax.servlet.jsp.jstl.tlv;version="1.1.2",         technologies
  org.apache.taglibs.standard.resources;version="1.1.2",   Packages
  org.apache.taglibs.standard.tag.common.core;            for servlets
➥   version="1.1.2",
  org.apache.taglibs.standard.tag.rt.core;
➥   version="1.1.2",                              Packages for the JSTL
  org.apache.taglibs.standard.tei;version="1.1.2",    implementation
  org.apache.taglibs.standard.tlv;version="1.1.2"
```

With these packages loaded, we can use JSTL within our JSP pages to display information we obtain from calls to OSGi services referenced using Spring DM facilities. Listing 8.6 shows how to initialize JSTL in JSP pages and which tags to use for iterations and for printing information contained in objects.

Listing 8.6 Implementing a JSTL view in a JSP file

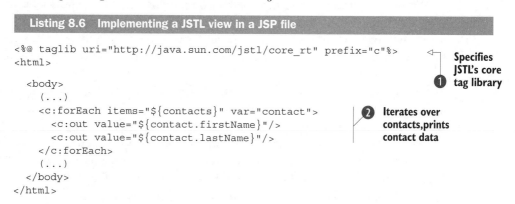

```
<%@ taglib uri="http://java.sun.com/jstl/core_rt" prefix="c"%>     Specifies
<html>                                                             JSTL's core
                                                               ➊   tag library
  <body>
    (...)
    <c:forEach items="${contacts}" var="contact">     ➋  Iterates over
      <c:out value="${contact.firstName}"/>               contacts, prints
      <c:out value="${contact.lastName}"/>                contact data
    </c:forEach>
    (...)
  </body>
</html>
```

The first step in listing 8.6 consists of specifying the core tag library for JSTL ➊. Thereafter, we can print the contact list using the `forEach` tag to iterate through the list and the `out` tag to print the contact information ➋.

As you've seen, configuring and using Spring MVC within an OSGi environment with Spring DM is easy because Spring MVC uses the extension capabilities of Spring application contexts. Using existing OSGi services from web UIs in this way helps to improve application modularity.

Another kind of web framework uses a component-based approach on the server side to implement the MVC 2 pattern. Spring DM can be integrated into such a framework so that managed entities can get OSGi services configured by the framework.

8.2 *Using component-based web frameworks with Spring DM*

Component-based web frameworks, unlike action-based frameworks, use an event-based implementation and have the ability to attach functionality, located on the server, directly to UI components. Based on specific request-handling lifecycles, frameworks call the attached methods of managed beans on the server to obtain data and execute operations. Most frameworks of this kind provide integration with Spring and can therefore use Spring DM in an OSGi environment.

In this section, we'll discuss how to integrate such frameworks with Spring DM and then look at some examples using the most popular of these frameworks: JSF and Wicket. These frameworks are useful if you want to implement the MVC pattern on the server side using a component-based approach.

8.2.1 *Using Spring DM with component-based frameworks*

The key abstractions of action-based web frameworks are the managed entities and components, which allow you to implement server representations of web UIs and to handle events and actions on the server side. These operations can be done using external services. Integrating Spring DM with such frameworks is simply a matter of using the Spring DM-configured OSGi services within managed components.

When configuring Spring support for component-based frameworks, Spring DM's OSGi web application context must be specified in order for you to use Spring DM's osgi namespace. Using this namespace allows you to define and reference OSGi services in Spring application contexts, which is the first step in integrating Spring DM and component-based frameworks.

The second step involves injecting OSGi services configured with Spring DM into managed entities or components of the application. This can be done using either classic XML-based or annotation-based dependency injection.

Figure 8.2 illustrates integrating component-based web frameworks with Spring DM. You can use OSGi-aware Spring DM web application contexts and Spring DM's service support to reference business services from actions. The integration of these Spring DM features is based on framework extensibility features.

Having described the general concepts behind integrating Spring DM with component-based web frameworks, we'll now detail the implementation of these concepts using JSF and Wicket.

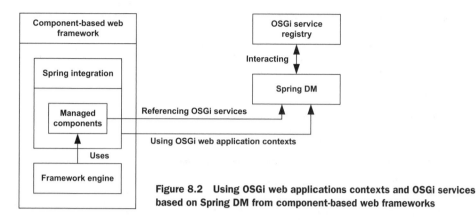

Figure 8.2 Using OSGi web applications contexts and OSGi services based on Spring DM from component-based web frameworks

8.2.2 Using JSF with Spring DM

JavaServer Faces (JSF) is part of Java EE and provides a server-side component-based framework for implementing the MVC pattern. It's intended to simplify the development and integration of UIs with their corresponding business entities and services. The request-handling lifecycle manages an in-memory UI representation and calls user entities as appropriate. Several implementations, such as the JSF reference implementation (RI) and MyFaces, are available as open source projects.

The integration of JSF with Spring DM is based on the JSF support provided by Spring itself. This support uses the Spring web application context and enables the configuration of JSF user entities directly in the application context.

In the following sections, we'll describe how to configure JSF in an OSGi environment and how to use Spring DM to process JSF-managed beans.

INSTALLING MYFACES

We'll use the MyFaces JSF implementation to show you how to integrate Spring DM with JSF. The first step is to provision the OSGi container with the necessary bundles.

The SpringSource EBR provides almost all you need to use the MyFaces framework in an OSGi environment. MyFaces requires a large number of dependencies, as shown in the repository. Table 8.2 lists all the necessary bundles for using MyFaces and its Spring integration, and table 8.3 lists the needed dependencies for MyFaces related to Tomcat.

Table 8.2 Bundles required to use MyFaces, available from the SpringSource EBR

Group ID	Artifact ID	Version
javax.annotation	com.springsource.javax.annotation	1.0.0
javax.el	com.springsource.javax.el	1.0.0
javax.persistence	com.springsource.javax.persistence	1.99.0
javax.servlet	com.springsource.javax.servlet	2.5.0
javax.servlet	com.springsource.javax.servlet.jsp	2.1.0
javax.servlet	com.springsource.javax.servlet.jsp.jstl	1.2.0

Table 8.2   Bundles required to use MyFaces, available from the SpringSource EBR *(continued)*

Group ID	Artifact ID	Version
org.apache.xmlcommons	com.springsource.org.apache.xmlcommons	1.3.4
javax.ejb	com.springsource.javax.ejb	3.0.0
javax.xml.rpc	com.springsource.javax.xml.rpc	1.1.0
javax.xml.soap	com.springsource.javax.xml.soap	1.3.0
javax.activation	com.springsource.javax.activation	1.1.1
javax.mail	com.springsource.javax.mail	1.4.1
javax.xml.ws	com.springsource.javax.xml.ws	2.1.1
javax.xml.bind	com.springsource.javax.xml.bind	2.1.7
javax.xml.stream	com.springsource.javax.xml.stream	1.0.1
org.apache.commons	com.springsource.org.apache.commons.beanutils	1.8.0
org.apache.commons	com.springsource.org.apache.commons.codec	1.4.0
org.apache.commons	com.springsource.org.apache.commons.collections	3.2.1
org.apache.commons	com.springsource.org.apache.commons.digester	1.8.1
org.apache.commons	com.springsource.org.apache.commons.logging	1.1.1
org.springframework	org.springframework.web	2.5.6

MyFaces version 1.2.2 requires to Tomcat 6 to work. Table 8.3 lists the bundles MyFaces requires for Tomcat 6.

Table 8.3   Bundles required to use MyFaces with Tomcat, available from the SpringSource EBR

Group ID	Artifact ID	Version
org.apache.catalina.springsource	com.springsource.org.apache.catalina.springsource	6.0.20.S2-r5956
org.apache.coyote.springsource	com.springsource.org.apache.coyote.springsource	6.0.20.S2-r5956
org.apache.jasper.springsource	com.springsource.org.apache.jasper.org.eclipse.jdt	6.0.16
org.apache.jasper.springsource	com.springsource.org.apache.jasper.org.eclipse.jdt.springsource	6.0.20.S2-r5956
org.apache.jasper.springsource	com.springsource.org.apache.jasper.springsource	6.0.20.S2-r5956
org.apache.el.springsource	com.springsource.org.apache.el.springsource	6.0.20.S2-r5956
org.apache.juli.springsource	com.springsource.org.apache.juli.extras.springsource	6.0.20.S2-r5956

We said "almost" previously because an error occurs when trying to use the provided MyFaces bundles. We need to patch the framework to make it work in an OSGi environment with Spring DM.

Why did we choose the MyFaces JSF implementation?

We chose to describe how MyFaces works with Spring DM here because this JSF implementation is commonly used by the Java community and it's the one that poses the fewest problems within an OSGi environment. However, this implementation can't be used directly in an OSGi environment and needs to be patched to fix an issue regarding the use of the `JspFactory` instance.

When using Tomcat 6, a configuration fragment is required to properly configure the web container for serving JSPs. The implementation of this fragment is described in section 9.4.2.

The bundles required by version 2.5.6 or later of the Spring Framework also need to be added to the OSGi container.

Problems with MyFaces 1.2.2 when used with Spring DM

There is a problem when using MyFaces 1.2.2 with Spring DM and Tomcat 6. MyFaces isn't able to initialize a `JspFactory` instance for JSP 2.1, and a `NullPointerException` exception occurs in its `Jsp21FacesInitializer` class:

```
java.lang.NullPointerException
    at org.apache.myfaces.webapp.Jsp21FacesInitializer
    .initContainerIntegration(...)
```

We opened an issue for this bug in the MyFaces JIRA under the identifier MYFACES-2442. The issue shows how to solve the problem by updating the `isJsp21` method of the `ContainerUtils` class in MyFaces. We provide, in the book's source code, a patched version of MyFaces 1.2.2 that fixes this bug.

Once MyFaces is installed, the next step is to configure it to use it with Spring DM.

CONFIGURING JSF SPRING INTEGRATION FOR SPRING DM

JSF uses the Spring application context of the web application to integrate with the Spring Framework, so when you're using Spring DM, OSGi service references are configured in the Spring configuration with Spring DM facilities. But configuring these references requires the use of a Spring application context that supports OSGi concerns. Specifying the `OsgiBundleXmlWebApplicationContext` class as the `contextClass` property of the web configuration enables this. The configuration within the web.xml file is the same as the one shown in listing 8.1.

You can configure the JSF web controller by using the `FacesServlet` class and the `StartupServletContextListener` listener in the context of the JSF implementation,

MyFaces. Again, this is configured in the web.xml file, as with any servlet. Listing 8.7 shows this configuration using the servlet and servlet-mapping XML elements.

Listing 8.7   Configuring the JSF front controller

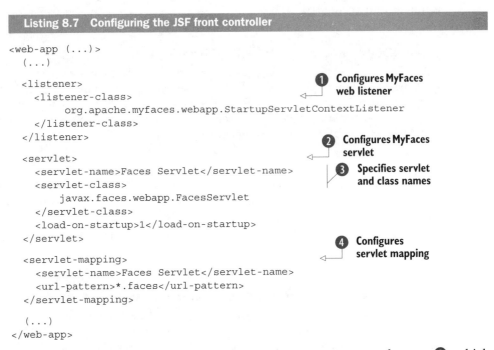

```
<web-app (...)>
  (...)
  <listener>
    <listener-class>                              ❶ Configures MyFaces
        org.apache.myfaces.webapp.StartupServletContextListener    web listener
    </listener-class>
  </listener>

  <servlet>                                       ❷ Configures MyFaces
    <servlet-name>Faces Servlet</servlet-name>       servlet
    <servlet-class>                               ❸ Specifies servlet
        javax.faces.webapp.FacesServlet              and class names
    </servlet-class>
    <load-on-startup>1</load-on-startup>
  </servlet>
                                                  ❹ Configures
  <servlet-mapping>                                  servlet mapping
    <servlet-name>Faces Servlet</servlet-name>
    <url-pattern>*.faces</url-pattern>
  </servlet-mapping>

  (...)
</web-app>
```

The JSF web controller is configured using the servlet XML element ❷, which allows its name and implementation class to be specified ❸. This servlet is responsible for handling all JSF requests by specifying a mapping for *.faces ❹. With MyFaces, the StartupServletContextListener web listener must also be added for its initialization ❶.

Because we need to use web scopes for beans with Spring JSF support, a dedicated request listener must be added in the web application configuration file. Listing 8.8 shows how to configure this using the listener XML element in the web.xml file.

Listing 8.8   Configuring the Spring request context listener

```
<web-app (...)>
  (...)
                                                  Specifies request
  <listener>                                      context listener
    <listener-class>
        org.springframework.web.context.request.RequestContextListener
    </listener-class>
  </listener>

  (...)
</web-app>
```

Finally, we need to configure Spring's JSF support. This support provides a variable resolver, which enables entities to be resolved directly within a Spring application context. Listing 8.9 shows how to configure this in the JSF XML configuration file, faces-config.xml.

Listing 8.9   Configuring the Spring JSF variable resolver

```
<faces-config>
  (...)
                                        Configures Spring
  <application>                         variable resolver for JSF
    <variable-resolver>           ◄
        org.springframework.web.jsf.DelegatingVariableResolver
    </variable-resolver>
  </application>

  (...)
</faces-config>
```

Everything is now configured for using Spring DM with JSF entities, so that OSGi services can be used in the JSF implementation. Now let's look at how to link these entities with Spring DM.

USING JSF WITH SPRING DM

The first step is to configure the OSGi services themselves, using Spring DM's facilities, in the Spring web application context of the web application. Our old friend, the `ref-erence` XML element, should be used to reference services, as shown in following snippet. These services can then be used in JSF entities defined by applications.

```
<beans (...)>
  (...)

  <osgi:reference id="contactService"
        interface="com.manning.sdmia.directory.service.ContactService"/>

  (...)
</beans>
```

The previous snippet shows how to reference an OSGi service using the Spring DM's facilities.

Once this configuration is done, we can implement our managed beans and inject OSGi services into them. With Spring's JSF support, every entity can now be defined within the Spring XML application context. For managed beans, we need to specify the appropriate scope. A `request` scope specifies that the bean is shared across the scope of a request.

Listing 8.10 shows how to inject an OSGi service configured with Spring DM into a managed bean within the Spring XML application context.

Listing 8.10   Configuring a JSF-managed bean

```
<beans (...)>
  (...)
                                        Specifies request    ❶
                                        scope for bean
  <bean id="contactManagedBean"
      class="com.manning.sdmia.jsf.bean.ContactManagedBean"
      scope="request">                                      ◄
```

```
<property name="contactService"
        ref="contactService"/>                    Injects OSGi
</bean>                                         ❷ service

(...)
</beans>
```

The `contactManagedBean` bean is a JSF-managed bean. When configuring such an artifact in a Spring XML configuration file, a web scope such as `request` or `session` must be specified because managed beans typically contain state for request handling. For the bean we're defining, we use `request` scope ❶. Because managed beans using Spring's JSF support are configured in Spring, we can inject OSGi services configured with Spring DM ❷.

The JSF bean is now properly implemented and configured, and we can create a simple JSP view to display our contact list in a table. Listing 8.11 shows how to use JSF `taglibs` to implement this feature.

Listing 8.11 Implementing the JSF view in a JSP file

```
<%@ taglib uri="http://java.sun.com/jsf/html" prefix="h"%>        ❶ Specifies
<%@ taglib uri="http://java.sun.com/jsf/core" prefix="f"%>           JSF taglibs

<f:view>
  <html>
    (...)
    <body lang="fr">
      <h:form>                                                   ❷ Specifies table
        <h:dataTable                                                component
                value="#{contactManagerBean.contacts}"             and links it to
                var="contact">                                     contact list
        <h:column>
          <f:facet name="header">
            <h:outputText value="First name"/>
          </f:facet>                                             ❸ Prints data
          <h:outputText value="#{contact.firstname}"/>             from contact
        </h:column>
        (...)
        </h:dataTable>
      </h:form>
    </body>
  </html>
</f:view>
```

Having defined the use of `taglibs` from JSF ❶, a table component can be specified using the `dataTable` XML element ❷. Its `value` attribute allows you to reference a method for the table data. In this example, the `getContacts` method is called, which delegates to a method from the injected OSGi service. For each column, we can then specify a value to display, such as the first name of a contact ❸.

As usual, when using external libraries in an OSGi environment, some extra packages must be specified in the `Import-Package` header of the manifest file for the component using JSF. Listing 8.12 shows the packages that need to be specified.

Listing 8.12 Packages to import for the MyFaces JSF implementation

```
Import-Package: (...)
  javax.faces;version="1.2.2",
  javax.faces.convert;version="1.2.2",            Packages
  javax.faces.event;version="1.2.2",              for JSF
  javax.faces.webapp;version="1.2.2",
  org.apache.myfaces.application;version="1.2.2",
  org.apache.myfaces.application.jsp;version="1.2.2",
  org.apache.myfaces.config;version="1.2.2",
  org.apache.myfaces.config.annotation;version="1.2.2",
  org.apache.myfaces.config.element;version="1.2.2",
  org.apache.myfaces.config.impl;version="1.2.2",
  org.apache.myfaces.config.impl.digester;version="1.2.2",
  org.apache.myfaces.config.impl.digester.elements;version="1.2.2",
  org.apache.myfaces.context;version="1.2.2",
  org.apache.myfaces.context.servlet;version="1.2.2",     Packages for
  org.apache.myfaces.convert;version="1.2.2",             MyFaces JSF
  org.apache.myfaces.el;version="1.2.2",                  implementation
  org.apache.myfaces.event;version="1.2.2",
  org.apache.myfaces.lifecycle;version="1.2.2",
  org.apache.myfaces.renderkit;version="1.2.2",
  org.apache.myfaces.renderkit.html;version="1.2.2",
  org.apache.myfaces.resource;version="1.2.2",
  org.apache.myfaces.taglib.core;version="1.2.2",
  org.apache.myfaces.taglib.html;version="1.2.2",
  org.apache.myfaces.util;version="1.2.2",
  org.apache.myfaces.webapp;version="1.2.2",
  org.springframework.beans.factory;version="2.5.6",
  org.springframework.osgi.web.context.support;version="1.2.0",
  org.springframework.util;version="2.5.6",               Packages for
  org.springframework.web.context;version="2.5.6",        Spring and
  org.springframework.web.context.request;version="2.5.6",  Spring DM
  org.springframework.web.jsf;version="2.5.6",
  org.springframework.web.jsf.el;version="2.5.6"
```

We've now seen how to use Spring DM with JSF through Spring's support for JSF. The integration between Spring DM and JSF allows us to use OSGi services within JSF managed beans.

We've now described JSF, but what if you want to use another component-based framework, such as Wicket? You'd have to know how to integrate this framework with Spring DM.

8.2.3 *Using Wicket with Spring DM*

Wicket is another widely used component-based web framework. It provides a proper separation of markup and logic, and a POJO data model with no XML configuration. The framework is based on powerful and reusable components written with plain Java and HTML code. The project is hosted by Apache and is available at http:// wicket.apache.org/.

In this section, we'll describe how to use this framework with Spring DM, which allows you to use a component-based approach with OSGi services on the server side. This integration leverages Spring's own integration with Wicket.

NOTE   If you want to go deeper with Wicket, we suggest reading *Wicket in Action* by Martijn Dashorst and Eelco Hillenius (Manning, 2008).

INSTALLING WICKET

The SpringSource EBR provides all you need to use the Wicket framework in an OSGi environment. Table 8.4 lists all the necessary bundles for using Wicket and its Spring integration.

Table 8.4   Bundles related to Wicket, available from the SpringSource EBR

Group ID	Artifact ID	Version
org.apache.wicket	com.springsource.org.apache.wicket	1.3.3
org.apache.wicket	com.springsource.org.apache.wicket.extensions	1.3.3
org.apache.wicket	com.springsource.org.apache.wicket.injection	1.3.3
org.apache.wicket	com.springsource.org.apache.wicket.spring	1.3.3
org.apache.wicket	com.springsource.org.apache.wicket.spring.injection.annot	1.3.3
javax.servlet	com.springsource.javax.servlet	2.5.0
net.sourceforge.cglib	com.springsource.net.sf.cglib	2.2.0

To install Wicket, all these components need to be provisioned to the OSGi container. Once Wicket is installed, you need to configure it so that you can use it with Spring DM.

CONFIGURING WICKET SPRING INTEGRATION FOR SPRING DM

Wicket's Spring integration is based on the application context associated with the web application itself. When using Spring DM, you can reference OSGi services in this application context, but this requires the use of a Spring application context that can interact with OSGi. Again, specifying the `OsgiBundleXmlWebApplicationContext` class for the web application context's `contextClass` property enables you to use Spring DM. The configuration in the web.xml file is the same as was shown in listing 8.1.

The Wicket web controller can be configured by using the `WicketServlet` class in the web.xml file as for any servlet. The `applicationFactoryClassName` parameter must be added to specify that we want to use the implementation that activates Spring support in Wicket.

Listing 8.13 shows this configuration using the `servlet` and `servlet-mapping` XML elements.

Listing 8.13   Configuring the Wicket frontend controller

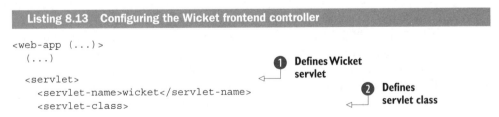

```
<web-app (...)>
  (...)
                                              ❶ Defines Wicket
  <servlet>                                       servlet
    <servlet-name>wicket</servlet-name>
    <servlet-class>                           ❷ Defines
                                                  servlet class
```

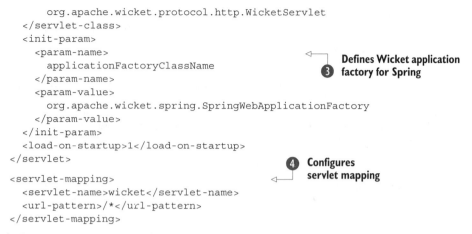

```
          org.apache.wicket.protocol.http.WicketServlet
    </servlet-class>
    <init-param>
      <param-name>
        applicationFactoryClassName
      </param-name>
      <param-value>
        org.apache.wicket.spring.SpringWebApplicationFactory
      </param-value>
    </init-param>
    <load-on-startup>1</load-on-startup>
  </servlet>

  <servlet-mapping>
    <servlet-name>wicket</servlet-name>
    <url-pattern>/*</url-pattern>
  </servlet-mapping>
```

❸ **Defines Wicket application factory for Spring**

❹ Configures servlet mapping

```
</web-app>
```

The Wicket web controller is configured using the `servlet` XML element ❶, which allows its name and its implementation class name to be specified ❷. Because we want to integrate Wicket with Spring DM, we must enable Wicket's Spring support. This is done using the `applicationFactoryClassName` ❸ and specifying the `SpringWebApplicationFactory` class . The last configuration is to specify the mapping for this servlet ❹.

Everything is now configured for using Spring DM in Wicket application entities so that they can use OSGi services to implement their functionality. In the next section, we'll look at how to link these entities with Spring DM.

USING SPRING DM WITHIN WICKET PAGES

In order to use OSGi services within Wicket entities, they must be configured themselves, using Spring DM's facilities, in the web application context of the web application. The `reference` XML element should be used to reference services, as shown in following snippet. These services can then be used in Wicket entities defined by applications.

```
<beans (...)>
  (...)

  <osgi:reference id="contactService"
        interface="com.manning.sdmia.directory.service.ContactService"/>

  (...)
</beans>
```

The preceding snippet shows how to reference an OSGi service using Spring DM's facilities.

Now that this configuration is done, we can implement our Wicket application entities. These must extend Wicket's `WebApplication` class and be configured as beans in the Spring application context.

Wicket provides two approaches for injecting OSGi services configured with Spring DM into Wicket entities:

- *Injection using Spring XML configuration files*—With its Spring support, Wicket allows the injection of any Spring bean within its application entities. Thereafter, page entities can obtain the corresponding application entities to get dependencies configured in Spring.
- *Injection based on annotations*—Wicket provides a mechanism that allows automatic injection of Spring dependencies based on the `SpringBean` annotation.

For the first approach, the injection of OSGi services is done directly in the Spring XML configuration in the bean corresponding to the application. Standard Spring configuration can be used, as shown in listing 8.14.

Listing 8.14   Configuring the Wicket `WebApplication` entity

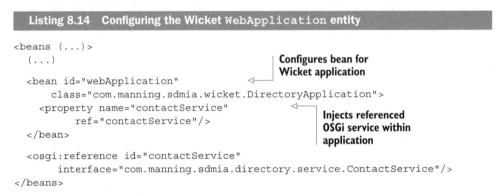

```
<beans (...)>
  (...)                                          Configures bean for
                                                 Wicket application
  <bean id="webApplication"           <--
      class="com.manning.sdmia.wicket.DirectoryApplication">
    <property name="contactService"        <--
          ref="contactService"/>               Injects referenced
  </bean>                                       OSGi service within
                                               application
  <osgi:reference id="contactService"
      interface="com.manning.sdmia.directory.service.ContactService"/>
</beans>
```

To be able to inject the service, the application class must contain the property corresponding to the service and its getter and setter methods to allow injection. Listing 8.15 shows the specification of a property referencing an OSGi service and the methods used for injection.

Listing 8.15   Implementation of the Wicket `WebApplication` entity

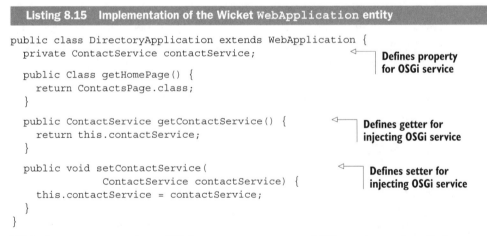

```
public class DirectoryApplication extends WebApplication {
  private ContactService contactService;         <--  Defines property
                                                      for OSGi service
  public Class getHomePage() {
    return ContactsPage.class;
  }

  public ContactService getContactService() {    <--  Defines getter for
    return this.contactService;                       injecting OSGi service
  }

  public void setContactService(                 <--  Defines setter for
            ContactService contactService) {          injecting OSGi service
    this.contactService = contactService;
  }
}
```

With these two steps done, Wicket pages can access OSGi services using their corresponding `WebApplication`. In fact, each page class can reference its page using its `getApplication` method. The following snippet shows how you can get a reference to an OSGI service configured with Spring DM in a page class:

```
public class ContactsPage extends WebPage {

  (...)

  public ContactService getContactService() {
    return ((DirectoryApplication)getApplication())
      .getContactService();
  }
}
```

Gets service reference from Wicket application

With this approach, references to configured OSGi services are made using the corresponding application class. Instances of the application class can be obtained using the getApplication method. We can then use the application class's accessor method to get the OSGi service instance.

The second approach is much more convenient and less intrusive. In fact, the injection of beans and OSGi services is implicit and is performed internally by Wicket. No injection needs to be explicitly done in the application class at all. We only need to configure an instance, as shown in the following snippet:

```
<beans (...)>
  (...)

  <bean id="webApplication"
        class="com.manning.sdmia.wicket.DirectoryApplication"/>

  <osgi:reference id="contactService"
        interface="com.manning.sdmia.directory.service.ContactService"/>
</beans>
```

Configures Wicket application class

References OSGi service with Spring DM

Some additional configuration is needed in the Wicket application class to enable automatic injection of Spring beans. This is done in its init method by passing the SpringComponentInjector class as parameter of the addComponentInstantiation-Listener method. The following snippet shows how to configure this in the application class:

```
public class DirectoryApplication extends WebApplication {
  public void init() {
    super.init();
    addComponentInstantiationListener(
              new SpringComponentInjector(this));
  }

  public Class getHomePage() {
    return ContactsPage.class;
  }
}
```

Configures automatic injection based on annotations

In this case, there's no need to define OSGi services as properties of the application class. Only pages that use them need to specify them as properties. These must then be configured using Wicket's SpringBean annotation. The presence of this annotation will tell Wicket to inject the corresponding instance present in the Spring XML configuration file in the associated property.

The following snippet shows how to configure this feature:

```
public class ContactsPage extends WebPage {
  @SpringBean(name="contactService")
  private ContactService contactService;

  (...)
}
```

As you can see, the annotation must simply be put on the property corresponding to the OSGi service.

We've described how to integrate Spring DM with Wicket by using Spring's Wicket support. The last thing we need to cover is the OSGi configuration of the component containing the Wicket application.

Because we want to use Wicket in an OSGi environment, we first need to specify some packages in the Import-Package header of the manifest file for bundles using Wicket entities. Some are related to Wicket itself, and others to Spring and Spring DM. Listing 8.16 shows all the packages that need to be specified in the Import-Package header.

Listing 8.16   Packages to import for Wicket

```
Import-Package: (...)
  org.apache.wicket;version="1.3.3",
  org.apache.wicket.application;version="1.3.3",
  org.apache.wicket.markup;version="1.3.3",
  org.apache.wicket.markup.html;version="1.3.3",                    Packages
  org.apache.wicket.markup.html.basic;version="1.3.3",             for Wicket
  org.apache.wicket.markup.html.list;version="1.3.3",
  org.apache.wicket.model;version="1.3.3",
  org.apache.wicket.protocol.http;version="1.3.3",
  org.springframework.context;version="2.5.6",                     Packages for
  org.springframework.osgi.web.context.support;version="1.2.0",    Spring and
  org.springframework.web.context;version="2.5.6"                  Spring DM
  org.apache.wicket.proxy;version="1.3.3",                         Packages for
  org.apache.wicket.spring;version="1.3.3",                        Wicket–Spring
  org.apache.wicket.spring.injection.annot;version="1.3.3",        integration
  org.apache.wicket.injection;version="1.3.3"
```

As you can see, using Spring DM with Wicket is pretty easy, thanks to Spring's support for Wicket. It allows you to access instances of OSGI services configured with Spring DM directly from within entities of a Wicket application.

Another category of web frameworks is AJAX frameworks. These allow you to add interactivity to web pages without having to reload them. Spring DM can be integrated with such frameworks in order to, for instance, remotely expose OSGi services. This allows for an improved user experience with web components by improving the interactivity provided by web user interfaces.

8.3   *Using AJAX frameworks with Spring DM*

AJAX frameworks are web frameworks that provide end-to-end support for implementing AJAX techniques from a JavaScript client on a web page to calling services on server side. These frameworks provide facilities for linking server abstractions to their JavaScript representations and to the application protocol used.

Most frameworks of this kind provide integration with Spring, allowing declarative configuration of services as remote services. Because of this support, integration with Spring DM is simple and consists of exposing OSGi services configured with Spring DM in an OSGi environment.

In this section, we'll describe the general concepts behind integrating these frameworks with Spring DM, then we'll look at examples of two of the most popular ones: DWR and GWT.

8.3.1 Using Spring DM with AJAX frameworks

Integrating Spring DM with AJAX frameworks involves exporting OSGi services referenced through Spring DM as remote services with the exporting facilities of these frameworks. These facilities typically only require some Spring configuration.

When configuring Spring support for this kind of framework, Spring DM's OSGi web application context must be specified so that the osgi namespace can be used. The other step is to use OSGi services, configured through Spring DM, in the exporters of the AJAX application. An *exporter* is a dedicated utility class that makes an existing service available remotely through a specific protocol. This can be done directly in the Spring application context.

Figure 8.3 shows the interactions necessary between Spring DM and AJAX-based web frameworks in order for them to work together.

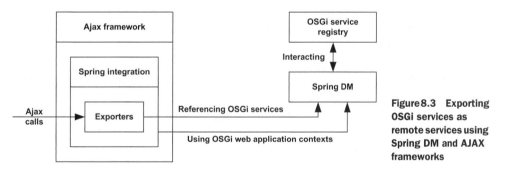

Figure 8.3 Exporting OSGi services as remote services using Spring DM and AJAX frameworks

That covers the general concepts involved in integrating Spring DM and AJAX frameworks. We'll now detail the implementation of these concepts using DWR and GWT.

8.3.2 Using DWR with Spring DM

As emphasized on the Direct Web Remoting (DWR) website (http://directwebremoting. org/), this framework aims to provide "easy AJAX for Java" by implementing all the steps in the chain for handling AJAX requests, from the JavaScript client to the Java server side.

On the client side, DWR provides JavaScript objects that represent objects on the server side. You're given the impression of being able to directly use the same objects on the client side as those developed on the server side. DWR provides creator abstractions that enable you to transparently expose objects as remote services accessible via AJAX.

The DWR framework also provides direct support for the Spring Framework, and this support allows every bean configured in Spring to be exported as a remote service. Integrating DWR with Spring DM involves exposing OSGi services configured through Spring DM as remote services.

With DWR, you can also expose a simple Spring bean that uses an OSGi service configured through Spring DM, but in this case you must be careful not to implement unnecessary additional classes.

INSTALLING DWR

To use DWR, you must provision the OSGi container with the bundles necessary for using DWR in an OSGi environment. The SpringSource EBR unfortunately only provides an old version of DWR (version 1.1.4) rather than the latest production version of the framework (version 2.0).

In chapter 6, we described how to OSGi-ify existing Java libraries and frameworks with the Bnd tool. Using this approach, we can create an OSGi bundle for version 2.0.5 of DWR. This bundle contains all you need to use the DWR framework in an OSGi environment, and it's included within the source code for this chapter.

Now we need to configure DWR's Spring integration to allow the use of Spring DM.

CONFIGURING DWR'S SPRING INTEGRATION FOR SPRING DM

DWR's integration with Spring is based on the application context associated with the web application itself. When using Spring DM, you can reference OSGi services in this application context, but using OSGi services configured with Spring DM requires the use of a Spring application context that can interact with OSGi.

To enable the use of Spring DM, specify the `OsgiBundleXmlWebApplicationContext` class for the `contextClass` property of the application context in the web.xml file. The appropriate configuration in the web.xml file is the same as described in listing 8.1.

You can configure the DWR web controller by using the `DwrSpringServlet` class. Again, this is configured in the web.xml file. Listing 8.17 shows this configuration using the `servlet` and `servlet-mapping` XML elements.

Listing 8.17 Configuring the DWR front controller

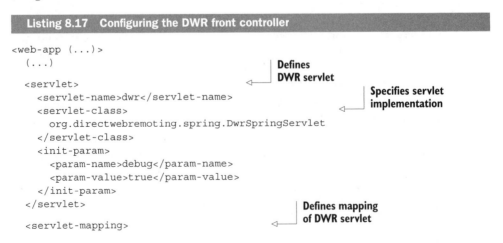

```
<web-app (...)>
  (...)
                                          Defines
                                          DWR servlet
  <servlet>
    <servlet-name>dwr</servlet-name>                   Specifies servlet
    <servlet-class>                                     implementation
      org.directwebremoting.spring.DwrSpringServlet
    </servlet-class>
    <init-param>
      <param-name>debug</param-name>
      <param-value>true</param-value>
    </init-param>
  </servlet>
                                          Defines mapping
                                          of DWR servlet
  <servlet-mapping>
```

```
    <servlet-name>dwr</servlet-name>
    <url-pattern>/dwr/*</url-pattern>
  </servlet-mapping>

  (...)
</web-app>
```

Everything is now configured for using Spring DM in DWR to expose OSGi services as remote services for AJAX calls. Next, we'll look at how we can use DWR facilities, such as its Spring 2 namespace and its creator mechanism.

USING SPRING DM WITHIN DWR

DWR version 2 provides an XML namespace that allows exposed beans to be configured directly by DWR in Spring XML configuration files. This namespace must be configured using standard XML techniques, like any other Spring XML namespace. Listing 8.18 shows how to configure the DWR XML namespace.

Listing 8.18 Configuring the DWR Spring namespace

```
<beans xmlns="http://www.springframework.org/schema/beans"
       xmlns:xsi="http://www.w3.org/2001/XMLSchema-instance"          ⟵  Defines DWR
       xmlns:dwr="http://www.directwebremoting                            XML namespace
  ⇒     .org/schema/spring-dwr"
       (...)
       xsi:schemaLocation="http://www.springframework.org/schema/beans
              http://www.springframework.org/schema/beans/spring-beans.xsd
          (...)
          http://www.directwebremoting.org/                                       ⟵
          schema/spring-dwr
              http://www.directwebremoting.org/schema/spring-dwr-2.0.xsd">
    (...)
</beans>                                             Defines location of namespace schema
```

We're now ready to export an OSGi service that has been configured through Spring DM. The service must be configured using the `reference` XML element of Spring DM, as described in section 5.1.2 of chapter 5.

Once the configuration described in listing 8.18 has been done in the Spring XML configuration file, we can use the `dwr` XML namespace to export the service for use by AJAX. Although DWR allows you to specify DWR configuration within a Spring bean's configuration, this can't be done with elements from Spring DM's `osgi` XML namespace. Instead, we use DWR's configuration element and its inner `create` element.

Listing 8.19 shows how to expose an OSGi service configured with Spring DM as a remote service for DWR.

Listing 8.19 Configuring a remote service with DWR

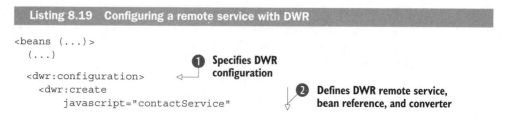

```
<beans (...)>
  (...)
                                    ❶  Specifies DWR
  <dwr:configuration>        ⟵         configuration
    <dwr:create                              ❷  Defines DWR remote service,
        javascript="contactService"             bean reference, and converter
```

```
          type="spring">
   <dwr:param name="beanName"
        value="contactService"/>
   <dwr:convert type="bean"
        class="com.manning.sdmia.directory.model.Contact"/>
   </dwr:create>
 </dwr:configuration>

 <dwr:controller id="dwrController" debug="true"/>

 <osgi:reference id="contactService"
        interface="com.manning.sdmia.directory.service.ContactService"/>

 (...)
</beans>
```

2 Defines DWR remote service, bean reference, and converter

3 Defines DWR controller

In order to export an OSGi service through DWR, you need to get hold of the OSGi service itself using Spring DM's reference XML element. To do so, you need to define the global configuration for DWR with the configuration **1** and controller **3** XML elements. You also need to add the specific configuration for the remote service by adding a create XML element **2** inside the configuration element. Name and type attributes must be set with the values contactService and spring, respectively, to specify the name of the JavaScript object created and to activate the Spring support. The bean name must also be specified, together with a converter entity, to indicate how to handle returned data objects.

Problems using DWR 2.0.5 with Spring DM

There is a problem when using DWR 2.0.5 with Spring DM to directly expose OSGi services configured as remote services. The problem occurs because DWR incorrectly determines the type of the service instance. DWR gets the implementation class that is hidden by the OSGi classloader because only the service interface is visible. When calling the service with DWR, the following exception then occurs:

```
java.lang.IllegalArgumentException: object isn't an instance of
declaring class
```

We opened an issue for this bug in the DWR JIRA under the identifier DWR-429. The issue shows how to solve the problem by updating the afterPropertiesSet method of the BeanCreator class in DWR. In the book's source code, we provide a patched version of DWR 2.0.5 that fixes this bug.

In some situations, developers don't want to directly expose OSGi services as remote services but prefer to implement an intermediate entity to expose. In this case, a classic Spring bean can be defined, and the OSGi service can be injected into it. This new bean can then be configured as a remote service and can use the OSGi service for its functionality.

In this situation, you can specify DWR's export configuration directly within the bean definition. Listing 8.20 shows how to do this.

Listing 8.20 Configuring the remote service with DWR

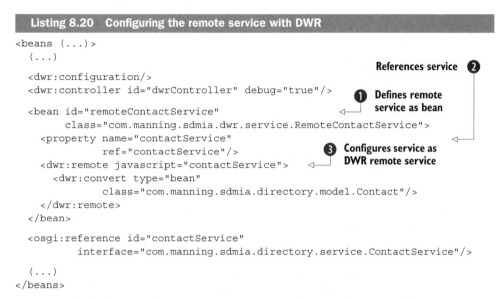

```
<beans (...)>
  (...)

  <dwr:configuration/>
  <dwr:controller id="dwrController" debug="true"/>

  <bean id="remoteContactService"
        class="com.manning.sdmia.dwr.service.RemoteContactService">
    <property name="contactService"
              ref="contactService"/>
    <dwr:remote javascript="contactService">
      <dwr:convert type="bean"
            class="com.manning.sdmia.directory.model.Contact"/>
    </dwr:remote>
  </bean>

  <osgi:reference id="contactService"
          interface="com.manning.sdmia.directory.service.ContactService"/>

  (...)
</beans>
```

References service ❷

❶ Defines remote service as bean

❸ Configures service as DWR remote service

As we saw before, the OSGi service must first be configured through Spring DM. The Spring bean is then defined using the bean XML element of Spring ❶, and the OSGi service is injected into it ❷. The remote DWR XML element is used ❸ inside this bean element, defining the remote DWR service with the same properties we saw previously.

As usual, when using external libraries in an OSGi environment some packages must be specified in the Import-Package header of the manifest file for the component using DWR. Some of these are specific to DWR's handling of remote calls and others to Spring and Spring DM's support for web application contexts. Listing 8.21 shows the packages that need to be specified.

Listing 8.21 Packages to import for DWR support

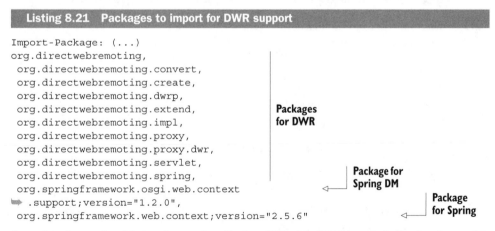

```
Import-Package: (...)
org.directwebremoting,
 org.directwebremoting.convert,
 org.directwebremoting.create,
 org.directwebremoting.dwrp,
 org.directwebremoting.extend,
 org.directwebremoting.impl,
 org.directwebremoting.proxy,
 org.directwebremoting.proxy.dwr,
 org.directwebremoting.servlet,
 org.directwebremoting.spring,
 org.springframework.osgi.web.context
➥ .support;version="1.2.0",
 org.springframework.web.context;version="2.5.6"
```

Packages for DWR

Package for Spring DM

Package for Spring

As we've shown in this section, using Spring DM with DWR is relatively simple, and it allows you to expose OSGi services configured with Spring DM for AJAX interactions.

Another useful framework with similar functionality is GWT, which specifically targets rich internet applications. In the next section, we'll deal with the integration between GWT and Spring DM, which like DWR allows you to use OSGi services with AJAX invocations.

8.3.3 Using GWT with Spring DM

The Google Web Toolkit (GWT) is a web framework that allows you to develop rich internet applications based on JavaScript and AJAX technologies and entirely written with Java.

The main feature of this framework is that it allows you to write applications exclusively in Java. The pieces related to web UIs are then compiled into JavaScript code. GWT provides efficient solutions for implementing AJAX-based applications and addresses related challenges such as asynchronous remote procedure calls (RPC), history management, bookmarking, internationalization, and cross-browser portability. If you want to go deeper into GWT, we suggest looking at *GWT in Action* by Robert Hanson and Adam Tacy. The second edition is to be published by Manning in early 2011.

Additional components, such as the GWT Widget Library (available from http://gwt-widget.sourceforge.net/), provide generic integration with Spring and allow GWT to be used easily with Spring DM. The GWT Widget Library is based on the remoting concepts of Spring, which allow any bean defined in Spring to be exposed as a remote service.

In following sections, we'll describe how to configure GWT and the GWT Widget Library in an OSGi environment and use them with Spring DM.

INSTALLING GWT

Unfortunately, as with DWR, the SpringSource EBR doesn't provide OSGi-ified versions of GWT and GWT Widget Library JAR files, so we need to create them ourselves using the Bnd tool. Table 8.5 lists all the files that need to be OSGi-ified.

Table 8.5 GWT JAR files that need to be OSGi-ified

Tool	Jar file	Version
GWT	gwt-user.jar	1.5.3
GWT	gwt-servlet.jar	1.5.3
GWT Widget Server	gwt-sl.jar	0.1.5b
Gilead	gilead-adapter4gwt.jar	1.2.3.823
Gilead	gilead-adapter-core.jar	1.2.3.823

To install GWT, the GWT Widget Library, and Gilead, all these components need to be provisioned to a OSGi container.

Once you've done that, everything is present within the OSGi container for using Spring DM with GWT to expose OSGi services as remote services for AJAX invocations. Let's look at how to use GWT to achieve this.

CONFIGURING GWT SPRING INTEGRATION FOR SPRING DM

Because we want to use the exporter mechanism provided by the GWT Widget Server framework to expose as Spring beans as remote GWT services, and this mechanism is based on Spring MVC, the global configuration is similar to that of Spring MVC. In fact, GWT provides a Spring MVC controller for handling GWT RPC calls.

Both Spring web application contexts—the global application context and the one linked to the `DispatcherServlet`—must be defined as described in the "Configuring Spring MVC for Spring DM" subsection of section 8.1.2, but a different mapping for the `DispatchServlet` servlet is necessary within the `servlet-mapping` XML element so that remote GWT calls can be made with URLs of the form /services/ *MY_SERVICE*.rpc. In order to allow access to URLs created directly from bean names, we need to configure the `BeanNameUrlHandlerMapping` class in the web application context of the Spring MVC servlet, as shown in following snippet:

```
<beans (...)>

  <bean id="handlerMapping" class="org.springframework.web.servlet
  .handler.BeanNameUrlHandlerMapping"/>

  (...)
</bean>
```

This configuration enables us to use OSGi services configured through Spring DM when handling remote GWT RPC calls.

In the next section, we'll look at how to declaratively expose these kinds of services as remote services for GWT.

USING SPRING DM WITH GWT

As we saw previously, there are two distinct parts to GWT applications. In this section, we'll look at how to implement these two parts to export an OSGi service configured within Spring DM as a remote GWT service and call it from the client side through GWT remote interfaces.

For the JavaScript frontend making the remote call, we need to add two interfaces in order to be able to call the service from the rich web application. The first interface corresponds to the remote interface for the service and contains all the exposed methods of the service. The following snippet shows its content for our contacts example:

```
public interface ContactService extends RemoteService {
  List<Contact> getContacts();
  (...)
}
```

The second interface is a remote asynchronous interface with a variant of the same methods exposed in the remote interface:

```
public interface ContactServiceAsync {
  void getContacts(AsyncCallback<List<Contact>> callback);
  (...)
}
```

Notice that the remote interface extends the GWT `RemoteInterface` interface and must be present in the OSGi container. The corresponding packages must be imported in the bundle that defines the service.

Because these interfaces use external abstractions, such as the `Contact` class, the bundle containing them must also be a GWT module. This can be achieved by adding a GWT XML configuration file to these bundles. This file must be located at a level above the packages containing the classes.

By default, GWT modules have a particular structure for packages:

- The package named *client* contains all the classes for the client side and will be compiled into JavaScript code by GWT. This package must contain the classes needed to build UIs and remote interfaces to map AJAX APIs.

- The package named *public* contains all the files related to HTML and CSS technologies and images. An HTML file to launch the application must be defined here, and it must load the JavaScript resources generated by GWT for the application.

- The package named *server* contains all the classes for the server side. These classes won't be compiled into JavaScript but will be executed in the Java EE web container containing the web application. (In our example, this package isn't present because all classes are provided by the bundle containing the OSGi service used.)

The following snippet shows a sample structure for a GWT module called DirectoryApplication:

```
com/
  manning/
    sdmia/
      gwt/
        client/
        public/
        server/
      DirectoryApplication.gwt.xml
```

The elements in the preceding directory structure have the following roles:

- `client` package—Contains classes for the client side
- `public` directory—Contains HTML, CSS, and images, resources
- `server` package—Contains classes for the server side
- `DirectoryApplication.gwt.xml` file—The GWT descriptor for the module

The GWT framework also allows you to adapt this structure and do things such as define packages other than the `client` one as packages containing classes for the client side. This is useful, in our case, so that we can use the model classes of bundles in GWT user interfaces.

The following snippet shows the GWT configuration of the com.manning. sdmia.directory bundle containing the service interface and business implementation class for contacts. The file named Directory.gwt.xml is located in the com/manning/ sdmia/directory under the Java source folder, and it defines the GWT metadata for the module.

```
<module>
  <inherits name='com.google.gwt.user.User'/>
  <source path="model"/>
</module>
```

Because GWT allows modules to use other modules, you must add this module into the GWT XML module file of your web bundle, as shown in following snippet:

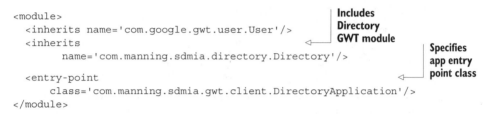

```
<module>
  <inherits name='com.google.gwt.user.User'/>
  <inherits
      name='com.manning.sdmia.directory.Directory'/>
  <entry-point
      class='com.manning.sdmia.gwt.client.DirectoryApplication'/>
</module>
```

Includes Directory GWT module

Specifies app entry point class

Exporting the OSGi service as a remote service for GWT RPC calls is quite easy, thanks to the GWT Widget Library and its GWTRPCServiceExporter facility, as shown in the following snippet:

```
<bean name="/contactService.rpc"
    class="org.gwtwidgets.server.spring.GWTRPCServiceExporter">
  <property name="service" ref="contactService"/>
  <property name="serviceInterfaces">
    <value>com.manning.sdmia.directory.service.ContactService</value>
  </property>
</bean>
```

In the preceding code, we added a bean of type GWTRPCServiceExporter to expose the OSGi service as a remote service for GWT. This enables any entity to be exported as a remote service. The interface to be exposed—the ContactService OSGi service in this example—must be injected into the exporter using its service property. The serviceInterfaces property controls which interfaces are exposed. In our example, we specified the interface of the OSGi service.

When it's all implemented and configured, we can call the getContact method of the GWT remote service from the GWT client code, as shown in listing 8.22.

Listing 8.22 Calling the service in client code

```
ContactServiceAsync contactService =
        (ContactServiceAsync) GWT.create(ContactService.class);

ServiceDefTarget endpoint = (ServiceDefTarget) contactService;
endpoint.setServiceEntryPoint(
        "../services/contactService.rpc");

contactService.getContacts(
        new AsyncCallback<List<Contact>>() {
```

Gets client service ❶ instance

❷ Sets service address

❸ Calls service asynchronously

```
public void onFailure(Throwable caught) {
  Window.alert(caught.toString());
}

public void onSuccess(List<Contact> contacts) {
  (...)
}
});
```

A client instance for the service must first be gotten using the GWT class's static create method ❶; the remote interface must be specified as parameter of this method. The returned instance corresponds to the asynchronous interface.

The address of the service must then be set on this instance using the ServiceDef-Target class and its setServiceEntryPoint method ❷. The service can then be asynchronously called ❸, and the result is returned through a callback. If the call is successful, the onSuccess method of the callback is called with the result; otherwise its onFailure method is called with the error.

As usual, when using external libraries in an OSGi environment, some packages must be specified in the Import-Package header of the manifest file of the component using GWT. Some of these packages are specific to GWT and the GWT Widget Library's handling of remote calls, and others to Spring and Spring DM's use of the web application context and its configuration. Listing 8.23 shows the packages that need to be specified:

Listing 8.23   Packages to import for GWT

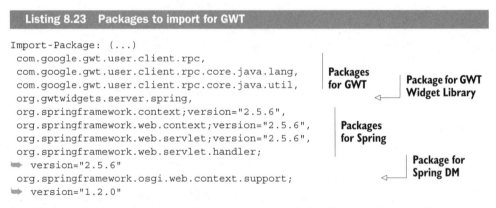

```
Import-Package: (...)
 com.google.gwt.user.client.rpc,
 com.google.gwt.user.client.rpc.core.java.lang,       Packages
 com.google.gwt.user.client.rpc.core.java.util,       for GWT      Package for GWT
 org.gwtwidgets.server.spring,                                     Widget Library
 org.springframework.context;version="2.5.6",
 org.springframework.web.context;version="2.5.6",     Packages
 org.springframework.web.servlet;version="2.5.6",     for Spring
 org.springframework.web.servlet.handler;
⇒ version="2.5.6"                                                  Package for
 org.springframework.osgi.web.context.support;                    Spring DM
⇒ version="1.2.0"
```

In this section, we've looked at how to integrate AJAX frameworks with Spring DM. This makes it possible to expose OSGi services as remote services for use by AJAX calls. These frameworks provide convenient mechanisms for declarative configuration in Spring web application contexts.

We've got one more web framework family to discuss—web services—which will also help you expose remote services. Once again, we'll see how to integrate frameworks of this kind with Spring DM.

8.4 Using web services with Spring DM

Web service frameworks provide remote access to services using web technologies such as SOAP and REST. They're generally responsible for handling underlying technology complexities and for routing requests to the right recipients. Most frameworks of this kind provide integration with Spring, which allows the use of dependency injection when configuring resources. Because of this support, integrating with Spring is generally easy and consists of injecting OSGi services configured through Spring DM into resource-handling abstractions.

In this section, we'll describe some general concepts related to integrating frameworks of this kind with Spring DM, and we'll take a look at examples of the most popular ones: Spring Web Services (Spring WS) and Restlet.

8.4.1 Using Spring DM with web service frameworks

The key abstractions of web service frameworks are request handlers (endpoints for Spring WS and resources for Restlet). These abstractions are responsible for handling requests and implementing functionality, which can be done by using other entities such as OSGi services. Integrating Spring DM with these frameworks is a simple matter of using OSGi services inside action implementations.

When configuring Spring support for this kind of framework, Spring DM's OSGi web application context must be specified so that the `osgi` namespace can be used. You also need to use OSGi services, configured through Spring DM, in the actions of the application. This can be done directly in the Spring application context using classic or annotation-based dependency injection.

Figure 8.4 shows the interactions between Spring DM and a web service framework that enable them to work together.

That's the general concept behind integrating Spring DM with web service frameworks. Now we'll consider the implementation details when using Spring WS and Restlet.

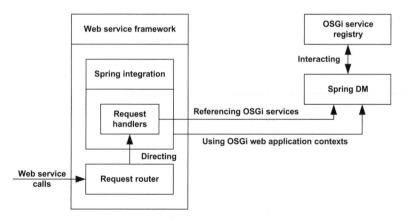

Figure 8.4   Using OSGi web application contexts and OSGi services based on Spring DM from web service frameworks

8.4.2 Using Spring WS with Spring DM

Spring WS is a Spring community project dedicated to implementing web services using SOAP. Leveraging Spring facilities such as dependency injection and annotations, it provides a contract-first approach to implementing web services. The framework naturally integrates with Spring DM because it uses Spring's web application context for its configuration.

> **Spring WS's contract-first approach**
>
> The *contract-first* approach used by Spring WS consists of first implementing web service contracts using the Web Services Description Language (WSDL) independent of the classes used to implement the services. This approach is the opposite of *contract-last*, which deduces these contracts from service implementation classes. The *contract-first* approach guarantees service interface stability, better performance, reusability, and versioning.

In following sections, we'll explain how to integrate Spring WS with Spring DM to use it in an OSGi environment, and how to use OSGi services configured through Spring DM in web service endpoints.

INSTALLING SPRING WS

Spring WS is part of the Spring portfolio, and, like other projects of this kind, is already available as OSGi bundles in the SpringSource EBR. In order to use it, additional XML components also need to be present in the OSGi container. Table 8.6 lists all the required OSGi components for using Spring WS in an OSGI environment with Spring DM.

Table 8.6   Bundles related to Spring WS, available from the SpringSource EBR

Group ID	Artifact ID	Version
org.springframework	org.springframework.web.servlet	2.5.6.SEC01
org.springframework	org.springframework.oxm	1.5.7.A
org.springframework	org.springframework.oxm.java5	1.5.7.A
org.springframework.ws	org.springframework.ws	1.5.7.A
org.springframework.ws	org.springframework.ws.transport	1.5.7.A
org.springframework.ws	org.springframework.ws.java5	1.5.7.A
org.springframework.ws	org.springframework.xml	1.5.7.A
javax.wsdl	com.springsource.javax.wsdl	1.6.1
javax.xml	com.springsource.javax.xml.bind	2.1.7
javax.xml	com.springsource.javax.xml.rpc	1.1.0
javax.xml	com.springsource.javax.xml.soap	1.3.0

Table 8.6 Bundles related to Spring WS, available from the SpringSource EBR *(continued)*

Group ID	Artifact ID	Version
javax.xml	com.springsource.javax.xml.stream	1.0.1
com.sun.xml	com.springsource.com.sun.xml.messaging.saaj	1.3.0
com.thoughtworks.xstream	com.springsource.com.thoughtworks.xstream	1.3.1
org.apache.ws	com.springsource.org.apache.ws.commons.schema	1.3.2
org.jdom	com.springsource.org.jdom	1.1.0
org.xmlpull	com.springsource.org.xmlpull	1.1.4

You'll notice that Spring WS version 1.5.7 uses Spring version 2.5.6.SEC01, which provides fixes over version 2.5.6. The bundles required by this version of the framework also need to be added to the OSGi container.

Everything is now present in the OSGi container for using Spring DM with Spring WS so that OSGi services can be used to handle web service requests. We'll describe in the next section how to configure the Spring WS framework with Spring DM.

CONFIGURING SPRING WS FOR SPRING DM

Like Spring MVC, Spring WS uses two Spring application contexts for its configuration.

The first application context corresponds to the association with the web application and should be used to configure entities that are independent from web issues, such as business logic or business layer abstractions. If the web service application uses Spring DM, this context is the perfect place to put OSGi service references to business services. To do this, you need to specify the OSGi-aware application context provided by Spring DM—its `OsgiBundleXmlWebApplicationContext` class. For more details, see the "Configuring Spring MVC for Spring DM" subsection of section 8.1.2.

The other application context is linked to Spring WS's frontend controller. This controller isn't the `DispatcherServlet` servlet that's used with Spring MVC but a context specific to Spring WS: the `MessageDispatcherServlet` servlet. Its configuration in the web.xml file is similar to Spring MVC's servlet. Listing 8.24 shows how to configure the servlet, as well as the configuration required for Spring DM.

Listing 8.24 Configuring the Spring WS front controller

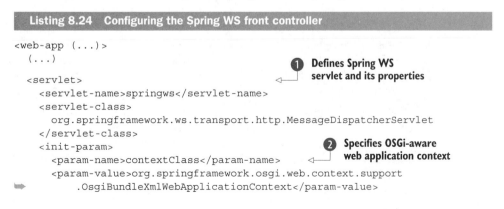

```
<web-app (...)>
  (...)

  <servlet>                                    ❶ Defines Spring WS
    <servlet-name>springws</servlet-name>        servlet and its properties
    <servlet-class>
      org.springframework.ws.transport.http.MessageDispatcherServlet
    </servlet-class>
    <init-param>                               ❷ Specifies OSGi-aware
      <param-name>contextClass</param-name>      web application context
      <param-value>org.springframework.osgi.web.context.support
        .OsgiBundleXmlWebApplicationContext</param-value>
```

```
    </init-param>
  </servlet>

  <servlet-mapping>
    <servlet-name>springws</servlet-name>
    <url-pattern>/*</url-pattern>
  </servlet-mapping>

  (...)
</web-app>
```

❸ Configures servlet mapping and its pattern

The configuration of the `MessageDispatcherServlet` servlet consists of two parts. The first is the configuration of the servlet properties using the `servlet` XML element ❶. Here we can specify the servlet's name, class name, and init parameters. We use the `contextClass` parameter ❷ to specify OSGi-aware behavior for this context with the `OsgiBundleXmlWebApplicationContext` class.

The last element is the configuration of the servlet mapping using the `servlet-mapping` XML element ❸. This specifies the criteria for calling Spring WS endpoints. In our case, the framework handles all the incoming requests on the web application.

We've finished configuring Spring WS so that we can use Spring DM in Spring WS's application context files. We'll now implement Spring WS endpoints using OSGi services configured through Spring DM.

USING SPRING WS WITH SPRING DM

Before implementing endpoints for handling web service requests, we must first configure OSGi services for use with Spring DM. This can be done using the `reference` XML element of the framework in the Spring XML configuration associated with the web application context, as shown in the following snippet:

```
<beans (...)>
  <osgi:reference id="contactService"
        interface="com.manning.sdmia.directory.service.ContactService"/>
</beans>
```

Based on this OSGi service, we can build a Spring WS endpoint to handle our web service requests. We implement a simple endpoint using the JDOM XML library to pull data from the request and build the response. The content of the response is built from the result of the injected OSGi service configured through Spring DM.

Spring WS endpoints

Endpoints are central abstractions of Spring WS because they handle web service requests. Spring WS allows requests to be routed to the right endpoint based on the XML content of the request. Different configuration approaches, including XML and annotations, are provided.

Spring WS also provides different kinds of endpoints. The first kind is based on DOM, which requires developers to handle the document structure for requests and responses themselves. A more advanced kind of endpoint provides marshalling, which allows automatic object-to-XML conversion (and vice versa) for building request and response content.

Listing 8.25 shows the implementation of a simple endpoint based on the JDOM library using an injected OSGi service.

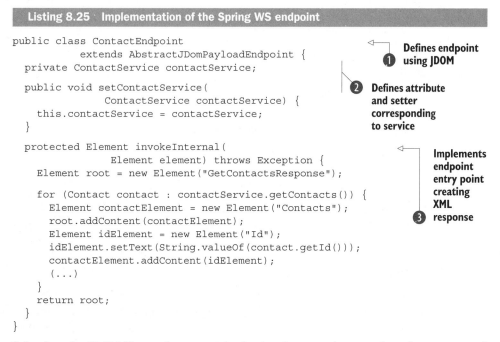

Listing 8.25   Implementation of the Spring WS endpoint

```
public class ContactEndpoint
            extends AbstractJDomPayloadEndpoint {
  private ContactService contactService;

  public void setContactService(
            ContactService contactService) {
    this.contactService = contactService;
  }

  protected Element invokeInternal(
              Element element) throws Exception {
    Element root = new Element("GetContactsResponse");

    for (Contact contact : contactService.getContacts()) {
      Element contactElement = new Element("Contacts");
      root.addContent(contactElement);
      Element idElement = new Element("Id");
      idElement.setText(String.valueOf(contact.getId()));
      contactElement.addContent(idElement);
      (...)
    }
    return root;
  }
}
```

❶ Defines endpoint using JDOM

❷ Defines attribute and setter corresponding to service

Implements endpoint entry point creating XML ❸ response

Selecting the JDOM library for our endpoint implementation requires that we extend the `AbstractJDomPayloadEndpoint` class ❶, which in turn requires that we implement the `invokeInternal` method ❸, which is the entry method of the endpoint. Spring WS passes the request content as the method parameter and takes the return element as the content of the response.

In our `ContentEndpoint` implementation, the Spring DM–configured OSGi service is injected into the `contactService` property using the associated setter method ❷. The handling of the request is then implemented in the `invokeInternal` method. Having created the root element of the response, we iterate over the results of the OSGi service call and build up the content of the response.

We then configure XML definitions for the provided services using a contract-first approach. These definitions represent the XML structure of exchanged messages and operations. Finally, we specify the routing of requests to endpoint handlers.

Listing 8.26 shows the configuration necessary for making it possible for the endpoint to handle requests.

Listing 8.26   Configuring schema, WSDL definition, and routing wih Spring WS

```
<beans (...)>
  (...)

  <bean id="schema"
      class="org.springframework.xml.xsd.SimpleXsdSchema">
```

❶ Configures XML schema for web service

```
    <property name="xsd" value="/WEB-INF/directory.xsd" />
  </bean>                                                              ❷ Configures
                                                                        service's WSDL
  <bean id="directory"                              ◁──┘
      class="org.springframework.ws.wsdl.wsdl11.DefaultWsdl11Definition">
    <property name="schema" ref="schema"/>
    <property name="portTypeName" value="Directory"/>
    <property name="locationUri"
        value="http://localhost:9080/springws/directory/"/>
    <property name="targetNamespace"
        value="http://www.manning.com/directory/definitions"/>
  </bean>

  <bean class="org.springframework.ws.server                          ◁──┐
⇒    .endpoint.mapping.PayloadRootQNameEndpointMapping">
    <property name="mappings">
      <props>
        <prop key="{http://www.manning.com/directory/schemas}
⇒              GetContactsRequest">contactEndpoint</prop>
      </props>
    </property>                                                     Configures
  </bean>                                                           endpoint to
                                                                   access service ❸
  (...)
</beans>
```

We first configure the XML definition of the entities used with Spring WS's `SimpleXsd-Schema` class ❶. This class is configured with the directory.xsd XML Schema file. The WSDL definition is then configured by using Spring WS's `DefaultWsdl11Definition` class ❷. The configuration of this class uses the previous schema and specifies the port type, name, location URI, and target namespace of the service. The last configuration step is to specify the routing of requests based on the root element of the XML messages by using the `PayloadRootQNameEndpointMapping` class ❸. In our example, a message containing a `GetContactRequest` XML element with namespace http://www.manning.com/directory/schema is handled by the endpoint with a bean name of `contactEndpoint`. We'll see this bean's configuration in listing 8.27.

The last step in implementing endpoints involves configuring the `ContactEndpoint` class and injecting into it the OSGi service configured through Spring DM. Listing 8.27 shows how to do this configuration using the same Spring XML configuration file that was used in the previous listing.

Listing 8.27 Configuring the Spring WS endpoint

```
<beans (...)>
  (...)                                            Defines endpoint
                                                   bean
  <bean id="contactEndpoint"            ◁──
      class="com.manning.sdmia.springws.endpoint.ContactEndpoint">
    <property name="contactService"     ◁──
        ref="contactService"/>                     Injects OSGi
  </bean>                                           service

  (...)
</beans>
```

As usual when using external libraries in an OSGi environment, some packages must be specified in the `Import-Package` header of the manifest file of the bundle using Spring WS. Listing 8.28 shows the extra packages that are required.

Listing 8.28 Packages to import for Spring WS

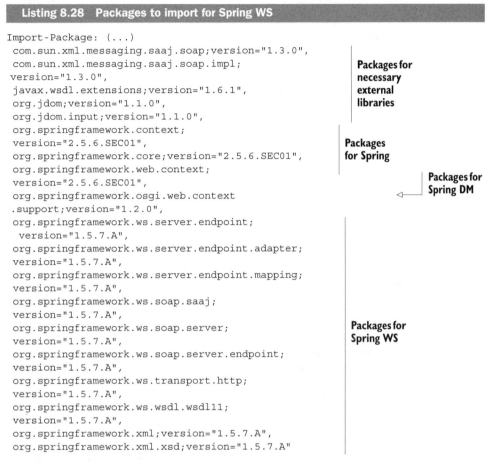

```
Import-Package: (...)
 com.sun.xml.messaging.saaj.soap;version="1.3.0",
 com.sun.xml.messaging.saaj.soap.impl;
version="1.3.0",
 javax.wsdl.extensions;version="1.6.1",
 org.jdom;version="1.1.0",
 org.jdom.input;version="1.1.0",
 org.springframework.context;
version="2.5.6.SEC01",
 org.springframework.core;version="2.5.6.SEC01",
 org.springframework.web.context;
version="2.5.6.SEC01",
 org.springframework.osgi.web.context
.support;version="1.2.0",
 org.springframework.ws.server.endpoint;
  version="1.5.7.A",
 org.springframework.ws.server.endpoint.adapter;
version="1.5.7.A",
 org.springframework.ws.server.endpoint.mapping;
version="1.5.7.A",
 org.springframework.ws.soap.saaj;
version="1.5.7.A",
 org.springframework.ws.soap.server;
version="1.5.7.A",
 org.springframework.ws.soap.server.endpoint;
version="1.5.7.A",
 org.springframework.ws.transport.http;
version="1.5.7.A",
 org.springframework.ws.wsdl.wsdl11;
version="1.5.7.A",
 org.springframework.xml;version="1.5.7.A",
 org.springframework.xml.xsd;version="1.5.7.A"
```

Packages for necessary external libraries

Packages for Spring

Packages for Spring DM

Packages for Spring WS

We've shown in this section that using Spring DM with Spring WS to implement SOAP-based web services is relatively simple. The integration between the two frameworks is natural and is based on the web application context provided by Spring DM. Once this web application context is configured, you can reference OSGi services through Spring DM in endpoint implementations.

REST technology allows us to implement another kind of web service without SOAP, and Restlet is a complete framework for providing such services. In the next section, we'll describe how you can use Spring DM with this framework so that OSGi services can be used to handle service calls.

8.4.3 *Using Restlet with Spring DM*

Restlet is a Java framework that allows you to implement Restful applications flexibly and to leverage of all the features of the web, the HTTP protocol, and the REST architectural approach. The framework provides support for a large number of extensions, including Spring. The Spring extension provides a convenient way of integrating Spring DM with Restlet so that OSGi services can be used in resource implementations.

In the following sections, we'll describe how to configure Restlet and the corresponding web application so that we can use Spring DM.

INSTALLING RESTLET

Unfortunately, as with DWR and GWT, the SpringSource EBR doesn't provide OSGi-ified versions of Restlet. The great news here is that Restlet already provides OSGi configurations for the JAR files contained in the distribution, so you don't need to create them yourself. Table 8.7 lists all the files that have been OSGi-ified.

Bundle ID	Version
org.restlet	2.0.0.SNAPSHOT
org.restlet.ext.servlet	2.0.0.SNAPSHOT
org.restlet.ext.spring	2.0.0.SNAPSHOT

Figure 8.7 Bundles related to Restlet, Spring, and Spring DM integration

The necessary dependencies for these bundles are CGLib, servlet, and various Spring bundles, all of which are already present in the standard Spring DM web configuration of an OSGi container.

You now have everything present in the OSGi container to use Spring DM with Restlet, which will allow you to use OSGi services to handle REST requests. We'll describe in the next section how to configure the framework with Spring DM.

CONFIGURING RESTLET FOR SPRING DM

Restlet's Spring integration is based on the application context associated with the web application itself.

When using Spring DM, the referencing of OSGi services can be done in the context configuration file. This requires the use of a Spring application context that supports OSGi; we can use `OsgiBundleXmlWebApplicationContext`, which we'll specify as the `contextClass` property of the application context. Listing 8.29 shows how to specify this class in the web.xml file.

Listing 8.29 Configuring the Spring web application context for Restlet

```
<web-app (...)>
  (...)

  <context-param>
    <param-name>org.restlet.application</param-name>     ❶ Specifies
    <param-value>application</param-value>                   Restlet
  </context-param>                                           application
                                                             identifier

  <context-param>
    <param-name>contextConfigLocation</param-name>
    <param-value>/WEB-INF/osgi-context.xml</param-value>
  </context-param>

  <context-param>
```

```
   <param-name>contextClass</param-name>
   <param-value>
      org.springframework.osgi.web.context.support
        .OsgiBundleXmlWebApplicationContext
   </param-value>
</context-param>

<listener>
   <listener-class>
        org.springframework.web.context.ContextLoaderListener
   </listener-class>
</listener>

(...)
</web-app>
```

As we saw earlier, the Spring listener for web applications is configured in the same way as a standard Java application by using the ContextLoaderListener class ❷. With Restlet, we also need to specify the Restlet application with the org.restlet.application parameter ❶.

You can configure the Restlet web controller by using the SpringServerServlet class. This is configured in the web.xml file like any servlet. Listing 8.30 shows this configuration using the servlet and servlet-mapping XML elements.

Listing 8.30 Configuring the Restlet front controller

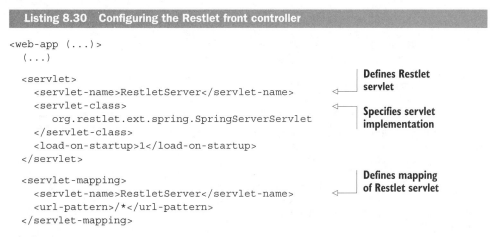

```
<web-app (...)>
  (...)

  <servlet>
    <servlet-name>RestletServer</servlet-name>
    <servlet-class>
       org.restlet.ext.spring.SpringServerServlet
    </servlet-class>
    <load-on-startup>1</load-on-startup>
  </servlet>

  <servlet-mapping>
    <servlet-name>RestletServer</servlet-name>
    <url-pattern>/*</url-pattern>
  </servlet-mapping>

</web-app>
```

The Restlet web controller corresponding to the SpringServletServlet class, is responsible to handle all REST requests and to route them to the right resource to be handle.

Everything is now configured for implementing REST resources using OSGi services configured through Spring DM. In the next section, we'll explain how to implement such resources using Restlet.

USING RESTLET WITH SPRING DM

Before implementing resources to handle REST requests, we must first configure OSGi services using Spring DM. As we saw before, this can be done using the reference XML element of the Spring DM framework.

By using our `ContactService` service, we can build a Restlet resource to handle our REST requests. We'll implement a simple resource using the JDOM XML library that builds response content as XML. The content is based on the results of calling the injected OSGi service that we configured through Spring DM. Listing 8.31 shows the implementation of our simple resource.

Listing 8.31   Implementing the Restlet resource

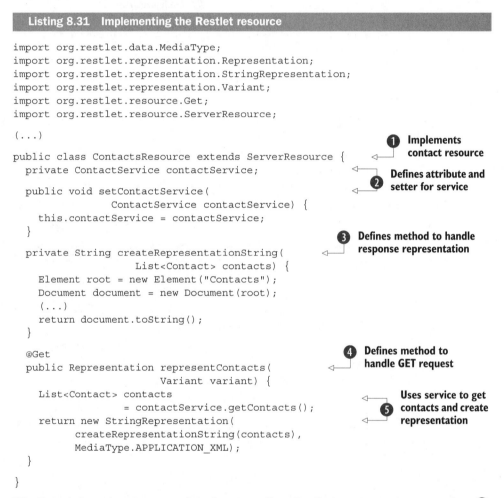

```
import org.restlet.data.MediaType;
import org.restlet.representation.Representation;
import org.restlet.representation.StringRepresentation;
import org.restlet.representation.Variant;
import org.restlet.resource.Get;
import org.restlet.resource.ServerResource;

(...)

public class ContactsResource extends ServerResource {          ①  Implements
  private ContactService contactService;                            contact resource

  public void setContactService(                                ②  Defines attribute and
              ContactService contactService) {                      setter for service
    this.contactService = contactService;
  }

  private String createRepresentationString(                    ③  Defines method to handle
                  List<Contact> contacts) {                         response representation
    Element root = new Element("Contacts");
    Document document = new Document(root);
    (...)
    return document.toString();
  }

  @Get                                                          ④  Defines method to
  public Representation representContacts(                          handle GET request
                      Variant variant) {
    List<Contact> contacts                                      ⑤  Uses service to get
                = contactService.getContacts();                     contacts and create
    return new StringRepresentation(                                representation
        createRepresentationString(contacts),
        MediaType.APPLICATION_XML);
  }

}
```

We first define the resource class by extending Restlet's `ServerResource` class ①. Annotations are used to specify which methods will be responsible for handling HTTP requests. In our example, the `Get` annotation specifies that the `representContacts` method ④ will handle REST using the HTTP GET method.

Within this class, the OSGi service configured through Spring DM is injected into the `contactService` property using the associated setter method ②. The handling of the request is then implemented in the `representContacts` method. Having obtained the results of the OSGi service call (#5), we build the response content (③ and ⑤) using the JDOM library.

The last step in implementing resources is to configure the Restlet application and specify the routing of REST requests to the appropriate handling resources. Listing 8.32 shows the configuration necessary for the resource to handle REST requests.

Listing 8.32 Configuring application and routing abstractions in Restlet

```
<beans (...)>
  (...)

  <bean id="application" name="application"          ❶ Defines and configures
    class="org.restlet.Application">                    Restlet application
    <property name="root" ref="router"/>
  </bean>

  <bean id="router"                                  ❷ Defines Restlet
    class="org.restlet.ext.spring.SpringRouter">        Spring router
    <property name="attachments">
      <map>
        <entry key="/contacts">        ❸ Configures link with
          <bean                           resource bean
            class="org.restlet.ext.spring.SpringFinder">
            <lookup-method name="create"
                    bean="contactResource" />
          </bean>
        </entry>
      </map>
    </property>
  </bean>

  (...)
</beans>
```

We first configure the Restlet application using the Application class ❶. This application is the one previously configured in the web.xml file, as described in listing 8.29. This configuration allows us to specify a router for handling REST requests by using its root property. With the Restlet Spring integration, the SpringRouter class must be used as the router ❷. This allows request URIs to be associated with the resources responsible for handling them via its attachments property. In our example, the /contacts URI is handled by the resource with the bean name contactResource. The configuration is done using Restlet's SpringFinder class ❸. We'll look at the configuration of this resource in listing 8.33.

Automatic converter registration with OSGi

In early Restlet 2 release candidates, the OSGi activator for Restlet didn't automatically register default converters at startup.

If an "Unable to find a converter for this object" message is displayed in traces when trying to call REST resources in OSGi, you can explicitly register default converters using the following code:

```
Engine.getInstance().registerDefaultConverters();
```

The last step in making resources work consists of configuring the `ContactResource` class and injecting into it the OSGi service configured through Spring DM. Listing 8.33 shows how to configure this in the same Spring XML configuration file we used in listing 8.32.

Listing 8.33   Configuration of the Restlet resource

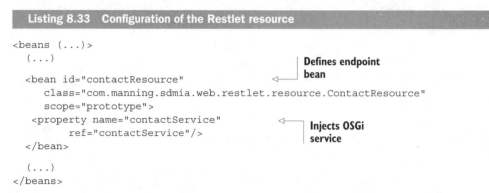

```
<beans (...)>
  (...)
                                                              Defines endpoint
  <bean id="contactResource"                                  bean
     class="com.manning.sdmia.web.restlet.resource.ContactResource"
     scope="prototype">
   <property name="contactService"                            Injects OSGi
        ref="contactService"/>                                service
  </bean>

  (...)
</beans>
```

As usual, when using external libraries in an OSGi environment, extra packages must be specified in the `Import-Package` header of the manifest file of the bundle using Restlet. Listing 8.34 shows the necessary packages.

Listing 8.34   Packages to import for Restlet

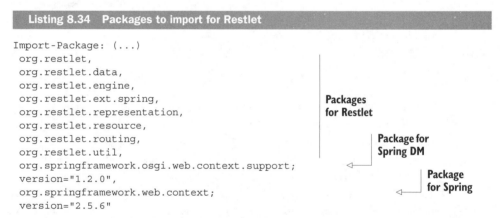

```
Import-Package: (...)
 org.restlet,
 org.restlet.data,
 org.restlet.engine,
 org.restlet.ext.spring,
 org.restlet.representation,                    Packages
 org.restlet.resource,                          for Restlet
 org.restlet.routing,
 org.restlet.util,                              Package for
 org.springframework.osgi.web.context.support;  Spring DM
 version="1.2.0",
 org.springframework.web.context;               Package
 version="2.5.6"                                for Spring
```

As we've shown in this section, using Spring DM with Restlet to implement REST applications is relatively straightforward. The integration between the two frameworks is natural and based on the web application context provided by Spring DM.

We've described in these sections how to integrate web service frameworks with Spring DM so that OSGi services can be used in endpoint and resource implementations. Often, the use of OSGi services configured through Spring DM is made possible by the Spring integrations that these frameworks provide.

8.5   *Summary*

In this chapter, we tackled another important data access issue related to developing enterprise applications: web data access. We focused on how to integrate Spring DM with several different kinds of web frameworks.

The Java EE community provides a large number of web frameworks, but we can categorize them into broad families based on their implementation and the issues they address. Classic web frameworks implement the MVC 2 pattern and can be action- or component-based. Other frameworks provide support for AJAX technology and web services.

Most of these frameworks provide integration with Spring, allowing their supporting classes to be configured directly in Spring web application contexts. This integration makes it easier to use Spring DM with these frameworks. Generally integration with Spring DM means that these web frameworks can be used in an OSGi environment and leverage OSGi services.

This chapter completes the trio of chapters dedicated to enterprise issues. They described global concepts of implementing enterprise applications with Spring DM in an OSGi environment. We also dealt with the most important issues of enterprise applications: data access and web issues. In the next part of the book, we'll focus on the advanced features of Spring DM and especially on advanced configuration.

Part 3

Advanced topics

You should by now have a deep understanding of what Spring DM is and does. You should be ready to embark on your first Spring DM project, if you have not done so already! As we all know, there is always more to learn, and deeper understanding often comes through a process of experience and trial and error.

This part of Spring Dynamic Modules in Action draws on our own experiences-and the mistakes we made-in developing with Spring DM, and it's devoted to more advanced Spring DM-related topics. It is likely that you will want to refer to this part as you encounter problems rather than necessarily read right through it.

Chapter 9 covers advanced Spring DM topics, including overall configuration of the Spring DM container and Spring DM patterns that we have found useful in real products that use Spring DM.

Chapter 10 covers the testing of OSGi applications that use Spring DM.

Chapter 11 discusses Spring DM's support for OSGi compendium services-in particular, configuration admin and eventing.

In chapter 12 we describe the Spring DM standard - the OSGi Blueprint specification and its relationship to Spring DM.

Following part 3 are four appendices which describe Spring DM development with Eclipse, OSGi development with Maven 2 and with the Pax tools, and Spring DM development with Ant and Ivy.

Advanced concepts

9

This chapter covers

- Globally configuring Spring DM's extenders to integrate the framework into managed environments
- Using Spring DM in a secured OSGi container
- Advanced OSGi patterns that involve Spring DM

We've looked at how OSGi bundles can leverage the power of Spring by using Spring DM. Indeed, increasing the power of bundles through Spring's features is a way to construct better, more modular OSGi applications. But OSGi applications always end up being deployed in OSGi containers, which we want to be robust, reliable, and stable. When we use Spring DM, its bundles are part of the infrastructure of the OSGi containers, so they must provide global configuration hooks (as apposed to per-bundle configuration) and they must be able to take advantage of some of the components that the environment provides.

In this chapter, we'll cover how we can globally configure Spring DM's extenders through fragment-based configuration. For the standard extender, settings range from thread management to the systematic registration of beans in Spring application contexts that Spring DM manages. The web extender also has its own settings that we can leverage; for example, to switch from one embedded web container to

283

another. We'll also introduce the OSGi security model and see how Spring DM can be integrated into a secured OSGi container.

We'll end this chapter with a description of two advanced patterns that can help implement elegant solutions in modular systems like OSGi. Spring DM helps in their implementation and also uses them internally.

By the end of this chapter, you'll be able to configure the global behavior of Spring DM (as opposed to the per-bundle configuration we mostly covered in previous chapters). You'll also learn how Spring DM can fit into and even benefit from the infrastructure that your OSGi environment provides.

This chapter covers some very advanced topics and settings of Spring DM and of OSGi, so you shouldn't feel overwhelmed by its content. The chapter isn't meant to be read sequentially; instead you should acquaint yourself with the types of configuration hooks Spring DM provides and come back to this chapter for the details when you need to use them.

Here's a quick overview of what the different sections of the chapter cover:

- Section 9.1 covers the extender's principles of configuration, and you should read this section.
- Section 9.2 (and 9.2.1) will familiarize you with what is configurable in Spring DM's standard extender. There's also a real-world example of configuration within SpringSource dm Server in section 9.2.9. Other subsections in section 9.2 dive into the details of configuration and are intended to be read on an on-demand basis.
- Section 9.3 follows the same pattern as section 9.2, but for Spring DM's web extender. The beginning of this chapter and section 9.3.1 provide the big picture, so you should read them first and come back to the remaining subsections when you need to configure the web extender.
- Section 9.4 covers how to use Tomcat 6.0 and Jetty with Spring DM. You can read the subsections according to your needs.
- Sections 9.5 and 9.6 deal with more cross-cutting topics: security and design patterns. You should read section 9.5 about security if you need to integrate Spring DM into a secured OSGi container or if you're curious about the Java and OSGi security models and how Spring DM fits into them. Read section 9.6 if you want to learn about modular design patterns. The patterns we describe both leverage the modular nature of OSGi and help to solve technical problems that only emerge in OSGi development.

As you can see, the topics are quite independent from each other, and you can skip to the ones that will help you with your particular needs.

9.1   *Configuring Spring DM core components*

We saw in chapter 4 that the behavior of Spring DM's extenders can be configured on a per-bundle basis, by using manifest headers, like `Spring-Context` or `Web-Context-Path`. Extenders then manage the application context of a specific bundle accordingly.

But sometimes we want global settings that apply to all Spring-powered bundles. For example, the duration Spring DM waits before failing the startup of an application context (because its dependencies aren't satisfied) can be configured at the extender level for all Spring-powered bundles. Setting this duration once means that you don't have to specify it for every bundle; this allows for centralized control over the bundles.

We may also want Spring DM to be integrated deeply into our OSGi environment and need to replace some of its inner components with our own, so we can benefit from a service the environment provides (like thread management). Luckily, Spring DM offers enough hooks for us to tune the behavior of its extender in a centralized way through fragment-based configuration.

In this section, we'll cover the basics of the fragment-based configuration and the features Spring DM lets us configure.

9.1.1   *Fragment-based configuration*

OSGi fragment bundles are meant to complement a host bundle. To tune Spring DM, we create fragments to complement its extender bundles. Each extender (standard and web) looks for Spring configuration files in its potential fragments. It can then use these files to bootstrap an OSGi-enabled Spring application context *for the extender* and use the beans declared there in place of its core components. By using an OSGi Spring application context, the fragment can leverage all the features of the Spring lightweight container, such as dependency injection, AOP, OSGi resource loading, and interaction with the OSGi service registry.

The fragment's host depends on the extender we want to augment (we'll see in sections 9.2 and 9.3 the exact line to include in the manifest of the fragment). What remains the same from one extender to the next is the location of the Spring XML configuration files: they must be in the META-INF/spring/extender directory of the fragment.

A fragment can contain several XML files or there can be several fragments. The target extender will search in its bundle space for all the .xml files in its META-INF/spring/extender directory and will bootstrap an application context from them. This implies that the composition of these files must define a consistent application context (consistent dependencies, no collision for the names of the beans, and so on). Figure 9.1 illustrates the fragment-based configuration of the extender in Spring DM.

Spring DM's extenders require specific beans to be defined in their fragments, which leads us to the nature of the contract between extenders and the application context they define.

9.1.2   *Features configurable through named beans*

Once one of Spring DM's extenders has bootstrapped its fragments' application context, it will pick up beans from that application context and use them in place of its default core components. The contract between the fragments and the extender is

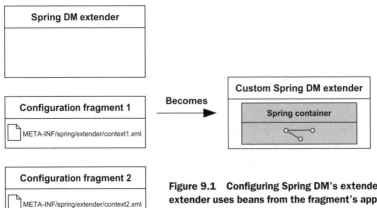

Figure 9.1   Configuring Spring DM's extender with a fragment. The extender uses beans from the fragment's application context for its core components.

driven by both the bean names and their types, so the fragments' configuration files must be very careful with the bean declarations and with the type that Spring DM expects for each bean.

We'll see in later sections (9.2.1 to 9.2.8 for the standard extender and 9.3.1 to 9.3.4 for the web extender) the list of names and types, but here is a quick overview of what Spring DM lets us configure for the standard extender:

- Creation and destruction of application contexts (asynchronous or synchronous, management of the threads, and so on), covered in sections 9.2.2 and 9.2.3 respectively
- Miscellaneous properties (timeout for dependency resolution, activation of annotation parsing), covered in section 9.2.4
- Event propagation, covered in section 9.2.5

And this is what we can configure for the web extender:

- Web container WAR deployer, covered in section 9.3.2
- Web application context path strategy, covered in section 9.3.3

From these lists, you can see that Spring DM is highly configurable. Let's move on to see how to tune the heart of Spring DM—its standard extender.

9.2   *Extending the standard extender*

The symbolic name of Spring DM's standard extender is `org.springframework.osgi.extender`, so a fragment meant to be attached to it must contain the following entry in its manifest:

```
Fragment-Host: org.springframework.osgi.extender
```

As stated in the previous section, such a fragment should contain a Spring configuration file in a META-INF/spring/extender directory. Here is a valid structure (following Maven 2 standards):

```
standard-extender-configuration
  src/
    main/
      resources/
        META-INF/
          spring/
            extender/
              standard-extender-configuration.xml
```

The standard-extender-configuration.xml file is a simple, standard Spring configuration file. It will contain bean declarations meant to override Spring DM's default core components. These beans will be created by the extender, which means its classloader will be used. The fragment is responsible for declaring all the necessary entries in its Import-Package headers. These entries will complement those of the extender and make the classes available for instantiation.

We'll now look at the beans that Spring DM lets us declare to override its default behavior. We'll provide samples and the corresponding Import-Package entries where appropriate.

9.2.1 *Beans usable for configuration*

Table 9.1 lists the beans that Spring DM's standard extender recognizes.

Table 9.1 Beans in Spring DM's extender available for overriding

Bean name	Type	Description
taskExecutor	TaskExecutor [a]	Manages threads and execution for the creation of Spring application contexts
shutdownTaskExecutor	TaskExecutor [a]	Manages threads and execution for the destruction of Spring application contexts
extenderProperties	Properties [b]	Defines simple properties related to the extender
osgiApplicationEvent-Multicaster	OsgiBundleApplicationContextEventMulticaster [c]	Propagates OSGi application contexts' events to interested parties
applicationContext-Creator	OsgiApplicationContext-Creator [d]	Allows customization of the creation of application contexts
Any bean name (only the type matters)	OsgiBeanFactoryPost-Processor [d]	Allows systematic processing of application contexts
osgiApplication-Contextlistener	OsgiBundleApplication-ContextListener [c]	Allows registration of a global application context listener

[a] From the org.springframework.core.task package
[b] From the java.util package
[c] From the org.springframework.osgi.context.event package
[d] From the org.springframework.osgi.extender package

The following sections are dedicated to the description, default behavior and overriding of each bean.

9.2.2   *Task executor for creating application contexts*

Within Spring DM, creating a Spring application context is a sensitive task, because there are many parameters to take into account: asynchronous versus synchronous creation, waiting for dependencies, and so on. Spring DM's extender handles some of these parameters in preparation for creation, but once the preparation is done, it delegates the creation to a `TaskExecutor`. Using a task executor allows the task submission to be decoupled from the way it will be run, because details such as the use of multiple threads and scheduling (to delay the execution) are part of the settings of the task executor implementation.

The `TaskExecutor` is a Spring interface, and even though you can use it in your own applications, it's most often used by frameworks that build on top of Spring (such as projects from the Spring portfolio). Spring comes with some simple `TaskExecutor` implementations, and it provides bridges to more sophisticated implementations, like the Java 5 `ThreadPoolExecutor` and Doug Lea's concurrent library (which was the base of the concurrency support added in Java 5). Using Spring's `TaskExecutor` abstraction is a nice way to get optimal portability, especially when a program needs to run under environments that have different task-execution support, like Java 1.4 and Java 5+.

By default, Spring DM uses a `SimpleAsyncTaskExecutor` to create Spring application contexts. A `SimpleAsyncTaskExecutor` has the following main characteristics:

- Execution is asynchronous (not in the same thread as the calling thread).
- A new thread is created for each task (threads aren't reused).

With a `SimpleAsyncTaskExecutor`, parallel processing can be controlled with the `concurrencyLimit` property, but Spring DM doesn't use this feature by default.

The `SimpleAsyncTaskExecutor` is suited for testing and development environments, but you should use another `TaskExecutor` implementation in production systems, especially if they're under heavy load where threads are valuable resources.

If you run Java 5 or above, Spring provides the `ThreadPoolTaskExecutor` (contained in the `org.springframework.scheduling.concurrent` package), which internally uses a `java.util.concurrent.ThreadPoolExecutor` and exposes its properties for configuration. A `ThreadPoolExecutor` manages a pool of threads and also maintains some basic statistics. It usually provides better performance than `SimpleAsyncTaskExecutor`: there is no creation overhead, because threads are reused from one task to another. A `ThreadPoolExecutor`, thanks to Spring's `ThreadPool-TaskExecutor` abstraction, can also be tuned to perfectly suit your resource requirements (and limitations).

Listing 9.1 shows what a configuration fragment of the standard extender should contain in its Spring configuration file if you want to override the default `taskExecutor` with a `ThreadPoolTaskExecutor`.

Listing 9.1 Overriding the default task executor with a Java 5 thread pool executor

```
<bean id="taskExecutor"
    class="org.springframework.scheduling.concurrent.
              ThreadPoolTaskExecutor">
  <property name="corePoolSize" value="10" />
  <property name="maxPoolSize" value="15" />
  <property name="keepAliveSeconds" value="30" />
  <property name="threadNamePrefix"
          value="CustomSpringOsgiExtenderThread-" />
</bean>
```

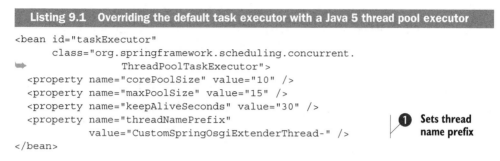 **❶ Sets thread name prefix**

When declaring the `ThreadPoolTaskExecutor`, as shown in listing 9.1, we must be careful with the bean name (`taskExecutor`) if we want Spring DM's extender to pick it up. The `corePoolSize` property defines the number of threads that the pool executor keeps alive, even if they're idle. If we don't want the pool to expand too much under heavy load, the `maxPoolSize` property will limit the number of threads. The `keepAliveSeconds` property defines the number of seconds extra idle threads (that is, if the number of threads exceeds the core size) will wait before terminating. We can also define the prefix used for names of newly created threads ❶; this can help with logging, when the thread name is included in the log message. The settings in listing 9.1 are just examples to show that the underlying `ThreadPoolExecutor` is flexible; you'll want to adapt them to your own needs.

NOTE Don't forget to import the `org.springframework.scheduling.concurrent` package from Spring's Context module in your configuration fragment if you use the `ThreadPoolTaskExecutor` bridge for the Java 5 thread pool executor.

Spring DM 1.2 and earlier is still compatible with Java 1.4, which is useful when the `java.util.concurrent` utilities aren't available. Spring provides the `ThreadPoolTaskExecutor` from the `org.springframework.scheduling.backportconcurrent` package, which uses Doug Lea's concurrent library under the covers. This allows the use of a thread pool, even if you're stuck on Java 1.4. Listing 9.2 shows the configuration of the concurrent-based `ThreadPoolTaskExecutor`.

Listing 9.2 Overriding the default task executor with Doug Lea's concurrent library

```
<bean id="taskExecutor"
    class="org.springframework.scheduling.backportconcurrent.
              ThreadPoolTaskExecutor">
  <property name="corePoolSize" value="10" />
  <property name="maxPoolSize" value="15" />
  <property name="keepAliveSeconds" value="30" />
  <property name="threadGroupName"
          value="CustomSpringOsgiExtenderThread-" />
</bean>
```

Doug Lea's concurrent library was the basis for the Java 5 `java.util.concurrent` utilities, so Spring's `TaskExecutor` bridges are configured in the same way.

NOTE Don't forget to import the `org.springframework.scheduling.` `backportconcurrent` package from Spring's Context module in your configuration fragment if you use the `ThreadPoolTaskExecutor` bridge for Doug Lea's library.

An OSGi-ified version of the concurrent library is available in the SpringSource EBR. It must be deployed along with the configuration fragment if you want to use the corresponding Spring `ThreadPoolTaskExecutor` bridge. Table 9.2 shows the Maven 2 identifier of the concurrent library in the EBR.

Table 9.2   Identifier of Doug Lea's concurrent library in the SpringSource EBR

Group ID	Artifact ID	Version
`com.springsource.edu.emory.mathcs.` `backport`	`edu.emory.mathcs.backport`	3.1.0

We've seen how to override the default task executor (and remember, don't use this default in a production environment!) with two robust implementations of a thread pool. By doing this, you'll get better thread management. But you're not limited to these two implementations: if your container comes with a component that manages threads, you can write your own implementation of `TaskManager` that delegates the work to this component. This `TaskManager` will then be a bridge between Spring DM and this management component.

NOTE Spring provides a `TaskManager` implementation for the CommonJ Work Manager API.

Let's now look at the task executor that's in charge of *destroying* application contexts.

9.2.3   *Task executor for destroying application contexts*

We explained in chapter 4 that the destruction of a bundle's application context is done synchronously, before the bundle is stopped; otherwise the application context could not shut down properly. We also explained that before stopping, Spring DM's extender computes a dependency graph to shut down in the right order all the application contexts it manages. Just like during creation, Spring DM's extender performs a preparation step before closing application contexts, but it ends up submitting the task to a `TaskExecutor`.

By default, Spring DM uses a `TimerTaskExecutor` to destroy Spring application contexts. These are the main characteristics of a `TimerTaskExecutor`:

- Execution is asynchronous and occurs in a unique thread, separate from the calling one.
- Tasks are executed sequentially, in the order of submission.

Spring DM uses this implementation mainly for the sequential execution of tasks it provides, and Spring DM does some synchronization work so that destructions occur synchronously. Unlike when using the `TaskExecutor` for creation, there is no benefit in overriding the destruction `TaskExecutor`. If for any reason you really need to do so, you must ensure that destructions occur sequentially—in the same order that Spring DM submits them.

We're done with the task executors that Spring DM uses for application context creation and destruction. Both are inner components of Spring DM, but you can override them with components of your own and even create a bridge between Spring DM and the container. In the next section, we'll look at how to set properties at the extender level and have them applied to all the bundles that Spring DM manages.

9.2.4 Extender properties

Spring DM's extender accepts some simple properties that can be gathered in an instance of `java.util.Properties`. Each of these properties has an equivalent when you create a Spring-powered bundle, but setting them at the extender level will affect all Spring-powered bundles. This is convenient when you want a unique but centralized configuration, instead of having a configuration for each bundle.

Table 9.3 lists the properties that Spring DM's extender accepts.

Table 9.3 Simple properties of Spring DM's extender

Name	Type	Description	Default
`shutdown.wait.time`	Long	Amount of time the extender waits for application contexts to shut down, in milliseconds.	`10,000` ms (10 s)
`process.annotations`	Boolean	Indicates whether the extender automatically processes OSGi service annotations.	`false`
`dependencies.wait.time`	Long	Amount of time the extender waits for dependencies to be resolved before failing the startup of an application context. Overridden if the bundle defines a value.	`300,000` ms (5 min)

The extender uses the `shutdown.wait.time` property when submitting an application context to its `TaskExecutor` for destruction. If an application context exceeds this duration, Spring DM considers it to have failed to shut down. It then stops the task and emits a logging message. The default duration (10 s) is a bit aggressive for slow bundles; making it longer is a good reason to override it.

The cascading shutdown problem

The most common reason that an application context might fail to shut down is because some remote resource involved in the shutdown is either slow or not responding. Service references from other bundles are particularly problematic because bundles often need to interact with other OSGi services to shut down properly—think of unregistering servlets or MBeans.

(continued)

If your code is written to only interact with these services when they're available, you can get into a situation where bundles successively fail to shut down because bundles that host services they require fail to shut down. For this and other reasons, it's generally best not to let Spring DM forcibly shut down your bundles. Instead, you should write your code in a way that ensures it won't exceed the shutdown timeout.

The `process.annotations` property allows for systematic detection of Spring DM's OSGi service annotations. You can also enable the processing of annotations on a per-bundle basis by declaring a `ServiceReferenceInjectionBeanPostProcessor` in the application context of a bundle. By default, annotation detection isn't activated, so you can set the property to `true` if you want to support annotations everywhere. As we mentioned earlier, it's better to do this in the extender configuration because that way you get support for service annotation–based dependencies.

Spring DM is able to defer the creation of application contexts if their mandatory dependencies aren't satisfied. You can globally set the duration of this postponement through the `dependencies.wait.time` property. The default value (5 min) is targeted at short update cycles (stop the current bundle, install a new version, start it, and test it). If you want more time between updates, you can lengthen the duration. Note that using the `timeout` directive of the `Spring-Context` header in a bundle overrides this global setting for that bundle.

The following snippet shows how to override all the properties by declaring an `extenderProperties` bean with Spring's `util` tag:

```
<util:properties id="extenderProperties">
  <prop key="shutdown.wait.time">20000</prop>
  <prop key="process.annotations">true</prop>
  <prop key="dependencies.wait.time">60000</prop>
</util:properties>
```

You should use the extender's properties when you need to set these properties globally. Moreover, this approach decouples your bundles from their environment and makes them less technology-specific.

9.2.5   *Propagating application context events*

Spring DM has its own event mechanism, which differs from Spring's, as it propagates events about the full lifecycle of application contexts to interested parties. These parties aren't known in advance and generally belong to application contexts other than the ones that emitted the events.

Spring DM uses an `OsgiBundleApplicationContextEventMulticaster` to broadcast events, and by default it uses an adapter that delegates to a `SimpleApplicationEvent-Multicaster` (a Spring class, and the default implementation used by Spring for its own event mechanism). This default implementation broadcasts events synchronously, in the same thread as the caller. This behavior is simple and fits the most common cases, but it can be problematic if some listeners take a long time performing their operations, because the propagation could then block the entire application.

Getting better control over the way events are propagated is a good reason to override the default event multicaster. You can either implement your own event multicaster or use a combination of what Spring and Spring DM offer for this. Listing 9.3 illustrates the second solution.

Listing 9.3 Overriding the default event-propagation mechanism

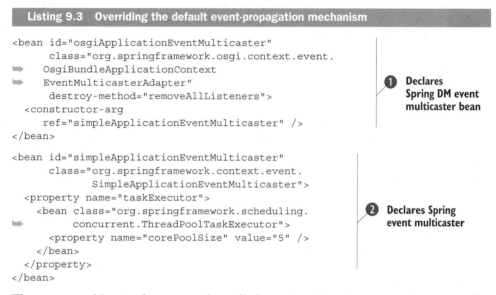

```
<bean id="osgiApplicationEventMulticaster"
      class="org.springframework.osgi.context.event.
      OsgiBundleApplicationContext
      EventMulticasterAdapter"
      destroy-method="removeAllListeners">
  <constructor-arg
    ref="simpleApplicationEventMulticaster" />
</bean>

<bean id="simpleApplicationEventMulticaster"
      class="org.springframework.context.event.
             SimpleApplicationEventMulticaster">
  <property name="taskExecutor">
    <bean class="org.springframework.scheduling.
          concurrent.ThreadPoolTaskExecutor">
      <property name="corePoolSize" value="5" />
    </bean>
  </property>
</bean>
```

❶ Declares Spring DM event multicaster bean

❷ Declares Spring event multicaster

The event multicaster bean must be called osgiApplicationEventMulticaster for Spring DM to pick it up **❶**. We use Spring DM's adapter that builds a bridge between its event mechanism and Spring's. This implementation needs a Spring ApplicationEventMulticaster for its constructor parameter. Thanks to the destroy-method attribute, the multicaster will release its listeners when the application context is destroyed.

Then we start defining the multicaster that will do the real job of propagation **❷**. It's the default implementation (SimpleApplicationEventMulticaster), but we override its inner TaskExecutor to use a thread pool.

With this configuration, event propagation will be done efficiently, without impacting the thread of the calling code. Nevertheless, you should check whether the default behavior suits your needs before overriding it like this.

9.2.6 *Overriding application context creation*

Spring DM's extender delegates the creation of Spring application contexts to an OsgiApplicationContextCreator. This interface is simple, but its implementation has a huge responsibility because it defines the creation of application contexts. This is its signature:

```
package org.springframework.osgi.extender;
(...)
public interface OsgiApplicationContextCreator {

  DelegatedExecutionOsgiBundleApplicationContext createApplicationContext(
    BundleContext bundleContext) throws Exception;

}
```

Notice that part of the interface contract is to create Spring DM's specific application contexts, `DelegatedExecutionOsgiBundleApplicationContext`. The other part of the contract finds Spring configuration files in the bundle context.

Spring DM's default behavior consists of using a `DefaultOsgiApplicationContextCreator` that implements the creation rules we saw in previous chapters:

- It looks for the `Spring-Context` header in the bundle manifest first.
- It falls back on scanning the META-INF/spring directory.

The way Spring DM creates a Spring application for an OSGi bundle can then be easily overridden by defining a new `OsgiApplicationContextCreator`. When doing so, you should follow one of the following three paths:

- Start from scratch and implement your own `OsgiApplicationContextCreator`.
- Use Spring DM's `ConditionalApplicationContextCreator`, which allows you to easily filter bundles that should have a Spring application context from those that shouldn't.
- Customize the `ConfigurationScanner` of the `DefaultOsgiApplicationContextCreator` that implements the `Spring-Context` header and META-INF/spring directory strategy.

There is little chance you'll have to write an `OsgiApplicationContextCreator` from scratch, so we'll focus on the second and the third options.

FILTERING POTENTIAL SPRING-POWERED BUNDLES

The `ConditionalApplicationContextCreator` class defines the `BundleContextFilter` interface and uses an instance of this interface to filter bundles. This filter is a barrier for bundles that shouldn't have a Spring application context bound to them, so that the application context creator focuses only on the creation of application contexts. All you have to do is define your own filter by implementing `BundleContextFilter`. If the filter doesn't discard the bundle, the `ConditionalApplicationContextCreator` delegates the application context creation to another `OsgiApplicationContextCreator` (a `DefaultOsgiApplicationContextCreator` by default, but you can inject any implementation).

Here's a simple implementation of `BundleContextFilter` that accepts only bundles from the current chapter of this book:

```
package com.manning.sdmia.ch09.stdextenderconf;

import org.osgi.framework.BundleContext;
import org.springframework.osgi.extender.support.
      ConditionalApplicationContextCreator.BundleContextFilter;
```

```
public class ManningBundleContextFilter implements BundleContextFilter {

    @Override
    public boolean matches(BundleContext bundleContext) {
        return bundleContext.getBundle().getSymbolicName()
                .startsWith(
            "com.manning.sdmia.ch09"
        );
    }

}
```

Filters bundles based on the beginning of their name

The following snippet shows how to declare the application context creator bean in the configuration fragment:

```
<bean id="applicationContextCreator"
      class="org.springframework.osgi.extender.support.
             ConditionalApplicationContextCreator">
    <property name="filter">
        <bean class="com.manning.sdmia.ch09.stdextenderconf.
                MagicBundleContextFilter" />
    </property>
</bean>
```

With the previous configuration, bundles are filtered *before* they have any chance to be scanned for the presence of the `Spring-Context` header or for Spring configuration files in the META-INF/spring directory. Indeed, after filtering, the `ConditionalApplicationContextCreator` uses a plain `DefaultOsgiApplicationContextCreator` that implements all the usual logic for scanning potential Spring-powered bundles.

Let's now see how we can configure the default application context creator.

OVERRIDING THE DEFAULT SCANNING PROCESS OF SPRING CONFIGURATION FILES

The `DefaultOsgiApplicationContextCreator` delegates the discovery of a bundle's Spring configuration files to an instance of `ConfigurationScanner`. Here's the declaration of this interface:

```
package org.springframework.osgi.extender.support.scanning;
(...)
public interface ConfigurationScanner {

    String[] getConfigurations(Bundle bundle);

}
```

The only provided implementation of `ConfigurationScanner`, `DefaultConfigurationScanner`, looks for the `Spring-Context` header in the bundle manifest and falls back on the META-INF/spring directory to find Spring application context files. It then hands the files to the application context creator, which uses them to load the application context.

> **NOTE** The configuration scanner is only in charge of locating the Spring configuration files. It doesn't interpret the directives of the `Spring-Context` header (asynchronous versus synchronous creation, timeouts, and so on).

Once you have implemented your own ConfigurationScanner, you can inject it into the default application context creator. The following snippet illustrates how to do so in the configuration fragment:

```
<bean id="applicationContextCreator"
      class="org.springframework.osgi.extender.support.
                DefaultOsgiApplicationContextCreator">
  <property name="configurationScanner">
    <bean class="com.manning.sdmia.ch09.stdextenderconf.
                MyConfigurationScanner" />
  </property>
</bean>
```

WHEN TO OVERRIDE THE APPLICATIONCONTEXTCREATOR

Overriding Spring DM's default mechanism for creating application contexts isn't a job for the faint-hearted. Here are some cases that justify it:

- Disabling the creation of specific Spring-enabled bundles (filtering bundles)
- Changing or augmenting the concept of Spring-enabled bundles (for example, scanning different locations or different manifest headers, basing the configuration on Java metadata, and so on)
- Supplying systematic default behavior (for example, creating a default Spring application context for non-Spring-enabled bundles, providing a parent application context to all contexts, and so on)

In any case, your customization of the creation process should still support the Spring-Context header and META-INF/spring couple, because it's the default and most accepted way to load Spring application contexts with Spring DM.

The principle of least surprise

You may have heard of the *principle of least surprise* (or sometimes *least astonishment*). Basically, it means that you should strive to make things work as a user would reasonably expect and that doesn't cause surprise. Function naming is an obvious example—you should name functions for the purpose they perform, rather than giving them obscure or counterintuitive names.

Although this may seem obvious, in highly configurable systems it can be tempting to "improve" on the default behavior. The problem with this is that the user won't be expecting it, and such changes can lead to problems because the way something works isn't the way the user expects it to work.

If you do override Spring DM's default behavior, try to make the changes as minimal as possible—your users will thank you!

Let's move on from application context creation to their postprocessing, which allows you to modify the definitions of Spring beans.

9.2.7 *Adding postprocessing to application contexts*

Spring DM's extender automatically detects any bean of type `OsgiBeanFactoryPost-Processor` declared in a bundle's OSGi application context. It then calls the `postProcessBeanFactory` method of these beans, passing the bean factory and the bundle context. This is particularly useful for working on bean definitions or even for adding beans to the application context in a systematic manner. This post-processing is done *before* the beans are created, meaning that the postprocessor works on *bean definitions* and not on the beans themselves.

By adding `OsgiBeanFactoryPostProcessors` in a configuration fragment of the extender, the scope is extended to *all* Spring-powered bundles. What you can achieve with `OsgiBeanFactoryPostProcessors` is close to infinite, so in this snippet we'll just show you how to output to the console the number of beans a Spring-powered bundle defines:

```
package com.manning.sdmia.ch09.stdextenderconf;
(...)
public class LoggingOsgiBeanFactoryPostProcessor implements
    OsgiBeanFactoryPostProcessor {

  @Override
  public void postProcessBeanFactory(BundleContext bundleContext,
      ConfigurableListableBeanFactory beanFactory) throws BeansException,
      InvalidSyntaxException, BundleException {
    System.out.println("Bundle "+
      bundleContext.getBundle().getSymbolicName()+" defines "+
      beanFactory.getBeanDefinitionCount()+" bean(s).");
  }

}
```

You need to register the postprocessor in the configuration fragment, and it will be called for the creation of the application context of each Spring-powered bundle:

```
<bean class="com.manning.sdmia.ch09.stdextenderconf.
              LoggingOsgiBeanFactoryPostProcessor" />
```

> **NOTE** Because Spring DM automatically detects OSGi bean factory postprocessors, you don't need to declare a bean with a specific name in the configuration fragment.

Spring and Spring DM's bean factory postprocessors can be used for any of the following:

- Logging
- Changing the definition of beans (for example, to get the final value of a property from a property file)
- Adding behavior to beans using Spring AOP
- Adding default singleton beans

Because Spring DM's bean factory postprocessors also have access to the bundle context, their operations can be bundle-specific.

9.2.8   *Overriding the default OSGi application context listener*

Spring DM's event mechanism allows you to interact with the lifecycle of the application context of each Spring-powered bundle. OSGi application context listeners are usually declared in Spring-powered bundles, and they must be exported as OSGi services if they want Spring DM to register them. Spring DM can register a default OSGi application context listener through a configuration fragment. By default, the extender registers an instance of `DefaultOsgiBundleApplicationContextListener` that logs events.

You can register your own implementation of an OSGi application context listener, but by doing so you'll lose the logging that Spring DM's default implementation performs, unless you reimplement it in your listener. This means there's no real benefit in overriding the default OSGi application context listener: its logging features are welcome, and you can easily declare listeners in a dedicated bundle and export them thanks to Spring DM.

Nevertheless, the following snippet shows how you can declare your own default application context listener:

```
<bean id="osgiApplicationContextListener"
      class="com.manning.sdmia.ch09.stdextenderconf.
          ConsoleApplicationContextListener" />
```

> **NOTE**   The default OSGi application context listener doesn't disable or replace listeners declared and exported in Spring-powered bundles.

This ends our tour of the configuration of the core components of Spring DM's extender. The extender is flexible and even allows you to override part of its most critical components. Some of them need to be overridden only in specific cases, and others (like the creation task executor or the extender properties) should always be considered for overriding in production environments. By overriding components, you can also plug Spring DM into your environment and make it work in a truly managed manner.

Let's now see a real-world example of the configuration of Spring DM's extender within SpringSource dm Server.

9.2.9   *How SpringSource dm Server customizes Spring DM's extender*

SpringSource dm Server is a true modular application server, both in its design and in the programming model it provides for its hosted applications. dm Server builds on top of OSGi, Equinox, Tomcat, and Spring DM. It provides monitoring capabilities like logging, trace, and service dumps, and it solves common pitfalls when running in an OSGi environment (like ORM or AOP). It also defines new units of packaging, more adapted to enterprise applications than plain OSGi bundles. Last but not least, it comes with a command-line utility, the dm Shell, which we'll use to find the configuration fragment of Spring DM's extender.

FINDING THE EXTENDER FRAGMENT WITH THE DM SHELL

If dm Server is running on your computer, you can access the dm Shell through SSH:

```
ssh -p 2401 admin@localhost
```

The default password is "springsource". Note you can access the dm Shell locally by adding the -shell flag to the start script.

Once connected, you'll see the splash screen on the console:

```
Using username "admin".
admin@localhost's password:

   @@@ ***
  @@@ *****              ._.                        ._.            ._. ._.
 @@@@ ******          _| |    ___    ___ .| |_     _  | | |
@@@@@@ ****          / _ | /     \  / _ /| |_  \ ./_  \ | | | |
@@@@@ ***           / /_/ || Y Y \ \__ \ |  Y  \ \_/ | |_| |_
  @@@ ***           \_____||_|_|__/ /____/ |__|_/ \__/ |___/|___/

Type 'help' to see the available commands.

:>
```

The bundle list command issues the names of dozens of bundles, but by looking at the list carefully, you can find Spring DM's extender bundle:

```
:> bundle list

Id    Name                                 Version                  State
0     org.eclipse.osgi                     3.5.1.R35x_v20091005     ACTIVE
(...)
3     org.springframework.osgi.core        1.2.1                    ACTIVE
4   S org.springframework.osgi.extender    1.2.1                    ACTIVE
5     org.springframework.osgi.io          1.2.1                    ACTIVE
(...)
```

Bundles that embed a Spring application context are flagged with an "S". The bundle examine command gives more information about the extender bundle and its fragments:

```
:> bundle examine 4

Id:            4
Name:          org.springframework.osgi.extender
Version        1.2.1
State:         ACTIVE
Spring Powered: true
(...)
Fragments:
    com.springsource.kernel.dmfragment 2.0.0.RELEASE [16]
```

This gives us enough information to open the dmfragment bundle, which is located in the lib/kernel directory of the dm Server distribution.

ANALYZING THE EXTENDER FRAGMENT

As of dm Server 2, only the TaskExecutor bean is overridden. dm Server provides its own implementation, ContextPropagatingTaskExecutor, for creating application contexts, which relies on a Java 5 thread pool with a core size of 15 threads. The main features of this implementation are the following:

- Interaction with dm Server's tracing service
- Customization of thread names, to help with logging (the thread name appears in the log)
- Setting of the thread context classloader to the caller's classloader for the task execution

By providing its own `TaskExecutor`, dm Server uses a portable and effective solution for creating Spring application contexts. The way dm Server customizes the Spring DM extender module is a real-world example of how you can configure Spring DM as you need for your own environment.

Now that Spring DM's standard extender no longer has any mystery for you, let's move on to configuring the web extender. We'll cover how to switch to the Jetty WAR deployer, how to change the strategy of the context path of web applications, and how to modify Spring DM's definition of web bundles. This proves especially useful when you want to finely tune the web container you're using with Spring DM web support.

9.3   *Extending the web extender and WAR deployer*

Just like the standard extender, Spring DM's web extender allows you to configure some of its core components through fragments. To be attached to Spring DM's web extender, a fragment must contain the following entry in its manifest:

```
Fragment-Host: org.springframework.osgi.web.extender
```

The packaging for a web extender's fragment is exactly the same as for the standard extender's: Spring configuration files must be in the META-INF/spring/extender directory. Let's see what the web extender lets us override.

9.3.1   *Beans available for configuration*

Table 9.4 lists the beans that Spring DM's extender recognizes.

Table 9.4   Beans in Spring DM's web extender available for overriding

Bean name	Type	Description
warDeployer	WarDeployer [a]	Installs OSGi bundles as web applications. Also handles the uninstallation.
contextPathStrategy	ContextPathStrategy [a]	Determines the context path for a web bundle.
warScanner	WarScanner [b]	Indicates whether or not an OSGi bundle is web-enabled.

[a] From the `org.springframework.osgi.web.deployer` package
[b] From the `org.springframework.osgi.web.extender.internal.scanner` package

The following sections are dedicated to the description, default behavior, and overriding of each bean.

9.3.2 *Overriding the WAR deployer*

Inside Spring DM's web extender, the WAR deployer is in charge of installing and uninstalling web bundles. An implementation of `WarDeployer` is specific to a web container and uses its API to achieve this integration. A WAR deployer can also start the web container, but the preferred way to start the container is to consume the container service from the OSGi repository, letting another bundle do the work of creating and configuring it.

By default, Spring DM uses the `TomcatWarDeployer` and, following the philosophy of WAR deployers, expects another bundle to start the servlet container. Spring DM also supports Jetty (6.0.x and 6.1.x) out of the box by providing the `JettyWarDeployer` class.

> **NOTE** Tomcat's servlet container is also referred to as Catalina.

To change the default WAR deployer, your configuration fragment must declare a `warDeployer` bean, of type `WarDeployer`. The following snippet shows how to switch to Jetty:

```
<bean id="warDeployer"
      class="org.springframework.osgi.web.deployer.jetty.
              JettyWarDeployer" />
```

To use Spring DM's web support, the WAR deployer isn't enough. You also need the following:

- The target container classes available in the OSGi container (which means an OSGi-ified version of the container)
- The container dependencies (Servlet API, optionally the JSP API and a JSP compiler)
- A bundle that starts the container and registers it on the OSGi service registry

We'll learn more about this process in section 9.4, which is dedicated to web containers. All you need to know for now is that you need to change the WAR deployer when switching from Tomcat to Jetty. Changing the default WAR deployer is simple; the difficult part comes when you need to provision the OSGi container with all the container's bundles.

9.3.3 *Overriding the context path strategy*

When deploying a web bundle to the embedded web container, the web extender relies on a `ContextPathStrategy` object to decide which context path the web application should be deployed on. This decision is based on the `Bundle` object.

The default is the `DefaultContextPathStrategy`, whose algorithm is based on the following steps:

- The value of the `Web-ContextPath` manifest header, if present
- The bundle location (without the extension), if present
- The bundle name, if present
- The bundle symbolic name, if present
- The bundle identity (assigned by the OSGi container)

The default context path strategy makes sense, but you might want to change it; for example, to change the order of the decisions or to use your own manifest headers. The following snippet shows a skeleton for implementing your own strategy:

```
package com.manning.sdmia.ch09.webextenderconf;

import org.osgi.framework.Bundle;
import org.springframework.osgi.web.deployer.ContextPathStrategy;

public class MyContextPathStrategy implements ContextPathStrategy {

  @Override
  public String getContextPath(Bundle bundle) {
    String contextPath;                              Computes
    (...)                                            context path
    return contextPath;
  }

}
```

Note that the context path must begin with a slash (/) and must not contain any whitespace. The following snippet shows how to declare the custom context path strategy in the configuration fragment:

```
<bean id="contextPathStrategy"
        class="com.manning.sdmia.ch09.webextenderconf.
                MyContextPathStrategy" />
```

Before overriding the context path strategy, try to take advantage of the default implementation, which has a flexible yet consistent algorithm. Also keep in mind the usual restrictions for context paths that also apply in an OSGi environment: uniqueness, no whitespace, and so on.

Now that you know how to choose the context path of your web application, let's see how we can easily choose which bundles should be web bundles, by changing the definition of a web bundle using Spring DM's WAR scanner component.

9.3.4   *Overriding the WAR scanner*

Spring DM's web extender relies on a `WarScanner` to decide whether or not a bundle is a web bundle. The `DefaultWarScanner` considers a bundle to be a web bundle if its location ends with `.war` or if it contains a WEB-INF directory.

If the default WAR scanner doesn't suit you, you can create your own implementation. You just have to make sure that the scanning is consistent with the structure of a web archive as a web container would expect it.

The following snippet shows the skeleton of a custom `WarScanner`:

```
package com.manning.sdmia.ch09.webextenderconf;

import org.osgi.framework.Bundle;
import org.springframework.osgi.web.extender.internal.scanner.WarScanner;

public class MyWarScanner implements WarScanner {

  @Override
  public boolean isWar(Bundle bundle) {
    boolean isWar;                          Implements WAR
    (...)                                   scanning and detection
    return isWar;
  }

}
```

To tell the web extender to use your `WarScanner` implementation, you must declare a `warScanner` bean in the configuration fragment, as illustrated in the following snippet:

```
<bean id="warScanner"
      class="com.manning.sdmia.ch09.webextenderconf.MyWarScanner" />
```

Simple!

This ends our study of the configuration of Spring DM's web extender. Its default behavior should fit most of your needs, except perhaps for the WAR deployer, which allows you to switch from one web container to another. That's why the next section is dedicated to WAR deployers and the configuration of their web containers.

9.4   *Configuring embedded web containers*

Spring DM provides out-of-the-box web support for two of the most popular Java web containers: Tomcat and Jetty. Tomcat is Spring DM's default choice, so we'll see in this section how to configure the web extender to use Jetty.

Tomcat and Jetty are both excellent web containers, and choosing one or the other is mostly a matter of taste or company policy (although Jetty has a longer track record with OSGi than Tomcat because it's often used as an implementation of the OSGi HTTP service). If you use Spring DM web support and don't have any opinion about Tomcat or Jetty, you can stick to Tomcat, because it's the default (and simplest) choice with Spring DM. Using Jetty will not give you any additional features.

When starting web containers, Spring DM uses a default configuration, which is convenient for demos but not sufficient when we have more specific requirements (such as starting the server on a port other than 8080, enabling SSL, and so on). We'll look at how to provide our own configuration for the web container, and we'll start by discussing the nuts and bolts of Spring DM web support, because this is a prerequisite to understanding how to configure it.

9.4.1   *The basics of Spring DM's web support*

Spring DM's web extender is in charge of detecting and deploying web bundles. We learned in section 9.3 that the web extender delegates most of the work to components that we can easily replace.

The WAR deployer is the most important of these components, because it handles the deployment and undeployment of web applications. A WAR deployer should not start and stop the web container: it should let another bundle handle this and subsequently look up the service to deploy web applications. This allows the management of applications to be decoupled from their target deployment environment. This is the behavior of the two WAR deployer implementations that Spring DM provides.

Spring DM also provides the corresponding bundles that start the web container. Figure 9.2 illustrates how the WAR deployer (embedded in the web extender) consumes the web container service that another bundle started and made available in the OSGi service registry.

Figure 9.2 illustrates another concept of Spring DM's web support: the fragment-based configuration. We already saw how to configure the web extender, allowing (among other things) the definition of the appropriate WAR deployer to use. The web container starter bundles that Spring DM provides can use a fragment to get a specific configuration file (`server.xml` for Tomcat and `jetty.xml` for Jetty).

Now that the configuration basics of Spring DM's web support are clear, we're going to apply them to configuring the two web containers that Spring DM supports out of the box: Tomcat and Jetty. This will allow us to switch from one web container to the other, and it will also allow us to configure them as we can when they're running standalone, outside of an OSGi environment.

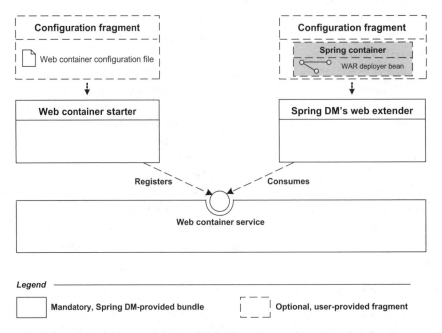

Figure 9.2   Spring DM's web support basics. The web container starter bundle starts the web service and registers it; the WAR deployer consumes this service. Users can configure the web container or change the WAR deployer using fragments.

9.4.2 Support for Tomcat

Apache Tomcat is arguably the most popular web container in the Java EE world and it's Spring DM's default web container. You learned in chapter 3 how to set up Tomcat 5.5, primarily because the distribution of Spring DM ships with this version. We'll discuss here how to use Tomcat 6.0 and then how to provide our own configuration for the web container.

USING TOMCAT 6.0

Tomcat 6.0 is a Servlet 2.5- and JSP 2.1-compliant web container (whereas Tomcat 5.5 is Servlet 2.4- and JSP 2.0-compliant). From Spring DM's repository, you can get a set of libraries that allow you to use Tomcat 6.0.16. Unfortunately, due to Tomcat and Jasper's (the JSP compiler's) design and package structure, JSP isn't supported.

Table 9.5 lists all the dependencies required to use Tomcat 6.0.16 with a limited set of dependencies from public and Spring DM repositories.

Table 9.5 Dependencies for Tomcat 6.0.16

Group ID	Artifact ID	Version	Origin
org.mortbay.jetty	servlet-api-2.5	6.1.14	Public repository
org.mortbay.jetty	jsp-api-2.1	6.1.14	Public repository
org.springframework.osgi	jasper.osgi	6.0.16-SNAPSHOT	Spring DM repository
org.springframework.osgi	catalina.osgi	6.0.16-SNAPSHOT	Spring DM repository
org.springframework.osgi	catalina.start.osgi	1.0.0	Spring DM repository

This solution uses a limited number of bundles, but although there are alternatives to the use of JSP, not supporting this standard Java EE view technology is a big limitation. Don't panic, you'll be able to use JSP with Spring DM, but doing so requires a solution with a larger set of bundles.

> **NOTE** The Jetty team makes OSGi-ified versions of the Servlet API and the JSP API available from the public Maven 2 public repositories; that's why we used them here. These JARs aren't specific to Jetty.

The SpringSource EBR contains all the bundles necessary for feature-complete support of Tomcat 6.0.24. Table 9.6 lists all these bundles.

Notice that both configurations use Spring DM's Tomcat starter.

Now you have a functioning Tomcat container in your OSGi environment, and you can use Spring DM's web extender to deploy web applications. Nevertheless, you'll want to customize the configuration of your web container, and that's what we'll discuss in the next section.

Table 9.6   Dependencies for Tomcat 6.0.24

Group ID	Artifact ID	Version	Origin
`javax.servlet`	`com.springsource.javax.servlet`	2.5.0	EBR
`org.apache.taglibs`	`com.springsource.org.apache.taglibs.standard`	1.1.2	EBR
`javax.servlet`	`com.springsource.javax.servlet.jsp.jstl`	1.1.2	EBR
`javax.servlet`	`com.springsource.javax.servlet.jsp`	2.1.0	EBR
`javax.el`	`com.springsource.javax.el`	1.0.0	EBR
`org.apache.el`	`com.springsource.org.apache.el`	6.0.24	EBR
`javax.activation`	`com.springsource.javax.activation`	1.1.1	EBR
`javax.xml.soap`	`com.springsource.javax.xml.soap`	1.3.0	EBR
`javax.xml.rpc`	`com.springsource.javax.xml.rpc`	1.1.0	EBR
`javax.ejb`	`com.springsource.javax.ejb`	3.0.0	EBR
`javax.persistence`	`com.springsource.javax.persistence`	1.0.0	EBR
`javax.mail`	`com.springsource.javax.mail`	1.4.1	EBR
`javax.xml.stream`	`com.springsource.javax.xml.stream`	1.0.1	EBR
`javax.xml.bind`	`com.springsource.javax.xml.bind`	2.0.0	EBR
`javax.xml.ws`	`com.springsource.javax.xml.ws`	2.1.1	EBR
`org.apache.coyote`	`com.springsource.org.apache.coyote`	6.0.24	EBR
`org.apache.juli`	`com.springsource.org.apache.juli.extras`	6.0.24	EBR
`org.apache.catalina`	`com.springsource.org.apache.catalina`	6.0.24	EBR
`org.apache.jasper`	`com.springsource.org.apache.jasper`	6.0.24	EBR

Table 9.6 Dependencies for Tomcat 6.0.24 *(continued)*

Group ID	Artifact ID	Version	Origin
`org.apache.jasper`	`com.springsource.org.apache.jasper.org.eclipse.jdt`	6.0.24	EBR
`javax.annotation`	`com.springsource.javax.annotation`	1.0.0	EBR
`org.springframework.osgi`	`catalina.start.osgi`	1.0.0	Spring DM repository

OVERRIDING THE DEFAULT CONFIGURATION

Spring DM's Tomcat bootstrap bundle is in charge of configuring and bootstrapping the Tomcat instance you use with Spring DM. For this purpose, it uses a default configuration file, conf/default-server.xml. Before using this file, it looks in its bundle space to find a conf/server.xml file. This means that we can use a fragment to provide our own configuration.

For example, by changing the default configuration, we can do any of the following:

- Use another port for HTTP (default is 8080)
- Add connectors (SSL for encryption or AJP for connecting a web server to the Tomcat engine)
- Configure clustering

To get attached to the Tomcat bootstrap bundle, the fragment must contain the following entry in its manifest:

```
Fragment-Host: org.springframework.osgi.catalina.start.osgi
```

For the bootstrap bundle to pick up the configuration file, the fragment must have the following structure:

```
tomcat-configuration-fragment
  META-INF/
    MANIFEST.MF
  conf/
    server.xml
```

The server.xml file can contain any configuration directives relating to Tomcat configuration (refer to the Tomcat reference documentation for an exhaustive description of the available options).

The following snippet shows how to start Tomcat on port 8090:

```
<Server port="8005" shutdown="SHUTDOWN">
  <Service name="Catalina">                          Starts Tomcat
    <Connector port="8090" />                         on port 8090
    <Engine name="Catalina" defaultHost="localhost">
      <Host name="localhost" unpackWARs="false" autoDeploy="false"
        liveDeploy="false" deployOnStartup="false"
        xmlValidation="false" xmlNamespaceAware="false"/>
```

```
      </Engine>
    </Service>
</Server>
```

Another facet of Tomcat configuration is the configuration of its Servlet container, also known by the name *Catalina*. We'll discuss this in the next section.

CONFIGURING CATALINA, TOMCAT'S SERVLET CONTAINER

The configuration of Catalina consists of providing a fragment to the Catalina bundle. This fragment can contain files that usually lie in the conf directory of any standard distribution of Tomcat 6.0. Catalina uses these files to automatically add behavior to web applications (such as using web.xml to register a `DefaultServlet` that serves static resources) or to apply a security policy to the web container. Without this extra configuration step, web applications in Tomcat are nearly unusable.

> **NOTE** The Catalina bundle provided by Spring DM already contains the Tomcat configuration files (web.xml, catalina.policies, and so on). This section is mainly intended to configure the Catalina bundle from the Spring-Source EBR.

The configuration fragment must contain the following entry in its manifest to get attached to the Catalina bundle from the SpringSource EBR:

```
Fragment-Host: com.springsource.org.apache.catalina
```

All the configuration files that the fragment contains are optional. Here's a sample structure of the fragment:

```
catalina-configuration-fragment
  META-INF/
    MANIFEST.MF
  conf/
    catalina.policy
    catalina.properties
    context.xml
    web.xml
```

The default web.xml file should always be added to the Catalina configuration because it contains important servlet declarations (you can find this file in the standard distribution of Tomcat).

Now that you're able to configure every aspect of Tomcat within a Spring DM environment, let's see how to configure the other web container that Spring DM supports: Jetty.

9.4.3 *Support for Jetty*

Jetty is a full-featured, Java EE-compliant web container that supports (in its 6.x version) the Servlet 2.5 and JSP 2.1 APIs. Starting with version 7, Jetty is part of the Eclipse foundation.

In this section, we'll cover how to use and configure Jetty 6.1 with Spring DM.

USING JETTY WITH SPRING DM

Spring DM supports Jetty out of the box thanks to a JettyWarDeployer implementation and Jetty bootstrap bundle. In section 9.3—dedicated to the configuration of Spring DM's web extender—you learned that, by default, Spring DM uses a Tomcat-WarDeployer and that you can switch to JettyWarDeployer using a fragment. Spring DM provides a working fragment that declares a Jetty WAR deployer bean, so switching to Jetty is just a matter of gathering the appropriate bundles.

Table 9.7 lists all the bundles necessary to make Jetty work (with JSP support) within Spring DM.

Table 9.7 Dependencies for Jetty 6.1

Group ID	Artifact ID	Version	Origin
org.mortbay.jetty	servlet-api-2.5	6.1.14	Public repository
org.mortbay.jetty	jsp-api-2.1	6.1.14	Public repository
org.mortbay.jetty	jetty	6.1.19	Public repository
org.mortbay.jetty	jetty-util	6.1.19	Public repository
org.springframework.osgi	jasper.osgi	6.0.16-SNAPSHOT	Spring DM repository
org.springframework.osgi	commons-el.osgi	1.0-SNAPSHOT	Spring DM repository
org.springframework.osgi	jstl.osgi	1.1.2-SNAPSHOT	Spring DM repository
net.sourceforge.cglib	com.springsource. net.sf.cglib	2.1.3	EBR
org.springframework.osgi	jetty.web.extender. fragment.osgi	1.0.1	Spring DM repository
org.springframework.osgi	jetty.start.osgi	1.0.0	Spring DM repository

Jetty core JARs are distributed as OSGi bundles, which is why they're available in public repositories.

Notice that Jetty uses Jasper (Tomcat's JSP compiler). As for Tomcat, Spring DM's Jetty bootstrap bundle bootstraps the server with a convenient default configuration. We're going to see how to provide our own configuration.

OVERRIDING THE DEFAULT CONFIGURATION

Jetty uses an XML file for its configuration. In Jetty's standard distribution, this file lies in the etc directory and is named jetty.xml. Spring DM's Jetty starter bundle searches its bundle space for an etc/jetty.xml file to configure its Jetty instance, and it defaults to etc/default-jetty.xml if it can't find one.

Our work consists of writing a fragment that attaches to the bootstrap bundle:

```
Fragment-Host: org.springframework.osgi.jetty.start.osgi
```

The fragment must have the following structure:

```
jetty-configuration-fragment
  META-INF/
    MANIFEST.MF
  etc/
    jetty.xml
```

Jetty uses its own lightweight container syntax for its configuration file—jetty.xml—making the configuration very flexible. The following snippet shows an excerpt of the jetty.xml file, for starting Jetty on port 8090:

```
<Configure id="Server" class="org.mortbay.jetty.Server">
  (...)
  <Call name="addConnector">
    <Arg>
      <New class="org.mortbay.jetty.nio.SelectChannelConnector">
        <Set name="host"><SystemProperty name="jetty.host" /></Set>
        <Set name="port">8090</Set>                                    ◁─── Starts Jetty
        <Set name="maxIdleTime">30000</Set>                                  on port 8090
        <Set name="Acceptors">2</Set>
        <Set name="statsOn">false</Set>
        <Set name="confidentialPort">8443</Set>
        <Set name="lowResourcesConnections">5000</Set>
        <Set name="lowResourcesMaxIdleTime">5000</Set>
      </New>
    </Arg>
  </Call>
  (...)
</Configure>
```

You can see that getting Jetty to work with Spring DM is easy, because integration in various environments is a strong focus of the Jetty team. So if you usually use Jetty as your web container, you can still do so when using Spring DM web support.

Because Spring DM can run with Tomcat or Jetty, the most popular web containers in the Java EE world, there's little chance you'll have to change your habits and learn to configure a new web container. This is another demonstration that Spring DM's foundations don't prevent it from being a flexible and customizable framework that can be used in many different environments.

Speaking about integration, perhaps your OSGi and Spring DM-powered applications will have to run on an OSGi environment you don't control, and this environment may be secured by its administrators to avoid third-party bundles. We'll see in the next section how Spring DM can run in a managed and secured environment, thanks to its support for the Java 2 security model.

9.5 *Support for Java 2 security*

As OSGi is all about modularity, you're likely to run many modules on your OSGi platform. Some of them will be yours, and others will have foreign origins, and you don't
want the latter to compromise the integrity of whole system or, worse, to execute some
malicious code. This is what the Java security model is about: being able to control
which instructions code can invoke. OSGi has its own security model, but it builds on
top of Java's. We'll give a primer on both models in this section.

What about Spring DM? Spring DM is just another set of modules, so perhaps you'll
need to run it in secured mode on your target environment. We'll see what this
implies.

9.5.1 *The Java security model*

Imagine you're developing a web controller in an enterprise application. Your mind is
filled with data access objects, HTTP requests, transactions, and business services. Why
not try something fun for relaxation? Put `System.exit(0)` in your web controller,
launch the server, and hit the controller URL with a browser. Bravo, you just stopped
the server! But what would have happened if your web controller had reached the
production server unchanged?

It's to avoid this kind of blunder that Java processes can be run in a secured mode,
where a security manager checks what permissions are granted to the code. By
default, Java processes—even sensitive ones like web containers—don't run in secured
mode.

> **NOTE** Covering the whole Java security model is beyond the scope of this
> book. Nevertheless, we'll give you the basics so that you can understand how
> OSGi uses Java security for the foundations of its own security model and
> what the OSGi security model implies for Spring DM. If you want to learn
> more about the Java security model, we invite you to consult the resources
> available on Sun's website.

The Java security model implies the three following actors:

- The *security manager,* which handles the checking
- The *permissions* (for reading/writing files, stopping the process, and so on)
- The *code,* which is identified with its codebase (the URL from which the source
  was loaded by the classloader).

A *policy* dictates what permissions are granted to the code. Policy configuration files
usually have a `policy` extension and contain the permission definitions. The following snippet shows how to give the permission to read files in the /etc/java/conf directory to the code that's loaded from the /var/lib/somejavalib/ directory:

```
grant codeBase "file:/var/lib/somejavalib/" {
  permission java.io.FilePermission "/etc/java/conf", "read";
}
```

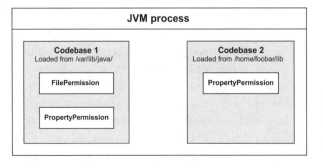

Figure 9.3   In the Java security model, code is given permissions depending on its codebase, which is identified by the URL from which the source was loaded.

The `java.io.FilePermission` class extends the `java.security.Permission` class, which any permission configured in a policy file must do. `Permissions` implement some of the logic of checking, and they get passed to the `SecurityManager`, which throws a `SecurityException` if the code isn't granted the permission.

Figure 9.3 illustrates the relationship between the codebase and permission in a secured JVM process.

How does the security manager get called? For built-in permissions (those included in the JDK), the checking is done in the class that needs protection. If you take a look at the classes in the `java.io` package, you'll see that they call the `SecurityManager`: they create `FilePermission` objects and hand them to the `SecurityManager`.

This checking is performed on the whole stack of the call. Usually, a call to a protected function is encapsulated in a deep succession of method calls, and each of them must be checked. If any frame of the stack doesn't have the correct permission, a `SecurityException` is thrown. This is the general rule, and, like any rule, it can be broken by *privileged* code.

Marking code as privileged enables the code to indirectly grant permissions to its calling code. For example, if some privileged code that has advanced file permissions gets called by code that doesn't have these permissions, no `SecurityException` will be thrown. The following snippet shows how to mark the code in the run method as privileged:

```
AccessController.doPrivileged(new PrivilegedAction() {
  public Object run() {
    (...)
  }
});
```

When should you use privileged code? When you want to grant permissions to trusted code that gets called by unknown code or by code you don't want to grant permissions to. The trusted code can then do its work without worrying about who calls it and without compromising the system, because its own permissions are carefully controlled.

Now that we've covered the basics of the Java security model, let's see how OSGi extends it for its own use.

9.5.2 The OSGi security model

The OSGi security model lets you configure permissions on a per-bundle basis, thanks to a dedicated framework service, the `ConditionalPermissionAdmin` (CPA). The CPA waits for conditions to be met and then checks permissions. Conditions can be based on either the location of a bundle or on the vendor that signed the bundle's code.

The OSGi API provides just these two kinds of permissions, but you can add your own because the system is extensible. Conditions are filter-based: you can define patterns to broaden them to a set of bundles. OSGi permissions use the exact same semantics as those for the Java security model (that's where both models meet).

Figure 9.4 shows how the OSGi security model builds on top of the Java security model.

The following snippet shows how to give a bundle (the condition is the location of the bundle) the permission required to read the contents of a directory (the `getConditionalPermissionAdmin` method encapsulates the lookup of the CPA service):

```
ConditionalPermissionAdmin cpa = getConditionalPermissionAdmin();
ConditionInfo conditionInfo = new ConditionInfo(
  BundleLocationCondition.class.getName(),
  new String[]{bundle().getLocation()}        Creates condition
);                                             and permission
PermissionInfo permissionInfo = new PermissionInfo(
  FilePermission.class.getName(),
  "/var/lib/somejavalib/", "read"
);
cpa.addConditionalPermissionInfo(
  new ConditionInfo[]{conditionInfo},          Adds permission
  new PermissionInfo[] {permissionInfo})}      to CPA
);
```

Notice that OSGi uses its own classes to represent conditions and permissions: `ConditionInfo` and `PermissionInfo`, respectively.

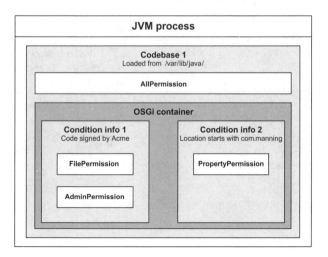

Figure 9.4 To secure an OSGi container, we usually give it all permissions and it then grants permissions to bundles, following rules dictated by the `ConditionInfo` and `PermissionInfo` objects.

The security layer of OSGi is optional, so you have to turn it on explicitly when you start the container. Otherwise there will be no CPA available. With Equinox, you can enable security and specify a policy file with system properties in the launch arguments:

```
java -Djava.security.manager
     -Djava.security.policy=my.policy
     -jar equinox.jar -console
```

Because the OSGi framework will handle all the security checking through the CPA, the policy file used to bootstrap the container just has to give it all permissions:

```
grant {
  permission java.security.AllPermission;
};
```

With these settings, all bundles will have all permissions by default. This isn't exactly what we want, but the OSGi specification gives us all the tools we need with the CPA. We're now on our own to make use of it.

A common way to set permissions in an OSGi container is to write a dedicated agent that listens to the installation of bundles and grants them permissions. It usually takes the form of a `BundleListener` and is started immediately after the system bundle.

You now know how to enable the OSGi security model and to set permissions on bundles. There is a last element in the OSGi security model that's worth mentioning: special permissions for framework- and service-related tasks.

In standard Java, there are `FilePermissions` for restricting access to the filesystem and `PropertyPermissions` for restricting access to system properties. As OSGi brings new concepts, it also comes with new corresponding permissions. Table 9.8 lists them (they all belong to the `org.osgi.framework` package and are subclasses of `java.security.Permission`).

Table 9.8 Permissions introduced by OSGi

Permission	Description	Actions
`AdminPermission`	Authority to perform operations on or get information about a bundle	`execute` (start/stop), `lifecycle` (update/uninstall), `metadata` (get headers/location), and so on
`BundlePermission`	Authority to require or provide a bundle and to receive or attach fragments	`require`, `provide`, `host`, `fragment`
`PackagePermission`	Authority to import or export a package	`import`, `export`
`ServicePermission`	Authority to register or get a service	`register`, `get`

Now that we've looked at the OSGi security model, we'll discuss how Spring DM fits into it.

9.5.3 *Integrating Spring DM into the OSGi security model*

When the OSGi container runs in secured mode, Spring DM needs to be granted some permissions, or it won't work properly. For example, one of the first jobs of Spring DM is to bootstrap Spring application contexts, and for this it inspects the content of bundles and their manifests. For this duty, Spring DM needs the `AdminPermission` on the bundles it manages (though, only if security is enabled).

Because Spring DM can be considered a trusted framework, it should be granted `AllPermission`. Nevertheless, if you need to run in a secured environment, table 9.9 lists the permissions that Spring DM needs for the different parts of its operation. Using this list, you can adjust the granted permissions according to the parts of the framework you're using.

Table 9.9 Permissions Spring DM needs to be granted

Permission	Target	Action	Usage
FilePermission	<<ALL FILES>>	read, write	For logging system and web extender for deploying WARs
RuntimePermission	*	accessDeclareMembers, setContextClassLoader	For reflection and setting the TCCL
ReflectPermission	*	suppressAccessChecks	For accessing nonpublic methods and fields with reflection
PropertyPermission	*	read, write	For the testing framework
AdminPermission	*	class, execute, listener, metadata, resolve, resource	For the extender to listen, introspect, and manage bundles
BundlePermission	*	host	For attaching a configuration fragment to extenders
PackagePermission	*	import, export	For importing and exported Spring DM's packages
ServicePermission	*	register, get	For publishing and looking up internal services

The usual way to grant the correct set of permissions is to start without any permissions at all and increase them little by little, until the system works correctly.

Since version 1.2, Spring DM has used privileged blocks to execute sensitive operations with its own permissions. This means that Spring DM-managed bundles can call some of the Spring DM code without being granted additional permissions, because the security checking will be based on Spring DM's permissions.

This ends our tour of securely integrating Spring DM into an OSGi environment. You have learned about both the Java and OSGi security models, and this should have given you the basics to understand how to tweak your system with the exact permissions required for Spring DM. You should also understand how Spring DM leverages the privileged blocks of code.

In the next section, we'll cover two advanced patterns related to OSGi and Spring DM.

9.6 *Advanced patterns*

Like any other technology, OSGi has its own patterns, which build on its specific features. Think about the fragment configuration pattern: a fragment gets attached to a host bundle and overrides the default behavior of the bundle. This pattern is specific to OSGi, as it uses the concept of an OSGi bundle fragment.

In this section, we'll cover two additional patterns: the implementation provider pattern, which helps enforce the modularity of a bundle, and the chained classloader pattern, which is designed to make aspect-oriented programming (AOP) work smoothly in an OSGi environment. We'll also see how Spring DM can help with the implementation of these patterns.

9.6.1 *Implementation provider pattern*

When using interface-based programming, we usually put all the interfaces of our API in a package that's made available to other bundles via an entry in the `Export-Package` manifest header. We can also provide a default implementation for each of our interfaces in an `impl` or `support` package. By adding this implementation package in our `Export-Packages`, other bundles can directly use these default implementations.

This practice works reasonably well, but it becomes dangerous when the default implementations expose too much of the owning bundle's internals: the bundle will probably need to share more packages, and its clients will need to add the corresponding entries in their `Import-Package` headers. This leads to tight coupling and to a system that's less modular overall. How can we make implementations available to consuming bundles without tightly coupling them? The answer lies in the factory pattern and the service layer of OSGi.

Let's consider an example: we want a component that's able to clean all the tables of a database. It needs to be portable and to work on several database systems. We'll define the `DatabaseCleaner` interface and provide implementations for H2, PostgreSQL, and Oracle.

Our bundle has the following structure:

```
com.manning.sdmia.db
  |
  |- DatabaseCleaner
  |- internal
     |- H2DatabaseCleaner
     |- PostgreSqlDatabaseCleaner
     |- OracleDatabaseCleaner
```

The bundle just defines an interface, because we forbid instructions like `new H2Database()` by not sharing the `internal` package. The missing piece of the puzzle is a `DatabaseCleanerFactory` interface, which would be exposed as an OSGi service and creates the appropriate database cleaner. Here is the definition of this interface:

```
package com.manning.sdmia.db;

public interface DatabaseCleanerFactory {

  public DatabaseCleaner create(DatabaseType dbType);

}
```

The `DatabaseType` enumeration defines the database system our bundle supports:

```
package com.manning.sdmia.db;

public enum DatabaseType {

  H2,Oracle,PostgreSQL

}
```

The bundle would end up with the following structure, with the new elements in bold:

```
com.manning.sdmia.db
  |
  |- DatabaseCleaner
  |- DatabaseCleanerFactory
  |- DatabaseType
  |- internal
     |- H2DatabaseCleaner
     |- PostgreSqlDatabaseCleaner
     |- OracleDatabaseCleaner
     |- DefaultDatabaseCleanerFactory
```

The design of our bundle is set. What we need now is to wire all the elements together: publish the `DefaultDatabaseCleanerFactory` (our default implementation) as an OSGi service; create the database cleaners when clients call the factory; provide the database cleaners with a connection to the database (probably retrieved from the OSGi service registry), and so on. These sound like tasks that Spring DM can fulfill.

The `DefaultDatabaseCleanerFactory` can rely on its owning Spring application context to provide `DatabaseCleaners`:

```
package com.manning.sdmia.db.internal;

(...)

public class DefaultDatabaseCleanerFactory implements      ⟵ Implements
                DatabaseCleanerFactory,                         DatabaseCleanerFactory
                ApplicationContextAware {

  private ApplicationContext appContext;

  @Override
  public DatabaseCleaner create(DatabaseType dbType) {      ⟵ Builds bean name
    String beanName = dbType+"DatabaseCleaner";                 from database type
    try {
      return appContext.getBean(                            Looks up database
        beanName,                                           cleaner in application
        DatabaseCleaner.class                               context
      );
```

```
    } catch (BeansException e) {
      return null;
    }
  }

  @Override
  public void setApplicationContext(
      ApplicationContext applicationContext)
      throws BeansException {
    this.appContext = applicationContext;
  }

}
```

The `DefaultDatabaseCleanerFactory` implements Spring's `ApplicationContextA-`
`ware` interface so that the Spring lightweight container automatically calls the `setAp-`
`plicationContext` method to pass a reference of the owning Spring application
context. Why should we rely on a lookup in the Spring container instead of using
dependency injection? Mainly because an explicit lookup allows us to honor the bean
scope as defined in the configuration (singleton, prototype, and so on) and to benefit
from features like dependency injection.

The last thing to do is to configure the application context of our Spring-powered
bundle:

```
<beans (...)>

  <bean id="databaseCleanerFactory"
        class="com.manning.sdmia.db.internal.
                 DefaultDatabaseCleanerFactory" />          Declares factory
                                                             and publishes it
  <osgi:service ref="databaseCleanerFactory"                as OSGi service
                interface="com.manning.sdmia.db.
                             DatabaseCleanerFactory" />

  <bean id="H2DatabaseCleaner"
        class="com.manning.sdmia.db.internal.
                 H2DatabaseCleaner"
        scope="prototype" />
                                                             Declares
                                                             database
  <bean id="PostgreSQLDatabaseCleaner"                       cleaners
        class="com.manning.sdmia.db.internal.
                 OracleDatabaseCleaner"
        scope="prototype" />
  (...)
</beans>
```

Notice that the database cleaner beans are prototypes. That's because they aren't
thread-safe, and a new instance is needed for each call to the factory. This illustrates
that we can rely on all the features of the Spring container without them having any
effect on the interface of our OSGi service.

To conclude, the implementation provider pattern prevents implementations
from leaking from a bundle. Clients can't create objects directly; they must use a factory implemented as an OSGi service. All the clients need to see are the interfaces of

> ### Anything else to hide behind the service?
> An implementation provider can encapsulate more than different implementations (as in our example here). Issues like dynamic class loading can be hidden behind the implementation provider, which relieves the client bundle from complex or even unpredictable configuration. The onus is purely on the provider, yielding a clear separation of concerns.

the bundle. Spring DM helps us publish the factory and lets the owning bundle leverage the power of the Spring container to wire its inner components.

9.6.2 *Chained classloader pattern for proxy-based AOP*

Proxy-based AOP implies the manipulation of bytecode, and OSGi doesn't make such manipulations particularly easy. The class of a proxy is generated dynamically and defined in a specific classloader, which must have privileged visibility, because it has to see all the classes and interfaces that are blended in the proxy class. Usually, these classes and interfaces have nothing in common; that's the whole point of AOP—separation of concerns, with the target object not knowing anything about its decorator. The creation of the proxy class is where all the parties meet, and OSGi doesn't like classloader gatherings!

Let's first see how proxy-based AOP works in a standard Java runtime. The following snippet uses the Spring AOP API to decorate a business service with a security aspect:

```
BusinessService targetService = new BusinessServiceImpl();
ProxyFactory proxyFactory = new ProxyFactory(
  targetService
);
proxyFactory.addInterface(BusinessService.class);
proxyFactory.addAdvice(new SecurityAspect());
BusinessService decoratedService = (BusinessService)
    proxyFactory.getProxy();
decoratedService.businessMethod();
```

Wraps target, adds aspect, and uses AOP proxy

The previous snippet works perfectly in a traditional Java application, because the default classloader used in the `ProxyFactory.getProxy` method (the thread context classloader) has full visibility and is able to use Spring API classes and the `BusinessService` interface to create the proxy class. But in OSGi, the visibility is restricted and the code of the previous snippet would fail. Solutions would typically consist of importing the appropriate packages or using dynamic imports. Unfortunately, both solutions are cumbersome, unmodular, and error-prone (in the case of dynamic imports).

Luckily there's another version of the `getProxy` method that accepts a `Class-Loader` as its parameter and uses it to generate the proxy class. By providing a classloader that has the correct visibility to the proxy factory (in bold in the following snippet), the creation of the proxy becomes possible:

```
ClassLoader customLoader = (...)
BusinessService decoratedService = (BusinessService)
➡    proxyFactory.getProxy(customLoader);
```

Unfortunately, this classloader doesn't exist. We need to build it so that it can see all the necessary classes (figure 9.5). This synthetic classloader is usually implemented by chaining the classloader of each entity.

Listing 9.4 illustrates the principle of a chained classloader.

Listing 9.4   Listing 9.4 Principle of a chained classloader

```
public class ChainedClassLoader extends ClassLoader {

  private Set<ClassLoader> loaders =
    new HashSet<ClassLoader>();

  public void addLoader(ClassLoader loader) {          Adds classloader
    loaders.add(loader);                                to the chain
  }

  @Override
  public Class<?> loadClass(String name)
      throws ClassNotFoundException {
    for (ClassLoader loader : loaders) {
      try {                                            Delegates loading
        return loader.loadClass(name);                  to each loader
      } catch (ClassNotFoundException cnfe) {

      }
    }
    throw new ClassNotFoundException(name);
  }
  (...)
}
```

Now that we have the chained classloader ready, we can modify our first snippet to make it work in OSGi:

```
BusinessService targetService = new BusinessServiceImpl();
ProxyFactory proxyFactory = new ProxyFactory(
  targetService
);
proxyFactory.addInterface(BusinessService.class);
proxyFactory.addAdvice(new SecurityAspect());
ChainedClassLoader loader = new ChainedClassLoader();     Chains classloaders
loader.addLoader(                                          with chained
  BusinessService.class.getClassLoader());                 classloader
loader.addLoader(SpringProxy.class.getClassLoader());
BusinessService decoratedService = (BusinessService)
➡    proxyFactory.getProxy(loader);
decoratedService.businessMethod();
```

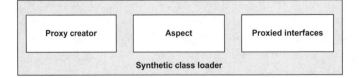

Figure 9.5   The synthetic classloader aggregates the class space of each entity for the creation of the proxy class.

The decorating now works, but the client module (the one that needs its business service decorated) has too many dependencies on the proxy creator API. We can easily encapsulate the decorating process in a dedicated module and provide it as an OSGi service. This makes the decorating code simpler for the client bundle:

```
OsgiProxyFactory proxyFactory = (...)

BusinessService service = (BusinessService) proxyFactory.
    createProxy(
  new BusinessServiceImpl(),
  new SecurityAspect(),
  BusinessService.class
);
```

Spring DM provides an implementation of the chained classloader pattern in the `org.springframework.osgi.context.internal.classloader` package of its core module. Like our `OsgiProxyFactory`, these utility classes aim to provide ready-to-use classloaders that hide the implementation details of the generation of proxy classes. We exposed only the basics here; you'll find that Spring DM's chained classloader is more sophisticated than ours.

We neglected one aspect in our chained classloader pattern: dynamics. What happens if the module that provides the aspect classes is stopped? Some dynamically created proxy classes rely on the aspects' definitions, and they should therefore be destroyed and recreated. Such a scenario would imply tracking and managing the created proxy classes, and this isn't part of Spring DM's feature set. Nevertheless, Spring-Source dm Server properly addresses this issue.

To conclude, the chained classloader is one way to merge the class space of entities that are unaware of each other in term of class visibility. It makes it possible to use proxy-based AOP in an OSGi environment, where visibility is restricted to only what bundles need to see.

Congratulations if you read this whole chapter in one go! You now have a strong foundation for customizing Spring DM's extenders, integrating the framework into managed and secured environments, and leveraging Spring DM to implement advanced OSGi patterns.

9.7 Summary

We saw in this chapter that Spring DM offers configuration hooks for both of its extenders. This configuration is based on the fragment configuration pattern: the extenders' bundles can be augmented with Spring configuration files that declare custom beans, which the extenders use in place of their default components. The scope of this configuration is global: the configuration applies to all the bundles that Spring DM manages. The extender configuration is also an entry point to the runtime environment: you can provide managed components to Spring DM and keep sensitive resources like threads under your control.

Spring DM can also run in a secured environment, where the OSGi container controls each bundle's permissions precisely. By providing the appropriate permissions to Spring DM's bundles, the framework can run properly without breaking the security rules of the OSGi environment.

Lastly, we saw that OSGi has its own design patterns. Knowing them can help you implement elegant design solutions without losing the benefits of modularity. It also allows you to avoid common pitfalls in OSGi environments, where the visibility of classes is restricted to what modules need to see. The implementation provider pattern is a way to keep a system modular, and Spring DM helps in the implementation of this factory-based pattern. The chained classloader pattern aims to merge the class space of modules that aren't aware of each other, allowing the use of proxy-based AOP in OSGi.

Testing with Spring DM

This chapter covers

- The concepts of testing, in both standard and OSGi environments
- When and how to use Spring DM's OSGi mocks for unit testing
- When and how to use Spring DM's support for OSGi integration testing

Testing is one of the most important activities in software development, not only because it ensures better quality in the end product, but also because good testing techniques can make a developer more productive. We introduced Spring DM's testing support early on in chapter 3 because manually testing the behavior of OSGi components in a target environment can be cumbersome, mainly because of tasks such as provisioning. You discovered then that Spring DM provides support for bootstrapping an embedded OSGi container and running JUnit test classes in it. This early coverage gave you the basics necessary to test your own OSGi bundles, and proved also that OSGi applications aren't particularly special in this regard: they can also be tested. In this chapter, we'll cover all the techniques and the tools that you'll need to test your OSGi components, and hence make your OSGi applications more reliable.

As software testing has its own vocabulary, this chapter starts by briefly describing the different kinds of tests (unit, integration, and system tests) and how they fit together. We'll then give some guidelines for testing Spring-based applications. This will give us enough of a basis to explain how OSGi applications (Spring-powered or otherwise) should be tested using Spring DM's testing support.

We'll then move on to cover unit tests and integration tests. Unit tests are for testing classes in an isolated manner. Most of the time, classes have dependencies on other classes or APIs (like the OSGi API), and these dependencies must be simulated by using mock objects (objects that mimic the behavior of real objects in a controlled way). That's where Spring DM can help, as it provides ready-to-use OSGi mocks. Automating integration tests for OSGi components is a difficult task, because it consists of testing how different OSGi components behave in an OSGi container. This implies bootstrapping and provisioning an OSGi container, and running the test instance *within* the OSGi container. Fortunately, Spring DM provides powerful and flexible testing support that takes care of all these steps. This testing support also leverages Spring and Spring DM features (like dependency injection and declarative interaction with the OSGi environment) and makes them available for use by the test classes. This is another incarnation of the bridge that Spring DM provides between the OSGi and the Spring worlds.

By the end of this chapter, you'll know everything you need to know about the practical testing of OSGi applications, and you'll have all the techniques necessary to test your OSGi components efficiently, thanks to the testing facilities that Spring DM provides. You'll also be able to take advantage of the hooks that Spring DM testing support provides for Spring-based OSGi applications.

Let's start with an overview of testing in software development.

10.1   Testing OSGi components with Spring DM

Testing OSGi applications isn't much different than testing standard applications, as long as you know the appropriate techniques and tools. So before diving into OSGi-specific testing practices, we'll remind you of the different kinds of tests we encounter in software development. We'll provide guidelines for unit-testing Spring-based applications, and this will give us enough of a basis to understand how to organize the testing of Spring DM applications.

10.1.1   General concepts

There are three different types of tests that are commonly encountered in software development:

- *Unit tests*—These verify and validate an individual programming unit (a class in an OOP language like Java). As a programming unit usually relies on other programming units, we usually resort to mocks and stubs to test it in isolation.
- *Integration tests*—These verify and validate that several programming units work as expected in collaboration.
- *System tests*—These verify a whole system by assembling all its components together (not covered in this book).

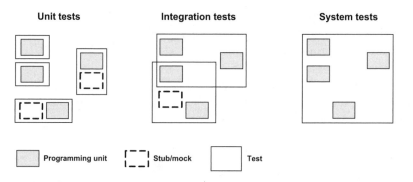

Figure 10.1 Unit tests, integration tests, and system tests are usually run sequentially, because testing programming units in collaboration is easier when they all behave as expected individually.

Testing programming units in collaboration is very difficult if they don't behave as expected individually. That's why it's vital to run unit tests before integration and system tests. Figure 10.1 shows how an application composed of four programming units can be tested. It reads from left to right to illustrate the order of testing.

We mentioned mocks and stubs, but we didn't really explain them. Mocks and stubs help with testing a programming unit in isolation by simulating the collaborators of the tested unit.

- *Stubs* are usually developed for one specific test and provide canned answers to the (limited) set of calls they're supposed to respond to. They can also record information about calls that the test uses for verification.
- *Mocks* are preprogrammed to answer to a sequence of calls and are usually able to tell if the sequence occurred correctly during the test.

Mock object libraries can be generic (like JMock or EasyMock), allowing you to create a mock object from any interface or class and dictate its behavior. They can also be specific to a particular technology, such as OSGi (like the mock object library provided by Spring DM), networking, database, and so on. Generic mock object libraries are very useful for mocking application classes (DAO, business services, and the like) but they can become cumbersome to use for mocking the same set of classes (like those specific to a technology) over and over. In contrast, specific mock libraries are more tailored.

Now that we know more about testing practices, let's look at some guidelines for testing Spring-based applications.

10.1.2 *Unit tests with Spring-based applications*

Thanks to its POJO programming model and its lightweight container, applications based on the Spring Framework are easy to unit test. Strict unit tests (which involve a class that doesn't use any dependencies) can be written with plain test frameworks like JUnit or TestNG. When testing a class that needs some dependencies (such as a Hibernate-based DAO, which needs a `SessionFactory` and so a `DataSource`), the Spring lightweight container is there to help assemble these different components together with an appropriate configuration (such as a test-dedicated Data-Source). By bootstrapping a Spring application context for testing the classes of a module, you can benefit from the wiring features of the lightweight container but also from features like transaction management, AOP, and so on. Figure 10.2 illustrates the organization of tests in a Spring-based module.

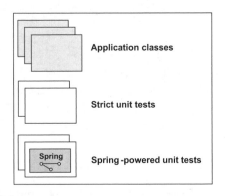

Figure 10.2   **In a Spring-based module, strict unit tests involve classes that don't use any dependencies. Tests can also embed a Spring application context when wiring or enterprise features are needed. Because Spring DM promotes a POJO programming model, these tests shouldn't imply the use of OSGi, even if the module is meant to be used in an OSGi environment.**

NOTE When a test implies complex operations, like bean wiring with Spring, transaction management, or AOP, we can already speak of integration tests. This terminology is a matter of point of view (the notion of a programming unit changes according to the view we adopt). From the module's point of view, we can call such tests integration tests, because we test the integration of inner components. From the whole system's point of view, such tests are internal to a module, whereas integration tests concern interactions between a set of modules.

What's the best way to write tests that leverage the Spring Framework? You could do it by hand—by bootstrapping a Spring application context at the beginning of the test—but you'd end up writing the same sequence of code for all your tests. The Spring Framework integrates well with test frameworks like JUnit and TestNG, thanks to the Spring `TestContext` Framework, which offers features like these:

- Automatic bootstrapping of a Spring application context for a test
- Caching of contexts if they're reused by several tests (to speed up test execution)
- Dependency injection of Spring beans in the test instance
- The possibility to react to the lifecycle of the test (to inject test data into a database before test execution, for example)

Coverage of the Spring `TestContext` Framework is out of the scope of this book, but let's take a quick peek at how it's used with the following code snippet (from the code samples for this chapter):

```
package com.manning.sdmia.directory.dao.jdbc;

import junit.framework.Assert;

import org.junit.Test;
```

```
import org.junit.runner.RunWith;
import org.springframework.beans.factory.annotation.Autowired;
import org.springframework.test.context.ContextConfiguration;
import org.springframework.test.context.junit4.SpringJUnit4ClassRunner;

import com.manning.sdmia.directory.dao.ContactDao;
import com.manning.sdmia.directory.domain.Contact;

@RunWith(SpringJUnit4ClassRunner.class)              Uses TestContext
@ContextConfiguration                                framework to
public class ContactDaoJdbcTest {                    manage Spring
                                                     application context
  @Autowired                                  Injects
  private ContactDao contactDao;              bean

  @Test public void getContacts() {
    (...)                                     Tests contact
  }                                           DAO

}
```

Remember that such tests should be written *before* testing the classes in an OSGi container: the core features of a module should be thoroughly tested in the module itself. Having fragile modules can make integration tests more difficult to write and makes diagnosing errors much harder.

Now that you have guidelines about testing the core features of modules, it's time to see how to test them in their target environment—OSGi, in our case. This is the goal of the next section, which covers how software testing applies to OSGi.

10.1.3 Testing OSGi components

Testing an OSGi component involves testing how it behaves when it interacts with the OSGi environment. It can either interact directly with the OSGi API or interact with the OSGi platform (by exporting or consuming services).

OSGi is all about modularity, and hopefully only carefully chosen parts of a component will interact with the OSGi environment. This means that most of the component's parts will be tested the usual way, with plain old unit and integration tests, by using the same techniques and tools we saw in the previous section. This is especially true when using Spring DM, as it enforces a POJO programming model where the framework handles most (if not all) of the interactions with the OSGi platform.

Application classes, like business services or DAOs, should be thoroughly tested as in a normal, non-OSGi environment. Then their basic operations (some of them, but not necessarily all) should be tested in an OSGi environment, to check that they behave as expected when used in their target environment and when they interact with other OSGi components. Automating these tests is challenging as it requires running the tests in an embedded OSGi platform. That's where Spring DM can help, because it provides this support, along with other testing facilities.

We'll introduce these testing tools in the next subsection. As testing OSGi applications can be quite different from testing standard applications in terms of project structuring, we'll also cover how to organize the layout of OSGi projects.

HOW SPRING DM CAN HELP TEST OSGI COMPONENTS

Tests for OSGi components can be roughly divided into two categories:

- *Unit tests*—When a part of the component relies on the OSGi API (BundleContext, ServiceTracker, and so on)
- *Integration tests*—When the component interacts with the OSGi environment (imports or exports packages, registers or consumes services, and so on)

For example, if an OSGi bundle has a BundleActivator that handles critical operations, writing a unit test for it is essential. Such a test can be written by using OSGi mocks: specific mock objects that implement the OSGi API and whose behavior can be modified programmatically. For testing a BundleActivator, we'd need at least a mock BundleContext. By using such a construct, the unit test doesn't need to be run on an OSGi platform—a plain old test framework is enough. Spring DM provides a set of OSGi mocks, which we'll study in section 10.2.

Integration tests imply interactions with the OSGi environment that can't be easily mocked. In OSGi integration tests we want to check several things, such as that a bundle can be started, which means that the platform resolved all the Java packages it imports or that a bundle published a service with the correct metadata (which can be part of its contract). These two tests can't be done with mock objects; they require a running OSGi platform. This means adapting test frameworks like JUnit to be able to bootstrap an OSGi platform, provision it, and run the test as if it were executing in OSGi. In doing this, OSGi integration tests can benefit from the array of tooling available for test frameworks (IDE and build tool launchers, XML/HTML reports, and so on) and thus don't need any special treatment. Spring DM provides such support, which turns the test into an OSGi bundle on the fly and runs its methods in an embedded OSGi platform. We cover this support in section 10.3.

Now that the purpose of OSGi tests is clearer, let's look at how to organize application projects to make their testing easier and more efficient.

HOW TO ORGANIZE OSGI TESTS

Depending on the nature of the test, test classes can be located in various places, and this has ramifications for the project's structure. We'll see how to organize standard non-OSGi tests, OSGi tests that use OSGi mocks, and OSGi integration tests.

Standard non-OSGi test classes (either unit or integration) usually reside in the same project as the classes they test. Let's take a data access bundle as an example: the tests consist of checking that all the DAOs do their data access job correctly (such as complex SQL queries). The test classes are located in a dedicated directory, separated from the actual application classes. The project also has all the necessary dependencies in its classpath (application classes like the domain layer, and technical libraries like Spring and Hibernate). There's no technical constraint that prevents the tests from being in the same project, which is convenient.

OSGi tests that use OSGi mocks can also be located in the same project as the classes they test (for example, an OSGi test that tests a bundle activator or any application class that relies on the OSGi API). As the scope of these tests is quite limited (there's no need for a full-blown OSGi platform running), the class tests are based on standard test tooling; the only difference is that they use OSGi mocks.

OSGi integration tests usually lie in a different project than the OSGi bundles they test. As these tests provision an OSGi platform with the bundles they test, the bundles being tested must be properly packaged before the tests can be run. The common sequence for OSGi integration tests is to build the to-be-tested bundles (compilation, "standard" tests, and packaging) and then run all the OSGi integration tests using a dedicated test project. Figure 10.3 illustrates the structure of an OSGi application and how to organize the tests.

With the support that Spring DM provides, OSGi integration tests end up being normal tests in that they can be run with common tools like Eclipse or Maven 2. The common way to organize the structure of an OSGi project is to use a Maven 2 module-based project: each bundle is a Maven 2 module, and Maven takes care of building the project in the right order. Once all the application bundles have been packaged and installed in the Maven 2 local repository, Maven 2 builds the last module, which is the integration test project. Note that the default behavior of Spring DM testing support is to provision the embedded OSGi platform from the Maven 2 local repository.

You now have a better understanding of software tests in an OSGi environment; it's time to apply this knowledge! The next two sections cover the techniques and tools that Spring DM provides for creating and running units tests with OSGi mocks (section 10.2) and OSGi integration tests (section 10.3).

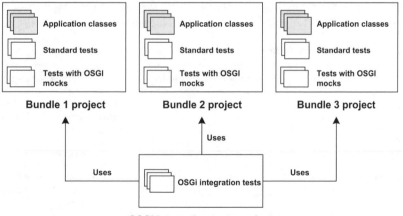

Figure 10.3   Standard tests and tests that use OSGi mocks are in the same project as the classes they test.; OSGi integration tests are in a separate project.

10.2   *Strict unit tests for OSGi components*

Even though Spring DM promotes a POJO-based programming model and handles most of the interaction with the OSGi environment, some parts of an OSGi bundle may still have to work with the OSGi API. These parts can be bundle activators or Spring beans that leverage the OSGi bridges that Spring DM offers (like the `BundleContext-Aware` interface introduced in chapter 4). Integration tests can be sufficient for testing these interactions as long as these OSGi-related tasks remain simple, but unit tests generally prove to be necessary when the interactions become more complex. This section introduces Spring DM's OSGi mock classes and provides some examples to illustrate their use.

10.2.1   *Spring DM's OSGi mocks*

Spring DM comes with a set of OSGi mocks that make OSGi unit testing easier. Generic mock libraries (like EasyMock or JMock) are another possible solution, but using them for mocking an API as complex as the OSGi Framework is very cumbersome. Spring DM itself is tested using a combination of its own OSGi mocks and mocks generated by EasyMock.

> **NOTE**   Spring DM's OSGi mocks are located in the `mock` module of the project.

The OSGi mocks that Spring DM provides are not meant to be a full-featured OSGi mock library, but rather internal tools that the Spring DM Framework makes available to others. Nevertheless, they make a good basis for OSGi unit tests—what's good for the goose is good for the gander.

Table 10.1 lists Spring DM's OSGi mocks, which all belong to the `org.spring-framework.osgi.mock` package. Table 10.1 also shows the corresponding emulated OSGi interfaces, which belong to the `org.osgi.framework` package.

Table 10.1   Spring DM's OSGi mocks

Spring DM class	Emulated OSGi interface	Description
`MockBundle`	`Bundle`	Maintains bundle metadata and delegates loading operations to its own classloader
`MockBundleActivator`	`BundleActivator`	Empty implementation
`MockBundleContext`	`BundleContext`	Maintains a bundle object, a list of service listeners, and a list of bundle listeners
`MockFilter`	`Filter`	Empty implementation
`MockServiceReference`	`ServiceReference`	Maintains service properties and handles OSGi properties like service ID, object class, and service ranking
`MockServiceRegistration`	`ServiceRegistration`	Maintains service properties

Spring DM's OSGi mocks maintain minimal features, but most of their methods are empty implementations. Users are encouraged to subclass the mock classes in their tests (as with anonymous classes) and override only the methods they need.

> ### Is there a full-featured OSGi mock library?
>
> Although generic mock libraries proliferate in the Java world, there's no de facto standard for mocking the OSGi Framework. The SpringSource dm Server team developed the OSGi test stubs library, which is still in its infancy at the time of this writing. Nevertheless, it looks promising and is already used in the dm Server test suite. A SpringSource Team Blog entry (http://blog.springsource.com/2009/06/23/osgi-test-stubs/) introduces the OSGi test stubs library.

Let's see how to use some of Spring DM's OSGi mocks.

10.2.2 *Spring DM's OSGi mocks in action*

Suppose you want to test a simple `BundleActivator`, like the one defined in listing 10.1.

Listing 10.1 A bundle activator to be unit tested

```
package com.manning.sdmia.ch10.internal;

import org.osgi.framework.BundleActivator;
import org.osgi.framework.BundleContext;
import org.osgi.framework.ServiceRegistration;
import com.manning.sdmia.ch10.dao.ContactDao;
import com.manning.sdmia.ch10.dao.jdbc.ContactDaoJdbc;

public class DirectoryDaoBundleActivatorSimple implements BundleActivator {

  private ServiceRegistration serviceRegistrationDao;

  @Override
  public void start(BundleContext bundleContext) throws Exception {
    serviceRegistrationDao = bundleContext.
                          registerService(                    Registers
      ContactDao.class.getName(),                             DAO as OSGi
      new ContactDaoJdbc(),                                   service
      null
    );
  }

  public void stop(BundleContext bundleContext) throws Exception {
    serviceRegistrationDao.unregister();                    Unregisters
  }                                                          service
}
```

The bundle activator's contract consists of registering a service and also taking care of the unregistration.

> **NOTE** The interactions with the OSGi service registry in the current section are purposefully simple so as to illustrate the use of Spring DM's OSGi mocks. You should always try to use Spring DM's declarative features for such tasks, because they're more reliable and flexible.

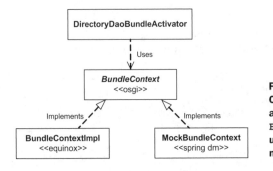

Figure 10.4   Depending on the environment (an OSGi platform like Equinox, or test), the bundle activator uses a different implementation of BundleContext. When running a unit test, we use the MockBundleContext, which doesn't need any runtime environment.

Figure 10.4 illustrates which implementation of bundle context the bundle activator will use when running on an OSGi platform (such as Equinox) and when running in a test. This is made possible by the use of the BundleContext interface.

Listing 10.2 illustrates how to test the bundle activator using Spring DM's mocks.

Listing 10.2   Unit testing the bundle activator with OSGi mocks

```java
package com.manning.sdmia.ch10.internal;

import java.util.Dictionary;
import org.junit.Assert;
import org.junit.Before;
import org.junit.Test;
import org.osgi.framework.BundleActivator;
import org.osgi.framework.BundleContext;
import org.osgi.framework.ServiceRegistration;
import org.springframework.osgi.mock.MockBundleContext;
import org.springframework.osgi.mock.MockServiceRegistration;
import com.manning.sdmia.ch10.dao.ContactDao;

public class DirectoryDaoBundleActivatorSimpleTest {

    int daoRegistered;

    @Before public void setUp() {                    ❶ Initializes
        daoRegistered = 0;                             test instance
    }
                                                              ❷ Declares
    @Test public void startAndStop() throws Exception {         test method
        MockBundleContext bundleContext =
            new MockBundleContext() {                  ❸ Declares mock
                                                          bundle context inline
            @Override
            public ServiceRegistration registerService(String clazz,
                    Object service, Dictionary properties) {
                if(service instanceof ContactDao) {
                    daoRegistered++;
                    return new MockServiceRegistration() {
                        @Override
                        public void unregister() {        ❹ Tracks
                            daoRegistered--;                 registrations and
                        };                                   unregistrations
                    };
                };
```

```
        } else {
          return super.registerService(clazz, service, properties);
        }
      }
    };

    BundleActivator bundleActivator =
      new DirectoryDaoBundleActivatorSimple();
    bundleActivator.start(bundleContext);
    Assert.assertEquals(1,daoRegistered);
    bundleActivator.stop(bundleContext);
    Assert.assertEquals(0,daoRegistered);
  }

}
```

⑤ Tests start and stop scenario

The unit test consists of checking that the daoRegistered variable (reinitialized before each test method at **❶** is correctly incremented and decremented. The test method **❷** tests both the start and stop methods of the activator. Because each needs the bundle context as a parameter, we declare a BundleContext variable and use Spring DM's Mock-BundleContext class for the implementation **❸**. We use an anonymous class to override the registerService method and increment the daoRegistered variable only if the OSGi service is a ContactDao. To track the unregistration of the service, we use a Mock-ServiceRegistration instance whose unregister method is also overridden to decrement the counter **❹**. At **❺**, we execute the start and stop methods of the bundle activator and check that the counter is properly updated.

We can push our bundle activator a little further and make it register the OSGi service only if a DataSource is available in the service registry. Listing 10.3 illustrates this slight modification.

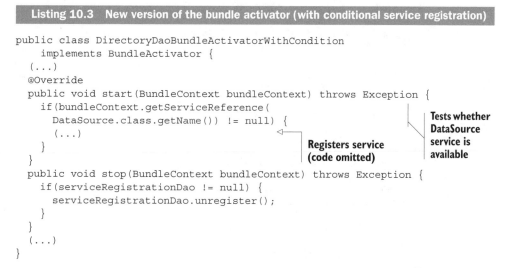

Listing 10.3 New version of the bundle activator (with conditional service registration)

```
public class DirectoryDaoBundleActivatorWithCondition
    implements BundleActivator {
  (...)
  @Override
  public void start(BundleContext bundleContext) throws Exception {
    if(bundleContext.getServiceReference(
      DataSource.class.getName()) != null) {            Tests whether
      (...)                                             DataSource
    }                          Registers service        service is
  }                           (code omitted)            available
  public void stop(BundleContext bundleContext) throws Exception {
    if(serviceRegistrationDao != null) {
      serviceRegistrationDao.unregister();
    }
  }
}
  (...)
}
```

Unit testing the new version of the bundle activator implies testing two paths (for whether or not the DataSource service is available), which means two test cases. It also implies overriding the getServiceReference method of the MockBundleContext and making it return either a dummy ServiceReference or nothing. Listing 10.4 illustrates this new test.

Listing 10.4   Unit testing the conditional service registration

```
public class DirectoryDaoBundleActivatorWithConditionTest {
  (...)
  @Test public void startAndStopWithDataSource()           Tests "DataSource
      throws Exception {                                    available" path
    BundleContext bundleContext = new MockBundleContext() {
      @Override
      public ServiceReference getServiceReference(String clazz) {
        return new MockServiceReference();                   Simulates
      }                                                      DataSource
      @Override                                              availability
      public ServiceRegistration registerService(String clazz,
          Object service, Dictionary properties) {
        // same implementation as before
      }
    };

    BundleActivator bundleActivator =
        new DirectoryDaoBundleActivatorWithCondition();
    bundleActivator.start(bundleContext);
    Assert.assertEquals(1,daoRegistered);
    bundleActivator.stop(bundleContext);
    Assert.assertEquals(0,daoRegistered);
  }

  @Test public void startAndStopNoDataSource()             Tests "DataSource
      throws Exception {                                    unavailable" path
    MockBundleContext bundleContext = new MockBundleContext() {
      @Override
      public ServiceReference getServiceReference(String clazz) {
        return null;                                         Simulates
      }                                                      DataSource
      @Override                                              unavailability
      public ServiceRegistration registerService(String clazz,
          Object service, Dictionary properties) {
        // same implementation as before
      }
    };

    BundleActivator bundleActivator =
        new DirectoryDaoBundleActivatorWithCondition();
    bundleActivator.start(bundleContext);
    Assert.assertEquals(0,daoRegistered);
    bundleActivator.stop(bundleContext);
    Assert.assertEquals(0,daoRegistered);
  }
}
```

This ends our tour of the OSGi mocks available in Spring DM. These mock objects should fulfill your needs when the interactions between your classes and the OSGi environment need comprehensive unit testing rather than more coarse-grained integration tests.

Speaking of integration tests, the next section covers Spring DM's integration test support for OSGi applications.

10.3 Integration tests for OSGi applications

When testing one or more OSGi bundles in their target environment (an implementation of an OSGi container), there are *a lot* of things that can go wrong, so checking them in an efficient way can save a lot of time, money, and sweat. The main challenge with OSGi integration tests is to keep close enough to developers' usual testing habits (such as using test frameworks like JUnit) while executing the test itself within a properly configured and provisioned OSGi container. Fortunately Spring DM takes up this challenge and provides a testing framework that smoothly fills the gap between OSGi and JUnit.

Section 10.3.1 covers the basics of Spring DM's integration test support through an example based on the data access layer of an enterprise application. We'll see in this section how to check common OSGi features, like the correct package exports for tested bundles and the consumption of registered OSGi services.

Section 10.3.2 then dives into more advanced features, like customizing the creation of the test bundle and changing the target OSGi platform.

10.3.1 Developing integration tests with Spring DM support

As shown previously in figure 10.3, OSGi integration tests should be located in a dedicated project. Creating this project is the first step when you start writing integration tests. In a typical Maven 2 modular project, the integration tests project is one of the submodules and should be built *after* the other submodules, so that the Maven 2 local repository is correctly filled with the modules' binaries (we'll see later in this section why the Maven 2 local repository is important when using Spring DM test support).

Once your test project is created, you're ready to benefit from Spring DM's test support. We'll see in this section how to create a simple integration test that only displays the OSGi platform we're running and what it's provisioned with. This first test seems simplistic, but it will illustrate how Spring DM runs the methods of the test within an embedded OSGi platform that it starts on the fly. Through testing this sample application, we'll see how to provision the embedded OSGi platform to test the visibility of Java classes and how to test that OSGi services are properly registered and functional.

CREATING A SIMPLE INTEGRATION TEST

Spring DM's integration test support lies in the test module of the project, so you'll have to add the corresponding JAR to your project, along with the other Spring DM binaries. Using Spring DM's test support is then as simple as inheriting from a test base class, as shown in listing 10.5.

WARNING If you use Spring DM 2, you need to override the `getTesting-FrameworkBundlesConfiguration` method of the test base class, as explained in section 3.4.4. This is because Spring DM depends on a release of the Spring Framework that isn't available in Maven 2 repositories anymore. The listings of this chapter don't override this method for brevity's sake, but the examples in the book's source code do.

Listing 10.5 A simple OSGi integration based on Spring DM's test support

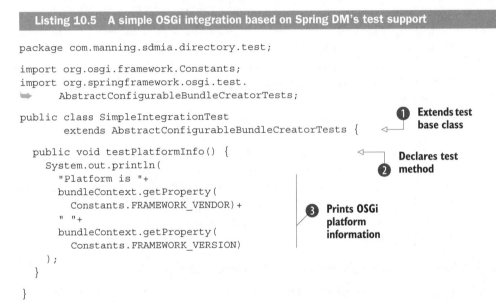

```
package com.manning.sdmia.directory.test;

import org.osgi.framework.Constants;
import org.springframework.osgi.test.
    AbstractConfigurableBundleCreatorTests;

public class SimpleIntegrationTest
        extends AbstractConfigurableBundleCreatorTests {          ❶ Extends test
                                                                     base class
    public void testPlatformInfo() {                              ❷ Declares test
        System.out.println(                                         method
          "Platform is "+
          bundleContext.getProperty(
            Constants.FRAMEWORK_VENDOR)+          ❸ Prints OSGi
          " "+                                      platform
          bundleContext.getProperty(                information
            Constants.FRAMEWORK_VERSION)
        );
    }

}
```

The `AbstractConfigurableBundleCreatorTests` class is the entry point for Spring DM's test support. All integration test classes must inherit from this class ❶. As for any test based on JUnit 3, every test method name must start with `test` if it is to be executed ❷. Our test method simply displays information about the running OSGi platform ❸. To do this, it uses the `bundleContext` property available in the `Abstract-ConfigurableBundleCreatorTests` class. We can use such a property because the test class is turned into an OSGi bundle on the fly by Spring DM test support.

Spring DM test framework and the Spring TestContext Framework

The Spring DM testing framework doesn't build on top of the Spring TestContext Framework (as of version 2.0.0.M1). It uses the JUnit 3.8 support from the Spring Framework, mainly because Spring DM prior to version 2.0 needed to support Java 1.4 (and the Spring TestContext Framework integrates with JUnit 4, which heavily uses Java 5 annotations). This ties you to JUnit 3.8 when using the Spring DM testing framework for OSGi integration test, but it doesn't prevent you from using the Spring TestContext Framework or any test framework for testing the core features of your modules.

If you run the test either in your IDE or on the command line with a tool like Maven 2, you should see something like the following on the console:

```
Platform is Eclipse 1.5.0
```

This tells us we are running under Eclipse Equinox, with the 1.5.0 version of the OSGi API (which means OSGi 4.2).

> **NOTE** Each OSGi integration test with Spring DM support must run in its own JVM. You can achieve this by using the "fork" option that tools like Maven 2 or Ant provide.

What happened exactly? What did Spring DM test framework do for us? Here are the steps the `AbstractConfigurableBundleCreatorTests` class accomplished:

- Started the OSGi platform
- Provisioned it with a minimal set of bundles
- Packaged the test into an on-the-fly bundle and installed it in the platform
- Executed the test methods inside the platform
- Shut down the platform

If you're curious and want to learn about the bundles that Spring DM provisioned the platform with, you can write a test method that lists the installed bundles:

```
public void testInstalledBundles() {
  for(Bundle bundle : bundleContext.getBundles()) {
    System.out.println(bundle.getSymbolicName());
  }
}
```

If you execute this method, you should see output like the following on the console:

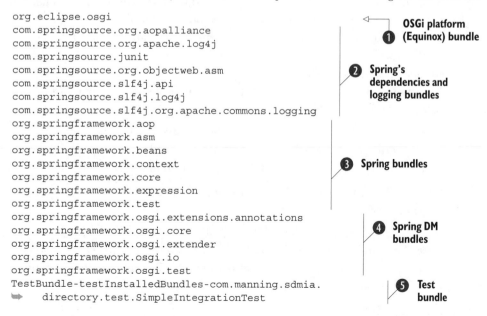

```
org.eclipse.osgi
com.springsource.org.aopalliance
com.springsource.org.apache.log4j
com.springsource.junit
com.springsource.org.objectweb.asm
com.springsource.slf4j.api
com.springsource.slf4j.log4j
com.springsource.slf4j.org.apache.commons.logging
org.springframework.aop
org.springframework.asm
org.springframework.beans
org.springframework.context
org.springframework.core
org.springframework.expression
org.springframework.test
org.springframework.osgi.extensions.annotations
org.springframework.osgi.core
org.springframework.osgi.extender
org.springframework.osgi.io
org.springframework.osgi.test
TestBundle-testInstalledBundles-com.manning.sdmia.
    directory.test.SimpleIntegrationTest
```

1 OSGi platform (Equinox) bundle

2 Spring's dependencies and logging bundles

3 Spring bundles

4 Spring DM bundles

5 Test bundle

The `AbstractConfigurableBundleCreatorTests` class provisioned the platform with several bundles we can divide into five categories: the system bundle (Equinox, at❶), Spring's dependencies and logging libraries ❷, Spring ❸, Spring DM ❹, and the test class itself ❺. Note that because Spring DM's extender is installed, any Spring-powered bundle should see its Spring application context bootstrapped.

But where do these bundles come from? By default, Spring DM provisions the embedded OSGi platform with bundles located in the Maven 2 local repository (see figure 10.5). This means that all the bundles listed in the previous console output must be available in the Maven 2 local repository (apart from the test bundle, which is created on the fly, and the system bundle, which must be on the classpath when running the test). This also means that, when provisioning Spring DM test instances from your Maven 2 local repository, the JARs you refer to must be OSGi-compliant bundles.

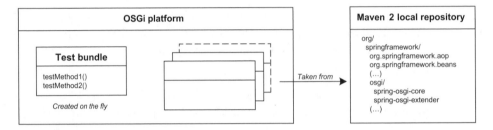

Figure 10.5   When running an integration test, Spring DM bootstraps an OSGi platform for the duration of the test. The test class is turned into an OSGi bundle on the fly and is used to provision the platform. By default, Spring DM provisions the platform with bundles taken from the Maven 2 local repository.

We've now seen the basics of Spring DM's test support. We're about to take advantage of the features provided by the class to test our OSGi bundles, Spring-powered or not, but before doing so, let's introduce the sample application that will be our guinea pig for the tests.

INTRODUCING THE SAMPLE APPLICATION

The sample application we'll use is part of a typical layered enterprise application. It consists of three bundles:

- *Directory domain*—Contains the domain classes (entities)
- *Directory DAO API*—Contains the DAO interfaces
- *Directory DAO JDBC*—A JDBC implementation of the DAO API

Figure 10.6 illustrates the relationships between the bundles and the interactions with the OSGi service registry.

The sample application gives us the opportunity to test the following:

- That the domain and DAO API bundles export their packages correctly
- That the DAO JDBC implementation bundle can see the domain and DAO classes and register the contact DAO

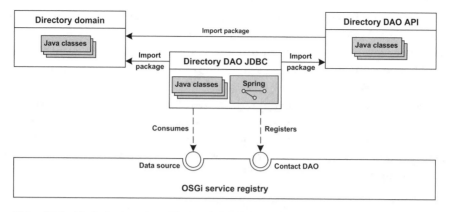

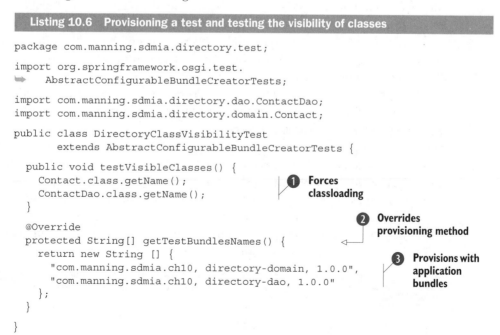

Figure 10.6 The to-be-tested application, composed of two API bundles and a Spring-powered implementation bundle that interacts with the OSGi service registry.

We'll start by testing the exporting of packages.

TESTING THE DOMAIN AND DAO API PACKAGES EXPORTATION

As shown in figure 10.6, our directory domain and directory DAO API bundles export packages that need to be visible to other bundles. An integration test can consist in provisioning an OSGi platform with both bundles and trying to import packages from them to ensure that these packages are correctly exported by our bundles. Note that such a test doesn't involve any Spring-powered bundles: Spring DM integration support works for any kind of bundle.

Listing 10.6 shows the integration test.

Listing 10.6 Provisioning a test and testing the visibility of classes

```
package com.manning.sdmia.directory.test;

import org.springframework.osgi.test.
    AbstractConfigurableBundleCreatorTests;

import com.manning.sdmia.directory.dao.ContactDao;
import com.manning.sdmia.directory.domain.Contact;

public class DirectoryClassVisibilityTest
      extends AbstractConfigurableBundleCreatorTests {

  public void testVisibleClasses() {
    Contact.class.getName();                    ❶ Forces
    ContactDao.class.getName();                      classloading
  }

  @Override                                              ❷ Overrides
  protected String[] getTestBundlesNames() {                 provisioning method
    return new String [] {
      "com.manning.sdmia.ch10, directory-domain, 1.0.0",   ❸ Provisions with
      "com.manning.sdmia.ch10, directory-dao, 1.0.0"           application
    };                                                        bundles
  }
}
```

The test method contains instructions that force the loading of a domain class and of a DAO interface ❶. Spring DM needs such explicit references to classes to detect needed Java imports and generate an appropriate manifest on the fly. The test class compiles, but what we want is to ensure that the loading of these classes works correctly in an OSGi platform. At ❷, we use one of `AbstractConfigurableBundleCreatorTests`'s hooks, the `getTestBundlesNames` method, to instruct Spring DM how to provision the OSGi platform. We need to return an array of `Strings`, each element corresponding to a bundle ❸. As stated before, Spring DM's test support heavily relies on Maven 2 concepts for provisioning, so bundles are located with their Maven 2 coordinates, using the following pattern:

```
[groupId], [artifactId], [version]
```

When running the test, you should get a green bar, because the OSGi platform is correctly provisioned and the test bundle can see the classes and interfaces it needs. You can comment out the provisioning part of the test and note that the test fails, as the domain class and the DAO interface are no longer available.

> **WARNING**   Always place your test classes in different packages than the ones you want to import. When Spring DM generates the manifest of the test bundle, it never imports packages that are in the test bundle. If the test class of our sample had been in the `com.manning.sdmia.directory.domain` package, Spring DM would not have imported it and the test would have failed.

What did we learn from this test? Spring DM scans the test class to detect dependencies and generate an appropriate manifest for the test bundle. Because the test methods are executed in the OSGi platform, these dependencies must be available. They're usually provided by bundles that the platform is provisioned with, so we need to override the `getTestBundlesNames` method to instruct Spring DM with bundles we want it to provision the platform with. We use a Maven-like method for this, by locating bundles with their coordinates.

We've just seen how to test a typical export/import package scenario. Let's see now how to test whether bundles correctly interact with the OSGi service registry.

TESTING THE DAO IMPLEMENTATION BUNDLE

There are several conditions to be fulfilled for our DAO implementation bundle to work correctly: some packages need to be exported (the domain package and the package of the DAO API), the bundle must import them correctly, and it must register a DAO as an OSGi service. Our integration tests will check that all these things work fine. (We wrote "integration tests", plural, because we'll explore different testing strategies. This will also give us the opportunity to explore features of Spring DM test support.)

Listing 10.7 shows the first version of our integration test.

Listing 10.7   Using a lookup on the OSGi registry to get the DAO

```
package com.manning.sdmia.directory.test.dao;

import junit.framework.Assert;

import org.osgi.framework.ServiceReference;
```

```
import org.springframework.osgi.test.
    AbstractConfigurableBundleCreatorTests;

import com.manning.sdmia.directory.dao.ContactDao;

public class ContactDaoLookupIntegrationTest
        extends AbstractConfigurableBundleCreatorTests {

  public void testGetContacts() throws Exception {
    ServiceReference ref =
        bundleContext.getServiceReference(
      ContactDao.class.getName()
    );
    Assert.assertNotNull(
      "a DAO should be registered",
      ref);
    ContactDao contactDao =
        (ContactDao) bundleContext.getService(
      ref
    );
    Assert.assertEquals(
      3,
      contactDao.getContacts().size());
  }

  @Override
  protected String[] getTestBundlesNames() {
    return new String [] {
      "com.manning.sdmia.ch10, " +
        "directory-domain, 1.0.0",
      "com.manning.sdmia.ch10, directory-dao, 1.0.0",
      "com.manning.sdmia.ch10, " +
        "directory-dao-jdbc, 1.0.0",
      "org.springframework, " +
        "org.springframework.jdbc, "+
        getSpringVersion(),
      "org.springframework, " +
        "org.springframework.transaction, "+
        getSpringVersion(),
      "com.h2database, h2, 1.1.118",
      "com.manning.sdmia.ch10, " +
        "ch10-datasource-tests, 1.0.0"
    };
  }
}
}
```

① Checks DAO OSGi service is present

② Tests DAO method

③ Adds application bundles

④ Adds Spring data access bundles

⑤ Adds database bundles

At **①**, we create a lookup to get the DAO from the OSGi service registry (we test that there's at least a service registered under the interface). The core of our test is rather simple **②**: we call a method to retrieve Contact objects and check the size of the list (this implies that we know how many Contact rows there are in the DataSource we're using—we'll see more about that later). Should we test more than that? If we suppose the DAO is correctly tested in its owning module, we don't need to do more in an integration test.

Then comes the provisioning. We start with the application bundles **③**: domain, DAO API, and JDBC-based DAO implementation. The latter uses the JdbcTemplate, so we also need to add some modules of the Spring Framework **④**. Note the use of the getSpringVersion method, which is convenient for provisioning the test OSGi container with the same version of the Spring Framework that Spring DM uses in the test support (there's also a `getSpringDMVersion` method). As the JDBC-based DAO implementation needs a `DataSource` service (as shown in figure 10.6), we need to provision the OSGi platform with a bundle that registers such a service. That's what we do at ❺, where we add a bundle meant for the test and another bundle for the corresponding database driver.

> **NOTE** The `DataSource` bundle is a Spring-powered bundle that bootstraps an in-memory database and registers the `DataSource` as an OSGi service—all of this with Spring and Spring DM. We don't show its full code here for the sake of brevity.

This is just fine: the OSGi platform is provisioned with everything we need to test that the DAO implementation bundle works correctly. We just have to run the test and wait for the green bar. But we want more! Spring DM promotes a POJO programming model, and the lookup on the service registry denies this. Wouldn't it be nice to have the DAO directly available (injected!) in the test? This is possible, because Spring DM allows tying an OSGi Spring application context to the test and injecting beans in it. Listing 10.8 shows what could be the configuration of this application context: it looks up the DAO on the OSGi registry with the `osgi:reference` XML element.

Listing 10.8   Spring application context for the test

```xml
<?xml version="1.0" encoding="UTF-8"?>
<beans (...)>

  <osgi:reference
    id="contactDao"
    interface="com.manning.sdmia.directory.dao.ContactDao" />

</beans>
```

The application context configuration leverages Spring DM's `osgi` namespace to look up the DAO and create a `contactDao` bean. This bean will be injected in the test instance at runtime, just by adding the corresponding property. This configuration may look like overkill for a single OSGi service, but it can save you a lot of tedious code when you have more services.

Listing 10.9 shows a new version of the test that benefits from the injection.

Listing 10.9   Injecting the DAO into the test via its Spring application context

```java
public class ContactDaoInjectionIntegrationTest
      extends AbstractConfigurableBundleCreatorTests {

  private ContactDao contactDao;

  public void setContactDao(ContactDao contactDao) {
    this.contactDao = contactDao;
  }

  public void testGetContacts() throws Exception {
    Assert.assertEquals(1,contactDao.getContacts().size());
```

❶ Tests DAO method

```
    }

    @Override
    protected String[] getTestBundlesNames() {
      (...)
    }

    @Override
    protected String[] getConfigLocations() {
      return new String[] {
        "/com/manning/sdmia/directory/test/dao/
➡      ContactDaoServiceDataSourceIntegrationTest
➡      -context.xml"
      };
    }
}
```

❷ **Declares Spring file for test**

The test now declares a `contactDao` property and the corresponding setter. Spring DM uses the latter to automatically inject the `contactDao` bean. This injection is made possible by the matching between the bean name in the application context and the name of the property in the test (the corresponding setter is mandatory). The test method is then simpler ❶, as it doesn't need the lookup anymore. We need to override the `getConfigLocations` method ❷ to tell Spring DM where to find the Spring configuration files.

We just saw how to look up an OSGi service via Spring DM and inject it in the test instance. This is made possible by the Spring application context that Spring DM ties to the test instance. The scenario we chose is a little complex, because it involves an OSGi lookup and then dependency injection in the test, but the application context of a test instance can be used for any operation. You could, for instance, retrieve the `DataSource` service and inject it in a bean that inserts data into the database. That's exactly what's done in the application context of the final version of our test:

```
<osgi:reference id="dataSource"
                interface="javax.sql.DataSource" />

<bean class="com.manning.sdmia.directory.test.dao.DatabaseInitializer">
  <constructor-arg ref="dataSource" />
</bean>
```

The `DatabaseInitializer` uses a `JdbcTemplate` to initialize the `DataSource`: this means that the package of the `JdbcTemplate` needs to be imported by the test bundle. This is the case for any package involved in the creation of the application context of the test. Spring DM has no way to know about such imports, so we must explicitly inform it about them. In our case, this can be done by declaring a dummy `JdbcTemplate` property in the test class:

```
public class ContactDaoServiceDataSourceIntegrationTest
      extends AbstractConfigurableBundleCreatorTests {

  private JdbcTemplate jdbcTemplate;

  (...)
}
```

Why not embed the DataSource in the test application context?

The DAO implementation bundle needs a `DataSource` available in the service registry to work correctly. We developed a dedicated bundle that creates and registers such a `DataSource` for our integration test, but wouldn't it be simpler to do this directly in the test application context, to avoid developing a dedicated bundle?

Yes it would be, but there's a reason we did what we did. By default, `AbstractConfigurableBundleCreatorTests` waits for the application context of each Spring-powered bundle to be created before running. This means the creation of the test application context is triggered *after* the creation of the Spring-powered bundles. Why should we care? Because of dependencies. If the `DataSource` service is a mandatory dependency of the DAO implementation bundle, Spring DM won't complete the creation of the corresponding application context. As the `DataSource` service is provided by the test application, which will start only after the creation of all application contexts, we're in front of a deadlock: the test doesn't run, it hangs.

What should we do then? We can make the `DataSource` service an optional dependency of the DAO implementation bundle, but if the `DataSource` must remain mandatory, this isn't an option. Another solution is to change the test's default behavior (waiting for the creation of the context of Spring-powered bundles) by overriding the `shouldWaitForSpringBundlesContextCreation` method and make it return `false`. If you choose this path, remember that the test methods can be run *before* all the Spring-powered bundles have completed their initialization. Creating the dedicated `DataSource` bundle doesn't seem like such a bad idea after all!

You're now aware of the basics of Spring DM's test support. We've covered how to test classic scenarios like package export/import and interaction with the OSGi service registry. This introduction should be enough for most of your OSGi integration tests.

In the next section, we'll learn more about the hooks that the `AbstractConfigurableBundleCreatorTests` class offers for running tests under different OSGi platforms or customizing the creation of the bundle test manifest (among other scenarios).

10.3.2 *Advanced features of Spring DM test support*

The `AbstractConfigurableBundleCreatorTests` offers reasonable defaults for the on-the-fly generation of the test bundle, the provisioning mechanics, and the underlying OSGi platform. But sometimes these defaults aren't appropriate, so you'll be happy to learn that the `AbstractConfigurableBundleCreatorTests` class offers hooks to override them. We're about to look at some of these hooks, which will allow us to dive further into the mechanics of test-bundle generation. We'll then apply this knowledge to customizing the creation of the test manifest and to changing the OSGi platform the test is run under.

HOOKS OF THE ABSTRACTCONFIGURABLEBUNDLECREATORTESTS CLASS

Before running the test methods, Spring DM turns the test instance into an on-the-fly bundle before provisioning the OSGi platform with it. Spring DM makes decisions regarding the content of the test bundle and its manifest (such as for import and export entries) that you can customize by overriding methods in your test class. Table 10.2 lists these methods as well as methods that change the default behavior of test execution.

Table 10.2   Test methods to override to change the behavior of the test execution

Method	Default value	Description
getRootPath	file:./target/test-classes	The root path used for located resources.
getBundleContentPattern	**/*	Comma-separated patterns to identify resources included in the bundle.
getManifestLocation	null	Location of the manifest file to use.
getSettingsLocation	[TestName]-bundle.properties	Location of the setting properties to use.
shouldWaitForSpringBundlesContextCreation	true	Whether or not to wait for the context creation of Spring-powered bundles before running the test.
getBootDelegationPackages	javax.*, org.w3c.*, org.xml.*, sun.*, org.apache.xerces.jaxp.*	The list of packages whose loading is delegated to the boot classloader.
getPlatformName	Platforms.EQUINOX	The OSGi platform to use for the execution of the test.

We can order the methods of table 10.2 into different categories. We'll start by covering those meant to customize the content of the test bundle, but first we need to study the principles of this customization.

Why customize the content of the test bundle?

Spring DM has reasonable defaults when it generates the test bundle—unfortunately they can't always be appropriate. The default root path is adapted to a standard Maven 2 layout, and not every Spring DM project uses Maven 2. By default, all the content of the root path is included in the test bundle, and narrowing the included files by using appropriate patterns can speed up bundle generation, which matters when the number of integration tests grows. Very specific integration tests may also need a very specific bundle manifest that Spring DM can't automatically generate.

Spring DM offers two ways to configure the content of the test bundle:

- Programmatically, by overriding methods from AbstractConfigurableBundleCreatorTests
- Declaratively, by using a properties file

Table 10.3 lists the customizable content of the test bundle and the corresponding elements (method or property keys) for both configuration approaches.

Table 10.3   Customizable items of the test bundle content

Item	Property	Method	Default value
Root path for located resources	`root.dir`	`getRootPath`	`file:./target/test-classes`
Comma-separated patterns to identify resources included in the bundle	`include.patterns`	`getBundleContentPattern`	`**/*`
Location of the manifest file to use	`Manifest`	`getManifestLocation`	`null`

Listing 10.10 shows how to customize the test bundle content *programmatically*.

Listing 10.10   Programmatically customizing the test bundle content

```
public class ProgrammaticContentTest
        extends AbstractConfigurableBundleCreatorTests {

  @Override
  protected String getRootPath() {                    Customizes bundle
    return "file:./bin/test";                         root directory
  }

  @Override
  protected String[] getBundleContentPattern() {      Customizes
    return new String [] {                            resources
      "/**/*.class",                                  included in
      "/**/*.xml"                                     bundle
    };
  }

  @Override
  protected String getManifestLocation() {            Indicates specific
    return "file:./src/test/resources/com/manning/    manifest location
      sdmia/directory/test/content/manifest.mf";
  }

  (...)

}
```

Note in listing 10.10 that the `getManifestLocation` method returns the manifest location using the Spring resource syntax. Let's move on now to the declarative customization.

By default, Spring DM's test infrastructure looks for a property file that has a similar name to the test case: for the test `com.manning.sdmia.MyTest`, the properties file must be named `com/manning/sdmia/MyTest-bundle.properties` and it must be located in the classpath of the test (the standard test, not the on-the-fly test bundle).

The following snippet shows a properties file that performs the equivalent of listing 10.10:

```
root.dir=file:./bin/test
include.patterns=/**/*.class,/**/*.xml
manifest=file:./src/test/resources/com/manning/
➥      sdmia/directory/test/content/manifest.mf
```

If the default name and location of the properties file doesn't suit you, you can override the `getSettingsLocation` method to give it a new location:

```
public class DeclarativeSettingLocationContentTest
      extends AbstractConfigurableBundleCreatorTests {

  @Override
  protected String getSettingsLocation() {
    return "/my/path/to/DeclarativeTest.properties";
  }

}
```

We've now covered the ways Spring DM offers to customize the content of the test bundle it generates. The manifest is one element of this configuration; let's see how we can create it instead of relying on its automatic generation.

CUSTOMIZING THE GENERATED MANIFEST

By analyzing the test class, Spring DM is able to generate an appropriate manifest for the on-the-fly bundle. This is particularly convenient when the test depends on classes that are exported by other bundles; Spring DM automatically adds the correct `Import-Package` entries. But sometimes the automatic manifest generation isn't enough, and we need to explicitly provide the manifest of the test bundle.

> **WARNING**   As the writing of OSGi manifests is a cumbersome and error-prone process, you should only write them yourself when you face a dead-end with Spring DM's automatic generation.

We saw previously how to indicate the location of a specific manifest file (either programmatically or declaratively), so let's see now what it should contain. Listing 10.11 illustrates this.

Listing 10.11   Customizing the test manifest

```
Manifest-Version: 1.0
Bundle-ManifestVersion: 2
Bundle-Name: com.manning.sdmia.directory.test.content
 .ProgrammaticContentTest
Bundle-SymbolicName: com.manning.sdmia.directory.test.content
 .ProgrammaticContentTest
Bundle-Description: on-the-fly test bundle
Bundle-Activator: org.springframework.osgi.test        ❶ Internal test
➥    .JUnitTestActivator                                  bundle activator
Import-Package: org.springframework.osgi.test,
 junit.framework,                                       ❷ Import necessary
 com.manning.sdmia.directory.domain                       packages
```

The manifest needs specific entries for the test to run correctly as an OSGi bundle in the Spring DM test framework. The first entry is the bundle activator ❶, and the second is the importation of packages related to the test infrastructure and the execution of the test methods ❷. The packages of the test infrastructure are mandatory for every Spring DM test. Packages that are used inside the test methods must also be specified. The manifest must also contain all the compulsory headers of an OSGi bundle, like `Bundle-SymbolicName`. The manifest must also meet the usual conditions of its folks (such as having no more than 72 characters on a line). With all these conditions, you can certainly understand that Spring DM's automatic manifest generation is worth using!

We thoroughly covered the customization of test bundles, so let's finish our tour of Spring DM's test support with the choice of the OSGi platform the tests run under.

CHOOSING THE OSGI PLATFORM

The Spring DM test framework supports three OSGi platforms: Equinox (the default), Felix, and Knopflerfish. This means that you can easily change the platform that tests are run under to check the portability of your applications.

Spring DM offers two ways to choose the OSGi platform:

- Programmatically, by overriding the `getPlatformName` method in the test class
- Declaratively, by specifying a system property

Listing 10.12 shows how to switch to Felix, using the programmatic approach.

Listing 10.12   Changing the platform programmatically in a test

```
package com.manning.sdmia.directory.test;

import org.osgi.framework.Bundle;
import org.osgi.framework.Constants;
import org.springframework.osgi.test.
    AbstractConfigurableBundleCreatorTests;
import org.springframework.osgi.test.platform.Platforms;

public class SimpleIntegrationTest
        extends AbstractConfigurableBundleCreatorTests {

  public void testPlatformInfo() {
    System.out.println(
      "Platform is "+
      bundleContext.getProperty(
        Constants.FRAMEWORK_VENDOR)+
      " "+
      bundleContext.getProperty(
        Constants.FRAMEWORK_VERSION)
    );
  }

  @Override
  protected String getPlatformName() {
    return Platforms.FELIX;
  }

}
```

Displays info on platform

Switches to Felix

The getPlatformName method should return public properties of org.springframe-work.osgi.test.platform.Platforms: EQUINOX, FELIX, and KNOPFLERFISH. This programmatic approach is simple, but it ties the test to the platform. Let's look at the declarative approach, which doesn't interfere with test classes.

The declarative approach consists in specifying a system property, org.spring-framework.osgi.test.framework. The property must take as a value the name of the OsgiPlatform class you want to use. Spring DM provides an implementation for each platform it supports.

How you specify the system property depends on the way you launch your tests. The declarative approach is meant to be used with build tools: running the whole test suite on different platforms becomes just a matter of configuration. Each build tool has its own way to set system properties. Let's see how to do it with Maven 2.

Maven 2 uses the surefire plug-in to run tests, and system properties must be set in the configuration of this plug-in. This happens to be in the build section of the POM, as shown in listing 10.13.

Listing 10.13   Setting the OSGi platform for tests with Maven 2

```
<build>
  <plugins>
    <plugin>
      <groupId>org.apache.maven.plugins</groupId>
      <artifactId>maven-surefire-plugin</artifactId>
      <configuration>
        <systemProperties>
          <property>
            <name>
            org.springframework.osgi.test.framework
            </name>
            <value>
            org.springframework.osgi.test.platform.FelixPlatform
            </value>
          </property>
        </systemProperties>
      </configuration>
    </plugin>
  </plugins>
</build>
```

Uses Felix for tests

Note that the platform binaries need to be in the classpath of the project; otherwise Spring DM won't be able to create the embedded instance. When using Maven 2, profiles are a good way to switch from one platform to another: you declare a profile for each platform with the corresponding dependencies and the surefire plug-in configuration.

You now know how to change the platform in Spring DM tests. Table 10.4 summarizes the constants (for the getPlatformName method) and the OsgiPlatform implementation (for the system property) for each platform Spring DM supports.

This ends our tour of the advanced features of Spring DM's testing framework. We looked at the basics of this testing framework and how to test classic classloading and

Table 10.4 Settings for the OSGi platforms Spring DM test framework supports

Platform	Constants *	Implementation class *
Equinox	`Platforms.EQUINOX`	`EquinoxPlatform`
Felix	`Platforms.FELIX`	`FelixPlatform`
Knopflerfish	`Platforms.KNOPFLERFISH`	`KnopflerfishPlatform`

* From the `org.springframework.osgi.test.platform` package

service import scenarios in section 10.3.1, and in this section we covered the different hooks of the `AbstractConfigurableBundleCreatorTests` class, customizing the content of the on-the-fly bundle and of its manifest and changing the OSGi platform the tests are run under. Thanks to all the features the testing framework offers, writing integration tests for OSGi and Spring DM applications is the same as for any application.

10.4 Summary

Testing OSGi-based applications isn't much different than testing traditional applications. Thanks to the POJO programming model that Spring DM promotes, most parts of OSGi components can be tested with common testing techniques and tools, without knowing they're meant to be run in an OSGi container. So adopting OSGi won't require that you lose your testing habits (build tools, continuous integration, and so on).

Nevertheless, OSGi brings with it a set of features like package visibility and services that need to be tested within an OSGi container. That's why Spring DM provides powerful testing support, which makes OSGi integration tests easier to write and run. More importantly, they're very similar to regular Java tests, because Spring DM builds on top of JUnit. This support takes care of bootstrapping an OSGi container, provisioning it with bundles that the test class specifies, and running the test methods *in* the container. The test is then run in an environment that mimics as much as possible the target environment.

Spring DM's testing support not only makes available all of OSGi's features to test classes, it also adds some Spring goodies like dependency injection to the test. Spring DM still fulfills its role as a bridge between the Spring and OSGi worlds.

We're now done with Spring DM's testing support; the next chapter is dedicated to another part of OSGi for which Spring DM provides support: compendium services.

11

Support for OSGi compendium services

This chapter covers

- How to use the main OSGi compendium services with Spring DM
- Spring DM's support for OSGi compendium services
- The benefits of using compendium services with Spring DM

The chapters in this part of the book cover advanced aspects of Spring DM. In the two previous chapters, we dealt with advanced configuration and unit tests. In this chapter, we'll describe features corresponding to additional OSGi specifications. Besides the core OSGi specification, the OSGi alliance provides an additional specification describing standardized services called *compendium services.*

The range of these services is wide—the services can be specific to environments other than enterprise applications. But some of them can be useful in the context of Spring DM because they allow for the centralization of certain behaviors and provide a level of indirection between the components and tools of an OSGi system. They can enable configuration and events to be externalized from Spring

351

DM. The framework offers mechanisms that can transparently link configured beans with these services.

In this chapter, we'll explain what compendium services are and the benefits of using them with Spring DM. Only the Configuration Admin Service and Event Admin Service compendium services are of interest to us in this context; Spring DM provides support for using them optimally and in a nonintrusive way. The Configuration Admin Service allows us to externalize configuration properties in a centralized repository independent of Spring DM, and the Event Admin Service handles events without knowledge of Spring DM.

11.1   Overview of compendium services

Before describing Spring DM's support for compendium services, we need to describe at a high level what compendium services are and the benefits they offer. Then we'll be able to see how Spring DM takes advantage of these services.

11.1.1   What are compendium services?

As you saw in the first chapters of the book, the core of the OSGi technology is a standard that's described in the OSGi core specification. OSGi also comes with the compendium services specifications that build on the features provided by the core specification.

> **NOTE**   We'll exclude from this description the Blueprint Service (a specification that was spawned from Spring DM), because chapter 12 covers it in depth.

Each compendium service addresses a particular requirement and can be used on any conformant OSGi platform. Only the APIs and their corresponding behavior are described in the specification. The implementations aren't standardized and are left up to providers. Table 11.1 lists the main services in the specification.

Table 11.1   The main OSGi compendium services

OSGi service	Description
Log Service	Standardizes the handling of log messages within an OSGi framework. When using this service, every message should be sent to it. The service is then responsible for dispatching logs to bundles that are subscribed to it.
Configuration Admin Service	Provides a standardized and flexible approach to both receiving configuration information and configuring the framework.
Device Access Service	Provides a mechanism for matching a driver to a new device and, when this occurs, allowing the bundle implementing the driver to be automatically downloaded. The service can be typically used to implement plug-and-play features.
User Admin Service	Runs as a database containing user information that's usable as a foundation for security features (authentication and authorization).
Declarative Service	Allows for declarative management of service registration and unregistration based on configuration files without having to directly use the core OSGi API.

Table 11.1   The main OSGi compendium services (continued)

OSGi service	Description
IO Connector Service	Implements the Connected Device Configuration (CDC) / Connected Limited Device Configuration (CLDC) `javax.microedition.io` package as a service.
Preferences Service	Provides access to a hierarchical database of properties, similar to the Windows registry or the Java `Preferences` class.
Component Runtime	Simplifies handling dynamic aspects of services by providing an XML-based declaration of the dependencies.
Deployment Admin	Provides facilities to handle an additional format for deployment: the deployment package. This package can combine bundles with arbitrary resources into a single deliverable that can be installed and uninstalled.
Event Admin Service	Provides a standardized and centralized service to manage events triggered by entities used within the OSGi container. It's based on an event channel called topic, which makes it possible for entities to subscribe to, receive, and send events.
HTTP Service	Allows the use of an embedded web container through a standard service, which provides support for interacting with the container in order to register and unregister resources.
Application Admin	Provides a way to manage OSGi bundles through an application model, providing the ability to start and stop applications like in a typical desktop or mobile phone application.

Some of the services in table 11.1 target embedded systems, where others can be used for those systems as well as for classic Java applications. In the context of this book, the Configuration Admin Service and Event Admin Service are particularly relevant, because they can provide additional functionality when using Spring DM. Spring DM also provides integration for some of them that makes their use easier while implementing their features in a standardized way.

The HTTP service seems to be suitable for the web part of enterprise applications, but it unfortunately doesn't allow the use of bundles as web applications and it has other limitations that make it inconvenient to use. The upcoming RFC 66 specification addresses this and is to be preferred in the future.

Let's now look at the two compendium services Spring DM provides support for: the Configuration Admin and Event Admin Services.

11.1.2   Spring DM's support for compendium services

In this section, we'll look at the benefits of using the compendium services with Spring DM. We'll first describe the two compendium services Spring DM provides support for, then we'll see how to declare the dedicated XML namespace that Spring DM provides for interacting with them.

CONFIGURATION ADMIN SERVICE

The most interesting compendium service in our context is the Configuration Admin Service. This service provides centralized configuration properties in an OSGi

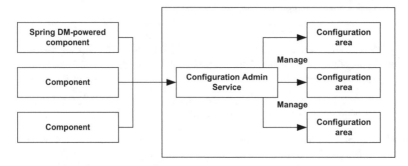

Figure 11.1   Interaction between components and the Configuration Admin Service in order to externalize configuration properties outside Spring DM

environment, which is particularly useful if you want to share these properties across different components from a central configuration repository. Figure 11.1 shows how this works.

Using the Configuration Admin Service within Spring DM consists of configuring the properties of beans. This strategy allows the configuration to be shared across components and beans that are parameterized from outside the owning components. Moreover, because the service is standardized, third-party configuration tools can be used to manage it. To some extent, the Configuration Admin Service is similar to the `PropertyPlaceholderConfigurer` Spring feature, which allows for properties to be externalized into property files.

Thanks to the `osgix` XML namespace (which will be described shortly), Spring DM can inject values retrieved from the Configuration Admin Service into beans' properties. The aim of Spring DM is to interact with the Configuration Admin Service in a nonintrusive way, without explicitly referencing it, thus enforcing the POJO programming model.

EVENT ADMIN SERVICE

Another interesting compendium service is the Event Admin Service, which provides a standardized way of exchanging events between components using a central dispatcher. The main advantage of this service is that consumers need not be aware of the event producers. Figure 11.2 shows how the Configuration Admin Service provides a central service for event management.

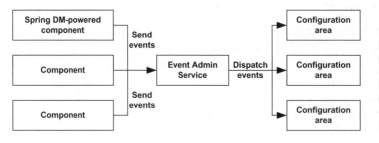

Figure 11.2 Interaction between components and the Event Admin Service in order to handle events—event consumers need no knowledge of Spring DM

The Event Admin Service is interesting because it can notify components of events triggered by Spring or Spring DM without being tied to the event management and the APIs of the two frameworks. Event listeners can be made independent of the tools that are sending events.

Although Spring DM doesn't currently provide support for the OSGi Event Admin Service, developing a bridge between this service and Spring DM's event management isn't too difficult. The only drawback is that you need to develop an asynchronous delivery mechanism if one is not supported by the tool triggering the initial event.

CONFIGURING THE OSGIX XML NAMESPACE

Spring DM's standard XML namespace mainly covers the interaction of Spring DM with the OSGi service registry, but it provides no support for compendium services. Spring DM introduces the `osgix` namespace for this purpose. This namespace enables us to interact directly with the Configuration Admin Service within a Spring XML configuration. The configuration of this namespace is done in the same way as the `osgi` namespace we introduced in chapter 3.

The `osgix` namespace identifier is `http://www.springframework.org/schema/osgi-compendium`, and the namespace is based on the `spring-osgi-compendium.xsd` schema. The namespace can be configured using all the usual facilities and mechanisms provided by XML, as shown in listing 11.1.

> **Listing 11.1   Configuring the XML namespace for compendium services**

```
<beans xmlns="http://www.springframework.org/schema/beans"
  xmlns:xsi="http://www.w3.org/2001/XMLSchema-instance"
  xmlns:osgix="http://www.springframework.org/schema/osgi-compendium"
  xsi:schemaLocation="
    http://www.springframework.org/schema/beans
    http://www.springframework.org/schema/beans/spring-beans.xsd
    http://www.springframework.org/schema/osgi-compendium
    http://www.springframework.org/schema/osgi-compendium/
    spring-osgi-compendium.xsd">
  (...)
</beans>
```

In this listing, the namespace is first linked to its identifier. The XML schema file is then associated with this identifier, allowing the XML parser to check the validity of the XML elements used in the namespace.

Now that we've seen how compendium services work with Spring DM and how to configure the corresponding XML namespace, let's delve into the details of using the Configuration Admin Service with Spring DM in order to externalize configuration properties.

11.2   *Spring DM's Configuration Admin Service support*

The main compendium service supported by Spring DM is the Configuration Admin Service because it provides support for centralizing configuration information. Spring DM allows XML elements of the `osgix` namespace to be used within a Spring configuration file, providing transparent integration between beans and configuration properties.

In this section, we'll first cover how to use the Configuration Admin Service to manage configuration properties. We'll then see how to link beans with configuration properties and implement managed services and managed service factories.

11.2.1 OSGi Configuration Admin Service

Before using Spring DM's `osgix` namespace to configure the Configuration Admin Service, we need to install the Configuration Admin Service bundle, reference the corresponding OSGi service, and update data within its configuration repository.

INSTALLING THE CONFIGURATION ADMIN SERVICE

As with every compendium service, you can distinguish between the components containing service interfaces and components providing implementations. The service's public API and implementation are commonly separated into different components. We'll use the implementation of the Configuration Admin Service provided by Equinox for this example.

The component containing the public API of a compendium service and its implementation in Equinox are both available in the SpringSource EBR as shown in table 11.2.

Table 11.2   Bundles related to the Configuration Admin Service from the SpringSource EBR

Group ID	Artifact ID	Version
`org.osgi`	`org.osgi.compendium`	4.1.0.build-200702212030
`org.eclipse.osgi`	`org.eclipse.equinox.cm`	1.0.0.v20080509-1800

Adding these two components to your OSGi container will install the Configuration Admin Service.

ACCESSING THE CONFIGURATION ADMIN SERVICE WITH SPRING DM

Now that the implementation bundle for the Configuration Admin Service is installed, you'll find that a service is present in the OSGi service registry under the name `org.osgi.service.cm.ConfigurationAdmin` corresponding to the service interface.

This service can be referenced using Spring DM like any other service—by using its `reference` XML element within a Spring XML configuration. It can then be injected into any bean, as shown in the following snippet:

```
<osgi:reference id="configurationAdminService"
        interface="org.osgi.service.cm.ConfigurationAdmin"/>

<bean id="configurationAdminManager" class="com.manning.sdmia
    .compendium.configuration.ConfigurationAdminManager">
  <property name="configurationAdminService"
        ref="configurationAdminService"/>
</bean>
```

In the previous snippet, after having referenced the `ConfigurationAdmin` OSGi service with Spring DM, we inject it into the `ConfigurationAdminManager` bean.

The `ConfigurationAdminManager` class configured in the preceding code now contains a configured reference to the current Configuration Admin Service, enabling the class to interact with it. Listing 11.2 shows the structure of the `ConfigurationAdminManager` class that would corresponds to the configuration described in previous snippet for dependency injection of the service.

Listing 11.2   Structure of the `ConfigurationAdminManager` class

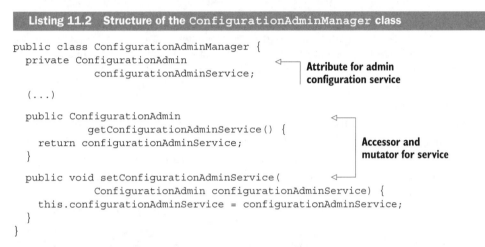

```
public class ConfigurationAdminManager {
  private ConfigurationAdmin
          configurationAdminService;          Attribute for admin
                                              configuration service

  (...)

  public ConfigurationAdmin
          getConfigurationAdminService() {
    return configurationAdminService;         Accessor and
  }                                           mutator for service

  public void setConfigurationAdminService(
          ConfigurationAdmin configurationAdminService) {
    this.configurationAdminService = configurationAdminService;
  }
}
```

Now that the `configurationAdminService` property has been set using dependency injection, all the methods of the class can be used to interact with the service. Before describing Spring DM's support for the Configuration Admin Service, we'll first look at how we can update configuration data.

INTERACTING WITH THE CONFIGURATION ADMIN SERVICE

The `ConfigurationAdmin` class allows you to interact with the Configuration Admin Service to access and modify configuration data. The service class provides access to this data through persistence identifiers. Its `getConfiguration` method allows you to get the configuration for a given identifier, represented by an instance of the `Configuration` class. This class gives access to a property dictionary and some methods for managing the configuration.

The following code provides demonstrates the use of these classes and methods.

```
Configuration configuration =
        configurationAdminService.getConfiguration("data.source.conf");
Dictionary<String, String> properties = configuration.getProperties();
if (properties==null) {
  configuration.update(new Hashtable());
}
```

The `Configuration` instance for the identifier `data.source.conf` is first retrieved using the `getConfiguration` method of the Configuration Admin Service. On this `Configuration` instance, the properties are gotten with the `getProperties` method.

If properties are `null`, they can eventually be initialized to an empty map by using the `update` method of the Configuration instance.

The Configuration Admin Service's persistence identifiers

Persistence identifiers act as primary keys for objects within the configuration repository, and they must be unique within this repository. They allow you to get the corresponding `Configuration` object by using the Configuration Admin Service's `getConfiguration` method.

Persistence identifiers should follow the symbolic name syntax of bundles, which uses a restricted character set. By convention, identifiers can be prefixed by the bundle identifier followed by a period (`.`). Package name syntax can also be used.

As you can see, properties for a given configuration identifier correspond to a map that can be updated. When it's created, this map is `null`, and you need to initialize it. You can then either use this map or specify a new one. In either case, the `update` method is used to save updates to configuration properties. The `Configuration` class also allows you to delete configuration properties by using its `delete` method.

Listing 11.3 shows how to set properties for a configuration identifier.

Listing 11.3   Updating properties for a given configuration identifier

```
Dictionary<String, String> properties
                  = configuration.getProperties();       ◁── Gets and initializes
if (properties==null) {                                       configuration
  properties = new Hashtable();                          ◁── properties if null
}
properties.put("jdbc.driverClassName",
               "org.h2.Driver");
properties.put("jdbc.url",                                    Sets properties
               "jdbc:h2:tcp://localhost/springdm-directory");  and updates
properties.put("jdbc.username", "sa");                        configuration
properties.put("jdbc.password", "");

configuration.update(properties);
```

You've now seen how to install, reference, and use the Configuration Admin Service to access and update configuration properties. It's time to look at how Spring DM's support for this service allows you to simplify and centralize the configuration of bean properties.

11.2.2   *Using properties defined by the Configuration Admin Service*

Spring provides support for configuring properties from different sources through the `properties` tag of its `util` XML namespace. Spring DM similarly allows you to configure properties stored in the Configuration Admin Service by using its `osgix` XML namespace.

This particular feature can be implemented using the `cm-properties` tag. This tag allows configuration properties for a persistent identifier to be retrieved, as shown in the following snippet:

```
<osgix:cm-properties id="dataSourceProperties"
                     persistent-id="data.source.conf"/>
```

This snippet defines a bean containing all properties specified in the Configuration Admin Service repository for the identifier `data.source.conf`.

The `cm-properties` tag also provides support for default values. By default, properties defined by the element are used if no corresponding keys are found in the Configuration Admin Service, but this behavior can be reversed by using the `local-override` attribute. This attribute's default value is `false`; setting it to `true` forces the use of the specified default, regardless of whatever data is present in the Configuration Admin Service.

The following snippet shows how to use default values with the `cm-properties` element when keys aren't present in the Configuration Admin Service repository.

```
<osgix:cm-properties id="dataSourceProperties"
                     persistent-id="data.source.conf">
  <prop key="jdbc.driverClassName">org.h2.Driver</prop>
</osgix:cm-properties>
```

This snippet sets a default value for the `jdbc.driverClassName` configuration key within the `cm-properties` XML element of the `osgix` namespace. Default values can be simply set within the XML element using the `prop` XML element.

Properties configured with the `cm-properties` XML element can be used with the `PropertyPlaceholderConfigurer` and `PropertyOverrideConfigurer` features of Spring. The `PropertyPlaceholderConfigurer` supports the externalization of values of property beans in properties files, and the `PropertyOverrideConfigurer` supports the defining of default values for these properties.

The following snippet shows how to use the Configuration Admin Service with the `PropertyPlaceholderConfigurer` to configure a data source.

```
<osgix:cm-properties id="dataSourceProperties"
                     persistent-id="data.source.conf"/>

<context:property-placeholder properties-ref="dataSourceProperties"/>

<bean id="dataSource" class="com.mchange.v2.c3p0.ComboPooledDataSource">
  <property name="driverClass" value="${jdbcDriverClassName}"/>
  <property name="jdbcUrl" value="${jdbcUrl}"/>
  <property name="user" value="${jdbcUsername}"/>
  <property name="password" value="${jdbcPassword}"/>
</bean>
```

Having configured properties with the `data.source.conf` identifier from Configuration Admin Service, this snippet uses them to configure the `PropertyPlaceholderConfigurer`. These properties can then be used to configure the different attributes of the data source.

In the preceding configuration, the configuration properties for the data source are retrieved from the Configuration Admin Service with the identifier `data.source.conf`. This approach allows global configurations to be defined across components in a centralized repository managed by the Configuration Admin Service. But be aware that modifying this configuration requires restarting all affected components so they can take into account the new values.

> ### The cm-properties tag and dynamics
> With early 2.0 versions of Spring DM, values contained in the properties corresponding to the `cm-properties` tag are lazily loaded on first access and remain unchanged after this. With the following version, this behavior will be changed to support dynamic updates occurring after first access.

As well as providing support for properties, Spring DM further supports the Configuration Admin Service by enabling tight integration between beans and the service. Spring DM provides managed entities for both the OSGi services and service factories.

11.2.3 *Support of managed entities*

The Configuration Admin Service provides a useful feature that allows components to be notified when updates occur within a dedicated configuration space. This feature can be implemented for both service and service factories through the use of the `ManagedService` and `ManagedServiceFactory` interfaces.

We'll first look at how to use this feature together with Spring DM by implementing these interfaces, and then we'll see how the framework leverages this feature by providing declarative support.

USING MANAGED RESOURCES DIRECTLY

Spring DM allows you to explicitly use the `ManagedService` and `ManagedServiceFactory` interfaces.

To do this, your services and service interfaces must implement one of these interfaces. The following snippet shows an example of such a service.

```
public class DataSourceManagedService implements ManagedService {
  (...)
  public void updated(Dictionary properties) {
    (...)
  }
}
```

Implementing the `ManagedService` interface allows the Configuration Admin Service to detect that the service is eligible for configuration updates. When updates occur, the `updated` method of the service will be called with the updated properties as the function argument.

After implementing the class of the managed service, the service needs to be configured and exported as an OSGi service using the facilities of Spring DM, as shown in listing 11.4.

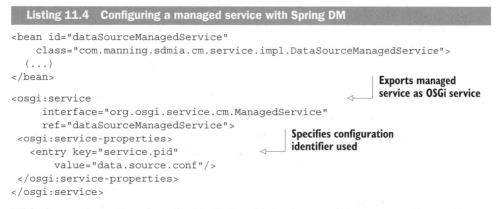

Listing 11.4 Configuring a managed service with Spring DM

```
<bean id="dataSourceManagedService"
    class="com.manning.sdmia.cm.service.impl.DataSourceManagedService">
  (...)
</bean>
<osgi:service
    interface="org.osgi.service.cm.ManagedService"
    ref="dataSourceManagedService">
 <osgi:service-properties>
   <entry key="service.pid"
       value="data.source.conf"/>
 </osgi:service-properties>
</osgi:service>
```

Exports managed service as OSGi service

Specifies configuration identifier used

With the configuration described in listing 11.4, when updates occur to the configuration with the identifier `data.source.conf` within the Configuration Admin Service, the `dataSourceManagedService` bean is notified and its `updated` method is called with the new properties as a parameter. The bean can then update the system according to the new configuration.

Although it's possible to support managed entities in this way, you're tied to the Configuration Admin Service API because you need to explicitly implement either the `ManagedService` or `ManagedServiceFactory` interfaces. Spring DM allows you to remove this dependency by providing declarative support for managed entities.

MANAGED SERVICE SUPPORT

The first case of declarative support for managed resources we'll consider is that for managed services. This feature doesn't require you to implement the `ManagedService` interface, but services can still be automatically notified when updates occur.

Two strategies are provided by Spring DM, but by default no strategy is used:

- *Container-managed*—Spring DM is responsible for reinjecting configuration data into the bean using setter methods corresponding to property keys. The bean is locked during the operation by a `synchronized` clause.
- *Bean-managed*—Spring DM notifies the bean that configuration updates are occurring but leaves it to the bean to actually update fields. In this case, there is no lock, and it's up to the class to decide how to update fields.

In both cases, the configuration of managed entities is done using the `managed-prop-erties` element of Spring DM's `osgix` XML namespace within the target bean's configuration, as shown in the following snippet:

```
<bean id="dataSourceService"
    class="com.manning.sdmia.cm.service.impl.DataSourceServiceImpl">
  <osgix:managed-properties
          persistent-id="data.source.conf"/>
</bean>
```

In this snippet, Spring DM uses the default container-managed strategy. It corresponds to explicitly specifying a value of `container-managed` for the `update-strategy` attribute of the `managed-properties` element.

This strategy sets all the fields of the DataSourceServiceImpl class with properties found in the configuration of the Configuration Admin Service under the persistent identifier data.source.conf. Property names must correspond to field names for a match to occur. Corresponding setter methods are used by Spring DM to inject values. If no property is found for a field, its value remains null. For example, if the bean has a field named jdbcDriverClassName and a property with the same name is present, the field will automatically be set with the value of the property.

Moreover, if a value is specified for a field using classic dependency injection, this value is overridden by the value found in the Configuration Admin Service.

Switching to the bean-managed strategy is simple, and is done by using the update-strategy attribute of the managed-properties XML element. In this case, its value must be bean-managed. Moreover, you need to specify with the update-method attribute which method will be called when updates occur. The method signature must accept a map as its only parameter and return void, as shown in the following snippet:

```
public class DataSourceServiceImpl {
  (...)

  public void updateDataSourceProperties(Map<String,?> properties) {
    (...)
  }
}
```

In the previous listing, the updateDataSourceProperties method of the Data-SourceServiceImpl class is called when configurations updates occur.

The configuration of the DataSourceServiceImpl class requires an inner managed-properties element containing both update-strategy and update-method attributes, as shown in the following snippet:

```
<bean id="dataSourceService"
      class="com.manning.sdmia.cm.service.impl.DataSourceServiceImpl">
  <osgix:managed-properties persistent-id="data.source.conf"
                     update-strategy="bean-managed"
                     update-method="updateDataSourceProperties"/>
</bean>
```

Within the managed-properties XML element, the update-strategy attribute is used to specify the bean-managed strategy and the update-method attribute for the method used for updates.

Now that we've seen Spring DM's convenient and declarative support for managing OSGi services through the use of the Configuration Admin Service, let's take a look at the support the Spring DM framework provides for managed service factories.

MANAGED SERVICE FACTORY SUPPORT

Spring DM's Configuration Admin Service support includes a managed service factory feature that handles configuration data for services with multiple instances. This approach is suitable when OSGi components need to configure OSGi services with different configuration values. The managed service factory allows you to link managed service instances with particular configurations for a persistence identifier.

With its support for managed service factories, Spring DM automatically creates and registers an OSGi service when a configuration element is added for managed service instances. Spring DM then manages updates and deletions according to the configuration. A `managed-service-factory` XML element is provided to configure Spring DM's support of managed service factories. This XML element refers to the corresponding configuration identifier within the Configuration Admin Service repository and uses an inner bean template to create OSGi service instances.

The following snippet describes how to use the `managed-service-factory` element in the context of the data source configuration from section 11.2.2.

```
<osgix:managed-service-factory id="dataSourceManagedServiceFactory"
                 factory-pid="data.source.confs">
  <bean id="dataSourceService"
    class="com.manning.sdmia.cm.service.impl.DataSourceServiceImpl">
    <!-- Default values -->
  </bean>
</osgix:managed-service-factory>
```

The first step consists in defining the `managed-service-factory` element and specifying the configuration identifier corresponding to the created factory. The next step is to configure the bean template to create OSGi services for a configuration element—this is done with a classical inner `bean` XML element. Default values can be defined in this template if necessary. These values will be overridden by values configured in the Configuration Admin Service repository with identifier `data.source.confs`.

Because Spring DM's managed service factory support acts as a service exporter, the `managed-service-factory` XML element owns similar attributes to those of the classic `service` element. Table 11.3 lists all the supported attributes for the `managed-service-factory` element.

Table 11.3 Supported attributes of the `managed-service-factory` XML element

Attribute	Description
`interface`	Specifies the interface you need to expose for the OSGi services. An inner `interfaces` XML element can be used to specify several interfaces.
`context-class-loader`	Specifies how the context classloader is managed when an operation is invoked on the exported service. Possible values are `unmanaged` (by default) for no management and `service-provider` to make the context classloader see elements of the bundle exporting the services.
`auto-export`	Specifies the strategy to autodetect interfaces exposed for the configured OSGi managed services. The same values as for the `service` element can be used. The `disabled` value allows the developer to specify interfaces by hand. The `interfaces`, `class-hierarchy`, and `all-classes` values autodetect interfaces based on different strategies. For more details, see section 5.3.1.
`update-strategy`	Defines the strategy for updating the managed service. By default (a value of `none`), no strategy is specified. Other values correspond to those for Spring DM's support of managed services: `bean-managed` lets the bean update fields and `container-managed` specifies updates done by Spring DM via setter methods. For more details, refer to the previous subsection in this chapter.

The following snippet shows a more advanced use of the `managed-service-factory` XML element, specifying a set of interfaces and an update strategy:

```
<osgix:managed-service-factory id="dataSourceManagedServiceFactory"
                    factory-pid="data.source.confs">
                    update-strategy="bean-managed"
  <osgix:interfaces>
    <value>com.manning.sdmia.cm.service.DataSourceService</value>
  </osgix:interfaces>
</osgix:managed-service-factory>
```

In the previous snippet and within the `managed-service-factory` XML element, the update-strategy attribute is used to specify the bean-managed update strategy and the interfaces XML element for the set of interfaces for the managed service factory.

We can also use the `managed-service-factory` XML element to specify a listener to be notified when service registrations and unregistrations occur. To configure this feature, an inner `registration-listener` XML elementmust be added. The registration-method and unregistration-method attributes specify which methods to call on the listener when service registration and unregistration occur. The following snippet shows how to configure the `registration-listener` element:

```
<osgix:managed-service-factory id="dataSourceManagedServiceFactory"
                    factory-pid="data.source.confs">
  (...)
  <osgix:registration-listener ref="dataSourceServiceListener"
            registration-method="onServiceRegistration"
            unregistration-method="onServiceUnregistration"/>
  </osgix:registration-listener>
</osgix:managed-service-factory>
```

The dataSourceServiceListener bean, referenced with the ref attribute in the preceding snippet, consists of a simple POJO with onServiceRegistration and onServiceUnregistration methods, as shown in listing 11.5.

Listing 11.5 The `DataSourceServiceListener` class

```
public class DataSourceServiceListener {
  public void onServiceRegistration(
            DataSourceService service, Map properties) {
    (...)
  }
  public void onServiceUnregistration(
            DataSourceService service, Map properties) {
    (...)
  }
}
```

Spring DM provides declarative support for the Configuration Admin Service, which enables transparent integration between beans configured in Spring DM and the configurations managed by this compendium service. This support makes it possible to centralize the configuration of bundles in a single configuration repository.

We'll now take a look at how to make Spring DM interact with the Event Admin Service, which provides standardized event management within the OSGi environment. This interaction enables you to handle Spring DM events without being linked with the framework.

11.3 Spring DM's Event Admin Service support

The Event Admin Service is another useful compendium service that allows for the standardized exchange of messages between components. At the moment, Spring DM doesn't support this service directly, but it's possible to implement a bridge between Spring and Spring DM events and the Event Admin Service.

We'll first explain how to install and use the service and the concepts behind linking Spring DM to the service. Then we'll see how to implement this bridge.

11.3.1 OSGi Event Admin Service

Before using the Event Admin Service with Spring DM, we need to know how to install it, how to reference the corresponding OSGi service, and how to send and receive events.

INSTALLING THE EVENT ADMIN SERVICE

The same bundle that provides support for the Configuration Admin Service can be used here, because it contains the public API for all compendium services. The bundle provided by Felix is available in the SpringSource EBR, as detailed in section 11.2.1.

Table 11.4 lists the components needed to install the Event Admin Service from the SpringSource EBR.

Table 11.4 Bundles related to the Event Admin Service from the SpringSource EBR

Group ID	Artifact ID	Version
org.osgi	org.osgi.compendium	4.1.0.build-200702212030
org.apache.felix	org.apache.felix.eventadmin	1.0.0

Adding these two components within your OSGi container will install the Event Admin Service.

ACCESSING THE EVENT ADMIN SERVICE USING SPRING DM

Once the implementation bundle for the Event Admin Service has been installed, a service will appear in the OSGi service registry under the name `org.osgi.service.event.EventAdmin` corresponding to the service interface.

This service can be referenced using Spring DM just like any other service, by using its `reference` XML element and then injecting the result into any bean. This is shown in the following snippet:

```
<osgi:reference id="eventAdminService"
        interface="org.osgi.service.event.EventAdmin"/>

<bean id="eventAdminManager" class="com.manning.sdmia
➥.compendium.event.EventAdminManager">
  <property name="eventAdminService" ref="eventAdminService"/>
</bean>
```

In the preceding snippet, the OSGi service for the Event Admin Service is referenced with the identifier `org.osgi.service.event.EventAdmin`. This service can be then injected in the `eventAdminManager` bean using its `eventAdminService` property.

The `EventAdminManager` class configured in the preceding snippet contains a configured reference to the installed Event Admin Service, enabling the class to interact with it. Listing 11.6 shows the structure of the class.

Listing 11.6   Structure of the `EventAdminManager` class

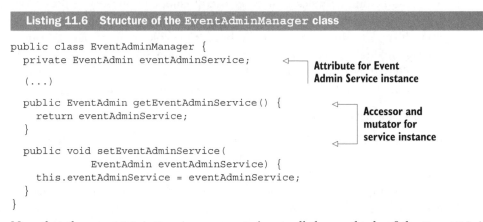

```
public class EventAdminManager {
  private EventAdmin eventAdminService;        ◁──┐ Attribute for Event
                                                  │ Admin Service instance
  (...)

  public EventAdmin getEventAdminService() {   ◁──┐
    return eventAdminService;                      │ Accessor and
  }                                                │ mutator for
  public void setEventAdminService(                │ service instance
          EventAdmin eventAdminService) {      ◁──┘
    this.eventAdminService = eventAdminService;
  }
}
```

Now that the `eventAdminService` property is set, all the methods of the `EventAdmin` interface can be used to interact with the service. Before describing how to implement a bridge between Spring DM and the Event Admin Service, we'll first see how to exchange events.

INTERACTING WITH THE EVENT ADMIN SERVICE

The Event Admin Service is primarily used to send events. This can be done explicitly using the `EventAdmin` service that we automatically registered. This service provides a `sendEvent` method that takes an event object to send an event. The following snippet shows how to send an event.

```
Event event = new Event(topicName, eventProperties);
eventAdmin.sendEvent(event);
```

The Event Admin Service can also implement event listeners based on the whiteboard pattern. These listeners must implement the `EventHandler` interface, and they have to be registered as OSGi services. When an event occurs, the Event Admin Service dispatches the event to all the registered implementations by calling their `handleEvent` method. The following snippet shows a sample implementation of the `EventHandler` interface.

```
public class SampleEventHandler implements EventHandler {
  public void handleEvent(Event event) {
    (...)
  }
}
```

Event data can be accessed using properties contained in the instance of the `Event` class passed as arguments to the `handleEvent` method. The class contains the event topic and its associated properties. The event topic has the same value as the `topic-Name` variable used to send the event.

Now that you know how to use the Event Admin Service to send and receive events, let's see how we can use it with Spring DM.

11.3.2 Linking Spring DM and the OSGi Event Admin Service

Spring DM and Spring raise a set of events during their normal operation. Applications, and components, in our case, can register event listeners to be notified of these events when they occur. These system elements then use their own strategies for implementing event handling and delivering messages.

In Spring, listeners are implemented as regular classes implementing the `ApplicationListener` interface. The scope of this event system is restricted to the owning Spring application context, and with this framework events are propagated synchronously.

In Spring DM, events are intended to be consumed by bundles other than the one that triggers them. Event handling is based on the whiteboard pattern, which allows for the decoupling of event producers from their consumers and provides support for registering and unregistering listeners dynamically. (This pattern was first described in section 4.1.5.) In the context of this pattern, delivery has important requirements because OSGi is dynamic and the implementation mustn't freeze the entire system. For this reason, Spring DM delivers events asynchronously to registered listeners.

In the next sections, we'll describe how to link Spring DM and Spring events to the Event Admin Service. When events occur in either framework, they're redirected to this service.

HANDLING SPRING DM EVENTS

A dedicated Spring DM listener receives any Spring DM events and forwards them to the Event Admin Service. To do so, the listener builds an event compatible with the Event Admin Service using data contained in the initial Spring DM event and then sends it using the `EventAdmin` service API.

This listener isn't provided by Spring DM and needs to be implemented. Figure 11.3 summarizes the steps for implementing the link between Spring DM events and the Event Admin Service.

First, like every Spring DM event listener, the bridge listener must implement Spring DM's `OsgiBundleApplicationContextListener` interface. Spring DM dispatches events to these listeners registered as services following the whiteboard pattern. The bridge listener references the `EventAdmin` service through the OSGi service registry and sends events to the Event Admin Service when it receives events from Spring DM. Every class registered as a listener on the Event Admin Service will then be notified.

This mechanism allows for third-party bundles to receive events and notifications from Spring DM without having to be tied to its use.

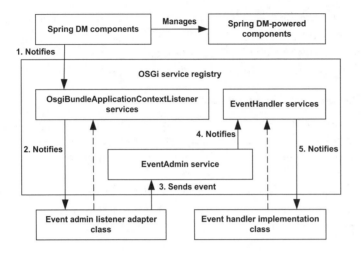

Figure 11.3 Linking Spring DM's event-handling mechanisms so that they forward events to the Event Admin Service

HANDLING SPRING EVENTS

With Spring, things are a little different because its event management is completely independent from OSGi, and event listeners must be directly defined within the Spring application context. Having detected all these configured classes, Spring notifies them when an event occurs. For our purposes, we can use a special Spring application listener that receives these events and forwards them to the Event Admin Service.

Figure 11.4 summarizes the steps for implementing the link between Spring events and the Event Admin Service.

First, like every Spring application event listener, the bridge listener must implement Spring's `ApplicationListener` interface. Spring dispatches events to these listeners configured within the Spring container. So far, nothing is specific to OSGi.

The bridge listener then references the `EventAdmin` service through the OSGi service registry and is sends events to the Event Admin Service when it receives events

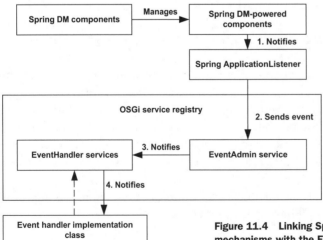

Figure 11.4 Linking Spring's event-handling mechanisms with the Event Admin Service

from Spring. Every class registered as a listener on the Event Admin Service will then be notified.

This mechanism allows for third-party bundles to receive events and notifications from Spring without having to be tied to the framework. Note that the bridge listener must deliver events asynchronously for the reasons discussed at the beginning of section 11.3.2.

Now that we've described how to have events triggered by Spring and Spring DM dispatched to the Event Admin Service, we'll focus on how to implement the bridge listener for Spring DM events.

11.3.3 *Implementing the bridge between Spring DM and Event Admin Service*

Handling Spring DM events consists of creating a listener class that implements Spring DM's `OsgiBundleApplicationContextListener` interface. Having registered this listener as an OSGi service, this class will then be able to handle Spring DM events and forward them to the Event Admin Service.

By implementing this interface, the class must also define the `onOsgiApplicationEvent` method. This method is called when an event is triggered and is responsible for handling it correctly.

Because the class provides the link with the Event Admin Service, it has an attribute of type `EventAdmin`. We'll configure this attribute later on by using the corresponding `EventAdmin` OSGi service referenced with Spring DM facilities.

Listing 11.7 shows the structure of this listener implementation.

Listing 11.7   A listener implementation linking Spring DM and the Event Admin Service

```
public class EventAdminAdapterListener
      implements OsgiBundleApplicationContextListener {
   private EventAdmin eventAdmin;

   public void onOsgiApplicationEvent(
                  OsgiBundleApplicationContextEvent event) {
     String topicName = buildTopicName(event);
     Properties eventProperties
                  = buildEventProperties(event);
     eventAdmin.sendEvent(new Event(
                  topicName, eventProperties));
   }
   (...)

   public void setEventAdmin(EventAdmin eventAdmin) {
     this.eventAdmin = eventAdmin;
   }
}
```

Implements Spring DM listener interface and method

Creates, configures and send event

Building the event for the Event Admin Service requires several steps, which are implemented in listing 11.6 by the `buildTopicName` and `buildEventProperties` methods within the `onOsgiApplicationEvent` method. We'll describe the implementation of `buildTopicName` and `buildEventProperties` methods shortly.

The first step in building the event is creating the name of the topic on which the event will be published. Topic names allow classification of topics using tokens separated by the slash (/) character. The following snippet shows how to use the class name of the Spring DM event to build the topic name:

```
private String buildTopicName(OsgiBundleApplicationContextEvent event) {
  String eventClassName = event.getClass().getName();
  return eventClassName.replace(".", "/");
}
```

Properties for the event then need to be specified—they should contain all the information describing the event. In our context, this information can be obtained from the event instance provided by Spring DM. Listing 11.8 shows how to build properties for an event compatible with the Event Admin Service.

Listing 11.8   Implementing `buildEventProperties` to build event properties

```
private Properties buildEventProperties(
            OsgiBundleApplicationContextEvent event) {
  Properties eventProperties = new Properties();

  eventProperties.put("event.timestamp",                    ◁──┐
                    event.getTimestamp());                       Sets general
  Object source = event.getSource();                             properties
  eventProperties.put("event.source.class",                 ◁──┘
                    source.getClass().getName());

  Bundle bundle = event.getBundle();
  eventProperties.put("event.bundle.id",                        Sets properties
                    bundle.getSymbolicName());                  related to bundle
  eventProperties.put("event.bundle.state",
                    bundle.getState());

  (...)

  return eventProperties;
}
```

Implementations of the `buildTopicName` and `buildEventProperties` methods provide all the information necessary to build an `Event` instance, which is the event class for the Event Admin Service. This instance can then be used when using the `sendEvent` method of the `EventAdmin` instance to send the event.

The last step consists of configuring the bridge listener. Because this listener uses the `EventAdmin` service, it first needs to be referenced using Spring DM's facilities. The listener itself can then be configured as a bean in the Spring application context and exported as an OSGi service with the same facilities. Once these configurations are done, the listener is ready to receive events from Spring DM and forward them to the Event Admin Service.

Listing 11.9 shows how to configure the bridge listener.

Listing 11.9 Configuring the bridge listener

```
<bean id="eventAdminAdapterListener"
        class="org.springframework.osgi
          .compendium.event.EventAdminAdapterListener">
  <property name="eventAdmin"
        ref="eventAdminService"/>
</bean>

<osgi:reference id="eventAdminService"
          interface="org.osgi.service.event.EventAdmin"/>

<osgi:service ref="eventAdminAdapterListener"
          interface="org.springframework.osgi
            .context.event.OsgiBundleApplicationContextListener"/>
```

Defines listener and injects
EventAdmin service

Registers listener as OSGi service

In this section, we saw how to implement and configure a bridge listener that receives and forwards Spring DM events to the Event Admin Service. This listener is primarily a Spring DM listener that builds a new Event Admin Service event from the initial Spring DM event and sends it to interested parties via the `EventAdmin` service.

Let's look now at how to implement listeners in Spring DM that can receive and handle events triggered by the Event Admin Service.

11.3.4 *Implementing OSGi event handlers*

Creating event listeners for the Event Admin Service involves implementing the `Event-tHandler` interface, which requires defining a `handleEvent` method that is called whenever an event occurs. The event is provided as parameter to this method.

Listing 11.10 shows how to implement such a listener.

Listing 11.10 An event listener implementation for the Event Admin Service

```
public class AdminEventHandler implements EventHandler {
  public void handleEvent(Event event) {
    String topicName = event.getTopic();
    String[] propertyNames = event.getPropertyNames();
    for (int cpt=0; cpt<propertyNames.length; cpt++) {
      String propertyName = propertyNames[cpt];
      String propertyValue = (String)event.getProperty(propertyName);
    }
  }
}
```

From the event instance passed as a parameter, we can get the topic names and the properties of the event and iterate through them.

Because the Event Admin Service follows the whiteboard pattern for finding all the registered listeners, the listener we just defined must also be defined as an OSGi service under the name `org.osgi.service.event.EventHandler`. Spring DM can be used to accomplish this. The `event.topics` service property can also be added when exporting the listener to specify which topic it's interested in. Wild-cards are allowed here.

> **TIP** Topic names support hierarchies and become more specific when going from left to right. You can take advantage of this to define an event handler that receives a set of event kinds. For example, specifying the expression `org/springframework/osgi/*` in the `event.topics` property of an event handler service will allow the handler to receive events whose names begin with `org/springframework/osgi/`. This means using hierarchies when creating event names is very important.

Listing 11.11 shows how to configure a listener for the Event Admin Service using Spring DM's facilities.

Listing 11.11   Configuring the Event Admin Service listener using Spring DM

```
<bean id="eventAdminHandler"
    class="org.springframework.osgi.compendium.event.AdminEventHandler"/>

<osgi:service ref="eventAdminHandler"
        interface="org.osgi.service.event.EventHandler">
  <osgi:service-properties>
    <entry key="event.topics" value="org/springframework/osgi/*"/>
  </osgi:service-properties>
</osgi:service>
```

The listener is configured as bean within the configuration and then registered as an OSGi service with Spring DM's `service` XML element. Within this element, the topic names are specified in service properties with the `event.topics` key.

Given the configuration in listing 11.10, all events with topic names beginning with `org/springframework/osgi` are sent to the listener corresponding to the `AdminEvent-Handler` class. For each event, the `handleEvent` method is called with the event instance passed as a parameter.

We've now seen how to use the Event Admin Service with Spring DM, even though this compendium service isn't directly supported by Spring DM.

11.4   Summary

In addition to its core specification, OSGi provides a specification describing a set of standardized services called *compendium services*. These services range from embedded technologies to web support, and some of them are useful in conjunction with Spring DM.

That's particularly the case with the Configuration Admin Service, which allows for the centralization of configuration properties. The configuration repositories can be managed by third-party tools. Using this service with Spring allows us to leverage configuration management and to share configurations across components. Spring DM provides non-intrusive support for automatically injecting configuration properties into beans.

The Event Admin Service is another interesting compendium service. It provides a standardized way of exchanging events between components—event producers and consumers don't need to be tied to a particular API. Although Spring DM doesn't provide support for this service, a bridge can be implemented to forward events triggered by Spring or Spring DM to the Event Admin Service. This allows components to be notified without having to use the API provided by these two frameworks.

The Blueprint Service (RFC 124) is the most recent addition to compendium services and it aims to standardize Spring DM. As a matter of fact, Spring DM 2 is now completely compliant with this specification because Spring DM 2 corresponds to the reference implementation of the Blueprint Service. In chapter 12, we'll take a look at all the concepts involved in this specification.

The Blueprint specification

12

This chapter covers

- Standardizing Spring DM though the Blueprint specification
- Discussing the Blueprint terminology
- Comparing Spring DM and Blueprint
- Using Blueprint

In the previous chapter, we looked at the OSGi compendium services and how they can be accessed from Spring DM. One of the most recent additions to the compendium services (introduced in OSGi 4.2) is the Blueprint Service specification (RFC 124)—a topic of great interest to us because it represents the standardization of Spring DM. In this chapter we'll describe and discuss the Blueprint specification and show how you can use it both standalone and together with Spring DM.

Because it's the reference implementation, Spring DM 2.0 fully supports Blueprint, and it's likely that many customers will choose to use Blueprint instead of Spring DM because of its standard status. Fortunately Blueprint isn't very different from Spring DM—all the concepts are the same. In fact, Blueprint can be thought of as a dialect of the Spring DM language, so you should have no trouble at all understanding and using it.

So without more ado, let's dive right in!

12.1 Standardization of Spring DM

Spring is what is known as a *de facto* standard—it's a standard simply because so many people use it. There is no Spring specification—Rod Johnson and his team at Interface21 simply implemented a clever solution to a thorny problem and documented what they did after the fact. The fact that so many people then used it serves to demonstrate how attractive and suitable the solution was.

Many standards that people are used to, however, such as Java EE and all its constituent components, are developed as open standards.

In this section, we'll discuss the history, goals, and scope of Blueprint, set in the context of open standards and their importance to the software industry.

12.1.1 The attraction of open standards

It's rare that anything remains a de facto standard for long. Widespread adoption usually indicates a ripe technology market that attracts other entrants. For customers, there is nothing worse than multiple technology offerings that do different similar things but that are generally incompatible with each other. The so-called "vendor lock-in" that results has historically been treated with a great deal of fear and loathing by customers and often causes the market as a whole to grow at a reduced rate.

Open standards are the solution to this problem. An open standard is generally open for anyone to implement and use (although the licensing terms vary), and vendors must then compete on quality of implementation. Customers meanwhile get to use technology from different vendors in a broadly similar way, not only reaping the benefits of common training, knowledge transfer, and support but also benefiting from increased competition in the marketplace and hence decreased costs.

That's why standards are good for customers, but interestingly they're often good for vendors as well because standards have been shown to grow the overall market.

The genesis of Blueprint

Spring DM's genesis was a little different from that of Spring. In late 2005 and early 2006, Adrian Colyer, Interface21's new CTO, discussed some ideas for integrating Spring with OSGi with one of your authors and Hal Hildebrand from Oracle. BEA at the time was fully committed to Spring and getting more interested in OSGi, and the ideas and prototype presented by Adrian Colyer seemed to hit the nail on the head with regard to these technologies.

Over the next few months Adrian Colyer developed his ideas with input, and some limited development effort, from both Oracle and BEA. As the nascent Spring DM took shape in code, a specification was written by Adrian Colyer to keep all the players headed in the same direction. Over time, the specification evolved into an internal standard agreed on by each of the three companies—Interface21, Oracle, and BEA. The implementation also evolved dramatically under the expert guidance of Costin Leau from Interface21.

(continued)

But there was a problem: the three players were concerned that the de facto nature of Spring and the proprietary nature of the Spring DM specification would mean that the uptake of Spring DM would be limited. Fortunately, at the same time a group was being formed inside the OSGi alliance tasked with developing specifications for enterprise customers—the so-called "Enterprise Expert Group." This was perceived as an ideal vehicle to take Spring DM from a proprietary standard to a published, open standard. Thus, with the full support of both BEA and Oracle, Adrian Colyer embarked on the tricky task of creating an open standard for Spring DM, which, because it relied so heavily on Spring itself, meant creating a partial standard for Spring too.

And so Blueprint was born.

12.1.2 Standards development

Most standards are developed by a standards organization because vendor-led standards will be viewed with suspicion by the competition. OSGi is no different, being developed by the OSGi Alliance.

OSGi standards require more than just a specification document describing what is supposed to happen. All OSGi standards also require a reference implementation (RI) and a technology compatibility kit (TCK), which is a suite of tests to check the conformance of any implementation. This means that anyone can implement the specification and then physically check whether it's conformant by running the TCK.

The Blueprint RI and TCK

In the case of Blueprint, the RI is Spring DM 2.0 and the TCK was developed independently by IBM. Generally it's wise for the RI and TCK to be developed by different companies so that there are no implicit erroneous assumptions in either specification or implementation.

12.1.3 Goals of the Blueprint specification

The original request for proposal (RFP) that spawned the Blueprint specification was called "A Component Model for OSGi." The intent of the specification was to standardize the groundwork laid by the Spring DM (back then, Spring-OSGi) project so that enterprise developers could target the OSGi platform.

In particular, the RFP identified several features lacking in the existing crop of OSGi specifications:

- There was no defined component model for the internals of a bundle
- There was a lack of rich configuration and assembly support
- There was no model for declaratively creating bundle cross-cutting concerns
- The reliance on OSGi APIs made out-of-container testing difficult

- There was no clear specification for the context classloader and what it saw in an OSGi context
- There was little component-level support for the dynamic nature of the OSGi platform

Of course, Spring DM already addressed these deficiencies, and initially there was a feeling that perhaps the Spring DM specification could simply be rubber-stamped for inclusion in the OSGi Alliance's suite of specifications. Over time, however, the Blueprint specification evolved to something more of a compromise as it became clear that to be self-contained it was not sufficient to simply standardize Spring DM; parts of Spring itself would need standardizing as well.

12.1.4 Scope of the specification

Initially the scope of the Blueprint specification was to replicate in a standard the scope of the Spring DM specification and project. But because of the need to standardize parts of Spring, it became necessary in the interests of time to trim down the scope to the bare essentials.

Out went some of the more esoteric extensions of Spring DM, out went the specification of namespace handlers, out went annotation support. In fact, out went anything that was deemed noncore, or that was in danger of requiring too much further expansion in order to be complete. In fact, as we look at the Blueprint way of implementing and accessing OSGi services, the biggest change you'll notice—apart from the change in naming—is the things that are missing.

The importance of Blueprint

Why are we discussing Blueprint at all? You may know already, because your organization may aggressively advocate and adopt open standards. All other things being equal, given the choice between an open or proprietary standard, most organizations will choose an open standard. Thus Blueprint, as the Spring DM standard, is likely to be quickly adopted by many organizations using Spring DM and also by organizations currently hesitant to use Spring DM. It's therefore likely that the growth of Blueprint will be rapid and at the expense of Spring DM.

This should not concern you—Spring DM and Blueprint are sufficiently similar that your education so far will set you in good stead for the future. Your job security will remain intact!

So let's get down to the nuts and bolts. What does Blueprint look like in actuality, and how do we use it?

12.2 A taxonomy of Blueprint

Perhaps it's easiest if we start by listing the Blueprint XML elements available and their Spring DM equivalents.

NOTE   Blueprint is now part of the OSGi 4.2 compendium specification, which can be found at http://www.osgi.org/Download/File?url=/download/r4v42/r4.cmpn.pdf, and the following discussion is based on this version of the specification.

The Blueprint namespace is http://www.osgi.org/xmlns/blueprint/v1.0.0 and the recommended namespace prefix is "bp". The following snippet shows the exact Blueprint namespace syntax:

```
<blueprint xmlns="http://www.osgi.org/xmlns/blueprint/v1.0.0"
        xmlns:xsi="http://www.w3.org/2001/XMLSchema-instance"
        xsi:schemaLocation="http://www.osgi.org/xmlns/blueprint/v1.0.0
    http://www.osgi.org/xmlns/blueprint/v1.0.0/blueprint.xsd">
```

Table 12.1 compares the Blueprint schema elements with their Spring DM equivalents.

Table 12.1   Blueprint XML elements and their Spring DM equivalents

Blueprint element	Spring DM element	Notes
blueprint	beans	At a superficial level, the use of blueprint instead of beans is the only major difference between Spring DM and Blueprint.
bean	bean	
reference	reference	
service	service	
reference-list	list	
type-converter	Java.beans. PropertyEditor	There is no direct equivalent to type-converters because Spring employs a number of schemes to convert source properties to a type compatible with the target.
	set	There is no support for set in Blueprint.

Simple! As you can see, the key elements supported by Spring DM are also supported by Blueprint and they have mostly the same names. So why don't we end the chapter right here? After all, you now have what you need to know in order to write Blueprint components.

Not quite so fast—there are a number of details in Blueprint that are subtly different from Spring DM.

12.2.1 *A Blueprint example*

Let's look at a Blueprint example. First, the metadata definition:

```
<blueprint>
  <service id="myService" interface="com.manning.sdmia.ch12.MyService"
    ref="myServiceImpl"/>
```

```
    <bean id="myServiceImpl"
        class="com.manning.sdmia.ch12.MyServiceImpl">
      <property name="message" value="Hello: "/>
    </bean>
</blueprint>
```

You can see that apart from the top-level `blueprint` tag, the XML looks identical to a Spring DM application context file. Even the syntax of properties is the same.

Blueprint has different terminology for these elements, however. Each top-level element is a *top-level manager* of a specific type and has a specific *component metadata* type, which we shall look at later. Managers manage component instances and they have a defined lifecycle similar to the lifecycle of Spring DM elements.

12.2.2 Blueprint bundles

Blueprint bundles are constructed in much the same way as Spring DM bundles. The only major difference is that the Blueprint container will look for metadata definitions in the bundle in OSGI-INF/blueprint/*.xml. Other artifacts and resources, such as classes and properties files, should be put in their regular bundle locations.

The `Bundle-Blueprint` manifest header can be used to modify the search location for Blueprint metadata, so the default search location could be represented by

```
Bundle-Blueprint: OSGI-INF/blueprint/*.xml
```

With these minor differences in mind, we're ready to build and run our first Blueprint bundle!

12.3   Blueprint manager syntax

We've already talked indirectly about the top-level managers that Blueprint supports, so it's time to look at the syntax of each of these individually. These are the available managers:

- *Bean manager*—Supports the creation of bean component instances
- *Service manager*—Supports the creation of OSGi service instances
- *Reference manager*—Supports the creation of OSGi service reference instances
- *Reference-list manager*—Supports the creation of collections of OSGi service references
- *Environment managers*—Supports access to environment-specific constructs, such as the Blueprint container, `BundleContext`, and the `Bundle` itself.

Each manager has corresponding XML syntax elements, and in many instances the XML syntax is identical to its Spring DM equivalent. We'll list the supported attributes for each in the following sections, but only describe in detail those that don't have a Spring DM equivalent. Let's look at these manager types in more detail.

12.3.1 Bean manager

Perhaps the most complex—and most important—manager is the bean manager. It deals with the complexities of creating and managing POJOs via the `bean` element, and as such it's the part of Blueprint that deals with standardizing parts of the core Spring framework itself.

The bean manager is also the manager that diverges most widely from Spring DM. The main reason for this isn't so much gratuitous renaming but the decision that Blueprint needed to be self-contained as a specification. As such, it isn't possible for the specification—or the XML schema—to reference external unspecified artifacts, such as the Spring Framework's schema. Instead, all XML elements and Java artifacts need to be described by the specification, so some needed to be changed in order to meet these goals.

The bean manager supports the following Spring attributes with their usual meanings: `id`, `depends-on`, `factory-method`, `init-method`, `destroy-method`, `class`, and `scope`. However, if a `factory-method` is specified, or a constructor other than the default is required, arguments can be supplied via a sequence of `argument` elements, rather than `constructor-arg`, which is used in Spring. The attributes for `argument` and `constructor-arg` are named the same with the same meanings.

The bean manager provides an extra attribute—`factory-ref`—which can be used to reference a manager to be used for construction.

Finally, properties can be specified via the `property` element as in Spring. Properties are defined either as values (`value`), as references (`ref`) to other managers, or as inlined definitions. Table 12.2 summarizes these elements.

Table 12.2   Blueprint bean manager XML elements and their Spring DM equivalents

Bean manager attribute or element	Spring bean attribute or element	Notes
`id`	`id`	
`depends-on`	`depends-on`	
`factory-method`	`factory-method`	Arguments are specified by `<argument/>` rather than `<constructor-arg/>`
`init-method`	`init-method`	
`destroy-method`	`destroy-method`	
`class`	`class`	Constructor arguments are specified by `<argument/>` rather than `<constructor-arg/>`
`scope`	`scope`	
`argument`	`constructor-arg`	
`property`	`Property`	Supports `ref`, `value`, and inline definitions
`factory-ref`		
`activation`	`lazy-init`	`activation="lazy"` is the equivalent of `lazy-init="true"`
	`*`	No other Spring elements are supported

Let's take a look at a couple of simple examples. First, an example using the standard constructor method:

```
<bean id="testServiceCtor" activation="eager"
  class="com.manning.sdmia.springdm.service.impl.TestServiceImpl">
  <argument index="0" value="foo"/>
</bean>
```

Next, an example using the factory method:

```
<bean id="testServiceFactory" activation="lazy"
      class="com.manning.sdmia.springdm.service.impl.TestServiceImpl"
      factory-method="createTestService">
  <argument index="0" value="bar"/>
</bean>
```

Finally, an example that references one bean from another:

```
<bean id="beanA"
      class="com.manning.sdmia.springdm.service.impl.TestServiceImpl"/>
<bean id="beanB"
      class="com.manning.sdmia.springdm.service.impl.NewServiceImpl">
  <property name="delegate" ref="beanA"/>
</bean>
```

Simple—and almost identical to Spring DM. Now we'll look at Blueprint's service manager.

12.3.2 Service manager

The Blueprint service manager supports the creation of OSGi services just like Spring DM's service element does. The attributes that the service manager supports are very nearly a simple subset of those in Spring DM's service element. The one difference is the syntax for activation which we've seen already.

For completeness we list them all in table 12.3. Note that, in particular, the `context-class-loader` attribute is missing from Blueprint.

Table 12.3   Blueprint service manager XML elements and their Spring DM equivalents

Service manager attribute or element	Spring DM service attribute or element	Notes
id	id	
depends-on	depends-on	
auto-export	auto-export	Identical values are supported
ranking	ranking	
activation	lazy-init	activation="lazy" is the equivalent of lazy-init="true"
interface	interface	

Table 12.3   Blueprint service manager XML elements and their Spring DM equivalents *(continued)*

Service manager attribute or element	Spring DM service attribute or element	Notes
ref	ref	
service-properties	service-properties	
interfaces	interfaces	
registration-listener	registration-listener	
	context-class-loader	

Let's take a look at another simple example that illustrates the service manager's use:

```
<service ref="testServiceFactory" auto-export="class-hierarchy">
  <service-properties>
      <entry key="service-id" value="theRealOne"/>
  </service-properties>
</service>
```

We can see in this example that we didn't need to specify an interface to export. Instead we relied on Blueprint to do the job for us via auto-export. This example is almost identical to similar examples for Spring DM, so the syntax should seem very familiar.

Now we'll look at Blueprint's service reference manager.

12.3.3   *Reference manager*

The Blueprint service reference manager supports the creation of references to other OSGi services, just as Spring DM's reference element does. The attributes and elements that the service reference manager supports are again largely the same as for Spring DM.

Again, we have id, depends-on, interface, filter, timeout, and reference-listener with their usual meanings. Again we have our friend activation instead of lazy-init, and instead of cardinality we have availability. Table 12.4 summarizes these elements.

Let's take a look at another simple example that illustrates the service reference manager's use:

```
<reference id="testService" filter="(service-id=theRealOne)"
➥        interface="com.manning.sdmia.springdm.service.TestService"/>
```

Now we'll look at Blueprint's reference-list manager and the differences between it and the Spring DM list equivalent.

Table 12.4   Blueprint service reference manager XML elements and their Spring DM equivalents

Bean service reference manager element or attribute	Spring service reference element	Notes
`id`	`id`	
`depends-on`	`depends-on`	
`interface`	`interface`	
`filter`	`filter`	
`timeout`	`timeout`	
`activation`	`lazy-init`	`activation="lazy"` is the equivalent of `lazy-init="true"`
`reference-listener`	`listener`	
`availability`	`cardinality`	"optional" equates to "`0..1`" "mandatory" equates to "`1..1`"
`component-name`	`bean-name`	
	`context-class-loader`	
	`interfaces`	

12.3.4 Reference-list manager

In a similar vein to the service reference manager, the service reference-list manager supports the creation of collections of OSGi service references. Just like in Spring DM, the collection semantics are dynamic, with the set of managed service references changing over time as services disappear and new ones become available.

The attributes that the reference-list manager supports are identical to those of the reference manager, with the addition of `member-type`. None of Spring DM's `comparator`, `comparator-ref`, or `greedy-proxying` are supported, nor is the set version of the reference list.

The missing interfaces

From the discussion of the reference manager, you'll notice that you can only specify a single interface for `reference` and `reference-list`. That's quite a problem, because you can't create a `reference` that can be cast to different support interfaces, as would be the case with the service object itself.

Another trick you can't use is interface-based capabilities. Under Spring DM, if you specify `greedy-proxying` for a `reference-list`, the proxied references will contain all of the supported interfaces of the underlying service. Thus, you could have some service objects that provide additional capabilities based on an additional interface, and the consumer of the `reference-list` could take advantage of this through a simple `instanceof` operation.

Another simple example shows just how similar the reference-list's use is to that of reference:

```
<reference-list id="testService"
        interface="com.manning.sdmia.springdm.service.TestService"/>
```

If you were to inject a component instance of this type into a bean, you'd see that the actual component type is `java.util.List`, with most, but not all, of the functionality that this implies. In particular, the returned list is read-only so that `java.util.List` operations that imply updates (such as `add()` or the `remove()` operation on an iterator) aren't supported and will throw an `UnsupportedOperationException`.

That finishes our tour of the main Blueprint managers. We have not, as yet, discussed the environment managers, but to do that we need to understand a little bit more about the Blueprint container and its metadata. First, though, let's look at a full example using Blueprint to reinforce our lessons so far and see the various managers in actual use.

12.3.5 *A Blueprint example*

This example can be found in the code samples, and it includes many of the snippets that we've already encountered.

In this example, we'll create two bundles, one exporting a bean as an OSGi service using Blueprint and the other importing this service using Blueprint. First of all, we need a Blueprint service to export. The metadata for this bundle is shown in listing 12.1.

Listing 12.1   Blueprint service metadata

```xml
<?xml version="1.0" encoding="UTF-8"?>
<blueprint xmlns="http://www.osgi.org/xmlns/blueprint/v1.0.0"
        xmlns:xsi="http://www.w3.org/2001/XMLSchema-instance"
        xsi:schemaLocation="http://www.osgi.org/xmlns/blueprint/v1.0.0
    http://www.osgi.org/xmlns/blueprint/v1.0.0/blueprint.xsd">

  <bean id="testService"
        class="com.manning.sdmia.springdm.service.impl.TestServiceImpl"/>

  <service ref="testService"
                auto-export="class-hierarchy">
    <service-properties>
        <entry key="service-id" value="theRealOne"/>
    </service-properties>
  </service>
</blueprint>
```

These metadata definitions require a definition of `TestService` and `TestServiceImpl`, and these are the same classes that we encountered in chapter 5.

Next, we need a reference to this service, which is shown in listing 12.2.

Listing 12.2   Blueprint service reference metadata

```xml
<?xml version="1.0" encoding="UTF-8"?>
<blueprint xmlns="http://www.osgi.org/xmlns/blueprint/v1.0.0"
        xmlns:xsi="http://www.w3.org/2001/XMLSchema-instance"
```

```
        xsi:schemaLocation="http://www.osgi.org/xmlns/blueprint/v1.0.0
    http://www.osgi.org/xmlns/blueprint/v1.0.0/blueprint.xsd">

  <bean id="testBean" class="com.manning.sdmia.springdm.SimpleTestBean"
            init-method="test">
    <property name="testService" ref="testService"/>
    <property name="testString" value="Hello World!"/>
  </bean>
  <reference id="testService" filter="(service-id=theRealOne)"
            interface="com.manning.sdmia.springdm.service.TestService"/>
</blueprint>
```

If we package each of these Blueprint XML documents in a bundle, putting the XML file in OSGI-INF/blueprint, we're done as far as the definitions go. Note that we don't need to provide a particularly special manifest file because the defaults are perfectly acceptable and there are no Blueprint packages that we need to import by default. We do need to import and export the `TestService` interface appropriately, but a tool like the Felix Bundle Plugin for Maven 2 will do this for us automatically.

The bundle set that we need to run the example is the same as for any regular Spring DM 2.0 application because Spring DM 2.0 is the RI for Blueprint, and Blueprint support is enabled by default.

We can start up Equinox and get the obligatory `"Hello World!"` message. There is no need to configure anything special for Blueprint—Spring DM automatically recognizes Blueprint bundles and starts them appropriately.

Now that we have a working Blueprint example, we can delve deeper into the structure of the Blueprint container, its associated metadata, and the mysterious environment managers.

12.3.6 The Blueprint container and its metadata

In order to understand the final managers that Blueprint defines—the environment managers—we first need to talk a little bit about the runtime model and Java interfaces supported by Blueprint.

We already mentioned that Blueprint managers manage component instances and are configured through component metadata. For example, a service reference manager (`bp:reference`) creates service references (the actual object that your application interacts with) configured through service reference metadata (such as the configured interface). The relationship between these elements is shown in figure 12.1.

Each of these elements also has a Java representation, so that it's possible to interrogate the managers, components, and associated metadata through Java. The entry

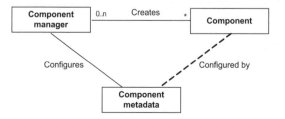

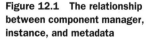

Figure 12.1 The relationship between component manager, instance, and metadata

point for this representation is the BlueprintContainer, which represents the configured state of the Blueprint container for a bundle. If you think of this as equivalent to Spring's ApplicationContext, you won't go far wrong.

The BlueprintContainer provides methods for getting both component instances and component metadata. Instances are returned as type Object and metadata as type ComponentMetadata with specific metadata elements represented as subtypes of this. For example, the configuration of a service reference is represented by ServiceReferenceMetadata. You can think of ComponentMetadata as being a little like Spring's BeanDefinition.

The definitions of BlueprintContainer and ComponentMetadata are shown in listing 12.3.

Listing 12.3 The BlueprintContainer and ComponentMetadata interfaces

```
package org.osgi.service.blueprint.container;
...
public interface BlueprintContainer {
  Set getComponentIds();
  Object getComponentInstance(String string);
  ComponentMetadata getComponentMetadata(String string);
  Collection getMetadata(Class aClass);
}
...
package org.osgi.service.blueprint.reflect;
...
public interface ComponentMetadata extends NonNullMetadata {
  int ACTIVATION_EAGER = 1;
  int ACTIVATION_LAZY = 2;

  String getId();
  int getActivation();
  List getDependsOn();
}
```

NOTE You don't need to worry about NonNullMetadata. It and its parent. Metadata, are just marker interfaces.

As you can see, the definition of BlueprintContainer is fairly limited and doesn't provide the rich array of abstractions that ApplicationContext has. Note also that this is strictly a read-only interface—you can't manipulate the components or their metadata at runtime.

Figure 12.2 summarizes the different metadata interfaces that are available. For details, you should consult the Blueprint documentation.

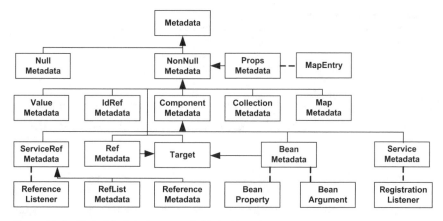

Figure 12.2 Metadata interfaces available in Blueprint

12.3.7 Environment managers

Now that we understand Blueprint components and metadata, we're in a position to delve into the details of environment managers. In the way that Spring DM's "*Aware" interfaces give us access to various Spring DM and OSGi artifacts, such as `Application-tionContext`, `Bundle`, and `BundleContext`, Blueprint environment managers give us access to Blueprint and OSGi artifacts that will be useful in our applications.

We saw that there is a close linkage between Blueprint's XML schema and its Java metadata model—each XML element has an equivalent in Java, usually defined on a subtype of `ComponentMetadata`. But there are some managers that aren't defined in XML at all; they only exist in the world of Java. These managers are predefined and give components access to important runtime artifacts for the bundle.

As you might expect, one of them is the `BlueprintContainer` itself, but the others are `Bundle`, `BundleContext`, and `Converter`. Even though they aren't defined in the XML schema for Blueprint, these artifacts can be referenced from the schema, so, for example, to get hold of the Blueprint container you might put this in your Blueprint context file:

```
<bean id="ex" class="com.manning.sdmia.ch12.EnvironmentExample">
  <property name="blueprint" ref="blueprintContainer"/>
</bean>
```

The name `blueprintContainer` is a special string recognized by the Blueprint container, and all of the environment managers have their own special reference strings. The effect of this snippet is to inject an instance of `BlueprintContainer` into the `blueprint` property of the `ex` bean. It provides the same functionality as Spring's `ApplicationContextAware` without the reliance on a special interface, but also without the magic injection support that it provides.

Table 12.5 summarizes the environment managers available and their corresponding XML keywords.

That completes our discussion of environment managers and our discussion of the static configuration aspects of Blueprint overall. We'll now turn our attention to the

Table 12.5 Blueprint environment managers

Manager class	XML keyword	Notes
`BlueprintContainer`	`blueprintContainer`	Similar to `ApplicationContextAware`
`Bundle`	`blueprintBundle`	No equivalent in Spring DM
`BundleContext`	`blueprintBundleContext`	Equivalent to `BundleContext-Aware` in Spring DM and also the magic bean `bundleContext`
`Converter`	`blueprintConverter`	No equivalent in Spring DM

runtime aspects of Blueprint and to what actually happens when you install a Blueprint-enabled bundle.

12.4 *Runtime support and lifecycle*

So far we've talked about defining Blueprint applications. In this section, we'll explore the runtime aspects of Blueprint, most of which are very similar to those of Spring DM.

Blueprint's runtime behavior is important to understand because it directly influences the runtime behavior of our applications. Blueprint also allows us to augment and introspect this behavior through the use of events and event listeners.

12.4.1 *Blueprint lifecycle*

The lifecycle of a Blueprint bundle is much the same as that of a Spring DM bundle, but with some of the state names changed. We won't regurgitate the entire lifecycle here because it's documented quite clearly in the OSGi compendium specification (section 121.3). Instead we'll discuss the key differences from Spring DM. These differences fall into three categories: lazy initialization, control directives, and events. We'll talk about each in turn.

LAZY INITIALIZATION

Blueprint allows Blueprint applications to be instantiated lazily. What this means is that if all the components in a Blueprint application are marked as having lazy activation, then the application itself is considered lazy. When an application is considered lazy, no initialization will be performed until a service request arrives. Only then will the appropriate components be instantiated with all of the classloading and other housekeeping that this implies. Of course, a little initialization needs to be performed so that declared services are actually registered in the service registry, but little else.

> ### Spring DM and lazy-init
>
> Although Spring DM supports lazy-init for beans, it doesn't support lazy-init for references or, more importantly, services. This means that although a bean can be declared lazy, in practice it will generally be eagerly initialized because the service that references it is always eagerly initialized.

The main reason for providing lazy initialization as a feature is performance. If no initialization is required, Blueprint bundles can be started very quickly indeed, contributing to lower startup times for the OSGi container as a whole.

CONTROL DIRECTIVES

Control of the lifecycle of Blueprint bundles is handled through manifest header entries, just as it is in Spring DM. Table 12.6 summarizes the control directives that are available and their Spring DM equivalents.

Table 12.6   Blueprint lifecycle control directives

`Bundle-SymbolicName` control directive	`Spring-Context` **control directive**	Notes
`blueprint.graceperiod`	`wait-for-dependencies`	Specifies whether or not the grace period is active
`blueprint.timeout`	`timeout`	Sets the timeout for the grace period in milliseconds

These properties would be used in a manifest entry like this:

```
Bundle-SymbolicName: mybundle;
        blueprint.graceperiod:=true; blueprint.timeout:=20000
```

Note that it isn't the `Bundle-Blueprint` that the directive is applied to, but rather the `Bundle-SymbolicName`.

In a similar vein, the service property names used when a Blueprint bundle has been started are subtly different. Spring DM publishes an `ApplicationContext`, whereas Blueprint publishes a `BlueprintContainer`. So, for instance, the service properties shown by Equinox might look like this:

```
    {org.osgi.service.blueprint.container.BlueprintContainer}
    ={Bundle-SymbolicName=com.manning.sdmia.blueprint-service,
    Bundle-Version=1.0.0.SNAPSHOT,
    osgi.blueprint.container.version=1.0.0.SNAPSHOT,
        osgi.blueprint.container.symbolicname=com.manning.sdmia.
    blueprint-service,service.id=31}
```

The service properties for these are shown in table 12.7.

Table 12.7   Blueprint container service properties

BlueprintContainer service property	ApplicationContext service property	Notes
`osgi.blueprint.container.` `symbolicname`	`org.springframework.context.` `service.name` and `Bundle-SymbolicName`	Although named differently, the same data is used
`osgi.blueprint.container.` `version`	`Bundle-Version`	Although named differently, the same data is used

Now that we've looked at how we can control the behavior of Blueprint bundles and access Blueprint-specific metadata, let's look at Blueprint's support for events.

LIFECYCLE EVENTS

Just as in Spring DM, components can register special listener services that the container will deliver Blueprint events to. In Spring DM, this is the `OsgiBundleApplicationContextListener`, which we looked at in section 4.1.5 in chapter 4. In Blueprint, components must register a service of type `BlueprintListener`. Let's take a look at the definition of this, together with the definition of `BlueprintEvent`, as shown in listing 12.4.

Listing 12.4   The `BlueprintListener` and `BlueprintEvent` classes

```
package org.osgi.service.blueprint.container;

public interface BlueprintListener {
  void blueprintEvent(BlueprintEvent blueprintEvent);
}

public class BlueprintEvent {
  public static final int CREATING = 1;
  public static final int CREATED = 2;
  public static final int DESTROYING = 3;
  public static final int DESTROYED = 4;
  public static final int FAILURE = 5;
  public static final int GRACE_PERIOD = 6;
  public static final int WAITING = 7;
  (...)
  public int getType();
  public long getTimestamp();
  public org.osgi.framework.Bundle getBundle();
  public org.osgi.framework.Bundle getExtenderBundle();
  public java.lang.String[] getDependencies() ;
  public java.lang.Throwable getCause();
  public boolean isReplay();
 }
```

Simple, yes, but this is one of the few instances where Blueprint goes a bit further than Spring DM and delivers some really useful functionality. First off, we can see that Blueprint events provide access to all of the states applicable to a Blueprint bundle and its container. `CREATING`, `CREATED`, `DESTROYING`, `DESTROYED`, `FAILURE`—these are all familiar concepts, but `GRACE_PERIOD` and `WAITING` are new. Let's look at how the OSGi 4.2 compendium specification defines these, because their behavior is a little subtle.

First off `GRACE_PERIOD`:

> The Blueprint Container has entered the grace period. The list of missing dependencies must be made available through the `getDependencies()` method. During the grace period, a `GRACE_PERIOD` event is sent each time the set of unsatisfied dependencies changes.

`GRACE_PERIOD` isn't so much a single state as a state that the container constantly re-enters as the set of unsatisfied dependencies changes. Clearly, one of the most useful things that can be accomplished with this functionality is the logging of unsatisfied dependencies.

Next, `WAITING`:

> The Blueprint Container is waiting on the availability of a service to satisfy an invocation on a referenced service. The missing dependency must be made available through the `getDependencies()` method which will return an array containing one filter object as a String.

This is the runtime equivalent of `GRACE_PERIOD`. The assumption is that all mandatory dependencies have already been satisfied and the container started, but at some later time one of the mandatory dependencies disappeared, so the container needs to be suspended. Originally it was proposed that the Blueprint container be shut down when this happens; fortunately sanity prevailed and the result was the `WAITING` state.

Spring DM and mandatory services

Spring DM has a similar state to `WAITING`. When a mandatory reference becomes unsatisfied, it will unregister all service beans declared by the `ApplicationContext` until such time as the reference is once again satisfied. However, Spring DM 1.2 doesn't post events while waiting for a dependency to be satisfied.

Finally, we need to mention the curious `isReplay()` function. What is this all about? Well, this is to support synchronous registration of `BlueprintListeners`. When a listener is registered, the Blueprint container will deliver the last known event for each Blueprint-managed bundle to the listener. Thus, new listeners can be assured of knowing the current state of the running system, even if they weren't present when the original lifecycle events were delivered. Of course, the last known event is essentially synthetic—the state transition that would have caused it is some way in the past—so these events are known as replay events.

EVENT ADMIN MAPPING

As we've seen, Blueprint has its own eventing infrastructure just like Spring DM. However, the OSGi-aware among you will realize that OSGi actually has its own eventing infrastructure already defined as a compendium service—`EventAdmin`. So where does `EventAdmin` fit into all of this? Well, Blueprint defines a mapping between Blueprint events and `EventAdmin` events, and if an implementation of `EventAdmin` is available in the OSGi container, Blueprint will signal events using that as well as its own infrastructure.

We discussed the OSGi `EventAdmin` service in section 11.3 of chapter 11. The `EventAdmin` topic used for Blueprint's events signaled on `EventAdmin` is org/osgi/service/blueprint/container/<event-name>, where <event-name> would be `GRACE_PERIOD` or one of the other Blueprint event names. All of the other Blueprint event information is then available as properties of the `EventAdmin` event.

The only material difference between the `EventAdmin` mechanism and Blueprint eventing is that `EventAdmin` doesn't support replay events—events are simply delivered at the time they're signaled. For further details, consult the Blueprint specification, section 121.12.1. In general, you'll want to use Blueprint's native eventing mechanism because it's faster, doesn't require `EventAdmin`, and is easier to understand.

That's enough about the Blueprint lifecycle. Let's now look at another runtime aspect of Blueprint—type conversion. Type conversion is important when you want to make the source and target of dependency injection be compatible and Blueprint's built-in conversion isn't sufficient for your needs.

12.4.2 *Type converters*

We've already mentioned in table 12.1 that type converters can be registered in Blueprint bundle configuration files, but what exactly do these components do, and how would you use them?

Spring applies certain rules for converting a source argument for dependency injection to a target type. The target type is dictated by the signature of the property mutator being used. For example, let's say we're given this class:

```
public class InjectionConversionExample {
  void setMyProp(Foobrilator foo)
};
```

And we have this XML configuration snippet:

```
<bean id="myfoo"
    class="com.manning.sdmia.chapter12.InjectionConversionExample">
  <property name="myProp" value="fooble"/>
</bean>
```

Spring must find a way of converting the string `"fooble"` (in the XML snippet) to an instance of a `Foobrilator` (for the class). It does this through a combination of built-in rules and looking for property editors for `Foobrilators`. For details, consult the Spring reference manual.

Blueprint is no different. Given the same declarations, Blueprint must find a way to convert from a String to a `Foobrilator` or die trying! Blueprint has some built-in rules for facilitating this conversion, which we summarize in table 12.8.

Table 12.8 Blueprint built-in conversion strategies

Source type	Target type	Description
Primitives	Wrapper type	Converts to wrapper types
String	Boolean	Converts to `Boolean`, also accepts yes/no, on/off
String	Character	Converts string of length 1 to `Character`
String	Locale	Converts locale name to `Locale`
String	Pattern	Creates pattern with `Pattern.compile()`

Table 12.8 Blueprint built-in conversion strategies *(continued)*

Source type	Target type	Description
String	Properties	Calls `Properties.load()` using the string as input
String	Enum	Converts to Enum using `Enum.valueOf()`
String	Class	Loads class using `Bundle.loadClass()`
String	<any>	Creates instance with `String` constructor if any

In our example, we'd hope that `Foobrilator` has a `String` constructor, because Blueprint would use that without any further need for conversion. However, if built-in conversion fails, Blueprint looks to the registered type converters to perform the conversion.

The definition of `Converter` is shown in listing 12.5.

Listing 12.5 Blueprint's `Converter` interface

```
package org.osgi.service.blueprint.container;

public interface Converter {
  boolean canConvert(Object object, ReifiedType reifiedType);
  Object convert(Object object, ReifiedType reifiedType)
        throws Exception;
}

public class ReifiedType {
  public Class getRawClass();
  public ReifiedType getActualTypeArgument(int i);
  public int size();
}
```

As you can see, a `Converter` specifies two functions: `canConvert()` to determine whether a type can be converted, and `convert()` to convert a type. If we were to write a converter for our `Foobrilator`, it might look something like listing 12.6.

Listing 12.6 A converter for a `Foobrilator`

```
public class FoobrilatorConverter implements Converter {
  public boolean canConvert(Object object, ReifiedType reifiedType) {
    return (reifiedType.getRawClass() == Foobrilator.class)
          && (object instanceof Foobumble);
  }
  public Object convert(Object object, ReifiedType reifiedType)
        throws Exception
  {
    return ((Foobumble)object).getTheFoobrilator();
  }
}
```

As we mentioned in table 12.5, Blueprint provides an environment manager called `blueprintConverter` that gives access to the built-in Blueprint `Converter`, and this can be used as a constructor argument to custom converters wishing to leverage Blueprint's built-in support.

Enough of type converters—we're done! You'll be pleased to know that we've now covered all the major differences between Blueprint and Spring DM. You should now be as proficient in Blueprint as you are already with Spring DM, and we think you'll agree that the two aren't so very different. If you understand Spring DM, then understanding Blueprint is straightforward.

Before we finish, however, we need to discuss what you may already be thinking— "I am using Spring DM now—how do I transition to Blueprint?" The answer, as we'll see, is very simple.

12.5   *Using Spring DM with Blueprint*

As we've already seen, Spring DM 2.0 supports Blueprint out of the box because it's also the RI for the Blueprint specification. But Spring DM 2.0 doesn't stop supporting the Spring DM mechanisms when it supports Blueprint, and this gives us some interesting possibilities.

Spring DM and Blueprint export and import services and classes using standard OSGi mechanisms. As far as anyone is concerned, the other end of a service reference could just as easily be defined using regular OSGi APIs as Spring DM or Blueprint. There is no reason why an application can't have both Blueprint and Spring DM bundles in the same container. The Spring DM 2.0 extenders support both, and they can interact easily because the only touchpoints are the OSGi service registry. This gives us a very useful way of transitioning existing applications from Spring DM to Blueprint— they can be migrated over time, a bundle at a time.

This means you can run both Blueprint and Spring DM bundles together at the same time. Spring DM 2.0 will start both extenders—one to manage Blueprint bundles and one to manage Spring DM bundles. Because the only interaction between bundles is through regular OSGi mechanisms—classes and services—each bundle will be blissfully unaware of the other types of bundles that it's interacting with. If an implementation should change, it won't affect the overall operation of the application as long as the class and service interaction points are maintained.

12.6   *Summary*

In this chapter we've discussed the Blueprint specification, the OSGi standard for Spring DM, and the OSGi component model that you may well be required to use in the near future. You should by now have realized that Blueprint is a lot like Spring DM without the bells and whistles. You can generally do in Blueprint most things that you can do in Spring DM—even the names are the same or similar!

The good news is that you can pick and choose which technology you want to use because Spring DM 2.0 supports both Blueprint and the Spring DM programming model. Spring DM 2.0 is the reference implementation for Blueprint, so you can be assured that it's 100 percent Blueprint-compliant.

Although Blueprint might seem like a slightly inferior technology to Spring DM, its use will become more important as server containers begin to support Blueprint without supporting Spring DM. For instance, IBM is working on a Blueprint implementation under the Apache Aries project, and it seems a pretty safe bet that their community edition application server will support Blueprint at some point in the future. Other containers already based on Spring DM, such as Oracle's CEP product and SpringSource's dm Server, will almost certainly support Blueprint as they move to the Spring DM 2.0 codebase.

Blueprint is here to stay. As a Spring DM expert, you should find its use straightforward, and by using it you'll be ensuring application portability for the future.

appendix A
Spring DM
development with Eclipse

Eclipse is a free integrated development environment (IDE). It's written in Java and was intended primarily for developing Java applications. The Eclipse platform is also extensible because it provides an advanced plug-in framework. The range of provided plug-ins is quite large, with plug-ins being available for many languages including C, C++, COBOL, Python, Perl, and PHP.

Eclipse is particularly suitable for OSGi development because it is based internally on this technology. The Eclipse IDE is built on Equinox, an OSGi 4 implementation that extends the specification with various extension points. Developing Eclipse plug-ins corresponds to creating extended OSGi components. Because Eclipse allows you to develop OSGi applications, implementing Spring DM applications is also possible.

A.1 Installing and configuring Eclipse for Spring DM

Using Eclipse to develop OSGi and Spring DM applications requires some setup to enable the plug-in development environment and provide Spring DM components access to the embedded OSGi environment. You need to install the plug-ins required for OSGi and Spring DM development and configure the OSGi environment.

A.1.1 Installing Eclipse

The Eclipse website offers a set of Eclipse distributions, each serving particular needs. All you need, in order to enable OSGi and Spring DM development in Eclipse, are Eclipse itself, the Java Development Tools (JDT), and the Plug-in Development Environment (PDE). We recommend that you use Eclipse Classic 3.5.2, which corresponds to the Galileo version of Eclipse. It can be found at http://www.eclipse.org/downloads/. Having retrieved the distribution, you simply have to decompress it.

In order to launch Eclipse, execute the eclipse.exe file under Windows or the eclipse file under Linux. In order to run Eclipse, you need to have the JDK installed on your computer.

> **NOTE** If you choose to install either the Eclipse IDE for Java Developers or Eclipse IDE for Java EE Developers distribution, instead of the Eclipse Classic distribution, the PDE isn't included. You'll need to install this tool separately by going to http://download.eclipse.org/eclipse/downloads/, selecting the desired version, and then downloading the archive from the PDE SDK section in the menu on the left. Having done this, unzip the file into your Eclipse installation directory and restart the IDE.

An additional plug-in called Spring IDE can also be installed because it provides useful facilities for developing Spring DM applications in Eclipse.

A.1.2   *Installing Spring IDE for Spring DM*

The Spring portfolio contains an interesting project that supports the development of Spring applications in the Eclipse IDE: Spring IDE. Spring IDE provides tooling that makes Spring development easier, especially the detection of errors in Spring XML and AOP configurations, thanks to its deep integration with Eclipse features.

You'll notice that version 2.0 of the SpringSource Tool Suite, now freely available, provides additional tools for OSGi development and can be used to analyze bundles and visualize their dependencies based on import and export package headers and service production and consumption. New versions of Spring IDE are now integrated into this tool.

INSTALLING SPRING IDE

You can install Spring IDE by using the update manager feature of Eclipse. To do so, select the Install New Software entry in the Help menu. You'll need to specify an update site, which must be http://dist.springsource.com/release/TOOLS/update/e3.5. This site contains all the Eclipse plug-ins for the latest stable version of Spring IDE. Figure A.1 shows the configuration window of the Eclipse update manager.

> ### Spring IDE and AOP
>
> If you want to use the visualizer features of Spring IDE, you need to install the Spring IDE/AspectJ Development Tools (AJDT) integration. This feature allows you to graphically see the impact of aspects on classes.
>
> You'll also need to install AJDT, whose update site is at http://download.eclipse.org/tools/ajdt/35/update.

When the update site is configured, Eclipse automatically inspects its contents and shows all the available modules. These are listed in table A.1.

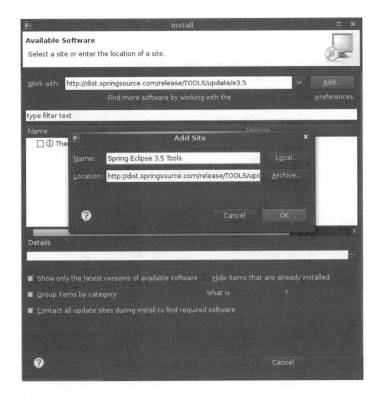

Figure A.1 Configuring the Spring IDE update site using Eclipse's update manager

Table A.1 Features of Spring IDE relevant to Spring DM

Feature	Description
Spring IDE core	Contains core features of Spring IDE for creating and editing Spring XML files, providing development tooling.
Spring IDE AOP extension	Contains extension features for checking AOP configuration and displaying the impact on classes.
Spring IDE OSGi extension	Contains extension features for OSGi and Spring DM. These provide support for the related XML namespaces.
Spring IDE AJDT integration	Contains integration with AJDT so that the Visualizer view can be used.

Figure A.2 shows the list of available modules from Spring IDE and the ones required in order to use Spring IDE to develop Spring DM bundles.

Once you've selected all the components, you can click the Next button and be guided by the Eclipse wizard. In the last step, the wizard asks you to confirm the installation of the previously selected extensions.

Once you restart Eclipse, you'll be able to use Spring IDE within your Eclipse IDE.

Figure A.2   Required
components of Spring
IDE in order to enable
its Spring DM support

SPRING DM SUPPORT FOR SPRING IDE

Spring IDE provides various levels of support for Spring DM. Support for the Spring DM namespaces is the central one of these levels. This support is useful both for creating namespaces and for detecting errors when developing Spring applications using these namespaces.

The following features of Spring IDE are dedicated to Spring DM:

- *Predefined target platforms*—Spring IDE registers predefined target platforms provisioned with the necessary bundles for Spring DM. These target platforms are accessible in the template list when adding a new target platform.
- *Creation of XML configuration files for Spring DM*—Spring IDE allows XML configuration files to be created and preconfigured with the requisite XML namespaces for Spring DM. This feature is natively present in Spring IDE, and Spring DM namespaces have simply been added to the list of available namespaces.
- *Support for Spring DM XML namespaces*—Spring IDE supports the XML namespaces of Spring DM at the structural level. Spring IDE will help you when adding tags and attributes for these namespaces. It also gives support for filling fields like `interface` and `ref` attributes when registering or referencing services, and checks whether the values are correct.

Let's now focus on how to configure Eclipse for developing Spring DM applications.

A.1.3   *Configuring the target platform*

The target platform corresponds to the set of OSGi components used for development and any OSGi components defined as projects within the workspace. Eclipse PDE uses these components for compilation and checks if imports can be resolved.

The target platform is based on a directory containing these components. By default, this is the plugins directory under the Eclipse installation directory, which contains all plug-ins associated with Eclipse. This is definitely much more than we need! We need to create a target platform containing only the relevant plug-ins.

Two approaches can be used to configure the target platform. The first consists in using the facilities provided by Eclipse PDE to specify all the components you need. Alternatively Spring IDE provides preconfigured target platforms for Spring DM. In the following subsections, we'll describe how to use these two approaches.

CONFIGURATION WITHOUT SPRING IDE SUPPORT

The first approach consists of creating an empty target platform and configuring it. To do this, we need to create a dedicated directory for gathering the necessary components, and it must contain the components required by Spring DM and their related dependencies. Best practice is to create this directory in the current workspace in a project called "target-platform". We then need to copy all the JAR files required by components into this directory. The bundles that need to be added for simple use are described in section 3.2.2 of chapter 3; for web use, see section 3.2.3.

Figure A.3 shows a simple Eclipse project containing bundles for provisioning the target platform of the current workspace.

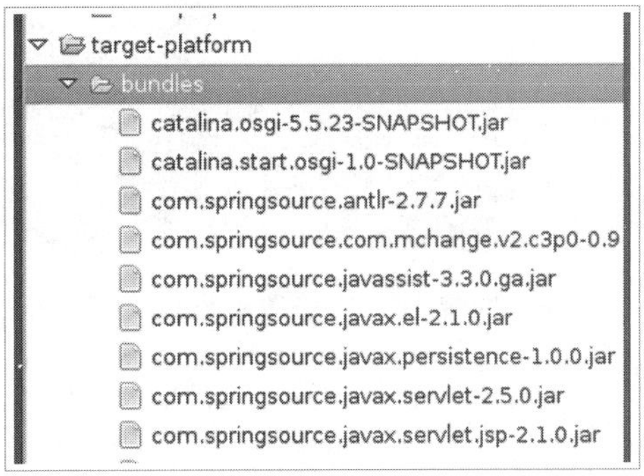

Now that we've created the directory and filled it with the required components, we need to tell Eclipse to use this directory as a target directory for the current workspace. This can be done by selecting the Windows > Preferences menu option and then selecting Plug-in Development > Target Platform in the navigation tree.

Figure A.3   A dedicated project used to provision the target platform

With the latest version of Eclipse, several target platform definitions can be specified and configured, but only one can be active—the one used for the current workspace. The default definition corresponding to the configuration for the running Eclipse is shown in figure A.4. This definition is activated by default.

A new target platform definition must be added using the Add button to use only the components that are necessary, and not include all of Eclipse itself. This target platform will use the bundles present in the previous target-platform project in the workspace.

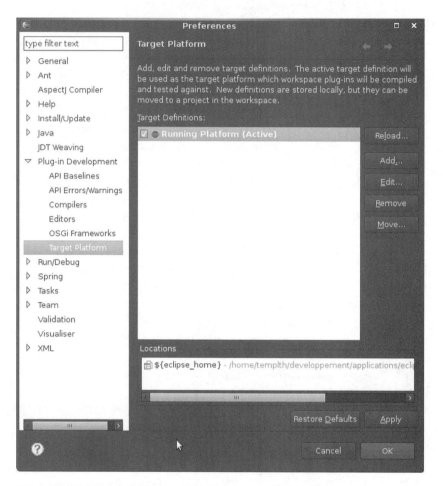

Figure A.4   The Target Platform configuration screen within Eclipse preferences

In the first screen of the Add wizard, select the option, Nothing: Start with an Empty Target Definition (see figure A.5) and click the Next button.

In the next screen, configure the target platform content (Figure A.6).

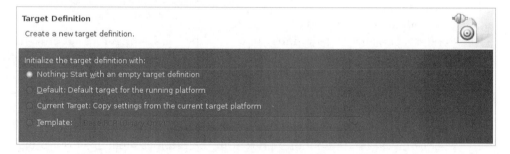

Figure A.5   Selecting an initialization approach for the target platform definition

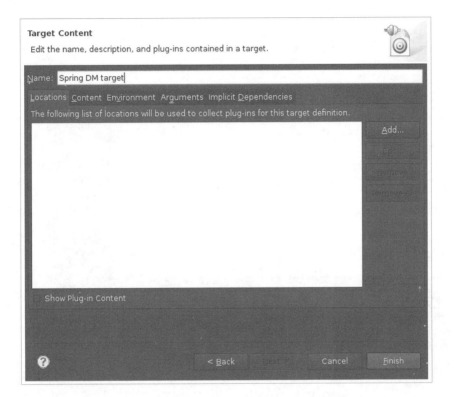

Figure A.6   Screen for configuring the content of the target platform

As you can see in figure A.6, no source is present. You need to add one by clicking the Add button. Several source types are available. For this example, choose the Directory type (see figure A.7), which allows you to select a directory from the filesystem (figure A.8). Only absolute filenames are allowed here.

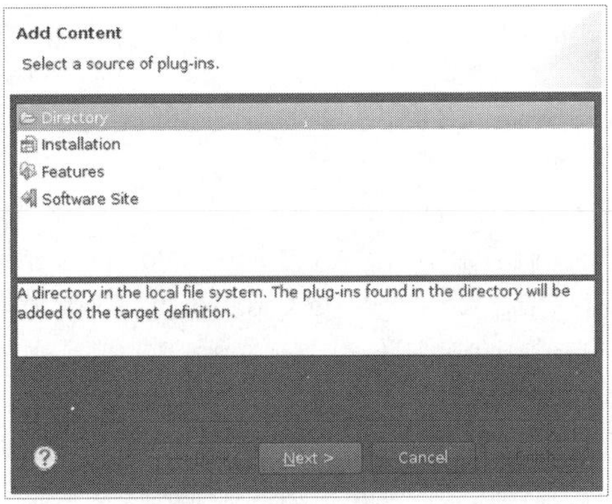

Figure A.7   Selecting the directory source kind

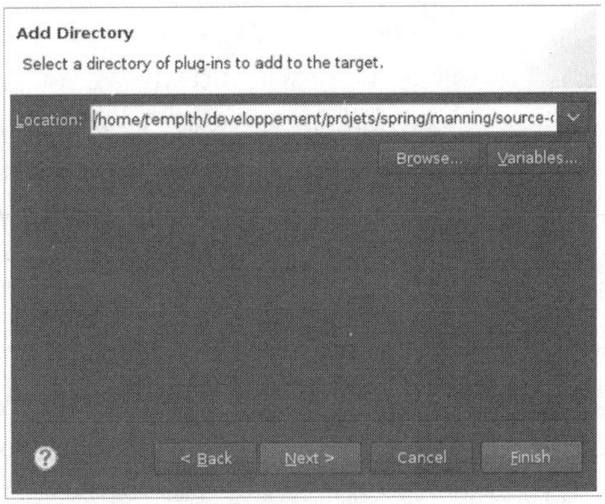

Figure A.8   Selecting the directory containing bundles for the target platform

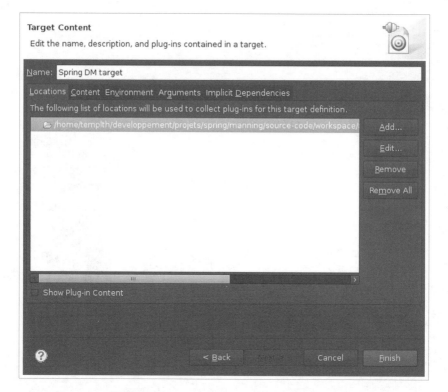

Figure A.9 The target platform content, including the configured directory source

The source should now appear in the list of target platform content (figure A.9).

You can now click the Finish button to end the configuration of the target platform. Your platform will now appear in the list of available target platforms.

The only remaining thing to do is to activate the target platform so you can use it in the current workspace. To do this, select the target platform from the list and check its check box. Then click the Apply button. The platform is now used for the workspace, as shown in figure A.10.

Now let's take a look at the support Spring IDE provides to make it easier to configure the target platform for developments using Spring DM.

USING SPRING IDE SUPPORT FOR THE TARGET PLATFORM

Spring IDE provides preconfigured target platforms for Spring DM. This means that Spring IDE automatically creates a directory for the target platform containing all the bundles required by a specific version of Spring DM.

With the Spring IDE's support for Spring DM, when creating the target platform, we need to select an appropriate template from the Template list in the Target Definition screen, as shown in figure A.11.

When we select a target platform template, Spring IDE automatically provides an installation source pointing to a directory containing all the bundles needed for

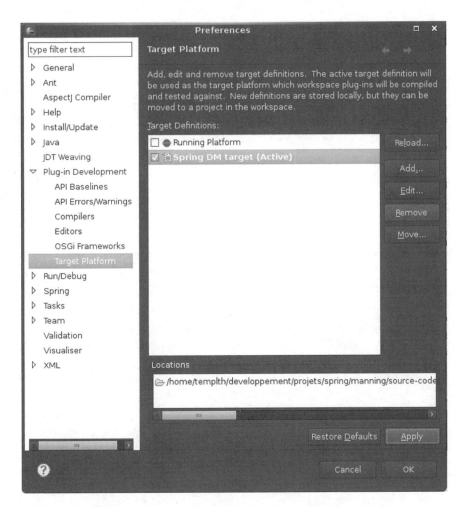

Figure A.10   The target platform for Spring DM activated for the current workspace

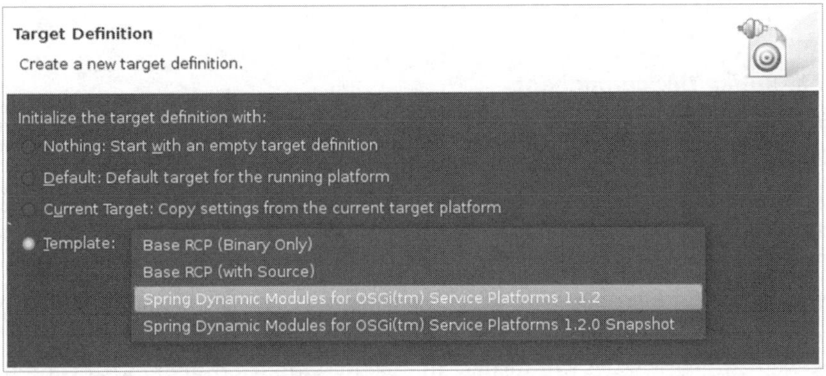

Figure A.11   Selecting a predefined target platform from Spring IDE for Spring DM

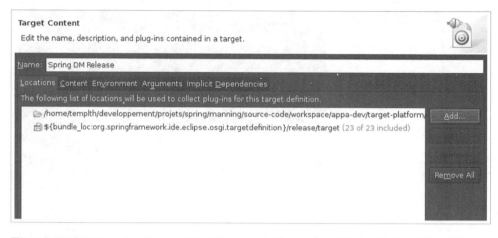

Figure A.12   Target content for a target platform created from a template provided by Spring IDE

Spring DM development. We can easily add other directories to specify additional bundles according to our needs. As we saw previously, the Add button in the Target Content screen can be used to add installation sources based on a directory.

Figure A.12 shows the target content for a target platform created from a template, where an additional source directory has been added.

You'll notice that all the steps we described in the previous subsection are the same here.

You've now seen how to install and configure the tools in Eclipse that simplify Spring DM development. Let's look at how we can use these tools to efficiently develop OSGi applications with Spring DM.

A.2   *Developing OSGi components*

Now that we have a functional environment in Eclipse for developing OSGi and Spring DM applications, it's time to implement bundles to be used by an application. We'll tackle the three classic kinds of bundles: simple Spring DM components, OSGi fragments, and Spring DM web components.

A.2.1   *Simple Spring DM components*

Let's look at how to develop an OSGi component with a Spring DM powered bundle whose development is entirely managed by the framework. As we described in chapter 1, this kind of bundle is a regular OSGi component containing additional Spring artifacts and specific headers in its manifest file.

In Eclipse, the first step consists of creating a plug-in project using the IDE. From the menus, select File > New > Other, or right-click on the project in an exploration view, such as the navigator view, and select New > Other.

A New Project wizard will display the list of supported elements ordered by category. The items that interest us are located in the Plug-in Development category. For a

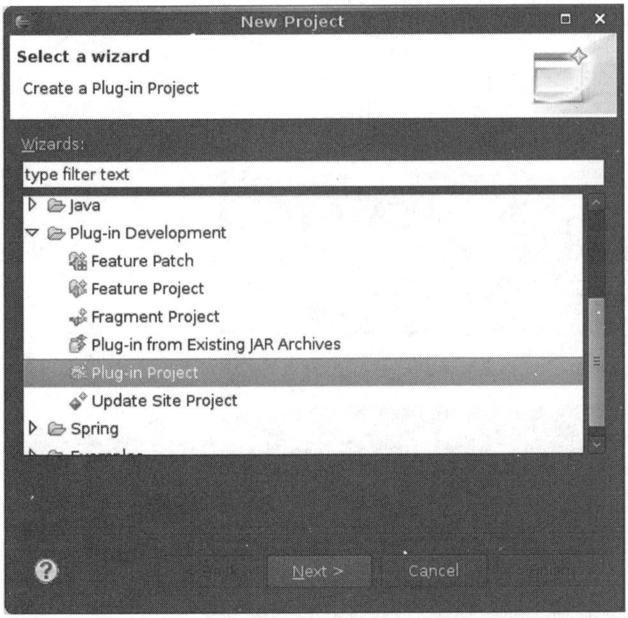

Figure A.13   A list of supported elements for artifact creation

simple Spring DM-powered bundle, select the Plug-in Project entry, as shown in figure A.13. Then click the Next button.

The next wizard screen allows you to configure information related to the project itself (name, source, and output folders) just as you would with a Java project—a plug-in project is first and foremost a Java project.

Other information you need to provide is related to OSGi itself. Here you can specify the link to the target container. You're developing an OSGi component without any Equinox- or Eclipse-specific features, so for the Target Platform select An OSGi Framework and choose Standard from the "drop-down list, as shown in figure A.14. Then click Next.

The Content wizard screen is displayed next, allowing you to specify general information for the manifest configuration, such as ID, Version, and Name. Because Spring DM doesn't use activators but is based on the extender pattern, you need to uncheck the Generate an Activator check box. Figure A.15 shows this screen with the specified configuration. Then click Finish to create the project.

Before starting development, you must remember to activate Spring IDE support for the project. Do this by right-clicking on the project and selecting Spring Tools > Add Spring Project Nature, as shown in figure A.16.

The newly created project is a regular Java project with OSGi support and it contains a MANIFEST.MF file within a META-INF directory. You can then create a spring directory inside this for Spring configuration XML files using Spring IDE features.

Spring IDE allows you to create a Spring DM XML file using a wizard that's accessed from the New > Others > Spring > Spring Bean Configuration File menu option. Hav-

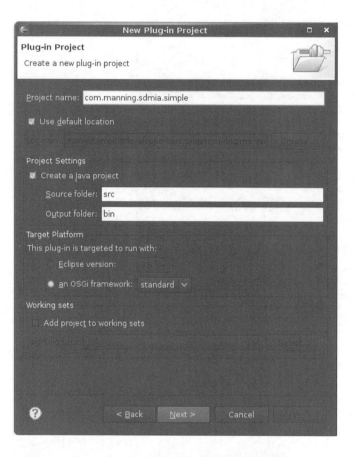

Figure A.14   Specifying information for the plug-in project

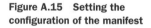

Figure A.15   Setting the configuration of the manifest

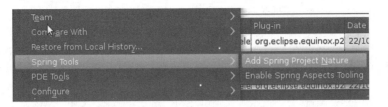

**Figure A.16
Activating Spring
IDE support using
the project's
context menu**

ing specified the file location in the first screen of the wizard, you will be asked for the XML namespaces to include, as shown in figure A.17.

For a simple Spring-powered bundle, you need to select the `osgi` namespace for the file containing OSGi configuration (commonly named osgi-context.xml). This approach generates an XML file with the contents shown in listing A.1.

Listing A.1   Content generated by the Spring DM configuration file wizard

```
<?xml version="1.0" encoding="UTF-8"?>
<beans xmlns="http://www.springframework.org/schema/beans"
    xmlns:xsi="http://www.w3.org/2001/XMLSchema-instance"
    xmlns:osgi="http://www.springframework.org/
        schema/osgi"
    xsi:schemaLocation="http://www.springframework.org/schema/beans
            http://www.springframework.org/schema/beans/spring-beans.xsd
```

**Configuring
osgi XML
namespace**

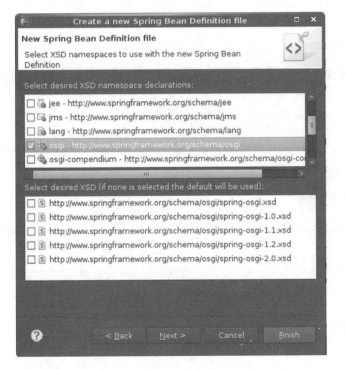

**Figure A.17   Selecting the
`osgi` namespace for Spring
DM configuration**

```
http://www.springframework.org/schema/osgi
    http://www.springframework.org/schema/osgi/spring-osgi.xsd">

</beans>
```

Configuring XSD file for
osgi XML namespace

You can then add Spring DM elements to the XML file, such as reference and service definitions, using Spring IDE's code-completion for the osgi XML grammar. Code-completion applies on the osgi XML grammar at different levels:

- Creates XML elements of the osgi XML namespace, as shown in figure A.18.

Figure A.18   Creating elements of the osgi namespace

- References bean identifiers from attributes of osgi namespace elements, as shown in figure A.19. This is supported natively by Spring IDE for all supported Spring namespaces.

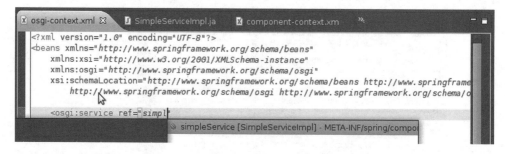

Figure A.19   Referencing beans by identifier from the osgi XML namespace

- Selects type attributes in osgi namespace elements, such as the interface attribute shown in figure A.20. Types are found in the bundle classpath and are dependent on the manifest configuration.

Figure A.20 Selecting types from the `osgi` XML namespace

Spring IDE and configuration set

By default, Spring IDE provides code-completion to find bean identifiers within a given Spring XML configuration file but not between files. With Spring DM, we typically have several files because best practice consists of separating OSGi-independent configuration from OSGi configuration.

To enable code-completion between files, a configuration set needs to be set up for the project, specifying configuration files that should be linked together. This can be done in the project configuration: in the Spring category, select the Beans Support entry and then the Config Sets tab.

We won't describe component development any further because this has been tackled throughout the book.

A.2.2   OSGi fragments

Although fragments aren't specific to Spring DM, they're very important to Spring DM because they allow system bundles to be configured, such as Spring DM extenders and trace bundles. Eclipse PDE provides a wizard to make the creation of fragments easy.

To access this wizard in Eclipse, select New > Others > Plug-in Development > Fragment project. This wizard is similar to the one for a regular bundle, the only difference being in the selection of the fragment host, as shown in figure A.21. A Browse button allows you to select this bundle from ones present in the target platform.

Once the bundle is created, you can use all the techniques we described previously to implement its functionality. Let's now look at the last kind of bundle that is usually involved in Spring DM development—the web bundle.

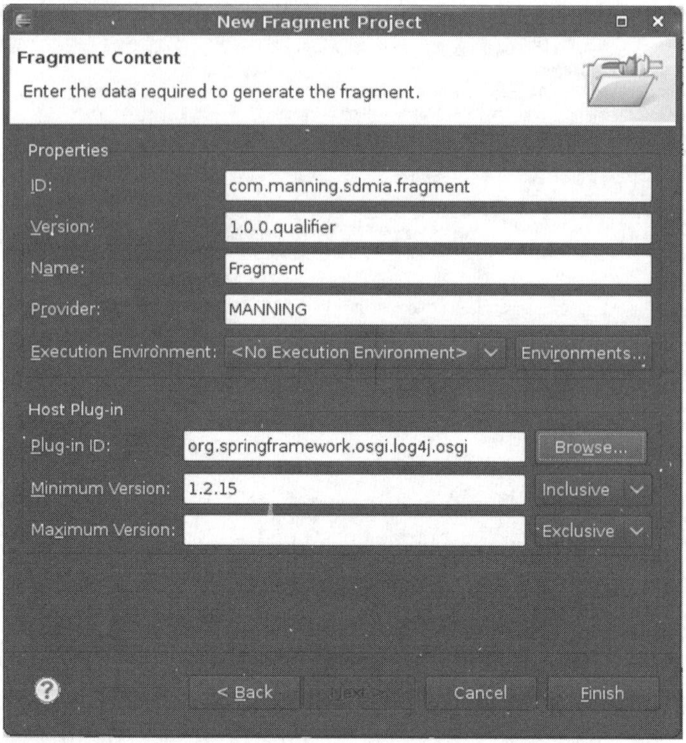

Figure A.21   Selecting a fragment host in the New Fragment Project wizard

A.2.3   *Spring DM web components*

The last Spring DM component type is the web component. In Eclipse, the same wizard used for creating a simple plug-in project should be used to create web components. The main difference is that a WEB-INF directory must be created in the project root, and classes for the bundle must be located in the WEB-INF/classes directory.

This is configured in OSGi using the `Bundle-ClassPath` header in the manifest file. The default output folder for the project must be changed to the WEB-INF/classes directory because by default it uses the bin directory. To change the directory, we need to select the Java Build Path in the properties of the project, click on the Source tab, and edit the Default Output Folder, as shown in figure A.22.

You've now seen how to develop different kinds of bundles for Spring DM applications and how PDE and Spring IDE help us in this task. It's now time to run our Spring DM applications in Eclipse IDE using the Equinox container.

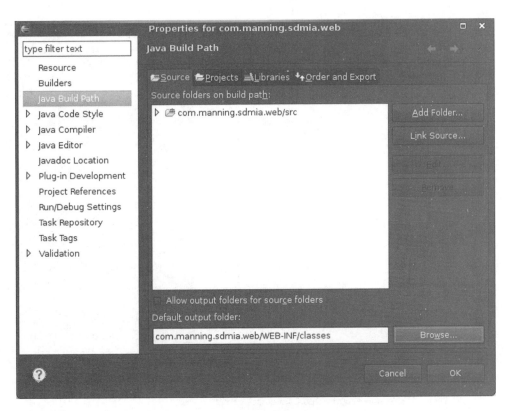

Figure A.22   Configuring the output folder for a Spring DM web bundle

A.3   *Executing in the Equinox container*

Once our bundles are created, configured, and developed, we need to execute them within Eclipse.

A.3.1   *Creating and configuring the Equinox container*

The first step toward executing Spring DM components in Eclipse consists of configuring the execution environment for an Equinox application. Eclipse provides a generic execution environment for different kinds of applications.

You can open configuration window by selecting the Run > Run Configurations menu option or by selecting the same option from the Run icon in the Eclipse toolbar, as shown in figure A.23.

In the Run Configurations window, Eclipse displays a tree on the left with all the supported kinds of applications. For this example, use the OSGi framework. You can add a new application by selecting Add from the context menu, as shown in figure A.24. This creates a new application with the default configuration.

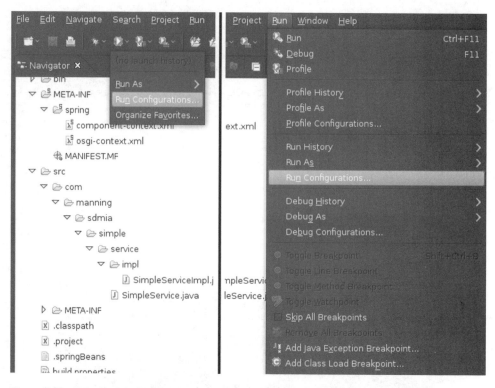

Figure A.23 Selecting the Run Configurations option

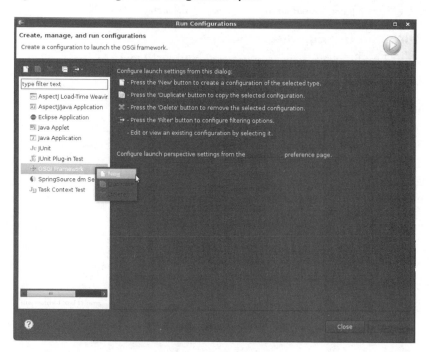

Figure A.24 Adding a new OSGi application within Eclipse

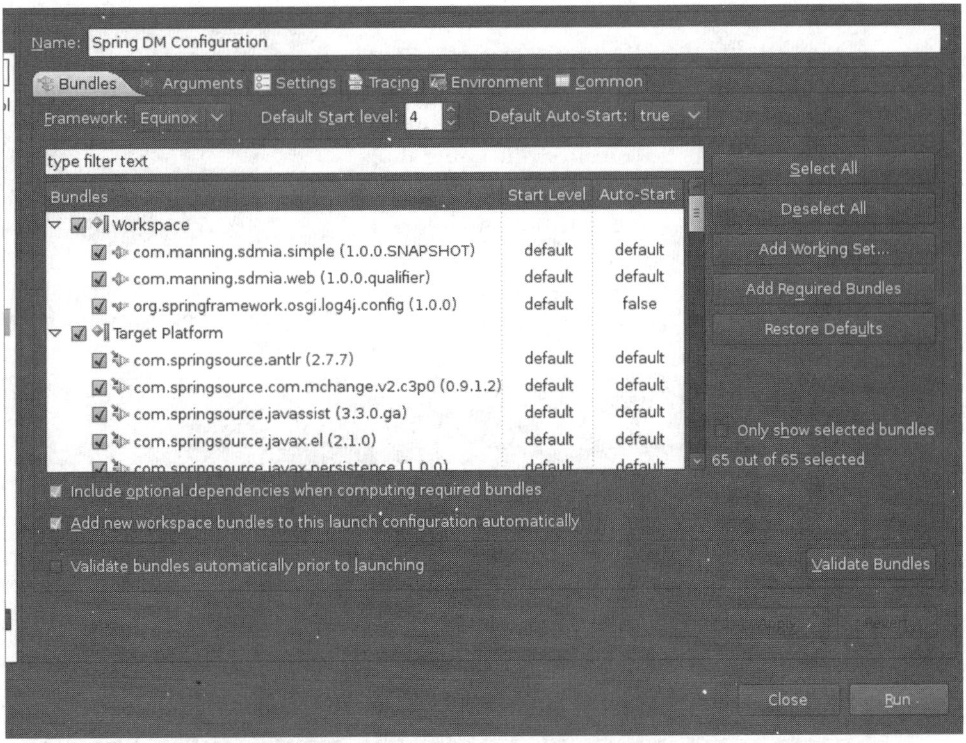

Figure A.25 Configuring the OSGi application with our Spring DM bundles

You can now change the name of the OSGi framework configuration, to "Spring DM Configuration", for example, in the Name field at the top of the panel (see figure A.25). The Equinox container is automatically provisioned with the bundles present in the workspace and all the bundles of the target platform. You can remove some of them, if desired, by using the Bundles tab in figure A.25.

Other settings are also available in this window, such as arguments provided to the JVM at startup in the Arguments tab, and the JVM and Equinox configuration used in the Settings tab. When you've finished our configuration, click the Apply button to save it. Figure A.25 shows the configuration window for the Spring DM application and the Bundles tab containing the bundles used.

Now that the application is configured, you can run it by launching your Spring DM application within Eclipse.

A.3.2 *Running the Equinox container*

The previously configured application can be run directly from the configuration window (figure A.25) using the Run button once its configuration is complete. But this window might not be open, so you can also run the application from the Run icon in the Eclipse toolbar or the Run menu, as shown in figure A.26.

When the application runs, its output appears in Eclipse's Console view at the bottom of the window. This output is the same as the output of the Equinox console and it's interactive. Figure A.27 shows the content of this view after launching the application.

To finish up, we'll see how to interact with the Equinox console to introspect the current bundles, show their states, and see which services they have registered.

Figure A.26 Launching the Spring DM application using the Eclipse toolbar

```
🅡 Problems  🗎 Javadoc  🗎 Declaration  ⊥ Outline  ▣ Console ✕

Spring DM Configuration [OSGi Framework] /usr/lib/jvm/java-6-sun-1.6.0.

1594 [Tomcat Catalina Start Thread] INFO  org.apache.catalina.core.StandardHost  - XML validat
1695 [SpringOsgiExtenderThread-2] INFO  org.springframework.osgi.service.exporter.support.Osgi
1701 [SpringOsgiExtenderThread-2] INFO  org.springframework.osgi.context.support.OsgiBundleXml
1817 [Tomcat Catalina Start Thread] INFO  org.apache.coyote.http11.Http11BaseProtocol  - Start
1825 [Tomcat Catalina Start Thread] INFO  org.springframework.osgi.web.tomcat.internal.Activat
1836 [WebExtender-Init] INFO  org.springframework.osgi.web.deployer.tomcat.TomcatWarDeployer
1851 [WebExtender-Init] INFO  org.springframework.osgi.web.extender.internal.activator.WarLoad
1954 [Tomcat Catalina Start Thread] INFO  org.springframework.osgi.web.tomcat.internal.Activat
2321 [Timer-2] WARN  org.apache.catalina.startup.DigesterFactory  - Could not get url for /jav
2322 [Timer-2] WARN  org.apache.catalina.startup.DigesterFactory  - Could not get url for /jav
2440 [Timer-2] INFO  org.springframework.osgi.web.deployer.tomcat.TomcatWarDeployer  - Success
```

Figure A.27 Console view after having launched the Spring application

A.3.3 Equinox console

Once you've launched an Equinox application, the console is immediately available from the Console view, together with a command prompt. This prompt isn't visible if traces haven't been displayed at container startup, but you can nevertheless enter commands.

To see all the available commands, type `help`. Table A.2 lists all the useful commands of the Equinox console.

Table A.2 Useful commands of the Equinox console

Category	Command	Description
Container management	`launch`	Launches the container.
	`shutdown`	Shuts down the container.
	`close`	Shuts down the container and stops the corresponding process.
	`init`	Uninstalls all the components present in the container.

Table A.2   Useful commands of the Equinox console *(continued)*

Category	Command	Description
Component management	`install`	Installs a component using a JAR file.
	`uninstall`	Uninstalls a component.
	`start`	Starts a component.
	`stop`	Stops a component.
	`refresh`	Refreshes a component.
	`update`	Updates a component.
Information display	`status`	Prints the status of the container by showing all components and services present.
	`ss`	Prints a list of present components with their states.
	`services`	Prints a list of services with hints of components that register and use them.
	`packages`	Prints a list of packages with hints of components that provide or use them.
	`bundles`	Prints a list of components with corresponding data.
	`bundle`	Prints detailed data (identifier, status, services and packages) of a component.
	`headers`	Prints all OSGi headers present in the manifest file of a component.
Problem diagnostics	`diag`	Prints non-resolved constraints of a component.

The main command is `ss` (for short status), which displays all the loaded bundles together with their internal identifiers, their states, and their symbolic names. The internal identifier is a number, and it can be used as input to commands like `bundle` and `diag`. Figure A.28 shows the output of the `ss` command for our application.

```
osgi> ss

Framework is launched.

id    State        Bundle
0     ACTIVE       org.eclipse.osgi_3.5.0.v20081201-1815
1     ACTIVE       com.springsource.javassist_3.3.0.ga
2     ACTIVE       org.springframework.bundle.osgi.web_1.1.2
3     ACTIVE       com.springsource.org.apache.commons.pool_1.4.0
4     ACTIVE       org.springframework.bundle.osgi.extender_1.1.2
5     ACTIVE       gwt_servlet_1.5.3
6     ACTIVE       com.springsource.org.apache.commons.io_1.4.0
7     ACTIVE       com.springsource.javax.el_2.1.0
8     ACTIVE       com.springsource.antlr_2.7.7
9     ACTIVE       gwtext_2.0.6
10    ACTIVE       com.manning.sdmia.web_1.0.0.qualifier
11    ACTIVE       com.springsource.net.sf.cglib_2.1.3
12    ACTIVE       com.manning.sdmia.simple_1.0.0.SNAPSHOT
13    ACTIVE       com.springsource.org.aspectj.weaver_1.6.1
14    ACTIVE       org.springframework.web_2.5.6
15    ACTIVE       com.springsource.org.hibernate.annotations.common_3.3.0.ga
16    ACTIVE       com.springsource.javax.servlet_2.5.0
```

Figure A.28   Output of the `ss` command for the Spring DM application

```
osgi> bundle 12
com.manning.sdmia.simple_1.0.0.SNAPSHOT [12]
  Id=12, Status=ACTIVE     Data Root=/home/templth/developpement/projets/spring/manning/source-
  Registered Services
    {com.manning.sdmia.simple.service.SimpleService}={org.springframework.osgi.bean.name=simpleS
    {org.springframework.osgi.context.DelegatedExecutionOsgiBundleApplicationContext, org.spring
  Services in use:
    {org.xml.sax.EntityResolver}={service.id=25}
    {org.springframework.beans.factory.xml.NamespaceHandlerResolver}={service.id=24}
  No exported packages
  No imported packages
  No fragment bundles
  Named class space
    com.manning.sdmia.simple; bundle-version="1.0.0.SNAPSHOT"[provided]
  No required bundles

osgi>
```

Figure A.29   Output of the `bundle` command for the bundle `com.manning.sdmia.simple`

Another useful command is `bundle`, which displays information about a bundle. This command accepts the internal identifier as a parameter. Figure A.29 shows the output of this command, and we can see that the `com.manning.sdmia.simple` bundle registers a service named `com.manning.sdmia.simple.service.SimpleService`, and that Spring DM automatically registered other services such as one for the Spring context itself.

A.4   Summary

PDE and Spring IDE provide interesting features for developing and executing Spring DM applications within Eclipse.

PDE offers tooling for selecting OSGi components to use within the OSGi container, creating new OSGi components, and configuring their content.

Spring IDE goes further by providing all the necessary tools to facilitate the development of OSGi components using Spring DM. Spring IDE can also be used to create Spring DM configuration files and for code-completion within these files.

appendix B
OSGi development
with Maven 2

Maven 2 is a popular and powerful build tool that spans the whole build lifecycle of a software project: compilation, automated tests, packaging, and deployment. It provides a dependency management system, supports many other tools via its plug-in architecture, and integrates well with continuous integration servers. Maven 2 also offers good support for OSGi-based development, which can then stay close to traditional development in terms of building, as long as you're aware of the good set of extensions and know to how use them.

Maven 2 is used throughout this book, so this appendix is intended for total Maven 2 beginners who want to test the code samples or adopt the tool for their own OSGi development. It's also intended for readers already familiar with Maven 2 who want to keep using their favorite build tool for their upcoming OSGi-based development. These people will be happy to discover that the use of OSGi doesn't need to disrupt their habits and that they'll be able to use Maven 2 in nearly the same way as before.

Readers totally new to Maven 2 should read this appendix from the beginning. Section B.1 covers how to install the tool, and section B.2 explains all the necessary basics of Maven 2: project creation, the POM file, build lifecycle, dependency management, and multimodule projects. Section B.2 could also be useful for people who want to brush up on their Maven 2 skills or learn some new tips and tricks.

Sections B.3 and B.4 introduce two different tools designed for creating OSGi-compliant bundles: the Felix Bundle Plugin and Bundlor. These sections are the core of this appendix, as they cover how to include OSGi ingredients in your Maven 2 builds. We chose to introduce Bundlor as well as the tool we used throughout the entire book—Felix Bundle Plugin—because it adopts a slightly different approach, and both deserve coverage.

By the time you reach the end of this appendix, you'll be comfortable using Maven 2 for your OSGi, Spring-powered applications.

B.1   Installing Maven 2

Maven 2 can be downloaded from its official website: http://maven.apache.org. It comes as an archive file that creates an apache-maven-2.2.1 directory where it's extracted. You then need to create an M2_HOME environment variable that contains the directory where you installed Maven 2.

> **NOTE** We'll use Maven 2.2.1. It runs only on Java 5 and needs a JDK installed (a JRE isn't sufficient).

To make the mvn command available in your shell, add M2_HOME/bin to your PATH environment variable: use $M2_HOME/bin if you're using a Linux-based OS; use %M2_HOME%\bin for Windows.

You can check that Maven 2 is properly installed by running the mvn --version command, which outputs some information about your system:

```
Apache Maven 2.2.1 (r801777; 2009-08-06 21:16:01+0200)
Java version: 1.6.0_16
Java home: /usr/local/jdk-6u16/jre
Default locale: fr_FR, platform encoding: UTF-8
OS name: "linux" version: "2.6.28-15-generic" arch: "i386" Family: "unix"
```

The output you get will certainly differ, but it ensures that Maven 2 is correctly installed on your computer.

We're now ready to create our first project with Maven 2 and ready to discover its basic features.

B.2   Creating a project the Maven 2 way

This section covers the basics of Maven 2. We'll see how to create a project with the mvn command-line tool, and this will give us the opportunity to discover the Maven 2 philosophy regarding project structure, build lifecycle, and dependency management.

B.2.1   Creating a simple project

Maven 2 provides *archetypes* for creating the skeleton of a project. There are different archetypes you can use, depending on the nature of the project you want to create: standard, web application, and so on.

We'll start by creating a standard Java project, using the default Maven 2 archetype. To do so, cd to a working directory and type the following command:

```
mvn archetype:generate
```

If this is the first time you've used Maven 2 on your computer, the command will trigger the downloading of different plug-ins that Maven 2 needs to create a project. Maven 2 is built on a core (the archive you downloaded previously) that can be easily extended with plug-ins, which provide most of Maven 2's features. The first time you run it can take a while, because your computer doesn't have any plug-ins installed. Once downloaded, plug-ins are stored in the local repository, and Maven 2 can reuse them for each subsequent run, as shown in figure B.1.

Once the downloading phase is done, the archetype generation kicks in and Maven 2 prompts you with the following questions:

- The number of the archetype to use—We want to use the "quickstart" archetype (the default), so type 15 and press Enter.
- The group ID of the project—Type com. manning.sdmia.appb and press Enter.
- The artifact ID of the project—Type maven101 and press Enter.
- The version of the project—The default (1.0-SNAPSHOT) is OK, so press Enter.
- The package of the project—The default (com.manning.sdmia.appb, which is the group ID) is OK, so press Enter.

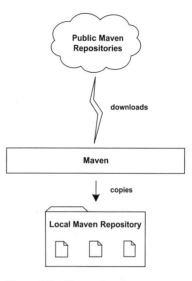

Figure B.1   **Maven downloads dependencies from public repositories on the internet and stores them on the local filesystem, in the local Maven repository.**

Maven 2 then asks you to confirm, so press Enter.

The project skeleton is then created in the maven101 directory (which is the artifact ID you entered). The group ID, artifact ID, and version that Maven 2 asked you to enter are important because they identify your project. They're sometimes called "GAV coordinates" or simply "coordinates," as they're one way to locate a project. We'll see later that coordinates are central to Maven 2 dependency management.

We're now ready to study the structure of the project we've just created.

B.2.2   *The Maven 2 project structure and the POM file*

We used maven101 as the artifact ID of our project, and that's why Maven 2 created it in the maven101 directory. The project directory has the following structure:

```
maven101
  pom.xml
  src/
    main/
      java/
        com/manning/sdmia/appb/App.java
    test
      java/
        com/manning/sdmia/appb/AppTest.java
```

The quickstart archetype created a project that follows Maven 2's standard project structure (a pom.xml file at the root of the project, a src/main/java directory for application classes, and a src/test/java directory for test classes). By using a standard layout, Maven 2 doesn't need extra configuration steps and allows developers to easily switch from one Maven 2 project to another. This approach is referred to as *convention over configuration* and is at the heart of Maven 2. Note that Maven 2's defaults can be easily overridden if they don't suit you.

Table B.1 lists the most important directories in the Maven 2 standard layout. Our project is simple and doesn't have all of them.

Table B.1   Maven 2 standard directory layout

Directory	Description
src/main/java	Application classes
src/main/resources	Application resources (non-Java files)
src/main/webapp	Web application files
src/test/java	Test classes
src/test/resources	Test resources (non-Java files)
target	Build output

Maven 2 didn't only create the skeleton of the project following its standard layout; it also created a pom.xml file at the root of the project. This file is at the core of Maven 2 configuration. Recall from chapter 3 that POM stands for Project Object Model, and the POM file of a project contains all the information to build the project, from compilation to deployment phases. Listing B.1 shows the POM file that Maven 2 created from the quickstart archetype.

Listing B.1   POM file created with the quickstart archetype

```
<project xmlns="http://maven.apache.org/POM/4.0.0"
         xmlns:xsi="http://www.w3.org/2001/XMLSchema-instance"
         xsi:schemaLocation="http://maven.apache.org/POM/4.0.0
         http://maven.apache.org/maven-v4_0_0.xsd">
  <modelVersion>4.0.0</modelVersion>
  <groupId>com.manning.sdmia.appb</groupId>
  <artifactId>maven101</artifactId>              Identifies
  <packaging>jar</packaging>                     project
  <version>1.0-SNAPSHOT</version>
  <name>maven101</name>
  <url>http://maven.apache.org</url>
  <dependencies>
    <dependency>
      <groupId>junit</groupId>
      <artifactId>junit</artifactId>             Sets JUnit as
      <version>3.8.1</version>                   dependency
      <scope>test</scope>
    </dependency>
  </dependencies>
</project>
```

The POM of the maven101 project is simple but representative of the Maven 2 philosophy. It contains two sections that deliver information about the project:

- The project identification, with the coordinates we entered during project creation. Note the `packaging` element, which specifies how to package the project (JAR, WAR, and so on).
- The project dependencies, which informs us that it depends on the JUnit library. Note that a dependency also has its own coordinates. Dependencies are an important feature of Maven, which we'll study in section B.2.4.

The POM file doesn't contain a section for the structure of the project: because we're following the standard directory layout, we don't need such information. This is one benefit of the convention over configuration approach. A POM file can grow and have lots of sections; we'll see some of them in the examples later in this appendix.

We've covered the basics of the Maven 2 project structure; now let's see the dynamic part: Maven 2 as a build tool.

B.2.3 *Compiling and packaging: the build lifecycle*

Maven 2 is best known as a build tool, so in this section we'll cover how to build our `maven101` project. Type the following command in the `maven101` directory to package the project:

```
mvn package
```

The execution might take a while, because Maven 2 downloads the artifacts (libraries and plug-ins) it needs to compile, run, test, and package the project. The console outputs a lot of messages; you should get something like the following at the end of the run:

```
(...)
-------------------------------------------------------
 T E S T S
-------------------------------------------------------
Running com.manning.sdmia.appb.AppTest
Tests run: 1, Failures: 0, Errors: 0, Skipped: 0, Time elapsed: 0.09 sec

Results :

Tests run: 1, Failures: 0, Errors: 0, Skipped: 0

[INFO] [jar:jar {execution: default-jar}]
[INFO] Building jar: /tmp/maven101/target/maven101-1.0-SNAPSHOT.jar
[INFO] ------------------------------------------------------------------
[INFO] BUILD SUCCESSFUL
[INFO] ------------------------------------------------------------------
[INFO] Total time: 6 seconds
[INFO] Finished at: Sun Sep 27 13:18:49 CEST 2009
[INFO] Final Memory: 14M/25M
[INFO] ------------------------------------------------------------------
```

This output informs us that Maven 2 launched the dummy unit test that the archetype created, packaged the project's compiled classes as a JAR, and that the build was successful (we didn't show the compilation phase for brevity). Note that Maven 2 fulfilled all the tasks without much input from us: downloading of the plug-ins, compiling, running tests (it added the JUnit library automatically to the classpath), and packaging. The project JAR file has been created in the target directory, under the name maven101-1.0-SNAPSHOT.jar (which follows the pattern ${artifactId}-${version}.${packaging}).

Users familiar with tools like Ant should be thrilled: thanks to the convention over configuration approach and the dependency management, setting up a project with Maven 2 needs many fewer configuration steps than with Ant. Maven 2 uses a more *declarative* approach than tools like Ant: we refer to the JUnit library (by its coordinates), not to a junit.jar file located in a specific directory. (Obviously Maven 2 ends up using a JAR file somewhere on the filesystem, which we'll see later, but we don't care much when we build the project). Ant uses a low-level approach (referring directly to a junit.jar file), which is more cumbersome but can be more flexible.

But what is the package option we used in the command line? It refers to a *phase* in the *default build lifecycle*. A build is composed of different phases, and when a phase is given in the command, Maven executes every phase up to and including the given phase. Table B.2 lists the most important phases of the default build in chronological order.

Table B.2 Main phases of the Maven 2 default build

Phase	Description
compile	Compiles the source code of the project
test-compile	Compiles the test source code of the project
test	Runs the tests of the project
package	Packages the compiled code and resource in the appropriate archive format (JAR, WAR, and so on)
install	Copies the generated package in the local repository
deploy	Copies the generated package in a remote repository for sharing with other developers

Maven 2 defines two other builds: clean (which deletes the target directory) and site (which generates the project's documentation). We can use phases from different builds in the same command line. The following snippet shows a commonly used command to deploy all the project artifacts (archive and documentation) from a cleaned project:

```
mvn clean deploy site-deploy
```

TIP Use the clean phase before critical tasks like packaging to ensure that the archive is built against a properly cleaned project.

Here are some other commands that are useful while doing Maven-based development:

- `mvn clean compile`—Cleans, then compiles project
- `mvn test`—Runs unit tests
- `mvn clean package`—Cleans and then packages project

Sometimes you'll need to run up to a particular phase without running previous phases. This can be done by skipping those phases. There's no uniform way to do so, but the plug-in that executes a phase can accept a command-line argument that prevents it from doing its job. We usually use system properties as plug-in arguments, with the `-Dargument.name` syntax. As an example, here is the command to package a project without running the unit tests:

```
mvn clean package -Dmaven.test.skip
```

To complete our tour of the Maven 2 command line, let's study a topic we've avoided so far: the exact syntax of command-line commands. Remember that we used the `mvn archetype:generate` command to start the creation of our project. This command uses the following syntax:

```
mvn plugin:goal
```

In the `mvn archetype:generate` command, we use the `generate` goal of the `archetype` plug-in. We've already said Maven 2 uses a plug-in-based architecture. Plug-ins provide features that can be called through their goals (goals can be seen as the equivalent of Ant tasks) . But when we built the project, we used build phases, and these don't follow the `plugin:goal` syntax. That's because phases can be considered shortcuts for plug-in goals. As an example, the `compile` phase is equivalent to the `compiler:compile` goal:

```
mvn compile
mvn compiler:compile
```

You've absorbed a lot of information about using Maven 2 so far, and that's only the beginning. You deserve what each developer seeks when starting to use a new tool: the Hello World! output. After packaging the `maven101` project, type the following command:

```
java -cp target/maven101-1.0-SNAPSHOT.jar com.manning.sdmia.appb.App
```

Congratulations on running your first Maven 2 project!

We're now about to cover one the most important features of Maven 2: its dependency management system.

B.2.4 *Introducing the dependency management system*

We hope we've talked enough about modularity in this book for you to understand that an application should not be built as a monolithic piece of software, nor should it reinvent the wheel each time it needs to do something new. An application should be divided into a consistent set of modules to encourage reuse, testing, and independent upgrades. It should also be able to leverage third-party libraries, which give strong foundations and keeps the focus on the main goal of the application.

OSGi is very powerful at enforcing modularity, but it does so at *runtime*, not while developing applications (unless you have some tooling like Eclipse PDE). For the development phase of a project, we need to rely on something else to handle modularity, and that's where Maven 2's dependency management system can help.

When splitting an application into modules, some modules depend on each other and on third-party libraries. We therefore need a strict way to identify the modules. There are also subtleties that can make the notion of a dependency tricky: if a module uses Hibernate, it needs the Hibernate binaries to compile and at runtime. This can be different for a module that uses Spring: it can only use the lightweight container, so it doesn't need the Spring binaries to compile but obviously does need them at runtime. We usually refer to this notion as the *scope* of the dependency.

Dependency management is a complex topic, and this section will cover how Maven 2 tackles it. This topic is relevant to modularity, one of OSGi's main concerns, but keep in mind that the scope differs: in this appendix, we're covering a build tool, whereas OSGi is a platform. The functionality of the two systems don't collide but rather are complementary.

DECLARING DEPENDENCIES

Dependencies are declared in the `dependencies` element of the POM file. Remember the POM of the `maven101` project, which uses the JUnit library for testing:

```
<dependencies>
(...)
  <dependency>
    <groupId>junit</groupId>
    <artifactId>junit</artifactId>
    <version>3.8.1</version>
    <scope>test</scope>
  </dependency>
(...)
</dependencies>
```

Adding a dependency is quite simple: just provide its coordinates. (In the next section, we'll cover where to find these coordinates.)

It's worth noting that Maven 2 provides support for the notion of *scope* that we mentioned previously. The JUnit library uses the *test* scope, which means Maven 2 will add JUnit to the classpath only when compiling and running the tests. Any reference to the JUnit API in the src/main/java directory will result in a compilation failure. Make sure you configure the scope of your dependencies, as it avoids having an inconsistent project. Table B.3 lists the main scopes that Maven 2 provides.

Note the notion of *dependency propagation* in the description of the `compile` scope. Maven 2 isn't only able to handle direct dependencies but a whole graph of dependencies. This notion is also referred to as *transitive dependencies*. We describe these in the next section.

Table B.3 Main Maven dependency scopes

Scope	Description
`compile`	Default scope. Dependencies are available in all classpaths (compilation, test) and are propagated to dependent projects.
`provided`	Same as `compile`, except that the dependency is expected to be provided at runtime (the application server provides the servlet API for a web application).
`runtime`	The dependency is required for normal use, but not for compilation.
`test`	The dependency is not required normally and is only available during the test phases.

TRANSITIVE DEPENDENCIES

Frameworks like Hibernate and Spring rely on other libraries or frameworks. When adding Spring or Hibernate to our application, we don't want to worry about these indirect dependencies. Maven 2 will provide them for us because it's able to figure out and retrieve the whole graph of dependencies from a single dependency.

Suppose we want to use the Spring Framework's lightweight container in our maven101 project. For this, we need to add the spring-context module:

```
<dependencies>
  <dependency>
    <groupId>org.springframework</groupId>
    <artifactId>spring-context</artifactId>
    <version>2.5.6</version>
  </dependency>
  (...)
</dependencies>
```

Note that we didn't specify any scope, which means Maven 2 will use the compile scope. By using the dependency plug-in and its tree goal, you can see the dependency tree of the project:

```
mvn dependency:tree
[INFO] Scanning for projects...
[INFO] Searching repository for plugin with prefix: 'dependency'.
[INFO] ------------------------------------------------------------------
[INFO] Building maven101
[INFO]     task-segment: [dependency:tree]
[INFO] ------------------------------------------------------------------
[INFO] [dependency:tree {execution: default-cli}]
[INFO] com.manning.sdmia.appb:maven101:jar:1.0-SNAPSHOT
[INFO] +- org.springframework:spring-context:jar:2.5.6:compile
[INFO] |  +- aopalliance:aopalliance:jar:1.0:compile
[INFO] |  +- commons-logging:commons-logging:jar:1.1.1:compile
[INFO] |  +- org.springframework:spring-beans:jar:2.5.6:compile
```

```
[INFO] |   \- org.springframework:spring-core:jar:2.5.6:compile
[INFO] \- junit:junit:jar:3.8.1:test
[INFO] ------------------------------------------------------------------
[INFO] BUILD SUCCESSFUL
[INFO] ------------------------------------------------------------------
[INFO] Total time: 3 seconds
[INFO] Finished at: Sun Sep 27 17:54:06 CEST 2009
[INFO] Final Memory: 9M/18M
[INFO] ------------------------------------------------------------------
```

The preceding output shows that Maven 2 not only added the Spring container dependency but also its own dependencies (other Spring modules and the Commons Logging library). How does Maven 2 know about that? The answer is that the spring-context module has its own POM, which carefully describes its dependencies.

When building the project, Maven 2 will add the transitive dependencies to the appropriate classpaths, according to the scope of the root dependency. As long as a dependency's POM is correctly written, Maven 2 can retrieve its whole dependency graph, with correct versions of all dependencies. Because Maven 2 manages these transitive dependencies, you shouldn't get any ClassNotFoundExceptions because you forgot to add an obscure library to your classpath, or experience weird behavior because you didn't add the correct version of a library.

We've revealed many features of Maven 2's dependency management. We're now going to describe how these features work by diving into one of its main mechanisms: repositories.

REPOSITORIES

When we ran Maven 2 for the first time, to create the maven101 project, it downloaded the plug-ins and dependencies it needed from a *remote repository*. Maven repositories contain artifacts (JAR, WAR, POM, and the like) and store them in directories with the following structure:

```
/${groupId}/${artifactId}/${version}/${artifactId}-${version}.${packaging}
```

Once downloaded, artifacts are stored on the filesystem, in the *local repository* of the computer. The default location for the local repository is ${user.dir}/.m2/repository.

> **NOTE**   The user directory location depends on your OS. It's c:\Documents and Settings\USERNAME for Windows XP, c:\Users\USERNAME for Windows Vista and 7, and /home/USERNAME for Linux-based systems.

What's really interesting about the concept of a local repository is that artifacts are then shared with all Maven 2 projects. This means that Maven 2 projects don't need to embed their dependencies, which saves disk space and avoids cumbersome and error-prone copy-and-paste operations.

Where does Maven 2 download artifacts from? The default remote repository is called the "central Maven 2 repository," and it's located at http://repo1.maven.org/maven2/. You can browse the central repository with your usual web browser, but this isn't a particularly convenient way to find artifacts. Here are two search engines

> ### Where should I place my local repository?
>
> You can override the default location of your local repository by editing the content of the `settings/localRepository` element in the M2_HOME/conf/settings.xml file. Note that this file is shared by all Maven 2 users on the computer. If you want your own configuration file, copy the global settings file in the ${user.dir}/.m2/ directory, and any change to it will override the global settings.
>
> Avoid spaces in the name of the local repository directory, as spaces prevent some (rare) plug-ins from working correctly.

that index remote repositories and provide a nice graphical interface for searching for artifacts:

- http://mvnrepository.com—The most famous of the repository search engines. It indexes the central repository and it's simple to use.
- http://mavensearch.net—A powerful search engine. It indexes several remote repositories (central, Codehaus, JBoss, and others) and understands Lucene-like queries.

By using these search engines, you can easily find the coordinates of your dependencies, and you'll just have to copy and paste the XML code from the search results into your POM.

But what should you do when artifacts aren't on the central repository? You can add repository entries in your POM that instruct Maven to look for artifacts in the default repository but also in these specific repositories. Repository entries can be added at the end of the POM, in a `repositories` element. Listing B.2 shows the necessary entries for the SpringSource EBR, which hosts Spring-related binaries and OSGi-ified versions of open source libraries.

Listing B.2 Adding the SpringSource EBR

```
<repositories>

  <repository>
    <id>com.springsource.repository.bundles.release</id>
    <name>SpringSource EBR - SpringSource Bundle Releases</name>
    <url>
    http://repository.springsource.com/maven/bundles/release
    </url>
  </repository>

  <repository>
    <id>com.springsource.repository.bundles.external</id>
    <name>SpringSource EBR - External Bundle Releases</name>
    <url>
    http://repository.springsource.com/maven/bundles/external
    </url>
  </repository>

</repositories>
```

The next step: repository management

Adding repositories to POM files is convenient, but it doesn't scale when you maintain lots of projects. A solution is to use a proxy that becomes the single entry point for Maven 2 and delegates artifact-lookup to a set of remote or local repositories. Such a proxy is usually in the local network of a company that wants to host its own artifacts for its development teams, or a company that want to share its artifacts with external developers. The proxy provides management features for administering repositories—that's why it's called a Maven repository manager. Nexus (http://nexus.sonatype.org/) is a powerful and open source implementation of a repository manager.

We've covered all the theory we need for managing dependencies with Maven 2. Let's put this into practice by adding some typical OSGi dependencies to a POM.

OSGI AND SPRING DM DEPENDENCIES

The OSGi Core and Compendium Services bundles are available in the central repository. The following snippet shows how to add them to a Maven 2 project:

```
<dependencies>

  <dependency>
    <groupId>org.osgi</groupId>
    <artifactId>org.osgi.core</artifactId>         Adds OSGi
    <version>4.2.0</version>                        Core API
    <scope>provided</scope>
  </dependency>

  <dependency>
    <groupId>org.osgi</groupId>
    <artifactId>org.osgi.compendium</artifactId>   Adds OSGi Compendium
    <version>4.2.0</version>                        Services API
  </dependency>

</dependencies>
```

Note that we used the `provided` scope for the OSGi Core API: we'd need the OSGi API only if our project needs it to compile (we hope it won't), but at runtime the OSGi platform *provides* the OSGi core classes.

Note also that we twice specified the 4.2.0 version of OSGi for the two bundles. Let's follow the DRY principle (Don't Repeat Yourself) by using a property in only one place to set the OSGi version:

```
<project (...)>
  (...)

  <properties>                                  Defines OSGi
    <osgi.version>4.2.0</osgi.version>      ◁── version property
  </properties>

<dependencies>

  <dependency>
```

```
    <groupId>org.osgi</groupId>
    <artifactId>org.osgi.core</artifactId>
    <version>${osgi.version}</version>
    <scope>provided</scope>
</dependency>

<dependency>
    <groupId>org.osgi</groupId>
    <artifactId>org.osgi.compendium</artifactId>
    <version>${osgi.version}</version>
</dependency>

</dependencies>
```

Uses OSGi version property

Adding Spring DM's bundles isn't so simple, because some of their dependencies are open source libraries that aren't distributed as OSGi bundles. The solution is to add the SpringSource EBR entries (shown in listing B.2) and then Maven will be able to find Spring DM's bundles and its dependency graph. The following snippet shows the necessary dependency entries in a POM:

```
<properties>
    <spring.dm.version>2.0.0.M1</spring.dm.version>
</properties>

<dependencies>

    <dependency>
        <groupId>org.springframework.osgi</groupId>
        <artifactId>spring-osgi-extender</artifactId>
        <version>${spring.dm.version}</version>
    </dependency>

    <dependency>
        <groupId>org.springframework.osgi</groupId>
        <artifactId>spring-osgi-test</artifactId>
        <version>${spring.dm.version}</version>
        <scope>test</scope>
    </dependency>

</dependencies>
```

Defines Spring DM version property

Adds Spring DM extender

Adds Spring DM test support

When will you need to add Spring DM bundles to your Maven 2 projects? Hopefully, you won't very often, as Spring DM promotes POJO-based programming and its API should not generally be present in your Java classes. However, you'll have to add these bundles for a special kind of Maven 2 project: integration test projects. As stated in chapter 10, Spring DM testing support relies on the Maven 2 local repository to provision the embedded OSGi container, so adding Spring DM as a dependency to the POM of an integration test project ensures that Spring DM's bundles and their dependencies are correctly downloaded and copied to the local repository.

WARNING Spring DM 2.0.0.M1 uses a version of the Spring Framework (3.0.0.RC1) which is no longer on Maven repositories. You'll need to override the dependencies on the Spring Framework in your POM file, as explained in chapter 3.

Having a dedicated project for integration tests leads us to module-based projects, a feature Maven 2 provides out of the box, and which is particularly relevant when working on OSGi applications.

B.2.5   *Splitting a Maven 2 project into modules*

So far we've covered using Maven 2 features on one project at a time, but when an application grows, it's usual to split it into smaller modules. Maven 2 is able to handle multimodule projects; the immediate benefits (regarding the build) are the possibility of sharing metadata between projects (by using POM inheritance) and building all the modules at once (by launching the build of the root module). The support Maven 2 provides for multimodule projects makes it an appropriate build tool for OSGi (and thus Spring DM) applications.

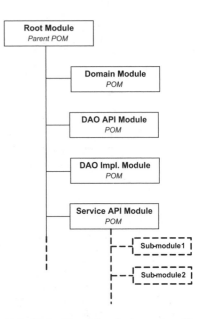

We'll see in this section that we can follow the typical structure of enterprise applications (studied in chapter 6), as illustrated in figure B.2. For brevity's sake, we'll limit our sample to the creation of the domain, DAO API, and DAO implementation bundles of the directory application. We'll end up with a nicely structured multimodule project, and the following sections on the Apache Felix Bundle and Bundlor will cover how to package these modules as OSGi bundles.

Figure B.2   Maven 2 projects can be split into modules, which allows information sharing and composite builds.

A multimodule project is defined by a *parent POM* referencing submodules. Let's take a working directory as the root of our project and create a pom.xml file with the following content:

```
<?xml version="1.0" encoding="UTF-8"?>
<project xmlns="http://maven.apache.org/POM/4.0.0"
  xmlns:xsi="http://www.w3.org/2001/XMLSchema-instance"
  xsi:schemaLocation="http://maven.apache.org/POM/4.0.0
  http://maven.apache.org/maven-v4_0_0.xsd">
  <modelVersion>4.0.0</modelVersion>

  <groupId>com.manning.sdmia.appb.directory</groupId>
  <artifactId>parent</artifactId>
  <packaging>pom</packaging>
  <version>1.0.0</version>
  <name>Directory Parent Project</name>

  <properties>
    <spring.dm.version>2.0.0.M1</spring.dm.version>
    <spring.version>3.0.2.RELEASE</spring.version>
  </properties>
```

Defines parent POM coordinates and nature

Declares global properties

```
<repositories>                    Declares
  (...)                           repositories
</repositories>
</project>
```

A parent POM gathers information that will be shared among its submodules; it's therefore a good location to centralize properties like framework version or repository locations. Let's create the domain module by using the `mvn archetype:generate` command from the project root directory and answer the following when prompted by Maven 2:

- Archetype to use: `quickstart` (the default)
- The group ID of the project: `com.manning.sdmia.appb.directory`
- The artifact ID of the project: `directory.domain`
- The version of the project: `1.0-SNAPSHOT` (the default)
- The package of the project: `com.manning.sdmia.appb.directory` (the default)

This creates a directory.domain directory that has the layout of a Maven 2 project. The parent POM has been modified to reflect that it now has a submodule:

```
<modules>
  <module>directory.domain</module>
</modules>
```

Let's have a look at the POM of the submodule we've just created:

```
<project (...)>
  <modelVersion>4.0.0</modelVersion>
  <parent>
    <artifactId>parent</artifactId>                              Inherits from
    <groupId>com.manning.sdmia.appb.directory</groupId>          parent POM
    <version>1.0.0</version>
  </parent>
  <groupId>com.manning.sdmia.appb</groupId>
  <artifactId>directory.domain</artifactId>
  <version>1.0-SNAPSHOT</version>
  <name>directory.domain</name>
  (...)
</project>
```

By using the `parent` element and providing the parent project coordinates, the submodule inherits all the metadata that resides in the parent POM. As with object-oriented inheritance, the submodule can override some settings by providing its own: that's exactly what it does with the group ID and the version. Because we want to closely tie the submodule to its parent, we must remove the `groupId` and `version` elements, and Maven 2 will use those of the parent POM (this will make our example simpler, but that's not the way to go if we plan on having a different release lifecycle for the submodules).

It's now time to see how Maven 2 lets us build our module-based project in one go. From the root of the project, type the `mvn clean install` command. The end of the output informs you that Maven 2 built the parent root module and the `directory.domain` submodule:

```
[INFO] -------------------------------------------------------------------
[INFO] Reactor Summary:
[INFO] -------------------------------------------------------------------
[INFO] Directory Parent Project ......................... SUCCESS [3.638s]
[INFO] directory.domain ................................. SUCCESS [3.974s]
[INFO] -------------------------------------------------------------------
[INFO] -------------------------------------------------------------------
[INFO] BUILD SUCCESSFUL
[INFO] -------------------------------------------------------------------
[INFO] Total time: 8 seconds
[INFO] Finished at: Sat Oct 03 10:05:14 CEST 2009
[INFO] Final Memory: 19M/34M
[INFO] -------------------------------------------------------------------
```

When you launch a Maven 2 command from the root of the project, it applies to all the modules. If you want the command to be launched only against the parent project, use the `--non-recursive` option:

```
mvn clean install --non-recursive
```

As stated previously, our sample multimodule project consists of three submodules: the domain, the DAO API, and a JDBC implementation of DAO. The creation steps for the two remaining modules are the same as for the domain module, so we won't dwell further on them (the whole project is available in the book's code samples).

> **NOTE** Our project is only one level deep, but Maven 2 can handle multimodule projects of any depth, meaning that a submodule can have submodules of its own.

You should now have a good overview of Maven 2's features and mechanics. There are many other interesting topics that we could cover, but as Maven 2 builds on a plug-in-based architecture, these topics are virtually endless. We have nevertheless covered enough material for creating standard projects, and it's time to get to the hot topic: OSGi with Maven 2. Packaging OSGi bundles is slightly different from packaging plain-vanilla Java archives, and Maven 2 doesn't provide native support for this. Fortunately, there are third-party plug-in solutions that smoothly integrate with Maven 2's build system.

In the next sections, we'll cover two powerful plug-ins that make packaging OSGi bundles with Maven 2 a breeze: the Apache Felix Bundle Plugin (which builds on top of Bnd) and the SpringSource Bundlor plug-in. These plug-ins are exclusive—you must use one or the other, not both—and having been introduced to both of them, you can choose the one that best suits your OSGi development with Maven 2. Our multimodule project will act as a guinea pig, and we'll use each tool's features for the OSGi-ification of its modules. This will also give you the opportunity to learn more about Maven 2, by discovering best practices and settings that commonly apply to projects.

B.3   *Using the Apache Felix Bundle Plugin*

The Apache Felix Bundle Plugin for Maven 2 builds on top of Bnd to package Maven projects as OSGi bundles. We already used this plug-in in chapter 3 to package our first Spring DM bundles and in chapter 6 to illustrate the OSGi-ification of third-party libraries. You can download the plug-in and access its documentation on its website: http://felix.apache.org/site/apache-felix-maven-bundle-plugin-bnd.html.

This section gives a more comprehensive (but nonexhaustive) introduction to this plug-in: the basic setup in a POM file, the default packaging behavior, and how to override this default behavior by using the set of instructions the plug-in provides. More advanced topics, like the way to benefit from the plug-in without changing the packaging of the project, how to externalize instructions from the POM, and the integration with the Eclipse Plug-in Development Environment are also covered. By the end of this section, you'll be able to efficiently use the plug-in for your own OSGi-based developments.

B.3.1 Setting up the plug-in

The most common way to use the Apache Felix Bundle Plugin is to change the packaging of the target Maven 2 project and declare the plug-in in the build/plugins section of the POM. Listing B.3 shows this basic setup for the domain module of our sample project.

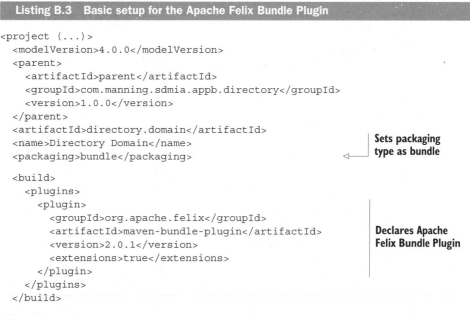

Listing B.3 Basic setup for the Apache Felix Bundle Plugin

```
<project (...)>
  <modelVersion>4.0.0</modelVersion>
  <parent>
    <artifactId>parent</artifactId>
    <groupId>com.manning.sdmia.appb.directory</groupId>
    <version>1.0.0</version>
  </parent>
  <artifactId>directory.domain</artifactId>
  <name>Directory Domain</name>                            Sets packaging
  <packaging>bundle</packaging>                      ◁──┘  type as bundle

  <build>
    <plugins>
      <plugin>
        <groupId>org.apache.felix</groupId>
        <artifactId>maven-bundle-plugin</artifactId>       Declares Apache
        <version>2.0.1</version>                           Felix Bundle Plugin
        <extensions>true</extensions>
      </plugin>
    </plugins>
  </build>

</project>
```

Listing B.3 shows how we changed the default packaging from jar to bundle. Maven 2 natively supports jar packaging, but that's not the case for bundle. In Maven 2, packaging types are an extension point, which means plug-ins can provide new ways to package projects. That's exactly what the Felix Bundle Plugin does: it provides the bundle packaging type. So we *need* to declare the Felix Bundle Plugin in the POM if we want Maven 2 to understand what the bundle packaging type is.

Note that we explicitly declared the version of the plug-in we want to use. This is a good opportunity to describe two practices that will make our Maven 2 build more robust:

- *Always specify the version of a Maven 2 plug-in.* Otherwise Maven 2 will use the latest version of the plug-in, which means Maven 2 could use a new version of a plug-in without warning you, and your build could break unexpectedly (if the new version isn't compatible with the previous one).

- *Centralize important information in the parent POM.* Now that you know the plug-in version is important information and that it'll be used in all modules, using a property defined in the parent POM is a good idea.

So, the version of the Felix Bundle Plugin has a place in the properties of the parent POM (shown in bold in the following snippet):

```
<properties>
  <spring.dm.version>2.0.0.M1</spring.dm.version>
  <spring.version>3.0.2.RELEASE</spring.version>
  <felix.bundle.plugin.version>
    2.0.1
  </felix.bundle.plugin.version>
</properties>
```

Because the domain module inherits from the parent POM, it can use the `felix.bundle.plugin.version` property when declaring the plug-in:

```
<plugin>
  <groupId>org.apache.felix</groupId>
  <artifactId>maven-bundle-plugin</artifactId>
  <version>${felix.bundle.plugin.version}</version>
  <extensions>true</extensions>
</plugin>
```

Now let's see what the Felix Bundle Plugin does with this packaging. If we launch the `mvn clean package` command from the domain submodule directory, it creates the JAR file in the target directory. What's in the resulting JAR? As expected, the JAR contains the compiled Java classes and the resources of the project. For this "normal" behavior, it's worth remembering how Bnd (the tool the Felix Bundle Plugin builds upon) works: it doesn't package Java classes and resources that are copied to a target directory; it scans the classpath and gathers what we tell it to gather into a JAR file and generates its manifest accordingly. Figure B.3 illustrates this mechanism.

In chapter 6, we took advantage of this mechanism to wrap an existing library by declaring it as a dependency in our Maven 2 project. We provided the Felix Bundle Plugin with the appropriate instructions to filter the classes of the library from the classpath. We won't leverage this feature directly here; we'll merely package the classes that are directly present in our project and focus on the generation of the manifest.

Speaking of the manifest, let's see what the Felix Bundle Plugin has generated. The following snippet shows an excerpt of the generated manifest (with the non-OSGi headers removed):

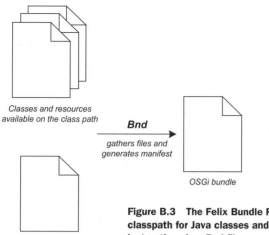

Classes and resources
available on the class path

Bnd

gathers files and
generates manifest

OSGi bundle

Bnd file

Figure B.3　The Felix Bundle Plugin builds on top of Bnd, which scans the classpath for Java classes and resources and gathers them according to instructions in a Bnd file.

```
Bundle-ManifestVersion: 2
Bundle-SymbolicName: com.manning.sdmia.appb.directory.domain
Bundle-Name: Directory Domain
Bundle-Version: 1.0.0
Export-Package: com.manning.sdmia.directory.domain
Import-Package: com.manning.sdmia.directory.domain;version="1.0"
```

Given that the project contains only one Java package (with the domain objects), the Felix Bundle Plugin did a pretty good job at adding relevant OSGi metadata without much information provided by us. This is one of the strengths of this plug-in: it uses reasonable default decisions. It nicely bridges Bnd and Maven 2, because it takes information from the POM and can perform the translation to OSGi metadata in the manifest.

The next subsection covers the details of the plug-in's default behavior.

B.3.2　Default behavior

By setting up the plug-in in the POM of the domain module, we've been able to produce an OSGi bundle with relevant metadata. Thanks to the Felix Bundle Plugin's default behavior, we didn't need to provide very much information. We'll cover this default behavior in the current section, and in section B.3.3 we'll see how to override it.

To generate the content of OSGi manifest headers, the plug-in retrieves information from the POM of the current project: group ID, artifact ID, name, and so on. We usually refer to this information with the ${property} syntax, where property can be the path to an XML element of the POM. For example, ${project.artifactId} refers to the artifact ID of the project. This property feature is natively supported by Maven 2, as it's part if its core features (it's another application of the DRY principle).

The default behavior of the plug-in for OSGi headers is outlined in table B.4.

Table B.4   Felix Bundle Plugin defaults for common OSGi headers

OSGi header	Default value	Description
`Bundle-ManifestVersion`	Hard-coded to be 2	The plug-in creates bundles for OSGi R4.
`Bundle-SymbolicName`	`${project.groupId}` + `"."` + `${project.artifactId}`	This is the most common case. The plug-in follows an algorithm to generate the most appropriate symbolic name.
`Bundle-Name`	`${project.name}`	This name is usually more descriptive (yet short) than the artifact ID.
`Bundle-Version`	`${project.version}`	The plug-in normalizes the version to the OSGi version format, so `1.0-SNAPSHOT` becomes `1.0.0.SNAPSHOT`.
`Export-Package`	The set of packages in the local Java sources of the current project	The default package and any package containing `impl` or `internal` are automatically excluded.
`Private-Package`	The set of packages in the local Java sources of the current project	Packages in both `Export-Package` and `Private-Package` are exported. Note that this isn't a standard OSGi header but an instruction that Bnd uses.
`Import-Package`	Everything the project's Java sources refer to	This is `'*'` in Bnd's notation. Exported packages are also imported to ensure a consistent class space.

If the default behavior doesn't suit your needs, instructions can be overridden in the dedicated configuration section of the plug-in.

B.3.3   *Configuring metadata generation with instructions*

Any Maven 2 plug-in can have a `configuration` element in its declaration where settings can be specified (this means the `configuration` element can contain any valid XML fragment). The Felix Bundle Plugin configuration schema has an `instructions` element where nested elements map to Bnd instructions.

The following snippet shows how to override the name of the generated bundle, using the `instructions` element in the configuration part of the plug-in (the `configuration` element) :

```
<plugin>
  <groupId>org.apache.felix</groupId>
  <artifactId>maven-bundle-plugin</artifactId>
  <version>${felix.bundle.plugin.version}</version>
  <extensions>true</extensions>
  <configuration>
```

```
    <instructions>
      <Bundle-Name>directory.domain</Bundle-Name>
    </instructions>
  </configuration>
</plugin>
```

Properties can (and should) be used in elements:

```
<configuration>
  <instructions>
    <Bundle-Name>${project.artifactId}</Bundle-Name>
  </instructions>
</configuration>
```

You can also mix static values and properties, as shown in the following snippet from the POM of the domain bundle:

```
<configuration>
  <instructions>
    <Export-Package>
    com.manning.sdmia.directory.domain;version="${project.version}"
    </Export-Package>
  </instructions>
</configuration>
```

Remember that the elements' values are Bnd instructions: they accept the powerful set of patterns that Bnd supports, like ! and *.

We're going to use the plug-in configuration for our sample project's JDBC DAO implementation module. It uses the domain package and relies on the Spring 3.0 API (when using the JdbcTemplate). Specifying the Spring version is important—it allows us to centralize the version range in the parent POM (note that a property definition can use another property) :

```
<properties>
  <spring.dm.version>2.0.0.M1</spring.dm.version>
  <spring.version>3.0.2.RELEASE</spring.version>
  <spring.version.range>
    [${spring.version},4.0)
  </spring.version.range>
</properties>
```

The following snippet illustrates the use of both kinds of properties (Maven 2 and user-defined) and of Bnd patterns for the plug-in configuration of the JDBC DAO implementation bundle:

```
<configuration>
  <instructions>
    <Import-Package>
      com.manning.sdmia.directory.*;version="${project.version}",
      org.springframework.*;version="${spring.version.range}",
      *
    </Import-Package>
    <Export-Package></Export-Package>
  </instructions>
</configuration>
```

The most important part of this configuration lies in the Import-Package instruction, which is composed of three expressions:

- The first expression specifies that any reference to classes in the com.man-ning.sdmia.directory packages and subpackages should use the same version of the current project. In our case, Bnd will generate two entries (one for the domain package and another for the DAO package) from this expression. It will also append the correct version directive.

- The second expression defines the import instruction for any Spring-related classes (org.springframework.*). It uses the version range property we defined earlier.

- The third expression specifies that any other references to Java classes in the project source code should be added to the manifest (*).

Because our bundle is a pure implementation bundle, it should not make any of its classes available. That's why we define an empty Export-Package instruction.

> **NOTE** Bnd not only analyzes the bytecode to generate the manifest, but, thanks to a dedicated built-in plug-in, Bnd searches for Spring configuration files in the META-INF/spring directory of the bundle and automatically adds to the Import-Package header the Java package of the beans declared in the files it found. Bnd scans most of the elements that have attributes relative to class or interface (such as bean@class) in most of the Spring namespaces (beans, aop, context, jee, lang, osgi, util, and webflow-config). There's similar support for Blueprint, but it's included in the Felix Bundle Plugin itself, not in Bnd.

You now know pretty much everything about the configuration of OSGi metadata using the Felix Bundle Plugin. By remembering the philosophy of the tool (building on top of Bnd, providing a bridge between Bnd and the POM, and using reasonable defaults), you can make the OSGi nature of your project nearly transparent for your build.

> **NOTE** We didn't cover the Embed-Dependency instruction, which allows embedding dependencies in the generated JAR. Chapter 6 covered most of its features with the OSGi-ification of Commons DBCP; we're focusing here on building OSGi projects, not converting existing non-OSGi libraries.

The next section covers how to configure the Felix Bundle Plugin without using the special bundle packaging type that it provides.

B.3.4   *Using the plug-in without changing the packaging type*

Sometimes changing the packaging type of a project isn't an option, so we need to find another way to make packaging plug-ins do their job. Maven 2 provides hooks in its lifecycle where plug-ins' goals can be launched.

Here are the two steps you need to follow to use the Felix Bundle Plugin without using the bundle packaging type:

- Ensure that the packaging type is set to `jar`.
- Tie the bundle goal of the plug-in to the package phase of the default lifecycle.

Listing B.4 illustrates the necessary configuration.

Listing B.4 Using the Felix Bundle Plugin without the `bundle` packaging type

```
<project (...)>
  <modelVersion>4.0.0</modelVersion>
  <parent>
    <artifactId>parent</artifactId>
    <groupId>com.manning.sdmia.appb.directory</groupId>
    <version>1.0.0</version>
  </parent>
  <artifactId>directory.domain</artifactId>
  <name>Directory Domain</name>              Sets packaging
  <packaging>jar</packaging>                 type as JAR

  <build>
    <plugins>
      <plugin>
        <groupId>org.apache.felix</groupId>
        <artifactId>maven-bundle-plugin</artifactId>
        <version>${felix.bundle.plugin.version}</version>
        <extensions>true</extensions>
        <executions>                              Makes execution
          <execution>                             happen during
            <id>bundle-manifest</id>              package phase
            <phase>package</phase>
            <goals>
              <goal>bundle</goal>            Sets plug-in's
            </goals>                         goal to launch
          </execution>
        </executions>
        <configuration>
          <instructions>                 Defines plug-in
          (...)                          configuration for
          </instructions>                OSGi metadata
        </configuration>
      </plugin>
    </plugins>
  </build>
</project>
```

The configuration illustrated in listing B.4 causes Maven 2 to trigger the `bundle` goal of the Felix Bundle Plugin when the build lifecycle reaches the `package` phase. This makes the OSGi packaging integrate smoothly with the Maven 2 lifecycle, without any modification to the packaging type of the project.

> **NOTE** This solution is a little bit more verbose, so you should stick to the bundle packaging whenever the packaging type isn't an issue.

So far we've covered all the settings necessary for the Felix Bundle Plugin in the POM of the target project. In the next section, we'll cover how to externalize the Bnd instructions in a dedicated file.

B.3.5   *Using a property file for externalization*

The Felix Bundle Plugin configuration accepts an _include element, which makes Bnd use the specified nested file when generating the bundle and its manifest. The following snippet illustrates the use of the _include element to use an osgi.bnd for the Bnd configuration:

```
<configuration>
  <instructions>
    <Bundle-Name>directory.dao.jdbc</Bundle-Name>
    <_include>osgi.bnd</_include>
  </instructions>
</configuration>
```

In the previous snippet, the osgi.bnd file lies at the root of the target project (besides its POM file) and must be a compliant Bnd file. We covered the format of these files in chapter 6, when converting the Commons DBCP library into an OSGi bundle. Here is a quick reminder: comment lines start with #, line continuations are indicated with the backslash character (\) at the end of the line, and patterns like ! or * are accepted. Maven 2 properties are also available in Bnd files.

The following snippet shows the osgi.bnd file for the DAO JDBC implementation bundle of our sample project:

```
Export-Package:
Import-Package: com.manning.sdmia.directory.*;
       version="${project.version}",\
 org.springframework.*;version="${spring.version.range}",\
 *
```

When should we use an externalized Bnd file instead of centralizing instructions in the POM? This is a matter of taste, but keeping instructions in a dedicated file can make sense, especially when the POM is big. Another good reason is upgrading from a build system that relies on plain Bnd to a Maven 2-based build: existing Bnd files will integrate smoothly with the new build system.

The Pax Construct (covered in appendix D) makes ingenious use of the externalized Bnd file: it defines a common configuration for the Felix Bundle Plugin in a parent POM, which all OSGi modules inherit from. This common configuration sets OSGi metadata like name, version, symbolic name, and so on, based on the POM information, and it includes an osgi.bnd file. Modules can then benefit from the common configuration for most of the metadata and use the osgi.bnd file for more specific metadata, like Export-Package or Import-Package. This solution provides a good balance between uniformity and specialization.

We're now getting close to the end of our coverage of the Felix Bundle Plugin. It's obviously a great help for OSGi developments with Maven 2, but it can go further by enhancing day-to-day development with Eclipse, as we'll see next.

B.3.6   *Integrating with the Eclipse PDE*

Maven 2 is a powerful build tool that comes with some useful features like dependency management. You'll be happy to learn that you can benefit from such features not only for building your project but also when developing with your IDE, like Eclipse. Let's get started by introducing the Maven Eclipse Plugin, which has changed the life of many Java developers.

Java, and especially Java EE, applications can have a lot of dependencies, and configuring your IDE to have all these dependencies in the project classpath can be *very* cumbersome and error-prone. By using a dependency management tool (which is what Maven 2 is), you gain a precise map of all these dependencies. There's only one step needed to use this map to configure your IDE, and that's what the Maven Eclipse Plugin is for. To try it, cd to a Maven 2 project that has numerous dependencies and type the following command:

```
mvn eclipse:eclipse
```

The command triggers the creation of the Eclipse configuration files for the project (like .project and .classpath). Maven 2 relies on the POM to create these files and uses information like the artifact ID and the dependencies to get a project that's ready to import into Eclipse.

> **NOTE** Maven 2 uses (in the .classpath file) a classpath variable, M2_REPO, that you'll have to create in Eclipse. It must point to your Maven 2 local repository.

Now that we're able to integrate a Maven 2 project into Eclipse, the next step is to integrate an OSGi project into the Eclipse Plugin Development using Maven 2 and the Felix Bundle Plugin. Appendix A covers how to develop OSGi and Spring DM applications within Eclipse, and you learned, among other things, that you need a META-INF/MANIFEST.MF file at the root of your Eclipse project to be able to provision an OSGi runtime configuration with it. We already know everything about the generation of the manifest with the Felix Bundle Plugin, so all we have to do is configure Maven 2 accordingly. This can be done in two steps:

- Add the root of the project as resource directory in the POM.
- Tell the Felix Bundle Plugin to generate the manifest in the META-INF directory.

Listing B.5 illustrates the configuration that must be done in the build element of the POM.

Listing B.5 Configuring the Felix Bundle Plugin for integration with Eclipse PDE

```
<build>
  <resources>
    <resource>
      <directory>src/main/resources</directory>        Adds standard
    </resource>                                          resource directory
    <resource>
      <directory>.</directory>                           Adds root as
      <includes>                                         resource directory
        <include>META-INF/**</include>                   Includes only
      </includes>                                        META-INF
    </resource>
  </resources>
```

```
<plugins>
  <plugin>
    <groupId>org.apache.felix</groupId>
    <artifactId>maven-bundle-plugin</artifactId>
    <version>${felix.bundle.plugin.version}</version>
    <configuration>
        <manifestLocation>META-INF</manifestLocation>    <──┐  Specifies where to
        <instructions>                                        │  generate manifest
        (...)
        </instructions>
    </configuration>
  </plugin>
</plugins>
</build>
```

Once you've modified the POM as shown in listing B.5, launch the `mvn clean package` command: it will trigger the generation of the manifest in the META-INF directory (don't forget to refresh the project in Eclipse!). Eclipse will then identify the project as an OSGi project and will let you add it in any OSGi framework runtime configuration. Note that Spring DM configuration files should be located in the META-INF/ spring directory for Eclipse to see them when running an OSGi framework from the IDE.

> **NOTE** If your project uses Blueprint, you should create the OSGI-INF/blueprint directory at the root of the project, place the Blueprint configuration files in it, and add an `include` element with `OSGI-INF/**` to the POM.

We've demonstrated here that any Maven 2 project can easily be configured to benefit from the Eclipse PDE tooling by using manifest generation provided by the Felix Bundle Plugin. Using both tools without losing the advantages of either is possible.

This concludes our presentation of the Felix Bundle Plugin, which is a powerful yet simple to use packaging tool for OSGi projects based on Maven 2. It builds on top of Bnd to generate the final OSGi bundle and doesn't need much configuration, thanks to its reasonable default behavior. Because it acts as a bridge between Maven 2 and Bnd, the Felix Bundle Plugin is suited for making an existing Maven 2 build OSGi-compliant or for upgrading an OSGi project to Maven 2.

The next section introduces an alternative to the Felix Bundle Plugin: Bundlor. This tool also integrates with Maven 2 but isn't based on Bnd and, as such, doesn't follow the exact same philosophy. It provides better support for some popular enterprise frameworks.

B.4   *Introducing Bundlor and its Maven plug-in*

Bundlor is a tool to ease the creation of OSGi-compliant manifests. It uses a template-based approach, where the developer writes a template that can contain standard OSGi headers as well as Bundlor-specific headers. Bundlor then takes as input the target JAR and this template to generate the manifest file, with the correct OSGi metadata. Bundlor scans the content of the JAR (class files, but also various resources like Spring configuration files) to detect dependencies and complements its analysis with the template, which drives part of the manifest generation. Figure B.4 illustrates this mechanism.

As you can see, Bundlor is more about manifest generation; it scans classes and resources available on the classpath to put them in the final bundle and generate the appropriate manifest.

Bundlor can be used from the command line or in build tools like Ant or Maven 2. Here, we'll study its integration within Maven 2, but thanks to its template-based approach, most of the content of this section is also valid for the other forms Bundlor takes.

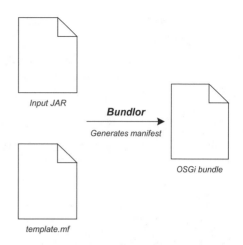

Figure B.4 **Bundlor takes an input JAR and a manifest template to generate a manifest with OSGi-compliant headers. It doesn't modify the content of the input JAR.**

Section B.4.1 covers the basic use of Bundlor in a Maven 2 project and how to properly set up the tool in a module-based project. Once you have grasped the basics of Bundlor, you'll learn about its specific headers in section B.4.2 and discover the real power of the template-based approach. Section B.4.3 then covers which sources (Java classes, Spring configuration files, and so on) Bundlor can scan to detect the dependencies of a JAR. By the end of this section, you'll know not only how to use Bundlor in your OSGi projects, but you'll have enough points of comparison to choose between the Felix Bundle Plugin and Bundlor.

Why not stick to the Felix Bundle Plugin and Bnd?

Bundlor is an alternative to Bnd. It has a Maven 2 plug-in, which can be used in place of the Felix Bundle Plugin. The SpringSource team created Bundlor mainly because Bnd lacks some features needed for the integration in an IDE (Bundlor is part of the SpringSource Tool Suite, and some functions build on top of it).

The code samples for this book use Maven 2 and the Felix Bundle Plugin, but we also provide this introduction to Bundlor because we think choice is good. Most Spring-related projects (Spring Framework, dm Server, and projects of the Spring portfolio) use Bundlor as their OSGi packaging tool. Spring DM used the Felix Bundle Plugin for its own build until version 1.2 but switched to Bundlor from version 2.0 on.

B.4.1 Setting up Bundlor in Maven 2

Bundlor's Maven 2 plug-in doesn't provide any new packaging type but rather a goal that must be launched after the packaging of the target JAR. This section covers how to set up Bundlor for simple use and then how to take advantage of Maven 2 features for a more efficient setup.

BASIC USE OF BUNDLOR IN MAVEN 2

Adding Bundlor to a Maven 2 project can be done in three steps:

- Add the SpringSource EBR to the POM.
- Add the Bundlor plug-in declaration to the POM.
- Create a template.mf file.

Listing B.6 illustrates the steps that deal with the project's POM.

Listing B.6   Configuring Bundlor in a POM

```xml
<?xml version="1.0" encoding="UTF-8"?>
<project (...)>
  <modelVersion>4.0.0</modelVersion>
  <parent>
    <artifactId>parent</artifactId>
    <groupId>com.manning.sdmia.appb.directory</groupId>
    <version>1.0.0</version>
  </parent>
  <artifactId>directory.domain</artifactId>
  <version>1.0.0</version>
  <name>Directory Domain</name>
  <packaging>jar</packaging>

  <build>
    <plugins>
      <plugin>
        <groupId>com.springsource.bundlor</groupId>          Declares
        <artifactId>                                          Bundlor plug-in
          com.springsource.bundlor.maven
        </artifactId>
        <version>1.0.0.RELEASE</version>
        <executions>
          <execution>
            <id>bundlor</id>                                  Inserts Bundlor's
            <goals>                                           transform task
              <goal>bundlor</goal>                            after package goal
            </goals>
          </execution>
        </executions>
      </plugin>
      <plugin>
        <groupId>org.apache.maven.plugins</groupId>
        <artifactId>maven-jar-plugin</artifactId>
        <version>2.3</version>                                Makes JAR plug-in
        <configuration>                                       use generated
          <useDefaultManifestFile>                            manifest
            true
          </useDefaultManifestFile>
        </configuration>
      </plugin>
    </plugins>
  </build>

  <pluginRepositories>
```

```
    <pluginRepository>
      <id>
        com.springsource.repository.bundles.release
      </id>
      <name>SpringSource EBR</name>
      <url>
      http://repository.springsource.com/
      maven/bundles/release
      </url>
    </pluginRepository>
  </pluginRepositories>
</project>
```

Adds SpringSource EBR as plug-in repository

Notice that listing B.6 doesn't provide any configuration for the plug-in. Bundlor accepts some optional configuration parameters, but only the template file is compulsory. The template must reside at the root of the project and be called template.mf.

The following snippet shows the template file for the domain module of our sample project:

```
Bundle-Name: ${project.artifactId}
Bundle-Version: ${project.version}
Bundle-SymbolicName: com.manning.sdmia.appb.${project.artifactId}
Bundle-ManifestVersion: 2
```

We can draw the following conclusions from our first Bundlor template:

- *Headers*—The template accepts standard OSGi headers. We'll see later that the template can also contain specific headers that help with generating the content of other headers in the final manifest.
- *Properties*—The template accepts properties with the usual ${property.name} syntax. In our case (Maven 2), properties come from the POM file. More generally, the origin of properties depends on the way Bundlor is used (command line, Ant, and so on).

It's time to generate our OSGi bundle with Bundlor. As shown in listing B.6, we use the transform goal of the Bundlor plug-in. This goal binds, by default, to the package lifecycle phase (which means the transform goal is launched just *after* the package phase), so we can use the mvn clean package command to generate the JAR.

The following snippet shows an excerpt of the manifest of the generated JAR (we kept only the relevant headers for brevity):

```
Manifest-Version: 1.0
Export-Package: com.manning.sdmia.directory.domain;version="1.0.0"
Bundle-Version: 1.0.0
Bundle-Name: directory.domain
Bundle-ManifestVersion: 2
Bundle-SymbolicName: com.manning.sdmia.appb.directory.domain
```

Notice that Bundlor substituted the values of the properties for the placeholders and automatically exported the package of the domain objects at the specified Bundle-Version. We'll learn more about Bundlor's default strategy for the Import- and

Export-Package headers in section B.4.2, but let's say for now that it exports every package of the JAR at the version specified for the Bundle-Version header and imports all referenced packages. We'll also see in section B.4.2 how to override and tune these default strategies.

We've introduced the basic use of Bundlor in Maven 2. We'll see in the next subsection how to leverage some features of both Maven 2 and Bundlor's plug-in for a more efficient configuration, especially in multimodule projects.

CONFIGURING BUNDLOR IN A MULTIMODULE PROJECT

If you use Bundlor for a multimodule project, it's a good idea to centralize some settings in the parent POM. Thanks to POM inheritance, submodules will then benefit from these settings.

Listing B.7 illustrates the centralization of the version of the plug-in and of the SpringSource EBR declaration.

Listing B.7   Centralizing plug-in version and repository in the parent POM

```
<project (...)>
  <modelVersion>4.0.0</modelVersion>
  <groupId>com.manning.sdmia.appb.directory</groupId>
  <artifactId>parent</artifactId>
  <packaging>pom</packaging>
  <version>1.0.0</version>
  <name>Directory Parent Project</name>

  <properties>
    <spring.dm.version>2.0.0.M1</spring.dm.version>
    <spring.version>3.0.2.RELEASE</spring.version>         ◁── Defines property
    <bundlor.version>1.0.0.RELEASE</bundlor.version>           for plug-in version
  </properties>

  <pluginRepositories>
    <pluginRepository>
      <id>
        com.springsource.repository.bundles.release
      </id>
      <name>SpringSource EBR</name>                    Specifies plug-in
      <url>                                            repository
      http://repository.springsource.com/
⇨     maven/bundles/release
      </url>
    </pluginRepository>
  </pluginRepositories>
</project>
```

The next step towards centralization is declaring the Bundlor plug-in and some default settings in the parent POM. Listing B.8 illustrates this step.

Listing B.8   Setting defaults in parent POM

```
<build>
  <plugins>
    <plugin>
```

```
      <groupId>com.springsource.bundlor</groupId>
      <artifactId>com.springsource.bundlor.maven</artifactId>
      <version>${bundlor.version}</version>
      <executions>
        <execution>
          <id>bundlor</id>
            <goals>
              <goal>bundlor</goal>
            </goals>
        </execution>
      </executions>
      <configuration>
        <bundleSymbolicName>
  com.manning.sdmia.appb.${project.artifactId}
        </bundleSymbolicName>
        <bundleVersion>
  ${project.version}
        </bundleVersion>
      </configuration>
    </plugin>
  </plugins>
</build>
```

Sets
common
manifest
headers

The declaration of the Bundlor plug-in in listing B.8 is similar to the one in listing B.6, except that it adds some configuration with the `bundleSymbolicName` and `bundleVersion` elements. Every submodule will benefit from this common declaration and will have to complement the manifest generation guidelines in its own template.mf file (typically with instructions dealing with imports and exports).

Note that we bound Bundlor's `bundlor` goal to the package phase in the parent POM in listing B.8. This means that each submodule that uses the parent POM must have a template.mf file in its base directory, or the build will fail. The parent project doesn't need a template.mf file because Bundlor doesn't attempt to transform artifacts with the `pom` packaging.

If a submodule doesn't need Bundlor (such as an integration test module), it can disable Bundlor with the `enabled` element:

```
<plugin>
  <groupId>com.springsource.bundlor</groupId>
  <artifactId>com.springsource.bundlor.maven</artifactId>
  <configuration>
    <enabled>false</enabled>
  </configuration>
</plugin>
```

We've covered the basic use of Bundlor in Maven 2 and the more advanced configuration suitable for multimodule projects. The next section delves into the most important feature of Bundlor: the manifest template.

B.4.2 *The template mechanism*

As stated previously, Bundlor uses a manifest template to generate an OSGi-compliant manifest. Bundlor copies any entries from the template into the final manifest, except for specific headers that provide it with instructions for generation. These specific headers help Bundlor grasp the essence of the bundle (imports, exports, version, and so on) and make the manifest generation less cumbersome and more reliable. This section introduces the headers Bundlor accepts in manifest templates and provides samples and guidelines for their use.

BUNDLOR'S SPECIFIC HEADERS

Table B.5 lists the specific headers that Bundlor uses to generate the final OSGi-compliant manifest.

Table B.5   Bundlor's specific headers and default behavior

Header	Description
`Excluded-Exports`	Packages that must be excluded from the `Export-Package` header (Bundlor exports by default all the packages of the input JAR).
`Excluded-Imports`	Packages that must be excluded from the `Import-Package` header (Bundlor imports by default all the packages referenced in the input JAR, either from the code or in special files).
`Export-Template`	Special `Export-Package` instructions, which accept patterns (such as `*`) and property substitution. By default, Bundlor exports all the packages at the specified `Bundle-Version`.
`Ignored-Existing-Headers`	Manifest headers from the input JAR's manifest that Bundlor should not include in the generated manifest.
`Import-Template`	Packages that should be added to the final `Import-Package` header. You can use this header to augment the imports that Bundlor automatically detects, to specify a version, or to mark imports as optional.
`Version-Patterns`	Version expansion patterns that can be reused in the template manifest. We'll detail this advanced feature shortly in the "Support for the version directive" section.

A typical Bundlor manifest template contains standard OSGi headers, whose values can take advantage of property substitution, as well as specific headers. Listing B.9 shows a manifest template that mixes both kinds of headers.

Listing B.9   A typical Bundlor manifest template mixes OSGi and specific headers

```
Bundle-Name: ${project.artifactId}
Bundle-Version: ${project.version}
Bundle-SymbolicName: com.manning.sdmia.appb.${project.artifactId}
Bundle-ManifestVersion: 2
Import-Template: com.manning.sdmia.directory.*;
        version="${project.version}",
  org.springframework.*;version="${spring.version.range}"
Excluded-Exports: com.manning.sdmia.directory.*
```

Let's next see how to use Bundlor's headers in order to understand the power of the tool.

USING BUNDLOR'S HEADERS

Apart from the `Version-Patterns` and `Ignored-Existing-Headers` headers, all Bundlor's headers accept a list of comma-separated packages. In these cases, Bundlor accepts the `*` pattern to match multiple packages and property placeholders:

```
Import-Template: com.manning.sdmia.directory.*;
    version="${project.version}",
  org.springframework.*;version="${spring.version.range}"
```

Matching multiple packages is useful when specifying the version for a set of packages or when setting them as optional.

A manifest template can also contain OSGi headers, like `Import-Package`, especially when Bundlor's default detection capabilities fail. Bundlor's headers are guidelines that the tool uses, but they only complement what it's able to detect. This means that if Bundlor can't detect some packages needed by the OSGi bundle, they shouldn't appear in the `Import-Template` header but in the `Import-Package` header, just like the `org.h2` package in the following snippet:

```
Import-Template: org.springframework.*;version="${spring.version.range}"
Import-Package: org.h2
```

Regarding exports, Bundlor has the following default behavior: it exports all the packages from the input JAR at the specified `Bundle-Version`. This behavior isn't always appropriate—especially for internal packages—and that's where the `Excluded-Exports` header comes in. We use the `Excluded-Exports` header for the JDBC DAO implementation module of our sample project, from which no class should leak:

```
Excluded-Exports: com.manning.sdmia.directory.*
```

Bundlor also provides the `Ignored-Existing-Headers` header to clean the generated manifest of unwanted headers present in the input JAR's manifest. The following snippet (taken from Spring DM's Bundlor configuration) shows the use of this header:

```
Ignored-Existing-Headers:
 Ant-Version,
 Archiver-Version,
 Unversioned-Imports,
 Tool,
 Ignore-Package,
 Private-Package,
 Created-By,
 Bnd-LastModified,
 Import-Package,
 Export-Package
```

We've covered Bundlor's support for import and export directives. The next subsection deals with an advanced feature that Bundlor provides for the OSGi `version` directive.

SUPPORT FOR THE VERSION DIRECTIVE

Bundlor is able to expand package versions using expansion patterns, which makes the manifest more dynamic. This is particularly useful when you want to specify a *version range* for imports.

Let's see this feature in action by defining version and version range properties in the POM (usually the parent POM):

```
<properties>
  <spring.version>3.0.2.RELEASE</spring.version>
  <spring.version.range>
    [${spring.version},4.0)
  </spring.version.range>
</properties>
```

You can use the `range` property in the manifest template and Bundlor will substitute the placeholder with the property value when generating the manifest:

```
Import-Template: org.springframework.*;
➥    version="${spring.version.range}"
```

This technique takes advantage of Maven 2's features and Bundlor's substitution capacity, but we can push it further to let Bundlor calculate the version range, based only on the `version` property (there's no need anymore to specify a property for the range). For a version property placeholder, Bundlor accepts not only the property name but also an *expansion pattern* that tells it how to generate the final version range. The following snippet illustrates the syntax of an expansion pattern with the previous `spring.version` property:

```
Import-Template: org.springframework.*;
➥    version="${spring.version:[=.=.=.=, +1.0.0)}"
```

The expansion pattern of the previous snippet specifies that the beginning of the range stays exactly the same as the value of the `spring.version` property (an = sign for each part of the version and the qualifier) and the end of the range should be one integer larger for the major number (+1) and 0 for the minor and micro numbers. The range generated by Bundlor is then [3.0.0,4.0.0).

Thanks to the `Version-Patterns` header, you can name an expansion pattern and use it for several imports. Instead of using the pattern itself in the property placeholder, you refer to its name. The following snippet shows how to define a `spring` pattern and use it in the `Import-Template` header:

```
Version-Patterns: spring;pattern="[=.=.=.=, +1.0.0)"
Import-Template: org.springframework.*;
➥    version="${spring.version:spring}"
```

Note that we could have defined more than one version pattern by separating them with commas.

Writing a manifest template should no longer be a problem for you. Bundlor provides a limited, yet powerful, set of headers that influence the generation of the manifest and makes it less cumbersome and more reliable.

As stated previously, the template mainly gathers guidelines for the generation. Bundlor builds its generation mechanism on these guidelines but also by scanning the input JAR. Understanding Bundlor's scanning capacities helps with writing consistent manifest templates, especially for the `Import-Package` header. What Bundlor is able to scan is the topic of the next section.

B.4.3 Bundlor's scanning capabilities for runtime dependencies

Bundlor's main goal in life is generating OSGi-compliant manifests, and to do so, it scans JAR files to determine their runtime dependencies. Bundlor can scan Java classes and also some commonly used file types (Spring configuration files, web.xml, and so on). This analysis, augmented by the manifest template, makes the manifest generation easier and more reliable, as the developer ends up giving only guidelines in the template and lets Bundlor do the tedious work.

This section covers the categories of files Bundlor is able to analyze, and for each of them gives the basics of Bundlor's capabilities. Consult the reference documentation at http://www.springsource.org/bundlor/ to find out which dependencies Bundlor can extract from the different kinds of files.

DETECTION FROM JAVA CLASSES

Bundlor scans all the Java classes of the input JAR and detects the dependencies by analyzing the bytecode. But Java classes are a specific case, because Bundlor also populates the `Export-Package` manifest header depending on the JAR content. By default, Bundlor exports any package that contains a class or a non-Java resource. (We already discussed this behavior.)

Detecting dependencies for the `Import-Package` manifest header is trickier, because there are many places in a Java class that another Java type can be referenced. For instance, if a class of the input JAR inherits from another class that comes from another bundle, the package that the parent class belongs to must be imported. The same goes for implemented interfaces, annotations, field types, method argument types, exceptions, and so on. Fortunately, Bundlor automatically detects all these references and imports the correct packages—you can (optionally) specify the version, with the help of the * wildcard to propagate it to subpackages.

DETECTION FROM SPRING CONFIGURATION FILES

Bundlor automatically detects Spring configuration files from Spring-powered bundles. To detect these files, Bundlor follows the same rules as Spring DM: files must be located in the META-INF/spring directory or specified in the `Spring-Context` manifest header.

Once Bundlor has detected Spring configuration files, it analyzes them to extract their dependencies. Most of Spring's namespaces are supported (`beans`, `aop`, `context`, `jee`, `jms`, `lang`, `oxm`, `osgi`, `util`, and `webflow`) and Bundlor is able to extract dependencies from attributes that await classes (such as `beans:bean/@class` or `util:list/@list-class`) or packages (such as `context:component-scan/@base-package`).

Despite its powerful scanning capacities, Bundlor can miss some dependencies. The following snippet reveals Bundlor's limitations:

```
<bean id="dataSource"
    class="org.springframework.jdbc.datasource.
    SimpleDriverDataSource">
  <property name="driverClass"
        value="org.h2.Driver" />
  <property name="url"
```

Catches this package

Misses this package

```
              value="jdbc:h2:mem:some-db" />
  <property name="username" value="sa" />
  <property name="password" value="" />
</bean>
```

Why does Bundlor miss the dependency toward the database driver? As stated before, Bundlor focuses on attributes that require classes or packages. It detects the package of the `SimpleDriverDataSource`, because it's in a `class` attribute, but misses the database driver because it's in a `value` attribute, which can contain anything. This means the manifest template must explicitly add the `org.h2` package to the dependencies. The following snippet shows what the manifest template would look like:

```
Import-Template: org.springframework.*;
⇨      version="${spring.version.range}"
Import-Package: org.h2
```

The case we've just exposed is rather unusual, and Bundlor will detect dependencies from Spring configuration files appropriately most of the time.

Let's see now what Bundlor can do for us when we're using Blueprint.

DETECTION FROM BLUEPRINT CONFIGURATION FILES

Bundlor scans for Blueprint configuration files in the OSGI-INF/blueprint directory or follows the `Bundle-Blueprint` manifest header. As with vanilla Spring configuration files, Bundlor scans attributes that require package or class name attributes (such as `bp:bean/@class`, `bp:service/@interface`, and `bp:list/@value-type`). Bundlor's Blueprint and Spring support are similar, and they suffer the same kind of limitations (for example, when specifying a class or package name in a `value` attribute).

DETECTION FROM JPA'S PERSISTENCE.XML

The JPA configuration file, persistence.xml, can refer to classes that don't belong to the owning bundle. Such classes are entity classes (which lie in dedicated domain bundles) or the persistence provider class (which lies in the JPA implementation bundle). Bundlor is able to detect a persistence.xml file in META-INF and scans it to extract classes from the `provider` and `class` elements.

The following snippet shows the content of a simple persistence.xml file:

```
<persistence (...)>
  <persistence-unit name="directory" transaction-type="local">
    <provider>
  org.eclipse.persistence.jpa.PersistenceProvider          Detects
    </provider>                                             persistence
    <class>                                                 provider package
  com.manning.sdmia.directory.domain.Contact    Detects entity
    </class>                                       packages
  </persistence-unit>
</persistence>
```

In this case, Bundlor will add the `org.eclipse.persistence.jpa` and `com.manning.sdmia.directory.domain` packages to the `Import-Package` manifest header of the owning bundle. Note that you should complete Bundlor's detection in the manifest template by specifying the exact version for each package.

Let's now see what Bundlor can do with a popular ORM tool, Hibernate.

DETECTION OF CLASSES FROM HIBERNATE'S MAPPING FILES

Hibernate's mapping files can refer to entity classes and implementation classes (user type, generator, and so on) that aren't located in the owning bundle. Bundlor scans files that end with .hbm and detects dependencies from attributes like `class/@name`, `generator/@class`, and so on. Bundlor also handles subtleties like unqualified entity class names by watching for the `package` attribute (the `package` attribute allows you to specify a package once in your Hibernate mapping files and then use unqualified Java class names in nested elements).

Let's take as an example the following snippet of a Hibernate mapping file:

```
<hibernate-mapping
    package="com.manning.sdmia.directory.domain">

  <class name="Contact" table="contact">
    <id name="id" column="contact_id">
      <generator class="sequence"/>
    </id>
    (...)
  </class>

</hibernate-mapping>
```

Bundlor will detect the `com.manning.sdmia.directory.domain` package, which is normal behavior because `Contact` is an unqualified class name (which refers to the package specified in the enclosing `hibernate-mapping` element), but it won't detect the class name hidden behind the `sequence` shortcut in the `generator` element.

Let's switch now from ORM tools to web applications, as Bundlor also scans web.xml files.

DETECTION OF CLASSES FROM THE WEB APPLICATION DESCRIPTION FILE, WEB.XML

When an OSGi bundle is a web application, it contains a web.xml file that can declare servlet listeners, servlet filters, or servlets. Servlets can come from the bundle itself, but most of the time they come from the bundle of the web frameworks used in the application (such as Spring MVC). The web bundle then depends on these classes, and the corresponding packages must be included in the `Import-Package` manifest header.

Bundlor detects any WEB-INF/web.xml file in a bundle and scans elements that can contain class names (such as `listener-class`, `filter-class`, `servlet-class`, and also nested `param-value` elements in elements that accept them). The following snippet shows an excerpt of a web.xml file that declares a listener to bootstrap a web OSGi-enabled Spring application context:

```
<web-app (...)>

  <context-param>
    <param-name>contextClass</param-name>
    <param-value>
  org.springframework.osgi.web.context.support.      Detects class
      OsgiBundleXmlWebApplicationContext             in parameter
    </param-value>
  </context-param>
```

```
<listener>
  <listener-class>
org.springframework.web.context.ContextLoaderListener
  </listener-class>
</listener>
```

**Detects
listener class**

```
</web-app>
```

From this web.xml file, Bundlor will detect and add to the `Import-Package` manifest header the `org.springframework.osgi.web.context.support` and `org.spring-framework.web.context` packages.

This concludes our exploration of Bundlor's capacities for detecting runtime dependencies. Applications aren't composed only of Java classes—they usually contain configuration files for various frameworks or standards. These files often refer to classes external to the owning bundle, and their packages must be included in its runtime dependencies. Bundlor can not only detect dependencies from Java classes but also from the files of several common enterprise frameworks, like Spring and Hibernate, and of various standards like Blueprint, JPA, and web applications. These detection features save you from the tedious and error-prone work of dependency tracking, but make sure you complete the template manifest with version ranges or directives like `optional` to obtain a consistent manifest.

B.5   *Summary*

OSGi brings new power to your Java applications, but it doesn't force you to change the way you're building them, especially if you rely on Maven 2. If you were a total newcomer to the world of Maven 2, you should by now be more comfortable with it and be able to use it for all your Java projects.

When it comes to OSGi, Maven 2 has built-in features like multimodule projects and dependency management that are particularly useful. Thanks to its plug-in-based architecture and the hooks it provides in its lifecycle, plugging tools like Bnd or Bundlor into projects is straightforward. You can then change the project packaging to switch from a standard JAR to an OSGi-compliant bundle by just adding a few lines of XML, and you can enjoy Maven 2 features like POM inheritance and property substitution.

This appendix provided in-depth coverage of the Felix Bundle Plugin and Bundlor, which are two powerful tools you can use to produce OSGi bundles with Maven 2. Which one should you choose? This is a matter of taste, and you now hold all the cards to make your own decision. Let's just say that the Felix Bundle Plugin, which builds on top of Bnd and also brings its own features, detects Java classes and resources that are available on the classpath and can gather them in the final JAR. Bundlor is more of a manifest generator, as it takes a JAR as an input, analyzes it, takes instructions from a template, and generates a manifest with OSGi-compliant headers.

Now that you know exactly how to add an OSGi flavor to your Maven 2 projects, perhaps you want to go a bit further. What is the next step? Appendix D, which covers two tools from the Pax family, can help you sharpen your OSGi development skills.

One of these tools, Pax Construct, is made of a set of Maven 2 plug-ins that streamline the Maven 2 build process for OSGi. They build on top of notions we introduced here: tools like the Felix Bundle Plugin and Maven 2 features like multimodule project management—they constitute a natural continuation of the topic of this appendix.

appendix C
Spring DM development with Ant and Ivy

We consciously chose to use Maven 2 throughout this book, mainly because that's the build tool we're the most familiar with, but also because Spring DM uses it for its own building and testing. Nevertheless Ant remains a very popular build tool, so here we'll provide enough information for you to get started with OSGi and Spring DM development using Ant.

The aim of this appendix is to reproduce part of what we did in chapter 3, but in an Ant and Ivy fashion: writing and packaging a Spring-powered bundle, then running the corresponding integration test. We won't focus on pure Spring DM topics—you should already be familiar with the core principles of Spring DM before reading this appendix.

Why would you want to use Ant instead of Maven 2? There are many reasons, the first being that Ant is your favorite build tool! Generally speaking, Ant can address complex builds, because it lets the user handle very technical tasks, whereas Maven 2 has a more declarative approach.

We'll start with the installation of Ant, and then dive into writing the bundle itself and compiling it with Ant. We'll then cover how to create an OSGi bundle using Bnd, which integrates nicely with Ant. Apache Ivy will help us handle our dependencies, and we'll see how to customize Spring DM's testing framework to make it work with Ivy. We'll finish by writing and running the integration test with Ant.

C.1 Installing Ant

Ant can be downloaded from its official website, http://ant.apache.org. It comes as an archive file that creates the directory apache-ant-1.8.1 when it's extracted.

> **NOTE** We're using Ant 1.8.1 here. For all Ant's tasks to work properly, you should use a JDK (not a JRE). Java 1.5 or later is strongly recommended.

Next, you need to create an ANT_HOME environment variable that contains the directory where you installed Ant. To make the ant command available in your shell, add the ANT_HOME/bin directory to your PATH environment variable (use $ANT_HOME/bin if you're using a Linux-based operating system or %ANT_HOME%\bin for Windows).

NOTE You should also set the JAVA_HOME environment variable to the directory where your JDK is installed. The *_HOME variable should not contain quotes nor end with / or \.

You can check that Ant is correctly installed by running ant -version, which outputs information about the version of Ant:

```
Apache Ant version 1.8.1 compiled on April 30 2010
```

Now that we're sure that Ant works, we're ready to create a Spring DM bundle and the corresponding Ant build file.

C.2   *Creating a Spring DM bundle with Ant*

Creating our bundle will involve three steps:

1 Creating the bundle's files (a Java class and a Spring configuration file)
2 Writing the Ant build file
3 Using Bnd's Ant task to package the project as an OSGi-compliant bundle

We'll look at each step in turn.

C.2.1   *Structure and content of the project*

Listing C.1 shows the structure of the project, which uses the standard Maven 2 layout. The bundle's Java class and Spring configuration file are displayed in bold.

Listing C.1   Spring DM bundle project structure

```
springdm-sample
  src/
    main/
      java/
        com/manning/springdmia/
          SpringDmSample.java
      resources/
        META-INF/
          spring/
            springdm-sample.xml
```

Listing C.2 shows the SpringDmSample class, which outputs a message on the console when an instance is created.

Listing C.2   The SpringDmSample class

```
package com.manning.sdmia;

public class SpringDmSample {
```

```
public SpringDmSample() {
  System.out.println("Spring DM sample created");
}

}
```

The Spring configuration file is in the META-INF/spring directory, which Spring DM's extender looks at when searching for an application context to bootstrap when the bundle is started. Our Spring application context will create an instance of SpringDm-Sample, which issues the message in listing C.2 on the console.

Listing C.3 shows the content of the Spring configuration file, springdm-sample.xml.

Listing C.3   The content of springdm-sample.xml

```
<?xml version="1.0" encoding="UTF-8"?>
<beans xmlns="http://www.springframework.org/schema/beans"
  xmlns:xsi="http://www.w3.org/2001/XMLSchema-instance"
  xsi:schemaLocation="http://www.springframework.org/schema/beans
  http://www.springframework.org/schema/beans/spring-beans.xsd">

  <bean id="springDmSampleBean" class="com.manning.sdmia.SpringDmSample" />

</beans>
```

That's it for the content of the project; let's now see how to build it with Ant.

C.2.2 *The Ant build file*

An Ant build file is an XML file located at the root of the project and usually called build.xml. If you run the ant command in a directory that contains a build.xml file, Ant will use it by default, whereas you'll have to provide the name of the file on the command line if it's not called build.xml.

An Ant build file consists of a succession of targets that can run from compilation to packaging to the creation of test reports. Here we're going to see how to compile our project and package it as a standard JAR.

First, we'll create a build.xml file at the root of the project. Its content is shown in listing C.4.

Listing C.4   Ant build file for compiling and packaging as a standard JAR

```
<?xml version="1.0" encoding="UTF-8"?>
<project name="springdm-sample" default="package" basedir=".">

  <property name="project.version" value="1.0.0"/>
  <property name="build.srcDir" value="src/main/java"/>
  <property name="build.resourceDir"
          value="src/main/resources"/>
  <property name="build.finalName"
          value="springdm-sample-${project.version}"/>
  <property name="build.dir" value="target"/>
  <property name="build.outputDir"
          value="${build.dir}/classes"/>
```

① Declares properties

```
<target name="clean"
        description="Clean the output directory">
  <delete dir="${build.dir}"/>
</target>

<target name="compile"
        description="Compile the code">
  <mkdir dir="${build.outputDir}"/>
  <javac destdir="${build.outputDir}"
         nowarn="false"
         debug="true"
         optimize="false"
         deprecation="true"
         target="1.5"
         verbose="false"
         fork="false"
         source="1.5">
    <src>
      <pathelement location="${build.srcDir}"/>
    </src>
  </javac>
  <copy todir="${build.outputDir}">
    <fileset dir="${build.resourceDir}"/>
  </copy>
</target>

<target name="package" depends="compile"
        description="Package as ordinary JAR">
  <jar jarfile="${build.dir}/${build.finalName}.jar"
       compress="true"
       index="false"
       basedir="${build.outputDir}" />
</target>
```

`</project>`

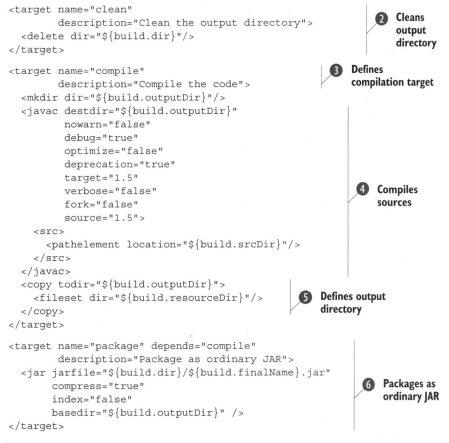

2 Cleans output directory

3 Defines compilation target

4 Compiles sources

5 Defines output directory

6 Packages as ordinary JAR

The build file starts with the declaration of a set of properties **1**. These properties are then used throughout the build file with the ${propertyName} syntax. The first target declared at **2** is for cleaning the output directory. We then define the compilation target at **3**, followed by the compilation itself **4** and then the copying of resources to the build directory **5**. The build file ends with the packaging of the project as a standard JAR at **6** (note that this target depends on the compile target).

You can build a JAR archive by launching the following command at the root of the project:

```
ant package
```

This produces the JAR file in the target directory. But don't we want to produce an OSGi-compliant bundle? The clean and compile targets are suitable for this, but we need to change the package target so that it uses a tool more appropriate to OSGi. In our case, we're going to use Bnd.

C.2.3   *Using Bnd with Ant to package the bundle*

We introduced Bnd in chapter 3, where we used it inside a Maven 2 plug-in. We also used it as a command-line tool in chapter 6. The good news is that Bnd can also work as an Ant task!

We'll look at how to make Bnd available to Ant builds and how to use the Bnd task inside a build file to produce an OSGi bundle.

INSTALLING BND FOR ANT

Ant can support new tasks by adding the corresponding libraries to its classpath. There are several ways to do this, but the easiest is to copy the library into the ANT_HOME/lib directory.

You can download Bnd from its web page (http://www.aqute.biz/Code/Bnd). The Bnd JAR contains the Ant task, so you only have to copy it to the ANT_HOME/lib to make the Bnd task available for all your builds.

Let's see now how to leverage this task.

PACKAGING THE BUNDLE WITH THE BND TASK

Using the Bnd task in Ant consists of two steps: importing the task and then using it with the bnd XML element. That's what listing C.5 illustrates.

> **Listing C.5   Using the Bnd Ant task to package an OSGi bundle**

```
<target name="package" depends="compile"
        description="Package the bundle with Bnd">

  <taskdef resource="aQute/bnd/ant/taskdef.properties" />

  <bnd files="build.bnd" classpath="${build.outputDir}"
      output="${build.dir}/${build.finalName}.jar" />

</target>
```

The package target is declared in the first line, the same way other targets are. But because the Bnd task isn't an Ant core task, we need to *define* it using a properties file that the Bnd JAR contains.

We can then use the task with the bnd element. Bnd isn't exactly a packaging tool: it scans the classpath (not a directory with class files) and gathers class files and resources into a JAR, following rules detailed in a configuration file (it also uses this file to generate the JAR manifest with the necessary OSGi metadata). That's why we use the classpath attribute to tell Bnd to scan the output directory, and the files attribute to indicate a configuration file.

> **NOTE**   Chapter 6 provides more details about Bnd's features and how to write configuration files.

The next step is to write the build.bnd file that the files attribute is pointing at. This file contains instructions that Bnd uses to generate the JAR. Listing C.6 shows the file content.

Listing C.6 The Bnd configuration file (build.bnd)

```
Bundle-Name=springdm-sample
Export-Package=com.manning.sdmia
Import-Package=*
Include-Resource=src/main/resources/
Private-Package=com.manning.sdmia
Bundle-SymbolicName=com.manning.sdmia.springdm-sample
Bundle-Version=${project.version}
```

Note that the Bnd configuration file can contain references to properties defined in the build file. We use this feature for defining the version of the bundle.

To package the bundle, launch the following command:

```
ant clean package
```

This produces a JAR in the same place as before, but this time it contains a manifest with the necessary OSGi metadata. You can try the bundle with the Equinox container we configured in chapter 3. Once the bundle is installed and started, the SpringDm-Sample should output a message to the console indicating that it has been created.

Testing the bundle manually—by installing it in an OSGi container—is cumbersome. That's why we introduced you to Spring DM's testing framework in chapter 3. The testing framework relies on Maven 2's local repository to provision an embedded OSGi container that the integration test then bootstraps. This is the default behavior, but as we're in an Ant appendix, we don't have a local Maven 2 repository, so we need to override the default behavior. Fortunately, Spring DM provides enough hooks in its testing framework to do this—we'll cover that in section C.4.

What we have to do immediately is retrieve the bundles we need for provisioning the OSGi container. For this we'll use a popular dependency management tool that integrates nicely with Ant: Apache Ivy.

C.3 *Provisioning with Apache Ivy*

Apache Ivy (http://ant.apache.org/ivy/) is a powerful dependency manager that's primarily used with Ant. What can Ivy help us with when developing a Spring DM bundle? It will download the bundles we need for our integration test. These bundles will then be used for compiling the project and provisioning the embedded OSGi container that the test framework launches.

We'll see in the following sections how to set up Ivy for Ant, how to configure the repositories Ivy will use to retrieve dependencies, and how to declare the dependencies in a configuration file before retrieving them from Ant.

C.3.1 *Installing Ivy for Ant*

Ivy is launched through an Ant task, so we need to make this task available to our Ant installation. All we have to do is download the Ivy distribution and copy the Ivy JAR to ANT_HOME/lib, just as we did with Bnd. Once this is done, all Ivy's tasks will be available to your Ant build.

We'll only use the `retrieve` task here, but before we do this, we need to configure the repositories Ivy will use for retrieving the dependencies.

C.3.2 *Configuring repositories for Ivy*

Ivy can be configured with an ivysettings.xml file located in the same directory as the Ant build file. This file can contain many configuration options, but we'll focus on *resolvers*.

In a nutshell, a resolver finds and downloads dependencies. We'll use a chained resolver here, which successively tries several remote repositories to download dependencies. Listing C.7 shows the content of the ivysettings.xml file.

Listing C.7 Configuring repositories in the ivysettings.xml file

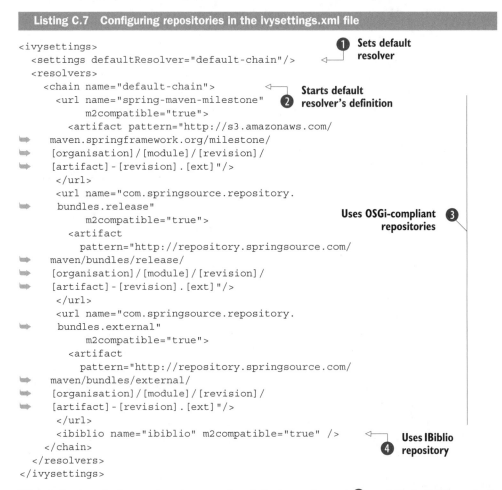

```
<ivysettings>
  <settings defaultResolver="default-chain"/>          ⬅  ❶ Sets default resolver
  <resolvers>
    <chain name="default-chain">                       ⬅  Starts default
      <url name="spring-maven-milestone"               ❷ resolver's definition
          m2compatible="true">
        <artifact pattern="http://s3.amazonaws.com/
➟   maven.springframework.org/milestone/
➟   [organisation]/[module]/[revision]/
➟   [artifact]-[revision].[ext]"/>
      </url>
      <url name="com.springsource.repository.
➟   bundles.release"
          m2compatible="true">                         Uses OSGi-compliant ❸
        <artifact                                       repositories
          pattern="http://repository.springsource.com/
➟   maven/bundles/release/
➟   [organisation]/[module]/[revision]/
➟   [artifact]-[revision].[ext]"/>
      </url>
      <url name="com.springsource.repository.
➟   bundles.external"
          m2compatible="true">
        <artifact
          pattern="http://repository.springsource.com/
➟   maven/bundles/external/
➟   [organisation]/[module]/[revision]/
➟   [artifact]-[revision].[ext]"/>
      </url>
      <ibiblio name="ibiblio" m2compatible="true" />    ⬅  Uses IBiblio
    </chain>                                             ❹ repository
  </resolvers>
</ivysettings>
```

The `default-chain` resolver is set as the default resolver at ❶ and its definition starts at ❷. The chain is made of three repositories that host only OSGi-compliant JAR files ❸ and the usual Maven 2 repository, IBiblio ❹. Note that this repository will be queried only if none of the previous ones can return a dependency, because it's the last element in the chain.

The next step consists of declaring the dependencies and modifying the Ant build files to make Ivy download them.

C.3.3 Retrieving Spring DM dependencies with Ivy

Ivy dependencies are declared in an ivy.xml file, located in the same directory as the Ant build file. Listing C.8 shows the structure of an Ivy dependency file.

Listing C.8 The structure of an Ivy dependency file

```
<ivy-module version="2.0">
  <info organisation="com.manning.sdmia"      Declares
      module="springdm-sample"/>              project's info
  <dependencies>

    <dependency org="org.springframework.osgi"
              name="spring-osgi-io" rev="2.0.0.M1" />
    <dependency org="org.springframework.osgi"
              name="spring-osgi-core"           Declares
              rev="2.0.0.M1" />                  dependencies
    <dependency org="org.springframework.osgi"
              name="spring-osgi-extender"
              rev="2.0.0.M1" />

  </dependencies>
</ivy-module>
```

Note that with Ivy, a dependency is identified by its organization, its name, and its revision number. Ivy also has the notion of type of dependency, but we'll only use JAR files here, which happens to be the default.

For brevity's sake, we won't include the whole set of dependencies needed for running our integration test; you can find the complete Ivy file in the code samples for this appendix. All you need to know is that these dependencies can be roughly divided into the following categories:

- Spring DM (I/O, core, extender)
- Spring Framework (core, lightweight container, AOP, and so on) and its dependencies
- Logging libraries
- Test libraries
- OSGi (the Equinox container that the testing framework will bootstrap in the test)

Our project now has the following structure:

```
springdm-sample
  src/
    main/
      java/
        com/manning/springdmia/
          SpringDmSample.java
      resources/
```

```
        META-INF/
           spring/
           springdm-sample.xml
     build.bnd
     build.xml
     ivy.xml
     ivysettings.xml
```

What we need to do next is to Ivy-enable our build file. Listing C.9 shows how to do so.

Listing C.9   Using Ivy in an Ant build file

```
<project name="springdm-sample" default="package" basedir="."
 xmlns:ivy="antlib:org.apache.ivy.ant">
 (...)
 <property name="lib.dir" value="./lib"/>

 <target name="resolve"
         description="Retrieve dependencies with ivy">
   <ivy:retrieve />
 </target>

</project>
```

Ivy comes with its own namespace that we declare in the root tag of the build file. This allows the use of the ivy:retrieve element in a target for retrieving dependencies. Let's run the resolve target to do so:

ant resolve

Here is part of the resulting console output:

```
Buildfile: build.xml

resolve:
[ivy:retrieve] :: Ivy 2.1.0 - 20090925235825 :: http://ant.apache.org/ivy/ ::
(...)
[ivy:retrieve]   [SUCCESSFUL ]
     org.eclipse.osgi#org.eclipse.osgi;3.5.1.R35x_v2009
0827!org.eclipse.osgi.jar (15141ms)
[ivy:retrieve] :: resolution report :: resolve 32266ms ::
      artifacts dl 81828ms
        ---------------------------------------------------------------------
        |             |                   modules          ||   artifacts   |
        |     conf    | number| search|dwnlded|evicted|| number|dwnlded|
        ---------------------------------------------------------------------
        |   default   |   22  |   22  |   0   |   0   ||   22  |   22  |
        ---------------------------------------------------------------------
[ivy:retrieve] :: retrieving :: com.manning.sdmia#springdm-sample
[ivy:retrieve]   confs: [default]
[ivy:retrieve]   22 artifacts copied, 0 already retrieved (5181kB/234ms)

BUILD SUCCESSFUL
```

What did Ivy do? It downloaded the dependencies from the various remote repositories, copied them into a directory to cache them, and then copied them into a newly created lib directory in the project directory. The project now has the following structure (with the library directory and its content shown in bold):

```
springdm-sample
  lib/
    spring-osgi-io-2.0.0.M1.jar
    spring-osgi-core-2.0.0.M1.jar
    spring-osgi-extender-2.0.0.M1.jar
    (...)
  src/
    main/
      java/
        com/manning/springdmia/
          SpringDmSample.java
      resources/
        META-INF/
          spring/
          springdm-sample.xml
  build.bnd
  build.xml
  ivy.xml
  ivysettings.xml
```

We're done with dependencies! It's time to take advantage of these dependencies to write the integration test and run it using Spring DM's testing framework.

C.4 Developing an integration test

As explained in chapter 3, Spring DM provides a test framework to run test cases in an embedded OSGi container. The test framework handles the bootstrapping of the OSGi container and turns the test into an on-the-fly bundle to run the test methods in an OSGi environment.

In section C.4.1 we'll see how to write the test and how to compile it by modifying the Ant build file. As the Spring DM test framework uses the Maven 2 dependency management system by default, section C.4.2 shows how to customize it to make it work with our Ivy-managed dependencies. Section C.4.3 then covers how to launch the test with Ant.

C.4.1 Writing and compiling the integration test

We'll stick to Maven 2's project layout by putting tests in the src/test/java directory of our project. The project now has the following structure (with the test directory and its content shown in bold):

```
springdm-sample
  lib/
    (...)
  src/
    main/
      java/
        com/manning/springdmia/
          SpringDmSample.java
      resources/
        META-INF/
          spring/
          springdm-sample.xml
```

```
test/
  java/
    com/manning/springdmia/
      SpringDmSampleTest.java
build.bnd
build.xml
ivy.xml
ivysettings.xml
```

Listing C.10 shows the backbone of our integration test. The test mainly consists of checking that our bundle has been installed and correctly started.

Listing C.10   The bundle integration test

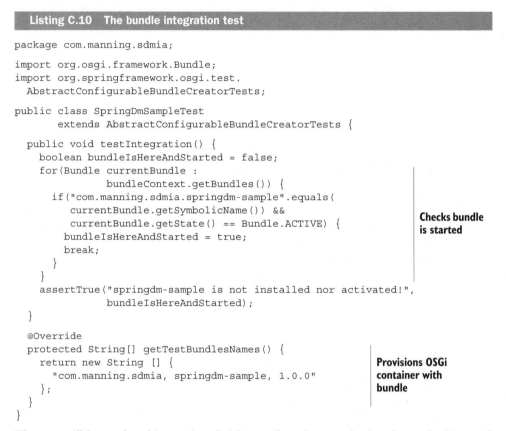

```
package com.manning.sdmia;

import org.osgi.framework.Bundle;
import org.springframework.osgi.test.
  AbstractConfigurableBundleCreatorTests;

public class SpringDmSampleTest
      extends AbstractConfigurableBundleCreatorTests {

  public void testIntegration() {
    boolean bundleIsHereAndStarted = false;
    for(Bundle currentBundle :
              bundleContext.getBundles()) {
      if("com.manning.sdmia.springdm-sample".equals(
        currentBundle.getSymbolicName()) &&
        currentBundle.getState() == Bundle.ACTIVE) {
        bundleIsHereAndStarted = true;
        break;
      }
    }
    assertTrue("springdm-sample is not installed nor activated!",
            bundleIsHereAndStarted);
  }

  @Override
  protected String[] getTestBundlesNames() {
    return new String [] {
      "com.manning.sdmia, springdm-sample, 1.0.0"
    };
  }
}
```

Checks bundle is started

Provisions OSGi container with bundle

The test will be updated in section C.4.2 to reflect that we don't rely on the Maven 2 local repository to provision the OSGi container that the test framework bootstraps. For now, we just need to compile the test. Listing C.11 shows the updates needed in the build file to compile the test.

Listing C.11   Compiling the test with Ant

```
<project (...)>

  <property name="build.testDir" value="src/test/java"/>
  <property name="build.testOutputDir"
          value="${build.dir}/test-classes"/>
```

❶ Defines properties for tests

```
<path id="classpath">
  <fileset dir="${lib.dir}">
    <include name="*.jar"/>
  </fileset>
</path>

<target name="compile-tests"
        depends="compile,resolve"
        description="Compile the test code">
  <mkdir dir="${build.testOutputDir}"/>
  <javac destdir="${build.testOutputDir}"
    (...) options eluded    >
  <src>
    <pathelement location="${build.testDir}"/>
  </src>
  <classpath>
    <path refid="classpath"/>
  </classpath>
  </javac>
</target>
```

2 Uses library directory for classpath

3 Sets targets to execute before test compilation

4 Refers to classpath

```
</project>
```

Modifications start at **1**, with the declaration of properties for the location of test source files and for the test output directory. We take advantage of our dependencies at **2**, by defining a dedicated path for our classpath. Note that the test compilation target depends on the resolve target **3**, which means that the dependencies will be retrieved before its execution. We refer at **4** to the classpath we created, as the test uses the OSGi API and the Equinox JAR (in the dependencies) provides this.

Compilation time! Launch the following command:

```
ant compile-tests
```

The test is almost ready to run, but before we do that, we need to tune the Spring DM test framework a little to use the Ivy-managed dependencies.

C.4.2 Customizing Spring DM's test framework to use Ivy's dependencies

By default, the test framework uses the Maven 2 local repository to provision the embedded OSGi container that it then bootstraps. What does the test framework provision the container with? With Spring DM's bundles (I/O, core, extender, and so on) and their corresponding dependencies (Spring Framework, logging, and the like). These bundles are referred to as *framework* bundles. It also provisions the container with the bundles that should be tested together with their own dependencies. Let's call them *application* bundles.

The main issue we're going to face is the way the test framework *locates* dependencies: we don't want it to search the Maven 2 local repository, but rather the directory we copied the dependencies to. Fortunately, the test framework offers a hook to customize the way bundles are found: the ArtifactLocator. Here is the definition of the ArtifactLocator interface:

```
public interface ArtifactLocator {
  Resource locateArtifact(String group, String id,
    String version, String type);
  Resource locateArtifact(String group, String id, String version);
}
```

With an `ArtifactLocator`, dependencies are identified by their group, ID, version, and type. Note the use of Spring's resource abstraction.

We'll provide a simple implementation that only uses the ID and the version to return a `Resource` from our lib directory. Listing C.12 shows the implementation of the `LocalFileSystemIvyRepository`.

Listing C.12 The `ArtifactLocator` for Ivy dependencies

```
package com.manning.sdmia;

import org.springframework.core.io.FileSystemResource;
import org.springframework.core.io.Resource;
import org.springframework.osgi.test.provisioning.ArtifactLocator;

public class LocalFileSystemIvyRepository implements ArtifactLocator {

  private String libDirectory = "./lib";

  private static final String fileSeparator =
    System.getProperty("file.separator");

  @Override
  public Resource locateArtifact(
      String groupId, String artifactId, String version) {
    return new FileSystemResource(libDirectory+fileSeparator+
      artifactId+"-"+version+".jar");
  }

  @Override
  public Resource locateArtifact(String groupId, String artifactId,
    String version, String type) {
    return locateArtifact(groupId, artifactId, version, null);
  }

  public void setLibDirectory(String libDirectory) {
    this.libDirectory = libDirectory;
  }

}
```

NOTE The `LocalFileSystemIvyRepository` is rather simple. Don't hesitate to write an implementation that suits your needs better.

How do we use our `LocalFileSystemIvyRepository` in our integration test? This can be done by overriding the `getLocator` method, as shown in listing C.13.

Listing C.13 Using a custom `ArtifactLocator` in an integration test

```
package com.manning.sdmia;

import org.osgi.framework.Bundle;
import org.springframework.osgi.test.
```

```
➡        AbstractConfigurableBundleCreatorTests;
import org.springframework.osgi.test.provisioning.ArtifactLocator;

public class SpringDmSampleTest
        extends AbstractConfigurableBundleCreatorTests {

  (...)

  @Override
  protected ArtifactLocator getLocator() {                    Uses custom
    return new LocalFileSystemIvyRepository();                 artifact locator
  }

}
```

Now, each time the testing framework needs a bundle, the request will be forwarded to our `LocalFileSystemIvyRepository`.

By default, Spring DM loads the necessary framework bundles and doesn't load any application bundles. You can change this behavior by overriding the `getTestFrameworkBundlesNames` and `getTestBundlesNames` methods. You're already familiar with `getTestBundlesNames`, because we overrode it to set the application bundles we wanted to install in the OSGi container in chapters 3 and 10. We also need to override the `getTestFrameworkBundlesNames` to make it consistent with our artifact locator, as shown in listing C.14.

Listing C.14 Customizing the set of framework bundles

```
package com.manning.sdmia;

import org.osgi.framework.Bundle;
import org.springframework.osgi.test.
➡        AbstractConfigurableBundleCreatorTests;
import org.springframework.osgi.test.provisioning.ArtifactLocator;

public class SpringDmSampleTest
        extends AbstractConfigurableBundleCreatorTests {

  (...)

  @Override
  protected String[] getTestFrameworkBundlesNames() {
    return new String[] {
      "org.aopalliance,com.springsource.org.aopalliance,1.0.0",
      "org.apache.log4j,com.springsource.org.apache.log4j,1.2.15",
      "org.junit,com.springsource.junit,3.8.2",
      "org.objectweb.asm,com.springsource.org.objectweb.asm,2.2.3",
      "org.slf4j,com.springsource.slf4j.api,1.5.6",
      "org.slf4j,com.springsource.slf4j.log4j,1.5.6",
      "org.slf4j,com.springsource.slf4j.org.apache.commons.logging,1.5.6",
      "org.springframework,org.springframework.aop,3.0.2.RELEASE",
      "org.springframework,org.springframework.asm,3.0.2.RELEASE",
      "org.springframework,org.springframework.beans,3.0.2.RELEASE",
      "org.springframework,org.springframework.context,3.0.2.RELEASE",
      "org.springframework,org.springframework.core,3.0.2.RELEASE",
      "org.springframework,org.springframework.expression,3.0.2.RELEASE",
      "org.springframework,org.springframework.test,3.0.2.RELEASE",
```

```
        "org.springframework.osgi,spring-osgi-annotation,2.0.0.M1",
        "org.springframework.osgi,spring-osgi-core,2.0.0.M1",
        "org.springframework.osgi,spring-osgi-extender,2.0.0.M1",
        "org.springframework.osgi,spring-osgi-io,2.0.0.M1",
        "org.springframework.osgi,spring-osgi-test,2.0.0.M1"
    };
  }
}
```

We're now done with the customization of the test framework: it uses our Ivy-managed dependencies instead of the Maven 2 local repository. We can't say it's been particularly easy, but Spring DM gives us enough hooks to achieve what we wanted!

Get ready for the last step: running the test with Ant.

C.4.3   *Running the test with Ant*

Ant has an optional task to launch JUnit tests, which is installed by default in the standard distribution. When it comes to running tests, Spring DM integration tests don't differ from plain JUnit tests, as shown in listing C.15.

> **Listing C.15   Running the integration tests with Ant**

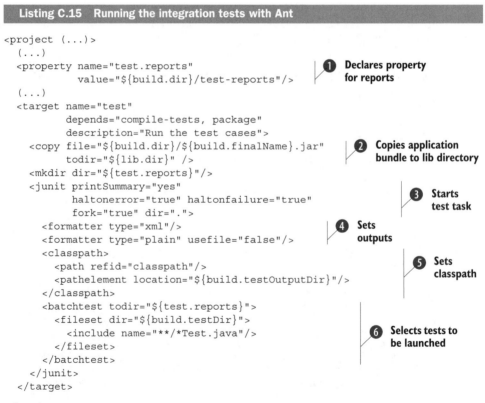

```
<project (...)>
  (...)
  <property name="test.reports"
            value="${build.dir}/test-reports"/>       ❶ Declares property
                                                          for reports
  (...)
  <target name="test"
          depends="compile-tests, package"
          description="Run the test cases">
    <copy file="${build.dir}/${build.finalName}.jar"   ❷ Copies application
          todir="${lib.dir}" />                            bundle to lib directory
    <mkdir dir="${test.reports}"/>
    <junit printSummary="yes"                          ❸ Starts
           haltonerror="true" haltonfailure="true"        test task
           fork="true" dir=".">
      <formatter type="xml"/>                          ❹ Sets
      <formatter type="plain" usefile="false"/>           outputs
      <classpath>                                      ❺ Sets
        <path refid="classpath"/>                         classpath
        <pathelement location="${build.testOutputDir}"/>
      </classpath>
      <batchtest todir="${test.reports}">
        <fileset dir="${build.testDir}">
          <include name="**/*Test.java"/>              ❻ Selects tests to
        </fileset>                                        be launched
      </batchtest>
    </junit>
  </target>

</project>
```

The JUnit Ant task can generate reports—that's why we define at ❶ a property for the directory where the reports should be generated. At ❷ we copy our bundle into the lib directory to make it available for provisioning (with our custom `ArtifactLocator`). The `junit` element at ❸ starts the JUnit task. It takes several options: formatters at ❹ (to set where the results of the tests should be printed–on the console and in XML files in our case), the classpath to use for launching the tests ❺, and the `batchtest` element specifying the set of tests that should be launched ❻.

We're now ready to run the test with the following command:

```
ant clean test
```

The command will trigger the compilation of the `SpringDmSample` class, the bundle creation, the retrieval of dependencies, the test compilation, and the test launching. Here's a part of the console output:

```
(...)
[junit] Running com.manning.sdmia.SpringDmSampleTest
[junit] Testsuite: com.manning.sdmia.SpringDmSampleTest
[junit] Tests run: 1, Failures: 0, Errors: 0, Time elapsed: 1,672 sec
[junit] Tests run: 1, Failures: 0, Errors: 0, Time elapsed: 1,672 sec
[junit] ------------- Standard Output ---------------
[junit] Spring DM sample created
[junit] ------------- ---------------- ---------------
[junit] Testcase: testIntegration took 1,609 sec

BUILD SUCCESSFUL
```

That's it! We managed to run our Spring DM integration test with a 100 percent Ant solution!

C.5 *Summary*

Even though we favored Maven 2 throughout this book, we haven't forgotten Ant users. Doing OSGi and Spring development with Ant isn't only possible, it's not too difficult at all.

The build file for the Spring DM sample is similar to that of any other project. Only the packaging task differs; for this we used Bnd to generate the OSGi metadata and create the bundle with the appropriate content. The biggest difference comes with integration tests, as Spring DM testing defaults to using the Maven 2 local repository for provisioning. Instead, we used Ivy to gather the necessary bundles and customize the test framework so that it used them from the project directory.

This gives you a shrink-wrapped solution for launching Spring DM-based integration tests but also enough knowledge to build your own solution. Also keep in mind that once the testing framework is correctly customized, running the integration tests is the same as for any other tests, because Spring DM tests are JUnit-based. Using Spring DM with Ant won't force you to change your build habits, and most of your build files can remain the same.

appendix D
OSGi development with the Pax tools

Pax (http://wiki.ops4j.org/display/ops4j/Pax) is an umbrella project for a set of OSGi-based tools. It is itself part of the Open Participation Software for Java (OPS4J) community, whose open source model is more decentralized and open than that of some other communities. Pax projects are all about OSGi: some provide basic yet very useful utility bundles, like Pax Logging or Pax URL, and others build on top of these utilities to provide more advanced tools, like Pax Web.

We'll focus here on two projects from the Pax family:

- Pax Runner—A tool for provisioning and launching an OSGi container
- Pax Construct—A Maven-based build-management system for OSGi

Both can be very helpful for any OSGi-related task, and they have built-in support for Spring DM. They're certainly the best tools for getting started quickly with OSGi, as they hide most of its underlying (and error-prone) aspects.

Throughout this book, we chose to follow a standard Maven-based approach, to show that you can use ordinary tools for OSGi development. We don't think relying on automatic tools without any understanding of what they do under the covers is a good approach, and it can put off people who want to know exactly what their tools do for them. But now that you have a good understanding of OSGi, you may want to be relieved of some of the more tedious tasks that it involves. In this case, you should definitely try Pax Runner and Pax Construct.

D.1 *Pax Runner*

Pax Runner aims to provision and launch an OSGi container. It's a command-line tool (which can be launched as a daemon process), and it accepts many options to

474

control the provisioning, the type of OSGi container (one of Equinox, Felix, or Knop-flerfish), and its own specific configuration.

With Pax Runner, you can easily try a set of bundles on different versions of the three open source OSGi 4 platforms, without worrying about having to get them from their respective websites. Pax Runner will download them automatically. You can also provision your entire platform, complete with all the Spring DM bundles and their dependencies, with a simple command-line argument, thanks to Pax Runner's pro-files, which define sets of bundles.

We'll first cover the basics of Pax Runner (installation, syntax, and miscellaneous options) and then look at advanced topics like profiles, configuration within a text file, and detailed aspects about the provisioning process.

D.1.1 Installing Pax Runner

You can download the distribution of Pax Runner from the website (http://paxrunner. ops4j.org/space/Pax+Runner). The distribution consists of a compressed file that you can unpack in any directory (from now on, we'll refer to this directory as PAX_RUNNER_HOME). You should add the PAX_RUNNER_HOME/bin directory to your PATH environment variable so that you can launch Pax Runner from anywhere.

NOTE We'll use Pax Runner 1.4.0 in this appendix.

Once the installation is done, you can start a command shell in an arbitrary working directory and type the pax-run command. The terminal will issue the following output:

```
  _____    _____
  \     \    \     \   __  __    __    __   __  __   _____
  |   __/\__  \  \  \  \/  /  |    _/  |  \/    \/   \/  _  \_   _  \
  |   |   /  __\_>   <  |   |   \  |  /   |   \   |   \   __/|   |  \
  |___|  (___/_/\_\ |___|_  /___/|___|  /___|  /\___  >_|
           \/      \/       \/        \/       \/      \/

Pax Runner (1.4.0) from OPS4J - http://www.ops4j.org
----------------------------------------------------

   -> Using config [classpath:META-INF/runner.properties]
   -> Using only arguments from command line
   -> Preparing framework [Felix 2.0.2]
   -> Downloading bundles...
   -> Felix 2.0.2 : 388030 bytes @ [ 60kBps ]
   -> Felix Shell (1.4.1) : 62616 bytes @ [ 39kBps ]
   -> Felix TUI Shell (1.4.1) : 12748 bytes @ [ 40kBps ]
   -> Using execution environment [J2SE-1.6]
   -> Runner has successfully finished his job!

Welcome to Felix
=================

->
```

What has Pax Runner done? It has downloaded the Apache Felix OSGi platform and launched it. This isn't a particularly complicated task, but Pax Runner handled everything for you. It also created a runner directory in the working directory for its internal functions (bundles, platforms configuration, and the like).

Let's see a preview of the available options and switch from Felix to Equinox (use shutdown to exit from Felix). Type the following command:

```
pax-run --p=equinox
```

> **NOTE** Windows users must use quotation marks for the option: "--p=equinox".

The terminal will issue the following output:

```
Pax Runner (1.4.0) from OPS4J - http://www.ops4j.org
--------------------------------------------------

 -> Using config [classpath:META-INF/runner.properties]
 -> Using only arguments from command line
 -> Preparing framework [Equinox 3.5.1]
 -> Downloading bundles...
 -> Equinox 3.5.1 : 1125860 bytes @ [ 78kBps ]
 -> Using execution environment [J2SE-1.6]
 -> Runner has successfully finished his job!

osgi>
```

As with Felix, Pax Runner downloaded Equinox and launched it. That's it for installing Pax Runner and its primary commands; let's now look in detail at the exact syntax of the tool's commands.

D.1.2 Pax Runner syntax

Pax Runner has a wide range of options, which vary from specifying the target OSGi platform to setting the working directory.

The pax-run command accepts any number of parameters. A parameter can be either

- An option, when it begins with --
- A provision spec

A provision spec is everything that doesn't start with --. The goal of a provision spec is self-explanatory: it describes where to find one or several bundles. We'll see later that Pax Runner supports many formats for provision specs.

Now, consider the following command:

```
pax-run --p=equinox --v=3.4.2 --clean file:./foo.jar
```

It contains

- Three options—p (for the platform), v (for the version of the platform), and clean (which doesn't take any value)
- One provision spec—the foo.jar bundle that lies in the current directory

Options and provision specs can appear in any order, so the following command is equivalent to the previous one:

```
pax-run --p=equinox file:./foo.jar --v=3.4.2 –clean
```

Windows users must enclose options that contain the equal sign (=) with quotation marks. Our first command would look like the following on a Windows/DOS shell:

```
pax-run "--p=equinox" "--v=3.4.2" --clean file:./foo.jar
```

We'll describe in the next sections the most important options and the kinds of provision specs that Pax Runner supports.

D.1.3 Pax Runner options

Pax Runner accepts a lot of options; table D.1 lists the most important ones.

Table D.1 Pax Runner options

Option	Description	Examples
platform	Sets the target OSGi framework	--platform=equinox --platform=e --platform=felix --platform=f --platform=knopflerfish --platform=k
p	Shortcut for platform	--p=equinox --p=e
version	Sets the version of the target OSGi platform	--version=3.5.0
v	Shortcut for version	--v=3.5.0
bootDelegation	Specifies Java packages for which the platform must delegate classloading to the boot class loader	--bootDelegation=sun.*,com.sun.*
systemPackages	Specifies additional Java packages to be exported by the system bundle	--systemPackages=javax.servlet
javaHome	Specifies the JVM to use for the platform process	--javaHome=/path/to/jdk1.5/
vmOptions	Sets options for the JVM of the platform process	--vmOptions="-Xms32m -Xmx64m"
profiles	Specifies profiles to be loaded when the platform starts	--profiles=log,config

Table D.1 Pax Runner options *(continued)*

Option	Description	Examples
`workingDirectory`	Sets the working directory of Pax Runner (defaults to `./runner`)	`--workingDirectory=/pax/dir/`
`clean`	Cleans the working directory before launching	`--clean`
`args`	Identifies a text file that contains the options	`--args=runner.args`

Table D.1 doesn't provide an exhaustive list of the options for Pax Runner, but these are the options you'll commonly use. Let's look at them in more detail.

CHOOSING THE TARGET PLATFORM

This section covers the `platform`, `p`, `version`, and `v` options, which let you select the target platform. Pax Runner lets you switch from one OSGi platform to another easily.

By default, it uses the latest version of Felix. If you want to use the latest version of Equinox, you can use the `platform` option:

```
pax-run --platform=equinox
```

If you don't want to type the whole word, the `p` option is a shortcut for `platform`:

```
pax-run --p=equinox
```

Each platform has an abbreviated name that you can use with either the `platform` or `p` option. The abbreviated name is `e` for Equinox, `f` for Felix, and `k` for Knopflerfish. That means the following commands are equivalent to the previous ones:

```
pax-run --platform=e
pax-run --p=e
```

This last command is less readable and less self-explanatory, but it's quick to type.

If you want to use a specific version of an OSGi platform, you must use the `version` option or its shortcut, `v`. The following command tells Pax Runner to use version 3.2.1 of Equinox:

```
pax-run --platform=equinox --version=3.2.1
```

You should consult Pax Runner's documentation to find out the exact versions that the tool supports for each platform. When you don't specify the version of the platform, the version used depends on the version of Pax Runner itself. If you use the latest version of Pax Runner, there's a good chance it'll use the latest version of the OSGi platforms.

When doing development, you can omit specifying the version, but you should always specify it when you use Pax Runner for a production system.

TUNING THE JVM PROCESS OF THE OSGI RUNTIME

Pax Runner runs the target OSGi platform in a new process, which means the OSGi runtime has its own JVM, different from the one that the Pax Runner command-line tool uses. This means you can explicitly set the JVM for the OSGi platform process, as well as its parameters (memory, debug, and so on).

To specify the home directory of the target JVM, you can use the `javaHome` option:

```
pax-run --javaHome=/usr/local/jdk1.5
```

To specify JVM options, use the `vmOptions` option:

```
pax-run --vmOptions="-Xms256m -Xmx512m"
```

You can, of course, use both:

```
pax-run --javaHome=/usr/local/jdk1.5 --vmOptions="-Xms256m -Xmx512m"
```

CHOOSING A WORKING DIRECTORY AND CLEANING IT OUT

Pax Runner uses a working directory to store installed bundles, platform artifacts, and configuration files. By default, Pax Runner creates this working directory in the current directory and calls it runner.

You can use the `workingDirectory` option (or its shortcut, `dir`) to change the default behavior and specify a directory where Pax Runner will store its files:

```
pax-run --workingDirectory=/tmp/pax-runner/
```

Note that Pax Runner always creates the working directory if it doesn't exist. Specifying a working directory can be useful for gathering downloaded artifacts and configuration; this avoids downloading the same files repetitively and saves disk space.

In contrast, you can use the `clean` option to delete the working directory. By doing this, all artifacts (bundles, frameworks, JARs, configuration files, and the like) will be removed, and Pax Runner will recreate the working directory. It will also trigger the redownloading of these artifacts. The following command tells Pax Runner to delete the default working directory with the `clean` option:

```
pax-run --clean
```

This ends our tour of the most common Pax Runner options. The `args` and `profiles` options, which allow you to specify options in a dedicated file and to provision the platform with a set of bundles, respectively, will be discussed later on their own.

In the next section, we'll cover one of the most interesting features of Pax Runner: provisioning.

D.1.4 *Pax Runner provision specs*

Provision specs are the other kind of parameter that the Pax Runner command line accepts. They specify how to get, install, and start OSGi bundles within the target OSGi platform. When it comes to provision specs, Pax Runner relies heavily on Pax URL, another project in the Pax family. Pax URL provides different URL handlers, in addition to those supported in Java.

In the previous samples, we saw that we can provision the OSGi platform with a bundle from the filesystem:

```
pax-run file:./foo.jar
```

We also saw how to get this bundle from a web server:

```
pax-run http://myhost/foo.jar
```

`file` and `http` refer to protocols. Java supports these two protocols natively—that's why we can use them as provision specs with Pax Runner. Thanks to Pax URL, Pax Runner supports other protocols: `mvn` to get bundles from the local Maven 2 repository, `obr` to retrieve bundles from an OSGi bundle repository, and so on.

Provision specs aren't only about protocols: Pax Runner can also scan directories or read text files that specify the location of bundles.

Pax Runner can also combine these different types of provision specs, which makes its provisioning capabilities powerful and flexible. In the following sections, we'll guide you through the most useful provisioning features of Pax Runner and provide you with guidelines for using them efficiently.

PROVISIONING FROM THE FILESYSTEM

We already know that we can provision the target platform with a single file. Let's just add that we can specify more than one file:

```
pax-run file:./foo.jar file:./bar.jar
```

Listing all the bundles can be cumbersome, especially when their number grows. Pax Runner is able to scan a directory and provision the platform with all the bundles that reside in that directory. All we have to do is give the path of the directory:

```
pax-run /path/to/bundles
```

We used the absolute path in the preceding example, but Pax Runner accepts relative paths too. You can also specify more than one directory:

```
pax-run /path/to/bundles currentbundles
```

You can also ask Pax Runner to scan immediate subdirectories by adding the asterisk (*) character at the end of the directory:

```
pax-run /path/to/bundles/*
```

PROVISIONING FROM A ZIP FILE

Pax Runner is able to get bundles from a zip file. All you have to do is give the path of the archive:

```
pax-run mybundles.zip
```

Pax will unpack the archive on the fly and provision the platform with the bundles it contains.

You have a great deal of flexibility in specifying the path to the archive: relative, absolute, or even remote. The following command tells Pax Runner to get bundles from a remote zip file:

```
pax-run http://myhost/mybundles.zip
```

Using a zip file is convenient when you want to distribute a set of bundles; Pax Runner makes the provisioning entirely transparent thanks to its automatic unpacking.

PROVISIONING FROM A LOCAL MAVEN 2 REPOSITORY

Pax URL defines a Maven 2 protocol, which is composed of the Maven 2 coordinates of an OSGi bundle (group ID, artifact ID, and version). Pax Runner leverages this protocol by provisioning the platform from the Maven 2 local repository (which defaults to the ${user.home}/.m2/repository directory).

The following command shows the use of the Maven 2 protocol:

```
pax-run mvn:com.manning.sdmia/paint/1.0.0
```

The syntax of the Maven 2 protocol is straightforward: `mvn:groupId/artifactId/version`. You can also specify the URL of a remote repository:

```
pax-run mvn:http://myhost/repository!com.manning.sdmia/paint/1.0.0
```

PROVISIONING FROM A TEXT FILE

When the number of bundles in your application grows, or when you want to mix different ways of provisioning the platform, the command line quickly becomes inefficient. Pax Runner lets you provide the location of your bundles in a text file.

Here is an example of a text file that contains two provision specs:

```
file:./foo.jar
mvn:com.manning.sdmia/paint/1.0.0
```

If the name of this file is bundle.txt, we can tell Pax Runner to use it simply by providing its name:

```
pax-run bundle.txt
```

Note that Pax Runner ignores empty lines and lines that start with #; this can help improve the readability of large provisioning text files.

These files can also contain the definitions of system properties, which will be available in the process of the OSGi platform. The following snippet shows a provisioning text file that combines mixed provisioning, empty lines, comments, and the assignment of system properties:

```
# bundle provisioning
file:./foo.jar
mvn:com.manning.sdmia/paint/1.0.0

# system properties
-Dmy.server.secured=true
-Dmy.server.secured.port=8443
```

PROVISIONING OPTIONS

We've seen so far that provisioning specs mainly consist of URLs, but even if the URL is the most important element, it's only one part of a provisioning spec. Pax Runner recognizes the following format for a provisioning spec:

```
bundle_url [@start_level] [@nostart] [@update]
```

These are the different parts of a provisioning spec:

- `bundle_url`—Any valid Pax URL (mandatory)
- `start_level`—An integer representing the start level of the bundle (optional)

- nostart—Indicates that the bundle must not be started (optional)
- update—Indicates that the bundle must be updated if it was already installed before (optional)

The following commands illustrate the use of these provisioning options:

```
pax-run file:./foo.jar@5
pax-run file:./foo.jar@nostart@update
pax-run file:./foo.jar@update
```

These options also apply to other protocols (http, mvn, and so on), as well as to the provisioning of text files.

You now have a good overview of Pax Runner's provisioning capabilities, and you can see that you're somewhat spoiled for choice; that's why we provide some guideline recommendations in the next section.

GUIDELINES FOR PROVISIONING

The main guideline of Pax Runner provisioning is to maintain consistency: avoid mixing different kinds of provision specs (command line, text files, and others). Your usage will be driven by your needs and context, and these will at least partly depend on whether you're using Pax Runner for development or distribution.

For day-to-day development, including the provisioning spec in the command line is useful: it's a handy way to quickly test a bundle on different OSGi platforms. You can then use the various protocols (file, or mvn if you use Maven 2) for building your bundles.

When distributing an OSGi application to end users, using zip provisioning is probably the most simple and straightforward way to go. The text file is more appropriate when the application needs more configuration (like system properties). As the text file also accepts all the protocols, it's well suited for development-based distributions (like the code samples of this book, which you can build with Maven 2 and then launch, thanks to a text provisioning file).

We advise you not to mix different kinds of provisioning specs, but there's one case when it can be useful. Imagine that you have written some Spring-powered bundles and you want to test them. The provisioning for Spring DM's bundles would always be the same, so you'll save yourself trouble if you include it in a text file and then specify your Spring-powered bundles on the command line. You'll then end up with your own reusable provisioning text file.

This is a rather manual way of gathering a provisioning definition in a text file and it leads us to the next topic: profiles. In Pax Runner, profiles allow us to quickly provision an OSGi platform, because they define consistent and ready-to-use sets of bundles.

D.1.5   *Pax Runner profiles*

In Pax Runner, a profile defines a consistent set of bundles that together provide one or more features. These features range from logging to web support to Spring DM support.

You can specify profiles with the `profiles` option. The following command provisions the container with the OSGi compendium bundle:

```
pax-run --profiles=compendium
```

You can specify more than one profile by separating them with a comma. The following command provisions the container with the Pax Logging and Pax Web bundles:

```
pax-run --profiles=compendium,log
```

You can also specify the version of the profiles by appending a slash (/) and then the version number:

```
pax-run --profiles=compendium/4.1.0
```

Because profiles generally gather the bundles for specific projects (Pax Logging, Pax Web, and the like), the profile version is usually the same as the target project version.

As of version 1.2.0, Pax Runner considers profiles to be like any other provision specs, which means that the `profiles` option can be omitted. The following snippet shows the equivalent of the three previous commands without using the `profiles` option:

```
pax-run compendium
pax-run compendium,log
pax-run compendium/4.1.0
```

Whether or not you use the `profiles` option is a matter of taste, even if readability and clarity matter. Thinking of the profile feature as a special kind of provision specification (which don't use any options) argues in favor of omitting the `profiles` option.

What makes profiles really interesting is that Pax Runner comes with a lot of them. Table D.2 lists some of the main ready-to-use profiles included in Pax Runner.

Table D.2   Main profiles available in Pax Runner

Profile	Description
`compendium`	Includes the OSGi Alliance Compendium bundle
`log`	Includes Pax Log, which provides support for popular enterprise logging libraries (Commons Logging, Log4j, SLF4J) in OSGi environments
`web`	Includes Pax Web, an implementation of OSGi HTTP service
`spring`	Includes the bundles of the Spring lightweight container
`spring.dm`	Includes the bundles of Spring DM

Profiles are defined through provisioning text files, which are hosted on a Pax Runner web server. Note that profiles can rely on each other: for example, the `spring.dm` profile "imports" the `spring` profile in its definition.

> **NOTE**   Prior to version 1.2.0, Pax Runner used to always include the OSGi Compendium bundle, but this is no longer the case. Including it is now up to the user, and even though some profiles depend on the Compendium bundle (like the `log` profile), it must still be explicitly added to the command line.

Pax Runner comes with a Spring DM profile, which makes provisioning an OSGi platform with Spring DM's bundles (and their dependencies) using Pax Runner as simple as the following command:

```
pax-run --profiles=spring.dm,compendium
```

OK, so we'll admit it. Using Pax Runner from the start in this book would have made your life (and ours!) much easier, and we'd have avoided the manual provisioning steps in the first chapters. We chose the hard way to show you what needs to be done and to illustrate what was happening under the covers. Nevertheless, if you want to quickly test your Spring-powered bundles, Pax Runner and its Spring DM profile are obviously a good solution.

The `profiles` option is just another Pax Runner option, so it can be used together with any others or even with the provisioning specs we've seen so far. This means you can complement the provisioning of one or more profiles with your own provisioning specs. Profiles are just another way for Pax Runner to simplify the provisioning of the target platform.

To further simplify the launching of Pax Runner, let's look at how to specify the entire command line in a file.

D.1.6   *Using a text file for the options*

We've seen so far that Pax Runner comes with a lot of options and provisioning capabilities. Launching OSGi applications can require a lot of options, and even though the provisioning can be specified in a file, the Pax Runner commands can become long and error-prone. That's why the `args` option exists: it specifies a text file that contains all the options, as well as the provisioning specs.

The following snippet shows how to specify all the command-line options and provisioning specs in a file:

```
# options
--p=equinox
--profiles=spring.dm,compendium
--bootDelegation=javax.swing.*
# provisioning
mvn:com.manning.sdmia.ch06/shape/1.0.0
mvn:com.manning.sdmia.ch06/paint/1.0.0
mvn:com.manning.sdmia.ch06/paint.circle/1.0.0
mvn:com.manning.sdmia.ch06/paint.square/1.0.0
mvn:com.manning.sdmia.ch06/paint.triangle/1.0.0
```

The syntax of the file is the following:

- There must be one option or provision spec per line.
- Empty lines are ignored.
- Commentary lines start with #.

Let's imagine the previous file is called paint.args and is located in the current directory. You can use it to launch Pax Runner with the following command:

```
pax-run --args=file:paint.args
```

You'll probably be happy to learn that using a text file for options is the default for Pax Runner: when you launch the pax-run command without any options, Pax Runner looks for a runner.args file in the current directory and uses it if it's available.

That means placing all the options in a text file is the way to go when distributing OSGi applications with Pax Runner. Imagine including all the advanced provisioning specs we saw earlier (filesystem, remote, zip, and so on) in a runner.args file, along with miscellaneous options (type and version of the platform, JVM options, and others) and letting Pax Runner trigger the platform and do the provisioning: the result is a simple, reliable, and portable way to launch your OSGi applications. It also applies to daily development tasks, when you want to quickly test bundles.

This ends our tour of Pax Runner, which you should consider an essential part of your OSGi tooling. As we mentioned earlier, Pax Runner can help distribute your OSGi applications. It's also very useful for day-to-day development, and we'll see in the next section that it's included as the default launch tool in Pax Construct, a set of Maven 2 plug-ins for OSGi development.

D.2 Pax Construct

Pax Construct is a tool for creating, building, managing, and deploying OSGi-based applications. It builds on top of a Maven 2 plug-in and comes with Unix and Windows scripts that encapsulate the Maven 2 plug-in goals.

Compared to plain Maven 2 and the Apache Felix Bundle plug-in, Pax Construct streamlines the Maven 2 build process for OSGi via its archetypes and its comprehensive module-based project layout. Whereas the Apache Felix Bundle plug-in offers a simple, yet powerful, new kind of packaging (based on Bnd), Pax Construct offers tooling for the whole build process, from creating a project through to packaging it and running it. (Note that Pax Construct also uses the Apache Felix Bundle plug-in.)

Why didn't we introduce Pax Construct earlier, or even use it throughout the book? Mainly because it's another layer between OSGi and the developer, and we wanted to focus on OSGi and Spring DM. Nevertheless Pax Construct is great for managing your OSGi build or for getting started with OSGi (if you don't want to be bothered with what happens under the covers).

In the following sections, we'll provide a comprehensive introduction to Pax Construct, from installation to creating a module-based project, creating Spring-powered bundles with Pax Construct's archetypes, and packaging and executing the application. We'll use a simple example based on a data source bundle and a database client bundle, which will give us the opportunity to illustrate most of the features of Pax Construct. By the end of this section, you'll know how and, more importantly, *when* to use Pax Construct.

D.2.1 Installing Pax Construct

At the heart of Pax Construct is a Maven 2 plug-in, but the Pax Construct's team provides a set of scripts that encapsulates the calls to the underlying plug-in. When using

Pax Construct, you can either stick to using a 100 percent Maven command approach or combine the scripts *and* the Maven command. We'll use the latter approach here, as the scripts offer useful shortcuts, especially for arguments, and they don't limit the capabilities of the tool.

You can download the Pax Construct scripts from the following website: http://www.ops4j.org/projects/pax/construct/. The distribution consists of a compressed zip file that you can unpack in any directory (which we'll refer to as PAX_CONSTRUCT_HOME from here on). You should then add the PAX_CONSTRUCT_HOME directory to your PATH environment variable so that you can launch Pax Construct scripts from anywhere.

> **NOTE** To run Pax Construct, you need Maven 2 installed on your computer. The scripts are available for Windows and Unix-based systems (Linux, Unix, and OS X). In this appendix, we'll use Pax Construct 1.4.

Table D.3 lists all the scripts available in Pax Construct; we'll use each of them and look at their options as our example progresses.

Table D.3 Pax Construct scripts

Script	Description
pax-create-project	Creates a module-based Maven 2 project, with Pax Construct's layout for OSGi applications
pax-add-repository	Adds a repository to the current POM
pax-create-bundle	Creates a Maven project with example sources and default packaging set to OSGi bundle
pax-import-bundle	Adds a bundle as a dependency (which will also be used to provision the platform)
pax-embed-jar	Embeds a third-party JAR into an OSGi bundle
pax-wrap-jar	Creates a Maven project to wrap an existing JAR as an OSGi bundle
pax-provision	Uses Pax Runner to run the current project in a target platform
pax-create-module	Creates a Maven module for an existing project
pax-move-bundle	Moves a bundle to a new directory
pax-remove-bundle	Deletes a bundle from the current project
pax-update	When run in the Pax Construct's install directory, updates the scripts to the last version
pax-clone	Clones an existing Pax Construct project so that it can be re-created elsewhere

Each Pax Construct script accepts its own set of parameters, as well as Maven 2 options. The script handles the parameters, whereas Maven 2 options are handed directly to the corresponding plug-in's goal. You must specify script parameters first, then Maven options. To clearly identify the two parts of the command, you must separate the parameters from the Maven options with two hyphens: --.

The following snippet shows a Pax Construct command that uses both parameters and Maven 2 options:

```
pax-import-bundle
    -g org.springframework.osgi -a spring-osgi-extender
    -v 1.2.0
    -- -DwidenScope -DimportTransitive
```

NOTE The Maven 2 options suffer from the same problem as Pax Runner options: on a DOS/Windows shell, you must enclose them within quotation marks when they use the equals sign.

Now that you have Pax Construct up and running on your computer and you know the basics, let's create our first project with this new tool.

D.2.2 *Creating a module-based project*

We're going to create a project using Pax Construct's archetype, which leverages the module-based layout of Maven 2 projects. To create the project, open a shell in a working directory and type the following command:

```
pax-create-project -g com.manning.smdia.paxconstruct -a dbapp
```

The execution of the script results in some typical Maven 2 output. The `-g` and `-a` parameters refer to the Maven 2 coordinates of the project (the group ID and the artifact ID, respectively). You could alternatively have typed the `pax-create-project` command, and you would have been prompted for the coordinates of your project, which is convenient when you don't remember the exact names of the parameters.

If you take a look at the content of the dbapp directory, you'll see a pom.xml file at the root and some directories that the archetype created. Don't feel overwhelmed by the apparent complexity of the project layout; we'll discuss each module when the time comes.

You can `cd` to the newly created dbapp directory and use the `pax-provision` command to launch your project in an OSGi container:

```
cd dbapp
pax-provision
[INFO] Scanning for projects...
[INFO] Reactor build order:
[INFO]   com.manning.smdia.paxconstruct.dbapp (OSGi project)
[INFO]   dbapp - plugin configuration
[INFO]   dbapp - wrapper instructions
[INFO]   dbapp - bundle instructions
[INFO]   dbapp - imported bundles
[INFO] ----------------------------------------------------------------
(...)
```

```
_____  _____  __ _____   _____  __  __  _____  __ _____   \
|    __/\_  \ \ \/ /  |   _/  |  \/  \ / \/  __\ _\    \
|    | / _ \_>  <   |   |  \  |  /   |  \  |  \  __/|  |\/
|____| (____/_/\_\  |____|  /____/|____|  /____|  /\____>__|
             \/      \/           \/          \/       \/      \/
```

Pax Runner (1.4.0) from OPS4J - http://www.ops4j.org

```
 -> Using config [classpath:META-INF/runner.properties]
 (...)
 -> Preparing framework [Felix 2.0.2]
 -> Downloading bundles...
 -> Felix 2.0.2 : 388030 bytes @ [ 26kBps ]
 -> Felix Shell (1.4.1) : 62616 bytes @ [ 23kBps ]
 -> Felix TUI Shell (1.4.1) : 12748 bytes @ [ 49kBps ]
 -> Using execution environment [J2SE-1.6]
 -> Runner has successfully finished his job!

Welcome to Felix
=================

 ->
```

With the `pax-provision` command, Pax Construct provisioned the default OSGi platform (Felix) with the content of your project and used Pax Runner to launch the platform. Because we haven't created any bundles so far, the platform instance contains only the bundles essential for Felix to run.

We're going to switch from Felix to Equinox. Type `shutdown` to exit from Felix, and edit the pom.xml file. In the `project/build/plugin` XML element, you'll find the declaration of the Pax plug-in and the option to switch to Equinox:

```
<plugin>
  <groupId>org.ops4j</groupId>
  <artifactId>maven-pax-plugin</artifactId>
  <version>1.4</version>
  <configuration>
    <provision>                              Sets Equinox as
      <param>--platform=equinox</param>  ◁── default platform
    </provision>
  </configuration>
  (...)
</plugin>
```

If you rerun the `pax-provision` command, Pax Runner will launch Equinox:

```
pax-provision
(...)
```

```
Pax Runner (1.4.0) from OPS4J - http://www.ops4j.org
----------------------------------------------------

 -> Using config [classpath:META-INF/runner.properties]
 (...)
 -> Preparing framework [Equinox 3.5.1]
 -> Downloading bundles...
 -> Equinox 3.5.1 : 1125860 bytes @ [ 56kBps ]
 -> Using execution environment [J2SE-1.6]
 -> Runner has successfully finished his job!

osgi>
```

Before creating our bundle subprojects, we need to instruct Pax Construct to provision our project with Spring DM.

D.2.3   *Setting up the project for Spring DM*

To tell Pax Construct to provision the project with Spring DM's bundles, we need to add Maven 2 dependencies. But as Spring DM refers to specific bundles that aren't available on standard Maven 2 repositories, we first need to add the SpringSource EBR to the project. We use the `pax-add-repository` command to achieve this:

```
pax-add-repository
    -i com.springsource.repository.bundles.release
    -u http://repository.springsource.com/maven/bundles/release
```

The `pax-add-repository` command has two mandatory parameters: the repository's identifier (`-i`) and the repository's URL (`-u`). With the previous command, we added the repository that contains the Spring Framework's and Spring portfolio projects' binaries. They're distributed as OSGi bundles but rely on external dependencies (such as Commons Logging and AOP Alliance), which are available as OSGi bundles on another repository, called the "External" repository. Here is the command to add it:

```
pax-add-repository
    -i com.springsource.repository.bundles.external
    -u http://repository.springsource.com/maven/bundles/external
```

> **NOTE** The `pax-add-repository` command adds `repository` entries in the POM of the current project.

We're now ready to add the Spring DM bundles to the project. For this we use the `pax-import-bundle` command:

```
pax-import-bundle -g org.springframework.osgi
    -a spring-osgi-extender -v 1.2.1
    -- -DwidenScope -DimportTransitive
```

Note that we used Maven 2 options in the previous command to add all of Spring DM's transitive dependencies (`widenScope` to include compile and runtime dependencies, and `importTransitive` to import any provided OSGi dependencies). Pax Construct gathers the declaration of these runtime dependencies in the provision/ pom.xml file.

We can now try to launch the project and see if Spring DM extender is properly deployed (we removed some unnecessary lines from the output for brevity):

```
pax-provision
(...)
   _____       \        _____
_____\  \_____ __ __ _____      \___ __ __ ___ __ _____
|      __/\_   \ \ \/ /  |     _/  |  \/   \ /   \/ _ \_ __ \
|   |     / _ \_>   <    |   |   \  |  /   |  \   |  \  ___/|  | \/
|___|    (____  /__/\_ \  |___|_  /____/___|  /___|  /\___  >_|
             \/      \/       \/         \/     \/     \/

Pax Runner (1.4.0) from OPS4J - http://www.ops4j.org
--------------------------------------------------
(...)
 -> Preparing framework [Equinox 3.5.1]
 -> Downloading bundles...
 -> mvn:org.springframework.osgi/spring-osgi-extender/1.2.1 : 120822 bytes
➡    @ [ 5253kBps ]
 -> mvn:org.springframework.osgi/spring-osgi-core/1.2.1 : 362889 bytes
➡    @ [ 12096kBps ]
 -> mvn:org.springframework.osgi/spring-osgi-io/1.2.1 : 35859 bytes
➡    @ [ 8964kBps ]
(...)
 -> Using execution environment [J2SE-1.6]
 -> Runner has successfully finished his job!

osgi> log4j:WARN No appenders could be found for logger
➡   (org.springframework.osgi.extender.internal.activator.
➡   ContextLoaderListener).
log4j:WARN Please initialize the log4j system properly.
osgi> ss

Framework is launched.

id     State      Bundle
0      ACTIVE     org.eclipse.osgi_3.5.1.R35x_v20090827
1      ACTIVE     org.springframework.osgi.extender_1.2.1
2      ACTIVE     org.springframework.osgi.core_1.2.1
3      ACTIVE     org.springframework.osgi.io_1.2.1
(...)
```

Here's what we can learn from the previous output:

- Pax Construct leveraged Pax Runner to provision the platform from the Maven 2 local repository.
- The Spring DM's bundles have been correctly installed (with their dependencies).
- There's a problem with Log4j.

Yet another problem with logging! Pax Construct included the SLF4J libraries and the binding for Log4j. It did a good job, but we need to provide our logging configuration in the form of a fragment, as we did in chapter 3. This gives us the opportunity to create our first bundle with Pax Construct.

> ### Do I really need all these bundles?
> If you take a closer look at the bundles loaded in the platform, you'll see that Pax Construct included a lot of them, some of which we won't need. That's a limitation of the tool: it can help you get started quickly, but you'll sometimes need to clean up after it. In our case, we'd need to remove some of the unnecessary dependencies. (We'll just live with them for the duration of this introduction to Pax Construct.)

D.2.4 Creating a bundle fragment for the logging configuration

To configure Log4j, we need to create a fragment that'll get attached to the Log4j bundle and will provide the log4j.properties configuration file. A fragment is a special kind of OSGi bundle, so we can use the `pax-create-bundle` script to create the skeleton of our bundle:

```
pax-create-bundle -p com.manning.sdmia
     -n dbapp.log4j.config
     -- -Dinterfaces=false -Dinternals=false
     -Dactivator=false
```

The `-p` and `-n` parameters refer to the package and the name of the bundle, respectively. We don't really need to fill in the package name, as our bundle will contain only the Log4j configuration file. We also include Maven 2 options to disable the creation of some classes and interfaces that the archetype creates by default.

The `pax-create-bundle` command creates a new module in the dbapp.log4j.config directory and declares it in the root POM. This module has the layout of a standard Maven 2 project. We need to perform the following tasks to organize our fragment:

- Delete the content of the src/main/java directory (our fragment contains only a configuration file).
- Create a src/main/resources directory and create a log4j.properties file in it.

Here is a sample of the Log4j configuration that'll cause Log4j to issue logging messages in a file:

```
log4j.rootLogger=INFO, FILE

log4j.appender.FILE=org.apache.log4j.FileAppender
log4j.appender.FILE.File=dbapp.log
log4j.appender.FILE.layout=org.apache.log4j.PatternLayout
log4j.appender.FILE.layout.ConversionPattern=%-4r [%t] %-5p %c %x - %m%n%M
```

Our bundle is a fragment, so we need to know its host bundle. We can learn this by issuing the `ss` command on Equinox:

```
osgi> ss
(...)
14       ACTIVE      com.springsource.org.apache.log4j_1.2.15
(...)
```

But where should we add the `Fragment-Host` header? Pax Construct uses the Felix Bundle Plugin internally, but in a slightly different way than we've used it so far (more about this later). The only thing you need to know right now is that Pax Construct's archetype created an osgi.bnd file in the module directory, and we can use it to include OSGi headers.

To attach our fragment to the Log4j bundle, add the following entry to the osgi.bnd file (and remove what the archetype added by default):

```
Fragment-Host: com.springsource.org.apache.log4j
```

From the root of the project, type the following Maven 2 command to install all the bundles and run the project (note that we don't use a Pax Construct script this time but Maven 2 commands):

```
mvn clean install pax:provision
```

The nasty warning should have disappeared, and by using the `ss` command, you can check that the Log4j bundle discovered its fragment:

```
osgi> ss
(...)
14      ACTIVE         com.springsource.org.apache.log4j_1.2.15
                       Fragments=25
(...)
25      RESOLVED       com.manning.smdia.paxconstruct.
➥    dbapp.log4j.config_1.0.0.SNAPSHOT
                       Master=14
```

The dbapp.log file lies in the runner directory, which is the default working directory of Pax Runner.

We're now ready to write our first Spring-powered bundle using Pax Construct, in which we'll define the data source of our database application.

D.2.5   *Creating the data source bundle*

Our simple database application needs a connection to a database; that's why we're about to create a bundle that will publish this connection as an OSGi service. We'll be using the `DataSource` interface for our connection, because it's a good example of a service: an object implementing `DataSource` can encapsulate advanced features, like pooling, behind a simple interface. Let's keep things simple for the moment: we'll use an in-memory database (H2) and a simple `DataSource` implementation that Spring provides (the persistent database and the connection pool will come later).

Let's create the data source bundle: `cd` to the base directory of the project, and launch the command shown in the following snippet:

```
pax-create-bundle -p com.manning.sdmia
➥    -n dbapp.datasource
➥    -- -Dspring
```

You should now be familiar with the basics of the `pax-create-bundle` script, but here we used a new Maven option, `spring`, that triggers the creation of ready-to-use Spring configuration files, located where Spring DM expects to find them: in the META-INF/ spring directory.

You can check that these files have been created in the dbapp.datasource/src/main/ resources directory (the project follows the standard Maven 2 layout). The archetype follows Spring DM's best practices and creates two Spring files: bundle-context.xml for the declaration of standard Spring beans and bundle-context-osgi.xml for interacting with the OSGi environment through Spring DM's namespaces.

NOTE You can safely delete the content of the dbapp.datasource/src/main/ java directory, where the archetype created some example classes.

Edit bundle-context.xml to declare the data source, as shown in the following snippet (delete the bean that Pax Construct declares by default in the file):

```
<bean id="dataSource"
      class="org.springframework.jdbc.datasource.SimpleDriverDataSource">
  <property name="driverClass" value="org.h2.Driver" />
  <property name="url" value="jdbc:h2:mem:dbapp" />
  <property name="username" value="sa" />
  <property name="password" value="" />
</bean>
```

Here we use a `SimpleDriverDataSource`, an OSGi-compliant `DataSource` implementation provided by Spring. It's not a connection pool because it creates a new connection on each call to `getConnection`, but its ease of configuration is suitable for development or testing.

WARNING Don't use `SimpleDriverDataSource` in a production environment for multithreaded or concurrent applications; use a real connection pool implementation instead.

Now that the data source has been created, edit the bundle-context-osgi.xml file to publish it as an OSGi service, using Spring DM's `osgi` namespace. This is shown in the following snippet:

```
<osgi:service ref="dataSource"
              interface="javax.sql.DataSource"/>
```

We're still in OSGi, so we need to explicitly import the packages that our bundle uses, which are the H2 driver package and the `SimpleDriverDataSource` package. This is done in the osgi.bnd file of the data source project, with the `Import-Package` manifest header:

```
Import-Package: org.h2,javax.sql,org.springframework.jdbc.datasource
```

We also need to provision the OSGi platform with the bundles exporting the packages we imported. These are the H2 library, the JDBC Spring module, and its dependency, the Spring Transaction module. We use the `pax-import-bundle` script for this:

```
pax-import-bundle -g com.h2database -a h2 -v 1.2.137
pax-import-bundle -g org.springframework
```

```
⮡    -a org.springframework.transaction -v 2.5.6.SEC01
pax-import-bundle -g org.springframework
⮡    -a org.springframework.jdbc -v 2.5.6.SEC01
```

You can now check that the data source is properly configured and published by launching the platform with the `mvn clean install pax:provision` command. The `ss` command should show the data source bundle:

```
osgi> ss
(...)
29     ACTIVE       com.manning.smdia.paxconstruct.dbapp.
⮡    datasource_1.0.0.SNAPSHOT
```

Even though our data source is a little simple, it's fully functional, and creating it has illustrated the support that Pax Construct provides for Spring DM projects. As a database is nothing without clients connecting to it, we'll create a Spring-powered client bundle next.

D.2.6   *Creating the database client bundle*

Our database client bundle will only display on the console the name of the database engine. Even if this appears simple, this bundle will be a full-blown Spring-powered bundle that leverages Spring DM's declarative service importing and dependency injection. Let's create the project by launching the following command from the root of our project:

```
pax-create-bundle -p com.manning.sdmia.dbapp.client
⮡    -n dbapp.client
⮡    -- -Dspring
```

It's time to create the `DataBaseClient` in the `com.manning.sdmia.dbapp.client` package (in the src/main/java directory of the newly created dbapp.client directory).

> **NOTE** You can safely delete the classes the archetype created in the source directory.

The following snippet shows the source code of the `DataBaseClient` class:

```
package com.manning.sdmia.dbapp.client;

import java.sql.Connection;
import javax.sql.DataSource;

public class DataBaseClient {

  private DataSource dataSource;

  public void init() throws Exception {
    Connection conn = null;
      try {
        conn = dataSource.getConnection();
        System.out.println("database is: "+          ⟵ Outputs database
          conn.getMetaData().getDatabaseProductName()       engine name
        );
      } finally {
```

```
      if(conn != null) {
        conn.close();
      }
    }
  }
}

  public void setDataSource(DataSource dataSource) {
    this.dataSource = dataSource;
  }
}
```

NOTE   To create the Eclipse configuration files so you can then import the projects into Eclipse, you can use the `mvn pax:eclipse` command.

The database client isn't very useful, but it'll tell us if our data source bundle is operational. It's a Spring bean we declare in the bundle-context.xml file, as the following snippet demonstrates (delete the bean that Pax Construct declares by default in the file):

```
<bean class="com.manning.sdmia.dbapp.client.DataBaseClient"
      init-method="init">
  <property name="dataSource" ref="dataSource" />
</bean>
```

Where does the preceding snippet's `dataSource` bean come from? From the data source bundle we created previously, of course! Thanks to Spring DM, we can import it from the OSGi service registry by leveraging the `osgi` namespace. The following snippet shows how to do that in the bundle-context-osgi.xml file:

```
<osgi:reference id="dataSource"
                interface="javax.sql.DataSource" />
```

To avoid any `import-package` surprises, modify the osgi.bnd file to import every package that the bundle source code refers to:

```
Import-Package: *
```

Where are the packaging instructions?

The bundle projects we've created so far with Pax Construct use a common parent POM that contains some instructions for the Felix Bundle Plugin. This POM is located in the project's poms/compiled directory. By doing this, Pax Construct centralized the generic parts of the packaging. As we already saw, these instructions can be modified on a per-bundle basis via the dedicated osgi.bnd file.

You're now ready to test the database client bundle by launching the `mvn clean install pax:provision` command from the root of the project. You should see the long-awaited message a couple of seconds after the `osgi>` prompt has appeared:

```
osgi> database is: H2
```

Another brick in the wall of our database application! This simple client is a way to check if the data source is up and running, so that's a good reason to play around with the data source service.

In the next section, we'll see how to replace our simple data source with a full-blown connection pool, made possible by the OSGi-ification of the DBCP library.

D.2.7   *Using a connection pool for the data source*

The `SimpleDriverDataSource` is good for testing, but it's not suitable for concurrent applications in production, so we're going to switch to a connection pool powered by Commons DBCP.

Unfortunately, DBCP isn't distributed as an OSGi bundle, so we'll have to wrap it. Fortunately, Pax Construct comes with a script that makes OSGi-ification easy. Once DBCP is OSGi-ified and included in our project, we'll modify the data source bundle to use it.

OSGI-IFYING DBCP WITH PAX CONSTRUCT

In chapter 6 we covered a state-of-the-art process for OSGi-ifying Commons DBCP using plain Bnd and the Felix Bundle Plugin for Maven 2. What we're about to do is more straightforward and ends up being a little less modular than the solution adopted in chapter 6, but the end justifies the means.

To wrap a library as an OSGi bundle, Pax Construct provides the `pax-wrap-bundle` script, which requires the Maven 2 coordinates of the target library. It can also handle a bunch of optional Maven 2 options, but we'll only look at a few of them (don't hesitate to check the reference documentation to learn more about them).

To start the OSGi-ification of Commons DBCP, `cd` to the root of the project and launch the following command:

```
pax-wrap-jar -g commons-dbcp
    -a commons-dbcp -v 1.2.2
    -- -DembedTransitive
    -DbundleName=dbapp.commons-dbcp
```

In this command, the most interesting option is `embedTransitive`: it tells Pax Construct to wrap in the resulting OSGi-ified bundle not only Commons DBCP but also all its dependencies. Commons Pool is the only dependency of Commons DBCP, so its class files will also be included in the wrapper. That's why our solution is less modular than the one adopted in chapter 6, where we wrapped each library in its own bundle. Wrapping two different libraries in the same bundle isn't particularly modular—it will be more difficult to upgrade one without also updating the other. Nevertheless, this rather unorthodox solution is sufficient for our simple database application.

How did Pax Construct wrap the library? It created a dbapp.commons-dbcp directory that contains a POM and osgi.bnd file. They provide all the instructions that the Felix Bundle Plugin needs to wrap DBCP and its dependency, Commons Pool.

Chapter 6 gives all the details, so you should refer to it for more information. What differs the most between the OSGi-ification in chapter 6 and the one done here is that here we embed Commons DBCP and its dependency, Commons Pool, together in the same OSGi-compliant JAR. This is the result of the `embedTransitive` option we used in the previous command, and this is reflected in the Bnd configuration file, osgi.bnd, that Pax Construct generates:

```
Embed-Dependency: *;scope=compile|runtime;type=!pom;inline=true
Embed-Transitive: true
```

> **NOTE** For wrapper projects, Pax Construct also uses a parent POM, which is in the poms/wrappers directory.

Because our DBCP bundle will connect to the H2 database engine, we must make the driver visible to DBCP, still in the osgi.bnd file:

```
Import-Package: org.h2;version="0.0.0";resolution:=optional,*
```

Our DBCP bundle is now ready; you can check if it can be deployed on Equinox by launching the project. It should appear in the ACTIVE state in the list of bundles:

```
31      ACTIVE      dbapp.commons-dbcp_1.2.2
```

The next step is to reconfigure the data source bundle to use the DBCP pool implementation.

CONFIGURING THE DATA SOURCE BUNDLE WITH THE CONNECTION POOL

Using a connection pool just requires an internal modification of the `dbapp.datasource` module: it has no impact on the bundles that use the data source service, because it's hidden behind the `DataSource` interface.

Switching from the `SimpleDriverDataSource` to a DBCP pool implies modifying the bundle-context.xml file of the `dbapp.datasource`, as shown in the following snippet:

```
<bean id="dataSource"
      class="org.apache.commons.dbcp.BasicDataSource"
      destroy-method="close">
  <property name="driverClassName" value="org.h2.Driver" />
  <property name="url"
            value="jdbc:h2:tcp://localhost/dbapp" />
  <property name="username" value="sa" />
  <property name="password" value="" />
</bean>
```

We use the default configuration of the DBCP pool here; don't hesitate to consult the reference documentation for the advanced settings (maximum number of connections, validation query, and the like). The database is no longer in memory; it now uses the H2 server engine, which is persistent.

> **NOTE** The code samples for this appendix contain a database directory containing the H2 binaries and the scripts to launch the database engine.

Because we replaced the `SimpleDriverDataSource` with DBCP's `BasicDataSource`, the bundle's imports must be updated accordingly in the osgi.bnd file:

```
Import-Package: org.apache.commons.dbcp,javax.sql
```

You can now test that the connection pool works correctly by building and launching the whole project. There's no difference for the client bundle; it still asks the data source service for a connection, but now this connection comes from a full-blown connection pool, which ensures the application scales under heavy load.

> **NOTE** You can change the database client to query the database (it contains a single table with some data in it). If you stick to Spring, this implies using a `JdbcTemplate` and adding the corresponding import. We leave this as an exercise; you can check the book's source code if you want to see how to implement this.

This ends our tour of Pax Construct, in which we've seen how to do OSGi development based on Maven 2. Even though we covered most of the Pax Construct scripts, we only scratched the surface of the tool—it offers many options and features. Pax Construct's approach, which uses a module-based Maven 2 project, allows us to start OSGi development quickly and offers consistent and comprehensive default settings. Pax Construct builds on top of tools like the Felix Bundle Plugin, which we covered in this book, and takes care of the tedious initial settings. This makes the projects created by Pax Construct ready to use on an OSGi platform.

D.3   *Summary*

Pax Runner and Pax Construct are two tools that each OSGi developer should know about. Even if you don't use them for all your projects, they're certainly a great help for distributing OSGi applications or quickly building OSGi projects.

Pax Runner makes it easy to launch and provision an OSGi container. It's very flexible, and operations like switching from one container to another or provisioning from the local Maven 2 repository are just a matter of command-line arguments. Pax Construct leverages many tools (Maven 2, the Felix Bundle Plugin, Pax Runner) to provide a consistent way of creating, building, and managing OSGi projects. It offers OSGi-oriented commands, like wrapping an existing library as an OSGi bundle, that streamline the development process.

Pax Runner and Pax Construct also offer support for Spring DM (with a dedicated profile for Pax Runner and an archetype for Pax Construct). This relieves the developer from tedious and error-prone tasks like provisioning, and it also adds some flexibility, like the possibility of choosing the framework version with a command-line argument.

We based most of the samples in this book on more traditional approaches (manual provisioning, Bnd, and the Felix Bundle Plug-in) because they make it easier to understand the underlying mechanisms. This also shows you that OSGi development isn't so different from traditional development and doesn't necessarily imply using different tools. Nevertheless, Pax Runner and Pax Construct are a consistent and logical evolution of the tooling of a well-informed OSGi developer. That's why they deserve a whole appendix in a Spring DM book.

index

RELATED MANNING TITLES

OSGi in Action
Creating Modular Applications in Java
by Richard S. Hall, Karl Pauls, Stuart
  McCulloch, and David Savage

  ISBN: 978-1-933988-91-7
  375 pages, $49.99
  October 2010

Spring in Action, Third Edition
by Craig Walls

  ISBN: 978-1-935182-35-1
  700 pages, $49.99
  December 2010

Spring in Practice
by Willie Wheeler and John Wheeler

  ISBN: 978-1-935182-05-4
  600 pages, $44.99
  March 2011

Spring Integration in Action
by Mark Fisher, Jonas Partner,
  Marius Bogoevici, and Iwein Fuld

  ISBN: 978-1-935182-43-6
  400 pages, $49.99
  December 2010

For ordering information go to www.manning.com

Groovy in Action, Second Edition

by Dierk König, Paul King,
  Guillaume Laforge, Jon Skeet

  ISBN: 978-1-935182-44-3
  700 pages, $49.99
  April 2011

Grails in Action

by Glen Smith and Peter Ledbrook

  ISBN: 978-1-933988-93-1
  520 pages, $44.99
  May 2009

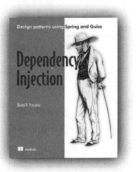

AspectJ in Action, Second Edition
Enterprise AOP with Spring Applications

by Ramnivas Laddad

  ISBN: 978-1-933988-05-4
  568 pages, $49.99
  September 2009

Dependency Injection
Design Patterns Using Spring and Guice

by Dhanji R. Prasanna

  ISBN: 978-1-933988-55-9
  352 pages, $49.99
  August 2009

For ordering information go to www.manning.com

YOU MAY ALSO BE INTERESTED IN

JUnit in Action, Second Edition
by Petar Tahchiev, Felipe Leme, Vincent Massol,
  and Gary Gregory

ISBN: 978-1-935182-02-3
504 pages, $49.99
July 2010

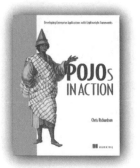

Java Persistence with Hibernate
Second Edition of Hibernate in Action

by Christian Bauer and Gavin King

ISBN: 978-1-932394-88-7
880 pages, $59.99
November 2006

POJOs in Action
*Developing Enterprise Applications
with Lightweight Frameworks*
by Chris Richardson

ISBN: 978-1-932394-58-0
592 pages, $44.95
January 2006

EJB 3 in Action
by Debu Panda, Reza Rahman, Derek Lane

ISBN: 978-1-933988-34-4
712 pages, $44.99
April 2007

For ordering information go to www.manning.com